THE DOMESDAY GEOGRAPHY OF
SOUTH-EAST ENGLAND

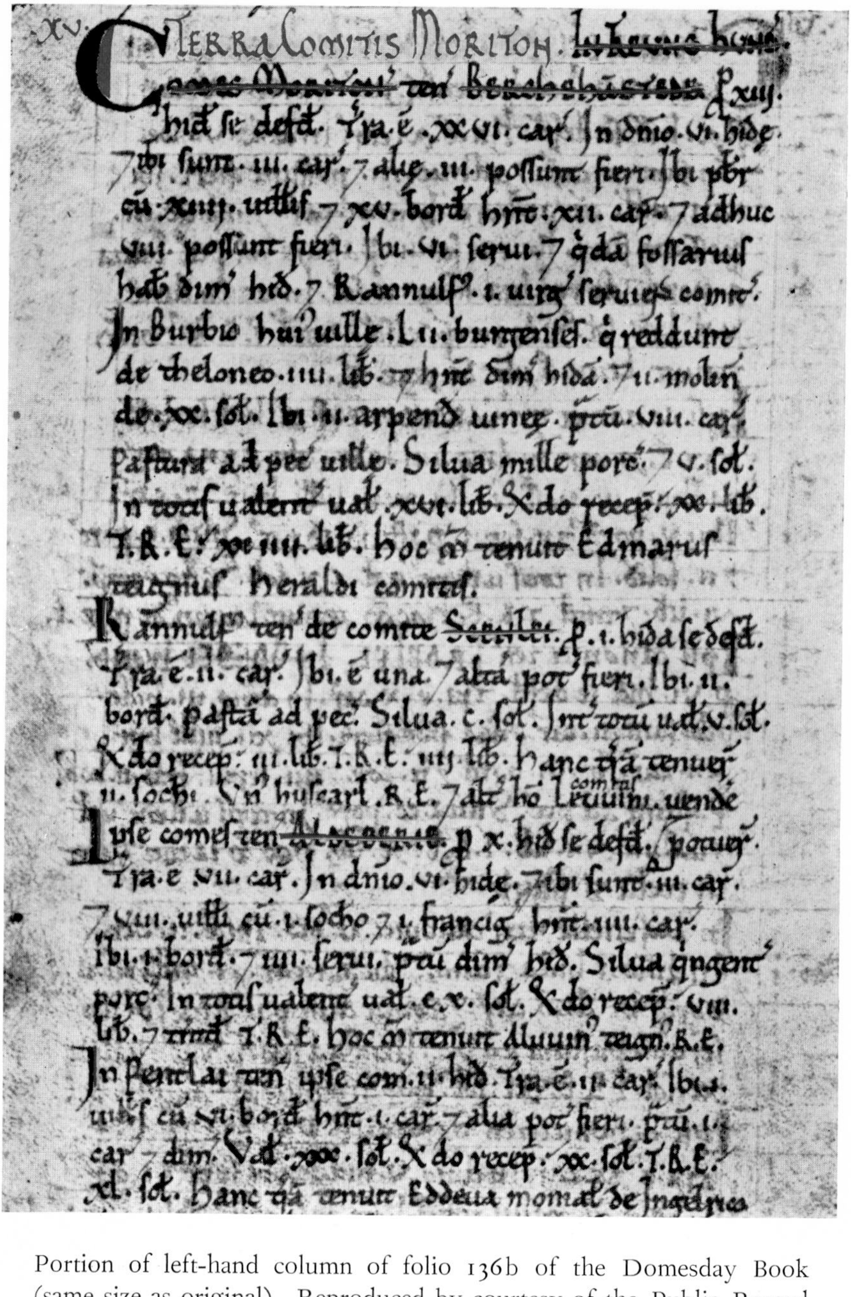

XV.

TERRA COMITIS MORITON. ...

[manuscript in abbreviated medieval Latin — best reading]

Comes Moriton ten ...

hid se defd. Tra .e. xxvi. car'. In dnio .vi. hide
7 ibi sunt .iii. car'. 7 alie .iii. possunt fieri. Ibi pbr
cu .xxiiii. uillis 7 xv. bord hnt .xii. car'. 7 adhuc
viii. possunt fieri. Ibi .vi. servi. 7 qda fossarius
hab dim' hid. 7 Rannulf' .i. uirg seruiens comite.
In Burbio hui uille .lii. burgenses. q reddu't
de theloneo .iiii. lib. 7 hnt dim hida 7 ii. molen
de .xx. sol. Ibi ii. arpend uinee. ptu .viii. car'
pastura ad pec uille. Silua mille porc'. 7 v. sol.
In totis ualent ual .xxvi. lib. 7 qdo recep .xx. lib.
T.R.E. xxiiii. lib. Hoc m tenuit Edmaruf
teign' heraldi comitis.

Rannulf' ten de comite Sciflet. p .i. hida se defd.
Tra .e. ii. car'. Ibi .e. una 7 alia pot fieri. Ibi ii.
bord. pastu ad pec. Silua .c. sol. In totu ual .v. sol.
7 qdo recep .ii. lib. T.R.E. .viii. lib. Hanc tra tenuer
ii. sochi. hn hucarl R.E. 7 alt ho Leuuini comitis uende

Ipse comes ten Alcoenie. p x. hid se defd. 7 potuer
Tra .e. vii. car'. In dnio .vi. hide. 7 ibi sunt .iii. car'.
7 viii. uilli cu .i. socho 7 i. francig hnt .iiii. car'.
Ibi .i. bord. 7 iiii. servi. ptu dim' hid. Silua qngent
porc. In totu ualent ual .c.x. sol. 7 qdo recep .viii.
lib. 7 tntd T.R.E. hoc m tenuit Aluuin teign R.E.

In Pentlai ten ipse com .ii. hid. Tra .e. ii. car'. Ibi i.
uills cu vi. bord hnt .i. car'. 7 alia pot fieri. ptu .i.
car 7 dim'. Val .xxx. sol. 7 qdo recep .xx. sol. T.R.E.
xl. sol. Hanc tra tenuit Eddeua mon̄al de Ingelrica

Portion of left-hand column of folio 136b of the Domesday Book
(same size as original). Reproduced by courtesy of the Public Record
Office. For extension and translation, see pp. 619-20.

THE
DOMESDAY GEOGRAPHY
OF
SOUTH-EAST ENGLAND

EDITED BY

H. C. DARBY

*Professor of Geography at University College
in the University of London*

AND

EILA M. J. CAMPBELL

*Lecturer in Geography at Birkbeck College
in the University of London*

CAMBRIDGE

AT THE UNIVERSITY PRESS

1962

PUBLISHED BY

THE SYNDICS OF THE CAMBRIDGE UNIVERSITY PRESS

Bentley House, 200 Euston Road, London, N.W. 1
American Branch: 32 East 57th Street, New York 22, N.Y.
West African Office: P.O. Box 33, Ibadan, Nigeria

©

CAMBRIDGE UNIVERSITY PRESS

1962

Printed in Great Britain at the University Press, Cambridge
(Brooke Crutchley, University Printer)

A century hence the student's materials will not be in the shape in which he finds them now. In the first place, the substance of Domesday Book will have been rearranged. Those villages and hundreds which the Norman clerks tore into shreds will have been reconstituted and pictured in maps, for many men from over all England will have come within King William's spell, will have bowed themselves to him and become that man's men.

From the concluding paragraph of F. W. MAITLAND'S
Domesday Book and Beyond (Cambridge, 1897)

CONTENTS

Part of folio 136b of the Domesday Book　　　　　　　*Frontispiece*

Preface　　　　　　　*page* ix

List of Maps　　　　　　　xi

Chapter I　BEDFORDSHIRE　　　　　　　I
　　　　　By EILA M. J. CAMPBELL, M.A.

　　II　HERTFORDSHIRE　　　　　　　48
　　　　　By EILA M. J. CAMPBELL, M.A.

　　III　MIDDLESEX　　　　　　　97
　　　　　By EILA M. J. CAMPBELL, M.A.

　　IV　BUCKINGHAMSHIRE　　　　　　　138
　　　　　By EILA M. J. CAMPBELL, M.A.

　　V　OXFORDSHIRE　　　　　　　186
　　　　　By E. M. JOPE, M.A. *and* I. B. TERRETT, B.A., PH.D.

　　VI　BERKSHIRE　　　　　　　239
　　　　　By EILA M. J. CAMPBELL, M.A.

　　VII　HAMPSHIRE　　　　　　　287
　　　　　By R. WELLDON FINN, M.A.

　　VIII　SURREY　　　　　　　364
　　　　　By C. W. LLOYD, M.A.

　　IX　SUSSEX　　　　　　　407
　　　　　By S. H. KING, M.A., PH.D.

X KENT *page* 483

By EILA M. J. CAMPBELL, M.A.

XI THE SOUTH-EASTERN COUNTIES 563

By H. C. DARBY, LITT.D.

Appendix I: Summary of the Domesday Book for the South- 611
    eastern Counties

Appendix II: Extension and Translation of Frontispiece 619

Index 621

PREFACE

This book is the third of a number covering the whole of Domesday England, and it is built upon the same plan as the *Domesday Geography of the Eastern Counties*, first published in 1952. The greater part of the preface to that volume is equally relevant to this one, and its argument must be repeated here. The Domesday Book has long been regarded as a unique source of information about legal and economic matters, but its bearing upon the reconstruction of the geography of England during the early Middle Ages has remained comparatively neglected. The extraction of this geographical information is not always as simple as it might appear to be from a casual inspection of the Domesday folios. Not only are there general problems of interpretation, but almost every county has its own peculiarities. There is, moreover, the sheer difficulty of handling the vast mass of material, and of getting a general view of the whole. The original survey was made in terms of manors, villages and hundreds, but the clerks reassembled the information under the headings of the different land-holders of each county. Their work must therefore be undone, and the survey set out upon a geographical basis.

The information that such an analysis makes available is of two kinds. In the first place, the details about plough-teams and about population enable a general picture of the relative prosperity of different areas to be obtained. In the second place, the details about such things as meadow, pasture, wood and salt-pans serve to illustrate further the local variations both in the face of the countryside and in its economic life. An attempt has been made to set out this variety of information as objectively as possible in the form of maps and tables. When all the maps have been drawn and all the tables compiled, we may begin to have a clearer idea of both the value and the limitations of the survey that has so captured the imagination of later generations.

But great though the bulk of the Domesday Book is, it is only a summary. The making of it not only omitted much, but has, too often, resulted in obscurity. No one works for long on the text before discovering how fascinating and tantalising that obscurity is. In reflecting over many Domesday entries we have been reminded, time and again, of some remarks in Professor Trevelyan's inaugural lecture at Cambridge in

1927: 'On the shore where Time casts up its stray wreckage, we gather corks and broken planks, whence much indeed may be argued and more guessed; but what the great ship was that has gone down into the deep, that we shall never see.' The scene that King William's clerks looked upon has gone, and the most we can do is to try to obtain some rough outline of its lineaments; this chapter in the history of the English landscape can only be a very imperfect one.

The Domesday Geography of Eastern England contained an introductory chapter which is not included here. Amongst other things that chapter explained that the counties are considered separately and that the treatment of each follows a more or less standard pattern. This method inevitably involves some repetition, but, after experiment, it was chosen because of its convenience. It enables the account of each county to be read or consulted apart from the rest, and it also has the advantage of bringing out the peculiar features that characterise the text of each county. For although the Domesday Book is arranged on a more or less uniform plan, there are many differences between the counties, both in the nature of their information and in the way it is presented. The relevance of each of the items to a reconstruction of Domesday geography is examined, and any peculiar features that occur in the phrasing of the Domesday text are also noted. All the standard maps have been reproduced on the same scale to facilitate comparison between one county and another. A final chapter sums up some of the salient features of the Domesday geography of the south-eastern counties as a whole. The treatment of the statistics for the boroughs is different from that in the earlier two volumes (see pp. 585–6 and 618 below), but this does not appreciably affect the maps.

The maps in this volume have been drawn by Mr G. R. Versey, but this is only a part of our debt to him. At all stages of the work he has helped to check the material and has given much general assistance. For help from time to time we are grateful to Sir Frank Stenton and Professor V. H. Galbraith. To our five fellow contributors we owe warm thanks for their courtesy and patience, and especially to Mr R. Welldon Finn for his comments on the proof of the whole book. Our debt to the officials of the Cambridge University Press is also great.

H. C. DARBY

EILA M. J. CAMPBELL

UNIVERSITY COLLEGE
LONDON
St Swithin's Day, 1961

LIST OF MAPS

FIG.		PAGE
1	South-eastern Counties	xviii
2	Bedfordshire: Domesday hundreds	3
3	Bedfordshire: Relief	5
4	Bedfordshire: Surface geology	7
5	Bedfordshire: Domesday place-names	10
6	Bedfordshire: Domesday plough-teams in 1086 (by densities)	18
7	Bedfordshire: Domesday plough-teams in 1086 (by settlements)	19
8	Bedfordshire: Domesday population in 1086 (by densities)	22
9	Bedfordshire: Domesday population in 1086 (by settlements)	23
10	Bedfordshire: Devastation *c.* 1070 (after G. H. Fowler)	27
11	Bedfordshire: Domesday plough-lands (by densities)	28
12	Bedfordshire: Domesday plough-team deficiency (by settlements)	29
13	Bedfordshire: Domesday woodland in 1086	32
14	Bedfordshire: Domesday woodland in 1086 (after G. H. Fowler)	34
15	Bedfordshire: Domesday meadow in 1086	35
16	Bedfordshire: Domesday meadow in 1086 (after G. H. Fowler)	37
17	Bedfordshire: Domesday fisheries in 1086	38
18	Bedfordshire: Domesday mills in 1086	40
19	Hertfordshire: Relief	49
20	Hertfordshire: Surface geology	51
21	Hertfordshire: Domesday place-names	53
22	Hertfordshire: Domesday plough-teams in 1086 (by densities)	64
23	Hertfordshire: Domesday plough-teams in 1086 (by settlements)	65
24	Hertfordshire: Domesday population in 1086 (by densities)	68
25	Hertfordshire: Domesday population in 1086 (by settlements)	69
26	Hertfordshire: Domesday plough-lands (by densities)	74
27	Hertfordshire: Domesday plough-team deficiency (by settlements)	75
28	Hertfordshire: Domesday woodland in 1086	78
29	Hertfordshire: Domesday meadow in 1086	79
30	Hertfordshire: Domesday fisheries in 1086	82
31	Hertfordshire: Domesday mills in 1086	84
32	Hertfordshire: Regional subdivisions	92

FIG.		PAGE
33	Middlesex: Domesday hundreds	98
34	Middlesex: Relief	99
35	Middlesex: Surface geology	100
36	Middlesex: Domesday place-names	102
37	Middlesex: Domesday plough-teams in 1086 (by densities)	110
38	Middlesex: Domesday plough-teams in 1086 (by settlements)	111
39	Middlesex: Domesday population in 1086 (by densities)	114
40	Middlesex: Domesday population in 1086 (by settlements)	115
41	Middlesex: Domesday plough-lands (by densities)	120
42	Middlesex: Domesday plough-team deficiency (by settlements)	121
43	Middlesex: Domesday woodland in 1086	124
44	Middlesex: Domesday meadow in 1086	126
45	Middlesex: Domesday fisheries in 1086	129
46	Middlesex: Domesday mills in 1086	130
47	Places contributory to London	133
48	Buckinghamshire: Domesday hundreds	139
49	Buckinghamshire: Relief	141
50	Buckinghamshire: Domesday place-names	144
51	Buckinghamshire: Domesday plough-teams in 1086 (by densities)	152
52	Buckinghamshire: Domesday plough-teams in 1086 (by settlements)	153
53	Buckinghamshire: Domesday population in 1086 (by densities)	158
54	Buckinghamshire: Domesday population in 1086 (by settlements)	159
55	Buckinghamshire: Domesday plough-lands (by densities)	162
56	Buckinghamshire: Domesday plough-team deficiency (by settlements)	163
57	Buckinghamshire: Domesday woodland in 1086	168
58	Buckinghamshire: Domesday meadow in 1086	171
59	Buckinghamshire: Domesday fisheries in 1086	173
60	Buckinghamshire: Domesday mills in 1086	176
61	Buckinghamshire: Regional subdivisions	181
62	Oxfordshire: Relief	188
63	Oxfordshire: Surface geology	191
64	Oxfordshire: Domesday place-names	195

FIG.		PAGE
65	Oxfordshire: Domesday plough-teams in 1086 (by densities)	202
66	Oxfordshire: Domesday plough-teams in 1086 (by settlements)	203
67	Oxfordshire: Domesday population in 1086 (by densities)	206
68	Oxfordshire: Domesday population in 1086 (by settlements)	207
69	Oxfordshire: Domesday woodland in 1086	215
70	Oxfordshire: Domesday meadow in 1086	216
71	Oxfordshire: Domesday pasture in 1086	219
72	Oxfordshire: Domesday fisheries in 1086	222
73	Oxfordshire: Domesday mills in 1086	226
74	Places contributory to Oxford	231
75	Oxfordshire: Regional subdivisions	235
76	Berkshire: Relief	240
77	Berkshire: Surface geology	241
78	Berkshire: Domesday place-names	246
79	Berkshire: Domesday plough-teams in 1086 (by densities)	254
80	Berkshire: Domesday plough-teams in 1086 (by settlements)	255
81	Berkshire: Domesday population in 1086 (by densities)	256
82	Berkshire: Domesday population in 1086 (by settlements)	257
83	Berkshire: Domesday woodland in 1086	263
84	Berkshire: Domesday meadow in 1086	266
85	Berkshire: Domesday fisheries in 1086	268
86	Berkshire: Domesday mills in 1086	270
87	Berkshire: Places contributory to Wallingford	275
88	Berkshire: Regional subdivisions	283
89	Hampshire: Relief	289
90	Hampshire: Surface geology	292
91	Hampshire: Domesday place-names	297
92	Hampshire: Domesday plough-teams in 1086 (by densities)	308
93	Hampshire: Domesday plough-teams in 1086 (by settlements)	309
94	Hampshire: Domesday population in 1086 (by densities)	312
95	Hampshire: Domesday population in 1086 (by settlements)	313
96	Hampshire: Domesday woodland in 1086	323
97	Hampshire: The Forest	325
98	Hampshire: Domesday meadow in 1086	339

FIG.		PAGE
99	Hampshire: Domesday fisheries in 1086	342
100	Hampshire: Domesday salt-pans in 1086	343
101	Hampshire: Domesday mills in 1086	347
102	Places contributory to Winchester	353
103	Hampshire: Regional subdivisions	358
104	Surrey: Domesday hundreds	365
105	Surrey: Relief	367
106	Surrey: Surface geology	368
107	Surrey: Domesday place-names	370
108	Surrey: Domesday plough-teams in 1086 (by densities)	378
109	Surrey: Domesday plough-teams in 1086 (by settlements)	379
110	Surrey: Domesday population in 1086 (by densities)	380
111	Surrey: Domesday population in 1086 (by settlements)	381
112	Surrey: Domesday woodland in 1086	388
113	Surrey: Domesday meadow in 1086	390
114	Surrey: Domesday pasture in 1086	392
115	Surrey: Domesday fisheries in 1086	393
116	Surrey: Domesday mills in 1086	395
117	Surrey: Places contributory to Southwark	399
118	Surrey: Regional subdivisions	402
119	Sussex: Domesday rapes	408
120	Sussex: Relief	409
121	Sussex: Surface geology	411
122	Sussex: Estates in the rape of Hastings attached to manors in the rape of Pevensey	412
123	Sussex: Domesday place-names	419
124	Sussex: Domesday plough-teams in 1086 (by densities)	432
125	Sussex: Domesday plough-teams in 1086 (by settlements)	433
126	Sussex: Domesday population in 1086 (by densities)	436
127	Sussex: Domesday population in 1086 (by settlements)	437
128	Sussex: Domesday woodland in 1086	447
129	Sussex: Domesday meadow in 1086	450
130	Sussex: Domesday pasture in 1086	452
131	Sussex: Domesday fisheries in 1086	454

FIG.		PAGE
132	Sussex: Domesday salt-pans in 1086	457
133	Sussex: Domesday mills in 1086	459
134	Sussex: Places contributory to Chichester	464
135	Sussex: Places contributory to Lewes	467
136	Sussex: Regional subdivisions	475
137	Kent: Domesday lathes	486
138	Kent: The lowy of Richard of Tonbridge	487
139	Kent: Relief	490
140	Kent: Surface geology	491
141	Western Kent: Eleventh-century place-names additional to those in the Domesday Book	496
142	Eastern Kent: Eleventh-century place-names additional to those in the Domesday Book	497
143	Kent: Domesday and other eleventh-century place-names	500
144	Kent: Domesday place-names	501
145	Kent: Domesday plough-teams in 1086 (by densities)	510
146	Kent: Domesday plough-teams in 1086 (by settlements)	511
147	Kent: Domesday population in 1086 (by densities)	514
148	Kent: Domesday population in 1086 (by settlements)	515
149	Kent: Domesday woodland in 1086	526
150	Kent: Domesday vills with denes in 1086	529
151	Kent: Domesday meadow in 1086	533
152	Kent: Domesday pasture in 1086	535
153	Kent: Domesday fisheries in 1086	538
154	Kent: Domesday salt-pans in 1086	540
155	Kent: Domesday mills in 1086	543
156	Kent: Places contributory to Canterbury	547
157	Kent: Places contributory to Rochester	551
158	Kent: Regional subdivisions	557
159	South-eastern Counties: Relief	564
160	South-eastern Counties: Soils	567
161	South-eastern Counties: *Tunc et Post* values in the west	570
162	South-eastern Counties: *Tunc et Post* values in the east	571
163	Depreciated values in the neighbourhood of Hastings	572

FIG.   PAGE

164   Depreciated values in the neighbourhood of Dover   573

165   South-eastern Counties: Domesday place-names   578

166   Relief and Domesday place-names in the London area   584

167   Surface geology and Domesday settlements in the London area   585

168   South-eastern Counties: Domesday population in 1086   586

169   South-eastern Counties: Domesday population in 1086   587
      (adjusted for serfs)

170   South-eastern Counties: Domesday plough-teams in 1086   589

171   South-eastern Counties: Distribution of serfs in 1086   592

172   South-eastern Counties: Distribution of serfs in 1086   593
      (adjusted for serfs)

173   South-eastern Counties: Sokemen, 1066–86   594

174   South-eastern Counties: Domesday woodland in 1086   599

175   South-eastern Counties: Domesday and later Forests   601

176   South-eastern Counties: Domesday meadow in 1086   603

177   South-eastern Counties: Domesday fisheries in 1086   605

178   South-eastern Counties: Domesday salt-pans in 1086   607

179   South-eastern Counties: Domesday vineyards in 1086   609

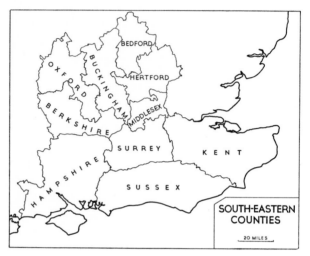

Fig. 1. South-eastern Counties.

CHAPTER I

BEDFORDSHIRE

BY EILA M. J. CAMPBELL, M.A.

There have been four other attempts to reassemble on a geographical basis the Domesday entries for Bedfordshire. The earliest was an analysis of the hidage alone in a communication to the *Gentleman's Magazine* in 1828.[1] The next to appear was *A Digest of the Domesday of Bedfordshire* by the Rev. William Airy.[2] Although Airy had completed his analysis by 1873, it was not published until after his death. It covered many items of information besides hidage, and it won the approval even of J. H. Round:

> It was, most happily, pointed out to the author [Airy] by the Rev. Joseph Hunter 'that what we want is not translations but analyses of the surveys of the several counties' (p. viii). To this most true remark we owe it that Mr Airy resolved to give us a 'digest' instead of that usual 'extension and translation', which is perfectly useless to the Domesday student.[3]

Round used Airy's analysis to demonstrate the prevalence of the five-hide unit in Bedfordshire.[4] Airy was followed by F. W. Ragg, who tried to reconstruct the original order of the vills in each hundred. Ragg's tabulation of the Bedfordshire assessments was used by F. H. Baring in his *Domesday Tables*;[5] Baring did not tabulate anew the 'teamlands, teams, values and men of each vill' but referred his readers to Airy's analysis.[6] But the most interesting of these earlier analyses is that by

---

[1] C.C., 'On the ancient division of counties into hundreds', *Gentleman's Magazine*, XCVIII, Pt. 2 (London, 1828), pp. 99–102.

[2] W. Airy, *A Digest of the Domesday of Bedfordshire, being an analysis of that portion of the Domesday Survey which relates to the county of Bedford, and a key to the facsimile edition of the same published by Government.* Edited by his son, the Rev. B. R. Airy (Bedford, 1881).

[3] J. H. Round, *Feudal England* (London, 1895; reprinted 1909), p. 55, quoting from W. Airy, *op. cit.* p. viii.

[4] J. H. Round, *op. cit.* pp. 55–7; see also *V.C.H. Bedfordshire*, I (London, 1904), pp. 191–3.

[5] F. H. Baring, *Domesday Tables for the counties of Surrey, Berkshire, Middlesex, Hertford, Buckingham and Bedford and for the New Forest, with an appendix on the Battle of Hastings* (London, 1909), pp. 172–91.

[6] *Ibid.* p. 173.

G. H. Fowler, who assembled the entries anew, 'reconstituting every vill and hundred as far as possible'.[1] He arranged the information given for each holding in a set of tables, the value of which cannot be overestimated. His analysis was accompanied by a set of nine maps on a scale of 2 miles to the inch; these maps are a most interesting experiment and are the more valuable because he wrote the accompanying text with an eye on the physical features of the county. Fowler's work marked a distinct advance in Domesday analysis, and his maps, although not above criticism, will always remain a most interesting pioneer achievement. He was very conscious of the many difficulties which one encounters in analysing the Domesday folios:

It is [he wrote] probably humanly impossible, in such detailed work as these Tables and the subsequent computations, for a single-handed student to escape error. The mere copying and rearrangement is difficult enough to achieve with any accuracy; as the greatest living Domesday Scholar complains 'No one who has not analysed and collated such texts for himself can realise the extreme difficulty of avoiding occasional error. The abbreviations and the formulæ employed in these surveys are so many pitfalls for the transcriber, and the use of Roman numerals is almost fatal to accuracy.'[2]

The Domesday county of Bedford corresponds more or less to the modern county, but there are some important differences. In the north-west, five places—Farndish (216, 216b, 225b), Podington (215b, 216, 225b), Newton Bromswold (210, 220b), Rushden (210, 212b, 225b), and Stanwick (210b, 221b)—were surveyed partly under Bedfordshire and partly under Northamptonshire; only Farndish and Podington are now in Bedfordshire. There was a similar intermingling along the Huntingdon-shire border; there, the Domesday village of Keysoe, consisting of four holdings, was described partly under Bedfordshire (212b, 216b) and partly under Huntingdonshire (205b, 207b), but the second of the Huntingdonshire entries tells us that a holding of one virgate 'lay in Bedfordshire but paid geld in Huntingdonshire' (*Jacet in bedefordscira sed geldum dat in huntedscire*). The Bedfordshire village of Pertenhall was surveyed under Huntingdonshire (203b, 208) because it rendered geld and service there; the first entry notes: *Haec terra sita est in Bedefordescire sed*

---

[1] G. H. Fowler, *Bedfordshire in 1086: An analysis and synthesis of Domesday Book* (Quarto Memoirs of the Bedfordshire Historical Record Society, Aspley Guise, 1922).
[2] *Ibid.* p. 4, quoting from J. H. Round, *Feudal England*, p. 20.

geldum et servitium reddit in hontedunescyre (203 b).[1] In 1086 Everton seems to have straddled the boundary between the two counties (207, 217 b), and only the second holding has been reckoned in Bedfordshire. Of the unidentified *Hanefelde* (211 b), rubricated under Stodden hundred in the

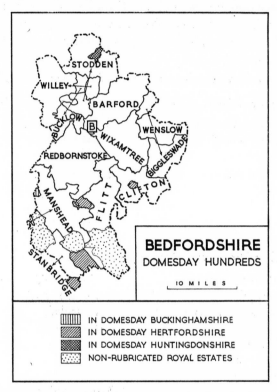

Fig. 2. Bedfordshire: Domesday hundreds.

B indicates the Domesday borough of Bedford, assessed at half a hundred. Those royal estates, unrubricated in the Domesday Book, are shown as part of the respective hundreds in which they later appeared (see p. 6).

Bedfordshire folios, we are told that it 'lay always in Kimbolton' (in Huntingdonshire) but by right was always assessed in Bedfordshire (*jacuit semper in Chenebaltone, sed Warram dedit semper iuste in Bedefordscira*); in the present analysis *Hanefelde* has been assumed to be a lost place

---

[1] Both entries refer to the same holding at Pertenhall; the second tells us only that 'King Edward had the soke' (*habebat rex Edwardus socam*).

in Bedfordshire.[1] One-sixth of a hide belonging to Easton, a berewick of Spaldwick in Huntingdonshire, was recorded as paying geld in Bedfordshire (208).[2] Swineshead, transferred to Bedfordshire as recently as 1888, was naturally surveyed under Huntingdonshire (205b, 206, 208), while Tilbrook, which only became a part of Huntingdonshire in that year, was entered under Bedfordshire (211b). In the west, the eleventh-century settlement of Edlesborough straddled the border between Bedfordshire

The Domesday County and the Modern County of Bedford

A. *Transferred from Domesday Bedfordshire to Modern Counties*

To Buckinghamshire
 Edlesborough (part)

To Hertfordshire
 Holwell

To Huntingdonshire
 Easton (part)
 Tilbrook

To Northamptonshire
 Newton Bromswold (part)
 Rushden (part)
 Stanwick (part)

B. *Transferred from Other Domesday Counties to Modern Bedfordshire*

From Hertfordshire
 Barwythe
 Caddington (part)
 Kensworth
 Meppershall (part)
 Polehanger
 Westoning

From Huntingdonshire
 Keysoe (part)
 Pertenhall
 Swineshead

From Northamptonshire
 Farndish (part)
 Podington (part)

---

[1] W. Airy thought that this holding might have been in the neighbourhood of Honey Hill near the boundary between the modern parishes of Kimbolton and Pertenhall (*op. cit.* pp. 47–8). There was also another holding in *Hanefeld* (218b).

[2] Some confusion has arisen about Easton (*Estone*). There are a number of other entries in the Bedfordshire folios relating to an *Estone* (210 *bis*, 211b *quater*, 213, 216 *bis*, 216b), and Round suggested that these referred to the Huntingdonshire village—see (1) J. H. Round in *V.C.H. Bedfordshire*, I, p. 215; (2) F. M. Stenton in *V.C.H. Huntingdonshire*, I, p. 322. But 'there is no doubt that "Estone", Beds., was Little Staughton' in Bedfordshire; see Ada Russell in *V.C.H. Huntingdonshire*, III (London, 1936), p. 42.

and Buckinghamshire (149b, 215), but the village now lies wholly in that county. In the south, six Bedfordshire villages were surveyed partly or wholly under Hertfordshire—Barwythe (138), Caddington (136, 211),[1] Kensworth (136),[2] Meppershall (142, 216b),[3] Polehanger (137b) and Westoning (132b).[4] Holwell (210b, 211) was transferred to Hertfordshire

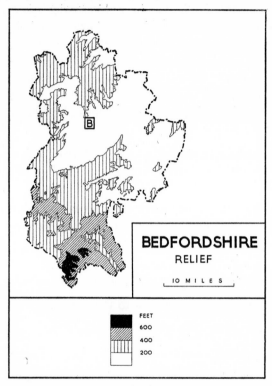

Fig. 3. Bedfordshire: Relief.

B indicates the Domesday borough of Bedford.

[1] Caddington became wholly part of Bedfordshire in 1888.
[2] Transferred to Bedfordshire in 1888.
[3] The Bedfordshire entry for Meppershall (216b) notes: *pro iiii hidis se defendit in Bedefordescire. Terra est iiii carucis. In Herefortscire ipsa villa se defendit pro iii hidis et una virgata. Terra est iii carucis.* The Hertfordshire entry (142) states: *Haec terra est appreciata in Bedefordscyre cum alia terra.*
[4] The entry for Westoning concludes with the statement: *Hoc manerium tenuit Heraldus comes et jacuit et jacet in Hiz* (i.e. Hitchin in Hertfordshire). *Sed Wara huius manerii jacuit in Bedefordscire T.R.E. in hundredo de Maneheue* (i.e. Manshead) *et ibi est Manerium et fuit semper, et post mortem R.E. non se adquietavit de gildo regis.*

as late as 1894. Thus, while some of these changes reflect ancient fiscal or tenurial arrangements, others are due to relatively recent adjustments of the county boundary. They are summarised in the table on p. 4.

Within the Domesday county there were nine hundreds and three half-hundreds.[1] In addition there were the borough of Bedford (209), assessed as a half-hundred 'for the host and for ship service' (in expeditione et in navibus)[2] and the royal demesne, assessed at 95 hides in 1086.[3] Thus it seems, as F. W. Ragg suggested, that Domesday Bedfordshire comprised the equivalent of twelve hundreds.[4] Fig. 2 shows one attempt to reconstruct the Domesday hundreds of the county. We hear incidentally of a pre-Domesday hundred, the mysterious Odecroft, which is mentioned only once in the Bedfordshire folios;[5] at the end of the entry for Sewell we read:

> In Odecroft hundredo jacuit T.R.E. Radulfus taillebosc in manerio houstone (i.e. Houghton Regis) eam apposuit concedente Willielmus rege per crementum quod ei dedit (209 b).

In a similar manner, Biscot had been taken out of Flitt hundred and placed in Luton, a royal manor without hundredal rubrication:

> Hanc apposuit Radulfus talliebosc in Loitone manerio regis per crementum quod ei dedit et foris misit de hundredo ubi se defendebat T.R.E. Et contra sumpsit alias v hidas de alio hundredo et posuit in Flictham hundredum (209 b).

Seventeen hides had also been added to Leighton Buzzard (209).

---

[1] The hundreds were: Barford, Biggleswade, Clifton, Flitt, Manshead, Redbornstoke, Stodden, Willey and Wixamtree. The half-hundreds were: Bucklow, Stanbridge and Wenslow.

[2] Bedford is not styled burgus but it is entered at the beginning of the Bedfordshire folios (209), and the burgesses of Bedford are noted as land-holders on folios 209 and 218.

[3] The 1086 assessment of the royal estates amounted to 95 hides—Biscot, 5 hides (209 b), Houghton Regis, 10 hides (209 b), Leighton Buzzard, 47 hides (209), Luton, 30 hides (209), and Sewell, 3 hides (209 b); only Biscot is rubricated under a hundred heading, and it is placed in Flitt hundred; see: (1) G. H. Fowler, op. cit. p. 55; (2) J. H. Round in V.C.H. Bedfordshire, I, p. 217.

[4] Noted by J. H. Round in V.C.H. Bedfordshire, I, p. 217. It is interesting to note that Maitland accepted that there were twelve Domesday hundreds, but he tells us that he took this figure from Stubbs; see F. W. Maitland, Domesday Book and Beyond (Cambridge, 1897), pp. 459 and 459, n. 2.

[5] G. H. Fowler suggested that the name may be represented today by Woodcroft manor in Luton (Bedfordshire in 1086, p. 56). See also V.C.H. Bedfordshire, II (London, 1908), p. 354; III (London, 1912), p. 391 n.

SETTLEMENTS AND THEIR DISTRIBUTION

The total number of separate places mentioned in the Domesday Book for the area included within the modern county of Bedford seems to be 145, including the borough of Bedford.[1] This figure, however, may not

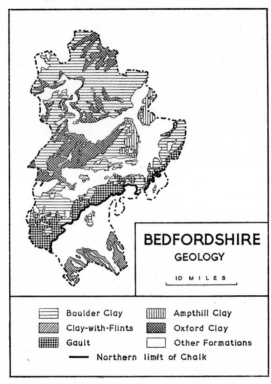

Fig. 4. Bedfordshire: Surface geology.

Based on (1) G. D. Nicholls, 'An introduction to the geology of Bedfordshire', *Bedfordshire Naturalist* (1947), no. 2, pp. 9–16 (Beds. Nat. Hist. Soc. and Field Club, Bedford, 1948); (2) Geological Survey One-Inch Sheets (New Series) 203 and 238, and Quarter-Inch Sheet 16.

accurately reflect the actual number of separate settlements in the county in 1086. In the first place, we cannot tell whether Upper Dean and Lower Dean, adjoining villages today, were distinctive units in the eleventh

[1] Bedford is not specifically styled *burgus*, but 'the burgesses of Bedford' are noted on fos. 209 and 218.

century;[1] their distinctive appellations are later in date.[2] The Deans may well have been separate settlements in 1086, but they have been counted as one in the present total of 145. On the other hand, Great Barford (213b *quater*) and Little Barford (210b, 216b) have been counted as separate places although their appellations are not recorded in the Bedfordshire folios; but they are not adjoining villages, and they were rubricated under different hundreds.[3] Then, again, it is possible that some of the large manors, e.g. Leighton Buzzard (209) and Luton (209), may have included more than one settlement apiece when the survey was made.

The total of 145 includes a few places regarding which very little information is given; the record may be incomplete, or the details may have been included with those of a neighbouring village. Thus Pertenhall (203b, 208) answered for 1 virgate (*i virgatam terrae ad geldam*),[4] had land for 1 plough-team, and was worth 5s. in 1086, as in 1066, but we are told nothing about its population or its other resources. The entry for Elvedon (216b) tells us that it was assessed at 1 hide and 1 virgate, that there were 1½ plough-lands which were being worked, that there was meadow for 1 plough-team and wood for 34 swine, and that its value, which had fallen from 15s. *T.R.E.* to 10s. *quando recepit*, had not recovered by 1086; but there is no mention of any people. Of Shirdon (216), which answered for 1 virgate, we know only that its value fell from 2s. in 1066 to 12d. in 1086. Then, again, we are told nothing at all about the resources or value of a holding of 1 virgate in Sudbury (216), save that it belonged to the

[1] There are four Domesday entries for *Dene* (209b, 210, 211b, 218b).

[2] Upper Dean was known as *Overdeane* in 1430 and Lower Dean as *Netherdeane* in 1539; the curious *Middeldene* of 1287 has not survived. For the history of these names, and of all other names mentioned in this chapter, see A. Mawer and F. M. Stenton, *The Place-Names of Bedfordshire and Huntingdonshire* (Cambridge, 1926).

[3] Cockayne Hatley is *Hatelai* in the Bedfordshire folios (217b, 218). There are two other villages nearby with the surname *Hatelai*, i.e. Hatley St George and East Hatley, but they are on the other side of the county boundary and were surveyed under Cambridgeshire in the Domesday Book; they are rubricated under different hundreds, so that separate settlements are presumably implied. But at one time the three parishes must have formed a single unit. Today the Domesday *Cravenhest* (213) is represented by Gravenhurst and its hamlet Little Gravenhurst, but Gravenhurst (*alias* Upper Gravenhurst) and Little Gravenhurst were separate parishes in 1888. The two Aspleys of today, Aspley Guise and Aspley Heath, represent the Domesday *Aspeleia* (213); Aspley Heath was constituted a civil parish only in 1885.

[4] The normal formula in the Huntingdonshire folios in which Pertenhall was surveyed.

church of St Neots.[1] No statement is made about the population of Gladley (217), yet its resources included 1 plough-land on which 4 oxen were at work, meadow for 1 plough-team, woodland for 100 swine, and a mill rendering 16s.

Not all the Domesday names appear on the present-day map of Bedfordshire villages. Some are represented by hamlets, others by individual farms or houses. Thus *Salchou* (213) is now the hamlet of Salph End in the parish of Renhold, and *Chauelestorne* or *Calnestorne* (212, 213b, 215 *bis*) is the hamlet of Chawston in Roxton. *Polehangre* (137b) is represented by Polehanger Farm in Meppershall, and *Putenehou* (212b) has given its name to Putnoe Farm in Goldington. *Segenehou* (i.e. Segenhoe, 216) survives in the name of a house in Ridgmont. The Domesday *Chenemondewiche* (210b) survived, until 1804, in the name of Kinwick Field in Sandy.[2] These are but some of the changes in the Bedfordshire villages. To them must be added two unidentified names, *Cudessane* (211b, 214)[3] and *Hanefelde* (211b, 218b). Whether these names will yet be identified or whether the places they represent have completely disappeared, leaving no record or trace behind, we cannot say.[4]

On the other hand, a few villages on the modern map of Bedfordshire are not mentioned in the Domesday Book. Their names do not appear until the twelfth or thirteenth century, and presumably, if they existed in 1086, they are accounted for under the statistics of neighbouring settlements. Thus the earliest record of Dunstable is from 1123, but, as W. Airy noted, its locality may well have been described in the Domesday entries for Houghton Regis (209b) and Sewell (209b), from which the parish of Dunstable was formed at a later date.[5] Souldrop dates only from 1196,[6] and

---

[1] It is possible that the unassigned holding of 2 hides and 3 virgates rubricated under Barford hundred on fo. 217b may refer to another holding in Sudbury; see J. H. Round in *V.C.H. Bedfordshire*, I, p. 258, n. 3.

[2] See (1) G. H. Fowler, 'Domesday Notes II—Kenemondwick', *Pubs. Beds. Hist. Rec. Soc.* v (Aspley Guise, 1920), pp. 61–73, especially p. 73; (2) E. Gibons and E. Arden, 'Map of the Parish of Sandy in the County of Bedfordshire'; a copy of this map accompanies the relevant Parliamentary Inclosure Award of 1804 [Bedfordshire Muniments, *MA 14*].

[3] See J. H. Round in *V.C.H. Bedfordshire*, I, p. 216.

[4] There are also six anonymous holdings entered in the Bedfordshire folios; they are rubricated under the hundreds of Barford (217b), Biggleswade (214b), Manshead (214), Stodden (218b) and Willey (210, 218b) respectively.

[5] W. Airy, *op. cit.* p. 45; see also J. H. Round in *V.C.H. Bedfordshire*, I, p. 194 n.

[6] Airy assigned an anonymous holding in Willey hundred (210) to Souldrop; see (1) W. Airy, *op. cit.* p. 45, and (2) J. H. Round in *V.C.H. Bedfordshire*, I, p. 225 n.

Wrestlingworth from about 1150, but G. H. Fowler showed that the resources of the latter were included in the account of Cockayne Hatley (217b).[1] Billington and Stanbridge in Manshead hundred date respectively from 1196 and 1165, and Chellington from 1242.[2] Whether or not some of the missing names refer to estates that were in fact in existence in 1086 we cannot say, but it is clear that others refer to settlements which were founded at a later date; most of the post-Domesday names are in the Chilterns.

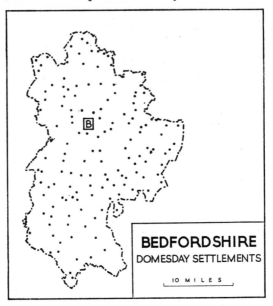

BEDFORDSHIRE
DOMESDAY SETTLEMENTS

10 MILES

Fig. 5. Bedfordshire: Domesday place-names.

B indicates the Domesday borough of Bedford.

The distribution of Domesday settlements is surprisingly even (Fig. 5). Villages were as frequent on the hills in the west as in the low-lying Vale of Bedford. But, in detail, three lines of villages stand out on the map; two follow the valleys of the rivers Ouse and Ivel, and the third is associated with the belt of loamy soils developed on the conspicuous level surface below the northward-facing scarp slope of the Chilterns. Villages in the Chilterns themselves were mainly in the valley of the Ver.

[1] G. H. Fowler, *Bedfordshire in 1086*, p. 58. But note that Wrestlingworth has not been included as a separate village in the present count of 145 settlements.

[2] J. H. Round thought that an unassigned holding in Willey hundred (210) might possibly relate to Chellington (*V.C.H. Bedfordshire*, I, p. 225, n. 4).

THE DISTRIBUTION OF PROSPERITY AND POPULATION

Some idea of the nature of the information in the Domesday folios for Bedfordshire, and of the form in which it was presented, may be obtained from the account of the village of Cockayne Hatley (*Hatelai*) in the half-hundred of Wenslow. Both the Countess Judith and Azelina, the widow of Ralf Taillebois, held land in Hatley, and so there are two separate entries:

Fo. 217b. Manor. In Hatley, Countess Judith holds 3 hides and 2½ virgates as 1 manor. There is land for 6½ plough-teams. In demesne [are] 1 hide and half a virgate, and there [are] 2 plough-teams. There, 8 villeins with 4½ plough-teams. There, 8 bordars and meadow for 2 plough-teams. Wood for 4 swine. It is worth £6. 5s. When received 100s. *T.R.E.* £6. This manor Earl Tostig held and it belongs to (*jacet in*) Potton, the countess's own (*proprio*) manor, and there a certain sokeman had 1 virgate. He could assign and sell [his land] and put himself under another lord (*ad alterum dominum recedere*).

Fo. 218. Manor. In Hatley, Azelina holds as her marriage portion (*de maritagio suo*) 5 hides and 1½ virgates. There is land for 8 plough-teams. In demesne 1 hide and 1 virgate, and there [are] 2 plough-teams. There, 8 villeins and 4 bordars with 6 plough-teams. There, 1 serf and 1 mill [rendering] 18s. Meadow for 2 plough-teams, wood for 4 swine, and 3s. from render (*de redditu iii solidi*). In all it is worth £6. When received 100s. *T.R.E.* £6. This manor Ulmar, a thegn of King Edward, held, and there were 2 sokemen, his men, there. They had 2½ virgates, and could assign and sell to whom they wished (*et cui voluerunt dare et vendere potuerunt*).

These entries do not include all the items of information that appear elsewhere in the Bedfordshire folios. There is no mention, for example, of pasture. But although not comprehensive, they are representative and straightforward, and they do contain the five recurring standard items that relate to a village as a whole: (1) hides, (2) plough-lands, (3) plough-teams, (4) population and (5) values. The bearing of these five items of information upon regional variations in prosperity must now be considered.

(1) *Hides*

The Bedfordshire assessment is stated in terms of hides and virgates and, very occasionally, of acres.[1] Fractions of both hides and virgates are

---

[1] In one of the four entries relating to Great Barford (213b), the scribe first wrote *iii car'* (i.e. 3 carucates) but corrected it to *iii hid* (i.e. 3 hides).

common; thus at Chalgrave there was one holding of a one-third (*terciam partem*) of a virgate (212) and another of 8 hides and two-thirds (*ii partibus*) of one virgate (216b). The form of the statement varies, as the following representative entries show:

Dean (210): *tenet in Dene ii hidas et dimidiam virgatam.*
Luton (209): *pro xxx hidis se defendit.*
Biddenham (210b): *habet in Bidenham dimidiam hidam.*

The first of these variations is the one most frequently used. In some entries the phrase 'of land' appears, e.g. at Stanford (212b) we are told that Hugh de Beauchamp held 1 hide and half a virgate of land (*i hidam et dimidiam virgatam terrae*).

Normally only the 1086 assessment is stated, but the figures may refer to 1066 as well. One entry, i.e. for a holding at Totternhoe (215b), tells of a reduction in assessment after the Norman invasion—*pro xv hidis se defendit T.R.E. Sed postquam rex Willielmus venit in Anglia; nunc se defendit nisi pro x hidis, et homines qui v hidas tenuerunt et tenent omnes consuetudines regis et gablum retinuerunt et retinent.*[1] For two royal estates, i.e. Biscot (209b) and Sewell (209b), we are given only the *T.R.E.* figure, presumably because Ralf Taillebois had since 'added' (*apposuit*) the former to Luton, and the latter to Houghton Regis. The entry for Leighton Buzzard (209) states assessments for both 1086 and 1066 (*pro xlvii hidis se defendit modo. T.R.E. non erant nisi xxx hidae*); that for Houghton Regis (209b) does not refer to any change in the composition of the estate, and notes only *pro x hidis se defendit.*

When an estate was held directly, and not by an under-tenant, the hidage of the portion in demesne (*in dominio*) was generally stated;[2] thus of Kinwick (210b), rated at 3 hides 3 virgates, we read: *In dominio i hida et iii virgatae et ibi sunt ii carucae.* Five entries mention what are called 'carucates' (*carucatae terrae*) in demesne; and in four of these, we are told specifically that the carucates were in addition to the hides of the assessment: Bolnhurst (*extra hidas,* 211), Chalgrave (216b), Clapham (*praeter*

---

[1] J. H. Round thought that this reduction should 'not be taken as an act of the authorities' (*V.C.H. Bedfordshire,* 1, p. 249, n. 5).

[2] This suggests an exemption from the payment of geld—see (1) J. H. Round, (i) 'Danegeld and the finance of Domesday' in P. E. Dove (ed.), *Domesday Studies,* 1 (London, 1888), pp. 96–8; and (ii) in *V.C.H. Bedfordshire,* 1, p. 229, n. 2; (2) F. W. Maitland, *Domesday Book and Beyond,* p. 55; (3) F. H. Baring, *Domesday Tables,* pp. 133–4.

hidas, 212) Little Staughton (*praeter hidas*, 216) and Toddington (*praeter hidas*, 212).[1]

The Bedfordshire folios record many examples of the five-hide unit: thus Wilden (209b) was assessed at 5 hides, Biggleswade (217) at 10 hides, Stotfold (213) at 15 hides, and Luton (209) at 30 hides. Even when a village was divided amongst a number of owners, the same feature can frequently be demonstrated. Wymington, for example, consisted of six holdings which together amounted to 10 hides:

William Spech (214b)	3 virgates
Alfred of Lincoln (215b)	3 hides
Walter the Fleming (215b)	4 hides
Walter the Fleming (215b)	half a hide
Five brothers with their mother (218b)	3 virgates
Turchil (218b)	1 hide

The number of settlements assessed in 1086 at either 5 or 10 hides amounts to 67 out of a total of 145;[2] there were two villages assessed at 15 hides each, two at 20 hides apiece, and one at 30 hides.[3] There were also three villages rated at 2½ hides each. In addition to these, there are many vills with a hidage that is not an exact multiple of 5. These too, did we but know all the complications, might well be examples of the five-hide unit. Dean, Streatley and Sutton are examples of such discrepancies:

Dean

			Hides	Virgates
(1)	*Fo.* 209b	Bishop of Coutances	4	0
(2)	*Fo.* 210	Bishop of Lincoln	2	0½
(3)	*Fo.* 211b	William de Warenne	2	0
(4)	*Fo.* 218b	Eleven sokemen	0	7¼
(5)	*Fo.* 218b	Goduin Dere of Bedford	0	0½
		Total	10	0¼

---

[1] G. H. Fowler has discussed the relationship between carucates in demesne, plough-lands and plough-teams—*Bedfordshire in 1086*, p. 60. For the possibility that these 'carucates' may have been plough-lands, see p. 148 below.

[2] The borough of Bedford was assessed at a half-hundred *T.R.E.* and the same in 1086 'for the host and for ship service' (see p. 42 below).

[3] Leighton Buzzard (209) had been assessed at 30 hides *T.R.E.*, i.e. before Ralf Taillebois added estates to it; see p. 6 above.

Streatley

		Hides	Virgates
(1) *Fo.* 212	William of Eu	1	0
(2) *Fo.* 213	Hugh de Beauchamp	4	1
(3) *Fo.* 214b	Nigel of Albini	4½	0
(4) *Fo.* 214b	William Spech	0	0⅔
(5) *Fo.* 218b	A reeve	0	0⅔
	Total	9	3⅓

Sutton

		Hides	Virgates
(1) *Fo.* 212	Eudo the steward	0	3
(2) *Fo.* 217b	Countess Judith		
	(*a*) Torchil	1½	0
	(*b*) Alwin	1	0
	(*c*) Levegar	½	0
	(*d*) Robert		3½
	(*e*) Sueting and Robert		1½
	(*f*) Turbert	2	0
	(*g*) Goduin	0	3
	(*h*) Ederic	½	0
(3) *Fo.* 218b	Alwin	0	1½
	Alwin	1	0
	Total	9	2½[1]

But, as J. H. Round noted, we must allow for trivial slips on the part of the Norman scribes and 'for possible errors in the baffling work of identification at the present day'.[2] It is also possible that some villages were grouped in blocks for the purpose of assessment, as in Cambridgeshire[3] or Leicestershire.[4] But the absence of information about these groups makes it difficult to be definite about the full extent of the five-hide unit in Bedfordshire.[5] Only one of the Domesday hundreds amounted to an

[1] J. H. Round gave a total of 9 hides 0½ virgates for Sutton—see *Feudal England,* p. 57. But see also *V.C.H. Bedfordshire,* I, p. 192.

[2] *Feudal England,* p. 57.

[3] For the Cambridgeshire blocks, see H. C. Darby, *The Domesday Geography of Eastern England* (Cambridge, 2nd ed., 1957), p. 276.

[4] For the blocks of Leicestershire, see D. Holly in H. C. Darby and I. B. Terrett (eds.), *The Domesday Geography of Midland England* (Cambridge, 1954), p. 320.

[5] For some possible combinations see F. H. Baring, *op. cit.* p. 178.

exact multiple of 5 hides; this was Clifton with a total of 100 hides.[1] But the totals of the other hundreds deviate only slightly from a multiple of 5.[2]

Whatever the origin of this system of assessment, there is little doubt that in 1086 it was artificial and bore little, if any, relation to agricultural realities. We cannot say whether the assessment of a village was ever adjusted to its arable capacity, but it is clear that by 1086 any correspondence between assessment and agricultural resources had become distorted. The variation among a representative selection of five-hide vills speaks for itself:

	Plough-lands	Teams	Population
Clapham (212)	30	28	37
Colmworth (213b)	10	10	26
Flitton (215)	6	4	10
Haynes (213)	8	8	24
Salford (213)	5	5	17
Steppingley (214b)	7	7	16
Wilden (209b)	16	10	33

These villages, each consisting of only one holding, are assessed alike, but their plough-lands vary from 5 to 30 in number, and their teams from 4 to 28. The same feature is seen when the hundred totals are compared. In the Domesday hundred of Stodden, for example, the ratio of plough-lands to hides is 1½:1, but it is only 0·9:1 in Clifton hundred.[3]

The assessment of the county seems to have amounted to 1,197½ hides and 25 acres, but it must be remembered that this estimate refers to the area covered by the modern county,[4] and includes the assessment of the

---

[1] This total omits one holding in Meppershall assessed in Hertfordshire but valued in Bedfordshire; the Bedfordshire entry for Meppershall (216b) tells us that the vill comprised two holdings, one of 4 plough-lands assessed at 4 hides in Bedfordshire and another of 3 plough-lands assessed at 3 hides and 1 virgate in Hertfordshire; the Hertfordshire folios (142) tell of a holding of 3 hides and 1 virgate in Meppershall and notes 'This land is appraised in Bedfordshire with other land' (*Haec terra est appreciata in Bedefordscyre cum alia terra*).

[2] See the tables in F. H. Baring, *Domesday Tables*, pp. 176, 179.

[3] F. H. Baring, *ibid.* p. 179.

[4] Maitland estimated the number of hides in the Domesday county at 1,193 hides (*Domesday Book and Beyond*, p. 400); W. J. Corbett and F. H. Baring both counted 1,215 hides—see: (1) W. J. Corbett, 'The Tribal Hidage', *Trans. Roy. Hist. Soc.* N.S., XIV (London, 1900), p. 218; (2) F. H. Baring, *Domesday Tables*, p. 179. Baring's corrected total, which included the three estates gelding in Hertfordshire (i.e. Westoning, part of Meppershall and Polehanger), amounted to 1,223⅜ hides (*ibid.* p. 176). G. H. Fowler (*op. cit.* p. 37) gave three totals, but they are not comparable either with the totals of Maitland, Corbett and Baring or with the present count.

borough of Bedford; the borough (209) was assessed at half a hundred *T.R.E.* and remained at this figure in 1086 'for the host and for ship service' (*modo facit in expeditione et in navibus*).[1] The number of additional carucates in demesne would seem to have been 26.

(2) *Plough-lands*

Plough-lands are systematically entered for the Domesday villages of Bedfordshire. The formula employed is simply 'there is land for *n* plough-teams' (*terra est n carucis*). Occasionally when there was only a small amount of arable on a holding it was measured in terms of oxen; thus one holding at Stanford (218b) had land for 3 oxen (*terra iii bobus*); and another in the same village had land for half-an-ox (*terra est dimidio bovi*).[2] There is one entry, that for a holding at Odell (211), which omits the statement about plough-lands, but which tells of teams at work.[3] Where the number of teams on a holding was less than that of the plough-lands, there is usually a statement to the effect that additional teams 'might be' or 'could be' employed, either on the demesne or on the lands of the peasantry or on both. It says, in effect, that the land could carry more teams than were at work, and it indicates therefore the possibility of further cultivation. Here are some sample entries that illustrate the variety of phrasing:

Arlesey (210b): *Terra est viii carucis. In dominio sunt iii carucae et viii villani habent iiii carucas et quinta potest fieri.*

Crawley (214): *Terra est v carucis. In dominio ii carucae et iii carucae villanorum possunt fieri.*

Sewell (209b): *Terra est ii carucis. Ibi est i caruca et dimidia et adhuc dimidia potest fieri.*

Wilden (209b): *Terra est xvi carucis. In dominio nulla est modo et iii possunt fieri. Villani habent x carucas et adhuc iii possunt fieri.*

---

[1] The entry adds: 'The land of this vill was never hidated, nor is it now except for one hide which belonged to the church of St Paul in almoin *T.R.E.*, and now belongs of right' (*Terra de hac villa nunquam fuit hidata nec modo est praeter unam hidam quae jacuit in ecclesia S[ancti] Pauli in elemosina T.R.E. et modo jacet recte*).

[2] For the meaning of *dimidius bos* or *semibos*, see p. 20n. below.

[3] No plough-lands or teams are mentioned for the portion of Meppershall entered under Hertfordshire (142). The Bedfordshire entry (216b) reads: *pro iiii hidis se defendit in Bedefordescire. Terra est iiii carucis. In Herefortscire ipsa villa se defendit pro iii hidis et una virgata. Terra est iii carucis. Inter totum vii carucae sunt. In dominio v hidae et iii carucae et adhuc ii possunt fieri. Ibi v villani habent ii carucas.*

Woburn (211): *Terra est xxiiii carucis. Hugo de Bolebec tenet de eo. Ibi in dominio ii carucae et alia duae possunt esse. Ibi viii villani habent vi carucas et adhuc xiiii possunt fieri.*

The *potest fieri* formula, or one of its variants, is to be found in Domesday entries relating to 69 of the 145 settlements of Bedfordshire.[1]

There are a few entries which record the lack of plough-teams in another way. Thus one of the holdings at Wymington (218b) had land for 1 plough-team, but the entry goes on to say that the team itself was not there, *Terra est i carucae sed non est ibi.* But occasionally for the smaller holdings, the text leaves us to assume the absence of teams. It merely says, as for a holding at Beeston in Sandy (218b), 'There is land for half a plough-team' (*Terra est dimidiae carucae*), and it omits any mention of teams that were not there or that might be employed. Some entries, on the other hand, specifically tell us that the land was being worked; for example, the entry for a holding at Dean (211b) notes: *Terra est iii carucis et ibi sunt.*

The exact meaning of the plough-land statement is not clear. It may refer to conditions in 1066, and the discrepancy between plough-lands and plough-teams may indicate incomplete recovery after lean years when the land had been wasted or had gone out of cultivation.[2] In most of these entries, the value shows a reduction between 1066 and 1086, which would support this contention. But, on the other hand, on a few holdings the ploughs were fewer than the plough-lands, and yet the values had risen— which seems unlikely if the plough-land is taken as a measure of the arable of 1066. This was the situation on some holdings in the three villages of Langford, Sandy and Stratton:

	Plough-lands	Teams	Value 1066	Value 1086
Langford (215b)	16	13	£15	£15. 10s.
Sandy (212)	16	11	£10	£12
Stratton (217)	8	7	100s.	£12

But this is not conclusive evidence, because even when plough-lands and plough-teams number the same, the value fluctuates, being sometimes

[1] There is no statement about either plough-lands or plough-teams in the entry for Bedford itself (209).

[2] Only two entries in the Bedfordshire folios specifically mention waste (*vastata, devastata*); see p. 44 below.

DD

greater and sometimes less than in 1066. Whether the plough-land entry refers to conditions in 1066 or not, the fact of understocking remains. An estate deficient in teams was not being tilled up to capacity; the arable of 1086 was capable of extension.

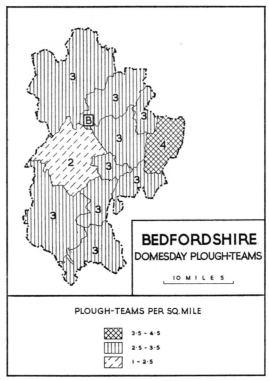

Fig. 6. Bedfordshire: Domesday plough-teams in 1086 (by densities).

B indicates the Domesday borough of Bedford.

On three estates the reverse was true; there were more plough-teams than plough-lands. One holding at Wyboston (212) had only 5 plough-lands but 6 teams, 2 on the demesne and 4 with the peasants. There was also an excess team on a holding at Astwick (213b), and another on a holding at Marston Moretaine (214). Perhaps these discrepancies are due to scribal errors but we cannot be certain. Occasionally it is the sum of the actual and potential teams that is in excess of the plough-lands. Thus at Harlington (214), an estate with only 10 plough-lands, 8½ teams were at work, and we are told that another 2 could be added.

The total number of plough-lands recorded for the area covered by the modern county is $1,605\frac{3}{16}$. If, however, we assume that plough-lands equalled teams on those holdings where a figure for the former is not given, the total becomes $1,609\frac{11}{16}$. With a similar assumption, Maitland's total for

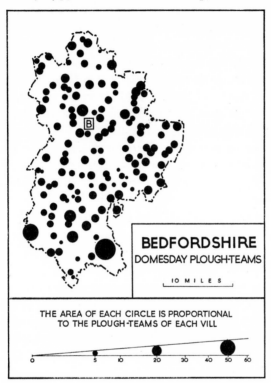

Fig. 7. Bedfordshire: Domesday plough-teams in 1086 (by settlements).

B indicates the Domesday borough of Bedford.

the Domesday county amounted to 1,557 plough-lands.[1] There have been two other estimates, but neither was for the area included within the modern county and so is not comparable with the present figures.[2]

[1] F. W. Maitland, *Domesday Book and Beyond*, pp. 401, 410.
[2] These were made by Baring and Fowler respectively. Baring's estimate of plough-lands only, based on Airy's analysis, was 1,579 (see F. H. Baring, *Domesday Tables*, p. 179). Fowler gave three totals for plough-lands, but his figures are not directly comparable with those of either Maitland or Baring, or with the present figures; see G. H. Fowler, *Bedfordshire in 1086*, p. 37.

(3) Plough-teams

The Bedfordshire entries for plough-teams, like those of other counties, usually draw a distinction between the teams on the demesne and those held by the peasantry. The latter are generally described as being held by so many villeins; thus at Edworth (212) we read: *In dominio iii carucae et viii villani habent v carucas. Ibi ii bordarii et v servi.* But an entry for Stondon reminds us that bordars also might have plough-teams: *Terra est ii carucis et dimidiae. In dominio ii carucae et iii bordarii cum dimidia caruca* (218). Small amounts of plough-land were, as we have noted above, measured in terms of oxen, and we hear also of oxen at work. There is one curious entry; on one holding at Stanford (218b) there was land for half an ox, and half an ox was there (*Terra est dimidio bovi et ibi est semibos*).[1]

For some holdings, the number of plough-teams at work is not stated, thus of Priestley (218) we read 'There is land for 1 plough-team' but we are not told whether the team was there. Similarly the entry for a holding at Milton Ernest (218b) tells of 'land for 2 oxen', but it does not go on to say whether there were any oxen at work. Such omissions illustrate the margin of error that must always be remembered when dealing with Domesday statistics. While the omissions are important for individual localities, they amount to only a minute fraction of all the teams recorded for the county. Taken as a whole, the record of teams provides a reasonable index of the arable land of the Bedfordshire villages in 1086.

The present analysis has yielded a total of $1,402\frac{3}{16}$ plough-teams for the modern county. Maitland's total for the Domesday county was 1,367 plough-teams.[2]

(4) Population

The bulk of the population was comprised in the three categories of villeins, bordars and serfs. In addition to these were the burgesses (see p. 42 below) together with a small miscellaneous group which included sokemen, cottars, knights and a solitary *francigena*.[3] The details of the

---

[1] The meaning of *semibos* is not certain. Maitland believed that it referred to the work done by a sixteenth of a plough-team (*op. cit.* p. 142). Alternatively it may have meant a heifer (J. H. Round in *V.C.H. Bedfordshire*, I, p. 264 n.).

[2] F. W. Maitland, *op. cit.* p. 401. G. H. Fowler (*op. cit.* p. 37) gave three totals but they are not comparable with either Maitland's figure or the present total.

[3] The *francigena* is recorded at Barwythe (138). The Bedfordshire folios also record 2 *francigenae* and 6 *angli* holding land at Riseley (210); but these, like other under-

groups are summarised below. There have been three other estimates
of population, by Ellis,[1] by Baring[2] and by Fowler[3] respectively, but they
are comparable neither with one another nor with the present estimate,
which has been made in terms of the modern county. Definite accuracy
rarely belongs to a count of Domesday population, and all that can be
claimed for the present figures is that they indicate the order of magnitude
involved. These figures are those of recorded population, and must be
multiplied by some factor, say 4 or 5, in order to obtain the actual
population; but this does not affect the relative density as between one
area and another.[4] That is all that a map, such as Fig. 9, can show.

Recorded Population of Bedfordshire in 1086

A. Rural Population

Villeins	1,888
Bordars	1,156
Serfs	480
Miscellaneous	101
Total	3,625

Details of Miscellaneous Rural Population

Sokemen . .	90	Priest	1
Cottars . .	6	Francigena	1
Knights (Milites)	2	A certain man (quidam) . .	1
		Total . . .	101

B. Urban Population

BEDFORD Unspecified number of burgesses (see p. 42 below).

It is impossible for us to say how complete were these Domesday
statistics, but it does seem as if some people were not enumerated. Thus
at two holdings in Blunham (212b, 217b) there were plough-teams and

---

tenants, have been excluded from the present count; similarly the 2 *francigenae* holding
land at Southill (215) have not been counted.

[1] Sir Henry Ellis, *A General Introduction to Domesday Book*, II (London, 1833),
p. 422. This estimate amounted to 3,875, but it included tenants-in-chief and under-
tenants, and moreover was in terms of the Domesday county.

[2] F. H. Baring, *op. cit.* p. 179. Baring's count, made from Airy's analysis, included
1,875 villeins (including sokemen), 1,153 bordars, and 479 serfs. These figures are also
for the Domesday county.

[3] G. H. Fowler, *op. cit.* p. 37.

[4] But see p. 589 below for the complication of serfs.

meadow, but apparently no men. At Wilden (209b) we are told that an unspecified number of villeins had 10 plough-teams (*Villani habent x carucas*), but only 20 sokemen, 12 bordars and 1 serf are enumerated; or, again, the entry for the bishop of Lincoln's estate at Dean (210) notes

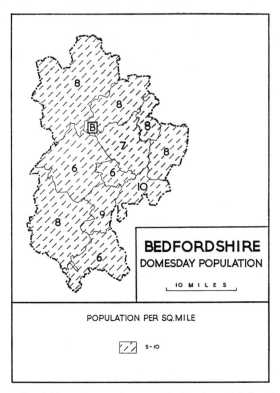

Fig. 8. Bedfordshire: Domesday population in 1086 (by densities).
B indicates the Domesday borough of Bedford.

that the villeins had 1½ teams (*villani habent i carucam et dimidiam*), but enumerates only 8 bordars and 2 serfs.[1] No statement at all is made about population in five of the eight entries for Cople (214 *quater*, 217b) or in one for Harrowden (211). It is impossible to be certain about the significance of these omissions, but they do suggest unrecorded inhabitants.

Villeins comprised the most important element in the population and

---

[1] The term *villani* may have covered the peasantry in general.

amounted to 52 per cent of the total. But, since the miscellaneous group in Bedfordshire is so limited, the category of villeins may well have included men who, in the folios for some other counties, are styled priests, Englishmen (*angli*) and *francigenae*.[1] Bordars amounted to about 32 per

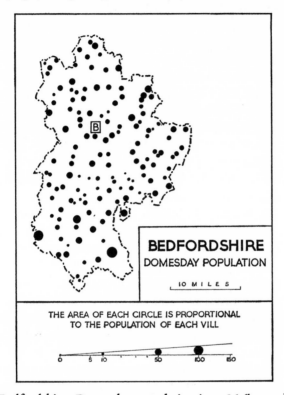

Fig. 9. Bedfordshire: Domesday population in 1086 (by settlements).

B indicates the Domesday borough of Bedford.

cent. No cottars are enumerated in the Bedfordshire folios, although they appear for Bedfordshire holdings surveyed in the Hertfordshire folios. The distinction between bordars and cottars is not clear, and it may be significant that 5 villeins, 4 bordars and 2 serfs are entered for the portion

---

[1] The entry for Shelton (210) is incomplete because it notes: *Ibi xiiii et v bordarii et iii servi*; these 14 unspecified men have been counted as villeins in the present analysis because an earlier statement in the entry tells of villeins having plough-teams (*In dominio ii carucae et villani habent iiii*).

of Meppershall surveyed under Bedfordshire (216b), and 3 villeins and 4 cottars for the portion recorded under Hertfordshire (142).[1] Some 13 per cent of the population were serfs, and G. H. Fowler showed that there was a close connection between serfs and demesne lands. He found that in the first 150 entries following the account of the royal estates, 246 serfs were recorded, and all but 20 of these were on holdings with demesne teams; moreover, most of the 20 could also have served their lord on adjacent holdings.[2]

The largest and most interesting element in the miscellaneous category is that of sokemen, and a number of entries tell us how many there were in 1066 as well as in 1086. It is not possible to be precise about the totals at the earlier date because we cannot always be sure whether a sokeman recorded on a holding in 1086 had also been there in 1066. With this reservation, the sokemen of 1066, specifically described as such, amounted to between 600 and 700, but twenty years later they numbered only 90.[3] The reduction in the free peasantry may have been even greater than this contrast implies, because the thegns on many Bedfordshire holdings in 1066 seem to have been more akin to sokemen than to the thegns of other counties.[4] They are enumerated in small groups, e.g. the 4 thegns at Wyboston (212)[5] and the 9 at Husborne Crawley (214). Altogether there had been upwards of 100 thegns in the county in 1066, but none appears for 1086.

Among the smaller groups in the miscellaneous category there were the 6 cottars, entered for holdings surveyed under Hertfordshire, and 2 priests (*presbyteri*); priests are not entered in the Bedfordshire folios and only 3 churches (see p. 41), but a priest is noted at Barwythe described in the Hertfordshire folios (138). Only 2 knights (*milites*) are entered, one at Sundon (211b) and the other at Yelden (210).[6] The one *francigena* (i.e.

---

[1] For a discussion of the differences between bordars and cottars, see (1) F. W. Maitland, *Domesday Book and Beyond*, pp. 39 *et seq.*; (2) P. Vinogradoff, *English Society in the Eleventh Century* (Oxford, 1908), pp. 456 *et seq.*

[2] G. H. Fowler, *op. cit.* p. 76.

[3] Sir Henry Ellis (*op. cit.* p. 422) estimated the 1086 sokemen at 107; but his count was for the Domesday county and is, therefore, not comparable with the present total. For a similar reduction in the number of sokemen in the adjoining county of Cambridge, see H. C. Darby, *The Domesday Geography of Eastern England*, p. 290.

[4] See below, pp. 157 and 595.

[5] Another holding at Wyboston was held *T.R.E.* by 12 sokemen (214b).

[6] Knights holding land as under-tenants, e.g. at Edworth (212) and Oakley (215), have been excluded from the present count.

foreigner or Frenchman) was at Barwythe (138), and a 'certain man' had a plough-team (*Ibi quidam i carucam habet*) at Streatley (214b).

(5) *Values*

The value of an estate is normally given in a round number of pounds or shillings for three dates—1066, 1086 and an intermediate date when an estate changed hands. Occasionally the formula *valet et valuit semper* occurs, e.g. in the entry for a holding at Great Barford (213b), and it has been taken as giving information for all three dates. But when the word *semper* is omitted, the statement is assumed to refer to conditions in 1086 and 1066 respectively, as in the entry for an estate at Goldington (210). There are a few entries in which only one value is given, e.g. Broom (214) and a holding at Stondon (210b). No value was entered for a holding of 1 virgate at Sudbury (216). Westoning (132b), surveyed in the Hertford-shire folios, was not separately valued, but may have been appraised with Hitchin.[1] Similarly a holding at Riseley (212b), described as a berewick of Keysoe, was presumably valued with its parent estate. We are specifi-cally told that a holding at Warden (217) was valued with its parent— *Haec terra jacet in Bichelesuuade* (i.e. Biggleswade) *et ibi est appreciata*.

The values are usually entered as plain statements of money, but the entries for three royal estates, Leighton Buzzard (209), Luton (209) and Houghton Regis (209b), indicate considerable differences in the method of reckoning. In view of the circulation of debased coins, some values were reckoned by weight (*ad pensum*), and were also tested by assay; the latter was known as 'white' money. There was another complication. On these three royal estates, the valuation was made partly in kind, that is in produce and entertainment. Their respective entries tell also of archaic renders that had been commuted into money payments. These interesting entries are best set out in full:

Leighton Buzzard (209): In all it renders yearly £22 by weight, and the expense of half a day's [provision] for the king (*dimidiam diem ad firmam regis*) in grain and honey and other things pertaining to the feorm (*in frumento et melle at aliis rebus ad firmam pertinentibus*). For the use of the queen (*Ad opus reginae*) 2 ounces of gold; and for 1 packhorse (*summario*) and for customary payment for the dogs (*consuetudine canum*) 70s. and 100s.

[1] See p. 5 n. above.

by weight and 40s. of white silver (*de albo argento*). This Ivo Taillebois imposed in addition; and 1 ounce of gold for the use of the sheriff yearly.

Luton (209): In all it renders yearly £30 by weight, and half a day's [provision] in grain and honey and for other customary dues (*aliis consuetudinibus*) pertaining to the king's feorm (*ad firmam regis pertinentibus*). For the queen 4 ounces of gold; and for a packhorse and other small dues (*aliis consuetudinibus minutis*) 70s.; and for customary payment for the dogs £6. 10s.; and for the additional payment which Ivo Taillebois imposed £7 by weight and 40s. of white silver (*albi argenti*); and 1 ounce of gold for the sheriff.

Houghton Regis (209b): In all it renders yearly £10 by weight, and half a day's [provision] in grain, honey, and for other things (*aliis rebus*) pertaining to the king's feorm. For small dues and for 1 packhorse 65s.; and for the customary payment for the dogs 65s.; and for the queen 2 ounces of gold. For the additional payment which Ivo Taillebois imposed £3 by weight and 20s. of white silver (*de albo argento*); and 1 ounce of gold for the sheriff.

All these complications make it difficult to compare the values of some manors with one another.

An outstanding feature of the Bedfordshire valuation is the decrease in the 'value' of many holdings in the years after 1066. The values of a large number were only some 25 per cent to 50 per cent of what they had been, and a few holdings had suffered even more (Figs. 161–2). F. H. Baring[1] and G. H. Fowler[2] both attributed the falls in values at the intermediate date to the passage of the Norman armies. Fowler mapped the percentage decrease for each vill[3] and drew lines round those places in the centre and south of the county with an intermediate value of 55 per cent or less. His map (redrawn here as Fig. 10) suggests that the royal estates and the borough of Bedford were the chief objectives of the Norman forces.[4] The

---

[1] F. H. Baring, *op. cit.* pp. 210–11. See also p. 569 below.

[2] G. H. Fowler, *op. cit.* p. 79.

[3] Baring seems to have based his conclusions on the values of the main estates only, but Fowler (*op. cit.* p. 79) summed the values of every holding in a vill and calculated the percentage changes in value.

[4] Subsequently Fowler tested his conclusions for Bedfordshire against the evidence furnished by the Domesday folios for neighbouring counties; see G. H. Fowler, 'The devastation of Bedfordshire and the neighbouring counties in 1065 and 1066', *Archaeologia*, LXXII (London, 1922), pp. 41–50, especially Map 2. It should be noted that Fowler did not contend that every reduction to half-value was necessarily due to

majority of the holdings had recovered in part or fully by 1086, and a few were even more prosperous than before. But the value of some, e.g. a holding at Felmersham (216b), remained constant between 1066 and c. 1070, only to fall appreciably by 1086. One holding at Beeston (216b)

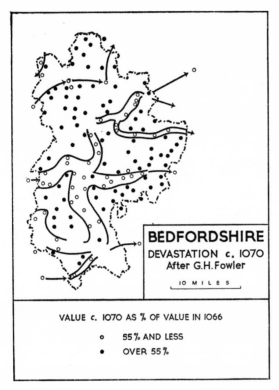

BEDFORDSHIRE
DEVASTATION c. 1070
After G.H.Fowler
10 MILES

VALUE c. 1070 AS % OF VALUE IN 1066

o 55% AND LESS

• OVER 55%

Fig. 10. Bedfordshire: Devastation c. 1070 (after G. H. Fowler).

This map is redrawn from Map viii in G. H. Fowler, *Bedfordshire in 1086: An analysis and synthesis of Domesday Book* (Quarto Memoirs of the Bedfordshire Historical Record Society, Aspley Guise, 1922).

was wasted (*devastata est*) and unvalued in 1086, but it had been worth 10s. at the intermediate date and as much as 20s. in 1066. On the other hand, a 'wasted' holding at Wyboston was nevertheless worth 16d.— *Vastata est tamen xvi denarios valet* (210b).

William's armies: 'fire, or murrain, or in the north of the county Morkere's raid from Northampton to Oxford in 1065, may have accounted for outlying cases' (*Bedfordshire in 1086*, p. 79).

Generally speaking, the greater the number of plough-teams and men on an estate, the higher its value, but it is impossible to discern any

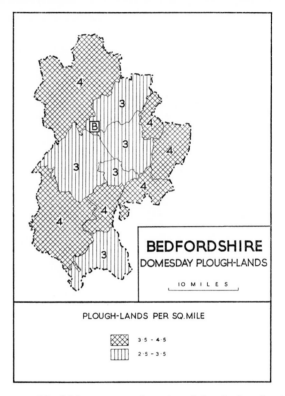

Fig. 11. Bedfordshire: Domesday plough-lands (by densities).

B indicates the Domesday borough of Bedford.

constant relationships as the following figures for six holdings, each yielding 60s. in 1086, show:

	Teams	Population	Other resources
Clophill (214)	8	11	Meadow, Wood
Flitton (215)	4	11	Meadow, Wood
Everton (217b)	2	9	Meadow
Gravenhurst (213)	3	11	Meadow, Wood
Holcot (214b)	3	14	Mill, Wood
Kinwick (210b)	4	6	Meadow, Mill

It is true that the variations in the arable, as between one estate and another, did not necessarily reflect variations in total resources, but even taking the other resources into account the figures are not easy to explain.

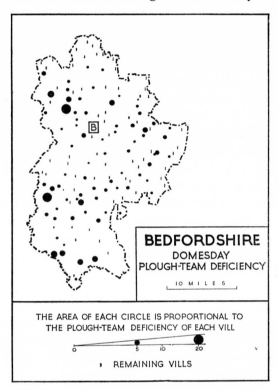

Fig. 12. Bedfordshire: Domesday plough-team deficiency (by settlements).

B indicates the Domesday borough of Bedford.

Conclusion

The Domesday hundreds of the county have been adopted as the main basis for constructing the density maps, but some modifications have been made. Thus in the north, the three interlocking hundreds of Bucklow, Stodden and Willey have been combined to form one unit, and in the south-west the hundreds of Manshead and Stanbridge have been grouped with a part of the royal demesne to form another unit.

The eleven units thus formed provide a rough and ready basis for distinguishing variations over the face of the county. This does not enable us to arrive at as perfect a regional division as a geographer would like, but we must be content with its limitations, bearing in mind the difficulties inherent in constructing any density maps from Domesday statistics.

Of the five standard formulae, those relating to plough-teams and population are the most likely to reflect something of the distribution of wealth and prosperity throughout the county in 1086. Taken together, they supplement one another; and when the distributions of plough-teams and population are compared, certain common features stand out. The most prominent is the general uniformity of both teams and men throughout the county (Figs. 6 and 8). Plough-team densities ranged from 2·3 to 3·9 per square mile, and those of population from 5·6 to 9·7 per square mile. These figures agree in general with those of the adjoining parts of the neighbouring counties, but they do not reflect the physical contrasts within the county. The land seems to have been fairly uniformly ploughed throughout in 1086. Figs. 7 and 9 are supplementary to the density maps; but, as we have seen, it may be that a few symbols should appear as two or more smaller symbols because some Domesday names may have covered two or more separate settlements, e.g. Upper and Lower Dean.[1] Fig. 11, showing the distribution of plough-lands, confirms in a general way the other two. Comparison of the plough-land and plough-team maps shows that the land of some hundreds was not being tilled up to capacity. Fig. 12 shows that in general the villages with the greatest deficiency of teams were on the uplands of Chalk and of Lower Greensand respectively (Fig. 4), but any attempt at a detailed correlation with relief or soil breaks down.

WOODLAND

Types of entries

The amount of woodland on a holding was normally indicated by the number of swine which it could support, and the usual formula was 'wood for *n* swine' (*silva n porcis*). The number ranged from under 5 to over 2,000. The largest amount recorded under a single name was enough for 2,050 swine at Luton, made up of two holdings with 2,000 and 50 swine respectively (209): the smallest amount was enough for only 2 swine at Polehanger (137b). The round figures of some of the larger entries (e.g. 400, 500, 600, 1,000 and 2,000) suggest that they were estimates rather than precise

[1] See p. 7 above.

amounts, but, on the other hand, the very detailed figures of a few entries suggest an attempt at exactness (e.g. 2, 4, 6, 12, 16 and 34). It does not necessarily follow that these figures indicate the actual number of swine grazing in a wood; the swine were used merely as units of measurement. A slight variation of the normal formula occurs in the entry for Cople, which runs: *Silva est super totam Chochepol c porcis* (213b).

While swine formed the normal unit of woodland measurement in Bedfordshire, there are a few entries which describe its value in other ways, sometimes by stating renders in kind—renders of rams, of a load of oats, and of iron for plough-shares.

Cranfield (210b): *Silva mille porcis et ferrum carucis.*
Harlington (214): *Silva cccc porcis et i aries et i summa avenae de silva.*
Segenhoe (216): *Silva ccc porcis et de consuetudine. silvae x arietes per annum.*
Westcote near Wilshamstead (214): *Silva c porcis et ferrum carucis.*

The more usual method of paying rent for woodland in 1086 was by a money render, and 13 villages in the county made a money payment in addition to providing pannage for swine:

Caddington (136): *Silva c porcis et ii solidi.*
Cainhoe (214): *Silva c porcis et ii solidi.*
Clapham (212): *Silva cc porcis et vi denarii.*
Clophill (214): *Silva cc porcis et xii denarii.*
Cockayne Hatley (218): *Silva iii porcis et de reddita iii solidi.*
Eaton Bray (209b): *Silva ccc porcis et xii denarii inde.*
Kensworth (136): *Silva c porcis et de reddita silvae ii solidi.*
Luton (209): *Silva ii miliū (sic) porcorum et de consuetudine x solidi et viii denarii.*
Meppershall (216b): *Silva cc porcis et de consuetudine silvae x solidi.*
Salford (213): *Silva cl porcis et de alia consuetudine x solidi.*
Silsoe (216): *Silva c porcis et ii solidi.*
Stanford (212b): *Silva lx porcis et ii solidi.*
Westoning (132b): *Silva cccc porcis et iii solidi.*

The woodland of one Bedfordshire village, recorded in the Huntingdonshire folios, was given in terms of acres:

Keysoe (205b):[1] *v acrae silvae pastilis* (i.e. pasturable woodland).

[1] The other holdings in Keysoe were surveyed under Bedfordshire (212b, 216b); one of these had 'wood for 200 swine' (212b), but the other had none entered in the Domesday Book (216b).

The woodland at Swineshead, also described in the folios for Huntingdon-shire, was expressed in terms of linear measurements, the normal method of measuring wood in that county:

(205 b): *Silva pastilis i leuga longa et iiii quarentenis lata.*
(206): *Silva pastilis i leuga longa et i quarentena lata.*

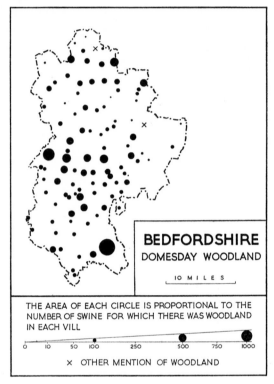

BEDFORDSHIRE
DOMESDAY WOODLAND

10 MILES

THE AREA OF EACH CIRCLE IS PROPORTIONAL TO THE
NUMBER OF SWINE FOR WHICH THERE WAS WOODLAND
IN EACH VILL

0   10   50   100   250   500   750   1000

× OTHER MENTION OF WOODLAND

Fig. 13. Bedfordshire: Domesday woodland in 1086.

Where the woodland of a village is entered partly in terms of swine
and partly in some other way, only the swine total is shown.

One further exceptional method of measuring wood must be noted; the two entries for Southill each tell of half a hide of wood (*dimidiam hidam silvae*, 215 b, 216).

Claims for woodland which had been seized unlawfully are set out in entries relating to Houghton Conquest, Sandy and Little Staughton. At Houghton Conquest (217b) half a virgate and 30 acres of woodland and arable (*dimidiam virgatam et xxx acras inter silvam et planum*) were in dispute. Another claim of 3 acres of woodland (*iii acras silvae*) is set out in the entry for Sandy (212). In the entries relating to Little Staughton claims for 20 acres of woodland (*xx acras silvae*) and 60 acres of arable and woodland (*lx acras inter planum et silvam*) are noted (210 *bis*). The entry for Sandy and the first of the entries for Little Staughton do not mention wood among the other resources of their holdings. Finally there was a park for the beasts of the chase (*parchus ferarum silvaticarum*) at Stagsden (212b).[1]

It is not possible to tell how complete was the Domesday record of wood in the county. Very little is entered for estates rubricated under Biggleswade and Wenslow hundreds respectively.[2] Indeed, only two of the twelve villages in Biggleswade had any recorded—Dunton with enough for 60 swine (216) and Langford for 16 swine (215b). In Wenslow hundred only Hatley had any recorded—wood for 8 swine and 3s. from rent (217b, 218); but, as we have seen, the entry for Sandy mentions a claim for 3 acres of wood (212). It is interesting that, although wood is not recorded for the holding in Everton rubricated under Wenslow hundred (217b), 40 acres of underwood are entered for the adjoining Huntingdonshire village of Everton, described in the folios for that county (207). Perhaps the Bedfordshire clerks recorded woodland only when it provided pannage for swine.

Distribution of woodland

When the returns are plotted on a map (Fig. 13) the county appears to have been but very slightly wooded in comparison with the adjoining counties of Buckinghamshire and Hertfordshire. There was a belt of fairly heavily wooded country across the centre of the county. In the south-east the large swine total entered under Luton (209) suggests that the Chilterns also supported a large amount of woodland in 1086. On the other hand, there seem to have been only small amounts in the Ouse valley below Bedford and the lower reaches of the Ivel valley.

Fig. 13 may be compared with a map of Domesday woodland published by G. H. Fowler in 1922.[3] Fowler attempted to convert the Domesday

---

[1] Three of the holdings at Stagsden had woodland for a total of 180 swine (209b, 212b, 217), but none is recorded for the fourth holding (211).

[2] For a table of the swine totals of the Domesday hundreds, see F. H. Baring, *Domesday Tables*, p. 177.   [3] G. H. Fowler, *Bedfordshire in 1086*, Map VI.

swine totals into modern acres and so obtain a quantitative estimate of the
wood cover in 1086. He converted the swine totals to statute acres on the
assumption that $1\frac{1}{2}$ statute acres of woodland were required to support a
Domesday pig.[1] He then expressed these acreages as percentages of the
total areas of the modern parishes, and drew a map, grouping the percentages by a system of graduated tints. He himself was very careful to

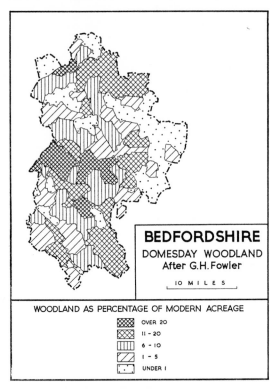

Fig. 14. Bedfordshire: Domesday woodland in 1086
(after G. H. Fowler).

This map is redrawn from Map vi in G. H. Fowler, *Bedfordshire in 1086: An analysis
and synthesis of Domesday Book* (Quarto Memoirs of the Bedfordshire Historical
Record Society, Aspley Guise, 1922). The percentages were calculated on the assumption that $1\frac{1}{2}$ statute acres of woodland were required to support a Domesday pig.

point out the 'difficulties and dangers of the method',[2] and it certainly
raises many problems. But, as an early attempt at mapping Domesday

---

[1] G. H. Fowler, *Bedfordshire in 1086*, pp. 62–3.   [2] *Ibid.* p. 107.

data, Fowler's map is a most interesting experiment. In general Figs. 13 and 14 confirm each other.

Types of entries

The Domesday meadow of Bedfordshire was measured in terms of plough-teams, i.e. by stating the number of teams of 8 oxen the meadow

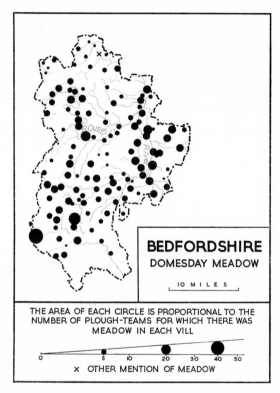

Fig. 15. Bedfordshire: Domesday meadow in 1086.

Where the meadow of a village is entered partly in terms of plough-teams and partly in some other way, only the plough-team total is shown.

was capable of feeding. The usual formula was *pratum n carucis* or *pratum n bobus*. The amount of meadow recorded ranged from enough for only 2 oxen on a holding at Henlow (218)[1] to sufficient for as many as 43 teams

[1] There were four other holdings at Henlow (214b, 215b, 218 *bis*) with meadow for a total of 11½ teams.

at Leighton Buzzard (209). The amount of meadow was always equal to or less than the number of plough-teams at work. Profits from the meadow were noted for three villages:

Biggleswade (217): *pratum x carucis et v solidi de feno.*
Langford (215 b): *pratum xvi carucis et ii solidi desuper plus.*
Sutton (217b): *Pratum i carucae et dimidiae et xvi denarii.*
Sutton (217b): *Pratum dimidiae carucae et xii denarii.*
Sutton (218b): *pratum ii carucis et xii denarii.*[1]

The meadow of the Bedfordshire estates surveyed under either Huntingdonshire or Northamptonshire was recorded in acres (*n acrae prati*), the customary unit of measurement in those counties.[2]

Distribution of meadowland

The distribution of meadow shown in Fig. 15 reflects fairly faithfully the surface geology (Fig. 4). Villages with the greatest amounts of meadow were in the Gault clay vale and along the banks of the rivers Ivel and Ouse respectively. The Vale of Bedford is drained by many streams, and both the Ivel and the Ouse are bordered by not inconsiderable tracts of alluvium. Villages with little or no meadow were in three main areas—on the upland in the extreme north-west of the county, on the ridge of high ground between Leighton Buzzard and Woburn, and in the Chilterns.

Fig. 15 may be compared with a map of Domesday meadow prepared by G. H. Fowler in 1922. Fowler attempted to convert the Domesday measurements into modern acres, and so obtain a quantitative estimate of the meadow in 1086.[3] In general his map (redrawn here as Fig. 16) agrees with Fig. 15, but his method raises many difficulties of which he himself was not unaware.

PASTURE

Pasture is not regularly mentioned in the Bedfordshire folios, in marked contrast to those for the adjoining counties of Cambridgeshire and Hertfordshire, in which the statement 'pasture for the livestock of the vill'

---

[1] Six other holdings at Sutton had between them enough meadow for 7¼ teams (212, 217b *quinquiens*) but none was recorded for two holdings in the village (217b, 218b).

[2] Keysoe (205 b) had 4 acres, and Swineshead (205 b, 206) had 19 acres. In the Bedfordshire folios, meadow at Keysoe is entered in terms of teams (212b).

[3] On the basis of later evidence, Fowler assumed that 3 statute acres of meadow provided feed sufficient for one ox (*Bedfordshire in 1086*, pp. 61–2 and 106–7).

(*pastura ad pecuniam villae*) is repeated monotonously. This formula occurs only twice in the Bedfordshire folios—for Potton (217b) and Sandy (212)—though the Hertfordshire entries for Barwythe (138), Caddington (136), Kensworth (136) and Westoning (132b) tell of

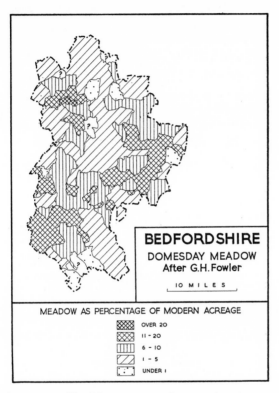

Fig. 16. Bedfordshire: Domesday meadow in 1086
(after G. H. Fowler).

This map is redrawn from Map v in G. H. Fowler, *Bedfordshire in 1086: An analysis and synthesis of Domesday Book* (Quarto Memoirs of the Bedfordshire Historical Record Society, Aspley Guise, 1922). The percentages were calculated on the assumption that 3 statute acres of meadow were sufficient to support a Domesday ox. The queries indicate areas for which G. H. Fowler did not give a percentage.

pasture for the livestock. Caddington is surveyed partly under Hertford-shire (136) and partly under Bedfordshire (211), and the former entry mentions pasture while the latter does not; this suggests that the scribe who rearranged the Bedfordshire returns by fiefs omitted the information.

For three Bedfordshire villages a money render is stated and, for one of these, pasture for sheep is also mentioned:

Henlow (214b): *De pastura x denarii.*
Kempston (217): *de pastura ii solidi.*
Langford (215b): *De pastura vi solidi et adhuc pastura est ad ccc oves.*

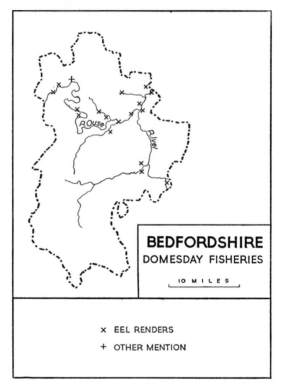

Fig. 17. Bedfordshire: Domesday fisheries in 1086.

The crosses indicate renders of eels from mills. The 'other mention' was of a fish-stew (*vivarium piscium*) on the holding of Osbern the fisherman at Sharnbrook.

These entries may imply that some grazing in each of the three places was not subject to free common right, but had to be paid for.[1] But whether this be so or not, one thing is certain, there was rarely more pasture in an eleventh-century village than was needed for the livestock.

[1] For a discussion of the pasture entries in the Bedfordshire folios, see G. H. Fowler, *op. cit.* p. 63.

FISHERIES

Fisheries (*piscariae*), as such, are not recorded in the Bedfordshire folios, but 17 of the settlements with mills rendered eels (*anguillae*) as well as making a money payment; presumably the eels were from fisheries connected with the mill-leats. The number of eels returned ranged from 50 at Stanford (212b)[1] to 400 at Stotfold (213);[2] these numbers are very small compared with the huge renders of the Cambridgeshire Fenland where villages often rendered many thousands apiece.[3] In addition to the 17 villages rendering eels, we hear of a fish-stew (*vivarium piscium*) on the holding of Osbern the fisherman (*piscator*) at Sharnbrook (216b) on the river Ouse.[4]

Fig. 17 shows the distribution of the fisheries, mainly along the Ouse below Bedford and along the Ivel. It is interesting to note that no eels were rendered in connection with mills situated on either the Ouzel or the Lea.

MILLS

Mills are mentioned in connection with 63 of the 145 Domesday settlements within the area covered by modern Bedfordshire. For each locality the number of mills is given, and also their annual value ranging from 1 mill worth only 16*d.* on a holding in Sharnbrook (216b)[5] to the 7 mills at Luton (209) which returned 110*s.* between them. Mills at 17 places rendered money and eels;[6] the 2 mills at Eaton Socon (212), for example, yielded 36*s.* 6*d.* and 100 eels. The total of 63 does not include Shillington where there was a broken-down mill yielding nothing (*fractum molinum*

---

[1] This number came from the 2 mills on the estate of Eudo the steward at Stanford; a payment of 29*s.* was also made. Two other mills at Stanford yielded 23*s.* 4*d.* between them (213b, 215, 218).

[2] The 4 mills at Stotfold rendered £4 and 400 eels.

[3] For a discussion of the Cambridgeshire entries, see H. C. Darby, *The Domesday Geography of Eastern England*, pp. 304–7.

[4] There still exists at Sharnbrook, and at nowhere else on the Ouse, 'a kind of dock on the left bank, some 120 feet by 40 feet, which if controlled by a sluice would form an excellent stew-pond' (G. H. Fowler, *op. cit.* p. 72).

[5] This was on the holding of Osbern 'the fisherman'; there was also a mill rendering 16*s.* on the holding of Albert of Lorraine (216b).

[6] Renders of eels were made by mills at: Bromham (213b, 217), Cardington (212b), Channel (212b), Clifton (212b), Eaton Socon (212), Goldington (212b), Great Barford (213b), Harrold (217), Little Barford (210b), Oakley (215), Odell (215b), Putnoe (212b), Roxton (215), Stanford (212b), Stotfold (213), Tempsford (210), Willington (213).

quod nichil reddit, 210b), nor does it include the unidentified *Cudessane*, one of the entries for which tells us that there could have been a mill— *i molinum potest ibi fieri* (211b).

Fractions of mills are mentioned in connection with only three places in Bedfordshire. At Bletsoe there was half a mill rendering 10s. on the

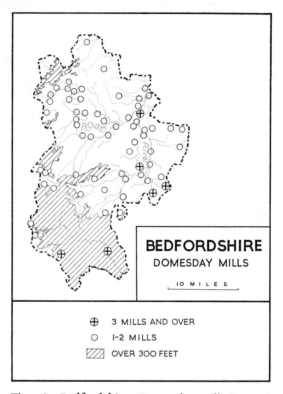

Fig. 18. Bedfordshire: Domesday mills in 1086.
The broken-down mill at Shillington and the mill that 'could be' at *Cudessane* are not shown.

holding of Hugh de Beauchamp (213), and another half mill, also yielding 10s., on the holding of Countess Judith (217); presumably there was one mill in Bletsoe rendering a total of 20s. Half-mills, each yielding 5s., are recorded for two holdings in Stanford (213b, 215), where there were 3 other mills rendering 42s. 4d. and 50 eels (212b, 218). But it is not always possible to combine the fractions; thus at Northill there was 1 mill rendering 14s. on the holding of Eudo the steward (212b) and a moiety of a mill rendering 13s. on the holding of William Spech (215), but there is no record of the other half.

Most of the villages with mills had only one or two apiece, as the following table shows:

Domesday Mills in Bedfordshire

1 mill	41 settlements	4 mills	4 settlements
2 mills	16 settlements	7 mills	1 settlement
3 mills	1 settlement		

Note that this table does not include the broken-down mill at Shillington nor the mill that 'could be' at the unidentified *Cudessane*.

The group of 7 mills was at Luton on the Lea. Stanford (212b, 213b, 215, 218), Stotfold (213), Tempsford (210, 212 *bis*) and Totternhoe (215b, 216) had each 4 mills; those at Stanford, Stotfold and Tempsford were on the river Ivel, and those at Totternhoe on the river Ouzel.

The mills were water-mills, and Fig. 18 shows how they were aligned along the rivers Ouse, Ivel, Lea, Ouzel and the Salford Brook and their larger tributaries. W. Austin tried to relate the mills of Domesday Bedfordshire to mills working in the county at the beginning of the present century.[1] Fowler also considered in detail the possible sites of the Domesday mills,[2] and came to the conclusion that many of the mills situated on brooks draining the uplands were *molendina hiemalia*, which were worked only in winter when there was enough water to turn the wheels; he suggested that this might account for their low values.[3]

CHURCHES

The Bedfordshire folios, unlike those of Huntingdonshire, do not regularly mention churches (*ecclesiae*). There were, in fact, only four churches entered—for Bedford (209, 210b), and for each of the three royal estates of Houghton Regis (209b), Leighton Buzzard (209, 210b) and Luton (209). The church of St Paul at Bedford with its endowments

[1] W. Austin, 'The Domesday water mills of Bedfordshire', *Pubs. Beds. Hist. Rec. Soc.* III (Aspley Guise, 1916), pp. 207–47, with map.
[2] G. H. Fowler, *Bedfordshire in 1086*, pp. 107–8 and Map VII.
[3] *Ibid.* p. 71.

(*cum adjacentibus*) was worth 100s.; that at Luton, with 5 hides of land belonging to it (*cum v hidis terrae quae ad eam pertinent*), rendered 20s. yearly (*ecclesia xx solidos per annum reddit*), apart from its endowment of land which was worth 60s. (209). The church at Houghton Regis with the land belonging to it seems to have been worth only 12s. yearly (209b), but that at Leighton Buzzard with the 4 hides of land pertaining to it was worth £4 (209, 210b).

The villages of Everton are described partly under Bedfordshire (217b) and partly under Huntingdonshire (207), and we hear of 'a church and a priest' (*Ibi presbyter et ecclesia*) in the Huntingdonshire entry.[1] A priest is also entered for Barwythe (138), surveyed under Hertfordshire. The only priests recorded in the Bedfordshire folios were under-tenants, and we cannot say if the land that they held was glebe;[2] very possibly some of them, at least, may have 'held in a secular rather than a religious capacity'.[3] One thing, however, is clear; the Domesday record of churches in the county in 1086 is incomplete; but, as neither priest nor church as such paid geld, it may well be that the Bedfordshire commissioners did not think it worth while to enumerate churches,[4] and may have enumerated the priests with the villeins.

URBAN LIFE

The Domesday description of the county begins with a very brief statement about Bedford (209):

> Bedford *T.R.E.* was assessed as a half hundred, and it is so now for the host and for ship service (*in expeditione et in navibus*). The land of this 'vill' (*Terra de hac villa*) was never hidated (*nunquam fuit hidata*) nor is it now, except for one hide which belonged to (*jacuit in*) the church of St Paul in almoin (*in elemosina*) *T.R.E.* and now belongs [thereto] of right (*modo jacet recte*). But Bishop Remigius put it out of almoin (*extra elemosinam*) of the church of St Paul unjustly, as the men say, and now holds (it) and all that belongs to it. It is worth 100s.

In this entry we are not specifically told that Bedford was a borough (*burgus*), nor are burgesses mentioned. But, on the same folio, the bur-

---

[1] The church in Huntingdonshire now serves the Bedfordshire village.

[2] Priests held land as under-tenants at Great Barford (213b), Biddenham (210, 211), Bolnhurst (209b), Cople (214), Harrowden (211), Riseley (213), Thurleigh (215) and Turvey (218b).

[3] G. H. Fowler, *Bedfordshire in 1086*, p. 65.

[4] *Ibid.* p. 65.

gesses (*Burgenses*) of Bedford are entered among the land-holders of the county, and on a later folio the holdings of the burgesses at Biddenham (218), a village nearby, are set out. One of these burgesses was a certain Ordwi, and an earlier entry for Biddenham (210b) tells us that he was the under-tenant in 1086 and had seized the land from its previous holder when he was reeve of the borough (*prepositus burgi*). Osmund and Ansfrid, canons of St Paul's church in Bedford, together held 4 virgates in Biddenham (211). There is also a reference to the church of Bedford on folio 210b where we are told that 'with its endowments' (*cum adjacentibus*) it was worth 100s. The Domesday account of Bedford and its inhabitants is thus exceedingly meagre, and we can deduce nothing about its size or its activities. It was assessed as a half-hundred 'for the host and for ship service'.[1]

Although we are not told anything about the activities of the burgesses in Bedford itself, they were at any rate dealing in land in Biddenham. One of them, Goduin, increased his holding of half a hide there by buying half a hide and the fourth part of a virgate after 1066—*Dimidiam unius hidae et quartam partem unius virgatae emit postquam rex W[illelmus] in anglia venit* (218); another, Ordwi, not only bought land after 1066 but also 'held a mortgage' (*in vadimonio tenuit*) on land in 1066 (218).

MISCELLANEOUS INFORMATION

There is very little miscellaneous information recorded in the Bedfordshire folios. We hear of a park for the beasts of the chase (*parchus ferarum silvaticarum*) at Stagsden (212b) and of 2 acres of vine (*ii acras vineae*) at Eaton Socon (212).[2]

Markets

The entries relating to markets in the Bedfordshire folios are three in number:

Arlesey (212): There is a market yielding 10s. (*Mercatus est ibi de x solidis*).
Leighton Buzzard (209): The toll from the market pays £7 (*Theloneum de mercato reddit vii libras*).
Luton (209): From toll and market 100s. (*De theloneo et mercato c solidi*).

---

[1] Round thought that this statement implied a contribution of ten men for either land or sea service—see J. H. Round, 'Danegeld and the finance of Domesday' in P. E. Dove (ed.), *Domesday Studies*, I (London, 1888), pp. 117–21.

[2] The more usual unit for measuring vineyards in the Domesday Book was the Norman arpent; see p. 609 below.

The market at Arlesey was on the land of William of Eu; Leighton Buzzard and Luton were royal manors.

Waste

Only two entries tell us specifically that the land was wasted:

Beeston (216b): This land is waste, but when Turstin received it, it was worth 10s. *T.R.E.* 20s. (*Haec terra devastata est sed quando Turstinus recepit valebat x solidos. T.R.E. xx solidos*).

Wyboston (210b): It is waste yet it is worth 16d. (*Vastata est tamen xvi denarios valet*).

The other holdings at Beeston (212b *ter*, 215, 218, 218b) and at Wyboston (212, 213b, 214b, 216, 218) possessed the usual agricultural resources, but, with one exception (Wyboston, 213b), had all fallen in value.

REGIONAL SUMMARY

The main physical contrast in Bedfordshire is between upland and vale (Fig. 3), but the difference is not as great as might be expected owing to the widespread distribution of superficial deposits, principally Boulder Clay (Fig. 4). The Domesday densities of plough-teams and population alike were remarkably uniform throughout the county but, taking the other agricultural resources into account, it is possible to discern differences between various localities.

The area to the north of the Chalk is occupied by outcrops of Gault, Lower Greensand, Oxford Clay and Oolite, which are alike masked extensively by Boulder Clay; the soils are various, ranging from strong clays to sandy loams. Most of the region lies below 250 feet in height, but in the south-west the Lower Greensand forms a broad upland which rises to over 500 feet. The region is drained by the Ouse and the Ivel and by their many small tributary streams. The density of teams ranged between 2·3 and 3·9 per square mile; that of population between 5·6 and 9·7. Generally the villages had sufficient wood to support between 100 and 250 swine each, but some villages had larger amounts, ranging up to 500 swine and even to a thousand. There was also a fair amount of meadow; the larger streams are bordered by alluvium, and their valleys must have been frequently flooded in the eleventh century. No fisheries were recorded, but many mills on the Ouse rendered eels. Generally the region was well supplied with mills.

The southern part of the county is underlain by chalk. Immediately to the south of the Gault vale, the Lower Chalk outcrop forms a conspicuous bench, often three miles in width. From this well-marked belt of easily worked, loamy soils, rises the abrupt scarp slope of the Chilterns to a crest line of over 600 feet; the crest reaches nearly 800 feet in the neighbourhood of Whipsnade. From the crest the dip slope extends south-eastwards, and its gently sloping surface is broken by the valleys of the Lea, the Ver and the Gade. There is open downland only in the Luton area; elsewhere the chalk dip-slope is covered with superficial deposits, mainly Clay-with-flints. Generally the densities of Domesday plough-teams and population were similar to those of the rest of the county. The scarp-foot zone was marked by a line of prosperous villages, each with many plough-teams and substantial amounts of meadow and wood. Settlements were less closely spaced on the dip-slope, but they included the royal manor of Luton with its 88 plough-teams and with enough wood to support more than 2,000 swine. The villages of the dip-slope had little or no meadow—even Luton had enough for only 4 of its plough-teams. Many of the villages of scarp zone and dip-slope alike had mills; Luton itself had 7 mills, presumably on the Lea.

BIBLIOGRAPHICAL NOTE

(1) It is interesting to note that D. Lysons and S. Lysons listed the Domesday manors of Bedfordshire at the beginning of their 'topographical account' of the county which was the first part of their *Magna Britannia*, 1 (London, 1813), pp. 3–5.

(2) The standard text of the Bedfordshire folios is that of the Rev. F. W. Ragg in *V.C.H. Bedfordshire*, 1 (London, 1904), pp. 219–66. This contains a valuable series of identifications and footnotes and is preceded by an introduction by J. H. Round (pp. 191–218).

(3) There have also been four analyses of the Bedfordshire folios:

(i) C.C., of Biggleswade, 'On the ancient divisions of counties into hundreds', *Gentleman's Magazine*, XCVIII, Pt 2 (London, 1828), pp. 99–102. This is an analysis of the hidage of the holdings in Domesday Bedfordshire, and is the earliest known attempt to reconstitute the Domesday vills of any county. It was quoted by G. Lipscomb in his *History of Buckinghamshire* 1 (London, 1847), p. 4.

(ii) REV. W. AIRY, *A Digest of the Domesday of Bedfordshire, being an analysis of that portion of the Domesday Survey which relates to the county of Bedford, and a key to the facsimile edition of the same published by Government* (Bedford, 1881). This analysis, which was designed to accompany the facsimile edition of the folios published by the Ordnance Survey Office (Southampton, 1862), was published some years after the author's death (1874) by his son, the Rev. B. R. Airy. At the end of the analysis there is a summary table of the Domesday vills arranged in alphabetical order (pp. 101–2).

(iii) F. H. BARING, *Domesday Tables for the counties of Surrey, Berkshire, Middlesex, Hertford, Buckingham and Bedford and for the New Forest* (London, 1909). The tables for Bedfordshire (pp. 180–91) were derived 'almost entirely' from a table drawn-up by the Rev. F. W. Ragg (*op. cit.* p. 173); their main value is that they contain a list of the holders of land in the county, arranged on a vill basis. The assessment of each holding is given, but no attempt is made to tabulate either population or resources.

(iv) G. H. FOWLER, *Bedfordshire in 1086: An analysis and synthesis of Domesday Book* (Quarto Memoirs of the Bedfordshire Historical Record Society, Aspley Guise, 1922). This analysis is accompanied by nine maps: I, 'The Hundreds in 1086'; II, 'Norman Estates i'; III, 'Norman Estates ii'; IV, 'Saxon Estates'; V, 'Meadow-Land'; VI, 'Woodland'; VII, 'Water Mills'; VIII, 'Area of Devastation in 1066, showing the probable route of the Norman columns'; IX, 'Distribution of Socland, *T.R.E.*' This is a pioneer work of the first importance.

(4) The following articles deal with various aspects of the Domesday study of the county:

F. H. BARING, 'The Conqueror's footprints in Domesday', *Eng. Hist. Rev.* XIII (London, 1898), pp. 17–25. Reprinted 'with some additions and alterations' in F. H. Baring, *Domesday Tables*, pp. 207–16 (see above).

W. AUSTIN, 'The Domesday water mills of Bedfordshire', *Pubs.Beds. Hist. Rec. Soc.* III (Aspley Guise, 1916), pp. 207–47, with map. This is an interesting discussion of the probable sites of the mills entered in the Bedfordshire portion of the Domesday Book.

G. H. FOWLER, 'Domesday Notes', *Pubs. Beds. Hist. Rec. Soc.* I (Aspley Guise, 1913), pp. 63–73. This paper discusses the identification of the Domesday *Chainhalle* and *Estone*.

G. H. FOWLER, 'Domesday Notes II—Kenemondwick', *Pubs. Beds. Hist. Rec. Soc.* V (Aspley Guise, 1920), pp. 61–73.

G. H. FOWLER, 'The devastation of Bedfordshire and the neighbouring counties in 1065 and 1066', *Archaeologia*, LXXII (London, 1922), pp. 41–50, with three maps. In this article, Fowler tested his conclusions for Bedfordshire, published in *Bedfordshire in 1086* (Quarto Memoirs of the Bedfordshire

Historical Record Society, Aspley Guise, 1922), against the corresponding record for Northamptonshire, Oxfordshire, Buckinghamshire, Huntingdonshire, Hertfordshire, and a part of Cambridgeshire.

(5) A valuable aid to the Domesday study of the county is A. Mawer and F. M. Stenton, *The Place-Names of Bedfordshire and Huntingdonshire* (Cambridge, 1926).

CHAPTER II

HERTFORDSHIRE

BY EILA M. J. CAMPBELL, M.A.

For three Hertfordshire entries we have another version of the Domesday returns in the *Inquisitio Eliensis* which describes most of the estates held or claimed by the abbey of Ely in 1086.[1] In Hertfordshire the abbey held land at Hadham, at Hatfield and at Kelshall. The information given in the *Inquisitio Eliensis*[2] is often fuller than that recorded in the Domesday Book, and the *I.E.* account of Hatfield has been set out below (p. 55) for comparison with the Domesday version.

The present-day county of Hertford, in terms of which this study is written, corresponds more or less to the Domesday county, but there are some differences along the border with Bedfordshire. In the eleventh century Caddington lay athwart the Hertfordshire-Bedfordshire boundary, and was surveyed partly in one and partly in the other county (136, 211); the parish became wholly part of Bedfordshire in 1888. In the same year the adjoining village of Kensworth, described in the Hertfordshire folios (136), was also transferred to Bedfordshire. One holding in the village of Meppershall was surveyed under Hertfordshire (142), although it was 'appraised in Bedfordshire with other land' (*Haec terra est appreciata in Bedefordscyre cum alia terra*); and it is interesting to recall that this holding remained a detached portion of Hertfordshire until the end of the nineteenth century.[3] The resources of three other Bedfordshire villages, Barwythe (138), Polehanger (137b) and Westoning (132b), were also included under Hertfordshire. Of Westoning, we are told that it belonged and belongs to Hitchin (in Hertfordshire), but it was assessed in Bedfordshire (*jacuit et jacet in Hiz. Sed Wara hujus manerii jacuit in Bedefordscire*). Holwell (210b, 211) was surveyed under Bedfordshire and was not trans-

---

[1] The abbey of Ely held land in the six counties of Cambridge, Essex, Hertford, Huntingdon, Norfolk and Suffolk.

[2] For the *I.E.* entries see N. E. S. A. Hamilton (ed.), *Inquisitio Comitatus Cantabrigiensis* (London, 1876), pp. 124–5.

[3] 'It remained to our own times assessed for land tax and income tax in Hertfordshire, though for all other purposes in Beds.'—J. H. Round in *V.C.H. Hertfordshire*, I (London, 1902), p. 341 n.

ferred to Hertfordshire until 1894. Thus, while some of these anomalies are due to relatively recent modifications in the boundary between the two counties, others reflect ancient fiscal or tenurial arrangements.[1]

One other Domesday entry must be noted here. In the Essex folios

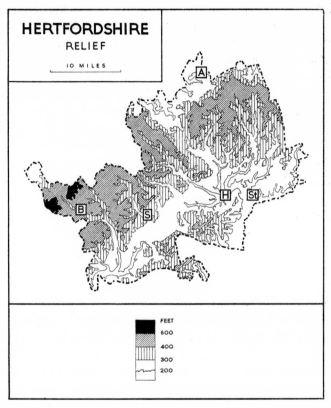

Fig. 19. Hertfordshire: Relief.

Domesday boroughs are indicated by initials: A, Ashwell; B, Berk-hamsted; H, Hertford; S, St Albans; St, Stanstead Abbots.

(vol. II, fo. 2b), holdings at the Hertfordshire settlements of Amwell, Hertford and Hoddesdon are described as berewicks in 1066 of Hatfield

[1] The hamlet of Stoke in Amersham in Buckinghamshire remained a detached portion of Hertfordshire until the nineteenth century; it is not named in the Domesday Book (*V.C.H. Buckinghamshire*, III (London, 1925), p. 150). Nettleden is also not named in the Domesday Book; it was transferred from Buckinghamshire to Hertfordshire in 1895 (see p. 140 below).

Broadoak in Essex, but there is no reference to this association in the Hertfordshire folios.[1]

Within the Domesday county there were nine hundreds, including Hitchin styled a half-hundred. The hundreds ranged in size from Hitchin with 67¾ hides 8 acres to Broadwater with as many as 230 hides 95 acres.[2] Two hundreds were not compact territorial units but aggregations of the widely scattered estates of great landowners. Thus Cashio (*Albanestou*) consisted of one compact area in the south-west and several widely scattered estates; Dacorum (*Danais*, *Daneis*) also had detached portions. Such complications make it difficult to draw a straightforward map of the hundreds of the county.

SETTLEMENTS AND THEIR DISTRIBUTION

The total number of separate places mentioned in the Domesday Book for the area included within the modern county of Hertford seems to be 168,[3] including the five places for which burgesses are recorded—Hertford, Ashwell, Berkhamsted, St Albans and Stanstead Abbots. This figure, however, cannot accurately reflect the actual number of separate settlements in the county in 1086. In the first place, when two or more adjoining villages bear the same surname today, it is not always clear whether more than one unit existed in the eleventh century. Only when there is specific mention of a second village in the Domesday Book itself, has it been included in the total of 168. Thus the separate existence of Much Hadham and Little Hadham is indicated by the Domesday names *Hadham* (133b, 135 *ter*) and *Parva Hadham* (133b), and of Great Offley and Little Offley by *Offelei* (132b, 139), and *altera Offelei* (132b).[4] There is

---

[1] J. H. Round (in *V.C.H. Essex*, 1 (London, 1903), p. 338) wrote: 'They appear to have been all comprised in that great manor of Amwell (lying just between Hertford and Hoddesdon) which Domesday enters as held by Ralf (de Limesi) and as having been held by Harold (*fo.* 138).'

[2] The larger total for Broadwater suggests that it may have been reckoned as two hundreds. The *I.E.* version has the rubrication *In duobus hundredis de Bradewatre*, and lists 16 jurors instead of the usual 8 (N. E. S. A. Hamilton (ed.), *op. cit.* pp. 100 and 125).

[3] This total excludes the anonymous manor of Eudo the steward in Hertford hundred (139), and an anonymous 'berewick' (*Bereuuicha*) belonging to Tring (137).

[4] Three pairs of adjoining villages have been counted as separate settlements in the total of 168, because their respective units are rubricated under different hundreds: Great Gaddesden (*Gatesdene*, Dacorum hundred, 139); Little Gaddesden (*Gatesdene*, Tring hundred, 136b); Abbots Langley (*Langelei*, Broadwater hundred, 140); Kings Langley (*Langelei*, Tring hundred, 136b); King's Walden (*Waldenei*, Hitchin hundred, 132b); St Paul's Walden (*Waldene*, Cashio hundred, 135b).

no indication, on the other hand, that, say, the Great and Little Munden of today existed as separate villages; the Domesday information about them is entered under one name *Mundene* (137), or *Mundane* (139), though they may well have been separate settlements in the eleventh century. The same applies, for example, to the two Ayots (135, 137b, 142b), the

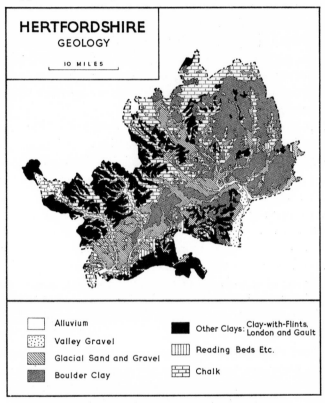

HERTFORDSHIRE
GEOLOGY

IO MILES

	Alluvium		Other Clays:	Clay-with-Flints, London and Gault
	Valley Gravel		Reading Beds Etc.
	Glacial Sand and Gravel		
	Boulder Clay		Chalk

Fig. 20. Hertfordshire: Surface geology.

Based on Geological Survey One-Inch Sheets (New Series) 204, 238, 239, 255 and 256; (Old Series) 46 N.E., 46 S.E., and 47.

two Wymondleys (132, 134, 137b, 140b), and the three Pelhams (133b *quinquiens*, 134 *bis*).[1] The distinction between the respective units of each of these groups appears later in time. Thus the names Ayot St Lawrence and Ayot St Peter *olim* Montfitchet, so far as the evidence goes, date from

[1] Ayot St Lawrence, Ayot St Peter; Great Wymondley, Little Wymondley; Brent Pelham, Furneux Pelham, Stocking Pelham.

the thirteenth century, the former from the dedication of the church, the latter from the Montfitchet family.[1] Then again it is possible that some of the larger manors, e.g. Bishops Hatfield (135), may have included more than one settlement apiece when the Survey was made.

The total of 168 includes a few places regarding which very little information is given; the record may be incomplete, or the details may have been included with those of a neighbouring village. Thus the entry for *Eia* (i.e. Rye, 134b) tells us that the holding answered for half a hide and mentions payments from meadow, a mill and weirs, but says nothing about any inhabitants. Or, again, the entry for Charlton (132b) notes only a plough-team, 2 cottars and a mill, and we are left in doubt about its other resources.

Not all the 168 names appear as names of villages on the present-day map of Hertfordshire. Some are represented by hamlets, by individual houses and farms, by fields or even by localities. Thus *Hailet* (i.e. Hailey, 140) is now a hamlet in the parish of Great Amwell, and *Berchedene* (137, 141b) is that of Berkesden Green in Aspenden. *Alsieswiche* (138) has given its name to Alswick Hall in Layston, *Henamesteda* (135b) to Hanstead House in St Stephens,[2] and *Pentlai* (136b) to Pendley Manor in Tring. *Celgdene* (133b) is represented by Chaldean Farm in Much Hadham, and *Flesmere* or *Flexmere* (133, 141) by Flexmore, a field-name in King's Walden; *Wlwenwiche* (137b, 141) has given its name to two fields, Great Woolwicks and Little Woolwicks, in Stevenage. *Eia* (Rye House and Rye Meads, 135b) is today a small area of land, nearly surrounded by the rivers Stort and Lea, in the parish of Stanstead Abbots; *Titeberst(h)* (i.e. Theobald, 134, 135 *bis*, 135b, 139, 140) survives in a street-name in Aldenham. These are but some of the changes in the Hertfordshire villages. To them must be added a number of unidentified names: *Bricewolde* (142), *Hainstone* (138, 139b), *Haslehangra* or *Helsangre* (134b, 141b), *Lampeth* (134), *Lewarewiche* (133b), *Rodehangre* or *Rodenehangre* (140, 142b),[3] *Sapeham* (138) and *Stiuicesworde* (139b). Whether these will

---

[1] For the history of these, and of all other names mentioned in this chapter, see J. E. B. Gover, A. Mawer and F. M. Stenton, *The Place-Names of Hertfordshire* (Cambridge, 1938).

[2] F. W. Ragg assigned this entry to Hemel Hempstead (*V.C.H. Hertfordshire*, I, p. 313). But see J. E. B. Gover, A. Mawer and F. M. Stenton, *op. cit.* p. 97; Hemel Hempstead is *Hamelamestede* (136b).

[3] *Rodehangre* may have adjoined Norton, with which it was given in 1007 to St Albans abbey by King Æthelred II; see *V.C.H. Hertfordshire*, III (London, 1912), p. 53.

yet be located or whether the places they represent have completely disappeared leaving no record or trace behind, we cannot say.[1]

On the other hand, some villages on the modern map are not mentioned in the Domesday Book. They are scattered here and there throughout the county, and their names do not emerge until the twelfth and thirteenth centuries, and, presumably, if they existed in 1086, they are accounted for

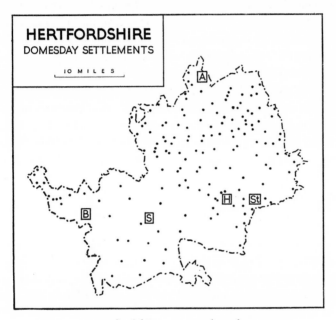

Fig. 21. Hertfordshire: Domesday place-names.

Domesday boroughs are indicated by initials: A, Ashwell; B, Berkhamsted; H, Hertford; S, St Albans; St, Stanstead Abbots.

under the statistics of other settlements. Thus Baldock was founded by the Knights Templar in the twelfth century and the earliest record of the name is from 1135; Royston first appears in 1184, and Nuthampstead in 1255. The most striking change in the distribution of settlements, between Domesday and later times, has taken place in the south of the county, where a prong of Hertfordshire projects into Middlesex. Villages situated

[1] In the present analysis *Scenlai* (135b), *Scenlei* (136b) and *Senlai* (139b) have all been plotted at Shenley, although they appear to be rubricated under different hundreds, namely Cashio, Tring and Dacorum.

in this district are not named in the folios for either county, and it seems that the area was still heavily wooded in 1086. Later manorial history suggests that the locality of the Barnets was surveyed with the resources of St Albans.[1] Those of Totteridge were probably included in the entry for Bishops Hatfield, of which it was certainly an outlying portion at a later date.[2]

The outstanding feature of Fig. 21 is the contrast between the north and south of the county. Towards the north-east, upon the East Hertfordshire plateau with its medium soils derived from Chalky Boulder Clay, there were many villages closely spaced. There were also many villages on the gravel soils in the neighbourhood of Hitchin. But in the south and west of the county, villages were relatively few and widely separated. They lay mainly in the valleys of the Colne, the Gade and the Ver; the intervening upland areas, extensively covered with Clay-with-flints, seem to have been devoid of settlements. The heavy soils of the London Clay formation in the extreme south of the county were also devoid of villages.

THE DISTRIBUTION OF PROSPERITY AND POPULATION

Some idea of the nature of the information in the Domesday folios for Hertfordshire, and of the form in which it was presented, may be obtained from the entry relating to Bishops Hatfield in Broadwater hundred. It is situated on the river Lea, some six miles to the south-west of the town of Hertford. The village was held entirely by the abbot of Ely, and so is described in a single entry (135). The corresponding version in the *I.E.* is given for the purpose of comparison.[3]

BISHOPS HATFIELD

A. *Domesday Book*

The abbot of Ely holds Hatfield. It is assessed at 40 hides (*pro xl hidas se defendit*). There is land for 30 plough-teams. In demesne 20 hides, and there are 2 plough-teams, and there could be 3 more. There, a priest with (*cum*) 18 villeins and 18 bordars have 20 plough-teams, and there could be 5 more. There

---

[1] At a time when the boundary between the two counties was still undetermined, East and High Barnet were included in Hertfordshire because they belonged to the abbey of St Albans—whereas Friern Barnet was left in Middlesex because it belonged to the Knights of St John of Jerusalem. See *V.C.H. Hertfordshire*, II (London, 1908), pp. 331, 338.   [2] *V.C.H. Hertfordshire*, III, p. 148.

[3] See N. E. S. A. Hamilton (ed.), *op. cit.* p. 125.

12 cottars and 6 serfs, and 4 mills yielding (*de*) 47*s*. and 4*d*. Meadow for 10 plough-teams. Pasture for the livestock. Wood for 2,000 swine, and 10*s*. from dues of wood and pasture. Altogether, it is and was worth £25; *T.R.E.* £30. This manor belonged and belongs to the demesne (*jacuit et jacet in dominio*) of the church of Ely.

B. *Inquisitio Eliensis*

The abbot of Ely holds Hatfield, *T.R.E.* and now assessed at 40 hides. There is land for 30 plough-teams. [There are] 2 plough-teams and 20 hides in demesne, and 3 plough-teams could be made. 20 plough-teams with the men, and there could be 5 more. 18 villeins each with (*de*) 1 virgate, and a priest [who has] half a hide, and 4 men with (*de*) 4 hides. And Adam, son of Robert, son of William, 2 hides under the abbot. 12 bordars with (*de*) half a hide, and 6 other bordars with (*de*) half a hide, 12 cottars, 6 serfs; 4 mills yielding (*de*) 46*s*. 4*d*. Meadow for 10 plough-teams; pasture for the livestock of the vill. Wood for 2,000 swine. From wood and pasture (*De bosco et pastura*) 10*s*.; and 26 cattle (*animalia ociosa*), 360 sheep, 60 swine. Altogether it is worth £25, when received £25; *T.R.E.* £30. This manor belonged and belongs to the church of Ely in demesne.

The general items relating to the village as a whole, entered in the Domesday Book, are five in number: (1) hides, (2) plough-lands, (3) plough-teams, (4) population, and (5) values. Their bearing upon regional variations in prosperity must now be considered.

(1) *Hides*

The Hertfordshire assessment is stated in terms of hides and virgates and, occasionally, in geld acres. The normal formula runs 'assessed at *n* hides' (*se defendit pro n hidis*). An alternative and frequently used statement is that an under-tenant holds *n* hides (*tenet n hidas*). Only the 1086 assessment is generally entered, but a few entries also record that for 1066.[1] The entry for one holding at Munden gives only the 1066 figure (137).[2] The borough of Hertford (132), assessed at 10 hides in 1066, was not rated twenty years later (*Pro x hidis se defendit T.R.E. et modo non facit*).

Hides in demesne (*in dominio*) are regularly recorded for estates held by tenants-in-chief and not held of them by under-tenants; such hides in demesne were apparently exempted from geld.[3] The entry for Sawbridge-

---

[1] See p. 58 below. [2] There was another holding in Munden (139).
[3] For example, the demesne land of the barons was exempted from the great levy of 1084; see J. H. Round, 'Danegeld and the finance of Domesday' in P. E. Dove (ed.), *Domesday Studies*, I (London, 1888), pp. 96–8.

worth (139b) is exceptional in that the holdings of the peasantry are set out in great detail;[1] and there is a trace of similar detail in a claim mentioned at the end of the account of Hailey (140).

In Hertfordshire, as in Bedfordshire and Cambridgeshire, there is evidence of the artificial character of the assessment and of the five-hide unit. Fifteen places in the modern county were rated at 5 hides, nineteen at 10 hides,[2] and seven at 15 or more hides. This means that about one-quarter of the villages in the area included within the present-day county were assessed at either 5 hides or some multiple of 5; in addition one village, Albury (133b), was assessed at 2½ hides. Frequently, the five-hide unit is at once apparent because a number of villages each consisted of one holding only; thus Bygrave (135) was held by the bishop of Chester for 5 hides, Aldbury (136b) by the count of Mortain for 10 hides, Cheshunt (137) by Count Alan for 20 hides, and Hatfield (135) by the abbot of Ely for 40 hides. But even where a village was divided amongst a number of lords, the same feature is often apparent when the entries are assembled. Here, in illustration, are the holdings in three representative villages each divided among several tenants-in-chief:

Datchworth

Land-holder	Folio	Hides	Virgates
(1) The archbishop of Canterbury	133	1	0
(2) The abbot of Westminster	135	3	1
(3) Geoffrey de Bech	140		2½
(4) Peter de Valognes	140b		½
Total		5	0

Watton

Land-holder	Folio	Hides	Virgates
(1) The archbishop of Canterbury	133	2½	0
(2) The abbot of Westminster	135	1	0
(3) Count Alan	136b	1½	0
(4) Derman and Alward	142	5	0
Total		10	0

[1] The holdings of the peasantry are regularly detailed in the Middlesex folios, see pp. 106–110 below.
[2] This figure of nineteen includes Hertford (132) and St Albans (135b).

Bengeo

Land-holder	Folio	Hides	Virgates
(1) Count Alan	137	0	1
(2) Hugh de Beauchamp	138b	6	0
(3) Geoffrey de Mandeville	139b	3	1
(4) Geoffrey de Bech	140b	5	1
(5) Geoffrey de Bech	140b	6½	0
(6) Geoffrey de Bech	140b	1	1½
(7) Geoffrey de Bech	140b	0	5½
(8) Geoffrey de Bech	140b	0	3½
(9) Peter de Valognes	141	0	0½
	Total	25	0[1]

It is, of course, true that many villages were assessed neither at 5 hides nor at some multiple of 5 hides, but, as in Cambridgeshire, some of the irregular assessments can be grouped into blocks which show that the same principle was at work.[2] Here, for example, are the assessments within the Domesday hundred of Tring for 1066:

	Hides				Hides	
Tring (137)	39	40	Miswell (136b, 138)	14½		20
Shenley (*Scenlei*, 136b)[3]	1		Gubblecote (136b)	1½		
Aldbury (136b)		10	Puttenham (134)	4		
Berkhamsted (136b)	13		Tiscot (137b)	4		5
Boarscroft (136b)	1½	15	In Tring hundred (139)[5]	1		
Polehanger (137b)[4]	½			Total		100
Wigginton (136b)	7⅔					
Dunsley (136b, 142)	⅓	10				
Pendley (136b)	2					

---

[1] 'So far as single Vills are concerned, Bengeo affords a good illustration of the way in which scattered fractions work out in combination'—J. H. Round, *Feudal England* (London, 1895; reprinted 1909), p. 59.

[2] For the Cambridgeshire blocks, see H. C. Darby, *The Domesday Geography of Eastern England* (Cambridge, 2nd ed., 1957), p. 276.

[3] In the present analysis, the three entries—*Scenlei* (Tring hundred, 136b), *Scenlai* (Cashio hundred, 135b) and *Senlai* (Dacorum hundred, 139b)—have been grouped together under Shenley. The table above, however, gives only the Tring assessment.

[4] Now in Bedfordshire (see p. 48 above).

[5] For this entry, see p. 58 below.

The origins of this system of assessment are obscure, but its implications for a geographical analysis of the Domesday Book are clear enough; by 1086 the assessment in detail 'bore no definite relation to area, plough lands or value'.[1] The variation among a representative selection of ten-hide vills speaks for itself:

	Plough-lands	Teams	Popula-tion	Values		
				1066	Inter-mediate	1086
Aldbury (136b)	7	7	15	£8	£8	110s
Aston (134)	15	9	27	£20	£14	£18
Bayford (133)	20	18	34	£20	£8	£16
Hemel Hempstead (136b)	30	24	23	£25	£25	£22
Sandridge (135b)	13	12	29	£12	£12	£18
Walkern (142)	12	10	33	£16	£8	£10
Wheathampstead (135)	10	8	37	£30	£16	£16

A few entries give two assessements, 1066 and 1086; all of these show exemption. Thus the assessment of Abbots Langley was reduced from 5½ hides to 3 hides (135b), and that of Flamstead fell from 4 hides to 2 hides (138). One entry for Miswell (138) tells us that 'it was assessed at 14 hides T.R.E. and now at 3 hides 2½ virgates, yet there are always 14 hides' (*pro xiiii hidis se defendit T.R.E. et modo pro iii hidis et ii virgatis et dimidia tamen sunt semper xiiii hidae*). Of Great Gaddesden (139), rubri-cated under Dacorum hundred, we read that 'it was assessed at 6 hides T.R.E., and now at 3 hides. But one of these is assessed in Tring hundred, and it is reckoned there' (*pro vi hidis se defendit T.R.E. et modo pro iii hidis. Sed una ex istis se defendit in Treunge hundret et hic apprecianda est*). It is difficult to account for these exemptions, and Round attributed them to special favour.[2] But we cannot be certain. Some may have been due to a regrouping of estates. Thus, we hear that the count of Mortain had taken certain appendages in Dunsley (136b), Gubblecote (136b), Pendley (136b) and Wigginton (136b) from Tring; 'these 2 hides are (part) of the 7 hides which the count of Mortain took from Tring' (*Hae ii hidae sunt de vii hidis quas sumpsit comes moritoniensis in Treunge*) runs the entry for

---

[1] J. H. Round in *V.C.H. Hertfordshire*, I, p. 290.
[2] *V.C.H. Hertfordshire*, I, p. 290.

Pendley.[1] We hear nothing of this rearrangement in the account of Tring (137); perhaps it helps to explain the reduction in Tring's liability from 39 hides *T.R.E.* to 5 hides 1 virgate in 1086, but we cannot be certain.

The assessment seems to have amounted in 1066 to 1091 hides 2⅓ virgates 407 acres which, reckoned at 120 acres to the hide, comes to nearly 1095 hides. In 1086 the gelding hides seem to have totalled 1031⅙ hides 407 acres, or approximately 1035 hides. But it must be remembered that these totals refer to the area of the modern county and include the figures for the boroughs.[2] Maitland estimated the number of hides in the Domesday county at 1,050,[3] and W. J. Corbett at 1,118.[4] Baring's total was 1,108 hides.[5] However, these totals are not comparable either with each other or with the present figures. Furthermore, the nature of some of the entries makes exact calculation exceedingly difficult, and, as Maitland himself wrote, 'two men not unskilled in Domesday might add up the number of hides in a county and arrive at very different results, because they would hold different opinions as to the meaning of certain formulas which are not uncommon'.[6] All the present totals can do is to indicate the order of magnitude involved; J. H. Round's comment on the assessment

---

[1] The sum of the holdings exceeds the total of 7 hides mentioned:

Place	Saxon holder	Hidage
Dunsley	Ingelric	⅓ hide
Gubblecote	Eddeva	1½ hides
Pendley	Eddeva	2 hides
Wigginton	(i) Brictric	3½ hides
	(ii) Godwin	3⅓ hides

[2] The figures for the boroughs are:

	1066	1086
Hertford (132)	10 hides	not rated
Ashwell (135, 139b, 141, 141b)	not stated	8¾ hides
Berkhamsted (136b)	not stated	13 hides
St Albans (135b)	not stated	10 hides
Stanstead Abbots (138b, 139b, 140b, 142b)	not stated	18½ hides

[3] F. W. Maitland, *Domesday Book and Beyond* (Cambridge, 1897), p. 400.

[4] W. J. Corbett, 'The Tribal Hidage', *Trans. Roy. Hist. Soc.* N.S. XIV (London, 1900), p. 218.

[5] Baring excluded the figures for Meppershall, Polehanger and Westoning; see F. H. Baring, *Domesday Tables for the counties of Surrey, Berkshire, Middlesex, Hertford, Buckingham and Bedford and for the New Forest* (London, 1909), pp. 98, 107.

[6] *Op. cit.* p. 407.

of the Domesday county applies equally to the area included within the modern county:

The one definite statistical fact that emerges for Hertfordshire in Domesday is that its assessment was low, being in proportion to its area little more than half of that which is found in Bedfordshire and Bucks, although the discrepancy is less marked when we compare the total assessment with the total of recorded ploughlands.[1]

(2) Plough-lands

Plough-lands are regularly entered for the villages of Hertfordshire. The normal formula runs 'there is land for *n* plough-teams' (*terra est n carucis*), and it then goes on to say how many teams were held in demesne and how many were held by the peasantry. Where there was only a very small amount of arable land in a holding, it is frequently stated in terms of oxen; thus each of the two holdings in Dunsley (136b, 142) had 'land for one ox' (*Terra est i bovi*), and a holding in Stanstead (142b) had 'land for 6 oxen' (*Terra est vi bobus*). Where the number of teams on a holding was less than that of the plough-lands, there is usually a statement to the effect that additional teams 'might be' or 'could be' employed, either on the demesne, or on the holdings of the peasantry, or on both. It says, in effect, that the land could carry more teams than were at work, and it indicates therefore the possibility of further cultivation. Here are two sample entries that illustrate the variety of phrasing:

> (1) Kings Langley (136b): *Terra est xvi carucis. In dominio nulla est, sed ii possunt fieri. Ibi unus francigena cum iiii villanis et v bordariis habent* (*sic*) *ii carucas et xii carucae possunt fieri.*
>
> (2) Minsden (132): *Terra est viii carucis. In dominio ii hidae et ii virgatae et dimidia et ibi sunt iii carucae. Presbyter cum viii villanis et ii cottariis habent* (*sic*) *iii carucas et adhuc ii possunt fieri.*

The *potest fieri* formula is to be found in the entries relating to as many as two-thirds of the Domesday settlements of Hertfordshire. Even so, occasionally it would seem that the Domesday scribe omitted the formula when he should have inserted it; thus on the bishop of London's estate at Much Hadham there were 22½ plough-lands but only 21 teams, yet no reference is made to the possibility of another 1½ teams, either on the

---

[1] *V.C.H. Hertfordshire*, I, p. 290.

demesne or among the peasantry (133b). Or, again, the entry for Ware (138b) seems to be incomplete;

Terra est xxxviii carucis. In dominio xiii hidae et ibi sunt iii carucae et aliae iii possunt esse. Ibi xxxviii villani cum presbytero et preposito villae et cum iii francigenis et ii anglicis hominibus habent xxvi carucas et dimidiam.

Nothing is said about the 5½ teams which are needed if the number of actual and possible teams is to equal the number of plough-lands; perhaps the scribe omitted the statement, but we cannot be certain.

There are also entries in which the Domesday folios record the lack of plough-teams in another way. One of the holdings at Ashwell (141b) had land for 1 plough, but the entry goes on to say that the team itself was not there: *Terra est i carucae sed non est ibi*. A variation of wording sometimes occurs, as in the entry for one of the holdings at Aldenham (136), where we read *Terra est i caruca sed deest caruca*. Quite often, however, on the smaller holdings the Domesday scribe leaves us to assume the absence of teams. It merely says, as of one holding at Broadfield (135), *Terra est iii bobus*, and omits to tell us whether the land was being worked.[1]

It is possible that the plough-land statement refers to conditions in 1066, and that the discrepancy between plough-lands and plough-teams indicates incomplete recovery after lean years when the land had been wasted or had gone out of cultivation. In most of these entries, the value shows a reduction between 1066 and 1086, which would support this contention, as in the following five villages:

	Plough-lands	Teams	Value 1066	Value 1086
Aston (134)	15	9	£20	£18
Kimpton (134b)	10	9	£15	£12
Kings Langley (136b)	16	2	£8	40s.
Puttenham (134)	4	3	£4	60s.
Wheathampstead (135)	10	8	£30	£16

Very occasionally in Hertfordshire, however, the teams were fewer than the plough-lands and yet the values had risen slightly. This was the situation at Hexton and at Rickmansworth as set out overleaf:

[1] The six entries for Theobald in Aldenham together record a total of 2½ plough-lands, but they omit any mention of teams or of oxen at work (134, 135 *bis*, 139, 140).

	Plough-lands	Teams	Value 1066	Value 1086
Hexton (133)	½	½	40d.	20d.
Hexton (136)	12	7	£16	£17. 10s.
Hexton (140)	1½	½	40s.	30s.
Rickmansworth (136)	20	17	£20	£20. 10s.

But, even when plough-lands and plough-teams number the same, the value fluctuates, being sometimes greater but generally less than that for 1066. Whether the plough-land statement refers to conditions in 1066 or not, the fact of understocking remains. An estate with fewer teams than team-lands was not being tilled up to capacity; the arable of 1086 was capable of extension.

There is only one example of overstocking in the county, i.e. at East-wick (140b) where there were 4 plough-lands but 5 teams, 3 on the demesne and 2 with the peasantry. Perhaps this excess is nothing more than a scribal error.[1] At Bennington (141) the total of actual and possible teams exceeds the plough-lands, but the apparent excess is explained by a statement in the entry for the holding of Peter de Valognes in Box (141); he also held Bennington. On his holding in Box there was land for 2 plough-teams, but this was worked by teams from Bennington—*Haec terra jacet et appreciatur in Belintone et colitur propriis carucis* (141).

The total number of plough-lands for the area included in the modern county amounts to 1,706½, as compared with 1,360¼ plough-teams.[2] Maitland's figures for the Domesday county were 1,716 plough-lands and 1,406 teams.[3]

[1] The entry for Cheshunt (137) tells of 33 plough-lands, but the total of actual and possible teams is only 23. The figure 33 may be a scribal error, but in the present analysis the number of plough-lands at Cheshunt has been counted as 33.

[2] The figures for the boroughs are: Ashwell, 19½ plough-lands and 13¼ teams (135, 139b, 141, 141b); Berkhamsted, 26 plough-lands and 15 teams (136b); Hertford, no information (132); St Albans, 16 plough-lands, 15 teams (135b); and Stanstead Abbots, 17¼ plough-lands, 11½ teams (138b, 139b, 140b, 142b). For the complication of these places see pp. 585–6 below.

[3] *Op. cit.* p. 401. F. H. Baring's total of 1,712 plough-lands is not comparable either with that of Maitland or with the present count (*Domesday Tables*, p. 107).

(3) *Plough-teams*

The Hertfordshire entries, like those of other counties, usually draw a distinction between the teams on the demesne and those held by the peasantry. Sometimes, however, only demesne ploughs are recorded; thus the entry for Boarscroft notes: *Terra est i caruca et ibi est in dominio* (136b). The entry for one holding in Bengeo carefully emphasises the fact that there are only demesne teams—*Terra est iii carucis. Ibi non sunt carucae nisi dominicae carucae* (140b). Sometimes we hear only of teams with the peasantry, e.g. at Bendish (136) and at Charlton (132b). Occasional entries seem to be defective. Thus, information about a team on the demesne at Caldecote seems to be wanting; the entry runs: *Terra est v carucis. In dominio iii virgatae et quarta pars unius virgatae. Ibi ix villani cum presbytero habent ii carucas et dimidiam et i caruca et dimidia potest (sic) fieri* (138). But sometimes, as we have noted above (p. 61), the fact that there is no team at work is clearly recorded, as in the entry for *Eia* (i.e. Rye) which notes: *Terra est dimidiae carucae sed non est ibi* (134b). Two entries tell us that the plough-lands were worked by teams from elsewhere. Eudo the steward worked his demesne in Barley (139) with teams from Newsells—*Terra est ii carucis. In dominio i hida et dimidia et xx acrae et laborat cum propriis carucis de Nuesselle. Ibi iiii villani habent i carucam*—but the entries for Newsells on the same folio (134 *bis*) do not refer to this arrangement. We have already noted (p. 62) that Peter de Valognes worked his demesne in Box with teams from Bennington (141).

The present analysis has yielded a total of 1,360¼ plough-teams for the modern county, including the figures for the boroughs.[1] Maitland's total for the Domesday county was 1,406 plough-teams.[2]

(4) *Population*

The main bulk of the population was comprised in the four categories of villeins, bordars, cottars and serfs. In addition to these main groups there were the burgesses (see p. 85 below) together with a miscellaneous group that included sokemen, freemen, *francigenae*, knights, priests, traders and others. The details of the groups are summarised on p. 70. The

---

[1] See p. 62, n. 2 above.
[2] *Op. cit.*, p. 401. F. H. Baring's total of 927 teams is not comparable either with that of Maitland or with the present count (*Domesday Tables*, p. 107).

estimate of Sir Henry Ellis was made in terms of the Domesday county and included tenants-in-chief, under-tenants and burgesses.[1] F. H. Baring's count is likewise not comparable with the present totals.[2] In any

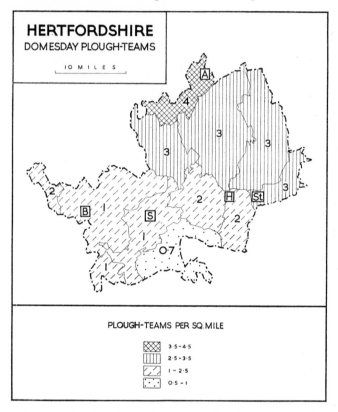

Fig. 22. Hertfordshire: Domesday plough-teams in 1086 (by densities).

Domesday boroughs are indicated by initials: A, Ashwell; B, Berk-hamsted; H, Hertford; S, St Albans; St, Stanstead Abbots.

case, one thing is certain; no one who counts Domesday population can claim definite accuracy. Finally, one point must always be remembered. The figures are those of recorded population, and must be multiplied by

[1] Sir Henry Ellis, *A General Introduction to Domesday Book*, II (London, 1833), p. 456. His grand total for the county amounted to 4,927.

[2] Baring counted only villeins, bordars, cottars and serfs, and, in any case, his figures are not comparable with those of the present count—see p. 63, n. 2.

some factor, say 4 or 5, in order to obtain the actual population; but this does not affect the relative density as between one area and another.[1] This is all that a map such as Fig. 24 can roughly indicate.

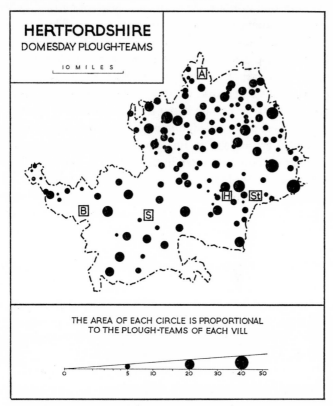

HERTFORDSHIRE
DOMESDAY PLOUGH-TEAMS

10 M I L E S

THE AREA OF EACH CIRCLE IS PROPORTIONAL
TO THE PLOUGH-TEAMS OF EACH VILL

0   5   10   20   30   40   50

Fig. 23. Hertfordshire: Domesday plough-teams in 1086
(by settlements).

Domesday boroughs are indicated by initials: A, Ashwell; B, Berkhamsted; H, Hertford; S, St Albans; St, Stanstead Abbots.

It is impossible for us to say how complete were these Domesday statistics, but it does seem as if some people had been left uncounted. In the entry for Ware (138b) we hear of 'other men' (*alii homines*) who had 3 mills rendering (*reddentes*) 10s., but nothing is said about either their status or their number; also at Ware there were 32 men, *inter villanos et*

---

[1] But see p. 589 below for the complication of serfs.

bordarios, and these have been counted as 16 villeins and 16 bordars. The entry for one holding at Meesden (134) notes *ibi i et i servus,* and from the order of the text the undescribed man seems to have been a cottar; he has been counted as one in the table on p. 70. Several entries, generally for small holdings, contain no reference to population. Thus the entry for *Eia* (i.e. Rye, 134b) does not mention any people, although it tells of a mill, weirs rendering 200 eels and of meadow producing 10s. from hay. Or, again, two of the four entries for Brickendon (140b, 142) each tells of a plough-team at work, but says nothing about the men working it. It is impossible to be certain about the significance of these omissions, but they do suggest unrecorded inhabitants. Some of the omissions may be due to scribal errors, and in this connection it is interesting to recall that the population figures entered in the *Inquisitio Eliensis* do not always agree with those in the Domesday folios. The main text of the *I.E.* is followed by a series of documents that includes an abstract setting out the teams and population of many of the Ely estates. Here are the comparative figures for the three Ely estates in Hertfordshire:

Hertfordshire: Domesday Book and I.E. Population Figures[1]

	Domesday Book	I.E. Main Version	I.E. Summary
Hadham	15 villeins	15 villeins	15 villeins
	15 bordars		7 bordars
		7 cottars	
	7 serfs	7 serfs[a]	7 serfs
Hatfield	18 villeins	18 villeins	18 villeins
	18 bordars	18 bordars	30 bordars[b]
	12 cottars	12 cottars	
	6 serfs	6 serfs	6 serfs
	1 priest	1 priest	
		4 men	
Kelshall	12 villeins	12 villeins	12 villeins
	9 bordars	9 bordars	9 bordars
	7 serfs	7 serfs	7 serfs[c]

[a] Another MS. has 8 serfs.   [b] 26 altered to 31 in one MS.
[c] Another MS. has 8 serfs.

[1] See N. E. S. A. Hamilton (ed.), *op. cit.* pp. 124–5, 173.

Villeins comprised nearly 40 per cent of the total recorded population. There was a half-villein (*villanus dimidius*) at Tiscott 137 b, and this term may mean either 'a man holding half a villein tenement or one whose land and services were shared between two estates'.[1] Bordars comprised 25 per cent, and cottars nearly 19 per cent of the recorded population. The distinction between them is not clear,[2] but in Domesday Hertfordshire they occurred together on many estates. Generally the bordars are linked with the villeins and other peasantry having plough-teams, but the cottars are usually coupled with the serfs. Like the serfs, who formed only 13 per cent of the population, the villeins, bordars and cottars present no special feature of interest for our purpose.

The miscellaneous group in Hertfordshire was fairly large and very varied. The most interesting category was that of sokemen, about whom details were given for 1066 as well as for 1086. But it is not possible to be precise about the number of sokemen in 1066 because we cannot always be sure whether a sokeman recorded at a place in 1086 had also been there 20 years earlier. Furthermore, men, who very possibly were of the rank of sokemen in 1066, are not always so described. Thus in the account of Wallington (137) we read: 'This land 2 sokemen, Eddeva's men, held and could sell.' On the same folio, an entry relating to a holding in Reed, on the other hand, notes: 'This land Turbern, one of Eddeva's men, held and could sell.' All three were 'men of Eddeva', but only two are specifically styled *sochemanni*. But it is clear that despite these doubts there were upwards of 250 sokemen in the county in 1066; twenty years later, this figure had been reduced to only 43. Even so, this reduction is not as striking as in the neighbouring county of Cambridgeshire.[3] It was greatest in the eastern half of the county; thus 74 sokemen were enumerated for 1066 on estates in Edwinstree hundred, but only two were enumerated for 1086. It is impossible to say what had become of the displaced sokemen, but the Domesday record itself occasionally suggests that they were reduced in status; thus on a holding in Datchworth (140), where there had been 3 sokemen in 1066, there were 3 villeins in 1086. On another in Barkway (141 b) 2 men (*homines*) held a virgate and a half

---

[1] L. F. Salzman in *V.C.H. Cambridgeshire*, 1 (London, 1938), p. 347.

[2] For a discussion of the differences between bordars and cottars, see: (i) F. W. Maitland, *op. cit.* pp. 39 *et seq.*; (ii) P. Vinogradoff, *English Society in the Eleventh Century* (Oxford, 1908), pp. 456 *et seq.*

[3] For a discussion of the reduction in the numbers of sokemen in Cambridgeshire, see H. C. Darby, *The Domesday Geography of Eastern England*, pp. 290 *et seq.*

of land which previously had been held by 2 sokemen. Sometimes we are told of the presence of a sokeman at both dates, as for a holding in Hoddesdon (137) where 'there was and is 1 sokeman holding half a hide' (*ibi fuit et est i sochemannus habens dimidiam hidam*). The entry for Bushey

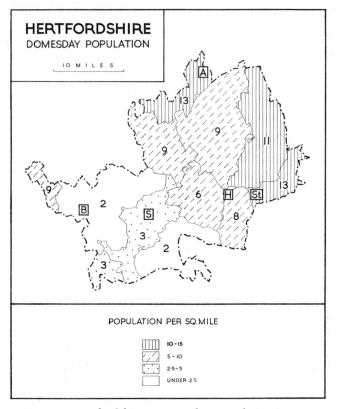

Fig. 24. Hertfordshire: Domesday population in 1086
(by densities).

Domesday boroughs are indicated by initials: A, Ashwell; B, Berkhamsted; H, Hertford; S, St Albans; St, Stanstead Abbots.

(139b), on the other hand, definitely tells us that a sokeman who held one hide of land had not been there in 1066—*Ibi est unus sochemannus qui non fuit ibi T.R.E.* It was Round who first noted that the bulk of the sokemen were found in the extreme north and east of the county, 'forming, as it were, a fringe from Lilley to Hoddesdon, with Essex and Cambridge as a kind of centre'.[1] In 1086 the freemen (*liberi homines*) were also greatly reduced in number; we hear of only 8, all on a holding in Barley (136). In 1066, a number of thegns (*teigni*) had also held land in the county.[2]

Of the other miscellaneous groups, the most numerous were priests and

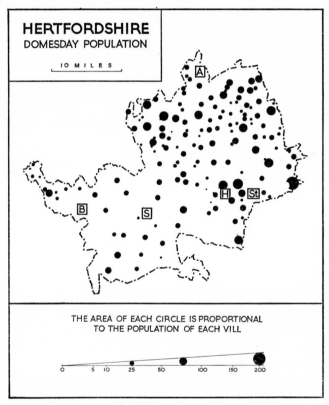

HERTFORDSHIRE
DOMESDAY POPULATION

10 MILES

THE AREA OF EACH CIRCLE IS PROPORTIONAL
TO THE POPULATION OF EACH VILL

0   5   10   25   50   100   150   200

Fig. 25. Hertfordshire: Domesday population
in 1086 (by settlements).

Domesday boroughs are indicated by initials: A, Ashwell; B, Berkhamsted; H, Hertford; S, St Albans; St, Stanstead Abbots.

francigenae; both classes seem to have partaken of the agricultural activities of the community because both are recorded as having plough-teams. Thus at Standon 29 villeins with a priest and 15 bordars and 2 sokemen and a certain Frenchman (*quidam francigena*) had 12 plough-teams (142b);

[1] *V.C.H. Hertfordshire*, I, p. 266.   [2] See p. 157 below.

and at Amwell 24 villeins with a priest, 4 Frenchmen and 7 bordars had 8 plough-teams (138). In all, 50 priests are mentioned; it is interesting to note that the Hertfordshire folios do not regularly record churches.[1] Unnamed knights (*milites*) and reeves (*prepositi villae*) appeared infrequently but in the same setting, e.g. a knight at Weston (138b) and a reeve at Bayford (133). These groups constituted almost all the miscel-

Recorded Population of Hertfordshire in 1086

A. *Rural Population*

Villeins	1,766
Bordars	1,120
Cottars	849
Serfs	591
Miscellaneous	176
Total	4,502

Details of Miscellaneous Rural Population

Francigenae	47	Freemen		8
Priests	47	Reeves		4
Sokemen	43	Englishmen		2
Knights (*Milites*)	12	*Rustici*		2
Traders	10	*Clericus*		1
		Total		176

B. *Urban Population*

Villeins, bordars, cottars, serfs and the sokeman are also included in the tables above.

HERTFORD	36 houses (*domus*); 18 burgesses. See p. 86 below.
BERKHAMSTED	52 burgesses; 14 villeins; 15 bordars; 6 serfs; 1 priest; 1 ditcher (*fossarius*). See p. 87 below.
ST ALBANS	46 burgesses; 4 *francigenae*; 16 villeins; 13 bordars; 12 cottars. See p. 87 below.
ASHWELL	14 burgesses; 24 villeins; 19 bordars; 17 cottars; 8 serfs; 1 priest. See p. 88 below.
STANSTEAD ABBOTS	7 burgesses; 4 *francigenae*; 1 sokeman; 4 villeins; 4 bordars; 7 cottars; 2 serfs; 1 reeve; 1 priest. See p. 89 below.

[1] The only entry which mentions a church is that for the borough of Hertford (132) which notes: 'Peter de Valognes has 2 churches and a house with them' (*Petrus de valongies habet ii ecclesias cum una domo*).

laneous population except for 2 *rustici* at Knebworth (139),[1] 2 Englishmen (*anglici*) at Ware (138b), and 1 clerk (*clericus*) on a holding in Sacombe (141). Finally there were 10 traders paying dues of 10s. (*Ibi x mercatores reddunt x solidos de consuetudinis*) at Cheshunt (137), which suggests that there may have been a market at this crossing-point on the river Lea, although none is recorded in the Domesday folios.

(5) *Values*

The value of an estate is normally given in a round number of pounds or shillings for three dates, 1066, 1086 and an intermediate date. Representative entries are:

> Cokenach (140): *Hoc Manerium valet lx solidos. Quando recepit xl solidos. T.R.E. c solidos.*
>
> Hemel Hempstead (136b): *In totis valentiis valet xxii libras. Quando recepit xxv libras et tantundem T.R.E.*
>
> Patmore (133b): *Valet et valuit semper iiii libras.*
>
> Stevenage (135): *In totis valentiis valet et valuit xii libras. T.R.E. xiii libras.*

Generally the values seem to have been entered with care, but no valuation is stated for a holding at Radwell (141), and the intermediate figure seems to have been omitted for a holding in Windridge—*Valet xl solidos. Quando recepit. T.R.E. l solidos* (135b). Occasionally the value of a berewick was included in that of its parent estate; Tring and its unnamed berewick were valued together (137), and a holding at Hoddesdon, said to be a berewick of Cheshunt, was also valued with its parent (137). Stevenage and its herdwick (*Harduich*) were also appraised together (135). One holding at Libury[2] 'was appraised in Watton' (*est appreciata in Watone*, 142), but another holding in the same village, called 'a berewick of Munden' (139) had its own set of values. A holding in Box (141) was appraised (*appreciatur*) in Bennington. Codicote and Oxwick were valued together (135b), and the entry tells us that they had been two manors *T.R.E.* but were only one in 1086—*Codicote et Oxewiche duo manerii fuerunt T.R.E. et modo est unum*. Hitchin and its appurtenances (*Hiz cum suis pertinentibus*) were valued together on fo. 133, but separate valuations of some of the appurtenant estates were also entered (132–3).[3]

---

[1] F. W. Ragg equated *rustici* with *villani* (*V.C.H. Hertfordshire*, I, p. 328).

[2] Libury is the Domesday *Stuterehele*.

[3] Individual valuations are given for: the holding belonging to the minster (*monasterium*) of Hitchin (132b), King's Walden (132b), Temple Dinsley (132b), Great

The 'values' are usually entered as plain statements of money, but there are entries which indicate considerable differences in the method of reckoning. We are specifically told that the values of some estates were reckoned by tale or number, when the coins were accepted at their nominal value. But in view of the circulation of debased coins, some values were reckoned by weight, and were also tested by assay; the latter was known as 'white' money. The relevant entries are:

Bayford (133): pays £16 by tale (*reddit xvi libras ad numerum*).

Dinsley (132b): pays yearly £14 burnt and weighed (i.e. assayed), and £5 by tale (*reddit per annum xiiii libras arsas et pensatas et v libras ad numerum*).

Hertford (132): This *suburbium* pays £20 burnt and weighed, and 3 mills pay £10 by tale (*Hoc suburbium reddit xx libras arsas et pensatas et iii molini reddunt x libras ad numerum*).

Tring (137): Its total value is £22 of white pennies weighed by the count (*In totis valentiis valet xxii libras de albis denariis ad pensum hujus comitis*).[1]

We also hear that an estate in Wormley (142) 'was sold for 3 marks of gold after King William came' (*fuit venditum iii markis auri post adventum regis Willelmi*).

There was another complication. On some royal estates, the valuation was made partly in service. Thus, in 1086, King's Walden, Temple Dinsley, Great Offley and Little Offley all rendered *avera* and *inward* in Hitchin (132b); likewise one *avera* was found (*Unam averam invenit*) by Weyley near Temple Dinsley (133). Round has shown that *avera*, and probably *inward* too, were essential carrying services with a horse, and that these services were commuted when the king did not visit the county.[2] Round also showed that in Domesday Hertfordshire *avera* was due at the rate of one per hide, and that the price of commutation was 4d. per *avera*.[3]

An outstanding feature of the Hertfordshire valuation is the decrease in the value of many holdings immediately after 1066. The values of a large number were only some 25 per cent to 50 per cent of what they had been,

Offley (132b *bis*), Little Offley (132b), Wellbury (133), Weyley (133 *bis*), Flexmore (133), *Leglega* (i.e. Leygreen, 133), Hexton (133) and Bayford (133); but there are no separate valuations for Wymondley (132), Minsden (132), Hitchin (132b), Weyley (132b), Wandon (132b) and Charlton (132b).

[1] I.e. silver pennies assayed by fire and weighed by the count's own standard; see J. H. Round in *V.C.H. Hertfordshire*, I, p. 320, n. 6.

[2] For a full discussion, see J. H. Round in *V.C.H. Hertfordshire*, I, pp. 269–74.

[3] *Ibid.* p. 269. It is interesting to note that in 1066 a sokeman in Lilley (140) 'rendered one *avera* or 3½d.' (*unam Averam in hiz reddidit vel iii denarios et i obolum*).

and a few holdings had suffered even more than this but none was completely devastated (*vastata*) (Figs. 161–2). F. H. Baring attributed these reductions to devastation by the Norman armies—'From Cambridgeshire and Bedfordshire the army entered Hertfordshire, where we find abundant signs of ravage on the eastern side'.[1] But we must also note that there was some destruction in the west. Some of the ravaged holdings had recovered fully or in part by 1086, and a few were even more prosperous than before; but by far the majority remained in their reduced condition.[2]

Generally speaking, the greater the number of plough-teams and men on an estate, the higher its value, but it is impossible to discern any constant relationships, as the following figures for seven estates, each yielding £4 in 1086, show:

	Teams	Population	Other resources
Aspenden (139)	3	10	Meadow, Wood
Bramfield (142)	4	11	Meadow, Pasture, Wood
Broxbourne (142b)	6	10	Meadow, Mill, Pasture, Wood
Digswell (139b)	8½	21	Mills, Pasture, Wood
Little Hadham (133b)	3	11	Meadow, Pasture, Wood
Patmore (133b)	3	13	Meadow, Wood
Wigginton (136b)	3	12	Meadow, Mill, Wood

It is true that the variations in the arable, as between one estate and another, did not necessarily reflect variations in total resources, but even taking the other resources into account the figures are not easy to explain. It is occasionally possible to correlate changes in value with economic changes as between 1066 and 1086. Where there was a decline in value, we frequently find the *potest fieri* clause in the statement about plough-teams, e.g. in the entries for Alswick (138), Hemel Hempstead (136b), and Wheathampstead (135), but it is unwise to draw any conclusions.

[1] *Domesday Tables*, p. 211.
[2] For the way in which this evidence fits into that of south-eastern England as a whole, see p. 569 below.

Conclusion

For the purpose of calculating densities, the hundreds themselves as far
as possible have been adopted, but a number of modifications have had
to be made in order to form units that correspond more closely with

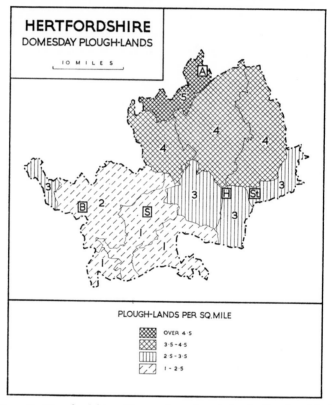

Fig. 26. Hertfordshire: Domesday plough-lands (by densities).

Domesday boroughs are indicated by initials: A, Ashwell; B, Berkhamsted; H, Hertford; S, St Albans; St, Stanstead Abbots.

differences in soil. The result of these modifications is twelve units which
form a useful basis for distinguishing variations over the face of the
county. It does not enable us to arrive at as perfect a regional division as
a geographer could wish for, but it must serve for our purpose.

From the preceding discussion of the five recurring formulae, it is clear that those relating to plough-teams and population are most likely to reflect something of the distribution of wealth and prosperity throughout the county in Domesday times. Taken together, they supplement one another to provide a general picture (Figs. 22 and 24). The essential

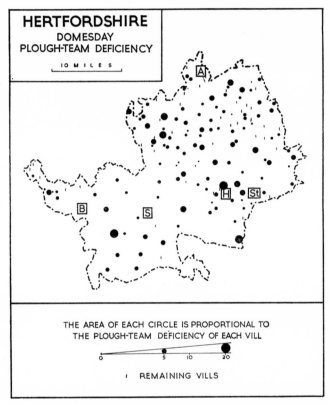

Fig. 27. Hertfordshire: Domesday plough-team deficiency (by settlements).

Domesday boroughs are indicated by initials: A, Ashwell; B, Berkhamstead; H, Hertford; S, St Albans; St, Stanstead Abbots.

feature of both maps is the contrast between the north and south of the county. The density of plough-teams ranged from nearly 4 per square mile in the north to under one in the south; that of population from 13 to only 2. The former area is largely covered by chalky Boulder Clay with its fertile loamy soils; streams are relatively frequent; villages were numerous. In the south, on the other hand, villages were widely separated, most of them in the few Chiltern valleys between which stretched inhospitable tracts of Clay-with-flints. Densities were lowest along the southern border of the county, on the inhospitable heavy soils of the London Clay.

Figs. 23 and 25 are supplementary to the density maps, but it is necessary to make one reservation concerning them. As we have seen on p. 50, it is possible that some Domesday names may have covered two or more settlements. A few of the symbols should therefore appear as two or more smaller symbols, but this limitation does not affect the main pattern of the maps. Generally speaking, they confirm and amplify the information of the density maps. In view of the doubtful nature of the plough-land entries, the implications of Fig. 26 are uncertain, but the map has been included for comparison with Fig. 22. Fig. 27 shows that generally the county may have been understocked in 1086.

WOODLAND

Types of entries

The wood of most Hertfordshire villages was measured in terms of the swine which it could support. The usual formula was 'wood for *n* swine' (*silva n porcis*), and the amount ranged from enough for one pig at a holding in Stanstead Abbots (139b) to sufficient for 2,000 swine at Bishops Hatfield (135). The round figures of many entries (i.e. 60, 100, 150, 400, 1000, 2,000) suggest estimates rather than precise amounts, but, on the other hand, there are detailed figures which possibly indicate a measure of exactness (e.g. 1, 2, 4, 15, 24, 55). One entry for Munden (137) notes that in addition to woodland for 150 swine there was 'another wood where 200 swine might feed' (*Altera silva unde cc porcis pascerentur*).

Another, but less frequent, way of indicating the amount of wood on a holding was by the formula 'wood for fences' (*nemus ad sepes*); the phrasing varied, as three representative entries show:

Offley (132b): *Silva cxx porcis. Nemus ad sepes.*
St Paul's Walden (135b): *Nemus ad sepes et domos.*
Hormead (138b): *Nemus tantum ad sepes.*

One entry for Graveley (140b) tells of 'underwood for fencing' (*Rispalia ad sepes*). Another for Weyley (133) mentions wood for fences, and tells of woodland for 50 swine (*silva ad l porcos*) that had been seized to the injury of the king.

Some woodland, in addition to providing pannage for swine, also made a money render, e.g. at Cottered—*silva c porcis et xii denarii* (133).[1] Sometimes the renders from wood and pasture, or from wood and meadow, were included in one sum; the full list is as follows:

Barkway (139b): *Pastura ad pecuniam. Silva l porcis. De pastura et silva ii solidi et iii socos* (i.e. plough-shares).

Bishops Hatfield (135): *Pastura ad pecuniam. Silva ii milibus porcorum et de consuetudine silvae et pasturae x solidi.*

Buckland (134b): *Pastura ad pecuniam. Silva xl porcis. De pastura et silva x solidi.*

Hertingfordbury (138b): *Pastura ad pecuniam villae. Silva cc porcis. De silva et pastura vii solidi.*

Pirton (138): *Pastura ad pecuniam villae. Silva quingentis porcis. De pastura et silva x solidi.*

Sawbridgeworth (139b): *Pastura ad pecuniam. Silva ccc porcis et de reddita earum iiii solidi.*

Stanstead Abbots (138b): *Pastura ad pecuniam villae. Silva c porcis. Ibi etiam vii burgenses qui reddunt cum aliis consuetudinibus prati et silvae xxiii solidos.*

Weston (138b): *Pastura ad pecuniam. Silva quingentis porcis. De bosco et pastura xiii solidi et iiii denarii.*

The entry for Abbots Langley (135b) tells us that the estate had been deprived of 1 hide of 'wood and field' (*inter boscum et planum*). Parks for the beasts of the chase—*parci bestiarum silvaticarum*—were recorded for Bennington (141), for St Albans (135b) and for Ware (138b).

Distribution of woodland

The contrast in prosperity between the north-east and the south-west is reflected in the distribution of woodland (Fig. 28). The villages of the south-west had large amounts; for example, Bushey (139b), Flamstead (138) and Tring (137) each had enough for 1,000 swine, Cheshunt (137), Hemel Hempstead (136b) and Rickmansworth (136) for 1,200 apiece, and Bishops Hatfield (135) for as many as 2,000. The villages of the north-east

---

[1] The entry for Shenley rubricated under Tring hundred (136b) runs: *silva c sol'*, but Round thought that in all probability *sol'* was here a scribal slip for *porc'* (*V.C.H. Hertfordshire*, I, p. 317n.). The full list of those places with money renders from wood is: Berkhamsted (136b), Bramfield (142), Cheshunt (137), Cottered (133), Hunsdon (143), St Albans (135b) and Tewin (141).

generally had very much smaller amounts: some had sufficient only for fences, and the swine totals of others were but small ones; thus Alswick (138) and Cockhampstead (137b) had wood for only 10 swine apiece. But three had substantially greater amounts—Meesden (133b) for 400

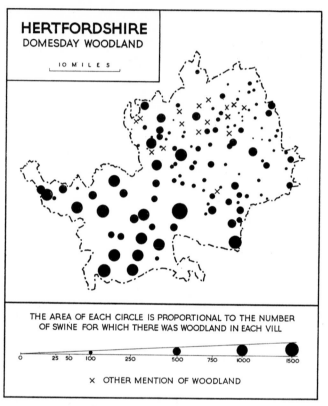

Fig. 28. Hertfordshire: Domesday woodland in 1086.

Where the wood of a village is entered partly in terms of swine
and partly in some other way, only the swine total is shown.

swine, Much Hadham (133b *ter*, 135) for 300, and Pelham (133b *quinquiens*, 134 *bis*) for 316. Generally the distribution of Domesday woodland in Hertfordshire reflects the surface geology (Fig. 20); the highest swine totals are found in connection with the heaviest soils, i.e. those derived from London Clay and from Clay-with-flints; the smallest amounts are found where the soils were relatively easily worked, on the chalky Boulder Clay.

Types of entries

The Domesday meadow of Hertfordshire was measured for the most part in terms of plough-teams, i.e. by stating the number of teams of

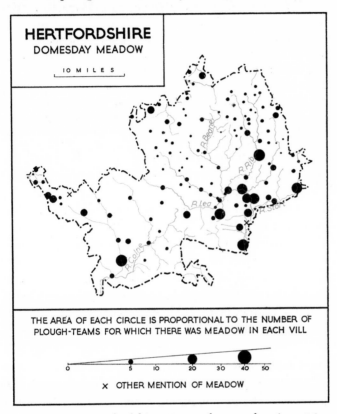

Fig. 29. Hertfordshire: Domesday meadow in 1086.

Where the meadow of a village is entered partly in terms of plough-teams and partly in some other way, only the plough-team total is shown.

8 oxen the meadow was capable of supporting. The usual formula was *pratum n carucis* or *pratum n bobus*. The amount was nearly always less than or equal to the number of plough-teams; but there were occasional exceptions, e.g. at Standon (142 b) there were 17 teams at work on 24 plough-lands and there was meadow for 24 teams. At Cheshunt (137) there was 'meadow for 23 teams and for the demesne horses' (*Pratum xxiii carucis*

et ad dominicos equos),[1] and at *Stiuicesworde* (139b) 'meadow for 1½ teams and for the use of the demesne' (*Pratum i carucae et dimidiae et ad dominicum opus*). A few entries mention a money payment; presumably the payment was from the sale of hay, but only three specifically say so:

> Amwell (138): *pratum xvi carucis. Pastura ad pecuniam villae. Silva cc porcis et de pastura et feno x solidi.*
> Broxbourne (142b): *Pratum vi solidi*[2] *et iiii solidi de faeno.*
> *Eia* (i.e. Rye, 134b): *pratum dimidiae carucae et de feno x solidi.*
> Hanstead (135b): *pratum iii carucis et xiii solidi.*
> Puttenham (134): *pratum iiii carucis et iiii solidi.*
> Stanstead Abbots (138b): *pratum xvi carucis. Pastura ad pecuniam villae. Silva c porcis. Ibi etiam vii burgenses qui reddunt cum aliis consuetudinibus prati et silvae xxiii solidos.*

It is difficult to explain these money payments, because not all the villages listed above had a surplus of meadow; thus Hanstead with 20 plough-lands and 16 teams at work had meadow for only 3 teams.

Finally mention must be made of two exceptional entries. The entry for Aldbury (136b) tells of 'meadow of half a hide' (*pratum dimidiae hidae*) and it is possible that this is a scribal slip for *pratum dimidiae carucae*.[3] The other exceptional entry is for Orwell Bury (141b) and it tells us that the village had no meadow—*Pratum nil*. This is particularly interesting in view of the fact that the entries for 37 of the 168 settlements in the county do not mention meadow; many holdings in the remaining 131 settlements also had none recorded.

Distribution of meadowland

Meadow was most abundant, as might be expected, along the alluvial valleys of the Lea and its tributaries, especially the Rib and the Stort (Fig. 29). In these valleys some villages had amounts sufficient for 20 or more teams. Thus in the Lea Valley, Cheshunt (137) had meadow for 23 teams, and Bayford (133) and Ware (138b) each had sufficient for 20 teams; Standon (142b) in the Rib valley had enough for 24 teams, and Sawbridgeworth (139b) in the Stort valley for 20 teams. Smaller amounts were to be found along the many small streams draining the eastern half

---

[1] The entry for Cheshunt mentions 33 plough-lands, but the sum of actual and possible teams is only 23, see p. 62n. above.

[2] This may have been a slip for *Pratum vi carucis*, as the village had 6 plough-lands.

[3] See J. H. Round in *V.C.H. Hertfordshire*, I, p. 318n.

of the county. In the south-west, along the valleys of the Colne, the Gade and the Ver, there was only one village with a substantial amount— Cassio (136, 139b) with enough for 23 teams.

PASTURE

Pasture is recorded for 116 out of the 168 Domesday settlements in Hertfordshire. The normal formula runs 'pasture for the livestock of the vill' (*pastura ad pecuniam villae*), but a few estates rendered money from pasture; the renders ranged from 8*d.* from one holding in Bengeo (140b) to 3*s.* at Tring (137).[1] Money renders from pasture and woodland were sometimes combined in one sum:

Barkway (139b): *Pastura ad pecuniam. Silva l porcis. De pastura et silva ii solidi et iii socos* (i.e. plough-shares).

Bishops Hatfield (135): *Pastura ad pecuniam. Silva ii milibus porcorum et de consuetudine silvae et pasturae x solidi.*

Buckland (134b): *Pastura ad pecuniam. Silva xl porcis. De pastura et silva x solidi.*

Hertingfordbury (138b): *Pastura ad pecuniam villae. Silva cc porcis. De silva et pastura vii solidi.*

Pirton (138): *Pastura ad pecuniam villae. Silva quingentis porcis. De pastura et silva x solidi.*

Sawbridgeworth (139b): *Pastura ad pecuniam. Silva ccc porcis et de reddita earum iiii solidi.*

Weston (138b): *Pastura ad pecuniam. Silva quingentis porcis. De bosco et pastura xiii solidi et iiii denarii.*

At Amwell (138) a money payment was made from hay and pasture— *pratum xvi carucis. Pastura ad pecuniam villae. Silva cc porcis et de pastura et feno x solidi.*

The distribution of villages with pasture is fairly general and presents no special features. But one question that naturally arises is what of the 52 villages with no record of pasture? Perhaps the Domesday scribe omitted to copy the statement *pastura ad pecuniam villae* which is repeated so monotonously elsewhere in the Hertfordshire folios. Or did the fallow field suffice for the livestock of these villages?[2] It is impossible to tell.

[1] The full list of entries recording money payments from pasture alone is: Bayford (133), Bengeo (140b), Brickendon (136b), Hemel Hempstead (136b), Miswell (138), and Tring (137); in each case the entry tells also of 'pasture for the livestock'.

[2] The entries for a few villages, e.g. Barley with 14 teams at work (134b, 136, 139*bis*,

6   D D

FISHERIES

Fisheries are mentioned or implied in connection with eight places in Hertfordshire. Only one entry specifically mentions a fishery (*piscaria*); one refers to fish (*pisces*), and two others record renders of eels from mills.

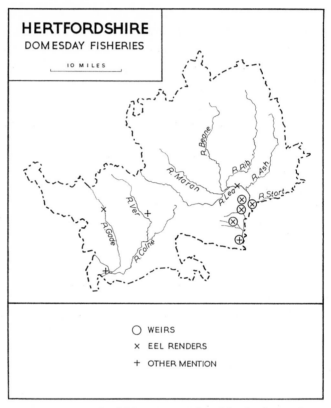

Fig. 30. Hertfordshire: Domesday fisheries in 1086.

Among the 'other mention' of fisheries is St Albans, with its *vivarium piscium*.

The remainder tell of weirs (*gurgites*), usually rendering eels, but, at Cheshunt, making a money payment. The relevant entries are:

140, 141 b), mention neither meadow nor pasture, and perhaps they had neither. A later document tells of villages elsewhere with no pasture except that upon the fallow field; see F. W. Maitland, *Domesday Book and Beyond*, pp. 399 n, 446.

Hoddesden (139): *De piscaria cl anguillae.*

Rickmansworth (136): *De piscibus iiii solidi.*

Hemel Hempstead (136b): *iiii molendina de xxxvii solidis et iiii denariis et ccc anguillis xxv minus.*

Ware (138b): *Ibi ii molendina de xxiiii solidis et cccc anguillis xxv minus.*

Rye (134b): *De gurgitibus cc anguillae.*

Hoddesden (137): *De gurgite c anguillae.*

Hoddesden (137b): *De gurgite xxi anguillae.*

Hoddesden (139b): *De gurgite xxii anguillae.*

Hailey (140): *De gurgite l anguillae.*

Wormley (137): *De dimidio gurgite l anguillae.*

Cheshunt (137): *De gurgite xvi denarii.*

There was also a fish-stew (*vivarium piscium*) at St Albans (135b).

Fig. 30 shows that the fisheries were mainly in the river Lea below its confluence with the Stort. The fishery at Hemel Hempstead was in the Gade and that at Rickmansworth was in the Colne, just below its confluence with the Gade.

MILLS

Mills are mentioned in connection with 73 out of the 168 Domesday settlements in Hertfordshire.[1] Their annual value is stated in terms of money, and this ranges from a mill yielding (*de*) 12*d.* at each of the villages of Braughing (137b) and Epcombs (142)[2] to 3 mills paying £10 by tale (*ad numerum*) at Hertford (132). At two places, Hemel Hempstead (136b) and Ware (138b), a render of eels as well as a money payment was made. Fractions of mills do not present any problem in Hertfordshire. At Digswell we hear of 1½ mills yielding 8*s.* 8*d.* on the holding of Geoffrey de Mandeville (139b) and of half a mill yielding 40*d.* on that of Peter de Valognes (141). Presumably there were 2 mills in the village of Digswell rendering a total of 12*s.* These were the only mill fractions in Hertford-shire in 1086. The entry for Ware is unusual: 'There are 2 mills yielding 24*s.* and 375 eels, and other men have 3 mills rendering 10*s.* yearly' (*Ibi ii molendina de xxiiii solidis et cccc anguillis xxv minus et alii homines habent iii molina reddentes per annum x solidos*).

More than one-half of the villages with mills had only one each. But there were some with 4, and two villages had 5 apiece. The table overleaf shows to what extent there was a clustering of mills:

---

[1] In addition there was a mill yielding 6*s.* 8*d.* on the unnamed manor of Eudo the steward in Hertford hundred (139).　　　　[2] Epcombs is the Domesday *Thepecāpe.*

Domesday Mills in Hertfordshire

1 mill	40 settlements	4 mills	9 settlements
2 mills	19 settlements	5 mills	2 settlements
3 mills	3 settlements		

This table excludes the mill on the anonymous holding of Eudo the steward in Hertford hundred (139).

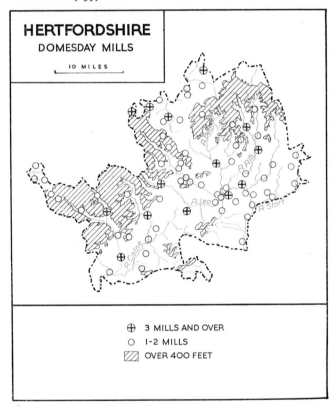

Fig. 31. Hertfordshire: Domesday mills in 1086.

There was also a mill on the anonymous holding of Eudo the steward in Hertford hundred.

One of the groups of 5 mills was at Ware (138b), either on the river Lea or on its tributary, the Ash. The other cluster was at Standon (142b) on the river Rib, another tributary of the Lea.

Fig. 31 shows the alignment of the mills along the rivers. But the general distribution, as opposed to the location of individual mills, is sometimes puzzling. Thus only 4 of the 34 villages in Edwinstree hundred seem to have had mills,[1] and only 3 of the 19 villages in the hundred of Odsey.[2] Yet these two hundreds were among those with the most plough-teams and with the highest recorded population. Was the grain of their villages ground elsewhere, or by hand? Or is the Domesday record of mills incomplete? We cannot tell.

CHURCHES

The entries relating to churches are only three in number:

> The borough of Hertford (132): Peter de Valognes has two churches with a house (*ii ecclesias cum una domo*) which he bought from Ulwi of Hatfield, rendering all customary dues (*reddentes omnes consuetudines*).
> Hitchin (132b): Of these 5 hides, 2 belong to the minster of this vill.
> Welwyn (142b): It belongs to the church of the vill.

The four churches mentioned in the folios can be but a very small fraction of the total number of churches in Domesday Hertfordshire. Some 50 priests are recorded in connection with 49 other places.[3] There was also a *clericus* at Sacombe (141). The priests of Hertfordshire, like those recorded in the Northamptonshire folios, are classed with the villeins and bordars. There were also a few priests holding land, e.g. at Roxford (140b) and at Welwyn (142b), but they have been excluded from the present total, as they may also have been holding land elsewhere.

URBAN LIFE

Five places in Hertfordshire seem to have been regarded as boroughs, although only two, Hertford and Ashwell, were specifically styled *burgus*. But we hear of a *burbium* in the 'villa' of Berkhamsted (*In Burbio hujus villae*), and of burgesses at St Albans and at Stanstead Abbots.[4] The information for all five places is very unsatisfactory, and it provides us

---

[1] One mill each at Affledwick (now Beauchamps) (137b), Berkesden (137), Hadham (133b), Widford (133b).

[2] Bygrave had one (135), Radwell two (134b, 141), and Ashwell a total of four (135b, 141).

[3] The only village with two priests was Weston (138b).

[4] The entry for a holding in Hoddesdon tells of Peter, a burgess, holding 2 hides (142); he appears in the account of the 'land of the king's thegns', but we are not told to which borough he belonged.

with hardly any indication of their commercial life and activities. Thus, there is no record of a market at any of them, but the entries for Ashwell, Berkhamsted and St Albans tell of 'tolls'. The Domesday evidence, slender as it is, has been set out below.

Hertford

The Domesday description of the county begins with an account of Hertford (132). We are told at once that in 1066 the borough was assessed at 10 hides but that it did not pay geld in 1086 (*modo non facit*). The entry then goes on to say that there had been 146 burgesses in the 'soke of King Edward'. No corresponding figure is entered for 1086, but we are given details of the ownership of some of their houses and are also told of 18 other burgesses (*Alios xviii burgenses*). The full list of properties mentioned is:

Count Alan	3 houses
Eudo the steward	1 house
Geoffrey de Bech	3 houses
Humfrey d'Ansleville	2 houses with 1 garden (*cum uno horto*)
Peter de Valognes	2 churches with 1 house[1]
Geoffrey de Mandeville	a certain holding (*occupatum quoddam*) and 7 houses
Ralf Baignard	2 houses
Hardwin de Scalers	15 houses

Finally, we are told the value of the township (*suburbium*) for the usual three dates. In 1066 it paid £7. 10s. by tale (*ad numerum*), but it was worth twice this amount when Peter de Valognes, the sheriff, received it. In 1086 it paid £20 assayed and weighed (*arsas et pensatas*) and its 3 mills paid (*reddunt*) £10 by tale.

The account of Hertford is particularly disappointing because the town must have acquired a certain importance after the building of the fort against the Danes at the beginning of the tenth century. Situated on the southern bank of the River Lea, near where the tributary streams of the Maran, the Beane and the Rib join it, Hertford was probably of commercial as well as strategic importance. Unfortunately we can only guess about its size and activities in 1086. The 34 houses (*domus*) and the

[1] For the churches, see J. H. Round in *V.C.H. Hertfordshire*, I, pp. 283, 299.

18 'other burgesses' seem to imply a total population of only some 250 people. But, on the other hand, if the 146 burgesses 'in the soke of King Edward' were also there in 1086, then the total population may have been of the order of 1,000 persons; but we cannot be certain.

St Albans

The entry (135b) relating to St Albans speaks of a *villa* and not of a *burgus*, and gives the impression that St Albans was a large agricultural community. But it tells also of 46 burgesses having half a hide, and records a payment of £11. 14s. from toll and other rents of the 'vill' (*de theloneo et de aliis redditis villae*). F. W. Maitland doubted whether the burgesses were 'really and physically' at St Albans, and he suggested that they may have been in London.[1] On the other hand, J. H. Round regarded St Albans as 'next in importance to Hertford' and suggested that the burgesses were 'clustered around the abbey's walls'.[2] But whatever the uncertainties about the legal status and commercial life of St Albans, its agricultural resources were substantial. The vill was assessed at 10 hides in 1086, and there were 3 hides in demesne. It had land for 16 plough-teams and there were 15 teams at work. Its other agricultural assets included woodland for 1,000 swine and with a render of 7s. besides, a park for the beasts of the chase (*unus parcus ibi est bestiarum silvaticarum*), meadow for 2 plough-teams, a fish-stew and 3 mills yielding 40s. The value of the vill had fallen to £12 after the Conquest from £24 T.R.E., but by 1086 it had largely recovered and was £20.

Its recorded population comprised 46 burgesses, 4 *francigenae*, 16 villeins, 13 bordars and 12 cottars. Assuming that the burgesses were physically as well as legally in the '*villa*', the recorded population amounts to 91 persons; this figure would imply a total population of some 500 persons. But we are only guessing, and the total number may well have exceeded this figure. Of the commercial life of St Albans we are told nothing beyond the fact that money was received from toll; this would seem to suggest the presence of a market, but we cannot be certain.

Berkhamsted

Like St Albans, Berkhamsted is called a *villa*, and its resources are surveyed in a single entry (136b) which is reproduced in the frontispiece

---

[1] *Domesday Book and Beyond*, p. 181.
[2] *V.C.H. Hertfordshire*, I, p. 296.

to this volume.[1] In 1086 the borough was held by the count of Mortain, and Round thought that it was probably 'his personal residence'.[2] The presence of a ditcher (*fossarius*) holding half a hide seems to indicate the existence and importance of the castle ditches, but a castle is not mentioned. Within the borough (*In Burbio huius villae*)[3] there were 52 burgesses having half a hide and rendering £4 from toll (*de theloneo*).

We can only guess at the commercial activities of the burgesses, but the entry suggests that the settlement was still primarily an agricultural community. Berkhamsted was assessed at 13 hides; there were 3 hides in demesne, the ditcher had half a hide, the burgesses half a hide, and Rannulf, a serjeant of the count (*serviens comitis*), 1 virgate. The agricultural resources included land for 26 plough-teams; only 15 teams were at work, but we are told that there could be 11 more, 3 on the demesne and 8 with the peasantry. There was woodland for 1,000 swine and yielding 5s. besides, meadow for 8 plough-teams, pasture for the livestock of the vill, and 2 arpents of vine (*Ibi ii arpendi vineae*). The value of the *villa* fell after the Conquest from £24 *T.R.E.* to £20. There was a further decrease in value, and in 1086 the *villa* seems to have been worth only £16.

The recorded population included, in addition to the 52 burgesses and the ditcher, a priest, 14 villeins, 15 bordars and 6 serfs, which gives a total of 89. This figure suggests that in 1086 Berkhamsted may have been a settlement of at least 500 people.

Ashwell

The main account of Ashwell is given on fos. 135–135 b and it is this entry which tells of a payment of 49s. 4d. from toll and other dues of the borough (*De theloneo et de aliis consuetudinibus*) and records the presence of 14 burgesses. Three subsidiary entries (139b, 141 and 141b) add some details about the agricultural resources of the settlement. The four entries are set out below:

(i) The abbot of Westminster's estate (135–135 b). 'The abbot himself holds Ashwell and it is assessed at 6 hides. There is land for 12 plough-teams. In

---

[1] Two other entries mention Berkhamsted; on fo. 136b we are told that half a hide of Wigginton had lain in (*jacuit in*) Berkhamsted and that Little Gaddesden had been a berewick of Berkhamsted (*fuit Beruuicha in Berchamstede*).

[2] J. H. Round in *V.C.H. Hertfordshire*, I, p. 280.

[3] This is an unusual expression. It would seem to refer to a *burbium*; note the *suburbium* of Hertford (p. 86 above). Or could it be a scribal error for *in burgo*?

demesne 2½ hides, and there are 2 plough-teams. A priest with 16 villeins and 9 bordars have 5 plough-teams [and] another 5 could be made. There, 14 burgesses and 9 cottars. From toll and from other dues of the borough 49s. 4d. There, 4 serfs and 2 mills rendering (de) 14s. Meadow for 6 plough-teams. Pasture for the livestock. Wood for 100 swine. In all it is and was worth (valet et valuit) £20. T.R.E. £22. Of this land (De hac terra) Peter the sheriff holds of the abbot half a hide, and Geoffrey de Mandeville 1 virgate and 1 mill rendering 10s. This manor belonged and belongs to the demesne (jacuit et jacet in dominio) of the church of St Peter of Westminster.'

(ii) The holding of Geoffrey de Mandeville (139b). 'In Ashwell Germund [de St Ouen] holds of Geoffrey 1 virgate. There is land for half a plough-team, and it is there with 2 bordars. Meadow for half a plough-team. It is and was always worth (Valet et valuit semper) 10s. This land Godeve [i.e. Godgifu] held of Asgar. She could not sell except with his consent (praeter ejus licentiam).'

(iii) The holding of Peter de Valognes (141). 'In Ashwell Peter holds 2 hides as one manor. There is land for 6 plough-teams. In demesne 3 virgates and there are there (ibi) 2 plough-teams, and 8 villeins with 8 bordars have 4 plough-teams. There, 2 cottars and 4 serfs and 1 mill rendering (de) 10s. Meadow for 1 plough-team. Pasture for the livestock. In all it is worth 100s. When received 60s., T.R.E. £7. This manor Elmer of Bennington, a thegn of King Edward, held.'

(iv) The holding of Hardwin de Scalers (141 b). 'In Ashwell Tetbald holds of Hardwin half a hide. There is land for 1 plough-team, but it is not there. There, 6 cottars. Meadow for half a plough-team. This land is worth 20s. When received it was worth 10s. T.R.E. 30s. Uctred held this land under Robert son of Wimarch; he could not sell without his leave (praeter ejus licentiam), so the men of the hundred testify.'

These four entries emphasise the agricultural character of the settlement at Ashwell; altogether, 13½ plough-teams were at work on 19½ plough-lands. The recorded population, including the 14 burgesses, amounts to 83 persons and implies a total population of between 400 and 500 people. Thus Domesday Ashwell seems to have been but a small borough with a significant agricultural element.

Stanstead Abbots

The Domesday account of Stanstead Abbots is given in four entries (138b, 139b, 140b and 142b). The first entry, the account of the holding of Rannulf brother of Ilger, tells us of 7 burgesses paying, with other dues from meadow and wood, 24s. (*Ibi etiam vii burgenses qui reddunt cum aliis consuetudinibus prati et silvae xxiiii solidos*). We cannot be sure that the burgesses were physically at Stanstead Abbots, but they may have been. One thing is certain. In 1086 Stanstead Abbots was still very much an agricultural community, differing but slightly from the surrounding villages. The four entries taken together tell of a settlement assessed at 18½ hides and with land for 17½ plough-teams; 11½ plough-teams were at work, and another 6 could be employed. There was also wood for 109 swine, meadow for 18¼ teams, pasture for the livestock of the vill, and a mill yielding (*de*) 10s. The recorded population consisted of 7 burgesses, 1 reeve (*prepositus*), 4 *francigenae*, 1 sokeman,[1] 1 priest, 4 villeins, 4 bordars, 7 cottars and 2 serfs, which would suggest a total population of under 200. But it is unwise to speculate.

MISCELLANEOUS INFORMATION

Very little miscellaneous information is given in the Hertfordshire folios. There is, for example, no mention of markets, but we hear of money renders from toll (*de theloneo*) at Ashwell (135b), at Berkhamsted (136b) and at St Albans (135b). The presence of 10 traders paying 10s. from customary dues (*Ibi x mercatores reddunt x solidos de consuetudinibus*) may indicate a market at Cheshunt (137).

Livestock

Livestock are mentioned in only one entry in the Hertfordshire folios— on the anonymous manor of Eudo the steward in Hertford hundred (139). From this one mention we obtain a glimpse of the numerous other requisites for stocking on an eleventh-century estate:

With this [land], when Humphrey took it from Eudo, he received 68 animals (*animalia*) and 350 sheep and 150 swine and 50 goats and 1 mare (*equam*) and 13s. 4d. of the king's rent (*de censu regis*), and between cloths and vessels (*inter pannos et vasa*) 20s.

The *Inquisitio Eliensis* records livestock. The relevant details for the three Hertfordshire estates which it describes have been tabulated below because they give some indication of the livestock commonly found on

---

[1] In 1066, there had been 14 other sokemen on the main estate (138b).

holdings in the eleventh century; they also serve to remind us of the great wealth of detail in the original return:[1]

Hadham	12 cattle	50 sheep	50 swine
Hatfield	26 cattle	360 sheep	60 swine
Kelshall	2 cattle	308 sheep	18 swine

Vineyards

There are three entries relating to vineyards in the Hertfordshire folios. At Berkhamsted (136b) and at Standon (142b) there were 2 arpents of vine (*ii arpendi vineae*), and at Ware (138b) there were 4 arpents of newly planted vine (*iiii arpendi vineae nuperrime plantatae*).

Other references

Although there are no direct references to hunting in the Hertfordshire folios, Bennington (141), St Albans (135b) and Ware (138b) had each a park for the beasts of the chase (*parcus silvaticarum bestiarum*).

REGIONAL SUMMARY

The evidence discussed above makes it clear that not all parts of Hertfordshire had offered equal opportunities to the Saxon colonists. Although the nature of the Domesday record permits only broad comparisons, it is clear that distinctive landscapes had already come into being. The essential difference in 1086 was between the relatively empty south and the well-populated north. But within each of these broad divisions there were variations, and altogether five regions have been recognised (Fig. 32). In addition to these five divisions the county includes a small portion of the clay vale below the Chiltern escarpment. This is similar in character to the Northern Claylands of Buckinghamshire (see p. 180 below), and is not separately described here.

(1) *The Chilterns*

In the south-west the county includes a portion of the Chiltern Hills and the scarp-foot zone beyond. From the crest of the escarpment, which reaches 800 ft. O.D. near Berkhamsted, a broad dip-slope extends south-eastwards to the Vale of St Albans. This sloping plateau surface is broken by a series of streams, e.g. the Gade and its tributaries, the Bulborne, the Ver and the Lea; and between their valleys the Chalk is extensively

[1] See N. E. S. A. Hamilton (ed.), *op. cit.* pp. 124–5.

overlain by superficial deposits, principally Clay-with-flints to the south of the Ver and brickearth to the north. Thus the region is one of varied soils, ranging from sticky clays to fertile loams.

Densities of plough-teams (mostly about one) and population (mostly about 2) were very low for the region as a whole, but there were some localities, notably those towards the Hitchin gap, with higher densities of both teams and men. There was little meadow, but substantial amounts of

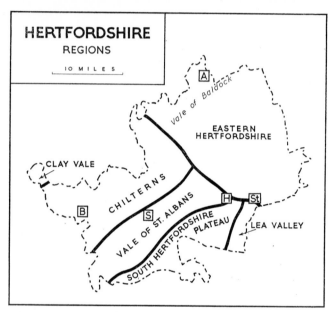

Fig. 32. Hertfordshire: Regional subdivisions.

Domesday boroughs are indicated by initials: A, Ashwell; B, Berk-hamsted; H, Hertford; S, St Albans; St, Stanstead Abbots.

wood especially to the south of the Lea; here, for example, Berkhamsted, Flamstead, Hemel Hempstead and Tring each had enough for 1,000 swine. Most of the valley villages had mills, and some had more than one apiece; the four mills at Hemel Hempstead rendered eels as well as a money payment.

(2) The Vale of St Albans

This undulating lowland, about 6 miles broad and 18 miles long, abuts on to the Chiltern dip-slope at about 350 ft. O.D.; it is flanked on the east by the low escarpment of the London Clay. The Vale coincides with a spread of drift material—chalky Boulder Clay, glacial sands and gravels, and the underlying Chalk is exposed only in the bordering slopes of the valleys. The soils over much of the area are intermediate in character (Fig. 160), yet the Domesday evidence gives the region fairly low densities for both teams (1·2) and men (3·0). All the villages had very substantial amounts of woodland, e.g. Cassio near Watford, Hanstead near St Albans and St Albans itself each had enough for 1,000 swine, and Hatfield for 2,000. Undoubtedly some of this woodland was in appurtenant holdings beyond the Vale, but we cannot tell how much. There was little meadow except at Cassio which had enough for 23 plough-teams. Nearly every settlement had a mill, and some had 3 or 4 mills apiece.

(3) *The South Hertfordshire Plateau*

The scarp edge of the South Hertfordshire plateau forms a conspicuous break of slope along the southern border of the Vale of St Albans. The dip-slope is heavily dissected by numerous small streams draining to the Colne and to the Lea. London Clay is exposed on the slopes and on the floors of the valleys; there are also patches of Boulder Clay, and the soils are predominantly heavy. The hill tops are capped by Pebble Gravel at heights of between 350 and 400 ft. O.D. Agriculturally this was an unrewarding region,[1] and it is not surprising that the densities of plough-teams and population were low, being under one and about two respectively. The countryside must have been very heavily wooded in the eleventh century, for its villages all had woodland for large numbers of swine—Bushey and Shenley each had sufficient for 1,000 swine—and, in addition, it probably supported the swine of the Lea valley villages, e.g. the 1,200 swine of Cheshunt. But there was hardly any meadow, although a few of the villages had mills.

(4) *The Lea Valley*

South of its confluence with the Stort, the Lea meanders across a flat, marshy flood plain. But on the Hertfordshire side of the river there is a series of gravel terraces covered with easily worked loamy soils. In 1086 these soils seem to have supported about 2 teams and 8 recorded people per square mile. There were substantial amounts of both meadow and

---

[1] For the sterility of the region in later times see H. Evershed, 'Agriculture of Hertfordshire', *Journ. Roy. Ag. Soc.* xxv (London, 1864), pp. 270–1.

woodland entered for the villages, but much of the wood must have been physically situated outside the region, on the heavy soils of the South Hertfordshire plateau. The villages all had a mill apiece, and some had weirs in the Lea; these provided an additional source of income from the fish trapped in them. The presence of ten traders at Cheshunt may indicate that the Lower Lea valley was already an important highway to London.

(5) *Eastern Hertfordshire*

The even distribution of Domesday names over this region tells its own story of fairly uniform agricultural development. The general prosperity, as indicated by the densities of plough-teams and population, resembles that of the adjoining areas of Cambridgeshire and Essex.[1]

East of the Hitchin gap the Chalk escarpment is masked by an extensive sheet of chalky Boulder Clay, and the crest of the escarpment is subdued; the East Anglian Heights reach a maximum height of only 549 ft. O.D. From this 'crest' the dip-slope extends southwards towards the Lea. Its surface has a mean altitude of about 350 ft., but it is broken by a series of streams that flow to join the Lea; the main valleys are those of the Beane, the Rib (and its tributary the Quin), the Ash and the Stort. The Chalk itself is only occasionally exposed in the sides of the deeper valleys, the floors of which are all drift-filled. The soils for the most part are deep calcareous loams, but they become heavier and less chalky in the south-east where the drift cover overlaps on to the London Clay formation. Plough-team and population densities per square mile were moderately high, being about 3 and 10 respectively. There was generally little wood-land, and many villages had only 'wood for fencing'; the 600 swine at Standon in the Rib valley and the 400 at Ware on the Middle Lea were exceptional. Ware also had a park for the beasts of the chase. The close network of streams suggests that there might have been a fair amount of meadow, but the quantity assigned to each vill was small; only Stanstead Abbots and Ware on the Lea, and Standon on the Rib had substantial amounts. There were but few mills in the region as a whole; the villages with mills were mostly along the middle course of the Lea where it is joined by the Beane and the Rib.

The scarp-foot zone of the East Anglian Heights is wider than that of

---

[1] For a discussion of these, see H. C. Darby, *The Domesday Geography of Eastern England*, pp. 313 and 260–1.

the Chilterns and forms a broad belt generally known as the Vale of Baldock. It differs from the rest of Eastern Hertfordshire because it is free from glacial drift, and its soils are chalk marls derived from the Lower Chalk formation. In the Vale the densities of plough-teams (3·7 per square mile) and of population (13·3 per square mile) were higher than the average for Eastern Hertfordshire as a whole. Its villages generally had small amounts of meadow, but little or no wood. Most had mills, presumably on the Ivel or on the Rhee.

BIBLIOGRAPHICAL NOTE

(1) It is interesting to recall that at the beginning of the eighteenth century Sir Henry Chauncy transcribed and translated the Hertfordshire entries—*The historical antiquities of Hertfordshire* (London, 1700)—and he reassembled the entries on a geographical basis. His history of the county was superseded by R. Clutterbuck's *The history and antiquities of the county of Hertford* (3 vols. London, 1815–27). Clutterbuck also translated the Domesday entries, generally giving a transcription of the Latin text.

(2) There was also a nineteenth-century translation of the Hertfordshire folios: William Bawdwen, *Dom Boc. A translation of the record called Domesday, so far as relates to the counties of Middlesex, Hertford, Buckingham, Oxford and Gloucester* (Doncaster, 1812).

The standard translation is that made by the Rev. F. W. Ragg in *V.C.H. Hertfordshire*, I (London, 1902), pp. 300–44; this is accompanied by one of J. H. Round's valuable introductions (pp. 263–99).

(3) F. H. Baring, *Domesday Tables for the counties of Surrey, Berkshire, Middlesex, Hertford, Buckingham and Bedford and for the New Forest* (London, 1909). The tables for Hertfordshire are full and are accompanied by a useful note.

(4) The following articles deal with various aspects of the Domesday study of the county:

O. C. PELL, 'Upon libere tenentes, virgatae, and carucae in Domesday....', *Comm. Camb. Antiq. Soc.* VI (Cambridge, 1891), pp. 17–40.

O. C. PELL, 'On the Domesday geldable hide....', *Comm. Camb. Antiq. Soc.* VI (Cambridge, 1891), pp. 65–176.

The strange ideas of Pell received the severest criticism, e.g. by J. H. Round in *Feudal England* (London, 1895; reprinted 1909), p. 64.

F. H. BARING, 'The Conqueror's footprints in Domesday', *Eng. Hist. Rev.* XIII (London, 1898), pp. 17–25. Reprinted with 'some additions and alterations' in F. H. Baring, *Domesday Tables*, pp. 207–16 (see above).

I. C. GOULD, 'Some notes on Wymondley in Domesday', *Trans. East Herts. Archaeol. Soc.* III (Hertford, 1906), pp. 12–13.

G. H. FOWLER, 'The devastation of Bedfordshire and the neighbouring counties in 1065 and 1066', *Archaeologia*, LXXII (London, 1922), pp. 41–50, especially Map 1, facing p. 50.

S. W. WOOLDRIDGE and D. SMETHAM, 'The glacial drifts of Essex and Hertfordshire, and their bearing upon the agricultural and historical geography of the region', *Geog. Journ.* LXXVIII (1931), pp. 243–69.

W. B. JOHNSON, 'Hertfordshire nine hundred years ago', *Hertfordshire Countryside*, VIII (Letchworth, 1953), pp. 68, 95. These notes include a count of Domesday population, pigs and mills.

(5) The *Inquisitio Eliensis* was printed in part by Sir Henry Ellis in vol. IV of the *Libri Censualis vocati Domesday Book* (London, 1816), pp. 497–528. It was reprinted by N. E. S. A. Hamilton in *Inquisitio Comitatus Cantabrigiensis* (London, 1876), pp. 97–195, and was discussed by J. H. Round in *Feudal England* (London, 1895; reprinted 1909). It is also discussed in many of the general works dealing with the Domesday Book; see H. C. Darby, *The Domesday Geography of Eastern England* (Cambridge, 2nd ed., 1957), pp. 3 *et seq.* and p. 22. See also R. Welldon Finn, 'The Inquisitio Eliensis reconsidered', *Eng. Hist. Rev.* LXXV (1960), pp. 385–409.

(6) A valuable aid to the Domesday study of the county is *The Place-Names of Hertfordshire*, edited by J. E. B. Gover, A. Mawer and F. M. Stenton (Cambridge, 1938).

CHAPTER III

MIDDLESEX

BY EILA M. J. CAMPBELL, M.A.

The Middlesex folios are exceptionally full. In addition to the usual statement about the hidage of an estate, we are also given not only the hidage
on the demesne, but also that of groups of peasant holdings or indeed
often of individual holdings. Generally, the compilers of the Domesday
Book omitted this detail but a solitary entry in the Hertfordshire folios,[1]
together with evidence afforded by the *Inquisitio Comitatus Cantabrigiensis*
and the *Inquisitio Eliensis*, suggests that such information was required
throughout the country.[2] Yet, despite their wealth of information, the
Middlesex folios are very disappointing because London itself is not
surveyed. Maitland thought that the compilers left space in the text for
an account of the city, and there is certainly space into which such an
account could have been inserted.[3] We hear incidentally of the burgesses
of London, for some are mentioned in the entries for rural manors not
only in Middlesex, but also in the neighbouring counties of Essex and
Surrey.[4]

The early nineteenth-century county of Middlesex, in terms of which
this study has been made, seems to have been the same as the Domesday
county. There was, apparently, no change until 1889 when certain parishes
in the south-east were detached to form part of the administrative county
of London. Historic Middlesex was defined on three sides by rivers—the
Thames, the Colne and the Lea—all occupying fairly wide, marshy valleys.
In the north, the boundary ran through the great stretch of woodland
which separated the county from Hertfordshire.

Within the Domesday county there were six hundreds, varying in size
from Edmonton with only 70 hides to Elthorne with 224½ hides (Fig. 33).
The arrangement of the six hundreds appears to have remained constant

---

[1] Sawbridgeworth (139b); see pp. 55–6 above.
[2] See (i) F. W. Maitland, *Domesday Book and Beyond* (Cambridge, 1897), pp. 476–7;
(ii) P. Vinogradoff, *English Society in the Eleventh Century* (Oxford, 1908), p. 168.
[3] F. W. Maitland, *op. cit.* p. 178, n. 1.
[4] See p. 132 below.

until the nineteenth century, except that Hampton (rubricated under
Hounslow in 1086) appears in subsequent records as part of Spelthorne;
the name Hounslow disappeared as a hundred name and was replaced
by Isleworth in the twelfth century.[1]

Settlements and their Distribution

The total number of separate places mentioned for Middlesex seems to be
62, including London, Westminster, referred to as *villa ubi sedet ecclesia
Sancti Petri* (128), and Bishopsgate, styled *ad portam episcopi* (128).[2]

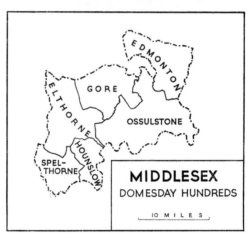

Fig. 33. Middlesex: Domesday hundreds.

The northern boundary of the county with Hertfordshire may
well have been indefinite (see p. 97).

This figure cannot accurately reflect the total number of separate settlements in the county in 1086. In the first place, when two or more adjoining
settlements bear the same surname today, it is not always clear whether
more than one unit existed in the eleventh century. Only when there is
specific mention of a second village in the Domesday Book itself, has it
been included in the total of 62. Thus the separate existence of East
Bedfont and West Bedfont seems to be indicated by *Bedefunt* (129, 130)

[1] O. S. Anderson, *The English Hundred-Names: The south-eastern counties* (Lund
and Leipzig, 1939), p. 56.
[2] The total of 62 excludes the unidentified *de nanesmaneslande* (i.e. of nomansland)
mentioned on fo. 127.

and *West bedefund* (130), but, on the other hand, there is no indication that, say, the Great and Little Stanmore of today existed as separate villages in 1086; the Domesday information about them is entered under only one name, *Stanmere* (129b, 130b), but they may well have been separate settlements in the eleventh century. Their distinctive appellations were first recorded in 1106, when Little Stanmore, alias Whitchurch, was styled

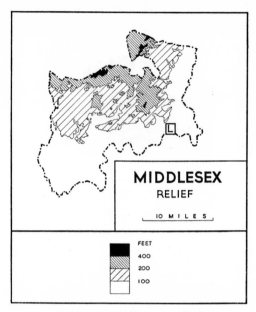

Fig. 34. Middlesex: Relief.

L indicates London.

alia Stanmera. Or again, explicit record of a distinction between Great and Little Greenford did not appear until 1254.[1] To these Domesday names which may have covered more than one settlement must be added those of large composite manors like Fulham (127b *ter*), Harrow (127) and Stepney (127 *quater*, 127b *septiens*, 130, 130b) which, as later evidence suggests, may well have included more than one locality apiece in 1086. In addition to the 62 named places, we hear of four unnamed berewicks

---

[1] Little Greenford has been known as Perivale since 1508. For the history of this name and of other place-names mentioned in this chapter see J. E. B. Gover, A. Mawer, F. M. Stenton and S. J. Madge, *The Place-Names of Middlesex* (Cambridge, 1942). In the Domesday Book there are four entries for *Greneforde* (128b, 129b *bis*, 130b).

belonging to Staines (128 b), but we cannot tell whether these four holdings were at places otherwise mentioned or whether they were separate places.

The total of 62 includes four places, besides the city of London itself, for which very little information is given; the record may be incomplete or the details may have been included with those of neighbouring vills. Thus the entry for Holborn (127) tells only of two cottars rendering 20*d.* yearly. Of Bishopsgate (128) we know only that the canons of

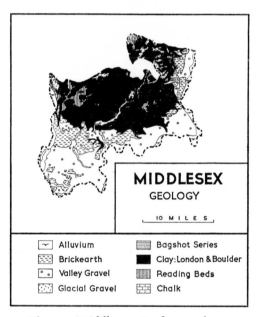

Fig. 35. Middlesex: Surface geology.

Based on Geological Survey One-Inch Sheets (New Series) 239, 255, 256, 269 and 270.

St Paul's had there 10 cottars with 9 acres for which they rendered 18*s.* 6*d.* yearly. Or, again, no separate details are recorded for South Mimms (*Mimes,* 129 b),[1] which is described as a berewick of Edmonton.[2] In addition to these three, the entry for *Exeforde* (i.e. Ashford, 129) notes a plough-land, a plough-team and meadow but no inhabitants.

Not all the 62 Domesday names appear on the present-day map of

---

[1] North Mimms (*Mimmine,* 135) was surveyed under Hertfordshire, in which county it still lies.

[2] The details for Edmonton have been divided equally with South Mimms.

Middlesex settlements; the growth of London and its suburbs during the last fifty years has obliterated several. Thus *Tolentone* (i.e. Tollington, 130b) survives only in the names of a park and two roads in the borough of Islington; and *Totehele* (i.e. Tottenhall, 128) is represented by Tottenham Court Road. The name *Rugemere* (i.e. Rug Moor, 127b) is now extinct, but it persisted until the eighteenth century as the name of a field in the extreme north-west corner of the parish of St Pancras, just east of the present Zoological Gardens. *Eia* (i.e. Ebury, 129b) is preserved in Ebury Bridge, Ebury Square and Ebury Street in the City of Westminster, and it is interesting to note that the Domesday vill of *Eia* was situated on an island in the marshy area now covered by the streets of Pimlico. The names of certain other Domesday settlements survived as the names of hamlets until the 1920's when they were engulfed by suburban development; thus Hatton (*Hatone*, 129, and *Haitone*, 130) was a hamlet in the parish of East Bedfont near the western edge of Hounslow Heath. Charlton (130b) and Kempton (129) in Sunbury, Dawley (129) in Harlington, and Colham (129) in Hillingdon are other Domesday settlements that were represented by hamlets until the 1930's. Only one name in the Middlesex folios cannot be identified—*Stanestaple* (128). F. H. Baring thought that it might have been in the vicinity of either Willesden or Hampstead;[1] more recently S. J. Madge has shown that it may have adjoined St Pancras.[2]

On the other hand, many settlements on the modern map of Middlesex are not mentioned in the Domesday Book. Some of their names appear in pre-Domesday documents. Others are not recorded until the twelfth, the thirteenth or even the fourteenth century, and presumably, if they existed in 1086, they are accounted for under the statistics of other settlements which are named. The places not recorded by name in the Domesday folios fall into three geographical groups. The first consists of those which were probably part of the great Domesday manor of Harrow (127): Roxeth and Wembley (both named in pre-Domesday documents), Preston (first recorded in 1194), Alperton (1199), Kenton and Pinner (1232), Harrow Weald and Sudbury (1282), and Roxborough (1334). The second group comprises Acton, Brentford, Ealing and Hammersmith, and it is

---

[1] F. H. Baring, *Domesday Tables for the counties of Surrey, Berkshire, Middlesex, Hertford, Buckingham and Bedford and for the New Forest* (London, 1909), p. 82.
[2] S. J. Madge, *The Early Records of Harringay alias Hornsey, from Prehistoric Times to 1216 A.D.* (Hornsey, 1938), p. 55.

possible that their resources were surveyed under Fulham (127b *ter*), for they were all part of the pre-Reformation 'Lordship of Fulham'.[1] Brentford is a pre-Domesday name, but Acton appears first in 1181, Ealing in 1130,[2] and Hammersmith in 1294; the last was a hamlet of Fulham as recently as 1834. The third group consists of Edgware, Hornsey, Finchley and Friern Barnet, to the north of London. Edgware is a pre-Domesday name, and C. F. Baylis has suggested that Edgware may have been described under either Stanmore or Kingsbury.[3] C. J. Féret identified Finchley as part of

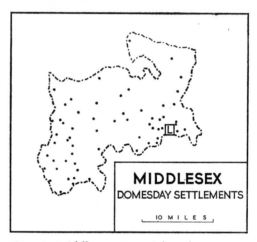

Fig. 36. Middlesex: Domesday place-names.

L indicates London.

the 'Lordship of Fulham',[4] and S. J. Madge has shown that one of the entries for Stepney can be assigned to Hornsey.[5] Sometimes, although a modern parish is not itself named in the folios, it contains the site of one or more Domesday settlements; thus the parish of Shoreditch contains Haggerston (130) and Hoxton (128 *bis*).

[1] See (1) C. J. Féret, *Fulham, Old and New*, I (Fulham, 1900), p. 13; (2) S. J. Madge, *The Medieval Records of Harringay alias Hornsey* (Hornsey, 1939), pp. 80–1.

[2] Although *Illing'* appears to date only from 1130, the *Gillingas* were in the locality in the seventh century.

[3] C. F. Baylis, 'The omission of Edgware from Domesday', *Trans. Lond. Mdx. Archaeol. Soc.* N.S. XI (London, 1954), pp. 62–6.

[4] *Op. cit.* p. 13. For a summary of evidence supporting this identification, see M. Robbins, 'A note on early Finchley', *Trans. Lond. Mdx. Archaeol. Soc.* XVIII (London, 1955), pp. 65–7.

[5] S. J. Madge, *The Early Records of Harringay alias Hornsey*, pp. 31–45, 49.

The distribution of Domesday place-names was naturally very uneven in a county with such marked physical contrasts as Middlesex (Fig. 36). Today, practically the whole of Middlesex is a built-up area, but in 1086 names were especially sparse over the heavy soils of the London Clay outcrop. Domesday villages were most numerous on the gravel terraces bordering the Lea and the Thames, and on the extensive loam-covered plain in the south-west of the county.

THE DISTRIBUTION OF PROSPERITY AND POPULATION

Some idea of the nature of the information in the Domesday folios for Middlesex, and of the form in which it was presented, may be obtained from the account of the village of Hanwell. The village was held entirely by the abbey of Westminster, and so it is described in a single entry (128b):

Manor: The abbot of St Peter [of Westminster] holds Hanwell. It is assessed at 8 hides (*se defendit pro viii hidis*). Land for 5 plough-teams. To the demesne belong 4 hides and 1 virgate, and 1 plough-team is there. The villeins have 4 plough-teams. There, 1 villein with (*de*) 2 hides, and 4 villeins with 1 hide, and 6 bordars with 3 virgates, and 4 cottars, and 2 serfs. There, 1 mill yielding (*de*) 2 shillings and 2 pence. Meadow for 1 plough-team. Wood for 50 swine. In all (*In totis valentiis*) it is worth 110s. When received, likewise (*similiter*). T.R.E. £7. This manor was and is in the demesne of St Peter.

This entry does not include all the kinds of information that appear elsewhere in the folios for the county. It does not mention, for example, the categories of population known as *francigenae* and priests. There is also no mention either of pasture or of fisheries. But, although not comprehensive, it is a representative and a straightforward entry, and it does set out the recurring standard items that are found for most villages. These are five in number: (1) hides, (2) plough-lands, (3) plough-teams, (4) population, and (5) values. The bearing of these five items of information upon regional variation in the prosperity of the county must now be considered.

(1) *Hides*

The Middlesex assessment is regularly stated generally in terms of a round number of hides, but sometimes in hides and virgates, and very occasionally in acres. Thus, at Hatton (*Hatone, Haitone*) there were two holdings, one of 'a hide and a half' (*i hidam et dimidiam*, 129) and the other of

'1 hide and 3 virgates and the third part of a virgate' (*unam hidam et iii virgatas et terciam partem de i virgata*, 130); and on fo. 127 we hear that the king held 12½ acres of land of nomansland (*xii acras terrae et dimidiam de nanesmaneslande*). The form of the statement varies, as can be seen from four representative entries:

- (i)   Hanworth (129): *Haneworde pro v hidis se defendit.*
- (ii) Hayes (127): *tenet Hesa pro lviiii hidis.*
- (iii) Islington (128): *In Isendone habent canonici S. Pauli ii hidas.*
- (iv) Twyford (127b): *In Tueverde tenet Durandus canonicorum S. Pauli de rege ii hidas terrae.*

Of these formulae, the second occurs most frequently. Only once is an assessment specifically stated for 1066—the entry for Harrow runs: *Pro c hidis se defendebat T.R.E. et modo facit* (127). But four other entries contain the formula *se defendebat semper*; thus Drayton was always rated at 10 hides (128), Isleworth at 70 hides (130), Tottenhall at 5 hides (128), and Willesden at 15 hides (127b). Every Domesday holding in Middlesex appears to have been assessed to geld in 1086. As in Bedfordshire, Buckinghamshire and Hertfordshire, hides in demesne (*hidae in dominio*) are generally entered for estates held by tenants-in-chief themselves and not held of them by under-tenants; presumably these hides 'in demesne' were separately recorded in view of some exemption from geld.[1] Once we hear of 'carucates' in demesne; the entry for Tottenham, assessed at 5 hides, notes—*In dominio sunt ii carucatae terrae praeter has v hidas* (130b). The two 'carucates' of land seem, therefore, to have been additional to the 5 hides of the assessment, and, according to Baring, it would appear that a special arrangement had been made by which the whole of the assessment for geld 'had been thrown on the villeins'.[2] But further investigation into the significance of hides and carucates in demesne is needed.[3]

The system of assessing villages in multiples of 5 hides is particularly prominent in Middlesex.[4] Generally it is very obvious; thus Charlton was assessed at 5 hides (130b), Kensington at 10 hides (130b), Northolt at 15 hides (129b), Hendon at 20 hides (128b), Ruislip at 30 hides (129b),

---

[1] See J. H. Round, 'Danegeld and the finance of Domesday' in P. E. Dove (ed.), *Domesday Studies*, I (London, 1888), pp. 96–8.

[2] F. H. Baring, *Domesday Tables*, p. 134.

[3] For the possibility that these 'carucates' may have been plough-lands, see p. 148 below.

[4] J. H. Round, *Feudal England* (London, 1895; reprinted 1909), p. 66.

Hampton at 35 hides (130), Isleworth at 70 hides (130), and Harrow at 100 hides (127). There are many other equally clear examples. The system is most easily recognised when a vill was in the hands of one landowner, but the same feature can also be seen when the several holdings of some villages are assembled from the different folios of the Domesday Book. Here, for example, are the different holdings in Ickenham and Islington respectively:

Ickenham

	Hides
(1) Earl Roger (129)	9½
(2) Geoffrey de Mandeville (129b)	3½
(3) Robert Fafiton (130)	2
Total	15

Islington

	Hides
(1) The canons of St Paul's (128)	2
(2) The canons of St Paul's (128)	2
(3) Geoffrey de Mandeville (129b)	½
(4) Derman of London (130b)	½
Total	5

Altogether the number of villages in the county assessed at either 5 or 10 hides is 19, and, if we include the larger assessments given in multiples of 5, the five-hide principle is readily apparent in one-half of the Middlesex villages;[1] Round showed that the principle is even more apparent when an attempt is made to reconstitute the hundreds.[2]

Whatever the origin of this principle, it is clear that in 1086 the assessment was artificial in character and bore no constant relationship to the agricultural resources of a vill. The variation among a representative selection of five-hide vills speaks for itself:

	Plough-lands	Teams	Population
Cranford (130b)	3	3	14
Hanworth (129)	3	4	10
Harefield (130)	5	5	25
Kempton (129)	5	4	19
Lisson (130b)	3	3	8
Tottenhall (128)	4	3½	8

[1] This number excludes the city of London itself, for which no information was recorded.   [2] *Feudal England*, pp. 66–7.

We cannot say whether consideration of area and value had ever entered into the assessment, but the Domesday figures bear the stamp of artificiality.

The total assessment of the county (apart from the city of London, for which no information was given)[1] seems to have been 880 hides; the present count has yielded a total of 879 hides 1 virgate and 21½ acres. Maitland's figure was 868 hides,[2] but it is clearly too low.[3] There have been four other estimates of the Middlesex assessment and they all agree that the corrected figure for the county should be 880 hides.[4] It was W. J. Corbett who first showed that the corrected total for the county could be neatly divided by hundreds into two groups, an eastern and a western:[5]

Eastern hundreds	Ossulstone	220	440
	Edmonton	70 220	
	Gore	150	
Western hundreds	Elthorne	225 330	
	Hounslow	105	440
	Spelthorne	110	
		Total	880

Besides this total of 880 hides,[6] there were 2 carucates of land in demesne at Tottenham (130 b) which seem never to have been rated for geld.[7]

The hidage in demesne for the county as a whole seems to have been 265½ hides 2½ virgates. In addition to stating the number of hides in demesne, the Middlesex folios give details of the amount of land held by

[1] F. W. Maitland showed that London seems to have gelded for 1,200 hides (*op. cit.* p. 409 n.).

[2] *Op. cit.* p. 400.

[3] On another page, Maitland wrote: 'we set so little reliance upon our own computation, that we are not very willing to institute a comparison' (*op. cit.* p. 456).

[4] In order of date of publication, they are: (1) W. J. Corbett, 'The Tribal Hidage', *Trans. Roy. Hist. Soc.* N.S. XIV (London, 1900), pp. 205, 218. (2) A. M. Davies, 'The Domesday hidation of Middlesex', *Home Counties Magazine*, III (London, 1901), p. 238. (3) F. H. Baring, *Domesday Tables*, pp. 80, 85. (4) Sir Montagu Sharpe, *Middlesex in the Eleventh Century* (Brentford, 1941), p. 22.

[5] *Op. cit.* p. 205.

[6] A. M. Davies's totals for the hundreds of Hounslow and Spelthorne are 70 and 147 respectively, but this discrepancy is due mainly to the fact that he includes the vill of Hampton in the latter (A. M. Davies, *art. cit.* pp. 236, 238). Round, to whom Morley Davies showed his paper, considered a division of the county into four blocks, originally equal in assessment, very probable.

[7] See p. 104 above.

the peasantry. In consistently recording this information the Middlesex record is unique.[1] One entry, i.e. for Harmondsworth (128b), is sufficient to show the kind of detail given:

pro xxx hidis se defendit. Terra est xx carucis. Ad dominium pertinent viii hidae et ibi sunt iii carucae. Inter franc'[2] et villanos sunt x carucae et vii adhuc possunt esse. Ibi quidam miles habet ii hidas et ii villani quisque i hidam et ii villani de i hida et xiiii villani quisque de i virgata et vi villani quisque de dimidia virgata et vi bordarii quisque v acris et vii cottari et vi servi.

In this entry there is a discrepancy between the sum of the detailed quantities listed (i.e. 8 hides in demesne, 2 hides with the knight and 7½ hides with the peasantry) and the assessment of the vill (i.e. 30 hides). Such discrepancy is encountered very frequently, and has given rise to some discussion. Vinogradoff made a detailed comparison between the figures in each entry,[3] and his results may be summarised thus:

Geld assessment greater than sum of particulars	51
Geld assessment equal to sum of particulars	6
Geld assessment less than sum of particulars	9

Both Vinogradoff and Maitland postulated a distinction between a fiscal hide used when the assessment of a holding as a whole was stated, and an agrarian hide used to measure the actual subdivisions. As Maitland wrote: 'it seems possible that in these Middlesex "particulars" we do at last touch real agrarian arrangements'.[4] Or as Vinogradoff put it: 'a geld-hide may have corresponded to one hide and a half or two hides distributed among the rustics'.[5] If, however, we try to compare these 'agrarian hides' with plough-lands we can observe no consistent relationship; 'in about an equal number of cases there are considerably more plough-lands than actual agricultural hides, and, on the other hand, more hides of actual occupation than plough-lands'.[6] Nor does comparison with actual teams suggest a relationship, as may be seen from the table on pp. 108–9. From the fact that the geld assessment generally exceeds the sum of the parti-

---

[1] See p. 97 above.

[2] ?*francos* or *francigenas*, see p. 119 below.

[3] P. Vinogradoff, *English Society in the Eleventh Century*; the figures have been taken from the tables on pp. 490–1.

[4] *Op. cit.* p. 478. See also R. Lennard, 'The economic position of the Domesday *villani*', *Econ. Journ.* LVI (London, 1946), pp. 244–64.

[5] *Op. cit.* p. 168.　　　　　　　　　　[6] *Ibid.* p. 171.

The Middlesex Assessment

(h = hides, v = virgates, a = acres, ns = not stated)

Folio	Entry	Geld	Particulars	Plough-lands	Plough-teams
127	Of (de) nomansland	? 12½ a	—	—	—
	Hayes	59 h	39½ h	40	28
	Harrow	100 h	60½ h, 13 a	70	49
	In hundred of Elthorne	2 h	—	1	1
	Stepney	32 h	30 h, ½ v	25	25
	In the same vill	5¼ h	1 h, 1½ v, 2½ a	4	4
	In the same vill	5 h	1½ h, 10 a	2½	1
127/127b	In the same vill	3½ h	1½ h	5	5
127b	In the same vill	1 h	—	1	1
	In the same vill	1¼ h	1 v, 28 a	1	1
	In the same vill	1½ h	14 a	1	½
	In the same vill	1½ + ¼ h	1 v, 5 a	1½	1
	In the same vill	1 h	—	1	0
	Fulham	40 h	49 h and cottars' gardens	40	30
	In the same vill	5 h	½ h, 8 a	3	2
	In the same vill	5 h	3½ v, 35 a	5	4
	Twyford	2 h	½ h, ½ v	1½	ns
	In the same vill	2 h	1 v, 6 a	1½	1
	Willesden	15 h	—	15	8
	Harlesden	5 h	4 h, 1 v	4	2½
	Rug Moor	2 h	—	1½	1
128	Tottenhall	5 h	—	4	3½
	St Pancras	4 h	—	2	1
	Islington	2 h	1 v	1½	1
	In the same vill	2 h	—	2½	2½
	Newington	2 h	10 a	2½*	2½*
	Hoxton	1 h	—	1	1
	Hoxton	3 h	—	3	3
	ad portam episcopi (i.e. Bishopsgate)	?	? 9 a	—	—
	Stanestaple	4 h	—	2	2
	St Pancras	1 h	—	1	1
	Drayton	10 h	7 h, 39 a	6	6
	In Villa ubi sedet ecclesia Sancti Petri (i.e. Westminster)	13½ h	13½ h, ½ v, 5 a	11	10
	In the same vill	3 h	—	2	2
	Hampstead	4 h	4 h	3	2
	In the same vill	1 h	—	½	½
128/128b	Staines	19 h	18 h, 119 a	24	24
128b	Sunbury	7 h	6½ h, ½ v	6	5
	Shepperton	8 h	7¾ h, 24 a	7	7
	Greenford	11½ h	11½ h	7	6
	Hanwell	8 h	8 h	5	5
	Cowley	2 h	2 h	1	1
	Kingsbury	2½ h	1 h, 1 v	2	2
	Hendon	20 h	16 h	16	11
	Harmondsworth	30 h	17 h, 2 v	20	13
	In Spelthorne hundred	1 h	—	½	ns

* The entry runs: *Ad ii carucas et dimidiam est ibi terra et modo sunt.* Vinogradoff omitted the details for Newington from his tables (*English Society in the Eleventh Century*, pp. 490–5).

The Middlesex Assessment (continued)

Folio	Entry	Geld	Particulars	Plough-lands	Plough-teams
	Tyburn (i.e. Marylebone)	5 h	2½ h, ½ v, 10 a	3	3
129	Hatton	1½ h	—	1	1
	Hanworth	5 h	2½ h	3	4
	Harmondsworth	1 h	—	1	½
	Harlington	10 h	4 h, 11 a	6	5
	Colham	8 h	9 h, 50 a	7	6
	Hillingdon	4 h	4 h, 10 a	2	1
	Dawley	3 h	1 h, 5 a	2	2
	Ickenham	9½ h	2 h, 3 v, 20 a	6	4
	Laleham	2 h	½ h	1½	1½
	Ashford	1 h	—	1	1
	East Bedfont	2 h	½ h, 8 a	1	½
	Feltham	12 h	10 h, ½ v	10	9
	Kempton	5 h	4 h, 3½ v	5	4
129 b	Stanmore	9½ h	8½ h, 11 a	7	3½
	Ebury	10 h	8 h, 2 v	8	7
	In the same (i.e. Ossulstone) hundred	1½ h	14 a	1	1
	Islington	½ h	—	½	½
	Greenford	3 h	½ h	1½	1
	In the same vill	½ h	—	¼	ns
	Ickenham	3½ h	1½ v	2	2
	Northolt	15 h	15 h	10	8
	Edmonton	35 h	28½ h, 40 a	26	26
	Enfield	30 h	26¾ h, 30 a	24	20
	Ruislip	30 h	21 h, 1 v, 28 a	20	15
129 b/130	Kingsbury	7½ h	2 h, 2½ v, 25 a	7	7
130	Stanwell	15 h	14 h, 28 a	10	13
	East Bedfont	10 h	3 h, 2 v, 13 a	5	5
	West Bedfont	8 h	5 h, 10 a	4	4
	Hatton	1 h 3⅓ v	2 v, 5 a	1	½
	Isleworth	70 h	31 h, 1½ v	55	34
	Hampton	35 h	28½ h	25	20
	Harefield	5 h	4 h, 1½ v, 8 a	5	5
	Haggerston	2 h	—	2	3
	In Elthorne hundred	2 h	—	1	½
	Stepney	4 h	1½ h, ½ v, 26 a	3	3
130/130 b	Ickenham	2 h	—	1	0
130 b	Stepney	3½ h	3¼ h, 19 a	2	2
	Laleham	8 h	8 h	5	5
	Charlton	5 h	5 h, 8 a	4	1½
	Stanmore	9½ h	5¼ h, 15 a	7	4
	Cranford	5 h	2 h, 1 v, 2 a	3	3
	Chelsea	2 h	2 h, 15 a	5	3
	Kensington	10 h	3 h, 3½ v	10	9
	Tollington	2 h	1 h, 2½ v, 9 a	2	3
	Islington	½ h	—	½	ns
	Tottenham	5 h*	6 h, 3 v, 60 a	10	14
	Lisson	5 h	5 h, 2 a	3	3
	In Spelthorne hundred	½ h and ⅓ of ½ h	—	½	0
	Greenford	½ h	—	½	0
			Totals	676¼	546

* Besides the 5 hides of the assessment, there were 2 carucates of land in demesne (see above, p. 104).

culars, Vinogradoff inferred 'that the county was, as a rule, assessed in a much heavier manner than the occupation of the soil at the time of Domesday would have warranted'.[1] Some day someone may be able to throw more light on these dark matters, but, in the meantime, we can only conclude that the Middlesex hidage, in spite of its unusual and curious detail, does not help us in a geographical view of the county in 1086.

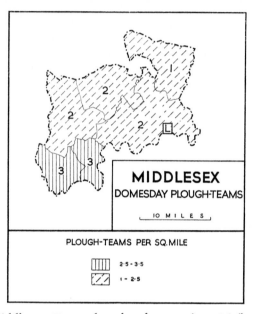

Fig. 37. Middlesex: Domesday plough-teams in 1086 (by densities).

L indicates London.

(2) *Plough-lands*

Plough-lands are systematically entered in the Middlesex folios, and the normal formula is simply 'there is land for *n* plough-teams' (*terra est n carucis*); but, sometimes, as in the entry for Shepperton (128b) the variant *terra est ad n carucas* is used. The entry for Sunbury (128b) states *Terra vi carucis est ibi*. Where the number of teams on a holding is less than that of plough-lands, there is usually a statement to the effect that additional teams 'might be' or 'could be employed', either on the demesne, or on the lands of the peasantry, or on both. It says, in effect, that the land could

[1] *Op. cit.* p. 169.

carry more teams than were at work, and it indicates therefore the possibility of further cultivation. Here are some sample entries that illustrate
the variety of phrasing:

(1) Hampstead (128): *Terra iii carucis. Ad dominium pertinent iii hidae et
    dimidia et ibi est i caruca. Villani habent i carucam et alia potest fieri.*
(2) Harrow (127): *Terra est lxx carucis. Ad dominium pertinent xxx hidae et*

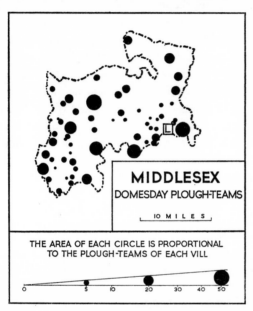

Fig. 38. Middlesex: Domesday plough-teams in 1086 (by settlements).

L indicates London.

*ibi sunt iiii carucae et v possunt[1] fieri. Inter franc' et villanos xlv carucae
et xvi plus possent esse.*

(3) Hayes (127): *Terra est xl carucis. Ad dominium pertinent xii hidae et ibi
    sunt ii carucae. Inter franc' et villanos sunt xxvi carucae et adhuc xii
    possent esse.*
(4) Tottenhall (128): *Terra est iiii carucis. Ibi sunt iii carucae et dimidia
    et adhuc dimidia potest fieri.*
(5) Westminster (128): *Terra est ad xi carucas. Ad dominium pertinent ix
    hidae et i virgata et ibi sunt iiii carucae. Villani habent vi carucae et i
    caruca plus potest fieri.*

[1] The MS. says *pot'*, but *possunt* must be meant.

The *potest fieri* formula, or one of its variants, is to be found in Domesday entries relating to 32 places and one anonymous holding. Generally, throughout the Middlesex folios there is what Baring calls 'at least a wish to make the sum balance', although the 'possible teams may perhaps sometimes be a mere assumption'.[1]

There are a few entries which record the lack of plough-teams in another way. Thus, for example, the entry for one holding at Greenford (130b) notes: *Terra est dimidia caruca sed non est ibi modo*. One of the holdings at Stepney (127b) had land for one plough-team, but the team was not there—*Terra est i caruca sed caruca deest*. Or, again, on a small unnamed holding in Spelthorne hundred (130b) there was land for 4 oxen but there were no oxen there (*Terra iiii bobus sed non sunt ibi*). Three other entries tell of a deficiency of teams—on holdings at Colham (129), at Isleworth (130), and at Sunbury (128b). Those for Colham and Sunbury make no reference to possible teams that might be employed; that for Isleworth does refer to possible teams with the peasantry, but omits to say anything about possible demesne teams. It may well be that entries like these result from scribal errors:

> Colham: *Terra vii carucis. In dominio vi hidae et ibi sunt iii carucae et villani habent iii carucas.*
> Isleworth: *Terra est lv carucis. In dominio vi hidae et dimidia et ibi sunt vi carucae. Inter franc' et villanos xxviii carucae et adhuc xi possunt fieri.*[2]
> Sunbury: *Terra vi carucis est ibi. Ad dominium pertinent iiii hidae et i caruca ibi est. Villani habent iiii carucas.*

A few entries in the Middlesex folios tell of plough-lands, but make no statement about actual or possible teams. Thus at Twyford (127b) we hear of land for 1½ plough-teams. Or, again, one of the entries for Greenford (129b) records 'land for 2 oxen', but does not tell us if the land was being worked. The entry for a holding at Islington (130b) merely notes: *Terra est dimidiae carucae. Ibi est unus villanus*; and another for an unnamed holding in Spelthorne hundred (128b) states: *Terra dimidiae carucae. Ibi est unus villanus qui tenet eam.*

It is not possible to say exactly what is implied by the formula *terra n carucis*. On every holding in Middlesex where plough-lands exceeded plough-teams the value fell between 1066 and 1086, but this is not con-

---

[1] *Domesday Tables*, p. 80.
[2] For the expression *Inter franc' et villanos*, see p. 114.

clusive evidence for assuming that the plough-land figure refers to conditions in 1066. The 1086 values generally throughout the county were lower
than those of 1066, even when the number of plough-lands was the same
as that of teams, e.g. at Drayton (128), Staines (128) and Tyburn (128b).
Whether the plough-land figure refers to conditions in 1066 or not, the
fact of understocking remains. An estate deficient in teams was not being
tilled up to capacity; the arable of 1086 was capable of extension. But
some estates in the county seem to have been overstocked; on five estates,
plough-teams exceeded plough-lands:

	Plough-lands	Teams
Haggerston (130)	2	3
Hanworth (129)	3	4
Stanwell (130)	10	13
Tollington (130b)	2	3
Tottenham (130b)	10 (?+2)[1]	14

But it is difficult to be certain about the implications of this evidence.

At Feltham (129) it is the total of the actual and potential teams that
appears to be in excess of the number of plough-lands: *Terra est x carucis.
In dominio vi hidae et ibi est i caruca et iii carucae adhuc possent esse.
Villani habent viii carucas.* If the possible teams could be read not as
'three' but as 'a third team', the totals of plough-lands and teams would
be equal, but the verb is in the plural (*poss*'); there may, of course, be a
scribal error here. At first sight, the entry for Kensington (130b) is
similar; it tells of six possible teams, but clearly only a sixth is meant
(*et vi potest fieri*).

The present count has yielded a total of 676¼ plough-lands. Maitland's
estimate was 664,[2] and Baring's total was 676.[3] All three counts relate to
the Domesday county which, apparently, was the same as the early
nineteenth-century county in terms of which the present analysis has been
made.

(3) *Plough-teams*

The Middlesex entries, like those for other counties, draw a distinction
between the teams held in demesne by the lord of the manor and those
held by the peasantry. The formula employed for Staines (128) is typical:
Ad dominium pertinent xi hidae et ibi sunt xiii carucae. Villani habent xi

[1] The entry states: *Terra est x carucis. In dominio sunt ii carucatae terrae praeter
has v hidas et ibi sunt ii carucae. Villani habent xii carucas.*
[2] *Op. cit.* p. 401.   [3] *Op. cit.* p. 85.

carucas. But the variant *villanorum xxii carucae* occurs in the entry for a holding at Stepney (127). The statement *Inter franc' et villanos n carucae* occurs in the entries for East Bedfont (130), Fulham (127b), Harmondsworth (128b), Harrow (127), Hayes (127), Isleworth (130), Ruislip (129b) and Stanwell (130).[1] There are a few minor variations. Thus the entry for Newington (128) runs: *Ad ii carucas et dimidiam est ibi terra et modo sunt*; this form also occurs in the entries for the unidentified *Stanestaple* (128) and for one of the holdings at Islington (128).

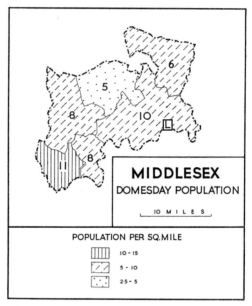

Fig. 39. Middlesex: Domesday population in 1086 (by densities).

L indicates London.

Four entries seem to be defective; they mention plough-lands but not teams; they relate to holdings at Greenford (129b), Islington (130b) and Twyford (127b), and to an unnamed holding in Spelthorne hundred (128b). But these defective entries amount to a minute fraction of all

[1] It is difficult to expand with certainty the Domesday *franc'*, Frenchman or freeman. Later in the entry for Fulham there is the statement: *Inter francigen' et quosdam burgenses Lundoniae xxiii hidae de terra villanorum. Sub eis manent inter villanos et bordarios xxx un'* (127b). Apparently, 31 villeins and bordars are meant.

the teams recorded for the county, and taken as a whole the Domesday record of teams provides a reasonable index of the arable land of the villages in 1086.

The present count has yielded a total of 546 plough-teams. Maitland's figure was 545 teams,[1] and Baring's 547 teams.[2] The discrepancy is slight, and it is almost impossible to arrive at a definitive figure when dealing with Domesday statistics.

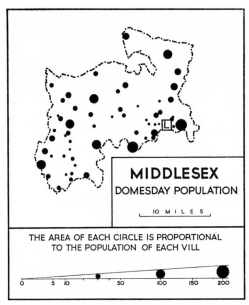

Fig. 40. Middlesex: Domesday population
in 1086 (by settlements).

L indicates London.

(4) *Population*

The bulk of the population was comprised in the four main categories of villeins, cottars, bordars and serfs. In addition to these were the burgesses, together with a small miscellaneous group that included knights (*milites*), *francigenae*, and 'men' (*homines*). Sokemen are not recorded for 1086, but 26 are entered for 1066.[3] The details of the several groups are

---

[1] *Op. cit.* p. 401.   [2] *Op. cit.* p. 85.
[3] In 1066 the sokemen were distributed thus: 5 at Enfield (129b), 2 at Greenford (129b), 1 at Harlington (129), 1 at Harmondsworth (128b), 4 at Hatton (129, 130),

summarised on p. 118. There are four other estimates of population, by
Sir Henry Ellis,[1] F. H. Baring,[2] M. E. Tanner,[3] and Sir Montagu Sharpe.[4]
None of these estimates agrees exactly with the present count. But, whatever the differences, one thing is certain; no one who counts Domesday
population can claim definite accuracy, and all that can be said of the
present figures is that they indicate the order of magnitude involved. These
figures are those of recorded population, and must be multiplied by some
factor, say 4 or 5, in order to obtain the actual population; but this does
not affect the relative density as between one area and another.[5] That is all
that a map, such as Fig. 39, can roughly indicate.

It is impossible to say how complete were these Domesday statistics, but
it does seem as if some people had been left uncounted. Certain entries
tell of plough-teams, but fail to enumerate the men working them; thus
at Rug Moor (127b) there was land for 1½ plough-teams and 1 team was
at work, but no inhabitants were recorded. Likewise no statement is made
about population in the entries for a holding of 1 hide at Ashford (129)
where there was a team at work and meadow for 1 plough-team; for a
holding of half a hide at Greenford (130b) where there was land for half
a team but no record of oxen at work; or for an unnamed holding of a
fraction of a hide in Spelthorne hundred (130b) where there was land
and meadow for 4 oxen, but again no record of oxen at work. Furthermore,
the entry for Westminster (128) mentions '25 houses of the knights of the
abbot and other men' (*xxv domus militum abbatis et aliorum hominum*), but
does not tell us the status of the 'other men'. The main entry for Fulham
(127b) refers to a total of 31 *inter villanos et bordarios*[6] dwelling under (*Sub
eis manent*) an unspecified number of *francigenae* and certain burgesses of
London (*Inter francigenas et quosdam burgenses Lundoniae*). At Isleworth

4 at Ickenham (129, 129b), 3 at East Bedfont (130), 2 at West Bedfont (130), 2 at
Fulham (127b) and 2 in Ossultone hd. (129b). There were also two unnamed thegns
(*teigni*) at Feltham (129); for unnamed thegns, see p. 157 below.
  [1] Sir Henry Ellis, *A General Introduction to Domesday Book*, II (London, 1833),
p. 468. The estimate of Sir Henry Ellis came to 2,302, but it included tenants-in-chief,
under-tenants and burgesses.
  [2] *Op. cit.* p. 85. Baring counted 1,174 villeins, 422 cottars, 363 bordars and 112 serfs.
These totals exclude the 32 cottars 'of the king' (127), the 10 cottars at Bishopsgate
(128), and the 24 'men' at St Pancras (128)—*ibid.* p. 85.
  [3] M. E. Tanner in *V.C.H. Middlesex*, II (London, 1911), p. 61.
  [4] Sir Montagu Sharpe, *Middlesex in the Eleventh Century*, p. 22.
  [5] But see p. 589 below for the complication of serfs.
  [6] In the present analysis these have been counted as 16 villeins and 15 bordars.

we hear of *francig'* and a certain Englishman (*quidam anglicus*) under whom dwelt (*Sub eis manent*) a combined total of 12 'villeins and bordars' (130).[1]

Villeins constituted the most important element in the population and amounted to over 50 per cent of the total. As Mr Reginald Lennard has emphasised, the Middlesex manors usually contained two or three classes of villeins, marked by uniform or nearly uniform holdings within each class.[2] Thus on the bishop of London's manor of Fulham there were 5 villeins each with 1 hide, 13 who held 1 virgate each, and 34 with only half a virgate each (127b). On some of the small estates all the villeins had equal holdings, as at Cranford, where there were 8 villeins each with a virgate (130b). On one holding at Stepney (127) there was a villein with (*de*) half a hide who paid yearly 4s. for his house (*reddit per annum iiii solidos de domo sua*), and another villein with half a hide rendered 8s. yearly. Cottars comprised 22 per cent of the total population and bordars 17 per cent.[3] On some estates the bordars and cottars also held small parcels of land,[4] e.g. at Staines where 36 bordars held between them 3 hides (128), at Kempton where there were 3 bordars with 1 virgate (129), or at Tottenham where 12 bordars each held 5 acres (130b). Some of the cottars also had small plots of land; thus at Staines there were 5 cottars each with 4 acres, and 3 others who held 9 acres, presumably shared between them (128). At Edmonton we read of 10 cottars and 4 villeins who seem to have held 1¼ hides between them (129b). In Westminster (128) there were 41 cottars who paid 40s. yearly for their gardens—*xli cotarii qui reddunt per annum xl solidos pro ortis suis*. These examples show the varying prosperity of the bordars and cottars in the county in 1086.[5] Of the 112 serfs in the county, the majority were to be found on estates rubricated under Elthorne and Spelthorne hundreds respectively, where they formed nearly 18 per cent of the total recorded

[1] These have been divided equally between villeins and bordars in the table on p. 118.

[2] R. Lennard, 'The economic position of the Domesday *villani*', *Econ. Jour.* LVI, p. 251.

[3] For a discussion of the differences between bordars and cottars, see (1) F. W. Maitland, *op. cit.* pp. 39 *et seq.*, and (2) P. Vinogradoff, *op. cit.* pp. 456 *et seq.*

[4] R. Lennard, 'The economic position of the bordars and cottars of Domesday Book', *Econ. Jour.* LXI (London, 1951), pp. 347–55.

[5] A Stepney entry on fo. 130 reads: *et bord' de dim' h et dim' virg'*. It is unlikely that a bordar held as much as this, and a numeral preceding *bord* seems to have been omitted from the text.

population;[1] for the county as a whole, the serfs amounted to less than 5 per cent of the total recorded population.

Recorded Population of Middlesex in 1086

A. Rural Population

Villeins	1,163
Cottars	464
Bordars	364
Serfs	112
Miscellaneous	74
Total	2,177

Details of Miscellaneous Rural Population

Men (*homines*) . . .	34	*Francigenae* . . .			9
Priests	18	*Francus*			1
Knights	11	*Anglicus* . . .			1
				Total	74

B. Urban Population

LONDON 46 burgesses at Staines and an unspecified number at Fulham; 32 burgesses attached to rural manors in Surrey. See p. 132 below.

47 *domus* attached to rural manors in Essex, and 59 to rural manors in Surrey. See p. 132 below.

The miscellaneous category was a small one. It included 34 'men' (*homines*)—24 paying 30s. yearly at St Pancras (128), 7 at Harrow (127) and 3 at Hillingdon (129).[2] Only 18 priests (*presbyteri*) were enumerated, and they were entered with the villeins, bordars and cottars; the details of their holdings were recorded with those of the other peasantry. The amount of land held by a priest in Middlesex ranged from half a virgate

---

[1] The distribution of serfs by hundreds was: 14 in Edmonton hundred, 42 in Elthorne hundred, 5 in Gore hundred, none in Hounslow hundred, 16 in Ossulstone hundred and 35 in Spelthorne hundred.

[2] Freemen (*liberi homines*) are not enumerated in the Middlesex folios, but there may be references to freemen in certain entries. The entries for eight estates contain the formula *Int' franc' et villanos sunt n carucae*, and it is difficult to tell whether the expansion of *franc'* should be *francos* or *francigenas*; the relevant entries are: East Bedfont (130), Fulham (127b), Harmondsworth (128b), Harrow (127), Hayes (127), Isleworth (130), Ruislip (129b) and Stanwell (130)—see p. 114 above.

at Kensington (130b), Shepperton (128b),[1] and Sunbury (128b) respectively to one hide at Colham (129) and at Harrow (127). The recorded priests were not equally dispersed among the settlements.[2] Unnamed knights (*milites*), too, appeared infrequently and in the same setting, e.g. at Harrow (127) and at Harmondsworth (128b). Only 9 *francigenae* were actually enumerated, but, as we have seen, there was also an unspecified number at Fulham (127b). One or more *francigenae* and a certain Englishman (*quidam anglicus*) at Isleworth (130) were styled *milites probati*. At Greenford (128b) there was a certain *franc'* who, in the present analysis, has been reckoned as a *francus*.

(5) Values

The value of an estate is generally entered in a round number of pounds for three dates, 1066, 1086 and an intermediate date. The formula *valuit et valet* occurs in seven entries—for holdings at Hampstead (128), Harmondsworth (129), Hoxton (128) and Islington (128, 130b), for an unnamed holding in Spelthorne hundred (130b), and for the king's holding *de nanesmaneslande* (127); it has been taken to apply to only two dates, 1066 and 1086. The 'values' are normally entered as plain statements of money; the only exception is the 1086 value for Tottenham (130b)—£25. 15s. and three ounces of gold (*iii uncias auri*).

An outstanding feature of the Middlesex valuation is the decrease in the value of many holdings after 1066. The values of a large number were only some 26 per cent to 50 per cent of what they had been, and a few holdings had suffered even more (Figs. 161–2). Some of these reduced holdings had recovered fully or in part by 1086, but by far the majority had not; the entry for Drayton (128) reads: *In totis valentiis vi libras. Quando recepit similiter. T.R.E. viii libras.* The statement *quando recepit similiter* occurs again and again in the Middlesex folios.

---

[1] The priest's holding at Shepperton was measured in acres, but it has been assumed that his 15 acres were the equivalent of half a virgate.

[2] The relation of priests to Domesday settlements (excluding London, for which no information was recorded) was:

Hundred	Settlements	Priests
Edmonton	4	2
Elthorne	15	7
Gore	4	4
Hounslow	2	1
Ossulstone	23	1
Spelthorne	13	3

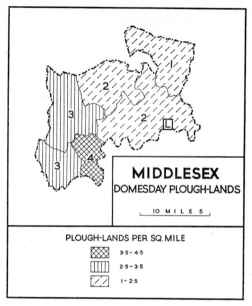

Fig. 41. Middlesex: Domesday plough-lands (by densities).

L indicates London.

Generally speaking, the greater the number of plough-teams and men on an estate, the higher its value, but it is impossible to discern any constant relationships as the following figures for three villages, each yielding £6 in 1086, show:

	Teams	Population	Other resources
Drayton (128)	6	17	Meadow, Mill Pasture, Weir
Feltham (129)	9	21	Meadow, Pasture
Sunbury (128b)	5	22	Meadow, Pasture

It is true that the variations in the arable, as between one manor and another, did not necessarily reflect variations in total resources, but even taking the other resources into account the figures are not easy to explain.

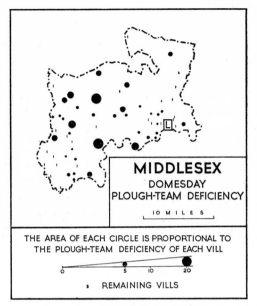

Fig. 42. Middlesex: Domesday plough-team deficiency (by settlements).

L indicates London.

Conclusion

The six Domesday hundreds of the county have been adopted as the basis for constructing the density maps. Of the five standard formulae, those relating to plough-teams and population are most likely to reflect something of the distribution of the wealth and prosperity throughout the county in the eleventh century. Taken together, they supplement one another to provide a general picture (Figs. 37 and 39). The essential feature of both maps is the contrast between the gravel soils of the south and the heavy claylands of the north. The density of plough-teams ranged up to 3·0 per square mile in the south, and down to 1·2 in the north. The density of 1·9 for Ossulstone hundred does not do justice to the more closely settled localities bordering the Thames, but it is difficult to separate the figures relating to these from those for the hundred as a whole.[1] The contrast between north and south is also apparent on the population map

[1] For the complications of Fulham (127b) and Stepney (127 *quater*, 127b *septiens*, 130, 130b), see p. 99 above.

(Fig. 39), where the southern figures ranged from 7·8 to 10·6, and those in the north from 4·7 to 8·1.

Figs. 38 and 40 are supplementary to the density maps, but it is necessary to make one reservation concerning them. As noted on p. 98, it is possible that some Domesday names may have covered more than one settlement. A few of the symbols should, therefore, appear as two or more smaller symbols, but this limitation does not affect the main patterns of the maps. Generally speaking, they confirm and amplify the information of the density maps. In view of the doubtful nature of the plough-land evidence, the implications of Fig. 41 are uncertain. Taken with Fig. 42, they suggest that generally throughout Domesday Middlesex the land was not being tilled up to capacity. But in detail the deficiency was greatest, as might be expected, on the heavy soils of the London Clay and least on the loamy soils of the riverine gravels (compare Figs. 42 and 35).

WOODLAND

Types of entries

The amount of woodland on a holding in Middlesex was normally indicated by the number of swine it could support and the usual formula was 'wood for *n* swine' (*silva n porcis*). The number ranged from 15 at Dawley (129) to as many as 2,000 each at Harrow (127), at Edmonton (with its berewick at South Mimms, 129b) and at Enfield (129b). The round figures of all the entries may indicate that they were estimates rather than precise amounts, e.g. 30, 70, 200 and 500. It does not necessarily follow that the figures indicate the actual number of swine grazing in a wood; swine may have been used merely as units of measurement.

Some woodland, in addition to providing pannage for swine, also made a money render; and occasionally the renders from wood and pasture are combined in a single sum. The full list is:

Chelsea (130b): *Silva lx porcis et lii denarii.*
Edmonton (129b): *Silva ii milibus porcorum et xii solidi de redditis silvae et pasturae.*
Enfield (129b): *Silva ii milibus porcorum. De silva et pastura xliii solidi.*
Fulham (127b): *Silva mille porcis et xvii denarii.*
Hayes (127): *Silva cccc porcis et iii solidi.*
Hendon (128b): *Silva mille porcis et x solidi.*
Isleworth (130): *Silva quingentis porcis. De herbagia xii denarii.*
Lisson (130b): *Silva c porcis. De herbagia iii denarii.*

Stanmore (129b): *Silva octingentis porcis et de Herbagia xii denarii.*
Stanestaple (128): *Silva cl porcis et x solidi.*
Stepney (127): *Silva quingentis porcis et xl solidi.*
Stepney (127): *Silva cl porcis et iii solidi et dimidius.*
Stepney (130): *Silva lx porcis et iiii solidi.*
Tollington (130b): *Silva lx porcis et v solidi.*
Tottenhall (128): *Silva cl porcis et xx solidi de Herbagia.*
Tyburn (128b): *Silva l porcis. De herbagia xl denarii.*

While swine formed the normal unit of measurement, there are entries which indicate the presence of enough woodland to supply timber for fencing:

Cranford (130b): *Nemus ad sepes.*
Rug Moor (127b): *Nemus ad sepes et iiii solidi.*
St Pancras (128): *Nemus ad sepes.*
Stepney (127b): *Nemus ad sepes faciendas.*
Stepney (130b): *Nemus ad sepes.*
In Ossulstone hundred (129b): *Nemus ad sepes.*

Finally, at Enfield (129b) there was a park (*parcus est ibi*), presumably an early indication of the Chase of later days, and at Ruislip (129b) there was a park for the beasts of the chase (*Parcus est ibi ferarum Silvaticarum*).

Distribution of woodland

The main fact about the distribution of woodland in Domesday Middlesex was its location on the claylands in the northern half of the county. Several villages here had pannage for 1,000 swine, and three had each enough for twice this number. It is difficult to say to what extent Fig. 43 gives a complete picture of eleventh-century woodland in the county. There may have been extra-manorial wood or non-profit yielding wood that escaped mention in the Domesday Book, and in this connection the widely-spaced villages of northern Middlesex must be borne in mind. Some hint of the early nature of the woodland to the north of London comes from the twelfth-century description by William fitz Stephen: 'a great forest with wooded glades and lairs of wild beasts, deer both red and fallow, wild boars and bulls'.[1] Through this heavily-shaded country

---

[1] F. M. Stenton, H. E. Butler, M. B. Honeybourne and E. Jeffries Davis, *Norman London: An Essay* (Historical Association, London, 1934). The essay on Norman London by Sir Frank Stenton is a revised and enlarged version of that published by the Historical Association in 1915.

ran the boundary between Middlesex and Hertfordshire. The name Enfield Chase, where in Domesday times there was a park, serves to remind us of the former state of the countryside.

There was, on the other hand, relatively little wood on the lighter soils in the south of the county. In the south-west, only two villages had wood —Staines with enough for 30 swine (128 b) and Stanwell with sufficient for 100 swine (130). In the south-east, amounts were also generally small, but

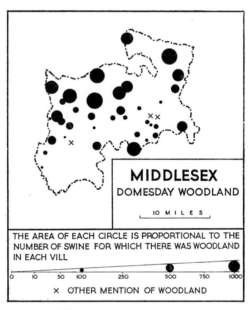

MIDDLESEX

DOMESDAY WOODLAND

10 MILES

THE AREA OF EACH CIRCLE IS PROPORTIONAL TO THE NUMBER OF SWINE FOR WHICH THERE WAS WOODLAND IN EACH VILL

| 0 | 10 | 50 | 100 | 250 | 500 | 750 | 1000 |

× OTHER MENTION OF WOODLAND

Fig. 43. Middlesex: Domesday woodland in 1086.

Where the wood of a village is entered partly in terms of swine and partly in some other way, only the swine total is shown.

there were two exceptions—Fulham with wood for 1,450 swine (127 b *ter*) and Stepney with enough for 770, and also other wood (127 *quater*, 127 b *septiens*, 130, 130 b). But, as we have seen, the Fulham entry may have included the resources of Finchley, and one of the Stepney entries may have referred to the Hornsey district.[1]

The English Place-Name Society's volume for Middlesex enables us to compare the distribution of Domesday woodland with that of place-names

[1] See p. 102 above.

and field-names that show the former presence of wood.[1] In the north of the county there are many names incorporating *wudu, hyrst, weald, gehaeg,* and the like. In south-west Middlesex, on the other hand, there is a marked absence of these elements, and instead there are many names ending in *ham* and *tun.*

MEADOW

Types of entries

The Domesday meadow of Middlesex was measured in terms of plough-teams, i.e. by stating the number of teams of 8 oxen the meadow was capable of feeding. The usual formula was *pratum n carucis,* but smaller quantities were recorded in terms of oxen—*pratum n bobus.* The amount of meadow in each vill varied from only enough for 2 oxen at Hendon (128b) to enough for as many as $45\frac{1}{8}$ teams at Fulham (127b *ter*). The amount was always equal to or less than the number of plough-lands. On some estates there was more meadow than teams; thus at Charlton there was meadow for 4 teams, but only $1\frac{1}{2}$ teams were at work on the 4 plough-lands (130b). Generally, however, the teams for which there was meadow were fewer than the teams at work. No meadow was recorded for 22 of the 62 settlements in the county.

Profits from meadow were entered for seven villages:

Ebury (129b): *Pratum viii carucis et de feno lx solidi.*
Edmonton (129b): *Pratum xxvi carucis et xxv solidi de super plus.*
Enfield (129b): *Pratum xxiiii carucis et xxv solidi de super plus.*
Hampton (130): *Pratum iii carucis et x solidi.*
Staines (128b): *Pratum xxiiii carucis et xx solidi de super plus.*
Stepney (127b): *Pratum ii carucis et ii solidi.*
Tottenham (130b): *pratum x carucis et xx solidi de super plus.*

Distribution of meadowland

The three bounding rivers of the county, the Colne, the Lea and the Thames, with their wide stretches of alluvium, were bordered by sub-stantial amounts of meadow (Fig. 44). Along the Lea the villages of Edmonton (129b),[2] Enfield (129b) and Tottenham (130b) had between

---

[1] J. E. B. Gover, A. Mawer, F. M. Stenton and S. J. Madge, *The Place-Names of Middlesex.* Maps in folder at end of volume.
[2] The entry for Edmonton also covered its berewick, South Mimms. On Fig. 44, the meadow has been divided equally between the two vills.

them sufficient for a total of 60 teams; downstream, near its confluence with the Thames, Stepney had enough for 33 teams (127 *quater*, 127b *septiens*, 130, 130b).[1] Along the Colne, Harmondsworth (128b, 129) had meadow for 20 teams and Staines (128b) for 24 teams, and there were smaller amounts entered for other villages in the area. Nearly all the villages along the Yeading and the Brent also had small amounts. Along the Thames itself, amounts ranged up to enough for $45\frac{1}{8}$ teams at Fulham

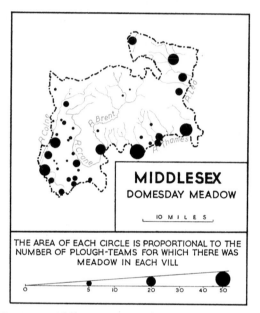

Fig. 44. Middlesex: Domesday meadow in 1086.

Where the meadow of a village is entered partly in terms of plough-teams
and partly in some other way, only the plough-team total is shown.

(127b).[2] Hendon (128b) and Kingsbury (128b, 130), in the heart of the northern claylands, had enough for only 6 oxen between them; this must have been on the small patches of alluvium that border Silk Stream and Dollis Brook, the two small headstreams of the Brent. No meadow

---

[1] The Domesday vill of Stepney seems to have included the locality subsequently known as Hackney, where there is a very extensive spread of alluvium; see S. J. Madge, *The Early Records of Harringay alias Hornsey*, pp. 31, 35.

[2] But we cannot be certain that all this meadow was in the immediate vicinity of the village itself; see p. 102 above.

is recorded for the great manor of Harrow (127) where 49 teams were at work on 70 plough-lands. Perhaps it had none, but we cannot be sure that the Domesday record is complete.

PASTURE

Pasture is recorded for 47[1] out of the 62 Domesday settlements of Middlesex. The usual formula is the bare statement that there was 'pasture for the livestock of the vill' (*pastura ad pecuniam villae*). There are, however, a number of variants which are set out below:

Ebury (129b): *De pastura vii solidi.*

Edmonton (129b): *Pastura ad pecuniam. Silva ii milibus porcorum et xii solidi de redditis silvae et pasturae.*

Enfield (129b): *Pastura ad pecuniam villae. Silva ii milibus porcorum. De silva et pastura xliii solidi.*

Isleworth (130): *Pastura ad pecuniam villae.... Silva quingentis porcis. De herbagia xii denarii.*

Lisson (130b): *Pastura ad pecuniam villae. Silva c porcis. De herbagia iii denarii.*

St Pancras (128): *Pastura ad pecuniam et xx denarii.*

Stanmore (129b): *Pastura ad pecuniam villae. Silva octingentis porcis et de Herbagia xii denarii.*

Stanmore (130b): *Pastura ad pecuniam villae et ii solidi.*

Stepney (127): *Pastura ad pecuniam villae et xv solidi.*

Tottenhall (128): *Silva cl porcis et xx solidi de Herbagia.*

Tyburn (128b): *Pastura ad pecuniam villae. Silva l porcis. De herbagia xl denarii.*

In Ossulstone hundred (129b): *Pastura ad pecuniam et xiii denarii.*

Finally, we are specifically told that there was no pasture (*Pastura non est*) at one holding in Stepney (127b).

The distribution of villages with pasture was fairly general and presents no special feature. But it is difficult to be certain about the villages without record of any. Take, for example, the estates of Gore hundred. Two of them, Harrow (127) and Stanmore (129b, 130b), had pasture for their livestock but no meadow; the other two, Hendon (128b) and Kingsbury

---

[1] This number includes South Mimms, a berewick of Edmonton (129b); the resources of South Mimms are not separately surveyed, but 'pasture for the livestock' is entered under Edmonton.

(128b, 129b), had very small amounts of meadow but apparently no pasture. We cannot but wonder whether the Domesday scribe sometimes omitted the statement *pastura ad pecuniam villae.* Perhaps the Domesday settlements without record of pasture had none other than that provided by the fallow field. One thing is certain: in the eleventh century, as in the thirteenth, there was rarely more pasture than was required for the livestock.[1]

FISHERIES

Fisheries are mentioned, or implied, in connection with twelve places in Domesday Middlesex. For three places *piscinae* are entered:

Enfield (129b): *De Piscinis viii solidi.*
Harefield (130): *De iiii piscinis mille anguillae.*
Harmondsworth (128b): *Ibi iii molini de lx solidis et quingentis anguillis et de piscinis mille Anguillae.*

Generally, only the presence of a weir (*guort, gort, gurges*) was noted; eels were rendered from only one weir, but presumably the money payments from the others were derived from fish trapped at them. Weirs were recorded for eight places:

Drayton (128): *De i gurgite xxxii denarii.*
Fulham (127b): *De dimidio gurgite x solidi.*
Hillingdon (129): *De i guort v solidi.*
Isleworth (130): *Unus gort et dimidius de xii solidis et viii denariis.*
Shepperton (128b): *i guort de vi solidis et viii denariis.*
Staines (128b): *i guort de vi solidis et viii denariis et i guort quod nil reddit.*
Stanwell (130): *Ibi iii molini de lxx solidis et cccc Anguillis xxv minus. De tribus gortibus mille Anguillae.*
Tottenham (130b): *De uno gort iii solidi.*

Fulham and Isleworth were adjoining villages and may have shared a weir between them. The payments from weirs varied; thus the half-weir at Fulham rendered 10s., but the one and a half at Isleworth paid only 12s. 8d. At Staines one weir yielded 6s. 8d., but the other rendered nothing. Only one village, Hampton, seems to have paid dues for seines and drag nets in the Thames—*De sagenis et tractis in aqua temisiae iii solidi* (130).

---

[1] In the thirteenth century, we hear of villages without any pasture save such as was afforded by the fallow field, as at Tillingham in Essex, mentioned in the Domesday of St Paul's; see W. H. Hale (ed.), *The Domesday of St Paul's of the year MCCXXII* (Camden Society, London, 1858), p. 59.

Finally we hear indirectly of a different type of fishing in one of the references to London; the entry for Walkingstead (34) in Surrey tells of contributory properties in London rendering herrings.

Fig. 45 shows that most of the fisheries recorded for Middlesex were in the west of the county, in the Colne and its tributary the Pinn. There were also some in the Thames itself and in the Lea.

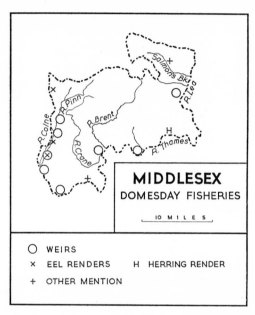

Fig. 45. Middlesex: Domesday fisheries in 1086.

MILLS

Mills are mentioned as existing in 1086 in connection with only 15 out of the 62 Domesday settlements in Middlesex. Their annual value was normally stated, and this ranged from a mill yielding 2s. 2d. at Hanwell (128b) to one yielding 66s. 8d. at Stepney (127). At two places the rent was paid partly in money and partly in eels from the mill-pond; at Harmondsworth (128b) 3 mills rendered 60s. and 500 eels (*de lx solidis et quingentis anguillis*), and at Stanwell (130) 4 mills gave 70s. and 400 eels less 25 (*de . . cccc Anguillis xxv minus*). These entries point to the practice of reckoning eels by the stick of 25 eels. Only one half-mill was specifically recorded in the Middlesex folios; it was at Colham, where there were two

9

others, but we are not told anything about the other half-mill (129). One of the mills entered under Stepney (127b) had been set up since 1066; the entry runs: *In eadem villam tenet Edmundus fitz Algot' de episcopo i molinum quod valet xxxii solidos et vi denarios, quando recepit similiter sed non fuit ibi T.R.E.*

Fig. 46. Middlesex: Domesday mills in 1086.

Nearly one-half of the villages with mills had only one mill. The following table shows to what extent there was a grouping of mills:

Domesday Mills in Middlesex

Under 1 mill 2 settlements[1]	4 mills 1 settlement
1 mill 6 settlements	6 mills 1 settlement
2 mills 2 settlements	7 mills 1 settlement
3 mills 2 settlements	

The group of 7 mills was at Stepney (127 *quater*, 127b *septiens*, 130, 130b) just above the confluence of the Lea and the Thames, and that of 6 mills was at Staines (128b) just above the confluence of the Colne and the Thames.

---

[1] In the present analysis the mill entered under Edmonton has been divided between Edmonton and its berewick of South Mimms (129b).

The mills were water-mills, and Fig. 46 shows their alignment along the Colne and the Lea. There were also a few along some of the smaller streams, notably the Brent, the Yeading and the Dollis Brook. None seems to have been situated on the Thames itself; that at Isleworth was on the Crane above its confluence with the Thames. As only 15 settlements had mills recorded in the Middlesex folios, one wonders where the inhabitants of the others ground their corn. Did they grind it elsewhere, or by hand? Or is the Domesday record incomplete? These are questions which we cannot answer.

URBAN LIFE

The Domesday treatment of towns is erratic, and often very disappointing. This is especially true in the case of London, because there can be little doubt that in 1086 the city of London 'stood alone above all other English towns in wealth and power, and its citizens were very conscious of the fact'.[1] It is, therefore, particularly unfortunate that there is no account of London's life and activities in the Domesday Book, especially as space would seem to have been left for such an account on folio 126.[2] But although no account is given of the city, there are references to its burgesses not only in the Middlesex folios, but also in those of Essex and Surrey; these references are set out on p. 132 (see also Fig. 47).

The entry for Staines does not specifically mention that its 46 burgesses were in London, but we cannot assume from this omission that Staines itself was a Domesday borough. Maitland was quite definite that it was not, and that the burgesses recorded *de iure* in Staines were *de facto* in London:

Were those burgesses really in Staines, and was Staines a borough? No, they were in the city of London. The Confessor had told his Middlesex thegns how he willed that St Peter and the brethren at Westminster should have the manor (*cotlif*) of Staines with the land called Staninghaw (*mid ðam lande Stœningehaga*) within London and all other things that had belonged to Staines. Is not the guess permissible that Staining Lane in the City of London, wherein stood the church of St Mary, Staining was so-called, not 'because stainers lived in it', but because it once contained the haws of the men of Staines?... The burgesses who *de iure* 'are in' one place are often *de facto* in quite another place.[3]

[1] F. M. Stenton *et al.*, *op. cit.* p. 5.
[2] *Ibid.* p. 5.
[3] F. W. Maitland, *op. cit.* p. 181; see also A. Ballard, *The Domesday Boroughs* (Oxford, 1904), p. 6.

References to London in Domesday Folios

(1) MIDDLESEX

    (*a*) Fulham (127b): *Inter francigenas et quosdam burgenses Lundoniae xxiii hidae de terra villanorum.*

    (*b*) Staines[1] (128b): *xlvi burgenses qui reddunt per annum xl solidos.*

(2) ESSEX

    (*a*) Barking (vol. II, 17b–18): *In Londonia xxviii domus quae reddunt xiii solidos et viii denarios et dimidia ecclesia quae T.R.E. reddebat vi solidos et viii denarios et modo non reddit.*

    (*b*) Thurrock (vol. II, 63): *vii domus sunt Londoniae quae jacent huic manerio et in hac firma.*

    (*c*) Waltham (vol. II, 15b): *Londoniae sunt xii domus pertinentes Manerio quae reddunt xx solidos et una porta quam rex dedit antecessori episcopi quae etiam reddit xx solidos.*

(3) SURREY

    (*a*) Banstead (31b): *in Lundonia una masura dominica fuit.*

    (*b*) Beddington (34b–35): *In Lundonia xv masurae quae pertinent huic manerio reddunt et xii solidos iii denarios.*

    Beddington (36b): *De isto manerio [   ] ablatae sunt xxi masurae quas comes Rogerius tenet. In Lundonia, xiii. In Sudwerche viii. Reddunt xii solidos.*

    (*c*) Bermondsey (30): *In Lundonia xiii burgenses de xliiii denariis.*

    (*d*) Bletchingley (34b): *In Lundonia et Sudwerche[2] vii mansurae de v solidis et iiii denariis.*

    (*e*) Chivington (34b) *In Lundonia duas masuras de x denariis.*

    (*f*) Lambeth (34): *xix burgenses in Londonia[3] qui reddunt xxxvi solidos.*

    (*g*) Mortlake (30b): *In Lundonia fuerunt xvii mansurae reddentes lii denarios.*

    (*h*) Walkingstead (34): *Huic manerio pertinent xv masurae in Suduuerca et in Londonia de vi solidis et ii millen' allecium.*

Westminster (128) is not described as a borough in the Domesday Book, but clearly the foundation of its church was marking it out from the surrounding villages. The complete entry is as follows:

In the vill where lies the church of St Peter (*In Villa ubi sedet ecclesia Sancti Petri*) the abbot holds of this place (*ejusdem loci*) 13 hides and a half. There is

---

    [1] See p. 131 above.

    [2] *et Sudwerche* interlined in the MS.; in the present analysis the number of *mansurae* have been divided equally between London and Southwark (see p. 399 below).

    [3] *In Londonia* interlined in the MS.; in the present analysis the number of *mansurae* have been divided equally between London and Southwark (see p. 399 below).

land for 11 plough-teams. To the demesne belong (*pertinent*) 9 hides and 1 virgate and 4 plough-teams are there. The villeins have 6 plough-teams and 1 plough-team more could be made. There, 9 villeins each with (*de*) 1 virgate, and 1 villein with (*de*) 1 hide, and 9 villeins each with (*de*) half a virgate and 1 cottar with (*de*) 5 acres and 41 cottars who pay yearly 40s. for their gardens (*qui reddunt per annum xl solidos pro ortis suis*). Meadow for 11 plough-teams. Pasture for the livestock of the vill. Wood for 100 swine and 25 houses of

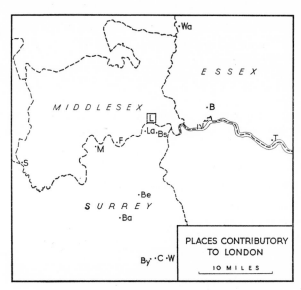

Fig. 47. Places contributory to London (L).

Middlesex: Fulham (F), Staines (S).
Essex: Barking (B), Thurrock (T), Waltham (Wa).
Surrey: Banstead (Ba), Beddington (Be), Bermondsey (Bs), Bletchingley (By), Chivington (C), Lambeth (La), Mortlake (M), Walkingstead (W). The entry for Mortlake refers to a period before 1086.

the knights of the bishop and of other men who pay 8s. yearly (*xxv domus militum abbatis et aliorum hominum qui reddunt viii solidos per annum*). In all it is worth £10. When received likewise (*similiter*). T.R.E. £12. This Manor was and is in the demesne (*in dominio*) of the church of St Peter of Westminster.

In the same vill (*In eadem villa*) Baynard holds 3 hides of the abbot (*de abbate*). There is land for 2 plough-teams and they are there in demesne and 1 cottar. Wood for 100 swine. Pasture for the livestock. There, 4 arpents of vine newly planted. In all, it is worth 60s. When received 20s. *T.R.E.* £6. This land belonged and belongs to (*jacuit et jacet in*) the church of St Peter.

Figs. 166 and 167 provide some indication of the relation of Westminster to the surrounding villages and to London itself.

MISCELLANEOUS INFORMATION

Very little miscellaneous information is recorded in the Middlesex folios. There is, for example, no mention of markets. Gardens (*orti*) are mentioned at Westminster (128).

Vineyards

There are seven entries relating to vineyards, and their extent is indicated by the arpent, an ancient Gallic unit of measurement.[1] Round, with the Essex vineyards in mind, thought that the Normans reintroduced the vine into England.[2] The use of the phrase *noviter plantatae* in two of the Middlesex entries may lend support to this view:

Colham (129): *i arpennus vineae.*
Harmondsworth (128b): *i arpennus vineae.*
Kempton (129): *viii arpenni vineae noviter plantatae.*
Kensington (130b): *iii Arpenni vineae.*
Staines (128–128b): *ii arpenni vineae.*
Westminster (128): *Ibi iiii arpenni vineae noviter plantatae.*
?Holborn[3] (127): *Willelmus camerarius reddit vicecomiti regis per annum vi solidos pro terra ubi sedet vinea sua.*

Parks

There are two references to parks:

Enfield (129b): *parcus est ibi.*
Ruislip (129b): *Parcus est ibi ferarum Silvaticarum.*

---

[1] F. W. Maitland, *op. cit.* p. 375.
[2] *V.C.H. Essex,* i (Westminster, 1903), p. 382. See also F. W. Maitland, *op. cit.* pp. 375–6.
[3] This entry follows a statement about Holborn, and it is not clear whether the vineyard was also at Holborn. S. J. Madge assigned it to Westminster (*The Early Records of Harringay alias Hornsey* (Hornsey, 1938), p. 39). Sharpe assigned it to Newgate—'Middlesex in Domesday Book', *Trans. Lond. Mdx. Archaeol. Soc.* N.S. VII (London, 1937), p. 524.

Churches

Churches are not mentioned in the Middlesex folios, apart from that of Westminster itself (128); but we hear of the minster (*monasterium*) of Staines in the Buckinghamshire folios; in 1066 three thegns of East Burnham (145 b) paid 'yearly 5 ores by custom to the church of Staines'. Eighteen priests were recorded for the county in 1086. The entry for Barking in the Essex folio (ii, 17 b–18) refers to half a church at London, that used to render 6s. 8d. but now does not.

REGIONAL SUMMARY

In order to appreciate the landscape of eleventh-century Middlesex we must look beneath the expanse of bricks and mortar that covers most of the county today and see the ground beneath (Fig. 35). Only then can the distinctive landscape of the Domesday county be appreciated. In 1086 the main regional contrast was between the heavy claylands of the north and the loam and gravel tracts of the south. The north had low densities of plough-teams and population but much woodland; the south had relatively high densities of both teams and men but only a little wood. Within each of these areas there were variations.

The northern half of the county consists of an undulating surface (London Clay) which slopes southwards from over 350 ft. o.d. near the boundary with Hertfordshire to below 100 ft. in the south where the ground is very flat. This sloping surface is broken in the north by a series of ridges, and elsewhere by isolated hills; the ridges and hills alike are capped by sands and gravels (Claygate and Bagshot Beds, Plateau and Pebble Gravels), and rise steeply from the plain. Further variety is given to the area by the gravel terraces overlooking the Lea in the east, and by the lobe of Boulder Clay in the neighbourhood of Finchley. But despite this variety, it is the London Clay formation that provides the dominating feature of the soils of the region. These soils are very heavy and cold, and in their natural state are often ill-drained. It is not surprising, therefore, that the Domesday densities of plough-teams and men were generally low. Densities of both teams and men were higher on the fertile loams and brick-earths in the Lea valley. Here, there was also abundant meadow on the broad belt of alluvium bordering the river. Most of the villages beyond the Lea valley had little or no meadowland, for the streams that traverse the London Clay are without wide alluvial belts. There was, on the other hand, much wood. Many settlements had wood for more than 500 swine, and several had enough for more than 1,000 swine apiece; Enfield (129b) and Ruislip (129b) also had parks. But the wood thinned out along the southern margin of the outcrop of London Clay.

In marked contrast to the northern half of the county, the southern portion is covered by deep loamy soils, easily tilled and very attractive to the early cultivator. The southern half of the county is low-lying, being everywhere below 100 ft. O.D.; it corresponds to the spread of river gravels bordering the Thames between the Colne and the Lea. This expanse of gravels is widest in the south-west, where the ground is remarkably level. It is not surprising that the Domesday prosperity of the region, as indicated by plough-teams and population, was well above that of the northern claylands; the proximity of London, too, accounted in part for the greater prosperity of the south-east. There was also, as we have seen (p. 124 above), more wood in the south-east than in the south-west, but we cannot be sure how much more. Most of the villages had meadow, and many had mills. The presence of vineyards added to the distinctive characteristics of the region.

BIBLIOGRAPHICAL NOTE

(1) It is interesting to note that the Rev. Daniel Lysons quoted the Middlesex evidence in his account of Middlesex in vol. II of *The Environs of London* (London, 1795).

Early in the next century came a translation of the text: William Bawdwen, *Dom Boc. A translation of the record called Domesday, so far as relates to the counties of Middlesex, Hertford, Buckingham, Oxford and Gloucester* (Doncaster, 1812).

(2) There are two other nineteenth-century translations of the Middlesex text:

(*a*) *A Literal Extension of the Latin text, and an English Translation of Domesday Book in relation to the county of Middlesex* (London, 1862). This was made to accompany the facsimile copy of the Domesday folios for the county photo-zincographed under the direction of Col. Sir Henry James, R.E., F.R.S., at the Ordnance Survey Office, Southampton (1861).

(*b*) G. H. de S. N. Plantagenet-Harrison, *Facsimile of the original Domesday Book, or the Great Survey of England A.D. 1080 (sic), in the reign of William the Conqueror*, Pt. I, Middlesex (London, 1876); this was accompanied by a translation made by the editor. No further volumes were published.

(3) F. H. Baring, *Domesday Tables for the counties of Surrey, Berkshire, Middlesex, Hertford, Buckingham and Bedford and for the New Forest* (London, 1909). The tables for Middlesex are of a high degree of accuracy, but the accompanying text is slight.

(4) Various aspects of Domesday Middlesex are discussed in the following:

E. Griffith, 'Middlesex in the time of the Domesday Survey', *Trans. Lond. Mdx. Archaeol. Soc.* I (London, 1860), pp. 175–82.

H. C. Coote, 'Notices of Deorman of London, a Domesday tenant in capite', *Trans. Lond. Mdx. Archaeol. Soc.* III (London, 1870), pp. 153–6.

F. Seebohm, 'The Domesday survey of the villa of Westminster', *The English Village Community* (Cambridge, 1926; 1st ed., London, 1883), pp. 97–101.

A. M. Davies, 'The Domesday hidation of Middlesex', *Home Counties Magazine*, III (London, 1901), pp. 232–8.

Sir Montagu Sharpe, 'The Domesday survey of Middlesex', *Home Counties Magazine*, X (London, 1908), pp. 315–16.

Sir Montagu Sharpe, 'Middlesex parishes and their antiquity', *Trans. Lond. Mdx. Archaeol. Soc.* N.S. VII (London, 1937), pp. 91–8.

Sir Montagu Sharpe, 'Middlesex in Domesday Book', *Trans. Lond. Mdx. Archaeol. Soc.* N.S. VII (London, 1937), pp. 509–27.

Sir Montagu Sharpe, *Middlesex in the Eleventh Century* (Brentford, 1941).

R. Lennard, 'The economic position of the Domesday *villani*', *Econ. Journ.* LVI (London, 1946), pp. 244–64.

R. Lennard, 'The economic position of the bordars and cottars of Domesday Book', *Econ. Journ.* LXI (London, 1951), pp. 341–71.

(5) Other works of interest in the Domesday study of the county are as follows:

G. J. Turner, 'William the Conqueror's march to London in 1066', *Eng. Hist. Rev.* XXVII (London, 1912), pp. 209–25.

H. Braun, 'The hundred of Gore and its moot-hedge', *Trans. Lond. Mdx. Archaeol. Soc.* N.S. VII (London, 1937), pp. 218–28.

S. J. Madge, *The Early Records of Harringay alias Hornsey, from Prehistoric Times to 1216 A.D.* (Hornsey, 1938).

S. J. Madge, *The Medieval Records of Harringay alias Hornsey* (Hornsey, 1939).

C. F. Baylis, 'The omission of Edgware from Domesday', *Trans. Lond. Mdx. Archaeol. Soc.* N.S. XI (London, 1954), pp. 62–6.

M. Robbins, 'A note on early Finchley', *Trans. Lond. Mdx. Archaeol. Soc.* XVIII (London, 1955), pp. 65–7.

(6) A valuable aid to the Domesday study of the county is *The Place-Names of Middlesex*, edited by J. E. B. Gover, A. Mawer, F. M. Stenton and S. J. Madge (Cambridge, 1942).

CHAPTER IV

BUCKINGHAMSHIRE

BY EILA M. J. CAMPBELL, M.A.

The Buckinghamshire folios raise few points that are of unusual interest in a geographical analysis of the Domesday Book. The entries, as Domesday entries go, are relatively straightforward. But there is one complication. The present-day county, in terms of which this study is written, is not the same as the Domesday county. The main difference is in the west, along the boundary with Oxfordshire. Here the Buckinghamshire village of Ibstone straddled the boundary between the two counties, and was surveyed partly under Buckinghamshire (152b) and partly under Oxfordshire (160b). The eleventh-century *Boicote* (160), represented today by Boycott Farm in Stowe, was also entered under Oxfordshire; this holding was not transferred to Buckinghamshire until 1844. *Duchitorp* (i.e. Tythrop in Kingsey, 155b) was also described under Oxfordshire, and it also remained for certain purposes in that county until the nineteenth century.[1] *Eie* (151b), entered in the Buckinghamshire folios, survives in the names of Kingsey[2] and Towersey,[3] two parishes which have been interchanged between Buckinghamshire and Oxfordshire on more than one occasion. The most recent adjustment of the county boundary, made in 1932, placed Kingsey in Buckinghamshire and Towersey in Oxfordshire; in the present analysis, *Eie* has been identified with Towersey.[4] In the north-west, Lillingstone Lovell (160, 160b) was entered under

[1] See A. M. Davies, 'The hundreds of Buckinghamshire and Oxfordshire', *Records of Buckinghamshire*, xv (Aylesbury, 1947–52), p. 238.

[2] Known as *Eia Magna* in 1196; the name Kingsey seems to date from the following year—see M. Gelling and D. M. Stenton, *The Place-Names of Oxfordshire*, I (Cambridge, 1953), p. 111; see also pp. 187–8 below.

[3] The first part of this name is derived from the Tours family who held land in the neighbourhood in the 13th century. It was called 'Tour's island' to distinguish it from the neighbouring 'King's island' or Kingsey. For the history of this place-name and of all other Buckinghamshire place-names mentioned in this chapter, see A. Mawer and F. M. Stenton, *The Place-Names of Buckinghamshire* (Cambridge, 1925).

[4] See J. H. Round in *V.C.H. Buckinghamshire*, IV (London, 1927), pp. 64 and 105. Later manorial history suggests that in 1086 Kingsey was part of the royal manor of Brill (*ibid.* p. 64).

Oxfordshire, of which it remained a detached portion until 1844, when it was transferred to Buckinghamshire;[1] Caversfield, recorded in the Domesday Book under Buckinghamshire (148), was transferred to Oxfordshire

Fig. 48. Buckinghamshire: Domesday hundreds.

in the same year. In the east of the county, the eleventh-century village of Edlesborough was described partly under Bedfordshire (*Edingeberge*, 215) and partly under Buckinghamshire (*Eddinberge*, 149b), but the

---

[1] The resources of the adjoining village of Lillingstone Dayrell were entered in the Buckinghamshire folios (147b). In the present analysis the Lillingstones have been counted as separate settlements in 1086, since they seem to have lain in different hundreds. The earliest record of the appellation 'Dayrell' is 1166; Lillingstone Lovell was styled *Magna* Lillingstone in 1255.

twentieth-century parish is wholly within the latter.[1] Nettleden, transferred from Buckinghamshire to Hertfordshire in 1895, is not named in the Domesday Book, but its resources may have been included with those of Pitstone.[2]

Within the Domesday county there were eighteen hundreds, varying in size from Bunsty, Risborough and Waddesdon, each with exactly 100 hides, to Aylesbury and Desborough with nearly 150 hides apiece. Some of the Domesday hundreds were not compact territorial units. Fig. 48 shows one attempt to reconstruct the Domesday hundreds of the county.[3]

SETTLEMENTS AND THEIR DISTRIBUTION

The total number of separate places mentioned in the Domesday Book for the area included within the modern county of Buckingham seems to be 207, including the boroughs of Buckingham and Newport Pagnell. This figure, however, cannot be an accurate one. In the first place, there are many instances of two or more adjoining villages bearing the same surname today, and it is not always clear whether more than one unit existed in the eleventh century. Only where there is specific mention of a second village in the Domesday folios, has it been included in the total of 207. Thus, the existence of Great and Little Kimble in the eleventh century is indicated by the mention of *Chenebella* (147) and *parva Chenebelle* (151), and of the two Burnhams by *Burneham* (151) and *Eseburneham* (145b). But there is, on the other hand, no indication that, say, the three Brickhills of today existed as separate villages in 1086; the Domesday folios name only *Brichella* (145, 145b, 147, 148 *bis*)[4] and their distinctive appellations do not appear until the twelfth and thirteenth centuries.[5] The same applies, for example, to the two Hampdens (148b), the two Missen-

---

[1] The portion of the eleventh-century village surveyed under Bedfordshire was assessed at 10 hides, that under Buckinghamshire at 20 hides.

[2] See (1) *V.C.H. Buckinghamshire*, III (London, 1925), p. 406; (2) *V.C.H. Hertfordshire*, II (London, 1908), p. 317.

[3] For an earlier reconstruction of the Domesday hundreds, see A. Morley Davies, 'The ancient hundreds of Buckinghamshire', *Home Counties Magazine*, VI (London, 1904), map on p. 143; this map was reprinted in *V.C.H. Buckinghamshire*, I (London, 1905), p. 227. It was reprinted with corrections (for some of which the author was indebted to F. H. Baring) in *Records of Buckinghamshire*, IX (Aylesbury, 1909), facing p. 114.

[4] But on fo. 145b, the name seems to appear in the plural *Brichellae*.

[5] Bow Brickhill (*Bolle*, 1198), Great Brickhill (*Magna*, 1247), and Little Brickhill (*Parva*, 1198).

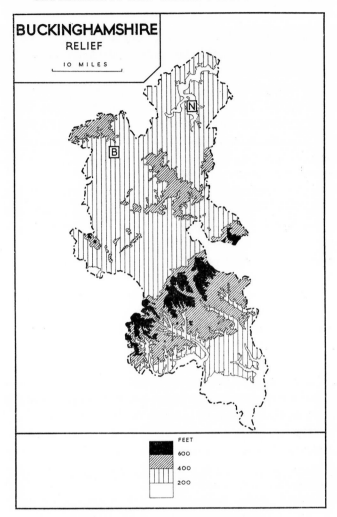

Fig. 49. Buckinghamshire: Relief.

Domesday boroughs are indicated by initials: B, Buckingham;
N, Newport Pagnell.

dens (146, 147, 150b, 151b), the two Risboroughs (143b *bis*) and the two
Wycombes (143b, 144b, 146, 149).[1] The distinction between the respective

[1] Great Hampden, Little Hampden; Great Missenden, Little Missenden; Princes
Risborough, Monks Risborough; West Wycombe, High (*alias* East, Chipping or
Great) Wycombe.

units of each of these groups appears later in time. Thus Great, *alias* Princes, Risborough, was first styled *Magna* in 1235,[1] and Little (or Monks) Risborough was called *Parva* about two years later.[2] In addition to the many dual place-names, there is the difficulty of anonymous holdings; thirteen entries in the Buckinghamshire folios were not assigned to precise localities, and so we cannot tell whether they lay in places mentioned elsewhere in the folios or whether they were in places that go unrecorded by name in the Domesday Book.[3] Finally there is the problem of the large manors, e.g. Burnham (151), which may have covered more than one settlement apiece in 1086.

The total of 207 includes two places about which very little information is given. The entry for *Sudcote* in Stone (151) tells of a virgate and 6 acres, with land for half a plough-team, worth 6s.; and Crawley (149) is mentioned only incidentally (see p. 177 below).

Not all the 207 Domesday names have survived as the names of villages on the present-day map of Buckinghamshire. Some are represented by hamlets, others by the names of farms. Thus *Opetone* or *Upetone* (149b, 148) is now the hamlet of Upton in Dinton, and *Estone* (146b, 149b) is that of Aston in Ivinghoe.[4] *Evresel* (153) is represented by Evershaw Farm in Biddlesden, and *Hortone* (146b, 149b, 150) by Horton Farm in Ivinghoe. These are but some of the changes in the Buckinghamshire villages. There are no unidentified Domesday place-names in Buckinghamshire, but the exact location of four, *Dileherst* (144), *Haseleie* (151b), *Sortelai* (150, 153), and *Sudcote* (151), is not known today.[5]

On the other hand, some villages on the modern map are not mentioned in the Domesday Book. Their names do not appear until the twelfth and

[1] Great Risborough was first called 'Princes' in 1343, when it passed into the hands of the Black Prince.

[2] The appelation 'Monks' appears to date only from 1346, although the estate belonged to Christ Church, Canterbury, even in pre-Domesday times.

[3] The relevant entries are: in Burnham hd. (144), in Cottesloe hd. (147), in Ixhill hd. (152b), in Lamua hd. (145, 148b, 149b), in Moulsoe hd. (149, 150b, 151 *bis*), in Stone hd. (148b), in Waddesdon hd. (150b), and in Yardley hd. (152).

[4] There are five other entries for *Estone* in the Buckinghamshire folios. *Estone* rubricated under Cottesloe hundred (145b) has been identified with Aston Abbots, *Estone* in Aylesbury hundred (150b) with Aston Clinton, and *Estone* in Ixhill hundred (144b) with Aston Sandford; the entries under *Estone* on fols. 150 and 152 have also been assigned to Aston Sandford because the hundredal rubrication of these folios appears, from later manorial history, to be incorrect.

[5] In the present analysis they have been plotted in the parishes of Taplow, Thornton, Quainton, and Stone respectively.

thirteenth centuries, and, presumably, if they existed in 1086, they are accounted for under the statistics of other places. Thus Beaconsfield, first mentioned in 1184, may have been surveyed with Burnham (of which it was subsequently a member),[1] Cold Brayfield with Lavendon,[2] Westcott with Waddesdon,[3] and Stokenchurch with Aston Rowant in Oxfordshire (159).[4]

The essential feature of the distribution of Domesday place-names is the contrast between the north and south of the county (Fig. 50). North of the Chiltern escarpment, settlements were numerous and fairly evenly distributed. The northern edge of the escarpment was marked by a line of villages set in the belt of loamy soils at its foot. To the south, in the Chilterns themselves, there were but few villages; they lay in the valleys of the Chess, the Misbourne and the Wye, and the intervening upland areas, extensively covered with Clay-with-flints, were devoid of Domesday place-names. Beyond the Chilterns, in the extreme south of the county, the spread of glacial gravels to the north of Burnham was also devoid of villages, in marked contrast to the well-settled river gravels bordering the Thames and the Colne.

THE DISTRIBUTION OF PROSPERITY AND POPULATION

Some idea of the nature of the information in the Domesday folios for Buckinghamshire, and of the form in which it is presented, may be obtained from the entry relating to the village of Medmenham situated on a gravel terrace overlooking the Thames (150b). The village was held entirely by Hugh de Bolbec, and so it is described in a single entry:

Manor. Hugh himself holds Medmenham. It is assessed at 10 hides (*pro x hidis se defendit*). There is land for 10 plough-teams. In demesne [there are] 4 hides and there are 2 plough-teams, and 10 villeins with 8 bordars have 8 plough-teams. There, 4 serfs. From fisheries 1,000 eels. Meadow for all the plough-teams (*pratum carucis omnibus*). Wood for 50 swine. In all (*Inter totum*) it is and was worth 100s. T.R.E. £8. This manor Ulstan, a thegn of King Edward, held, and could sell to whom he wished.

[1] *V.C.H. Buckinghamshire*, III, p. 157.
[2] *V.C.H. Buckinghamshire*, IV, p. 324.   [3] *Ibid.* p. 114.
[4] *V.C.H. Buckinghamshire*, III, p. 96. In post-Domesday times, Stokenchurch was a detached portion of Oxfordshire, but it was transferred to Buckinghamshire in 1896. Within Stokenchurch was Abefeld which A. M. Davies identified with one hide assigned to Lewknor in Oxfordshire (158)—Abefeld and Achamsted, *Records of Buckinghamshire*, XV, pp. 166 and 169.

This entry does not include all the kinds of information that appear in the folios for Buckinghamshire. It does not mention, for example, a mill. But, although not comprehensive, it is a fairly representative and straight-forward entry, and it does set out the recurring standard items that are

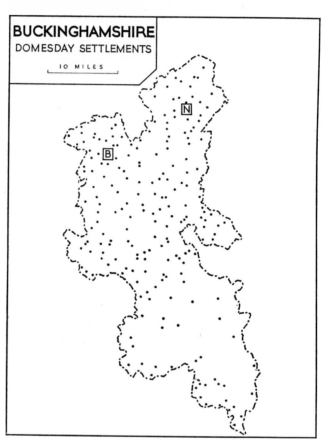

Fig. 50. Buckinghamshire: Domesday place-names.

Domesday boroughs are indicated by initials: B, Buckingham; N, Newport Pagnell.

found for most villages. These are five in number: (1) hides, (2) plough-lands, (3) plough-teams, (4) population, and (5) values. The bearing of these five items of information upon regional variations in the prosperity of the county must now be considered.

(1) *Hides*

The Buckinghamshire assessment is stated in terms of hides and virgates. Acres are sometimes mentioned,[1] and the measurement once descends to feet; thus on one holding at Lathbury (145) there was 1 hide less 5 feet (*i hidam v pedes minus*). Fractions of both hides and virgates are common. The form of the statement varies, as can be seen from three representative entries:

(i) Waldridge (144b): *In Wadruge tenet Helto de episcopo ii hidas et i virgatam.*

(ii) Stoke Mandeville (143b): *Remigius episcopus Lincoliæ (sic) tenet Stoches; pro octo hidis se defendit.*

(iii) Beachampton (147b): *In Becentone tenet Hugo de Walterio v hidas pro uno manerio.*

The first formula is the one most frequently used. Although normally only one assessment is stated, five entries specifically state that the rating was always the same—*pro n hidis se defendit semper.*[2] One other statement should be noted; at the end of the account of Oakley (149), a vill assessed at 5 hides and 3 virgates, we read: 'these 5 hides and 3 virgates are 8 hides' (*Haec v hidae et iii virgatae sunt viii hidae*). Perhaps this baffling statement conceals a reduction in liability.

There are many examples of the five-hide unit as the basis of the assessment in Buckinghamshire:[3] thus Ditton was assessed at 5 hides (148b), Hughenden at 10 hides (144b), Dinton at 15 hides (144), Hambleden at 20 hides (152b), Bledlow at 30 hides (146), and Haddenham at 40 hides (143b). Even when a village was divided among a number of owners, the same feature can often be demonstrated; three examples are given on p. 146. The number of settlements assessed in 1086 at either 5 or 10 hides amounts to 86 out of a total of 206, and 28 at a greater multiple of 5 hides (e.g. 15, 20, 30, 40 or 60 hides); there were also two villages rated at $2\frac{1}{2}$

---

[1] The acres are, of course, not units of area, but geld-acres, i.e. units of assessment.

[2] The entries for Aylesbury (143), Brill (143b), Risborough (143b), Wendover (143b) and Wormingham (145); the first four of these were royal estates, the last a manor of the bishop of Coutances.

[3] See J. H. Round (1) *Feudal England* (London, 1895; reprinted 1909), p. 66; (2) in *V.C.H. Buckinghamshire*, I, p. 208. In the latter work (p. 208), Round referred to a reconstruction of the hundred groupings by the Rev. F. W. Ragg, but the tables said by Round to have been compiled by Ragg do not appear to have been published.

Littlecote

	Hides	Virgates
(1) Walter Gifard (147)	2	2
(2) William, son of Ansculf (148b)	1	2
(3) Miles Crispin (150)	1	0
Total	5	0

Amersham

	Hides	Virgates
(1) Bishop of Bayeux (144)	0	2
(2) Count of Mortain (146)	0	2
(3) Geoffrey de Mandeville (149b)	7	2
(4) Hugh de Bolbec (150b)	0	2
(5) Turstin Mantel (151b)	0	2
(6) Gozelin the Breton (152)	0	2
Total	10	0

Chesham

	Hides	Virgates
(1) Bishop of Bayeux (144)	0	2
(2) Bishop of Bayeux (144)	1	2
(3) Hugh de Bolbec (150b)	8	2
(4) Turstin Mantel (151b)	0	2
(5) Alsi (153)	4	0
Total	15	0

hides each. We cannot be far wrong in saying that the five-hide principle is readily apparent in over one-half of the Buckinghamshire villages.

In addition to these, there are many vills with a hidage that is not an exact multiple of 5. These, too, did we but know all the complications, might well be examples of the five-hide unit. The entries relating to Clifton and Pitstone are examples of such discrepancies (see p. 147).

We have, as Round remarked, to allow for slight errors on the part of the Domesday scribes and for the difficulties of identification at the present day.[1] It is, moreover, possible that some of the villages were grouped in blocks for the purpose of assessment, as in Cambridgeshire.[2]

[1] *Feudal England*, p. 57.
[2] For the Cambridgeshire blocks, see H. C. Darby, *The Domesday Geography of Eastern England* (Cambridge, 2nd ed., 1957), p. 276.

Clifton

	Hides	Virgates
(1) Bishop of Coutances (145 b):	1	2
(2) Bishop of Coutances (145 b):	1	0
(3) Robert de Todeni (149):	4	0
(4) Robert de Todeni (149):		3
(5) Countess Judith (152b):	1	0½
(6) Countess Judith (152b):	1	2
Total	9	3½

Pitstone

	Hides	Virgates
(1) Count of Mortain (146):	3	1
(2) Count of Mortain (146):	3	1
(3) Count of Mortain (146):	1	1
(4) Walter Gifard (147):	5½	0
(5) Miles Crispin (150):	5	0
(6) Miles Crispin (150):	2	0
Total	20	1

But the absence of information about these groups makes it impossible to be definite about the full extent of the five-hide unit in Buckinghamshire.

Whatever the origin of this system of taxation, there is little doubt that, by 1086, the assessment was artificial, and that it bore little, if any, relation to the resources of a village. The variation among a representative selection of ten-hide vills speaks for itself:

	Plough-lands	Teams	Population
Adstock (148)	7	6	7
Chetwode (145)	5	4½	15
Dunton (144b)	8	5	10
Fawley (147)	14	14	19
Quarrendon (149b)	10	12	28

We are specifically told that the two holdings at Ibstone, entered in the Oxfordshire folios (160b *bis*), did not pay geld:

(i) *Herveus tenet de rege i hidam in Ypestan. Terra i carucae. Ibi est unus villanus et iii acrae prati. Valuit et valet xx solidos. Non geldat haec terra.*

(ii) *Isdem Herveus tenet Ebestan. Ibi i hida. Terra i carucae. Valet x solidos. Ulf tenuit. Haec ii terrae*[1] *nec geldum nec aliud servitum reddidunt regi.*

[1] This statement seems to refer not only to the second holding at Ibstone but also to one at Bix in Oxfordshire.

Nothing is said about the geld liability of a holding of 2 hides at Ibstone entered in the Buckinghamshire folios (152b).

Buckinghamshire, like Hertfordshire and Middlesex, is one of the counties for which the hidage of the demesne is regularly entered. Baring concluded that hides 'in demesne' were recorded in view of an exemption from geld of land held by the tenant-in-chief himself, and not held of him by an under-tenant;[1] but in the Buckinghamshire folios the hidage of the demesne is also recorded for four estates held by under-tenants.[2] Three entries mention 'carucates in demesne', and a fourth records, or seems to record, both carucates and hides in demesne:

> Newport Pagnell (148b): *Ipse Willelmus [filius Ansculfi] tenet Neuport; pro v hidis se defendit. Terra est ix carucis. In dominio iiii carucatae terrae et ibi sunt iiii carucae et v villani habent v carucas. Burgenses habent vi carucas et dimidiam; aliorumque hominum extra v hidas laborantes.*[3]

> Tickford (149): *Ipse Willelmus [filius Ansculfi] tenet Ticheforde; pro v hidis se defendit. Terra est viii carucis. In dominio duae carucatae terrae et ibi ii carucae. Praeter v hidas. Ibi vi villani cum iiii servis habent vi carucas.*

> Turweston (151): *Willelmus de Felgeres tenet Turvestone; pro v hidis se defendit. Terra est viii carucis. Praeter has v hidas in dominio sunt iii carucatae terrae et ibi una caruca et adhuc ii possunt esse et vi villani cum iiii bordariis habent v carucas.*

> Hanslope (152): *Winemarus tenet Hammescle; pro x hidis se defendit. Terra est xxvi carucis. In dominio sunt v hidae et, praeter has, v carucatae terrae et ibi sunt ii carucae et adhuc iiii possunt fieri. Ibi xxxvi villani cum xi bordariis habent xviii carucas et adhuc ii carucae possunt esse.*

These entries are difficult. At Newport Pagnell, at Tickford and at Turweston, the carucates in 'demesne' equalled in number the demesne teams in 1086 and may perhaps indicate the number of plough-lands in

---

[1] F. H. Baring, *Domesday Tables for the counties of Surrey, Berkshire, Middlesex, Hertford, Buckingham and Bedford and for the New Forest* (London, 1909), pp. 133–5. See also J. H. Round, 'Danegeld and the finance of Domesday' in P. E. Dove (ed.), *Domesday Studies*, I (London, 1888), pp. 96–8.

[2] For the estates held of the count of Mortain by the monks of Grestain at Ickford (146) and at Marsh Gibbon (146b), and for those held of the bishop of Bayeux by Tedald at *Hanechedene* (Radnage, 144b) and Marlow (144b); see F. H. Baring, *op. cit.* p. 134. For the identification of *Hanechedene*, see G. R. Elvey, 'Buckinghamshire in 1086', *Records of Buckinghamshire*, XVI (Bedford, 1953–60), p. 344.

[3] The text seems defective.

demesne.[1] But the entry for Hanslope with a record of hides 'in demesne' as well as carucates 'in demesne' suggests other possibilities.[2]

The total number of hides (including non-gelding hides) seems to amount to 2,125 hides 3¾ virgates 3 acres less 5 feet (*minus v pedes*), but it must be remembered that this total refers to the area covered by the modern county and includes the figures for the boroughs.[3] Maitland estimated the number of hides in the Domesday county at 2,074.[4] F. H. Baring[5] and W. J. Corbett[6] also totalled the Buckinghamshire assessment, but their figures are comparable neither with each other nor with the present total. There were also 14 carucates in demesne.[7]

(2) Plough-lands

The normal formula runs: 'There is land for *n* plough-teams' (*Terra est n carucis*). Only once does the phrasing vary, i.e. the entry for Buckingham with Bourton[8] notes: *Terra est octo carucarum* (143). The arable of a few small estates was measured in terms of oxen; thus on one holding at Wavendon (153) there was land for 4 oxen (*Terra est iiii bobus*). Once in the Buckinghamshire folios, in an entry for a holding at Beachendon (144b), the words *Terra est* are followed by a lacuna.[9] Where the number of teams on a holding is less than that of the plough-lands, there is usually a statement to the effect that additional teams 'might be' or 'could be employed', either on the demesne or on the lands of the peasantry or on both. It says, in effect, that the land could carry more teams than were at

---

[1] See p. 563 below.

[2] F. H. Baring thought that the record of both hides and carucates in this entry was but a scribal error—'It looks as if in the MS. from which the compiler worked "præter has (10 hidas) 5 carucatæ terræ" was written over the "5 hidae" as a correction and the scribe copied both into Domesday.'—*Domesday Tables*, p. 135 n.

[3] The figures for the boroughs are: Buckingham *cum* Bourton (143), 1 hide; Newport Pagnell (148b), 5 hides.

[4] F. W. Maitland, *Domesday Book and Beyond* (Cambridge, 1897), p. 400.

[5] F. H. Baring, *Domesday Tables*, p. 143. Baring made an earlier estimate for Buckinghamshire in 'The hidation of some southern counties', *Eng. Hist. Rev.* XIV (London, 1899), p. 291, but it was incorrect as he himself realised: see (1) *Eng. Hist. Rev.* XV (London, 1900), p. 199; and (2) *Domesday Tables*, p. 131 n.

[6] W. J. Corbett, 'The Tribal Hidage', *Trans. Roy. Hist. Soc.* XIV (London, 1900), p. 218.

[7] This figure assumes that the information for Hanslope is correct and does not include a scribal error; see above.   [8] *cum Bortone* is interlined.

[9] It was a small estate of one virgate, and was worth only 5s. in 1086 as in 1066. No population or teams are mentioned.

work, and it indicates therefore the possibility of further cultivation. Here are some sample entries that illustrate the variety of phrasing:

(1) Akeley: *Terra est iiii carucis. In dominio sunt quattuor boves et ii carucae possunt fieri. Ibi ii villani cum iiii bordariis habent ii carucam et dimidiam* (147b).

(2) Biddlesden: *Terra est octo carucis. In dominio ii hidae et ibi est una caruca et duae plus possunt fieri. Ibi iiii villani et v bordarii habent ii carucas et iii possunt fieri adhuc* (143b).

(3) Farnham: *Terra est viii carucis. In dominio v hidae et ibi sunt ii carucae et v villani cum iii bordariis habent iiii carucas et adhuc duae possunt esse* (151b).

(4) Ivinghoe: *Terra est xxv carucis. In dominio v hidae et ibi sunt iii carucae et quarta potest fieri. Ibi xxviii villani cum iiii bordariis habent xx carucae et adhuc potest una fieri* (143b).

(5) Shipton: *Terra est vii carucis. In dominio iii hidae et ibi sunt ii carucae et aliae ii possunt esse. Ibi iiii villani cum i bordario habent ii carucas et tercia potest fieri* (151).

(6) Wavendon: *Terra est ii carucis et dimidiae. In dominio est una et ii villani cum iii bordarii habent i carucam et adhuc possunt facere dimidiam* (146b).

The *potest fieri* formula, or one of its variants, is to be found in entries relating to well over one-third of the Domesday settlements of Buckinghamshire. Even so, it seems that the scribe may sometimes have omitted what he should have inserted. Thus at Aston Abbots (145b) there were 12 plough-lands, but only 9 'actual' and 2 'possible' teams are mentioned; it seems that the scribe may have omitted to say that another could have been made on the holding of the peasantry. Or, again, on one estate at Wycombe (143b) there were 23 plough-lands, but only 22 teams at work, and there is no reference to the possible addition of another team.

There are a few entries in which the Buckinghamshire folios record the lack of plough-teams in another way. One of the holdings at Horsenden had land for half a plough-team, but the entry goes on to say that the team itself was not there, *Terra est dimidiae carucae sed non est ibi caruca* (144). One of the ten holdings at Lavendon had 3 plough-lands which were not being worked—*Terra est iii carucis sed non sunt ibi nisi iiii bordarii* (152b). Plough-lands on holdings at Brickhill (145), Clifton (152b) and Milton Keynes (148) were in a similar plight. Quite often on the smaller holdings, the Buckinghamshire text leaves us to assume the absence of teams. It merely says, as for a holding at Hardmead (150b), *Terra est ii bobus*, and it omits any mention of oxen that were not there; or, again, as for an anonymous holding of Walter the Fleming in Moulsoe hundred (151), *Terra est i carucae.* We can only assume that most of these laconic entries mean what they say, and so indicate understocked holdings.

It is possible that the plough-land figure refers to conditions in 1066, and that the discrepancy between plough-lands and plough-teams indicates incomplete recovery after lean years when the land had been wasted or had gone out of cultivation. In most of the entries which record excess plough-lands, the value shows a reduction between 1066 and 1086, which would support this contention. But, on the other hand, on a few holdings the teams were fewer than the plough-lands, and yet the values had risen— which seems unlikely if the plough-land is taken as a measure of the arable of 1066. This was the situation, for example, on holdings at the five villages listed below:

	Plough-lands	Teams	Value 1066	Value 1086
Barton Hartshorne (145)	5	3	60s.	£14
Farnham (151b)	8	6	£4	100s.
Ivinghoe (143b)	25	23	£15	£18
Oving (145)	9	7	£7	£10
Wycombe (143b)	23	22	£12	£15

This is not conclusive evidence because, even when plough-lands and plough-teams are the same, the value fluctuates, being sometimes greater and sometimes less than in 1066. Whether the plough-land entry refers to conditions in 1066 or not, the fact of understocking remains. An estate deficient in teams was presumably not being tilled to capacity; the arable of 1086 was capable of extension.[1]

At some half-dozen places, however, the reverse was true. There were more plough-teams than plough-lands. At Wooburn, for example, there were only 9 plough-lands but 12 teams, 2 on the demesne and 10 with the peasants (144); or, again, for Upton near Slough only 10 plough-lands were entered, but as many as 17 teams, 2 on the demesne and 15 with the peasants (143b). Sometimes it is the total of the actual and possible teams that is in excess of the plough-lands. Thus on one holding in Milton Keynes, there seems to have been an excess of half a team, for the Domesday entry notes: *Terra est x carucis. In dominio ii carucae et dimidiam et dimidia*

---

[1] For the widespread deficiency of teams, see p. 165 below.

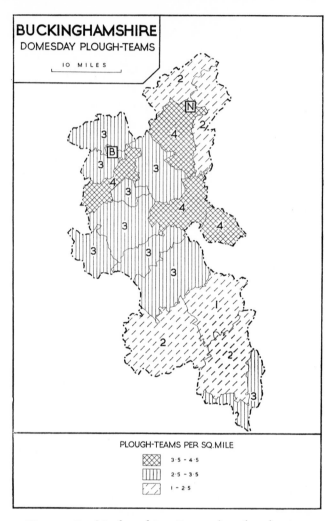

Fig. 51. Buckinghamshire: Domesday plough-teams
in 1086 (by densities).

Domesday boroughs are indicated by initials: B, Buckingham;
N, Newport Pagnell.

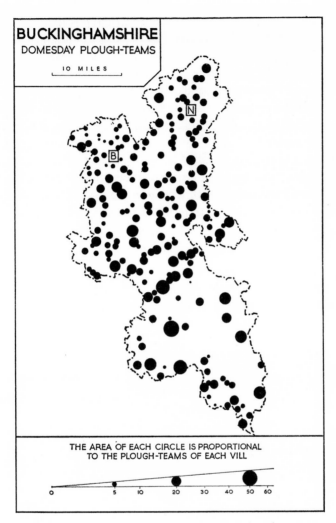

Fig. 52. Buckinghamshire: Domesday plough-teams
in 1086 (by settlements).

Domesday boroughs are indicated by initials: B, Buckingham;
N, Newport Pagnell.

potest fieri. Ibi xviii villani cum vi bordarii habent viii carucae (153). On one of the five holdings at Swanbourne actual and possible teams exceeded plough-lands by one team (143b), but on another holding in the same village the plough-lands exceeded in number the teams at work, but nothing is said about a possible team, either on the demesne or with the peasants (147).[1] Some of these discrepancies may be arithmetical errors, but we cannot be certain. Whatever be the explanation of the occasional overstocking of estates in general, the Buckinghamshire folios throw no light on the matter.[2]

A total of 2,299¾ plough-lands[3] is recorded for the area covered by the modern county. But we must also remember that no figure for plough-lands is given in one entry for Beachendon (144b).[4] There have been two other estimates, but each was in terms of the Domesday county.[5]

(3) *Plough-teams*

The Buckinghamshire entries like those for other counties draw a distinction between the teams held in demesne by the lord of a manor, and those held by the peasantry. The entry for Edgcott (147b), for example, is typical: 'In demesne there are 2 [plough-teams], and 10 villeins with

---

[1] The details of the plough-land and plough-team figures for the five holdings in Swanbourne are:

| | | Plough-teams | | | |
| | | Demesne | | Peasants | |
Landowner	Plough-lands	Actual	Possible	Actual	Possible
The king (143b)	4	1	1	1½	1½
Count of Mortain (146b)	5	1	4	—	—
Walter Gifard (147)	7	2	—	4	—
Walter son of Ansculf (148b)	¼ (i.e. 2 oxen)	—	—	—	—
Geoffrey de Mandeville (149b)	2	1	—	1	—

[2] For a discussion of possible causes of apparent overstocking on some Domesday estates in Lincolnshire, see H. C. Darby, *The Domesday Geography of Eastern England*, pp. 40–3.

[3] This total includes the figures for the boroughs—Buckingham *cum* Bourton with 12 plough-lands (143), and Newport Pagnell with 9 plough-lands (148b).

[4] See p. 149 above.

[5] Maitland counted 2,244 plough-lands, but his totals were for the Domesday county and excluded the figures for Buckingham and possibly for Newport Pagnell; see F. W. Maitland, *op. cit.* pp. 401 and 409. Baring's total was 2,293 plough-lands (*op. cit.* p. 143).

9 bordars have 6 plough-teams' (*In dominio sunt ii [carucae] et x villani cum ix bordariis habent vi carucas*). Occasionally, e.g. in the entries for Dadford (151b, 153), only demesne teams seem to be recorded;[1] there are also some in which we hear only of the teams of the peasantry such as those for Bradenham (153) and Lude (144) respectively. Very occasionally, oxen are mentioned; thus on one holding at Hardmead, there were two at work—*Terra est ii bobus et ibi sunt* (149); but on another holding in the same village (150b), with land for 2 oxen, we are not specifically told that the land was being tilled. On the other hand, in a few entries we are definitely told that the land was not in cultivation, e.g. the entry for one of the Horsenden estates runs: *Terra est dimidiae carucae sed non est ibi caruca* (144).

A total of 2,056 teams are recorded for the area included in the modern county.[2] Maitland estimated the number for the Domesday county at 1,952;[3] Baring's total came to 2,046 teams.[4]

(4) *Population*

The bulk of the population was comprised in the three main categories of villeins, bordars and serfs. In addition to these main groups were the burgesses (see p. 177 below), together with a small miscellaneous group that included sokemen, cottars and *buri*.[5] The details of these groups are summarised on p. 160. There are two other estimates of population, by Sir Henry Ellis[6] and F. H. Baring[7] respectively. The present estimate is not comparable with either of these because it is in terms of the modern county. In any case, one thing is certain; no one who counts Domesday population can claim definite accuracy. All that can be said for the present figures is that they indicate the order of magnitude involved. The figures are those of recorded population, and must be multiplied by some factor, say 4 or 5, in order to obtain the actual population; but this does not affect

---

[1] *In dominio* is implied but not specifically mentioned.

[2] This total includes the figures for the boroughs—9½ for Buckingham *cum* Bourton (143), 15½ for Newport Pagnell (148b).

[3] *Op. cit.* p. 401.   [4] *Op. cit.* p. 143.

[5] Priests are not regularly recorded for Buckinghamshire; see p. 177 below.

[6] Sir Henry Ellis, *A General Introduction to Domesday Book*, II (London, 1833), p. 427. This estimate amounted to 5,420, but it included tenants-in-chief, under-tenants and burgesses, and moreover was in terms of the Domesday county.

[7] *Op. cit.* p. 143. Baring counted 2,900 villeins, 1,322 bordars and 855 serfs, but his count was also in terms of the Domesday county.

the relative density as between one area and another.[1] That is all that a map such as Fig. 53 can roughly indicate.

It is impossible for us to say how complete were these Domesday statistics, but it does seem as if some people had been left uncounted. One entry for Leckhampstead (149b) omits the number of villeins; the scribe left a space for the number to be inserted but it was never filled in. On one holding at Shenley (152) the villeins are said to have a plough-team, but their number is not stated (*villani habent i carucam*). Or, again, the entry for Newport Pagnell (148b) tells of 'other men working outside the 5 hides' (*aliorumque hominum extra v hidas laborantes*),[2] and reference is made later in the entry to a money render from 'men who dwell in the wood' (*et adhuc iiii solidi de hominibus qui manent in silva*), but neither their status nor their number is specified.[3] Finally, there are some small Domesday holdings that omit all reference to population, e.g. the entry for a holding at Addington (150b) where there was half a team at work, but no mention is made of the men working the land. It is impossible to be certain about the significance of these omissions, but they all suggest unrecorded inhabitants.

Villeins constituted the most important element in the population, and amounted to 57 per cent of the total. Bordars comprised only 25 per cent. A peculiar feature of the Buckinghamshire folios is that they do not regularly enumerate cottars, an important category in the population of the adjoining counties of Hertfordshire and Middlesex. The only cottars recorded in Buckinghamshire are the ten on the estate belonging to the church of the borough of Buckingham (143); it may be that the *bordarii* included men who in neighbouring counties were styled *cotarii*.[4] Serfs accounted for some 16 per cent of the population, and like the villeins and bordars present no features of special interest for our purpose.

The remaining categories of population are small in number, but are of considerable interest. The largest and most interesting group is that of sokemen, about whom details are given for 1066 as well as for 1086. But it is not possible to be precise about the number of sokemen in 1066 because we cannot always be sure whether a sokeman recorded at a place in 1086

---

[1] But see p. 589 below for the complication of serfs.

[2] Newport Pagnell was assessed at 5 hides.

[3] For the full entry, see p. 179 below.

[4] For a discussion of the difference between bordars and cottars, see (1) F. W. Maitland, *op. cit.* pp. 39 *et seq.*; (2) P. Vinogradoff, *English Society in the Eleventh Century* (Oxford, 1908), pp. 456 *et seq.*

had also been there 20 years earlier. Thus, at Tickford (149) there were 5 sokemen rendering (*reddunt*) 27s. in 1086, but in 1066 there had been 5 thegns holding 3½ virgates of the estate; and we are left with the suspicion that the 5 sokemen of 1086 represent the 5 thegns of 1066. In some other counties, e.g. Hertfordshire and Middlesex, men styled thegns usually held at least half a hide, but in Buckinghamshire there seem to have been two 'grades' of thegn. F. H. Baring first pointed out that many of the thegns in the north of the county held only very small parcels of land, often less than a virgate apiece, and seem to have been little more than sokemen;[1] they were also often enumerated in groups like the sokemen of Bedfordshire and Hertfordshire. It may be, as the entry for Tickford would seem to suggest, that to the scribe of the Buckinghamshire folios the terms sokeman and thegn were comparable. If this were so, it would explain the very small number of sokemen in the county in 1066, particularly in the Danelaw portion; there were only 37 sokemen as opposed to upwards of 200 thegns. Twenty years later, only 20 sokemen were recorded but there may have been more; at the end of the entry for Stoke Mandeville (143b) we hear of payments in grain from sokemen in the eight hundreds 'around Aylesbury' (*in circuitu Elesberie*).[2] Some entries suggest that many of the Buckinghamshire sokemen were depressed, as were those of Cambridgeshire and Hertfordshire. Thus, at a holding at Wycombe (146), there was a bordar in 1086 where there had been 1 sokeman in 1066; and on another, at Waldridge (144b), there were 2 villeins where earlier there had been 2 sokemen. It would, of course, be unsafe to assume that the 2 villeins represented the 2 sokemen, but the figures in this example, and in others, are curious. Fifteen of the 20 sokemen enumerated in 1086 were on holdings in the two most northerly hundreds of Bunsty and Moulsoe, yet in 1066 only one sokeman was recorded for Bunsty hundred (at Olney, 145b) and none at all for Moulsoe hundred.

The other miscellaneous categories are those of *buri* (i.e. four at Wycombe, 149)[3] and *vavassores* (i.e. two paying 32s. 6d. at Caldecote, 146b).[4] There was also a smith (*faber*) at Ibstone (152b), a *francigena* at Weston Underwood (145b), and a saltworker of Droitwich rendering

---

[1] *Domesday Tables*, pp. 136–7.
[2] But see P. Vinogradoff, *op. cit.* pp. 441–2.
[3] Maitland discussed the status of the *buri*, *burs* or *coliberti* and showed that they were to be found especially in the counties of Wessex and Western Mercia (*op. cit.* pp. 36–7). See also p. 314 below.
[4] *Ibid.* p. 81.

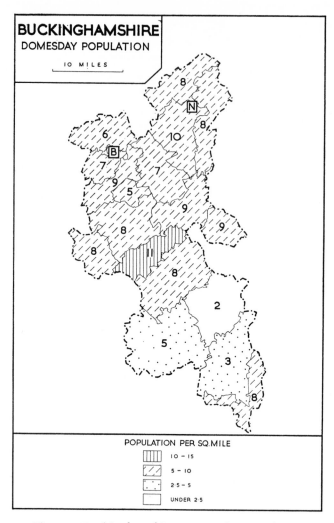

Fig. 53. Buckinghamshire: Domesday population
in 1086 (by densities).

Domesday boroughs are indicated by initials: B, Buckingham;
N, Newport Pagnell.

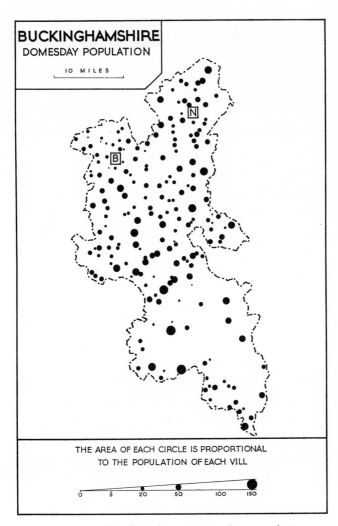

Fig. 54. Buckinghamshire: Domesday population
in 1086 (by settlements).

Domesday boroughs are indicated by initials: B, Buckingham;
N, Newport Pagnell.

loads of salt (*Adhuc unus salinarius de Wicg (sic) reddit summas salis*) at
Risborough (143 b); but, as he was probably at Droitwich, he has not
been counted in the total below. Finally mention must be made of two
men for the guard of Windsor (*duos Loricatos in custodiam de Windesores*)
who had been dispossessed at Drayton Parslow (151 b); they have not been
counted as their fate and status in 1086 are uncertain.[1]

Recorded Population of Buckinghamshire in 1086

A. Rural Population

Villeins	2,901
Bordars	1,314
Serfs	842
Miscellaneous	38
Total	5,095

Details of Miscellaneous Rural Population

Sokemen	20	*Vavassores*		2
Cottars	10	*Francigena*		1
Buri	4	Smith (*Faber*)		1
		Total		38

B. Urban Population

Villeins, bordars, cottars and serfs are also included above.

BUCKINGHAM   26 burgesses; ? 27 other burgesses; 3 villeins; 14 bordars;
(with Bourton)   10 cottars; 2 serfs. See p. 178 below.

NEWPORT PAGNELL unspecified numbers of burgesses, 'other men' (*aliorumque
hominum*), and men 'who dwell in the wood' (*qui manent
in silva*); 5 villeins; 9 serfs. See p. 179 below.

(5) Values

The value of an estate is normally given in a round number of pounds or
shillings for three dates, 1066, 1086 and an intermediate date. The entry
for Taplow (144) is typical: *In totis valentiis valet viii libras. Quando*

---

[1] The knight at Caldecote (148 b), the two knights at Loughton (152), and the two
Englishmen at Soulbury (153) have been reckoned as land holders and so have been
excluded from the table above.

recepit lx solidos. T.R.E. ix libras. But occasionally the statement varies, and the formulae *valet et valuit* and *valet et valuit semper* are used:

Dinton (144): *In totis valentiis valet xv libras et valuit semper.*
Horsenden (144): *Valet et valuit iii solidos. T.R.E. v solidos.*
Tickford (149): *Valet c solidos. Quando recepit vi libras et tantundem T.R.E.*

Occasionally the intermediate value is omitted, e.g. the entry for a holding at Chesham (150b) notes only: *In totis valentiis valet x libras iii solidos minus. T.R.E. xii libras.*

The 'values' are usually entered as plain statements of money, but there are eight entries which indicate considerable differences in the method of reckoning. We are specifically told that the values of some estates were reckoned by tale or number, when the coins were accepted at their nominal value. But in view of the circulation of debased coins, some values were reckoned by weight, and were also tested by assay; the latter was known as 'white money'. These variations are listed below:

Aylesbury (143): In all it pays (*In totis valentiis reddit*) £56 assayed and weighed (*arsas et pensatas*), and from the toll £10 by tale (*ad numerum*). *T.R.E.* it used to pay (*reddebat*) £25 by tale.
Brill (143b): In all it pays yearly £38 of blanched silver (*Inter totum reddit per annum xxxviii libras de albo argento*, and for the forest (*pro foresta*) £12 assayed and weighed. *T.R.E.* it used to pay £18 by tale.
Buckingham with Bourton (143):[1] In all (*In totis valentiis*) *T.R.E.* it used to pay £10 by tale. Now (*Modo*) it pays £16 of blanched silver.
Hambleden (152b): In all it pays yearly £35 by tale. When the queen was alive £15. *T.R.E.* £16. (*In totis redditionibus per annum reddit xxxv libras et ad numerum. Quando vivebat regina xv libras. T.R.E. xvi libras.*)
Risborough (143b): In all (*Inter totum*) it pays yearly £47 of blanched silver less (*minus*) 16d. *T.R.E.* it used to pay £10 by tale.
Swanbourne (143b): In all it pays 30s. of blanched silver. *T.R.E.* 30s. by tale.
Upton near Slough (143b): In all it pays £21 assayed and weighed. *T.R.E.* it used to pay £15 by tale.
Wendover (143b): In all (*In totis valentiis*) it pays yearly £38 assayed and weighed. *T.R.E.* it used to pay £25 by tale.

A feature of the Buckinghamshire valuation is the decrease in 'value' of many holdings in the years after 1066. The values of a number were

---

[1] For the complication of this entry, see p. 178 below.

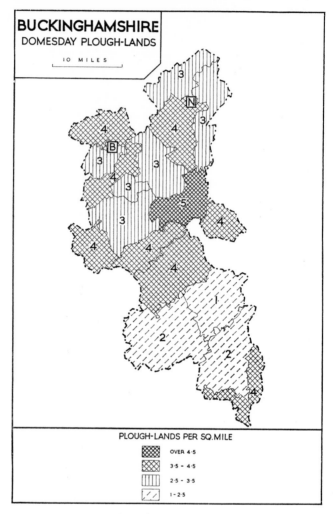

Fig. 55. Buckinghamshire: Domesday plough-lands
(by densities).

Domesday boroughs are indicated by initials: B, Buckingham;
N, Newport Pagnell.

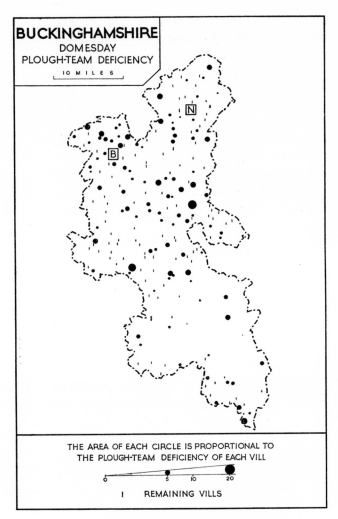

Fig. 56. Buckinghamshire: Domesday plough-team
deficiency (by settlements).

Domesday boroughs are indicated by initials: B, Buckingham;
N, Newport Pagnell.

only some 25 per cent to 50 per cent of what they had been, and a few had suffered even more (Figs. 161–2); but only one Buckinghamshire estate, Stowe (144b), was completely wasted at the intermediate date—*Valet xl solidos. Vastam recepit. T.R.E. lx solidos.* F. H. Baring attributed the falls in value of some of the estates at the intermediate date to the passage of the Norman armies.[1] By 1086 the majority of the holdings in the county had recovered fully or in part, and some were even more prosperous than before. No valuation was made of wasted holdings at Biddlesden (146b) and Cheddington (150b), but a value was entered for a waste holding in Chesham—*Valet et valuit semper v solidos* (151b).

Generally speaking, the greater the number of plough-teams and men on an estate, the higher its value, but it is impossible to discern any constant relationships, as the following figures for six estates, each yielding £6 in 1086, show:

	Teams	Population	Other resources
Cublington (152)	9	21	Meadow
Datchet (152b)	8	25	Fisheries, Meadow, Wood
Eton (151)	8	23	Fisheries, Meadow, Mills, Wood
Fawley (147)	14	19	Meadow, Wood
Slapton (146)	6	26	Meadow
Worminghall (145)	5	26	Meadow, Wood

It is true that the variations in the arable, as between one estate and another, did not necessarily reflect variations in total resources, but even taking the other resources into account the figures are not easy to explain. When there was a decline in value between 1066 and 1086, we sometimes find the *potest fieri* clause in the statement about plough-teams, e.g. for Denham (145b), Little Kimble (151) and Twyford (151b). But the clause occasionally appears even when there was an increase in value, e.g. at Ivinghoe (143b) and Oving (145). It would be unwise therefore to attempt any correlations.

Conclusion

The eighteen Domesday hundreds have been adopted as the main basis for constructing the density maps, but some modifications have been made. In 1086 several of the hundreds were dispersed; e.g. Risborough

---

[1] *Op. cit.* pp. 210–11. See also p. 569 below.

hundred was divided into two by a 'tongue' of Desborough hundred (Fig. 48). Some of the hundreds have been regrouped to make the units correspond more closely to significant changes in soil. The result of these modifications is not as perfect a regional division as a geographer would wish, but it is as satisfactory a division as can be obtained from the material available.

Of the five recurring formulae, those relating to plough-teams and population are the most likely to reflect something of wealth and prosperity throughout the county in 1086 (Figs. 51 and 53). Taken together, they supplement one another; and, when they are compared, certain common features stand out. The most prominent of these features is the contrast between north and south. The densities of both teams and population were very low in the Chilterns, being generally about one-third or less than those in the northern hundreds. This contrast reflected the distinction between the closely-settled northern lowlands and the empty areas of the wooded Chilterns and of the Burnham gravel plateau. In the extreme south, on the fertile terraces of the Thames and the Colne, the densities reached those commonly found in the north.

Figs. 52 and 54 are supplementary to the density maps; but, as we have seen on p. 140 above, it is possible that some Domesday names may have covered two or more settlements, e.g. Monks Risborough and Princes Risborough are represented in the Buckinghamshire folios by only one name. A few of the symbols, therefore, should appear as two or three smaller symbols. Fig. 55, showing the distribution of plough-lands, confirms Figs. 51 and 53 in a general way. Comparison of Figs. 51 and 55 shows that in several areas the land was not being tilled to capacity. Further comment on this is provided by Fig. 56 which shows the plough-team deficiency for individual settlements. This deficiency was sometimes quite appreciable.

WOODLAND

Types of entries

The amount of woodland on a holding in Buckinghamshire was normally indicated by the number of swine which it could support, for the swine fed upon acorns and beech-mast, and so provided a convenient measure. The usual formula was 'Wood for *n* swine' (*Silva n porcis*), and the numbers recorded under a single place-name ranged from only 16 at Ditton (148b) up to as many as 2,000 at Wendover (143b). The round figures of many entries may indicate estimates rather than actual amounts, but, on the other hand, there are detailed figures that suggest exactness, e.g. the 806 swine (*Silva octingentis porcis et vi*) entered under Akeley (147b). At Oakley (149) we are told that there was woodland for 200 swine, were it not in the king's park—*Silva cc porcis nisi esset parcus regis in quo jacet*. We cannot tell how complete was the Domesday record of wood in the eleventh-century county. No mention of wood is made for the Buckinghamshire villages rubricated under Cottesloe hundred;[1] this omission may be due to an error either in the original returns, or in the compilation of the Domesday Book. It is difficult to believe that the 15 Domesday vills in this hundred were without wood.[2]

Although swine form the normal unit of measurement in the Buckinghamshire folios, several entries indicate the presence of woodland in other ways. Three entries, i.e. those for Kimble (147), Claydon (148) and the church of Buckingham with Bourton (143), tell of 'Wood for fencing' (*Nemus ad sepes*).

Eleven entries mention a money payment from woodland:

Caldecote (146b): *Silva xxiiii porcis et xxviii denarii de consuetudinibus.*
Ivinghoe (143b): *Silva sexcentis porcis et x solidi.*
Lenborough (144b): *De silva iiii solidi per annum.*
Marlow (150): *Silva cc porcis et xii denarii.*
Missenden (147): *Silva quingentis porcis et de reddita silvae quattuor ore (sic) per annum.*
Tyringham (148b): *Silva cc porcis et xxvi denarii de minutis consuetudinibus.*
Wendover Dean (153): *Silva xxx porcis et x solidos reddit.*
Winslow (146): *De silva x solidi per annum.*
Wooburn (144): *Silva cc porcis et vii solidi et iiii denarii.*
In Moulsoe hundred (149): *Silva cl porcis et xvi denarii.*

The entry for Newport Pagnell records 'woodland for 300 swine and with a yield of 2s.' and a further payment of 4s. from men who dwelt therein— *Silva ccc porcis et ii solidi et adhuc iiii solidi de hominibus qui manent in silva*

---

[1] F. H. Baring, *Domesday Tables*, p. 133.
[2] The complete list of villages rubricated under Cottesloe hundred is: Aston Abbots (145b), Burston (146 *bis*, 147, 150), Crafton (145b, 146), Cublington (152), Grove (152), Hardwick (146, 150, 151), Helsthorpe (146, 152), Hollingdon (148b, 150, 152b), Linslade (150b), Littlecote (147, 148b, 150), Mentmore (146b), Soulbury (148, 150, 150b, 152, 153 *bis*), Whitchurch (147), Wing (146) and Wingrave (146, 150 *ter*, 152b). There was also an anonymous holding (147).

(148b). Five estates made renders of iron for plough-shares from the profits of the wood:

Aston Clinton (150b): *Silva ccc porcis et ferra carucis dominicis.*
Bledlow (146): *Silva mille porcis et de reddita silvae ferra carucis sufficienter.*
Burnham (151): *Silva sexcentis porcis et ferrum carucis.*
Chesham (150b): *Silva octingentis porcis et ferrum carucis.*
Hampden (148b): *Silva quingentis porcis et de reddita silvae ferra ii carucis.*

The woodland of the three Buckinghamshire estates described in the Oxfordshire folios was recorded in terms of linear dimensions, the usual method of measuring woodland in that county; each of the two entries for Lillingstone Lovell (160, 160b) mentions 'Wood 10 furlongs in length and 5 furlongs in breadth' (*Silva x quarentenis longa et v quarentenis lata*) and the entry for Boycott (160) tells of 'Wood 4 furlongs in length and 2 in breadth'.

The royal forests of eleventh-century Buckinghamshire for the most part go unmentioned in the Domesday Book. There is only one actual reference to forest; at the end of the entry for Brill (143b) we are told that the estate rendered annually for the issues of the forest £12 assayed and weighed (*pro foresta xii libras arsas et pensatas*); earlier in the entry we hear of wood for 200 swine. At Oakley (149) nearby we are told that the woodland would have fed 200 swine were it not in the king's park— *Silva cc porcis nisi esset parcus regis in quo jacet*; this statement has been taken to mean that the king had placed the wood under forest law.[1] There were also two references to eyries of hawks; the entries for the two estates at Chalfont (144, 151b) each note one (*una area accipitris*). There was also a park for the beasts of the chase (*parcus ibi bestiarum silvaticarum*) at Long Crendon (147). But these scattered references do little justice to the Norman love of the chase.

Distribution of woodland

Domesday Buckinghamshire was a well-wooded county (Fig. 57).[2] There was a considerable amount of wood in the Chilterns and in the

---

[1] Both entries presumably refer to Bernwood Forest, close by; Oakley was subsequently styled '*in Bernewode*'—see (1) A. Mawer and F. M. Stenton, *The Place-Names of Buckinghamshire*, p. 126; (2) J. H. Round in *V.C.H. Buckinghamshire*, I, p. 223.

[2] The frequency of place-name elements in Buckinghamshire that denote the former presence of wood should be noted. See A. Mawer and F. M. Stenton, *op. cit.*

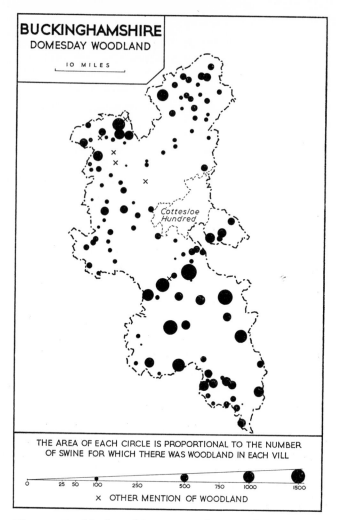

THE AREA OF EACH CIRCLE IS PROPORTIONAL TO THE NUMBER
OF SWINE FOR WHICH THERE WAS WOODLAND IN EACH VILL

X OTHER MENTION OF WOODLAND

Fig. 57. Buckinghamshire: Domesday woodland in 1086.

Where the wood of a village is entered partly in terms of swine and partly in some
other way, only the swine total is shown. No wood is entered for any of the Cottesloe
villages (see p. 166).

Burnham area to the south. The scarp-foot zone is marked by a line of villages each with substantial swine totals, and many of the villages lying to the south-east of the Chiltern crest had wood for over 1,000 swine apiece; thus, for example, Chalfont (144, 151b–152) had enough for 1,200, Chesham (144 *bis*, 150b, 151b, 153) for 1,650, Marlow (144b, 150, 151, 152b) for 1,250, and Wycombe (143b, 144b, 146, 149) for 1,500, and there were several other villages each with enough for between 500 and 1,000 swine. We must suppose that the woodland of these villages lay on the heavy soils of the Clay-with-flints, that mask so much of the Chiltern dip-slope, and on the infertile gravels of the area between the Colne and the Wye in the south-east. There was also another concentration of wood in the extreme north of the county, in the neighbourhood of Buckingham and of Newport Pagnell, but the individual village totals were generally smaller than in the southern half of the county. Between this northern area and the Chilterns, the country seems to have been fairly open. The clays of this area would seem to have been largely cleared of wood by 1086, as is indicated by the relatively high plough-team densities found here (Fig. 51). But in looking at Fig. 57 we must remember that there was no mention of wood for estates rubricated under Cottesloe hundred in the Buckinghamshire folios, and that the Domesday record of wood may be incomplete.

MEADOW

The Domesday meadow of Buckinghamshire was measured for the most part in terms of plough-teams, i.e. by stating the number of teams of 8 oxen the meadow was capable of feeding. The usual formula was *pratum n carucis*; but, very occasionally, when the amount was very small it was recorded in terms of oxen (*pratum n bobus*). The amount was always equal to or less than the number of plough-lands; there was never any excess; thus Denham, with 12 plough-lands but only 9 teams at work, had meadow for 12 teams (145b). The amounts recorded for any village ranged from enough for half a plough-team at Gawcott (144) and at Horton (150–150b)[1] respectively to sufficient for 37 at Wycombe (143b, 149).[2] Two entries, one for Drayton Parslow (144b) and the other for Stone (144), tell of *pratum carucis*, presumably for the teams at work. For one holding at

---

[1] This was Horton in Yardley hundred; Horton in Stoke hundred had sufficient for 3 plough-teams (151).

[2] No meadow is recorded for the two other holdings at Wycombe (144b, 146).

Lavendon (145b) the scribe noted: *Terra est i carucae et dimidiae et ibi sunt; pratum similiter.* At three holdings we are told that there was also meadow for the horses:

Dorney (149b): *pratum iii carucis et equis.*
Wooburn (144): *pratum vi carucis et ad equos.*
Wycombe (149): *pratum iii carucis et ad equos de curia et carucis villanorum.*[1]

The entry for Wyrardisbury (149b) tells of *pratum v carucis et fenum ad animalia curiae.* A payment of eight days' hay was made for the 'feorm' of the archbishop (*ad firmam archiespiscopi per octo dies fenum*) at Haddenham (143b), a Canterbury estate with meadow for 6 teams and 'pasture for the livestock'. Four entries mention a money payment, presumably for surplus hay:

Aylesbury (143): *Pratum viii carucis et de remanenti xx solidi.*
Newport Pagnell (148b): *pratum omnibus carucis et x solidi.*
Wendover (143b): *pratum iii carucis et de remanenti xx solidi.*
Weston Turville (144): *pratum x carucis et vi solidi.*

The amount of meadow at Tythrop (155b) and for one holding at Ibstone (160b) was recorded in terms of acres (*acrae prati*), the normal way of measuring meadow in the Oxfordshire folios, where these two estates were surveyed; Tythrop had 10 acres of meadow, and Ibstone 3.[2]

It would greatly help our mapping if we could convert the plough-team measurements into acres. On the basis of later evidence G. H. Fowler suggested that 3 statute acres of meadow provided sufficient meadow for one ox,[3] but this is not conclusive, and no attempt has been made to convert the teams into acres. For Buckinghamshire, as for Bedfordshire, Hertfordshire and Middlesex, we have merely plotted the plough-team figures.

Distribution of meadowland

The contrast between the north and the south of the county is readily apparent on Fig. 58. North of the Chilterns, on the well-watered clay-lands, individual amounts were generally small, but nearly every holding had some meadow, and a number of villages had amounts for 20 teams or

[1] At this estate in Wycombe, there were 3 plough-teams in demesne and 27 plough-teams with the peasants.
[2] No meadow is mentioned in the entry for a second holding at Ibstone surveyed on fo. 160b, or for the portion of the village entered under Buckinghamshire (152b).
[3] G. H. Fowler, *Bedfordshire in 1086* (Quarto Memoirs of the Bedfordshire Historical Record Society, Aspley Guise, 1922), pp. 61–2 and 106–7.

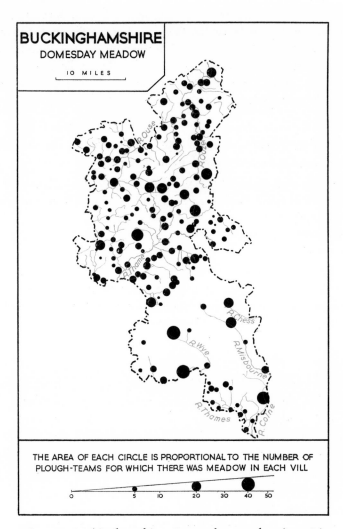

Fig. 58. Buckinghamshire: Domesday meadow in 1086.

Where the meadow of a village is entered partly in terms of plough-teams and partly in some other way, only the plough-team total is shown.

over. To the south, some of the settlements of the Chiltern valleys also had a great deal of meadow; Chesham on the Chess, Amersham on the Misbourne, and Wycombe on the Wye, each had sufficient for 20 teams or more. Along the southern boundary of the county, near the alluvial areas of the Colne and the Thames, there was hardly a village without some meadow; Iver on the Colne and Marlow on the Thames each had meadow for well over 20 teams.

PASTURE

Pasture, unlike meadow, was not regularly entered in the Buckinghamshire folios, and only four entries mention any:

Buckingham with Bourton[1] (143): *Pastura ad pecuniam villae.*
Haddenham (143 b): *Pastura ad pecuniam et ad firmam archiepiscopi per octo dies fenum.*
Barton Hartshorne (145): *De pastura xxx solidi*
Wing (146): *De pastura ferra ad v carucas.*

This meagre list stands in great contrast with the frequent mention of pasture in the folios for the neighbouring counties of Hertford, Middlesex and Oxford, and it is clear that these four entries cannot account for all the pasture in eleventh-century Buckinghamshire.

FISHERIES

Fisheries (*piscariae*) are recorded in connection with 16 places in Buckinghamshire, but the number of fisheries is not always specifically stated. The yields of the fisheries are normally expressed in terms of eels (*anguillae*); the 4 fisheries at Iver (149) rendered 1,500 eels and also supplied 'fish on Fridays for the use of the reeve of the vill' (*pisces per dies veneris ad opus prepositi villae*). Furthermore, two villages paid a money rent from their fisheries:

Denham (145 b): *iii piscariae reddunt iii solidos per annum.*
Wyrardisbury (149 b): *iiii piscariae in Tamesia de xxvii solidis iiii denarii minus.*

In addition to the 16 places for which *piscariae* are specifically mentioned, there are also 5 other places with mills rendering eels.[2]

The distribution of the places with fisheries, mentioned or implied, is

---

[1] *cum Bortone* interlined.
[2] The five places are: Haversham (148), Lavendon (145 b, 146 b), Olney (145 b), Stantonbury (150 b), and Winchendon (147).

shown on Fig. 59. Most of the fisheries were in the Thames which forms the southern boundary of the county, but a few were to be found along some of the streams that flow to join the Thames. The outstanding localities were Wyrardisbury (149b) on the Thames and Iver (149) on

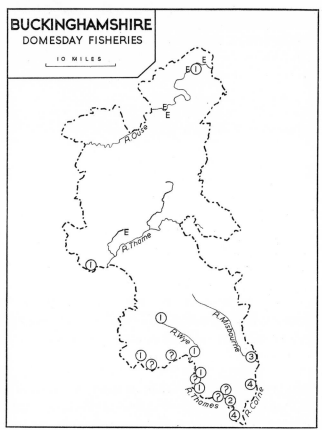

Fig. 59. Buckinghamshire: Domesday fisheries in 1086.
The figure in each circle indicates the number of fisheries.
E indicates renders of eels from mills.

the Colne, each with four fisheries, and Denham (145b), where the Misbourne joins the Colne, with three. In the north of the county fisheries were recorded for a few places along the Thame and the Ouse, but the entries for these northern localities, for the most part, record not *piscariae* but eel renders from mills.

WASTE

The 'waste' entries of Buckinghamshire are unimportant and there are only three for 1086:

Biddlesden (146b): *In Betesdene tenet isdem comes [Moritoniensis] iii virgatas. Terra est i carucae sed vastata est.*

Cheddington (150b): *In Cetedone tenet Hugo dimidiam hidam sed wastata est.*

Chesham (151b): *In Cestreham tenet Turstinus dimidiam hidam. Terra est i carucae sed wastata est. Valet et valuit semper v solidos.*

As the entry for Chesham indicates, it was possible for a Domesday holding to be worth something even when it was waste. At the intermediate date we hear of waste at Stowe (144b).[1]

MILLS

Mills are mentioned in connection with 78 out of the 207 Domesday settlements in Buckinghamshire. For each locality the number of mills was given, and, generally, their annual value was also stated. This was usually in shillings and pence, but occasionally partly in eels, or in ounces of silver, or in loads of malt. The annual value ranged from a mill yielding 20*d.* at Leckhampstead (147b)[2] to 9 mills yielding 95*s.* at Wycombe (143b, 149); a mill at Horsenden (146) paid nothing (*nil reddit*). The mills at five places rendered eels from the mill-leet as well as making a money payment, e.g. the mill at Winchendon (147) yielded 20*s.* and 80 eels (*i molinus de viginti solidis et quater viginti anguillis*).[3] At Aston Clinton (150b) 1 mill yielded 5 ounces of silver (*de v oris argenti*), and at Thornton (151b) the mill yielded 10 ounces (*de x oris*). The entry for one of the three holdings at Caldecote notes: *i molinus de v ores (sic) et iiii denariis* (146b).[4] On one holding at Chalfont (151b–152) there were 3 mills, one paying 5 ounces [of silver] and the other two nothing (*iii molendina. Unum reddit v ores et alii ii nil reddunt*).[5] The mill at Bledlow (146) yielded 24 loads of malt (*xxiiii summas brasiis*). No value was

---

[1] See above, p. 162.

[2] This was on the holding of Walter Gifard.

[3] Mills paying a rent partly in money and partly in eels are mentioned in the entries for Haversham (148), Lavendon (145b, 146b), Olney (145b), Stantonbury (150b) and Winchendon (147).

[4] There was also a mill entered for a second holding at Caldecote (148b), but not for the third holding there (153).

[5] The other holding at Chalfont (144) had a mill yielding 6*s.*

entered for a mill on one holding at Saunderton (144b),[1] or for the mill at Broughton near Moulsoe (148), but the latter was said to be 'in demesne' (*in dominio*). The entry for Wyrardisbury (149b) is defective—*ii molini de xl per Annum*—and we are left in doubt as to what was rendered by the mills. Finally, at the end of the entry for Farnham (151b), we are told: *Radulfus tailgebosc fecit supra terram Bertranni unum molinum qui non fuit ibi T.R.E. ut hundredum testatur.*

Fractions of mills do not present the problem in Buckinghamshire that they do in East Anglia; thus there were 1½ mills at Clifton Reynes (145b *bis*, 149, 152b *bis*) and 2½ at Lavendon (145b *quater*, 146b, 148, 152b *ter*, 153). As Clifton Reynes and Lavendon were neighbouring villages, perhaps they shared a mill. Two-thirds of the villages with mills had only one mill each, and there were only two large groups of mills in Domesday Buckinghamshire. That of 9 mills was at Wycombe (143b, 149) and that of 8 at Wooburn (144); both villages were in the valley of the Wye.

Domesday Mills in Buckinghamshire

1 mill	48 settlements	4 mills	3 settlements
2 mills	18 settlements	8 mills	1 settlement
3 mills	7 settlements	9 mills	1 settlement

Note that this table excludes the mill on the anonymous holding of William son of Ansculf in Moulsoe hundred (149).

Fig. 60 shows that the mills were generally aligned along the streams. In the south, they were along the Chess, the Misbourne, the Colne and the Wye, but there were only a few along the Thames. In the north, they were along the Thame and its tributaries, along the Ouse and along the Ouzel. But it is difficult to relate the mills entered for villages along the northern edge of the Chiltern escarpment to any stream; presumably they were along small streams draining to the Vale of Aylesbury to the north. Taking a more general view it is surprising to find so few mills in the central portion of the northern claylands. Not a single mill is entered for the hundred of Mursley, and only one each for the hundreds of Ashendon, Cottesloe and Waddesdon. Many Buckinghamshire villages are without record of a mill in the Domesday Book. Was the grain of these villages ground elsewhere, or by hand? Or is the Domesday record incomplete? These are questions that we cannot answer.

[1] On a second holding at Saunderton (150) there were 2 mills yielding 8s.

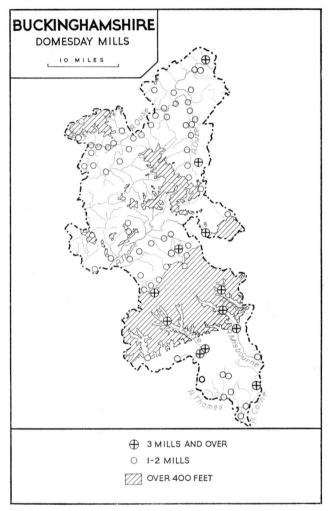

Fig. 60. Buckinghamshire: Domesday mills in 1086.
There was also a mill on an anonymous holding in Moulsoe hd.

CHURCHES

Churches are mentioned in connection with only four places in Bucking-
hamshire—Aylesbury, Crawley, Haddenham and the borough of
Buckingham itself. The entry for Aylesbury (143) tells us only that the
Bishop of Lincoln held the church of the manor, but on another folio

(143b) we hear of payments in grain to the church by the sokemen of the eight hundreds 'around' Aylesbury:

De octo hundredis qui jacent in circuitu Elesberie unusquisquam sochmannus qui habebat i hidam aut plus reddebat unam summam annonae huic ecclesiae. Adhuc etiam de unoquoquam sochmanno i acra annonae aut quattuor denarii soluebantur huic ecclesiae T.R.E. sed post adventum regis Willelmi redditum non fuit.

The other entries mentioning churches are as follows:

Buckingham with Bourton (143):[1] *Ecclesiam huius burgi tenet Remigius episcopus et terram iiii carucis quae ad eam pertinet.*

Haddenham (143b): *De hac terra tenet Gislebertus presbyter de Archiepiscopi iii hidas et i ecclesiam cum decima.*

Hardmead (149): *De hac terra jacet dimidia virga (sic) in monasterio Sancti Firmani de Cravelai* (i.e. Crawley) *et iacuit T.R.E.*[2]

It is clear from these entries that the Domesday record of churches in Buckinghamshire was incomplete. The folios also do not specifically enumerate priests (*presbyteri*), but they may have been included among the villeins.

URBAN LIFE

In the Buckinghamshire folios only one place, Buckingham with Bourton,[3] is specifically styled *burgus* (143). Burgesses are also mentioned in the entry for Newport Pagnell (148b) and, after some hesitation, we have regarded it as a borough in the present analysis.[4] Apart from the properties in Buckingham held by the lords of manors in Buckinghamshire itself, the folios tell of a certain burgess in Oxford 'belonging to' Risborough—*In hoc manerio jacet et jacuit quidam burgensis de Oxeneford reddens ii solidos* (143b). The Oxfordshire folios (154) mention this connection, and also tell of two houses (*mansiones*) belonging to Twyford, another Buckinghamshire estate:...*et terciam [mansionem] reddentem xxx*

---

[1] For Crawley, see p. 142 above.

[2] The monastery of St Firmin was at North Crawley; see J. H. Round in *V.C.H. Buckinghamshire*, I, p. 224.

[3] *cum Bortone* is interlined in smaller script in the MS.; there was a second entry for Bourton (147b).

[4] Round noted that its name, 'in spite of its rural character, implies a market of some kind' (*V.C.H. Buckinghamshire*, I, p. 222). But it should be noted that it was not listed as a borough by A. Ballard—*The Domesday Boroughs* (Oxford, 1904), p. 9. On the other hand, Alan Mawer and F. M. Stenton also concluded that it was a borough in 1086 (*op. cit.* p. 21).

denarios pertinentem ad Riseberge et ii alias de iiii denariis pertinentes ad Tuiforde in Buchingehamscire. Una ex his est vasta. The Buckinghamshire folios, on the other hand, do not mention this connection.

Buckingham

The Domesday description of the county begins with an account of the borough of Buckingham, which stands on a hill overlooking the Ouse. The entry (143) is remarkably similar in form to the entries for rural estates in the county, except that we are told of 26 burgesses; it is followed by an account of the land belonging to the church of the borough:

Buckingham with Bourton was assessed at one hide in the time of King Edward and now likewise (*et modo similiter facit*). There is land for 8 plough-teams (*Terra est viii carucarum*). In demesne are two and the villeins have 3½ plough-teams and a further 2½ might be added. There are 26 burgesses and 11 bordars and 2 serfs. There, 1 mill yielding (*de*) 14s. Meadow for 8 plough-teams. Pasture for the livestock of the vill. In all it used to pay *T.R.E.* £10 by tale (*ad numerum*). Now, it pays £16 of blanched silver (*de albo argento*).

Bishop Remigius holds the church of this borough and the land for 4 plough-teams which pertains to it (*ad eam pertinet*). There are 4 plough-teams and 3 villeins and 3 bordars and 10 cottars and one mill yielding (*de*) 10 shillings. Meadow for 2 plough-teams. Wood for the fences. It is and was worth £6. *T.R.E.* £7. Bishop Wluui (i.e. Wulfwig of Lincoln) held this church from King Edward.

There follows a long list setting out the dues paid by the burgesses to their lords, and sometimes by them to the king also; these burgesses numbered 27, and included one who had passed to the king with Earl Aubrey's land, but we are not told whether they were additional to the twenty-six burgesses enumerated earlier in the entry. Round thought that probably 'the latter dwelt on the king's land and should, therefore, be reckoned separately'.[1]

The picture that emerges is that of an essentially agricultural community. Of the occupations of the burgesses we are told nothing; nor is there mention either of a market or of a mint. It is impossible to tell how much of the information given under Buckingham with Bourton related to the latter.[2] There is also a separate entry for Bourton, later in the folios (147b):

[1] *V.C.H. Buckinghamshire*, I, p. 221.
[2] 'The *burh* which gave name to this place may well be the southernmost of the two built on either side of the river by Edward the Elder at the beginning of his

The same Hugh holds Bourton (*Burtone*) of Walter Gifard. It is assessed at 1 hide. There is land for 2 plough-teams. On the demesne is 1 [plough-team] and 2 villeins with 2 bordars have 1 plough-team. Meadow for 2 plough-teams. It is and was worth (*Valet et valuit*) 30s. T.R.E. 20s. This manor Alric, a thegn of King Edward, held and could sell.

The two entries taken together suggest that, in spite of the presence of 53 or 26 burgesses, Buckingham was an agricultural community, as primitive as any county borough could be.

Newport Pagnell

The Domesday entry for Newport Pagnell (148b) is very brief and may be incomplete:

William (i.e. William son of Ansculf) himself holds Newport. It is assessed at 5 hides. There is land for 9 plough-teams. In demesne 4 carucates of land (*iiii carucatae terrae*) and there are there 4 plough-teams and 5 villeins have 5 plough-teams. The burgesses have 6½ plough-teams and of other men working outside the 5 hides (*Burgenses habent vi carucas et dimidiam aliorumque hominum, extra v hidas laborantes*[1]). There 9 serfs and 2 mills yielding 40s. Meadow for all the plough-teams and 10s. Wood for 300 swine and 2s. and a further 4s. from men who dwell in the wood (*adhuc iiii solidi de hominibus qui manent in silva*) and from all other renders (*in omnibus aliis redditis*) it pays yearly 106s. 4d. In all it is worth and was worth £20. T.R.E. £24. This manor Ulf a thegn of King Edward held.

It will be noticed that the number of burgesses is not recorded, and we are left in doubt about the class and number of the 'other men working outside the 5 hides'. But, whether Newport Pagnell was a borough or not, it is clear that it was an agricultural settlement, the general character of which must have resembled that of neighbouring villages. Its name suggests that it had a market, but the Domesday entry itself does not mention one; perhaps market dues were included in the total of 'all other renders'.

MISCELLANEOUS INFORMATION

The Buckinghamshire folios give very little information of a miscellaneous character. There is no record of a market but we hear of 'a toll worth £10 by tale' (*de Theloneo x librae ad numerum*) at Aylesbury (143).

attack on the Danelaw, in 918 according to the *Chronicle*, more probably in 913. If so the name means "farm by the fort" rather than "fortified enclosure".'—A. Mawer and F. M. Stenton, *op. cit.* p. 60.   [1] The text seems to be defective.

Vineyard

At Iver (149) there were two arpents of vine (*ii arpendi vineae*).

Hunting

We hear but little of the Norman love of the chase in the Buckingham-shire folios, but a payment for the issues of the forest (*pro foresta*) was made at Brill (143b), and at Oakley (149) woodland had been placed in the king's park (*parcus regis*). There was a park for the beasts of the chase (*parcus ibi bestiarum silvaticarum*) at Long Crendon (147).

An eyry of hawks (*una area accipitris*) was noted in each of the two entries for Chalfont (144, 151b).

Saltworking

We hear indirectly of the Worcestershire saltworks in an entry for Risborough (143b) which tells of a saltworker of Droitwich rendering 'loads of salt' (*summas salis*).

REGIONAL SUMMARY

Buckinghamshire is traditionally divided into two.[1] In the northern half of the county the various geological formations are extensively covered by Boulder Clay. The economic prosperity of this half of the county was fairly uniform in 1086. On the other hand, conditions in the southern half of the county were more varied, and further subdivision has been made (Fig. 61).

(1) Northern Claylands

The northern half of the county, drained by the Ouse-Ouzel and the Thame systems of streams, lies mainly between 200 and 400 ft. above sea-level, but there are a few isolated hills rising above 500 ft. The soils are fairly mixed in character and quality, but are mainly derived from drift deposits, chiefly Boulder Clay.

The general prosperity of the region as indicated by the densities of plough-teams and population was relatively high. The density of plough-

---

[1] This fundamental division of the county into two major units was recognised by W. James and J. Malcolm in their *General View of the Agriculture of the County of Buckingham* (London, 1794). For a subdivision of the county based on twentieth-century land use, see D. W. Fryer, *Buckinghamshire* (London, 1942), p. 83, being Pt. 54 of *The Land of Britain*, ed. L. Dudley Stamp.

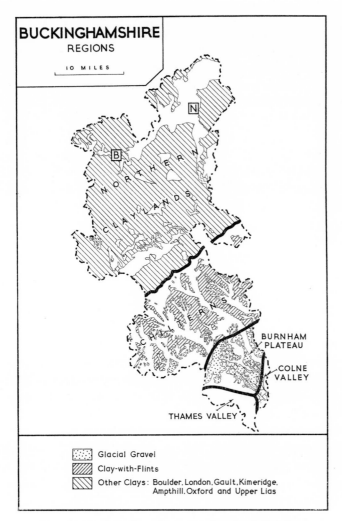

Fig. 61. Buckinghamshire: Regional subdivisions.

Domesday boroughs are indicated by initials: B, Buckingham; N, Newport Pagnell. The surface geology is based on Geological Survey One-Inch Sheets (New Series) 203, 238, 254, 255, 269.

teams ranged from 2·4 to 3·9 per square mile; that of population from 5·3 to 10·5. Villages were fairly evenly spaced, but both the Ouse and the Ouzel valleys were marked by a line of villages. All but a few of the villages had meadow, but a number were apparently without any wood.[1] Generally, even those villages with woodland had but small amounts. Many of the villages had mills, and renders of eels were made from mills in the Ouse and Thame valleys.

(2) *The Chilterns*

The Chilterns form the oustanding feature of the relief of the county. They are marked on the north by a steep escarpment which, for the most part, is about 300–700 ft. above sea-level but which rises to over 850 ft. in the neighbourhood of Ellesborough. From this northern edge, a wide dip-slope, falling to about 350 ft., extends south-eastwards. This sloping plateau surface is broken by a series of streams that flow to join the Colne and the Thames in valleys for the most part between 200 and 300 ft. below the level of the surrounding countryside. The main valleys are those of the Chess, the Misbourne and the Wye. Chalk underlies the whole of the region, but is rarely exposed at the surface except in the floors and steep slopes of the valleys. The intervening ridge tops are covered with Clay-with-flints, which give rise to a heavy clay-loam with many flints.

The densities of plough-teams and population are very much less than those of the Northern Claylands. Over the greater part of the area the plough-team density ranged from 1·0 to 2·2 per square mile; that of population from 2·2 to 4·7. The villages were in the valleys, and many of them had large numbers of plough-teams at work; thus, Chesham had 28 plough-teams, Hambleden had 30, Marlow had 40½, and Wycombe had 53½. Most of the villages had meadow, and a few had each enough for more than 20 plough-teams. All the Chiltern villages had very substantial amounts of woodland, and we can only suppose that the heavy soils of the Clay-with-flints were still closely wooded in 1086. Nearly every village had a mill, and there were some with 3 and 4 apiece; Wooburn had 8, and Wycombe 9. Several of the villages had fisheries either in the Wye or in the Thames itself.

Stretching below the Chiltern escarpment, there is a well-marked 'bench' which lies at about 250 ft. above sea-level. It has been excavated

---

[1] But see p. 166 above, for the possibility that the Domesday record of wood in Buckinghamshire is incomplete.

in the Lower Chalk, and its soils are rich loams, fertile and easily worked. This scarp-foot zone was marked by a line of prosperous villages, each with many teams at work. The densities of plough-teams and population were substantially higher than those of the dip-slope, but very similar to those of the Northern Claylands. The villages each had substantial amounts of meadow, much of which must, presumably, have been on the claylands beyond. Most of the villages had considerable amounts of woodland— several had enough for 1,000 or more swine apiece. There is little doubt that some of this woodland was in the clay vale to the north, and some in the Chilterns to the south. Nearly every village had its own mill, but it is difficult to locate the mills of these villages, for their streams were but small ones.

(3) The Burnham Plateau

This region lies between the valleys of the Wye and the Colne in the south-east of the county. The ground slopes southwards from about 350 ft. along the northern margin to some 150 ft. above sea-level in the south. This southward sloping surface is deeply dissected by many valleys draining to the Colne and the Thames. The underlying rock is Chalk in the north, but this is overlain successively by Reading Beds and by London Clay towards the south; all three formations are masked by superficial deposits of fluvio-glacial origin. The soils are very varied, and range from heavy clays to light sands. Agriculturally the region is unrewarding, and it is not surprising that the Domesday densities of plough-teams and population were low, being only 1·5 and 2·7 respectively. Even these low figures were due to the villages along its southern and eastern margins; the interior stands out as an empty tract on the map of Domesday place-names. It must have been a heavily wooded area in the eleventh century although only one village had enough wood to support more than 700 swine, but the wood of another rendered 'iron for the ploughs' in addition to providing pannage for 600 swine. The villages generally had small amounts of meadow, and mills and fisheries added to the prosperity of some.

(4) The Thames Valley

The Thames forms the southern boundary of Buckinghamshire, but only below its confluence with the Wye does its valley broaden sufficiently to be considered a region in itself. Below this point the vale opens out and the river flows over the gravels of a wide flood plain, until just east of

Wyrardisbury it is joined by the Colne. In places the gravels are covered by brickearth. The finely textured soils were both fertile and easily worked and are a key to the prosperity of the villages. The density of plough-teams reached 3·1 per square mile, and that of population as high as 8·4 per square mile. Every village had some meadow. The progress of cultivation had not entirely obliterated the wood, and some of the villages had enough to feed as many as 200 swine. The region was not well supplied with mills, but there were fisheries in the Thames.

(5) *The Colne Valley*

The river Colne, flowing southwards to join the Thames just east of Wyrardisbury, cuts through the London Clay and forms a band of alluvium, bordered by gravel patches. In 1086 the Buckinghamshire bank of the river was marked by a line of prosperous villages situated on the fertile gravels which were easy to till. Densities of teams and men were comparable with those of the Thames valley. The Colne valley was likewise rich in meadow. Its villages also had very substantial amounts of appurtenant woodland, which was probably to be found on the heavier clay soils to the west of the gravel patches. Mills were plentiful, and there were also fisheries in the Colne.

BIBLIOGRAPHICAL NOTE

(1) It is interesting to note that D. Lysons and S. Lysons listed the Domesday manors of Buckinghamshire at the beginning of their topographical account of the county which was the third part of their *Magna Britannia*, 1 (London, 1813), pp. 452–7.

G. Lipscombe made great use of the Domesday folios for Buckinghamshire in his history of the county—*The history and antiquities of the County of Buckingham* (London, 1847), 4 vols. He transcribed and translated portions of the text in his description of the parishes.

(2) There was an early nineteenth-century translation of the Domesday folios relating to Buckinghamshire: William Bawdwen, *Dom Boc. A translation of the record called Domesday, as far as relates to the counties of Middlesex, Hertford, Buckingham, Oxford and Gloucester* (Doncaster, 1812). This was superseded by the Rev. F. W. Ragg's translation in *V.C.H. Buckinghamshire*, 1 (London, 1905), pp. 230–77. This is accompanied by an introduction by J. H. Round (pp. 207–28).

(3) F. H. Baring, *Domesday Tables for the counties of Surrey, Berkshire, Middlesex, Hertford, Buckingham and Bedford and for the New Forest* (London,

1909). These tables are clearly set out and are accompanied by a useful note on each county.

(4) Various aspects of Domesday Buckinghamshire are discussed in the following:

(i) F. H. Baring, 'The hidation of some southern counties', *Eng. Hist. Rev.* xiv (London, 1899), pp. 290–9; the Buckinghamshire figures are, however, incorrect, as the author himself subsequently realised—'Note on the hidation of Buckinghamshire', *Eng. Hist. Rev.* xv (London, 1900), p. 199.

(ii) W. J. Corbett, 'The Tribal Hidage', *Trans. Roy. Hist. Soc.* N.S. xiv (London, 1900), pp. 187–230; the Domesday assessment of Buckinghamshire is discussed on pp. 218–19.

(iii) A. M. Davies, 'The ancient hundreds of Buckinghamshire', *The Home Counties Magazine*, vi (London, 1904), pp. 134–44. This is an interesting attempt to reconstruct the hundreds of Domesday Buckinghamshire and to relate them to the physical features of the county. It is accompanied by a map (p. 143), which is reproduced in *V.C.H. Buckinghamshire*, i (London, 1905), p. 227. This paper was reprinted in *Records of Buckinghamshire*, ix (Aylesbury, 1909), pp. 104–19.

(iv) A. M. Davies, 'Eleventh century Buckinghamshire', *Records of Buckinghamshire*, x (Aylesbury, 1916), pp. 69–74.

(v) A. M. Davies, 'Abefeld and Achamsted', *Records of Buckinghamshire*, xv (Aylesbury, 1947–52), pp. 166–71.

(vi) A. M. Davies, 'The hundreds of Buckinghamshire and Oxfordshire', *Records of Buckinghamshire*, xv (Aylesbury, 1947–52), pp. 231–49. This is a reappraisal of the Domesday evidence for Buckinghamshire, first used by the author in his paper of 1904 (*supra*), in the light of evidence furnished by the thirteenth-century Assize Rolls; in this paper he compares the Buckinghamshire hundredal divisions with those of Oxfordshire. The 1950 paper includes on p. 233 a reprint of the map of the Domesday hundreds of Buckinghamshire (first printed 1904).

(vii) G. R. Elvey, 'Buckinghamshire in 1086', *Records of Buckinghamshire*, xvi (Bedford, 1953–60), pp. 342–62.

(5) A valuable aid to the Domesday study of the county is A. Mawer and F. M. Stenton, *The Place-Names of Buckinghamshire* (Cambridge, 1925).

CHAPTER V

OXFORDSHIRE

BY E. M. JOPE, M.A., AND I. B. TERRETT, B.A., PH.D.

The uncertainties common to every portion of the Domesday Inquest are especially numerous in the Oxfordshire folios,[1] and they obscure many facts of geographical interest in the eleventh century. Unfortunately, there is no satellite source, comparable with, say, the Lindsey Survey or the Leicestershire Survey, to aid us in the interpretation of the material. We must rely, therefore, even more than usual, upon a variety of other sources in guiding the interpretation of the Oxfordshire folios; fortunately the county is one for which the Hundred Rolls survey of 1278–79 is especially full. But, even so, many difficult problems remain.

Before dealing with these, one complication must be mentioned. The present analysis has been made in terms of the modern county which does not correspond exactly to the area described in the Oxfordshire folios. The resources of many Oxfordshire villages were entered in the folios for other counties.[2] Cottisford (224b), Charlton on Otmoor (224b), Finmere (221), Glympton (221), Grimsbury near Banbury (227b), Hethe (221), Shipton on Cherwell (224b), Shelswell (221), and Worton (221) are all described solely in the Northamptonshire folios. Wootton, on the other hand, was described partly under Northamptonshire (221) and partly under Oxfordshire (154b), so was Heyford (158, 159b, 221). Sibford Gower (today entirely in Oxfordshire) was described partly under Northamptonshire (224b) and partly under Staffordshire (250). Spelsbury was described entirely under Warwickshire (238b). These were certainly administratively within Oxfordshire by 1278.

Other villages now in Oxfordshire, but entered in the Domesday folios of adjoining counties, did not become administratively part of the county until very recent times. Thus Shenington (163b) and Widford (164b),

---

[1] F. M. Stenton in *V.C.H. Oxfordshire*, 1 (London, 1939), p. 392.

[2] F. M. Stenton writes: 'It is not easy to explain the inclusion of many Oxford-shire villages in the surveys of other counties. Most of them were undoubtedly part of Oxfordshire in 1086, and were described under other counties because of some confusion in the distribution of the original returns to the Domesday Inquest among the clerks who wrote Domesday Book' (*ibid.* p. 392).

rubricated under Gloucestershire, remained detached portions of that county until 1844, when they were transferred to Oxfordshire, together with Caversfield, from Buckinghamshire (148). In that year too the parish of Little Faringdon, and parts of Langford and Shilton, were transferred from Berkshire. These were formerly part of the Lordship of Faringdon,[1] and in 1086 their resources seem to have been included in the entry for (Great) Faringdon in the Berkshire folios (57b).[2] Similarly, several villages described in the Oxfordshire folios have been transferred to adjoining counties since 1800. Thus Boycott (160) and Tythrop (155b) were not transferred to Buckinghamshire until 1833 and 1894 respectively. Caversham (157b) remained wholly within Oxfordshire until 1911, when it was divided between that county and Berkshire.[3] The resources of the Buckinghamshire villages of Lillingstone Lovell and Lillingstone Dayrell were described partly under Oxfordshire (160, 160b), and partly under Buckinghamshire (147b), and there can be little doubt that the Oxfordshire entries relate to Lillingstone Lovell, which remained a detached parish of that county until 1844. The parish of Mollington, which is still divided between Oxfordshire, Northamptonshire and Warwickshire, was described in the folios relating to them (157, 226 and 244); it is included wholly in Oxfordshire in this analysis. The origins of this 'complicated piece of administrative geography' date from before the Norman Conquest and have not yet been fully explained.[4] Towersey and Kingsey were described in the Buckinghamshire folios under *Eie* (151b); and in the eleventh century *Eie* probably straddled the boundary between Oxfordshire and Buckinghamshire.[5] Subsequently, Kingsey was part of Oxfordshire and Towersey was part of Buckinghamshire, but in 1932

---

[1] J. H. Round in *V.C.H. Berkshire*, I (London, 1906), p. 319.

[2] Part of Langford, however, had always been in Oxfordshire, and is so named and described in the Oxfordshire folios (154b). The church at Shilton (but not the bulk of the parish) also lay in Oxfordshire—*V.C.H. Berkshire*, I, p. 319; it is so shown on J. Cary's map of Oxfordshire (1797). Note that it is impracticable to assign any of the Faringdon figures to Oxfordshire, but the small amounts involved would not affect the densities.

[3] In the present analysis the Domesday resources of Caversham have been divided between the two counties: one-third of the totals for hides, plough-lands, plough-teams and population has been allocated to Berkshire, and the remainder to Oxfordshire. The meadow, the mill and the woodland have been plotted on the Berkshire maps (see p. 241 n. below).

[4] *V.C.H. Oxfordshire*, I, p. 392.

[5] Later manorial history, however, suggests that in 1086 Kingsey formed part of the royal manor of Brill; see *V.C.H. Buckinghamshire*, IV (London, 1927), p. 64.

Kingsey was transferred to Buckinghamshire, and Towersey became part of Oxfordshire. In the present analysis, all the resources are plotted at Towersey. One other complication must be noted. Ibstone, now in

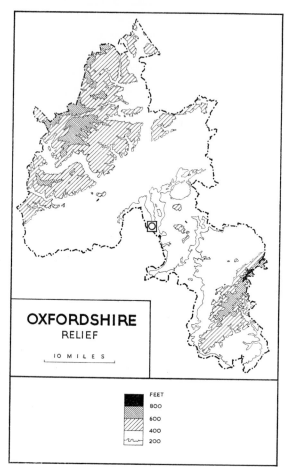

Fig. 62. Oxfordshire: Relief.

O indicates the Domesday borough of Oxford.

Buckinghamshire, was surveyed partly under that county (152b) and partly under Oxfordshire (160b). The village of Stokenchurch, transferred to Buckinghamshire as recently as 1896, was not named in the Domesday folios, but its resources may well have been included with those of Aston Rowant (*Estone*, 159).[1] These changes are summarised in the table on p. 190.

Occasional uncertainty arises from obvious errors and omissions. A few entries record teams but no people, or, maybe, people but no teams.[2] There are also several entries for which no name is entered. Sir Frank Stenton identifies one (157b) with a part of Bodicote.[3] H. E. Salter identified another in the d'Ivry fee (158b) with Combe and Chilworth in the parish of Great Milton.[4] The anonymous holding held of the King by William Levric (160) cannot be traced in other medieval records.

Another difficulty in handling the Oxfordshire material from a geographical point of view is the fact that the information about two places is occasionally combined in one statement, as in that for Bloxham and Adderbury (154b). For the purpose of constructing distribution maps the details of this and other combined entries have been divided equally among the pairs of villages concerned. This is not wholly satisfactory, but the error cannot be very great, especially as the respective 'halves' frequently come together again when the densities are averaged over an area covering a group of villages.

More serious than these uncertainties is the fact that the bishop of Lincoln's large manors of Dorchester (90 hides), Thame (60 hides), Great Milton (40 hides), Banbury (50 hides) and Cropredy (50 hides) each contained several subsidiary settlements and holdings which were not separately distinguished by name (155). Thus the resources of Charlbury (a pre-Domesday name) must have been included in the account of Banbury, some distance away; similarly, those of Epwell (another pre-Domesday name) must have been surveyed with the large manor of Dorchester in quite a different part of the county.[5] The entry for the great royal manor of Benson, or Bensington (154b), must likewise have included the details of several unnamed villages and hamlets (e.g. Stonor), for, in 1086, it extended from Benson southwards across the Chilterns to the Thames in the neighbourhood of Henley; Henley itself is a post-Domesday name.[6] Thus the absence of a place-name from the settlement

---

[1] *V.C.H. Buckinghamshire*, III (London, 1925), p. 96. See also p. 143, n. 4 above.

[2] For examples of these omissions, see pp. 203–5 below.

[3] *V.C.H. Oxfordshire*, I, p. 411, n. 2.

[4] *Ibid.* p. 415, n. 2.

[5] *Rotuli Hundredorum*, II, pp. 709 and 751 (Record Commission, 1818).

[6] M. T. Pearman, *A History of the Manor of Bensington* (London, 1896); see especially the map in the frontispiece and pp. 1–27.

The Domesday and the Modern County of Oxford

A. *Transferred from Domesday Oxfordshire to Modern Counties*

To Buckinghamshire

Boycott
Ibstone (part)
Lillingstone Lovell
Stokenchurch (not named in
　D.B., but see p. 143 n.)

To Berkshire

Caversham (part)

B. *Transferred from Other Domesday Counties to Modern Oxfordshire*

From Northamptonshire

Charlton on Otmoor
Cottisford
Finmere
Glympton
Grimsbury
Hethe
Heyford (part)
Mollington (part)
Shelswell
Shipton on Cherwell
Sibford Gower (part)
Wootton (part)
Worton

From Berkshire

Langford, Little Faringdon
　and Shilton (see p. 187)

From Gloucestershire

Shenington
Widford

From Warwickshire

Mollington (part)
Spelsbury

From Buckinghamshire

Caversfield
Towersey (*Eie*)

From Staffordshire

Sibford Gower (part)

map of the county (Fig. 64) does not necessarily mean that it was not in existence at the time of the Domesday Inquest.

Finally, the Domesday survey of Oxfordshire is so imperfectly rubricated that it is not possible to draw a map showing hundred boundaries. The only hundreds mentioned by name are: Dorchester, Pyrton, Lewknor, the half-hundred of Bensington, and the two hundreds described respectively as the first and second *Gadre* hundred.[1] Sir Frank Stenton con-

---

[1] Dr Helen Cam is doubtful if the *Primo* and *Secundo* Gadre of the Oxfordshire folios are hundred names; See Helen M. Cam, 'The hundred outside the North Gate of Oxford', *Oxoniensia*, I (Oxford, 1936), p. 115; a map showing the hundred boundaries a century after 1086 is given on p. 116.

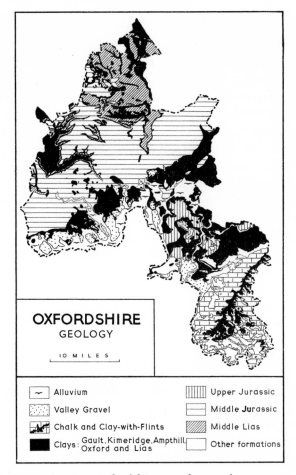

Fig. 63. Oxfordshire: Surface geology.

Based on Geological Survey One-Inch Sheets (New Series) 235, 236, 254, 268; the
Oxford special One-Inch Sheet; and Quarter-Inch Sheet 15. The main constituents of
the Middle Jurassic in Oxfordshire are Inferior Oolite and Great Oolite.

cluded that 'at least 22 divisions known as hundreds or half-hundreds
existed within the county in the 11th century, most of their names are unknown, and it is only from later evidence that any section of their
boundaries can be drawn'.[1]

[1] For a full discussion see F. M. Stenton in *V.C.H. Oxfordshire*, I, p. 374.

Settlements and their Distribution

The total number of separate places mentioned in the Domesday Book for the area within the modern county of Oxford seems to be approximately 251, including the borough of Oxford itself. This figure cannot accurately reflect the total number of settlements. In the first place, when two or more adjoining villages bear the same surname today, it is not always clear whether more than one existed in the eleventh century. Thus the existence of Great Rollright and Little Rollright in the eleventh century is indicated by the mention of *Rollandri majore* (160b) and *parva Rollandri* (155),[1] and of Upper Arncott and Lower Arncott by *Ernicote* (160) and *alia Ernicote* (156b).[2] The three Tews—Great, Little, and Duns—form a borderline case; the Domesday information about them is entered under one name only,[3] and their distinctive appellations date from the twelfth and thirteenth centuries. In the present total of 251, Great and Little Tew, being adjacent villages, have been counted as one settlement, but Duns Tew, which is separated from the other Tews by the parishes of Worton and Sandford St Martin, has been reckoned as a separate settlement.[4] Britwell Salome (*Brutwelle*, 159b) and Brightwell Baldwin (*Britewelle*, 155b; *Bretewelle*, 160b) have also been mapped as two distinct settlements in spite of their proximity and the similarity of their names; their names, although resembling one another in the Domesday folios, are distinct etymologically.[5] The manorial descent of properties has been used to separate the various holdings entered under the Miltons, Nortons, Stantons, Astons and Broughtons which are not adjacent, but which lie widely separated over the county.

Then again, other names in the folios for Oxfordshire seem also to have covered more than one adjoining settlement. Thus the 6 hides entered under Beckley (158b) are seen from a charter of A.D. 1005–12 to have

---

[1] There are also other entries for *Rollandri* (158, 160b).

[2] Nethercote in Lewknor is styled *altera Cote* (159, 159b), but *Cote* itself is not named; it may have been Cop Court (*Cobicote*, 1199) nearby in Aston Rowant. Nethercott in Tackley is *Hidrecote* (156).

[3] *Tewam* (155b, 156b), or its variants *Tewa* (156b, 158b), *Tuuam* (158), *Teowe* (156 *bis*), *Tewe* (156) and *Teova* (156b).

[4] This procedure is supported by the finding in 1952 of eleventh and twelfth century pottery in the churchyard extension at Duns Tew; see E. M. Jope, *Oxoniensia*, xvii/xviii (Oxford, 1954), pp. 219–20.

[5] For the history of all names mentioned in this chapter, see M. Gelling and D. M. Stenton, *The Place-Names of Oxfordshire*, 2 vols. (Cambridge, 1953–54).

been made up of 1 hide at Beckley itself and of 5 hides at Horton, a pre-Domesday settlement which is not named in the Oxfordshire folios.[1] Similarly the 10 hides entered under Whitchurch (159) must have included Hardwick, the separate existence of which is suggested by archaeological evidence from the eleventh century.[2] Archaeological evidence also suggests that the entries under the single name of Yarnton (155b, 156) referred to more than one adjacent settlement not separately distinguished by name;[3] the same is true of Kiddington (160, 161).[4] To these examples of Domesday names covering more than one settlement must be added the large composite manors already discussed.[5]

The total of 251 includes nearly a dozen places about which very little information is given; the record may be incomplete or the details may have been included with those of other villages. Launton, a pre-Domesday place-name, is mentioned only incidentally; we are merely told that 'the soke of 2½ hundreds belongs' to Kirtlington, 'except for 2½ hides in Launton which used to belong there' (154b).[6] Then again we hear of Ledwell (154b) but are told nothing about its population or about its teams or other resources; they may have been included with the totals for the parent manor of Bloxham and Adderbury. With these must be included those places with teams but no people or with people but no teams.[7]

Not all the 251 Domesday names appear as the names of villages on the present-day map of Oxfordshire. Some are represented by hamlets, by individual farms and houses, or by the names of topographical features. Thus *Bristelmestone* (156, 161) is now the hamlet of Brighthampton in the parish of Standlake, and *Hentone* (157b) that of Hempton in Deddington. *Galoberie* (158) survives in the name of Ilbury Farm at Deddington, and it is an interesting example of a flourishing medieval settlement which dwindled after the thirteenth century; by the sixteenth century its site was marked only by a mill, and the present day Ilbury Farm is a new settlement on the old site.[8] *Wistelle* (156, 158b) survives as Whitehill

---

[1] Cambridge University Library, Red Book of Thorney, I, fo. v, see also F. M. Stenton, *Anglo-Saxon England* (Oxford, 1943), p. 376, n. 1.

[2] E. M. Jope, *Oxoniensia*, XIX (Oxford, 1955), p. 14.

[3] E. M. Jope, *Oxoniensia*, X (Oxford, 1945), pp. 97–9.

[4] E. M. Jope, *Oxoniensia*, XIII (Oxford, 1948), pp. 67–9.

[5] See p. 189 above.

[6] In 1279 Launton was described as a hamlet and assessed at 5 hides; see *Rotuli Hundredorum*, II, p. 832.

[7] See pp. 203–5 below.

[8] We are indebted to Mr H. M. Colvin for this information.

Farm in Tackley. *Scildeswelle* (221) survives in the name of Shelswell House in Newton Purcell; in the seventeenth century the inhabitants of the hamlet were ejected in order that a country park might be laid out and a mansion built.[1] *Winehel(l)e* (159b, 161) survives in the names of two hamlets in Chinnor—Lower and Hempton Wainhill. *Stochelie* (154b) is represented today by Stockley Copse in Asthall. The site of Rofford (160b) in Chalgrove can still be traced on the ground, but that of Warpsgrove (156b) in the same parish is now obscured by the runways of an aerodrome. Several Domesday vills have completely disappeared from the ground as well as from the map. Of these, *Draitone* (158) in Bruern is an interesting example of the deliberate removal of a settlement by a Cistercian House to attain the solitude it desired.[2] The site of *Sexintone* (155b *bis*) in Bucknell has also completely disappeared, although it could still be traced just over a hundred years ago.[3] *Hunesworde* (157b) which has also disappeared, has been plotted in Stadhampton.[4] Finally, there are some Domesday names which cannot be identified with certainty—*Adlach* (161),[5] *Asce* (157b), *Bispesdone* (160),[6] *Pereio* (156)[7] and *Verneveld* (154b).[8]

[1] J. C. Bromfield, *History of the Deanery of Bicester* (London, 1882–94), Pt. v, p. 1 (under Shelswell).

[2] Nicolas Bassett founded Bruern Abbey in 1147, presumably on waste land (Bruern = heath). The removal of a settlement in this way was not an unusual practice of Cistercian Houses at this period. See H. M. Colvin, 'Deserted villages and the archaeologist', *The Archaeological News Letter*, iv (London, 1952), pp. 130–1.

[3] See (1) White Kennett, *Parochial Antiquities* (Oxford, 1695), p. 413; and (2) John Dunkin, *The History and Antiquities of the Hundreds of Bullington and Ploughley*, I (London, 1823), p. 202.

[4] For a discussion of the problem of identifying this entry, see (1) *V.C.H. Oxfordshire*, I, p. 428 (Note on 'Hunesworde'); (2) J. L. G. Mowat, *Notes on the Oxfordshire Domesday* (Oxford, 1892), p. 12, n. 7.

[5] The entry for *Adlach* may possibly refer to Standlake, or to Latchford in Great Haseley; neither is named in the Domesday Book.

[6] Sir Frank Stenton noted that there does not seem to be any place-name in Oxfordshire representing the form of *Bispesdone*—see *V.C.H. Oxfordshire*, I, p. 421, n. 4. See also J. L. G. Mowat, *op. cit.* p. 3, n. 13.

[7] H. E. Salter suggested that it is represented by *Piriho*, the name of a wood and of assarts in Stanton Harcourt in the thirteenth century; see *The Feet of Fines for Oxfordshire, 1195–1291*, transcribed and calendared by the Rev. H. E. Salter (Oxford, 1930), pp. 100–28. But *Parihale* was also the name of a wood held by the Knights Templars in the locality of Horspath—see (1) *Rotuli Hundredorum*, ii, p. 714; (2) H. E. Salter (ed.), *Eynsham Cartulary*, ii (Oxford, 1908), p. 97; and (3) J. L. G. Mowat, *op. cit.* p. 15, n. 4.

[8] The waste entered under *Verneveld* (154b) in the hundred of Bensington may perhaps be identified with the Fernfeld of Æthelred II's grant of A.D. 996 which would

Their statistics have been included in the totals for the county; but, owing to the absence of hundredal headings, they cannot be assigned to density units.

On the other hand, some villages and hamlets on the present-day map are not mentioned in the Domesday Book. The names of a few of them appear in pre-Domesday documents, and, as we have noted above, their

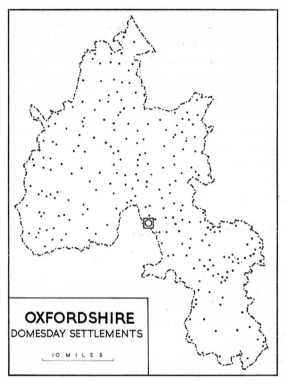

OXFORDSHIRE
DOMESDAY SETTLEMENTS

IO M I L E S

Fig. 64. Oxfordshire: Domesday place-names.

O indicates the Domesday borough of Oxford.

resources were doubtless included either with those of neighbouring vills, or in the surveys of the large manors into which certain of the royal and episcopal estates in Oxfordshire were grouped. But a number have not been identified with any Domesday entry. One of these is Culham, which had been in the possession of Abingdon Abbey since the tenth century.

place it in the neighbourhood of Nuffield and Swyncombe. See (1) M.T. Pearman, *op. cit.* pp. 7–9; (2) G. B. Grundy, *Saxon Oxfordshire* (Oxford, 1933), p. 7. Grundy could not identify in detail the bounds of the woodland set out in this grant.

The names of some other villages were not recorded until the twelfth or thirteenth century. Among these may be mentioned Tetsworth (1146), Standlake (1164), Souldern (1173), Newton Purcell (1198), and the new settlements that appeared in Wychwood Forest—Finstock (1150), Fawler (1205) and Leafield (1213). Or, again, in the wooded Chilterns there are Nuffield (1181), Pishill (1195)[1] and Nettlebed (1247).

Several empty areas stand out on Fig. 64. The extensive tract of royal forest probably accounts for the paucity of Domesday place-names to the south and east of Wychwood. The Chilterns are another empty area; here, there must have been several settlements concealed in the entry for the royal manor of Benson, but, even so, this countryside is unlikely to have been as closely settled as most of the rest of the county in the eleventh century; several parishes certainly bear post-Domesday names. The district to the south of Thame is another empty area; the name of Tetsworth parish does not appear until the twelfth century, but, of course, its territory may have been included within the Domesday accounts of Thame. Elsewhere, place-names are fairly evenly distributed.

THE DISTRIBUTION OF PROSPERITY AND POPULATION

Some idea of the information in the Domesday folios for Oxfordshire, and of the form in which it is presented, may be obtained from the entries relating to Dunthrop (*Dunetorp*). This Domesday vill is represented today by a cluster of farm buildings in the parish of Heythrop; the buildings lie some 400 yards to the east of the eleventh-century settlement, the site of which is clearly discernible in an air photograph of the neighbourhood. The Domesday village was held partly by the Bishop of Lisieux, and partly by the count of Evreux, and so its resources are described in two separate entries:

Fo. 156b. The same bishop holds 5 hides in Dunthrop. [There is] land for 8 plough-teams. Now in demesne [there is] 1 plough-team and 3 serfs; and 3 villeins have 1 plough-team. There [are] 15 acres of meadow. It was and is worth £3.

Fo. 157. The same count holds Dunthrop. There are 5 hides. [There is] land for 5 plough-teams. Now in demesne [there are] 2 plough-teams with 1 serf; and 4 villeins with 2 bordars have 2 plough-teams. There [are] 10 acres of meadow and 30 acres of pasture. It was worth 60s., now [it is worth] 100s.

[1] But pottery finds here suggest a settlement by 1086; see E. M. Jope, *Oxoniensia*, xvii/xviii (Oxford, 1954), pp. 221–2.

These two entries do not include all the items of information that are given for some other places; there is no mention, for example, of woodland, mills or fisheries. But they are representative enough, and they do contain the recurring standard items that are found in entry after entry. These standard items are: (1) hides, (2) plough-lands, (3) plough-teams, (4) population and (5) values. Their bearing upon regional variations in prosperity must now be considered.

(1) *Hides*

The Oxfordshire assessment is stated in terms of hides and virgates, and, occasionally, acres. There was, for example, a holding of 1½ hides and 6 acres of land at Barton (156), and in 1066 there had been another of 60 acres at Stockley (154b). The usual formula runs either 'there are *n* hides' or '*a* holds *n* hides in *b*'. The assessment is sometimes elaborately divided, e.g. the 2 hides and a third part of half a hide entered under Cornwell (161). In an entry for Adderbury (155) we are first told that there were 14½ hides, and then, later on, that 'the whole [is] 3 leagues and 3 furlongs in length and 1½ leagues in breadth' (*Totum iii leuuis et iii quarentenis longum et i leuua et dimidia latum*). It recalls the measurements in the folios for Norfolk, Suffolk and Yorkshire; but, on the other hand, *Totum* here may well be an error for *Silva*.[1] The number of hides in demesne is frequently given,[2] and reference is also made to 'inland' or ancient demesne.[3] An entry relating to Garsington (156b) makes an interesting reference to the open-field system: 'There 1 hide of inland which never paid geld lying scattered among the king's land' (*Ibi i hida de inland quae nunquam geldavit jacens inter terram regis particulatim*).

The system of assessing villages in multiples of 5 hides, so prominent in Bedfordshire, Buckinghamshire, Hertfordshire and Middlesex, is equally apparent in Oxfordshire. One of the villages rated at 5 hides is named Fifield (*Fifhide*, 157b).[4] The five-hide unit is at once apparent in those villages consisting of only one holding; thus Waterperry (158b) and

---

[1] This is suggested by the position of the statement which is between record of meadow and of value; the Oxfordshire wood was normally measured in terms of length and breadth.   [2] See above, pp. 12, 55, 104 and 148.

[3] For a discussion of 'inland', see *V.C.H. Oxfordshire*, I, pp. 393–4.

[4] This is the village of Fifield near Idbury in west Oxfordshire; another settlement of the same name near Benson is not named in the Domesday Book. Both appear as five-hide vills in the Hundred Rolls (*Rotuli Hundredorum*, II, pp. 732 and 751).

Pyrton (157) were rated at 10 hides and 40 hides respectively. But even
when a village was divided amongst a number of lords, the same
feature is frequently apparent when the several entries are assembled and
the village reconstituted:

Hensington

	Hides	Virgates
(1) Bishop of Bayeux (156)		5
(2) Roger d'Ivry (158b)	2½	
(3) William fitz Osbern (161)		5
Total	5	0

Baldon

	Hides	Virgates
(1) Bishop of Lincoln (155b)	5	0
(2) The same (155b)	2½	0
(3) Bishop of Bayeux (156)	1½	0
(4) The same (156)	1½	0
(5) Count of Evreux (157)	3½	0
(6) Milo Crispin (159b)	10	0
(7) Swegn the sheriff (160)	6	0
Total	30	0

Thirty-two villages in the modern county were rated at 5 hides, thirty-six
at 10 hides, seven at 15 hides, and seventeen at 20 or more hides. Altogether,
92 of 252 Domesday settlements in Oxfordshire were rated at either
5 hides, or at some multiple of 5; in addition, seven villages were rated at
2½ hides each. The figures for the Domesday county are different, but
they bear out the same general point.

There are many village assessments, however, that do not seem to fit
into this system; representative of these are Bicester (158) rated at
15½ hides, Wroxton (159b) at 17 hides, and Broadwell (160) at 24 hides
and 1 virgate. But it has been shown, for some other counties, that an
irregular assessment recorded for a single place may be part of a round
number of hides laid jointly on two or more villages. Few combinations
of this kind have been traced in Oxfordshire, yet, as Sir Frank Stenton
has remarked, 'it cannot be through chance that the irregular figures given
in the three entries [154b, 155 and 158] which relate to Bloxham and
Adderbury (34½ hides, 14½ hides and 1 hide) amount together to a neat
total of 50 hides. In any case, the 5-hide unit of assessment appears so

clearly on the surface of the Oxfordshire survey that it is hardly necessary to search for further illustrations of the system to which it belongs'.[1]

In the light of the artificial nature of the assessment, it is obvious that the hidage can in no way reflect the agrarian realities of a district. The figures certainly bear no relation to those of plough-teams and population, as the details for eight villages each assessed at 10 hides demonstrate:

	Plough-lands	Teams	Population	Other Resources
Ambrosden (157b)	16	16	38	Meadow
Chalgrove (159)	12	13	42	Meadow, Mills, Pasture
Charlton on Otmoor (224b)	15	15	32	Meadow, Pasture
Glympton (221)	6	11	26	Meadow, Mill, Wood
Leigh (158b)	10	14	42	Meadow, Mill, Wood
Merton (160)	12	7	27	Meadow, Wood
Newnham Murren (159b)	16	9	32	Meadow, Wood
Stoke Talmage (159)	$6\frac{1}{2}$	$6\frac{1}{2}$	22	Meadow, Pasture

The present count has yielded a total of $2,580\frac{2}{3}$ hides and 66 acres for the area covered by the modern county;[2] the assessment of the borough of Oxford is not given in Domesday Book. This figure can only be an approximate one, for any total depends upon the individual interpretation of a number of entries.[3]

(2) Plough-lands

Plough-lands are systematically entered in the Oxfordshire folios, and the normal formula runs: 'Land for n plough-teams' (Terra n carucis) or

---

[1] V.C.H. Oxfordshire, I, p. 374.

[2] It is even more difficult than usual to arrive at a satisfactory total for the hidage because of the doubts associated with five of the bishop of Lincoln's manors on fo. 155–155b: Banbury, Cropredy, Dorchester, Milton and Thame. The present total excludes the hidage in the second entry for each place on the assumption that it is included in the hidage of the first entry. It includes $\frac{2}{3}$ of the hidage for Caversham (see p. 187 below), and also the 4 hides juxta Oxford (see p. 229 below).

[3] F. W. Maitland's total for the Domesday county amounted to 2,412 hides (Domesday Book and Beyond (Cambridge, 1897), p. 400). W. J. Corbett's total for the Domesday county, plus the Oxfordshire villages entered in the Northamptonshire folios, was 2,494 ('The Tribal Hidage', Trans. Roy. Hist. Soc. N.S. XIV (London, 1900), p. 218). Sir Frank Stenton's total amounted to 2,509 (V.C.H. Oxfordshire, I, p. 393), but this also is not strictly comparable with the present total.

occasionally 'There is land for *n* plough-teams' (*Terra est n carucis*). The statistical usefulness of the Oxfordshire plough-land figures is considerably reduced by a number of omissions. No plough-lands are entered for Shenington (163b) and Widford (164b), for these are described in the Gloucestershire folios from which plough-lands are omitted. But ploughlands are also omitted—apparently in error—from some entries in the Oxfordshire folios themselves, e.g. those relating to Milton (155b), Kingston Blount (159b) and Wootton (154b). More important still, they are also omitted from the entries for seven of the nine manors held by King William in the county. But in three of these there is a statement about the number of teams in the time of King Edward. The relevant entries are:

> Bampton (154b): *Ibi sunt xxvii hidae et dimidia. In dominio sunt vi carucae et vi servi, et xl villani et xvii buri et xiii bordarii habent xvi carucas. T.R.E. habebant xxvi carucas.*
>
> Benson (154b): *Ibi sunt xii hidae una virgata terrae minus. T.R.E. erant ibi l carucae. Nunc in dominio viii carucae et v servi, et xxxii villani cum xxix bordariis habent xxiiii carucas.*
>
> Bloxham and Adderbury (154b): *Ibi sunt xxxiiii hidae et dimidia. T.R.E. erant ibi xlviii carucae. In dominio sunt modo xiii et xxvii servi, et lxxii villani cum xvi bordariis habentes   carucas.*[1]

These entries would seem to support the view that the plough-land formula indicates the number of plough-teams in 1066, rather than the extent of potential arable land.[2] In this connection the successive entries for Banbury, Cropredy and Eynsham respectively are interesting:

> Banbury (155): *Ibi sunt l hidae. De his habet episcopus in dominio terram x carucis et iii hidas preter inland. Homines villae habent xxxiii hidas et dimidiam. T.R.E. erant ibi xxxiii carucae et dimidia et totidem episcopus R[emigius] invenit. Nunc in dominio vii carucae[3] et xiiii servi, et lxxvi villani cum xvii bordariis habent xxxiii carucas.*
>
> Cropredy (155): *Ibi sunt l hidae. De his habet episcopus in firma sua xxv hidas et milites tantundem. Supra has l hidas est terra in dominio ad x carucas. Inter totum terra est xxx carucis. Episcopus invenit xxxv. Nunc in dominio vi carucae et xii servi, et lv villani cum xxii bordariis habent xxxiiii carucas.*

---

[1] The letter *r'* (*require*) appears in the margin at this point of the MS.

[2] Note also the entry for Waterstock (155b) which reads: *Terra est v carucis*, but in the margin there is added: *Ibi fuerunt v carucae T.R.E. In dominio iii.*

[3] At this point in the MS. four minims (*iiii*) have been altered to *vii*.

Eynsham (155): *Ibi sunt xv hidae et dimidia pertinentes eisdem ecclesiae. Terra est xviii carucis et totidem invenit. In dominio est terra ii carucis inland. Nunc in dominio iii carucis et iii milites cum xxxiiii villanis et xxxiii bordariis habent xv carucas.*

The indication here also is that we are dealing with teams before 1086. We must finally notice a short entry on fo. 157 which follows an entry for Cadwell (and may refer to the same place). Instead of saying *Terra i carucae*, as is usual, it states *Ibi fuit i caruca*. We can only wonder whether this variation shows that to the scribe plough-lands and past plough-teams were one and the same.[1]

The total number of plough-lands is greater than the number of teams, but the relation between the two figures varies a great deal in individual entries. Where teams are fewer than plough-lands, no reference is made to the missing teams, as in the folios for some counties, e.g. Buckinghamshire and Middlesex. The number of teams at work exceeded the number for which there was land at about one-quarter of the Domesday vills for which plough-lands were recorded. Generally, the excess was small, e.g. under 3 plough-teams. Two entries make specific reference to excess:

Brize Norton (160b): *Terra dimidiae carucae. Ibi tamen habet i carucam.*
Northbrook (159): *Terra dimidiae carucae. Ibi tamen est una in dominio et vi villani cum iii bordariis habent aliam.*

A certain degree of understocking, on the other hand, was apparent in nearly one-half of the villages for which plough-lands were recorded. Merton and Newnham Murren, noted in the table on p. 199, provide examples. At Swyncombe our attention is specifically drawn to the absence of teams: *Terra ii carucis et dimidiae. Nulla modo est* (159b).

The total number of plough-lands recorded for the area included in the modern county is 2,513¼.[2] But the plough-land figure is omitted from some entries, and we can attempt to make allowance for this either by assuming that there were plough-lands equal in number to the teams, or, in the case of four entries,[3] by taking the earlier figure for teams as indicating the plough-lands. With these adjustments, the number of plough-lands is increased to 2,860¼.[4]

---

[1] Note the variant in the entry for Duns Tew (156) reads: *Ibi sunt iii hidae et dimidia. Terra est totidem carucis.*

[2] This total includes the 5 plough-lands *juxta* Oxford—see p. 229 below.

[3] For Bampton, Banbury, Benson, Bloxham and Adderbury, see p. 200 above.

[4] F. W. Maitland's total for the Domesday county was 2,639 plough-lands, and he

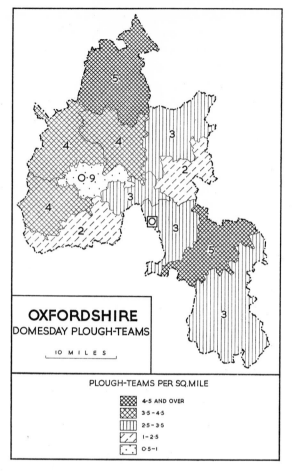

Fig. 65. Oxfordshire: Domesday plough-teams in 1086 (by densities).

O indicates the Domesday borough of Oxford.

(3) *Plough-teams*

The Oxfordshire entries for plough-teams and oxen are straightforward, and, like those of other counties, they usually differentiate between the teams at work on the demesne and those held by the peasantry. As we

seems to have made allowance for the missing figures in some entries (*op. cit.* pp. 401 and 410). Sir Frank Stenton's total amounted to 2,648½ plough-lands (*V.C.H. Oxfordshire*, I, p. 393), but this also is not strictly comparable with the present total.

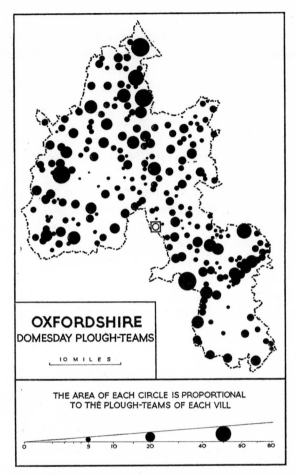

Fig. 66. Oxfordshire: Domesday plough-teams in 1086 (by settlements).

O indicates the Domesday borough of Oxford.

have seen, a few entries give plough-teams for a date earlier than 1086, but this is unusual.[1] Occasional entries are defective. Two villeins but no plough-teams appear in an entry for Britwell Salome (159b); at the unidentified *Asce*, a villein and three bordars were also without teams (157b); and on an unnamed holding belonging to William Levric (160)

---

[1] For 1066: Bampton (154b), Benson (154b), Bloxham and Adderbury (154b), Banbury (155). Note also Cropredy (155) where the bishop of Lincoln found (*invenit*) 35 plough-teams, and Cadwell (157) where there was (*fuit*) one team.

there were four bordars and two serfs, but again no teams. In a few
entries, demesne teams are not recorded, e.g. for Lashbrook (157b); and
in the account of Cutslow there is a blank in the MS. where the peasants
and their teams are usually entered (159). There is also a blank, as we have
seen, in the entry for Bloxham and Adderbury (154b).[1] The account of
Cottisford in the Northamptonshire folios, where 'actual' teams and
'possible' teams are normally very carefully recorded, also seems to be
incomplete: *Terra est x carucis. In dominio sunt iii et quarta posset esse.
Ibi sunt x villani et v bordarii* (224b). We can only conjecture to what
the peasants' teams amounted.

These omissions illustrate the uncertainty that must always be remembered when dealing with Domesday statistics. But while the doubts
are important for individual localities, they amount to only a small fraction
of all the teams recorded for the county. Taken as a whole, the record of
teams provides a reasonable index of the arable land of the Oxfordshire
villages in the eleventh century.

The total number of plough-teams amounted to 2,608,[2] but this refers
to the area included in the modern county and, in any case, a definitive
total is hardly possible.[3]

(4) *Population*

The bulk of the population was comprised in the three main categories
of villeins, bordars and serfs. In addition to these were the burgesses,
together with a small miscellaneous group that included freemen, 'men',
buri, knights, radmen, fishermen and others. The details of these groups
are summarised on p. 205. There are two other estimates of the Domesday
population of Oxfordshire, by Sir Henry Ellis,[4] and by Sir Frank Stenton,[5]
but they are comparable neither with one another nor with the present

---

[1] See p. 200 above. In the present analysis the teams on this royal holding have been
counted as 48, i.e. the number at work at the 'time of King Edward'. As the value of
the holding had risen from £28 to £33. 10s., it is probably not an under-estimate.

[2] This total includes the 5 plough-teams *juxta* Oxford—see p. 229 below.

[3] F. W. Maitland's total for the Domesday county was 2,467 teams—*op. cit.* p. 401.
Sir Frank Stenton's total amounted to 2,641 (*V.C.H. Oxfordshire*, I, p. 393), but
this also is not strictly comparable with the present total.

[4] Sir Henry Ellis, *A General Introduction to Domesday Book*, II (London, 1833),
p. 477. This estimate amounted to 6,775, but it included tenants-in-chief and under-
tenants, and, moreover, was in terms of the Domesday county.

[5] *V.C.H. Oxfordshire*, I, p. 393. The figures are 3,682 villeins, 2,933 bordars, 1,007
serfs and 23 freemen. The 2,933 bordars is obviously a misprint for 1,933.

estimate. In any case, definite accuracy rarely belongs to a count of Domesday population, and all that can be said for the present figures is that they indicate the order of magnitude involved. These figures are those of recorded population, and must be multiplied by some factor, say 4 or 5, in order to obtain the actual population; but this does not affect the relative density as between one area and another.[1] That is all that a map such as Fig. 67 can roughly indicate.

Recorded Population of Oxfordshire in 1086

A. Rural Population

Villeins	3,699
Bordars	1,966
Serfs	1,022
Miscellaneous	97
Total	6,784

Details of Miscellaneous Rural Population

Freemen	26
'Men with small gardens'	23
Buri	17
Francigenae	8
Knights	6
'Others' (*Alii*)	6
Radchenistres	5
Fishermen	4
Man (*Uno homo*)	1
Priest	1
Total	97

B. Urban Population

OXFORD   Possibly as many as 1,070 properties (including 593 wasted houses and 15 that paid nothing). Certainly 938 properties (including 559 wasted houses and one that paid nothing). See p. 228 below. In addition, there were 18 villeins close by (*juxta*) Oxford; these have been included in the tables above.

It is impossible for us to say how complete were these Domesday statistics, but it does seem as if some people were left uncounted. At Finmere there was land for 2 ploughs on which the bishop of Bayeux's men

---

[1] But see p. 589 below for the complication of serfs.

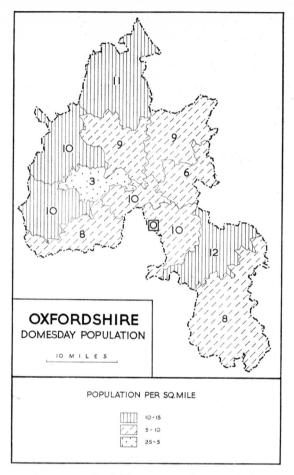

Fig. 67. Oxfordshire: Domesday population
in 1086 (by densities).

O indicates the Domesday borough of Oxford.

(*homines eius*) had 1 plough, but we are not told their number (155b).
Similarly, on a holding at South Newington there were men with half a
plough-team, but again we are not told how many (156). A few entries,
e.g. that for Stoke Lyne and Tusmore (157b), record teams but no
people. We cannot be certain about the significance of these omissions.[1]

---

[1] 'Five thegns' are noted at the end of the entry for Deddington, and this is followed
by a blank line with *rq'*(=*require*) in the margin (155b). Judging from the analogy of

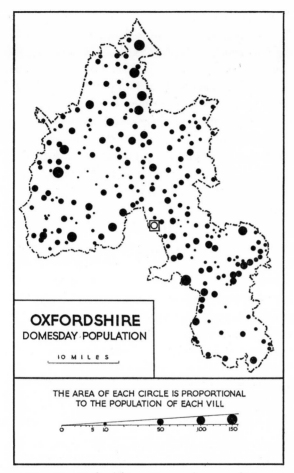

Fig. 68. Oxfordshire: Domesday population
in 1086 (by settlements).

O indicates the Domesday borough of Oxford.

Villeins constituted the most important element numerically in the
population, and amounted to 54 per cent of the total. Then came the
bordars who numbered 29 per cent. The serfs accounted for only 15 per
cent. The free element was extremely small; no sokemen and only 26 free-

other entries the missing line would have shown that the thegns were in possession of
the holdings in 1066. Twenty-eight other thegns are also entered for 1066 for Aston
(158), Bolney (161), Brize Norton (158b), Hampton (160b) and Idbury (159). There
were no thegns in 1086.

men (*liberi homines*) were enumerated. Of this very small group of free peasantry, 15 were recorded at Aston Rowant (159), 4 at Pyrton (157), 4 at Enstone (157) and 3 at Goring (158). The men with small gardens (*homines hortulos habentes*) were at Holywell outside the medieval city of Oxford (158b). The 17 *buri* were at Bampton (154b).[1] Only 6 knights are counted here,[2] but there were other knights enumerated among the under-tenants. The 5 radmen (*radchenistres*) were at Shenington, entered in the Gloucestershire folios (163b). Of the 4 fishermen, three were at Nuneham Courtenay (159) and the fourth at Dorchester (155). The only priest was at Great Milton, but nothing is said about a church there (155). The rest of the miscellaneous group calls for no special comment.

(5) *Values*

The value of an estate is generally given for only two dates, 1066 and 1086, but it is sometimes also stated for an intermediate date, described as when its new owner received it (*cum recepit*) or as 'afterwards' (*post*). The following examples illustrate the variation in formulae:

Britwell Salome (159b): *Valuit et valet iii libras.*
Crowell (157b): *Valuit vi libras. Modo vii libras.*
Broadwell (160): *T.R.E. valebat xxv libras et post xxx libras. Modo xxxi libras.*
Thame (155): *T.R.E. valebat xx libras. Cum recepit xvi libras. Modo xxx libras.*

The 1066 value, however, is not given for any of the royal estates (154b) and it is also omitted from the account of one holding at Great Milton (155b), and from that of Ardley (157); it is also omitted from entries that describe waste.[3] The values are usually reckoned in pounds or to the nearest 10s., although sometimes values of 5s. are given, e.g. for a holding at Thomley (159b); there are also one or two odd amounts, like the 23s. entered for Ludwell (156). One holding at Stoke (155), which was worth £6 in 1066, is noted in 1086 as rendering '£12 and 12 sticks of eels' (*modo reddit xii libras et xii stichas anguillarum*). The values of most of the royal manors (154b) were reckoned 'by tale' (*ad numerum*), that

---

[1] The *buri* were 'all one' with the *coliberti*, and in general stood between villeins and serfs, although more akin to the latter—see F. W. Maitland, *op. cit.* pp. 36–8 and 329. See also p. 314 below.

[2] One each at Brize Norton (158b), Mongewell (161), Wigginton (160), and three at Eynsham (155).   [3] See pp. 223–4 below.

was by count of coins. In 1086, the borough of Oxford (154) rendered £60 by tale of 20 [pence] to the ounce (*lx libras ad numerum de xx in ora*).

The values of about one-half of the Oxfordshire villages increased between 1066 and 1086, and the low figures for 1066 here, as in Northamptonshire, have been attributed to the ravages of the northern insurgents described in the *Anglo-Saxon Chronicle* for 1065.[1] Where triple valuations are available, they often show the same feature, e.g. the figures for Crowmarsh (157b) are: *T.R.E. et post valuit x libras. Modo xx libras.*[2] It is upon such evidence that F. H. Baring attempted to trace the routes followed by insurgents.[3] A decline in value between 1066 and 1086 is recorded for about 14 per cent of the villages, and some triple valuations also indicate a similar fall. The greatest decrease was at Lashbrook (157b) where the value dropped from £12 to £8 and then to 30s. Occasionally a value fell only to rise higher than ever; the figures for Thame (155) are £20, £16 and £30. Amidst this variation there were some estates that remained constant in value; Nuneham Courtenay (159) was worth £13 *T.R.E. et post et modo*.

Generally speaking, the greater the number of plough-teams and men on an estate, the higher its value, but it is impossible to discern any constant relationships, even when taking other resources into account. Conditions on the following seven holdings, each valued at £3 in 1086, illustrate the kind of variation that is encountered:

	Teams	Population	Other resources
Bix (157b)	4	6	Meadow, Wood
Bix (160b)	6	11	Meadow, Wood
Checkendon (160)	3	15	Meadow, Wood
Dunthrop (156b)	2	6	Meadow
Eaton (158b)	4	15	Meadow, Moor, Wood
Fulwell in Mixbury (158)	2	6	Mill, Pasture
Minster (160b)	1	4	Mill

[1] See H. C. Darby and I. B. Terrett (eds.), *The Domesday Geography of Midland England* (Cambridge, 1954), p. 397.

[2] The rise in value of a holding at Milton under Wychwood (161) from 20s. in 1066 to £7 in 1086 was doubtless an error; *libras* should probably read *solidos*; the intermediate value was 15s.

[3] F. H. Baring, 'Oxfordshire traces of the northern insurgents in 1065', *Eng. Hist. Rev.* XIII (London, 1898), pp. 295–7. See also G. H. Fowler, 'The devastation of Bedfordshire and the neighbouring counties in 1065 and 1066', *Archaeologia*, LXXII (London, 1922), pp. 41–50.

Even more mysterious is the entry for Swyncombe (159b). Here there was land for 2½ plough-teams but no team was at work (*Nulla modo est*), yet the value of the holding had risen from 40s. to 60s. There may be a perfectly reasonable explanation for such an oddity, but it is difficult to see what it is.

Conclusion

As it is impossible to reconstruct the Domesday hundreds of Oxfordshire, the densities have been calculated on the basis of twelve divisions. In forming them, variations of soil and surface features have been borne in mind, and the twelve divisions fit roughly into the four main regions adopted in the Regional Summary below. But a weakness of any division is the fact that we cannot resolve the large composite manors into their components.[1]

Of the five standard formulae, those relating to plough-teams and population are most likely to reflect something of the distribution of wealth and prosperity throughout the county in the eleventh century. Neither is without uncertainty, but taken together they supplement one another, and when they are compared certain common features stand out (Figs. 65 and 67). The highest densities per square mile of plough-teams (4·5 to 5) and population (11 to 12) were in the North Oxfordshire Upland and in the southern portion of the Central Claylands. The rest of the county had only moderate densities, but certain local differences are nevertheless apparent. The unit area occupied by Wychwood Forest stood out as a region of very low density both of teams (under one) and of population (about 3). The densities of the Ot Moor region were also fairly low, being 2·1 and 5·7 for teams and population respectively. It is less easy to explain why the area immediately to the north of the Thames above Oxford should have had such low densities, for here the soils are for the most part well-drained loams derived from river gravels; such soils usually attracted settlement and were cleared at a very early date. The considerable prosperity of the Cotswolds in the later Middle Ages was already apparent in 1086, and was reflected in both moderately high densities, 3 to 4 for teams and 9 to 10 for population.

It is not easy to generalise about the relative prosperity of the Chilterns in Domesday times, because the royal manor of Benson stretched across the upland from the village of Benson, situated on the fertile outcrop of

[1] See p. 189 above.

Upper Greensand at the scarp foot, to Henley on Thames; and it is not practicable to apportion its resources among the several villages and hamlets which it must have included. Other estates also (Pyrton for example) stretched across more than one geological outcrop. There can be little doubt, however, that the most prosperous localities were below the Chiltern escarpment, and that plough-team and population densities were lowest on the plateau surface to the east and south-east.

Figs. 66 and 68 are supplementary to the density maps, but it is necessary to make one reservation about them. As we have seen on p. 192 some Domesday names covered two or more settlements, and several of the symbols should thus appear as two or more smaller symbols. But this limitation does not affect the general character of the maps. Generally speaking, they confirm and amplify the information of the density maps.

WOODLAND AND FOREST

Types of entries

The amount of woodland (*silva*) on a holding in Oxfordshire was usually recorded by giving its length and breadth in terms of leagues and furlongs. The entries for Handborough and Mongewell are representative:

Handborough (159b): *Silva vii quarentenis longa et vi quarentenis lata.*
Mongewell (161): *Silva i leuua et dimidia in longitudine et iiii quarentenis lata.*

The use of perches in the entry for Sandford on Thames (156b), where there was 'wood 28 perches long and 30 perches broad' (*Silva xxviii perticis longa et xxx perticis lata*), is exceptional. The exact significance of these linear measurements is far from clear, and we cannot hope to convert them into modern acreages.[1] All we can do is to plot them diagrammatically as intersecting straight lines (Fig. 69). At Crowell (157b) there were '2 furlongs of woodland' (*ii quarentinae silvae*), and it has been suggested that such entries refer, not to linear dimensions, but to an areal league of 120 acres.[2] In any case, the map could be but little affected, and on Fig. 69 this entry has been plotted conventionally as a single line.

[1] See p. 595 below.
[2] R. W. Eyton, *A Key to Domesday: the Dorset Survey* (London, 1878), pp. 31–5. See also H. C. Darby and I. B. Terrett (eds.), *The Domesday Geography of Midland England*, pp. 26, 83, 135, 194, 244, and 291. For one furlong of spinney at Sandford St Martin, see p. 212 below. See also p. 219 below for similar pasture entries.

While leagues and furlongs form the usual units of measurement, there are a number of entries that refer to wood in other ways. In a few entries, the woodland is measured in terms of acres, and the amounts vary from as little as 6 acres on one holding in Hensington (161)[1] to as much as 40 acres on two holdings at Brightwell Baldwin (155b, 160b).

Information about coppice (*grava*), underwood (*silva minuta*), and spinney (*spinetum*) is occasionally given. Their extent is usually measured in acres; at Cropredy (155b), for example, there were '5 acres of coppice' and at South Weston (157) '4 acres of underwood'. Three of the entries mentioning coppice are especially curious:

Cowley (157b): *Grava ii acrae in longitudine et latitudine.*
Cowley (159b): *Grava iii acras (sic) in longitudine et in latitudine.*
Iffley (157b): *Grava ii acras (sic) in longitudine et in latitudine.*

The precise meaning of these entries must remain a matter for conjecture.[2] On a third holding at Cowley (160b) there was 'coppice 4 furlongs in length and 2 furlongs in breadth' (*Grava iiii quarentenis longa et ii quarentenis lata*). At Britwell Salome (159b *bis*) there were respectively 'underwood 3 furlongs in length and 1 furlong in breadth', and '6 acres of coppice'. The term spinney (*spinetum*) appears in six entries:

Cassington (156): *vii acrae spineti.*
Cassington[3] (156): *vii acrae spineti.*
Hook Norton (158): *Spinetum ii quarentenis longum et dimidia quarentena latum.*
Juxta Oxford (157): *viii acras (sic) spineti.*
Radford (161): *iii acrae spineti.*
Sandford St Martin (156b): *i quarentena spineti.*[4]

Occasionally we are given the render of the woodland when it bore mast (*cum oneratur*), as in the entry for Witney: *Silva iii leuuis longa et ii leuuis lata. Cum oneratur valet l solidos* (155).[5] The phrase also occurs in entries for Eynsham (155), Lewknor (156b), Newington (155), and in the composite entry for Bloxham and Adderbury (154b). The last is unusual

---

[1] On two other holdings (156, 158b) at Hensington there was a total of 11 acres of underwood (*minutae silvae*).

[2] For 'linear acres' see O. J. Reichel in *V.C.H. Devonshire*, 1 (London, 1906), p. 387.

[3] This may be a duplicate entry.

[4] For 2 furlongs of wood at Crowell, see p. 211 above.

[5] For the phrase *cum oneratur* see J. H. Round in *V.C.H. Warwickshire*, 1 (London, 1904), p. 292.

in mentioning a render of swine: *Silva xiii quarentenae et dimidia in longi-tudine et lx quarentinis lata.... De pasnagio xxiiii solidi et vii denarii, et xl porci cum oneratur et Aliquando lxvi porci.*

Renders of money from the pannage along with other dues were also mentioned for four places, all on fo. 154b:

Bampton: *De pasnagio et salinis de Wic et aliis consuetudinibus hominum ix librae et xiii solidi.*

Benson: *Inter prata et pascua et piscarias et silvas exeunt xviii librae et xv solidi et v denarii per annum.*

Kirtlington: *De pratis et pascuis et pasnagio et aliis consuetudinibus viii librae.*

Shipton under Wychwood: *De pratis et pasnagio et gablo et aliis consuetu-dinibus xii librae et xvii solidi.*

For none of these places is any measurement of wood entered; but for Shipton under Wychwood, and also for Wootton (154b), we are told that there was 'wood in the king's enclosure' (*Silva est in defensione regis*); at the former place it had rendered 50s. in 1066, and at the latter place, 10s., but we are told nothing of the renders in 1086. Lastly, in the entry for Bampton (154b) we read that in addition to the render mentioned above, Henry de Ferrers held a certain piece of woodland which Bundi the forester had held (*Henricus de fereires tenet quamdam silvam quam tenuit Bundi forestarius*), but no detail of its size is given.

Distribution of woodland

Fig. 69 shows a central belt of woodland to the north and east of the city of Oxford. It stretched from the Wychwood Forest area, on the dip-slope of the Cotswolds, southward across the Oxford Clay exposure to the forested area of Shotover and Stowood, and beyond to the broken outcrops of Kimeridge Clay; it is likely that both forested areas contained more wood than is indicated on Fig. 69. The Chilterns formed another wooded area. On Fig. 69 a belt of wood appears at the foot of the Chiltern escarpment, but it must be remembered that the manors of these villages extended southward over the dip-slope, and that the wood itself probably lay there—on Clay-with-flints soils.

Between the Chilterns and the central woodlands, there appears to have been a marked lack of wood on the heavy Gault Clay; and there was also very little wood on the Middle Lias loams of north Oxfordshire. Both these areas had relatively high plough-team densities, and much clearing must have taken place. Another area with little wood lay in the south-west of the county—along the Thames valley.

Forests

The only direct reference to forests occurs on fo. 154b:

In Shotover, Stowood, Woodstock, Cornbury and Wychwood are demesne forests of the king having 9 leagues in length and the same in breadth. To these forests belong 4½ hides, and there 6 villeins with 8 bordars have 3½ plough-teams. From these and all things belonging to the forests Rainald renders £10 yearly to the king.

The places lie in two groups to the east and the north-west of Oxford, and the single set of dimensions seems to imply some process of addition whereby the measurements of separate tracts were consolidated into one sum. Areas under forest law were not necessarily wooded, but, as has been said above, it is likely that the Domesday Book does not fully record the wood in these two forested districts. Fig. 69 has been made more complete by the addition of forest symbols.

Certain other entries contain what would seem to be indirect references to the forests. The woodland of Shipton under Wychwood (154b) and of Wootton (154b) was said to be 'in the king's enclosure' (*in defensione regis*), presumably in the royal forest. On the same folio, among various customary payments rendered by the county of Oxford, we read that £10 was paid 'for a hawk' (*pro accipitre*) and £23 'for the hounds' (*pro canibus*); the implication of these customary payments is that hunting was carried on in the county. One of the two holdings in Chadlington (160b), not far from the Wychwood area, was held by Siward the huntsman (*venator*), but we cannot be certain that he actually lived in the locality; the same applies to Bundi the forester who formerly had held wood at Bampton (154b).

MEADOW

Types of entries

The entries for meadow in Oxfordshire are comparatively straight-forward. For holding after holding, the same phrase is repeated monotonously, '*n* acres of meadow' (*n acrae prati*). The amount of meadow in each vill varied from as little as half an acre at Ludwell (158b)[1] to as much

---

[1] There were five holdings in this vill (156, 158b, 160, 160b *bis*), but meadow is recorded for only one of them.

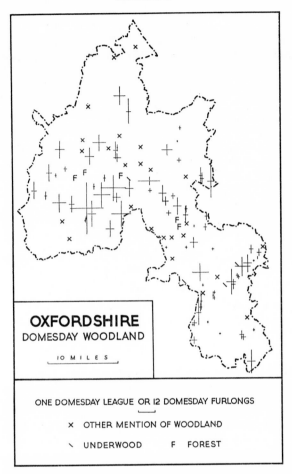

OXFORDSHIRE
DOMESDAY WOODLAND

10 MILES

ONE DOMESDAY LEAGUE OR 12 DOMESDAY FURLONGS

× OTHER MENTION OF WOODLAND

＼ UNDERWOOD   F FOREST

Fig. 69. Oxfordshire: Domesday woodland in 1086.

Where the wood (*silva*) of a village is entered partly in terms of linear dimensions and partly in some other way, only the dimensions are shown. 'Other mention' includes references to coppice (*grava*), spinney (*spinetum*), as well as miscellaneous references to wood (*silva*).

as 365½ acres at Great and Little Tew (155b *bis*, 156 *bis*, 156b).[1] Sometimes round figures like 20, 30 or 40 acres seem to indicate estimates but, on the other hand, the many detailed figures (e.g. 1, 2, 7½, 11, 43, 155) suggest actual amounts. Quantities of 100 acres or more are encountered at about two dozen places. As in the case of other counties, no attempt has been

[1] For the Tews, see p. 192 above.

made to translate the Domesday figures into modern acreages. The Domesday acres have been treated merely as conventional units of measurement, and Fig. 70 has been plotted on that assumption.

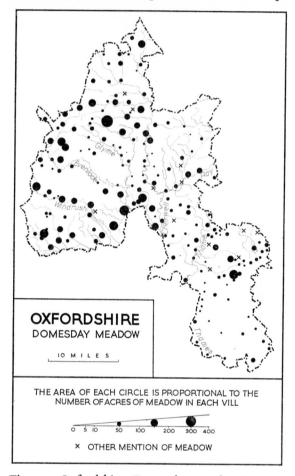

Fig. 70. Oxfordshire: Domesday meadow in 1086.

Where the meadow of a village is entered partly in terms of acres and partly in some other way, only the acres are shown.

While measurement in acres is normal, there are a number of entries that refer to meadow in other ways. The meadow of nine vills is given in terms of linear dimensions; that of five other vills in terms partly of acres, and partly of linear dimensions. The usual unit is the furlong, but perches are occasionally used. A complete list of the entries recording meadow in this way is set out below:

Adwell (159b): *Pratum i quarentena longum et una quarentena latum.*

Bloxham and Adderbury (154b): *pratum ii leuuis et v quarentenis longum et iiii quarentenis latum.*

Chalgrove (159): *pratum iii quarentenis longum et iii quarentenis latum.*

Charlton on Otmoor (224b):[1] *Pratum iiii quarentenis longum et ii quarentenis latum.*

Cogges (156): *Pratum xi quarentenis longum et ii quarentenis latum.*

Eaton (158):[2] *Ibi pratum x quarentenis longum et totidem latum.*

Hampton (158b):[2] *Pratum iii quarentenis longum et una et dimidia latum.*

Hempton (157b): *ii quarentenae prati latae et una leuua et dimidia longa.*

Hensington (158b):[2] *Pratum i quarentena longum et dimidia latum.*

Horley (158):[2] *Pratum i quarentena longum et xxx perticis latum.*

Kidlington (158): *Ibi pratum iii quarentenis longum et ii quarentenis latum.*

Lewknor (156b):[2] *Pratum iiii quarentenis longum et ii quarentenis latum.*

Wendlebury (159b–160): *prati viii quarentenae longae et ii quarentenae latae.*

There are also a few other variations, most of them involving money payments:

Anonymous holding (157): *vi acrae prati et pasturae.*

Bampton (154b): *De pratis lxv solidi.*

Benson (154b): *Inter prata et pascua et piscarias et silvas exeunt xviii librae et xv solidi et v denarii per annum.*

Broadwell (160): *Ibi ii molini cum piscaria et pratis reddunt xx solidos et cc acrae prati xv minus.*

Bromscott and Pemscott (158): *Ibi xlvii acrae prati reddunt x solidos.*

Cogges (156): *De feno x solidi.*

Deddington (155b): *ibi cxl acrae prati....De pratis x solidi.*

Dorchester (155): *De prato xl solidi.*

Dorchester (155): *De pratis et piscariis xxii solidi et viii denarii et ix stichae anguillarum.*

Grafton (157): *Ibi lxiii acrae prati et reddunt x solidos.*

Great Milton (155): *pratum de x solidis.*

Headington (154b): *De pratis et pascuis iiii librae.*

Kirtlington (154b): *De pratis et pascuis et pasnagio et aliis consuetudinibus viii librae.*

---

[1] Charlton on Otmoor is described in the Northamptonshire folios.
[2] Other entries for these places record meadow in terms of acres.

Shipton under Wychwood (154b): *De pratis et pasnagio et gablo et aliis consuetudinibus xii librae et xvii solidi.*

Taynton (157): *Inter quadrariam et prata et pascua reddunt xxiiii solidos et vii denarios.*

Thame (155): *De pratis lx solidi.*

The entry for Yarnton, where there were 180 acres of meadow, concludes by saying: *Totum T.R.E. valebat x libras. Modo cum piscaria et cum pratis valet xiiii libras* (155b). Finally, at Towersey (*Eie*) there was 'meadow for 7 plough-teams' (*pratum vii carucis*), the usual formula in the Buckinghamshire folios where it is entered (151b).

Distribution of meadowland

The main feature about the distribution of meadow was its alignment along the valleys of the Thames, the Windrush, the upper Evenlode, the Cherwell and their larger tributaries (Fig. 70). Several villages along these streams had nearly 100 or more acres of meadow apiece. Villages along the Thame and its tributaries usually had smaller amounts. Small amounts were also recorded for the villages situated along the spring line at the foot of the Chilterns; Pyrton (157) with 200 acres here was exceptional. There was very little meadow in the Chilterns, in the Wychwood Forest area, and in many parts of the Cotswolds. Where it was found in these areas, the amounts recorded for any one vill rarely exceeded 20 acres.

PASTURE

Type of entries

Pasture (*pastura* or occasionally *pascua*) is recorded for 105 out of the 251 Domesday settlements of Oxfordshire,[1] and it is generally measured either in terms of linear dimensions or in terms of acres. The former method is characteristic of some 46 places, and the following entries are typical:

Astrop (161): *Ibi iii quarentenae pasturae in longitudine et ii quarentenae in latitudine.*

Fulbrook (158b): *Pastura x quarentenis longa et iii quarentenis lata.*

Occasionally, the dimensions seem to be very precise and employ perches, as in the entry for Stoke Talmage (159) where there was 'pasture 13 furlongs in length and 1 furlong and 12 perches in breadth' (*Pastura*

---

[1] There was also pasture on an unnamed holding (157)—see p. 220 below.

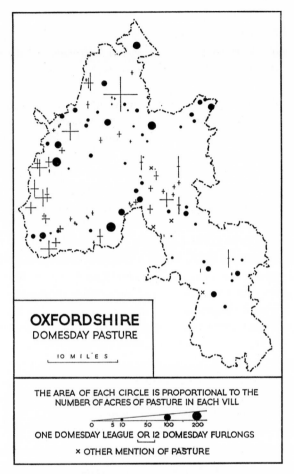

OXFORDSHIRE
DOMESDAY PASTURE

10 M I L E S

THE AREA OF EACH CIRCLE IS PROPORTIONAL TO THE
NUMBER OF ACRES OF PASTURE IN EACH VILL

0   5 10   50   100   200

ONE DOMESDAY LEAGUE OR 12 DOMESDAY FURLONGS

× OTHER MENTION OF PASTURE

Fig. 71. Oxfordshire: Domesday pasture in 1086.

Both acres and linear dimensions have been plotted for Black Bourton
and for Shipton on Cherwell (see p. 220).

xiii quarentenis longa et una quarentena et xii perticis lata). In three entries
one dimension only is given; there was 1 furlong of pasture at Iffley
(157b), 2 furlongs at Newington (155), and 3 furlongs on a holding at
Shipton on Cherwell (224b). The exact meaning of these entries is far
from clear, and they have been plotted as single lines on Fig. 71.[1] There

---

[1] See p. 211 above for 'areal leagues'.

are also two other entries, each of a composite nature, that differ some-what from those set out above:

>   Bloxham and Adderbury (154b): *Pascua in longitudine et latitudine ii leuuae.*
>   Bromscott and Pemscott (158): *iii quarentenae pasturae in longitudine et latitudine.*

Some have believed that such formulae imply not linear dimensions but areal leagues of 120 acres each.[1] On Fig. 71, however, the first entry has been plotted at Bloxham as intersecting lines of 2 leagues each, and the second entry at Bromscott as intersecting lines of 3 furlongs each. What-ever be the truth the pattern of the map cannot be much affected as there are only these two entries in which this doubt arises.

The pasture at another 53 places is stated in terms of acres (*n acrae pasturae*); the individual amounts vary from a mere 2 acres at Berrick Salome (159b) to as much as 200 acres at Lyneham (156b). It may well be that small amounts could not be expressed conveniently in terms of furlongs, so were given in acres. Round figures like 40, 60 or 100 acres seem to suggest that the amount had only been estimated, but, on the other hand, detailed figures, like $9\frac{1}{2}$, 24, 33 and 156 give the impression of being actual amounts. At two places each comprising more than one holding, both linear dimensions and acres occur:

>   Black Bourton (160): *Pastura iiii quarentenis longa et totidem lata.*
>   Black Bourton (161): *viii acrae pasturae.*
>   Black Bourton (161): *vi acrae prati et totidem pasturae.*
>   Shipton on Cherwell (156): *iii acrae pasturae.*
>   Shipton on Cherwell (224b): *iii quarentenae pasturae.*

A few other variations in the statement about pasture must be noted:

>   Anonymous holding (157): *vi acrae prati et pasturae.*[2]
>   Benson (154b): *Inter prata et pascua et piscarias et silvas exeunt xviii librae et xv solidi et v denarii per annum.*
>   Headington (154b): *De pratis et pascuis iiii librae.*
>   Kirtlington (154b): *De pratis et pascuis et pasnagio et aliis consuetudinibus viii librae.*
>   Taynton (157): *Pastura i leuua longa et dimidia leuua lata.... Inter quadrariam et prata et pascua reddunt xxiiii solidos et vii denarios.*[3]

---

[1] R. W. Eyton, *A Key to Domesday: the Dorset Survey*, pp. 31–5. See also C. S. Taylor, 'An analysis of the Domesday Survey of Gloucestershire', *Bristol and Gloucs. Archaeol. Soc.* (Bristol, 1889), p. 59.

[2] This is not included in the 53 places with pasture measured in acres.

[3] This is included in the 46 places with pasture measured in linear dimensions.

Finally, in the main entry for Oxford (154) we are told that 'all the burgesses of Oxford have pasture in common, without the wall, rendering 6s. 8d.' (*Omnes burgenses Oxenford habent communiter extra murum pasturam reddentem vi solidos et viii denarios*).[1]

Distribution of pasture

The main feature of the distribution, as shown on Fig. 71, is the concentration of pasture in (i) the western and northern parts of the Oxfordshire Cotswolds, and (ii) the western and northern part of the central claylands.[2] There is also a little in the south of the county below the Chiltern escarpment. Taking the distribution as a whole, it is difficult to discern any consistent geographical basis for it. We naturally wonder about the villages with no record of pasture. Did the fallow field, together with the hay from the meadow, suffice for their stock? It is impossible to say, but it does seem unlikely that well over one-half of the villages of the county were without pasture. In any case, pasture is one of the more erratic items of information that the Domesday Book provides. Mr L. F. Salzman's suggestion, made in connection with Cambridgeshire, may be relevant: 'Apparently there was rarely more pasture than was required for the stock; it was therefore not a source of income and it is more likely that it was omitted in many entries for that reason than that these estates were carrying stock with no permanent pasture for their support.'[3]

FISHERIES

Fisheries are mentioned or implied in connection with 26 places in Oxfordshire. Most of the entries give the number of fisheries (*piscariae*) and their money render which ranges from 16d. from one fishery at Walton to 33s. from two at Bampton. Occasionally, the render is stated in eels, or in both money and eels, and in two entries the eels are estimated in terms of the *sticha* or stick of 25. Entries for Benson, Broadwell, Dorchester and Yarnton give a joint render covering both fisheries and other resources. For Shifford and Stoke, eels are mentioned without any reference to a fishery. Fishermen are specifically mentioned at Dorchester,

---

[1] For a discussion of this entry, see F. W. Maitland, *op. cit.* p. 202.
[2] Around Ot Moor, Charlton (224b), Islip (160), Noke (161) and Oddington (160b) each had pasture 3 furlongs by 2 furlongs, which may suggest intercommoning. Beckley (158b) had as much as 1 league by 2 furlongs.
[3] *V.C.H. Cambridgeshire*, 1 (Oxford, 1938), p. 344.

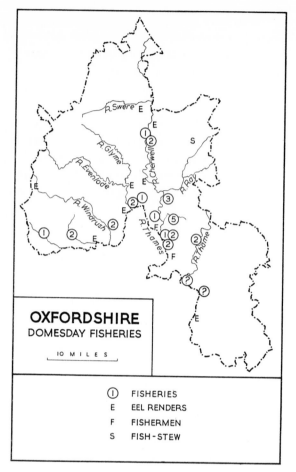

Fig. 72. Oxfordshire: Domesday fisheries in 1086.
The figure in each circle indicates the number of fisheries.

Nuneham Courtenay and at Oxford itself. The Nuneham Courtenay entry groups the fishermen with the villeins and, again, makes no reference to a fishery as such. Whether the fisherman who held a house at Oxford really lived in the city we cannot say. The entries for 20 of the 26 places are given on p. 223. A few of these entries link the fishery with the mill, and in some other entries the account of the fishery, although rendered separately, follows that of the mill. But in addition to these 20 places, there were 6 others with mills that rendered eels although their entries do not mention *piscariae*. These are set out on pp. 224–5, and are also included on Fig. 72. Not included in the above totals is the fish-stew (*vivarium piscium*) at Caversfield (148).

As might be expected, most of the fisheries were situated along the Thames and its main tributaries, particularly the Cherwell (Fig. 72).

Fisheries in Oxfordshire in 1086

(For eel renders from mills, see pp. 224–5 below.)

Aston (160): *Ibi molinum cum piscaria reddunt xxx solidos.*

Bampton (155): *Ibi ii piscariae de xxxiii solidis.*

Benson (154b): *Inter prata et pascua et piscarias et silvas exeunt xviii librae et xv solidi et v denarii per annum.*

Broadwell (160): *Ibi ii molini cum piscaria et pratis reddunt xx solidos.*

Cassington (156): *De molino et piscaria xv solidi et v denarii et clxxv anguillae.*

Cassington (156):[1] *De molino et piscaria xv solidi et v denarii et clxxv anguillae.*

Cowley (160b): *ii piscariae viii solidis.*

Cuddesdon (156b): *Ibi molinum et ii piscariae xii solidis.*

Dorchester (155): *Piscator reddit xxx stichas anguillarum.*

Dorchester (155): *De pratis et piscariis xxii solidi et viii denarii et ix stichae anguillarum.*

Eaton (158): *iii piscarias de xii solidis.*

Headington (154b): *v piscariae de xx solidis.*

Heyford (158): *ii piscariae de nongentis Anguillis.*

Iffley (157b): *Ibi piscaria iiii solidis.*

Nuneham Courtenay (159): *et xxxv villani cum iii piscatoribus habent xiiii carucas et reddunt xxx solidos.*

Oxford (154): *Wluuius piscator i mansionem de xxxii denariis.*

Sandford on Thames (156b): *De ii piscariis x solidi.*

Shifford (155): *et ccl anguillae.*

Stanton Harcourt (155b): *ii piscariae de xxx solidis.*

Stoke (155): *Valuit vi libras T.R.E. modo reddit xii libras et xii stichas anguillarum.*

Walton (159): *Ibi piscaria xvi denariis.*

Yarnton (155b): *Totum T.R.E. valebat x libras. Modo cum piscaria et cum pratis valet xiiii libras.*

WASTE

There are only a few references to wasted land in the Oxfordshire folios. Apart from the wasted properties in the borough of Oxford itself,[2] waste is

---

[1] This may be a duplicate entry.   [2] See p. 227 below.

mentioned in connection with four places and one anonymous holding; of these, only the unidentified *Verneveld* was wholly waste in 1086. The complete list of references is as follows:

Anonymous holding[1] (159b): *Idem tenet de rege ii hidas et dimidiam vastas. Terra iii carucis. Valebat xl solidos.*

Chastleton (156b): *Hae ii hidae vastae sunt et fuerunt cum una virgata terrae nec geldum nec aliamquam consuetudinem regi reddunt.*

Chastleton (157): *In Cestitone habet abbatia i hidam vastam.*

Chastleton (157b): *Idem tenet i hidam in Cestitone de feudo abbatiae. Vasta est.*

Noke (161): *Idem Robertus et Rogerus tenent dimidiam hidam vastam in Acam.*

South Newington (156): *In eadem villa tenet i hidam vastam. Terra est i caruca. Valuit xx solidos.*

Verneveld[2] (154b): *In Verneveld habet rex dimidiam hidam vastam.*

In the borough of Oxford (154), a large number of properties are described as waste, and others are said to render nothing.[3]

Besides these entries which specifically mention waste, there was at Rycote (157b) a holding of 4 hides with land for 4 ploughs, on which were 3 villeins; it had been worth £4, but in 1086 it rendered nothing (*Modo nihil reddit*). Although this holding is not described as waste, the fact that no plough-team was at work and that it rendered nothing suggests that it had gone out of cultivation.

MILLS

Mills are mentioned in connection with 116 out of the 251 Domesday settlements within the area included in present-day Oxfordshire.[4] For each locality the number of mills is given, and also their annual value, ranging from one mill yielding only 20*d.* at Brightwell Baldwin (155b) to another yielding 30*s.* at Wykham (155b). At six places the mills rendered eels as well as money:

Bladon (156): *Ibi ii molini de xiiii solidis et cxxv anguillis.*

Deddington (155b): *Ibi iii molini de xli solidis et c anguillis.*

Eynsham (155): *Ibi molinum de xii solidis et ccccl anguillis.*

---

[1] Unnamed entry; H. E. Salter suggested that this manor lay in Horspath—see *V.C.H. Oxfordshire*, I, p. 422, n. 3.

[2] See p. 194n. above for *Verneveld*.

[3] See p. 227 below.

[4] This number excludes 'the part of a mill' noted in the entry for the unnamed holding on the land of William Levric (160), and also the mill-site at Lashbrook (157b).

Somerton (155b): *Ibi molinum de xx solidis et cccc anguillis.*

Taynton (157): *Ibi ii molini de xxxii solidis et vi denariis et pro anguillis lxii solidis et vi denariis.*

Thrupp (159): *molinum de vi solidis et cxxv anguillis.*

Occasionally a joint render is given, covering both mills and some other resources. At Aston (160), at Cassington (156) and at Cuddesdon (156b), a single render covered both mill and fishery; at Broadwell (160) one render covered the mill, the fishery and the meadow; and at Cowley (157b) a mill and 1 virgate of land together yielded 35s. At Lashbrook (157b) the 'site of a mill rendered 10s.' (*Ibi sedes molini reddit x solidos*). At Oxford itself there were three mills, described as close to the wall (*juxta murum*); of these, one rendered 10s. (158), and the other two 40s. (160b). There is also record of a mill within the city (*infra civitate*) in 1066 (154), but no value is assigned to it.

Fractions of mills were sometimes noted. There was, for example, half a mill on each of three holdings of the bishop of Bayeux at South Newington (156), but we are told nothing of the missing halves.[1] Again, on an unassigned holding belonging to William Levric (160), 'part of a mill' rendered 40d. (*de parte molini xl denarii*), but we are told nothing about the remainder.

Mills are mentioned in two composite entries; at Bloxham and Adderbury (154b) there were 6 rendering 56s. 4d.,[2] and at Dean and Chalford (157b) there were 2 of 5s. The number of mills in each of these composite entries has been divided equally between the constituent villages, but this means that the table of mills set out below may not be accurate, for the number of mills in each category may be affected. And again, we cannot tell whether all the mills entered for a large manor, such as Dorchester, were at one place. But the general impression given by the table cannot be far wrong:

Domesday Mills in Oxfordshire

1 mill	62 settlements	4 mills	3 settlements
2 mills	34 settlements	5 mills	4 settlements
3 mills	12 settlements	6 mills	1 settlement

Note that this table does not include the anonymous holding with part of a mill nor the place with a mill-site.

[1] Two halves were each valued at 16d., and the third at 25d. Yet another entry (161) mentions a mill rendering 25d. Could this have been another half?

[2] Adderbury also had two other mills under its own name (155).

Six mills were entered for Shipton under Wychwood on the Evenlode; 5 mills for Adderbury (on the Sor Brook just above its confluence with the Cherwell), for Chalgrove (on the Thame), for Cropredy (at the con-

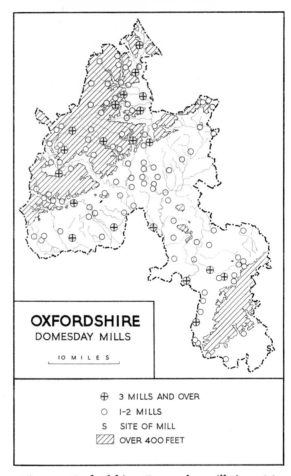

Fig. 73. Oxfordshire: Domesday mills in 1086.
There was also 'part of a mill' on the anonymous holding of William Levric.

fluence of the Highfurlong Brook and the Cherwell), and for Dorchester (on the Thame).

It is clear from Fig. 73 that the Domesday mills were closely associated with the principal rivers of the county; the majority were situated at heights below 400 ft. O.D. Well-marked linear distributions of mills are characteristic of the valleys of the Thames, the Cherwell, the Windrush and the Evenlode, and of many of their tributaries.

URBAN LIFE

The Domesday description of Oxfordshire begins with an account of the city (*civitas*) or vill (*villa*) of Oxford (154), the only place for which burgesses are mentioned.[1] It was situated at the southern tip of a tongue of gravel that slopes down to the alluvium of the Thames and the Cherwell on either side; the ford itself, according to H. E. Salter, was at Hinksey Ferry on the Thames.[2] The city is first mentioned in A.D. 912, and the Domesday account includes a possible reminiscence of its foundation as a borough in the mention of the '8 virgates that were subject to customs in King Edward's time'.[3]

The Domesday entry makes no attempt to state the total number of burgesses, but there are four relevant groups of figures:

(1) We are told, early in the entry, that in 1086 'both within and without the wall' there were 243 houses (*domus*) paying geld, and another 478 so wasted and destroyed that they could not pay (*ita vastae et destructae quod geldum non possunt reddere*). We can then start with the figure of 721.

(2) Then follows a list of 217 tenements called *mansiones murales*, which, in King Edward's time, were 'free of every custom except military service and the repair of the wall'. H. E. Salter argued that, as they did not contribute to the geld, they must be added to the earlier figure,[4] so making a total of 938. We must also note that, of these 217 tenements, 81 were described as waste (*vastae*) and one was said to render nothing.

(3) Then follows a further list of 67 *mansiones* and 13 *domus*. It is possible (though Salter did not consider it to be so) that these also

[1] There are subsidiary entries on fos. 57b, 62, 143b, 157, 158, 158b and 160b. The account of the laws and customs of Oxford at the foot of 154b probably relates to the county as a whole.

[2] See H. E. Salter: (1) 'The ford of Oxford', *Antiquity*, II (Gloucester, 1928), pp. 458–60; (2) *Medieval Oxford* (Oxford, 1936), p. 1.

[3] For the significance of the 8 virgates, see (1) J. Tait, *The Medieval English Borough* (Manchester, 1936), pp. 17 and 89; (2) H. E. Salter, *Medieval Oxford*, p. 27; (3) F. M. Stenton, *Anglo-Saxon England* (Oxford, 1943), p. 522.

[4] H. E. Salter, *op. cit.* p. 22.

were *mansiones murales*,[1] and so must be counted in, making a total of 1,018. We must again note that of these 80 tenements, 26 were waste and 14 rendered nothing.

(4) Finally comes a miscellaneous group comprising (i) the 42 inhabited houses (26 of which were too poor to render anything) together with the 8 waste houses all held by Robert d'Oilly;[2] (ii) the *haga* pertaining to Streatley; and (iii) the burgess at Whitehill who may have been at Oxford. The addition of this 52 brings the grand total to 1,070. We can probably omit the 13 *hagae* that belonged to Steventon in 1066, as they may be included in Robert d'Oilly's total of 50.[3]

This total of 1,070 may well be too large, but it is difficult to argue for less than the conservative total of 938. Whatever be the exact figure, it would seem that, earlier in the eleventh century, Oxford had had a population of, say, between 4,000 and 5,000. But in thinking of its size in 1086, we must make allowance for the wasted houses. In the conservative total of 938, the sum of 559 wasted houses, and another that paid nothing, is included; and in the grand total of 1,070, there are 593 wasted houses and another 40 that paid nothing. On this view, therefore, the population of Oxford in 1086 was only about one-half its former size. Perhaps this is too severe a reduction, for the 478 houses, 'so wasted and destroyed' that they could pay nothing, may not have absolutely disappeared. Whatever view we take, it is clear that the Oxford of 1086 was in reduced circumstances. The cause of the waste and poverty is not clear;[4] some of it was probably the result of clearance to provide a site for the castle that was built in 1070, but Domesday Book tells us nothing of this.[5]

We are given little or no idea of the activity associated with this community. Five churches are mentioned or implied, and these include St Frideswide's, St Mary's and St Peter's. There is also reference to

---

[1] We are told of Wluric's waste dwelling that nevertheless he would repair the wall if need be (*tamen si opus fuerit murum reparabat*).

[2] See p. 229 below.   [3] See p. 230 below.

[4] For a discussion, see H. E. Salter, *op. cit.* pp. 21–2; see also *V.C.H. Oxfordshire*, I, p. 389.

[5] For the topography of eleventh-century Oxford, see (1) E. M. Jope, 'Saxon Oxford and its region' in D. B. Harden (ed.), *Dark-Age Britain* (London, 1956), pp. 235–45; (2) Helen M. Cam, 'The hundred outside the North Gate of Oxford', *Oxoniensia*, I, pp. 113–28, reprinted in *Liberties and Communities in Medieval England* (Cambridge, 1944), pp. 107–23.

Suetman the moneyer,[1] and the account of the customs of the shire on fo. 154b records a render of £20 from the mint. No market is mentioned, but we are told of a render from toll (*theloneum*) in 1066, which may imply one; there is also record of a mill within the city in 1066. That there was a strong agricultural element in the community may be inferred from the fact that all the burgesses held, outside the wall, common pasture yielding 6s. 8d. (*communiter extra murum pasturam reddentem vi solidos et viii denarios*). This pasture, known as Port Meadow, is still so held.

This meagre picture of Domesday Oxford is slightly amplified by four entries that give a few details of what may perhaps be called the suburbs of the city:

(1) *Fo.* 157: The canons of St Frideswide hold 4 hides of the king close to (*juxta*) Oxford.[2] They held them in the time of King Edward. Land for 5 plough-teams. There, 18 villeins have 5 plough-teams, and 105 acres of meadow and 8 acres of spinney. It was, and is, worth 40s. This land never paid geld nor did it belong to any hundred.

(2) *Fo.* 158: The same Robert d'Oilly has 42 inhabited houses in Oxford, both within and without the wall (*tam intra murum quam extra*). Of these, 16 render geld and rent. The others render neither on account of poverty. And he has 8 waste houses and 30 acres of meadow close to the wall (*juxta murum*), and a mill [yielding] 10s. In all it is worth £10 and he holds it as one manor with the benefice (*cum beneficio*) of St Peter.

(3) *Fo.* 158b: The church of St Peter of Oxford holds 2 hides of Robert [d'Oilly] in Holywell. Land for 1 plough-team. There is one plough-team and a half, and 23 men having gardens. There [are] 40 acres of meadow. It was worth 20s. Now 40s. This land never paid geld nor did it render any dues.

(4) *Fo.* 160b: The same [Sawold] holds of the king 2 mills which the king gave him and his wife. They are close to the wall (*juxta murum*) and are worth 40s.

For the purpose of plotting the information, Holywell has been regarded as separate from Oxford. The other three entries have been taken as

---

[1] Coins struck by a man of this name are known from the reigns of the Confessor and the Conqueror—C. L. Stainer, *Oxford Silver Pennies* (Oxford, 1904), pls. IX and XII.

[2] This holding has been placed between Magdalen Bridge and Cowley—S. R. Wigram (ed.), *The Cartulary of the Monastery of St Frideswide at Oxford*, 1 (Oxford, 1895), p. 4. In the present analysis it has not been counted as a separate place.

referring to lands within the ambit, even if not within the walls, of the city itself.

One interesting feature that Oxford shares with a number of other Domesday boroughs is that some urban properties are recorded as belonging to rural manors in the villages around. The implications of this connection have been much debated and lie outside the scope of this chapter.[1] Here we can only record the facts. Most of these connections are entered in the main account of Oxford itself, but a few appear under their respective village headings. The full list is as follows (Fig. 74):

Entered under Oxford (154)		*Entered under rural manors*	
Bletchington	*i mansio*		
Bloxham	*i mansio*		
Burford	*i mansio*		
Hampton	*i mansio*		
Shipton under Wychwood	*i mansio*		
Taynton	*i mansio*		
Twyford	*i mansio; i vasta mansio*		
Risborough	*i mansio*	Risborough (143 b)	*i burgensis*
		Steventon (57 b)[2]	*xiii hagae et unum pratum*
		Streatley (62)	*i haga*
		Whitehill (158 b)[3]	*i burgensis*

This Domesday list is not complete. H. E. Salter showed from non-Domesday sources that of the fourteen houses held by the abbey of Abingdon, and entered in the main account, one was attached to Lyford in Berkshire[4] and another to Tadmarton in north Oxfordshire.[5] Or again,

---

[1] For a review of the controversy, see (1) C. Petit-Dutaillis, *Studies Supplementary to Stubbs' Constitutional History*, I (Manchester, 1923), pp. 78 *et seq.*; (2) Carl Stephenson, *Borough and Town* (Cambridge, Mass., 1933), pp. 81 *et seq.*

[2] The entry for Steventon in the Berkshire folios tells us that 13 *hagae* in Oxford had belonged (*pertinuerunt*) to the manor, but that in 1086 the men of the hundred believed that Robert d'Oilly had become the holder and that they knew no more about it because it was in another shire (57 b). These 13 may therefore be among the 50 tenements entered for Robert in the Oxfordshire folios (158).

[3] This entry does not specifically state that the burgess was at Oxford, but it seems likely.

[4] H. E. Salter, *Medieval Oxford*, p. 16.

[5] H. E. Salter, 'An Oxford mural mansion' in *Historical Essays in Honour of James Tait*, ed. by J. G. Edwards, V. H. Galbraith and E. F. Jacob (Manchester, 1933), p. 301.

it seems that one of Earl Hugh's seven houses was attached to Pyrton in south Oxfordshire.[1] Other connections may be likewise concealed in the terse Domesday summaries. For instance, the seven houses belonging to the archbishop of Canterbury may have been attached to his only Oxfordshire estate at Newington (155).

Fig. 74. Places contributory to Oxford.

For Steventon, see, p. 230, n. 3.

Two of the properties contributory to Oxford were in Buckinghamshire —at Risborough and Twyford; two were in Berkshire—at Streatley and, in 1066, at Steventon. This was somewhat unusual because contributory properties normally lay within the same county as their borough. Wallingford, just across the county boundary in Berkshire, was even more exceptional, for a large number of its houses were attached to Oxfordshire properties.[2] Here, in the valley of the Middle Thames, county boundaries seem to have been ignored by this system in 1086.

[1] H. E. Salter, *ibid.* pp. 301–2.　　　　[2] See p. 276 below.

Salt

MISCELLANEOUS INFORMATION

There are two references to the salt works of Droitwich:

Bampton (154b): *De pasnagio et salinis de Wic et aliis consuetudinibus hominum ix librae et xiii solidi.*
Great Rollright (160b): *iii summae salis ad Wich.*

A. Mawer and F. M. Stenton have traced the probable saltways from Droitwich, and in this connection it is interesting to note that one of the parishes adjoining the Rollrights is named Salford—i.e. 'salt ford'.[1]

Markets

The only market specifically mentioned was that at Bampton (154b) which rendered 50s. (*de mercato l solidi*); it may be relevant to notice that this entry also refers to salt at Droitwich. No market is assigned to Oxford itself, but we are told of a render from toll (*theloneum*) in 1066 (154).

Quarry

A quarry (*quadraria*) is noted in the entry for Taynton (157) where we are told that a payment of 24s. 7d. was made 'between the quarry and the meadows and the pasture'. The Great Oolite quarries at Taynton were worked for high quality freestone throughout the Middle Ages.[2]

Pottery

There was a pottery (*ollaria* or *potaria*, the latter is interlined in the MS.) yielding 10s. at Bladon (156). The exact site of the Domesday kilns has not been located, but pottery of eleventh-century types has been discovered at the nearby settlement of Yarnton, as well as in Oxford.[3]

Grain rents

Grain rent (*annona*) involved considerable sums and was taken within each manor, year by year, as a commutation of ancient corn-rents once

---

[1] A. Mawer and F. M. Stenton, *The Place-Names of Worcestershire* (Cambridge, 1927), pp. 7–8. See also M. Gelling and D. M. Stenton, *The Place-Names of Oxfordshire*, I, pp. 3–4.

[2] See (1) W. J. Arkell, *Oxford Stone* (London, 1947), pp. 54 *et seq.*; (2) E. M. Jope, 'Saxon Oxford and its region' in D. B. Harden (ed.), *op. cit.* pp. 251–4; (3) W. G. Hoskins and E. M. Jope, 'The medieval period' in A. F. Martin and R. W. Steel (eds.), *The Oxford Region* (Oxford, 1954), pp. 114–15.

[3] E. M. Jope, *Oxoniensia*, x (Oxford, 1945), pp. 99.

paid in kind. In Oxfordshire, these grain rents 'were only exacted from the seven great manors to which hundreds were annexed, and they may be regarded as distinctive of the ancient demesnes of the Crown in this county'.[1] The relevant entries occur consecutively on fo. 154b:

(1) Benson: *De annona unius anni xxx librae.*
(2) Headington: *De annona anni viii librae.*
(3) Kirtlington: *De annona anni xx librae.*
(4) Wootton: *De annona anni xl solidi.*
(5) Shipton under Wychwood: *De annona anni xv librae.*
(6) Bampton: *De annona Anni xv librae.*
(7) Bloxham and Adderbury: *De annona anni xxviii librae et x solidi.*

Churches

On fo. 155b, an incidental reference to the church at Eynsham (*ecclesia Eglesham*) appears under the entry for Yarnton. This is the only church, apart from those in Oxford itself, mentioned in the Oxfordshire folios. As already noted, only one priest is recorded, at Great Milton (155). Church-scot (*Circet*) is mentioned in the entries for Benson (154b) and Headington (154b).[2] At the former it was worth 11s. and at the latter 10s. 6d.

Other references

At Eaton (158b), not far from Ot Moor, there were '26 acres of moor' (*morae*)—a very unusual reference. A render from wool and cheeses (*De lana et caseis*) produced 40s. at Bloxham and Adderbury (154b). At Holywell (158b) there were 23 men with small gardens (*hortulos*). In 1066, there had been a render of 6 sesters of honey from the city of Oxford (154b). Finally, from the royal manor of Headington (154b) the king received 30s. as the commutation of a duty known as *Helueuuecha*, but the meaning of this service is not clear.[3] Headington also rendered 100s. and 25d. 'from other customs' (*de aliis consuetudinibus*).

REGIONAL SUMMARY

The present subdivision of Oxfordshire into four main regions follows closely that of Arthur Young in 1809.[4] From north to south, Young

---

[1] *V.C.H. Oxfordshire*, I, p. 375.
[2] For a discussion of church-scot, see F. W. Maitland, *op. cit.* pp. 321–2.
[3] See *V.C.H. Oxfordshire*, I, p. 375.
[4] A. Young, *View of the Agriculture of Oxfordshire* (London, 1809).

recognised the Redland District, the Stonebrash District, the District of Miscellaneous Loams and the Chiltern District. Within each of these areas there are variations, but the broad division into four must suffice for the purpose of summarising the geography of the county in the eleventh century (Fig. 75).

(1) *The North Oxfordshire Upland*

This is an undulating countryside for the most part above 400 ft. o.d., but rising towards the west where the hills of Epwell and Shenlow reach a maximum height of 743 ft. It slopes eastward down to the valley of the Cherwell, and it is much dissected by the right-bank tributaries of that river. The greater part of it is underlain by the ironstone of the Middle Lias formation to which its fields owe their rust-coloured appearance; this is the Redland district of Arthur Young. But there are some areas of heavier soil derived from the clays of the Lower and Upper Lias, and also some areas of lighter Oolitic soils.

Taken as a whole, it has some of the best land in the county, and this was reflected in its high densities per square mile for teams (about 5) and for population (about 11).[1] In this fertile land of many streams it is not surprising to find that there were some villages each with 3 or more mills. Moderate amounts of meadow lay along these streams, and in such a highly cultivated district but little of the original cover of wood remained by the eleventh century.

(2) *The Cotswolds*

Across the widest part of the county stretches a continuous belt of Oolitic Limestone which, as in Gloucestershire, forms a plateau surface sloping gently from north-west to south-east. It reaches its maximum height of 811 ft. o.d. in Rollright on the western boundary of the county, but most of it lies between 350 ft. and 600 ft. This surface is broken by the valleys of the Windrush, the Evenlode, the Glyme, the Cherwell and their tributaries. The Cherwell, and particularly the Evenlode, have cut down into the Lias below to expose clays that contrast with the thin light 'stonebrash' soils of the plateau itself.

The region as a whole was characterised by moderately high densities of teams (3 to 4) and population (9 to 10), and its general prosperity thus

---

[1] But it must be noted that this region included Banbury to which was attached a great royal estate which probably included the resources of Charlbury, a Cotswold village. If we could make allowance for this, the densities would be a little reduced.

resembled that of much of midland England. An exception to this, readily apparent on Figs. 65 and 67, was the Wychwood Forest area where the team and population densities respectively were 0·9 and 3. It was a fairly

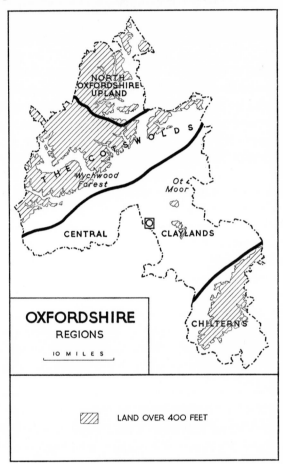

Fig. 75. Oxfordshire: Regional subdivisions.

O indicates the Domesday borough of Oxford.

well-wooded countryside except, surprisingly, to the east of the Cherwell. The valleys were marked by numerous villages, each with a tract of meadow, and some with 100 or more acres apiece. Along the streams, too, mills were frequent; and along the Cherwell, fisheries were relatively numerous.

(3) *The Central Claylands*

Between the Cotswolds and the Chilterns, in a belt some 18 or so miles wide, lies a lowland of Oxford, Kimeridge and Gault Clays. Its undulating surface rarely rises above 400 ft. O.D., and much of it lies below 200 ft.; the low-lying alluvial areas of the Thames, the Windrush, the Evenlode, the Ray and the Thame must frequently have been flooded as they are today. The region is divided by a line of discontinuous hills formed by outcrops of more resistant Corallian, Portland and Purbeck Limestones, sometimes capped by Lower Greensand. These hills lie to the east and south-east of Oxford itself, and rise in places to over 400 ft. O.D., reaching 562 ft. in Shotover Hill.

Within this region, some differences can be discerned—hence Arthur Young's term 'District of Miscellaneous Loams'. The most prosperous district was the Gault Vale in the south with densities of 4·8 for teams and 11·5 for population.[1] The least prosperous area was that to the north-east of Oxford where lay Ot Moor, and we are reminded of its presence by the Domesday entry of '26 acres of moor' at Eaton nearby. Ot Moor, too, may have provided pasture for the villages around. The rest of the area was intermediate between these two extremes. There was a moderate cover of wood in the north, and here too were the royal forests of Shotover and Stowood; the heavily tilled Gault Clay to the south, on the other hand, had but little wood left. Meadow, as might be expected in this area of clay and alluvial valleys, was fairly abundant and widely distributed. In the rivers themselves, particularly in the Thames, there were fisheries, but there were relatively few mills.

(4) *The Chilterns*

Overlooking the Central Claylands is the Chiltern escarpment which, in places, rises to over 800 ft. O.D. and reaches its highest point (837 ft.) not far from Watlington. From the crest, the ground slopes south and south-east to the Thames valley. The Chalk of this dip-slope is mostly masked by stiff Clay-with-flints. At the foot of the escarpment lies a narrow belt of loamy soils, developed on the outcrops of the Upper Greensand and Lower Chalk—the so-called Icknield Loam Belt.

[1] Here, again, it must be noted that this district included Dorchester, the centre of a large manor held by the bishop of Lincoln. The Dorchester entry probably included the resources of outlying estates elsewhere. If we could make allowance for this, the densities of the Gault vale would be a little reduced.

As certain Domesday estates straddled vale and upland alike, it is necessary to consider the whole of south Oxfordshire as one unit.[1] The moderate prosperity indicated by the densities for teams (3·3) and population (8·4) must therefore obscure considerable contrasts within the region. The impression given by the settlement maps (Figs. 66 and 68) may not be quite accurate, but they are probably correct in showing the upland as a relatively empty area, with most villages in the Icknield Loam Belt and in the Thames valley. Much of the woodland entered for these villages probably lay on the Clay-with-flints soils of the plateau. The picture is completed by small quantities of meadow (except for the 200 acres at Pyrton),[2] by mills and by an occasional fishery.

BIBLIOGRAPHICAL NOTE

(1) An early nineteenth-century edition of the text is William Bawdwen's *Dom Boc. A translation of the record called Domesday, as far as relates to the counties of Middlesex, Hertford, Buckingham, Oxford and Gloucester* (Doncaster, 1812).

A recent translation is that by Sir Frank Stenton in *V.C.H. Oxfordshire,* I (Oxford, 1939), pp. 396–426. It is accompanied by a most valuable introduction also by Sir Frank Stenton (pp. 373–95).

(2) Other works that deal with various aspects are:

JAMES PARKER, *The Early History of Oxford, 727–1100* (Oxford, 1885); this contains an elaborate account (pp. 221–304) of 'The description of Oxford in 1086 as given in the Domesday Survey', with a facsimile of part of the Survey.

J. L. G. MOWAT, *Notes on the Oxfordshire Domesday* (Oxford, 1892). This contains some mistaken identifications, but it is still useful.

F. H. BARING, 'Oxfordshire traces of the northern insurgents of 1065', *Eng. Hist. Rev.* XIII (London, 1898), pp. 295–7.

G. H. FOWLER, 'The devastation of Bedfordshire and the neighbouring counties in 1065 and 1066', *Archaeologia,* LXXII (London, 1922), pp. 41–50.

H. E. SALTER, *Medieval Oxford* (Oxford, 1936).

HELEN M. CAM, 'The hundred outside the North Gate of Oxford', *Oxoniensia,* I (Oxford, 1936), pp. 113–28; reprinted in *Liberties and Communities in Medieval England* (Cambridge, 1944), pp. 107–23.

E. A. G. LAMBORN, 'A problem of the Oxfordshire Domesday', *Notes and Queries,* CLXXXVII (London, 1944), pp. 203–5.

[1] See p. 211 above.   [2] See p. 218 above.

A. M. DAVIES, 'Abefeld and Achamsted', *Records of Buckinghamshire*, XV (Aylesbury, 1947–52), pp. 166–71.

A. M. DAVIES, 'The hundreds of Buckinghamshire and Oxfordshire', *Records of Buckinghamshire*, XV (Aylesbury, 1947–52), pp. 231–49.

W. G. HOSKINS and E. M. JOPE, 'The medieval period', being chap. 11 (pp. 103–20) of A. F. Martin and R. W. Steel (eds.), *The Oxford Region* (Oxford, 1954).

E. M. JOPE, 'Saxon Oxford and its region', being pp. 234–58 of D. B. Harden (ed.), *Dark-Age Britain* (London, 1956).

R. V. LENNARD, 'Estates and landlords: a sample county in Domesday England', being chap. 3 (pp. 40–73) of *Rural England, 1086–1135* (Oxford, 1959). The chapter is concerned with Oxfordshire.

(3) A valuable aid to the Domesday study of the county is Margaret Gelling and Doris M. Stenton, *The Place-Names of Oxfordshire*, 2 vols. (Cambridge, 1953–54).

CHAPTER VI

BERKSHIRE

BY EILA M. J. CAMPBELL, M.A.

The Domesday folios for Berkshire were selected for special treatment by Freeman in his *History of the Norman Conquest*;[1] and Round, in his *Victoria County History* introduction to the Domesday Survey, declared that 'the long account of the borough of Wallingford and the very important entry on the local institutions of Berkshire would alone afford material for lengthy disquisition'.[2] But these details, although of great interest to students of law and administration, contribute little to a picture of the countryside in the eleventh century. We are given much the same details as for the other counties of the Exchequer Domesday Book, and the entries, as Domesday entries go, are relatively straightforward. But the usual deficiencies of the text must not be overlooked. Some seventeen entries refer to anonymous holdings, and we cannot tell whether they were at places named elsewhere in the folios or in unnamed localities.[3] Then again, there are as many as twenty lacunae where the number of plough-lands was never filled in.[4] Occasionally entries were made in the margins of the manuscript.[5] But these are exceptions, and the text of the Berkshire folios is, in general, full and complete.

One further complication must be mentioned. The present-day county of Berkshire, in terms of which this study is written, differs from the Domesday county. The main difference is in the west along the border with Wiltshire. The folios of both counties contain entries for the Wilt-shire village of Shalbourne (57b, 73, 74 *bis*, 74b), and the Berkshire portion was not transferred to Wiltshire until 1895. In the same year, the nearby Bagshot, described only in the Berkshire folios (60b), also became

---

[1] E. A. Freeman, *The History of the Norman Conquest of England*, IV (Oxford, 1871), pp. 32–47, 728–36.
[2] J. H. Round in *V.C.H. Berkshire*, I (London, 1906), p. 285. Round's treatment of the Berkshire evidence was unusually geographical. He illumined the Domesday evidence with the local detail set down in the Chronicle of the abbey of Abingdon (*Chron. Mon. Abingdon* (Rolls Ser. 1858), 2 vols.).   [3] See below, p. 243.
[4] E.g. Warfield (57) and Windsor (56b); see p. 251 below.
[5] On fos. 60, 61, 61b, 62b.

part of Wiltshire. Not far away, *Standene* (72), now represented by Standen Manor and North Standen Farm in Hungerford in Berkshire, was surveyed in the Wiltshire folios;[1] so was *Cerletone* (71 b), or Charlton, also now in Hungerford. Further north, the ancient Berkshire lordship of Faringdon included outliers in other counties—Little Faringdon and

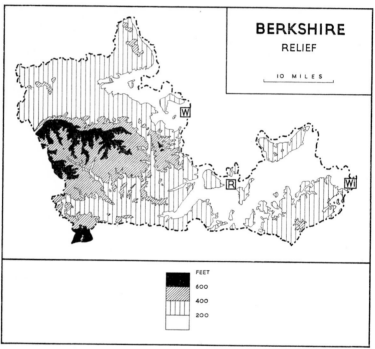

Fig. 76. Berkshire: Relief.
Domesday boroughs are indicated by initials: R, Reading;
W, Wallingford; Wi, Windsor.

parts of Langford and Shilton in Oxfordshire and part of Inglesham in Wiltshire. These outliers were transferred to Oxfordshire and Wiltshire respectively in 1844.[2] In the north-east of Berkshire, part of Caversham

---

[1] *V.C.H. Wiltshire*, II (London, 1955), pp. 149 and 152. See also *V.C.H. Berkshire*, IV (London, 1924), pp. 194–6. Charlton is now represented by Hopgrass Farm and other localities named after the Hopgrass family of the fourteenth century. The Wiltshire folios (72 b) contain a reference to Coleshill, surveyed under Berkshire (59 b, 61, 63)—*V.C.H. Wiltshire*, II, p. 156.

[2] See J. H. Round in *V.C.H. Berkshire*, I, p. 319. The eleventh-century Oxfordshire portion of Langford was surveyed on fo. 154 b. Little Faringdon, Shilton and

(157b) was transferred from Oxfordshire in 1911.[1] There have also been some minor adjustments in the south of the county along the border with Hampshire. In the west, the parish of Combe (46b) did not become part of Berkshire until 1895. Some miles to the east, the district of Stratfield was surveyed partly under Berkshire and partly under Hampshire. In 1894 a portion of Stratfield Mortimer in Berkshire was transferred to Hampshire,

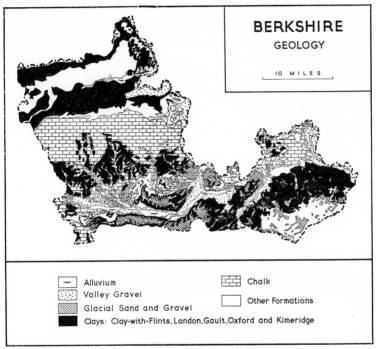

Fig. 77. Berkshire: Surface geology.

Based on Geological Survey One-Inch Sheets (New Series) 236, 254, 255, 267–9; the Oxford special One-Inch Sheet; and Quarter-Inch Sheet 19.

Inglesham are nowhere specifically named in the Domesday Book. See p. 187 above. It is impracticable to assign any of the resources of Faringdon (57b) to Oxfordshire and to Wiltshire in the present analysis; but in any case the small amounts involved would not affect the densities of teams and men in any of the localities concerned.

[1] In the present analysis the Domesday resources of Caversham have been divided between the two counties: one-third of the totals for plough-teams and population have been allocated for plotting and for the calculation of the density maps to Berkshire (Figs. 79 and 81), and the remainder to Oxfordshire (Figs. 65 and 67). The meadow, the mill and the woodland have been plotted on the Berkshire maps (Figs. 83 and 86); 7 of the 20 hides, and 7 of the 21 plough-lands, have also been included in the totals for Berkshire.

and became Mortimer West End. Stratfield Saye and Stratfield Turgis remained in Hampshire.[1] There is also a reference in the Hampshire folios to Swallowfield in Berkshire (48). Finally one other entry must be noted— that for the unidentified *Lonchelei* (61 b), rubricated under Reading hundred in the Berkshire folios;[2] we are told only that 'it belonged to and was appraised with Gatehampton in Oxfordshire but that it gave "scot" in Berkshire' (*Haec terra jacet et appreciata est in Gratentun quod est in Oxenefordscire et tamen dat scotum in Berchescire*). But nothing is said about this arrangement in the Oxfordshire folios.

Within the Domesday county there were some twenty-two hundreds, which seem to have ranged in size from Bray with only 18 hides in 1066[3] to Wantage with apparently as many as 239¾. But there are many uncertainties in the hundredal rubrication of the Berkshire estates, and it is not possible to draw a satisfactory map of the Domesday hundreds.

Settlements and their Distribution

The total number of separate places mentioned in the Domesday Book for the area included within the modern county of Berkshire seems to be 192, including the boroughs of Wallingford, Reading and Windsor. This figure cannot accurately reflect the total number of separate settlements in the county in 1086. In the first place, when two or more adjoining villages bear the same surname today, it is not always clear whether more than one unit existed in the eleventh century. Only once did the Berkshire scribe differentiate between the related units by designating one as 'the other' (*alia*); thus the separate existence of Great Coxwell and Little Coxwell in 1086 is indicated by the mention of *Cocheswelle* (57 b) and *alia Cocheswelle* (57 b). On the other hand, there is no indication that,

---

[1] The Domesday entries in the Berkshire and Hampshire folios have been assigned as follows: Stratfield Mortimer: 47, 62 b; Stratfield (Saye and Turgis): 45 b, 48 *bis*, 49 b.

[2] See p. 245 below. It may possibly be identified with the later Luckley (see *V.C.H. Berkshire*, I, p. 355), but it has not been so identified in the present analysis. See also F. H. Baring, *Domesday Tables* (London, 1909), p. 40.

[3] The Domesday hundred of Bray seems to have been co-extensive with the later parish of the same name; only one estate is actually rubricated under *Brai* hundred— Bray itself (*Brai*, 57). There was also a holding at *Bras* (? Bray, 63 b), assessed at 2 hides, entered under *Benes* hundred—see *V.C.H. Berkshire*, III (London, 1923), p. 137. In the present analysis the figures for *Bras* have been added to those of Bray and plotted at Bray. It has been suggested that *Bras* may represent Binfield, not named in the Domesday Book—see D. Lysons and S. Lysons, *Magna Britannia*, I (London, 1813), p. 167.

say, the Letcombe Regis and Letcombe Bassett of today existed as separate units in the eleventh century; the Domesday information about them is entered under the one name of *Ledencumbe* (57b, 62), although they may well have been separate settlements. The same applies, for example, to the Astons (56b, 60, 63), the Hagbournes (61b, 63), the Moretons (61 *bis*, 63), the Sheffords (62, 62b *bis*, 63), and the Wittenhams (59, 60).[1] The distinction between the respective units of each pair of names appears later in time.[2] In addition to the many dual place-names, there is the difficulty of anonymous holdings; as many as seventeen entries in the Berkshire folios were not assigned to precise localities, and so we cannot tell whether they lay in places mentioned elsewhere in the folios or whether they were in places that go unrecorded by name in the Domesday Book.[3] Finally, there is the problem of the great estates which covered more than one settlement apiece. Thus the entry for Sonning (58) covers not only Sonning itself but also Arborfield, Ruscombe, Sandhurst and Wokingham —all in the hundred of Charlton.[4]

The total of 192 includes a few places about which very little information is given. One of these is Abingdon. The various properties of the abbey of Abingdon in Berkshire are surveyed on fos. 58b–59b, but there is no record of Abingdon itself or of its monks and their agricultural activities. The entry for Barton (58b), however, tells of '10 traders dwelling before the door of the church' (*x mercatores ante portam ecclesiae manentes*) and it is possible that this entry covered Abingdon.[5] The resources of the

---

[1] Aston Tirrold and Aston Upthorpe; East and West Hagbourne; North and South Moreton; East (*alias* Great) and West Shefford; Long Wittenham and Little Wittenham.

[2] The same is true of White Waltham and Waltham St Lawrence, but they have been counted as two settlements in the total of 190; they are not adjoining parishes today, being separated by Shottesbrooke which was also named in the Domesday Book (63b). The figures in the three entries for Waltham (56b, 58, 59b) have been totalled and divided equally between the present-day villages of White Waltham and Waltham St Lawrence, but the church (59b) has been assigned to the former.

[3] This number includes the unnamed manor of Gilbert de Gand in *Roeberg* hundred (62); J. H. Round thought that it could be identified with Bradley and Langley near Hampstead Norris (see *V.C.H. Berkshire*, I, p. 357 n.), but it has been reckoned as an anonymous holding in the present analysis.

[4] See J. H. Round in *V.C.H. Berkshire*, I, p. 301. For a discussion of the Sonning area, see also F. M. Stenton, *Introduction to the Survey of English Place-Names* (Cambridge, 1924), p. 39.

[5] Barton lies to the east of Abingdon. In 1086 its resources included 37¾ plough-teams and its recorded population numbered 136 persons (including the 10 traders).

unidentified *Lonchelei* (61b) were presumably included with those of Gatehampton in Oxfordshire with which it was appraised;[1] similarly the resources of one holding at Bucklebury (63) were presumably surveyed with those of its parent estate at Hampstead Marshall.[2] There are also a number of entries which tell only of plough-lands, plough-teams and men and do not mention any other resources, e.g. the entries for Bessels Leigh (58b), Catmore (60), and Hodcott (61, 62b). Or, again, the entry for Beedon (58b) tells of 9 teams at work on 11 plough-lands and of a recorded population of 27, but does not mention any other resources. Such entries as these suggest that the Domesday record is incomplete. Only once are we specifically told that there was 'nothing else' (*nil aliud*)— in the entry for a holding of 2 hides at Benham (58b), with land for one plough-team, 20 acres of meadow and a recorded population of 5 bordars.

Not all the Domesday names appear on the present-day map of Berkshire villages. Some are represented by hamlets, others by the names of individual houses and farms, or even by the names of topographical features. Thus *Dudochesforde* (63b) is now the hamlet of Duxford in Hinton Waldrist, and the lost village of *Follescote* (62b) is represented by Fulscot Farm in the parish of South Moreton.[3] The name of *Seuacoorde* (58b), another lost village, is preserved today in the name of a piece of ground sloping down to the Seacourt Stream from Wytham Hill in the parish of Wytham.[4] The Domesday *Elentone* (61b) is represented by Maidenhead and Pinkneys Green, which were called Southealington and Northealington respectively in the seventeenth century.[5] *Wibalditone*, rubricated under Blewbury hundred (60b), was identified by Sir Frank Stenton with Willington Farm in Long Wittenham.[6] These are but some of the changes in the Berkshire villages. To them must be added eight

[1] See p. 242 above.

[2] But see *V.C.H. Berkshire*, I, p. 365 n.

[3] M. Beresford, *The Lost Villages of England* (London, 1954), p. 340.

[4] By 1439 all but two of the houses in Seacourt were uninhabited and in ruins; see *Calendar of Entries in the Papal Registers relating to Great Britain and Ireland, Papal Letters*, IX (London, 1912), p. 60, under Seckworth. See also (1) *V.C.H. Berkshire*, IV (London, 1924), pp. 421 *et seq.*; (2) R. L. S. Bruce-Mitford, 'The excavations at Seacourt, Berks., 1939', *Oxoniensia*, V (Oxford, 1940), pp. 31–41; and (3) M. Beresford, *op. cit.* pp. 68–9, 340 and 415.

[5] *Camden's Britannia newly translated into English with large additions and improvements*, published by E. Gibson (London, 1695), p. 144.

[6] F. M. Stenton, *The Place-Names of Berkshire* (Reading, 1911), p. 5. *Wibalditone* adjoined Appleford, of which one of the boundary marks was 'the old dike that lies between Wigbaldincgtune and Appleford'; see J. E. Field, 'Some notes on the Domesday

unidentified names, e.g. *Acenge* (63 b)[1] and *Lierecote* (63 b).[2] Whether these names will yet be located, or whether the places they represent have completely disappeared leaving no record or trace behind, we cannot say.

On the other hand, some villages on the modern map are not mentioned in the Domesday Book. The most striking absence of Domesday place-names is in the hundred of Charlton.[3] Here, for example, as far as record goes, Arborfield was first mentioned in 1220, Ruscombe in 1091, Sandhurst in 1175 and Wokingham in 1227;[4] the localities were in post-Domesday times tythings of the bishop of Salisbury's great manor of Sonning, and 'it is safe to conclude that they are all covered in Domesday by the name of the manor to which they belonged'.[5] In western Berkshire only a few modern place-names were not recorded in the Domesday folios. Hungerford was not named, but J. H. Round showed that it was part of the vill of *Eddevetone* (Eddington, 57b) and that the name Hungerford can be traced back 'to within a generation of Domesday'.[6] The Domesday *Seriveham* (Shrivenham, 57b) may have covered the localities represented in later times by Bourton, Longcot and Fernham, as they were all part of the parish of Shrivenham until 1863.[7]

survey of Berkshire', *Berks., Bucks. and Oxon. Archaeol. Journ.* x (Reading, 1904), p. 86. F. H. Baring, on the other hand, suggested that *Wibalditone* might probably be identified with Didcot (*Domesday Tables*, p. 40).

[1] *Acenge* may possibly be associated with Wasing, see editorial note, 'Berkshire Domesday', *Quarterly Journal of the Berks. Archeol. and Archit. Soc.* III (Reading, 1894), p. 167.

[2] The full list of unidentified Domesday place-names in Berkshire is: *Acenge* (63b), *Burlei* (60b, 63b *bis*), *Crochestrope* (60), *Ebrige* (63), *Lierecote* (63b), *Lonchelei* (61b), *Nachededorne* (57b), and *Ortone* (61b). F. H. Baring suggested that *Burlei* may be a scribal error for *Hurlei*, i.e. Hurley (*Domesday Tables*, p. 40); that *Crochestrope* may have been Westrop (*ibid.* p. 55); and that the scribe substituted the hundred name for the name of the vill in the entry under *Nachededorne*. It is unusual for so large an estate as *Nachededorne* to have disappeared without trace, and Baring concluded that the estate was at Ilsley (*ibid.* p. 39). It has also been presumed to have been at East (formerly Market) Ilsley—see D. Lysons and S. Lysons, *Magna Britannia*, I, p. 169.

[3] Sir Frank Stenton drew attention to the relative paucity of Early English place-names in the south-east of the county (*The Place-Names of Berkshire*, p. 2 and frontispiece).

[4] The dates in this paragraph are taken from E. Ekwall, *The Concise Oxford Dictionary of English Place-Names* (Oxford, 4th ed., 1960).

[5] *V.C.H. Berkshire*, I (1906), p. 301. For a discussion of this area, see also F. M. Stenton, *Introduction to the Survey of English Place-Names*, p. 39.

[6] *V.C.H. Berkshire*, I, pp. 314, 358 n.; see also F. M. Stenton, *The Place-Names of Berkshire*, p. 22.

[7] *V.C.H. Berkshire*, IV, p. 532.

In spite of the complications of lost place-names and additional settlements, the general distribution of Domesday place-names (Fig. 78) was remarkably similar to that of the modern villages except in the Sonning area. It was along the spring-lines of northern Berkshire that the villages clustered most closely in 1086.[1] North of the Berkshire Downs three lines of villages could be discerned. The first lay along the northern edge of the Corallian escarpment and overlooked the Thames; the second, sited on the outcrop of Upper Greensand, overlooked the Vale of White Horse;

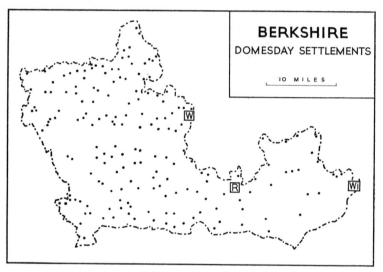

Fig. 78. Berkshire: Domesday place-names.

Domesday boroughs are indicated by initials: R, Reading;
W, Wallingford; Wi, Windsor.

and the third was along the well-marked bench at the foot of the great northward-facing escarpment of the Downs. The higher portions of the Downs themselves appeared as a villageless area; but in the south, where the Chalk surface is lower and broken by many surface streams, e.g. the Lambourn, the Pang and their tributaries, Domesday villages were quite numerous. So were they on the gravel terraces along the Kennet and the Loddon. But in the eastern part of the county, between Reading

[1] The concentration of settlements in the vales of northern Berkshire is even more striking on Sir Frank Stenton's map of the county in the Old English period. Out of a total of 99 sites, no fewer than 60 were in this region; see F. M. Stenton, *op. cit.* frontispiece.

and Windsor, the county was but lightly settled. It is true that the Sonning villages are absent from Fig. 78, but even with them, the pattern would still be a sparse one. This is not surprising in view of the stretches of Bagshot Sand and London Clay (Fig. 77), together with the presence of Windsor Forest itself.

THE DISTRIBUTION OF PROSPERITY AND POPULATION

Some idea of the nature of the information in the Domesday folios for Berkshire, and of the form in which it is presented, may be obtained from the account of Harwell in the hundred of Blewbury. The village was held by two landowners, the bishop of Winchester and Roger d'Ivry, and their respective holdings were as follows:

Fo. 58. The bishop [of Winchester] himself holds Harwell in the demesne of his bishopric. Bishop Stigand held [it] *T.R.E.* Then it was [assessed] at 15 hides; now [it is assessed] at 10 hides. There is land for 8 plough-teams. In the demesne are 2 plough-teams, and 18 villeins and 5 cottars with (*cum*) 6 plough-teams. There, 4 serfs, and a mill yielding (*de*) 30d., and 45 acres of meadow, and in Wallingford 3 closes (*hagae*) yielding (*de*) 15d. *T.R.E.* and afterwards it was worth £12. Now £16.

Fo. 62b. The same Roger [Roger d'Ivry] holds Harwell. Ulvric, a freeman, held [it] *T.R.E.* [It was] then [assessed] at 6 hides. Now [it is assessed] at 3 hides. There is land for 5 plough-teams. In the demesne are 2 plough-teams, and 7 villeins and 7 cottars with 2 plough-teams. There 2 serfs, and a chapel (*capella*). It was worth £12. Now £15.

Fo. 62b. The same Roger holds Harwell of the fee of Earl William. Achi, a freeman, held (it) *T.R.E.* Then [it was assessed] at 5 hides; now [it is assessed] at 2½ hides. There is land for 4 plough-teams. In the demesne is 1 [plough-team], and 5 villeins and 5 cottars with 1 plough-team, and 3 serfs [are] there. It was worth £5. Now £6.

These three entries do not include all the kinds of information that appear elsewhere in the folios for the county. There is no mention, for example, of woodland or of fisheries. But, although not comprehensive, the entries are representative enough, and they do contain the recurring standard items that are found for most villages. These are five in number: (1) hides, (2) plough-lands, (3) plough-teams, (4) population, and (5) values. The bearing of these five items of information upon regional variations in the prosperity of the county must now be considered.

(1) *Hides*

The Berkshire assessment is stated in terms of hides and virgates, and occasionally acres. It is normally given for two dates, 1066 (*T.R.E.* or *tunc*) and 1086 (*modo*); the entry for Watchfield is representative—*Tunc se defendit pro xx hidis. Modo pro x hidis* (59). There are a few entries which note only *Ibi n hidae*, e.g. Lambourn (57b) and Windsor (56b). There is no statement about the hidage of the royal estate at Swallowfield, but a space was left in the MS. (57). On the other hand, figures were entered for three dates for Brightwalton (59b)—*Tunc pro x hidis. Quidam tainus qui ante eum* (Earl Harold) *tenuit geldabat pro xv hidis. Modo pro nichilo.*

The ancient system of assessing villages in multiples of 5 hides, so prominent in Bedfordshire, Buckinghamshire, Hertfordshire, Middlesex and Oxfordshire, is equally apparent in Berkshire. Indeed, as Round wrote, 'the existence of the five-hide unit as the basis of all assessment [in Berkshire] needs no special demonstration; assessments in multiples of that unit are found thick upon the ground'.[1] Thus Stanford Dingley (61) was held for 5 hides, and Hatford (62) for 10 hides.[2] Even when a village was divided amongst a number of owners, the same feature can sometimes be demonstrated. Thus Chaddleworth was held by two lords whose holdings together had amounted in 1066 to 20 hides:

The abbey of Winchester (59b): 16 hides.[3]
Robert d'Oilly (62): 4 hides.

And the hidage of the four estates at Enborne totalled 20 hides:

	Hides	Virgates
(i) William Lovet (61)	3	1
(ii) William, son of Corbucion (61)	10	0[4]
(iii) Ghilo, brother of Ansculf (61b)	3½	0[5]
(iv) Roger de Laci (62b)	3	1[5]

[1] J. H. Round in *V.C.H. Berkshire*, I, p. 286; see also *Feudal England* (London, 1895; reprinted 1909), p. 65.
[2] Unlike the Oxfordshire village of Fifield (*Fifhide*, 157b), the two estates at the Berkshire village of Fyfield (*Fivehide*, 60b *bis*) were each assessed at 10 hides in 1066, but one gelded for only 5 hides in 1086 because King Edward had exempted it (*condonavit*).   [3] Reduced to 10 hides by 1086.
[4] Reduced to 8 hides by 1086.   [5] Reduced to 1 hide by 1086.

Altogether the number of villages assessed in 1066 at either 5 or 10 hides amounted to nearly 50 out of a total of 191.[1] There were also a number of other assessments of 15, 20, 40 and even 60 hides. Thus Stanford in the Vale was assessed at 40 hides (60b), and Barton at 60 hides (58b).[2] We cannot be far wrong in saying that in 1066 the five-hide principle was readily apparent in nearly one-half of the Berkshire villages. It is possible that some villages were grouped in blocks for the purpose of assessment as in some other counties, e.g. Cambridgeshire.[3] In any case, the absence of information about these groups makes it difficult to be definite about the full extent of the five-hide unit in Berkshire in 1066.

Berkshire is one of a block of counties in which the geld of many holdings was reduced after 1066.[4] Thus the liability of Littleworth (*Ordia*, 58) had been reduced from 31 hides to nothing (*modo pro nichilo*), that of the mysterious *Nachededorne* (57b) from 20 hides to '9 hides less 1 virgate', and that of Basildon (57) from 20 hides to 6. A number of complete exemptions from geld, mostly on land held by King William, are also recorded; thus we are told that Cookham (56b), assessed at 20 hides, had never gelded (*Tunc xx hidae sed nunquam geldabat*). Finchampstead, assessed at 5 hides, did not pay geld in 1086 but rendered 'farm' in Reading (*Tunc pro v hidis, modo non geldat sed reddit firmam in Radinges*, 57).

'It is tempting', wrote J. H. Round, 'to connect this phenomenon with the possible ravages of William's host in the early days of the Conquest, but the Berkshire evidence does not, apparently, point in that direction. Indeed the reductions had begun before William's time.'[5] Four entries tell us specifically that the reduction had been made before King Edward died:

Beedon (58b): *Tunc se defendit pro x hidis, modo pro viii hidis. Tamen fuit pro xv hidis, sed rex Edwardus condonavit pro xi hidis ut dicunt.*

Brightwalton (59b): *Tunc pro x hidis. Quidam tainus qui ante eum* (i.e. Earl Harold) *tenuit geldabat pro xv hidis. Modo pro nichilo.*

[1] It must be remembered that these figures relate to the area included within the modern county; the figures for the Domesday county are different.

[2] The whole manor of Barton was assessed at 60 hides in 1066, but it is said to have included land in other localities—Bayworth, Kennington, Shippon, Sugworth and Sunningwell, for which individual assessments are also recorded. The 60-hide manor of Sonning (58) also covered a number of localities—see p. 243 above.

[3] For the Cambridgeshire blocks, see H. C. Darby, *The Domesday Geography of Eastern England* 2nd ed., (Cambridge, 1957), p. 276.

[4] In P. E. Dove (ed.), *Domesday Studies*, I (London, 1888), pp. 100, 111–12, 114–16; see also in *V.C.H. Berkshire*, I, p. 286.

[5] *V.C.H. Berkshire*, I, p. 286.

Fyfield (60b): *Godric tenuit de rege Edwardo et tunc se defendit pro x hidis et modo pro v hidis quia rex Edwardus sic condonavit ut hundredum testatur.*

Stanford in the Vale (60b): *Tunc se defendit pro xl hidis et ut dicunt rex Edwardus condonavit pro xxx hidis. Modo geldat pro vi hidis.*

Generally speaking the reduction in liability was greatest on ecclesiastical estates. Abingdon Abbey secured very substantial reductions for its estates; for example, Barton (58b) was reduced from 60 hides to 40, Cumnor (58b) from 50 hides to 30, Uffington (59) from 40 hides to 14, and Watchfield (59) from 20 hides to 10. The reduction for the bishop of Salisbury's manor of Sonning (58) was even greater—from 60 hides to 24 hides. The abbey of Glastonbury's estate at Ashbury (59b) was reduced from 40 hides to 16 hides 2½ virgates. The bishop of Winchester's estates at Brightwell (58) and Woolstone (58) were each reduced from 20 hides to 10 hides, and his estate at Harwell (58) from 15 hides to 10. These are but some of the reductions in the liability of ecclesiastical estates in the county. The reductions on lay estates were less regular; thus only two of the six estates held in Berkshire by Geoffrey de Mandeville were reduced—Lambourn (62) and Streatley (62) from 30 and 25 hides respectively to 10 hides apiece. But the reductions on some lay estates were sweeping, e.g. Buscot (60), held by Earl Hugh of Chester, fell from 40 hides to 6. Very occasionally the Domesday Book explains the reduction; thus the liability of Clewer fell from 5 hides to 4½, because Windsor Castle was on half a hide (*castellum de Windesores est in dimidiam hidam*, 62b). But generally we can only attribute the many reductions to some form of beneficial hidation.

Interesting as these reductions are, they throw no light on the agricultural realities of the time. The assessment was conventional, and the exemptions by 1086 do not appear to have made it any less so. The variation among a representative selection of ten-hide vills in 1066 speaks for itself:

| | 1086 | Plough- | | Popula- | | Values | |
	Hidage	lands	Teams	tion	1066	*Post*	1086
Avington (62b)	2	[—]	6	17	£5	?	£5
Hatford (62)	10	6	4	17	£8	£5	£10
Sotwell (59b)	10	5	6	21	£8	£8	£12
Warfield (57)	10	[—]	8	13	£12	£12	£6
Woolley (61)	3½	6	6	22	£10	?	£6

The artificiality of the assessment is sometimes emphasised in the Domesday Book itself, e.g.:

Hagbourne (61 b): *Tunc et modo x hidae ibi sed pro vi hidis et dimidia se defendit.*

Hagbourne (63): *Ibi xv hidae sed tunc et modo se defendit pro xii hidis una virgata minus.*

Padworth (63 b): *Ibi vii hidae et dimidia sed tunc et modo geldat pro v hidis et dimidia.*

The present count has yielded an assessment of 2,507¾ hides 6 acres for the area covered by the modern county;[1] the assessment of the borough of Wallingford is not given in the Domesday Book. The gelding hides in 1086 seem to total 1,313⅛ hides 42 acres. Maitland's totals for the Domesday county were 2,473 hides and 1,338 hides respectively.[2] F. H. Baring's estimates for the Domesday county were 2,502 and 1,213 hides respectively.[3] The nature of some entries makes exact calculation difficult. All the figures can do is to indicate the order of magnitude involved, and none of these estimates is strictly comparable one with another.

(2) *Plough-lands*

The normal formula runs: 'there is land for *n* plough-teams' (*terra est n carucis*). There are two variants: once the scribe wrote 'This land is for 4 plough-teams' (*Terra haec est iiii carucis*) at the end of the entry for Shippon (58 b); once the amount was entered in terms of oxen—the entry for an anonymous holding in Wantage hundred notes: *Terra est v bobus. In dominio tamen est una caruca cum i cotario* (58). In each of 20 entries for 19 places the words *Terra est* are followed by a blank space where a figure was never inserted. There are also other entries which make no reference to plough-lands, although they state the number of teams at work, e.g. that for Yattendon (61) where there were 5 teams, and that for *Acenge* (63 b) with 6 teams at work.[4] Including the entries with lacunae,

---

[1] The gelding hides in 1066 seem to total 2,414¾ hides 6 acres.

[2] F. W. Maitland, *Domesday Book and Beyond* (Cambridge, 1897), pp. 400–1 and 409. On another page he declared: 'According to our reckoning, the Oxfordshire and Berkshire of Domesday Book have just about 2,400 hides apiece' (*ibid.* p. 505).

[3] F. H. Baring, *Domesday Tables*, p. 51. Baring's low total for 1066 is partly due to the fact that he did not include a figure for 1086 when the Domesday entry noted only *Ibi n hidis*, e.g. Windsor (56 b).

[4] Where teams but not teamlands are entered for the component parts of manors, we have assumed that the manorial figure for teamlands covers the parts.

there are altogether about 35 places with incomplete figures for plough-lands.[1]

The relation between plough-lands and plough-teams varies a great deal in individual entries. A deficiency of teams was frequent, being found for just over one-half of the Domesday settlements for which plough-lands were recorded. The deficiency was usually small, but in some villages it was considerable, e.g. at Lambourn where there was land for 69 teams but only 49 were at work (57b, 61b, 62, 63).[2]

The number of teams at work exceeded the number for which there was land for about just under one-quarter of the Domesday settlements for which plough-lands were recorded. The excess was generally small, but at Reading there were as many as 62 teams recorded, but only 47 plough-lands (58, 60).

It is impossible to say whether the number of plough-lands represents conditions in 1066, and the number of teams those in 1086. Changes in the values of estates do not throw any light on the problem. On those estates with fewer teams than plough-lands, it is true that the values sometimes fell, but quite often they remained the same, and occasionally they increased, as the following examples show:

		Plough-lands	Teams	Value 1066	Value 1086
Decrease in value	Eddington (57b)	6	3	£6	70s.
	Hampstead Norris (63)	12	10	£12	£10
Same value	Upton (63)	9	8	£13	£13
	Winkfield (59)	20	9	£4	£4
Increase in value	Hatford (62)	6	4	£7	£10
	Uffington (59)	14	12	£15	£26

This is not, of course, conclusive evidence, because other considerations apart from the amount of arable land entered into the value of an estate, and even when ploughs and plough-lands were equal, the value sometimes fluctuated.

The total number of plough-lands recorded for the area covered by the

[1] The figure 35 includes three places without information for either plough-lands or teams—Wallingford, Abingdon and *Lonchelei*.

[2] There is no mention of teams that could be added: the *potest fieri* formula found in the folios for some other counties, e.g. Buckinghamshire, Hertfordshire and Middlesex, is not employed in the Berkshire section of the Domesday Book.

modern county is 1,948⅛.[1] Maitland counted 2,087[2] and Baring 2,109[3] for the Domesday county; both these totals were on a rather different basis from the present estimate. In those entries where there was no mention of plough-lands, or where a space was left for the number, Maitland assumed that there were plough-lands equal in number to the recorded plough-teams.[4] A comparable total on the same basis for the present study is 2,132⅞ plough-lands. Baring also made allowance for the missing plough-lands but the exact basis of his estimate is not clear.

(3) *Plough-teams*

The Berkshire entries, like those of other counties, draw a distinction between the teams at work on the demesne and those held by the peasantry. Several entries seem to be defective. There is, for example, no information about demesne teams at Easthampstead (59b) or at Whistley (59). On the other hand, at one holding at Ardington (62), it is the peasants' teams that seem to have been omitted—*Terra est v carucis. In dominio est una, et vi villani et v servi.* But, for the most part, the record of teams seems to be fairly complete, and it is possible that the absence of teams may well have been but a transitory vicissitude which, caught in the cross-section of Domesday Book, has been preserved for all time; or, equally possibly, it may be due to a scribal error.

Half-teams are occasionally entered, but the moieties are stated not in terms of oxen but as simple fractions; thus, for example, on one holding in Lambourn (61b), the peasantry had 2½ plough-teams. Generally it is the villeins and bordars who are recorded as having plough-teams in Berkshire, but there is a solitary reference to 'a radman with his own plough' (*i racheneste cum sua caruca*) in the entry for Goosey (59).

The total number of plough-teams seems to be 1,891¾, but it must be remembered that this number refers to the area included in the modern county.[5] Maitland estimated the number for the Domesday county at 1,796.[6] Baring's total appears to be 1,881;[7] but, as we have seen, a definitive total is hardly possible.

---

[1] The total includes the figures for the boroughs; see pp. 278–80 below.
[2] F. W. Maitland, *op. cit.* p. 401.
[3] *Domesday Tables*, p. 51.
[4] F. W. Maitland, *op. cit.* p. 410.
[5] This total includes the figures for the boroughs; see pp. 278–80 below.
[6] F. W. Maitland, *op. cit.* p. 401.   [7] *Domesday Tables*, p. 51.

(4) *Population*

The bulk of the population was comprised in the four main categories of villeins, bordars, cottars and serfs. In addition to these main groups, there were the burgesses (see p. 273 below), together with a small miscellaneous group that included priests, *alodiarii*, *buri*, and *coliberti*. Neither

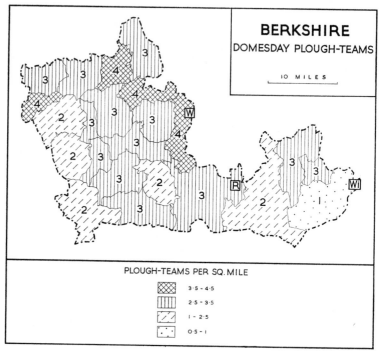

Fig. 79. Berkshire: Domesday plough-teams in 1086 (by densities)

Domesday boroughs are indicated by initials: R, Reading;
W, Wallingford; Wi, Windsor.

freemen nor sokemen are recorded for 1086, but a number of freemen are noted as having held land in the county on the eve of the Norman Conquest.[1] The details of the groups are summarised on p. 258. There are two other estimates of population, by Sir Henry Ellis[2] and by F. H.

[1] There were also 20 thegns; see p. 595 below.
[2] Sir Henry Ellis, *A General Introduction to Domesday Book*, II (London, 1833), p. 423. His grand total for the Domesday county came to 6,324, but it included tenants-in-chief, under-tenants, and burgesses.

Baring[1] respectively, but they are comparable neither with one another nor with the present estimate, which has been made in terms of the modern county. Definite accuracy rarely belongs to a count of Domesday population, and all that can be claimed for the present figures is that they indicate the order of magnitude involved. The figures are those of recorded population, and must be multiplied by some factor, say 4 or 5, in order to

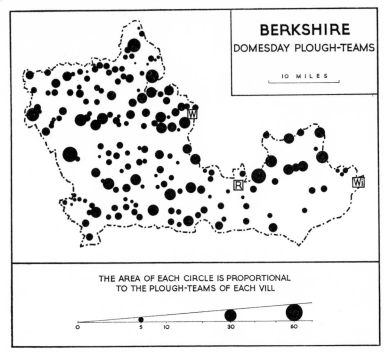

Fig. 80. Berkshire: Domesday plough-teams in 1086 (by settlements).

Domesday boroughs are indicated by initials: R, Reading;
W, Wallingford; Wi, Windsor.

obtain the actual population; but this does not affect the relative density as between one area and another.[2] This is all that a map, such as Fig. 81, can roughly indicate.

It is impossible for us to say how complete were these Domesday statistics. But it does seem as if some people had been left uncounted, for,

---

[1] *Op. cit.* p. 51. Baring counted 2,685 villeins, 2,593 bordars and cottars, and 793 serfs.
[2] But see p. 589 below for the complication of serfs.

as we have seen, a few entries seem to be defective and contain no reference to population.[1] We cannot be certain about the significance of these omissions but, on the whole, they appear to have been very few.

Villeins constituted the most important element in the population, and amounted to 44 per cent of the total.[2] Bordars and cottars comprised 31 per

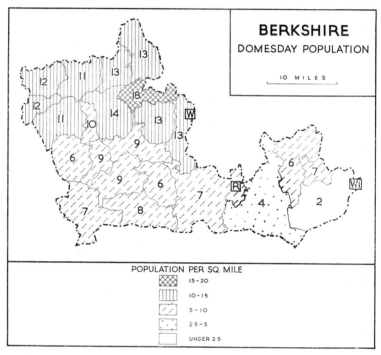

Fig. 81. Berkshire: Domesday population in 1086 (by densities).

Domesday boroughs are indicated by initials: R, Reading;
W, Wallingford; Wi, Windsor.

cent and 11 per cent of the peasantry respectively. The distinction be-tween them is not clear;[3] and it is interesting to note that in the Berkshire folios they are never enumerated together on the same holding. For four

[1] See pp. 243–4 above.

[2] There is one reference to 'land of the villeins' in the Berkshire folios: *In Winteham* (i.e. Wytham) *tenet Hubertus de abbate v hidas de terra villanorum fuerunt iiii et gelda-verunt cum hidis Manerii* (58b).

[3] For a discussion of the differences between bordars and cottars see (1) F. W. Maitland, *op. cit.* pp. 39 *et seq.*; (2) P. Vinogradoff, *English Society in the Eleventh Century* (Oxford, 1908), pp. 456 *et seq.*

hundreds, namely Beynhurst, Blewbury, *Eletesford* and Wantage, cottars were recorded, but not bordars; in all the other hundreds, apart from Ganfield, there were bordars but no cottars.[1] It seems probable that in the Berkshire folios the two terms were used as alternatives. Serfs amounted to about 13 per cent of the total population, and present no special feature of interest for our purpose.

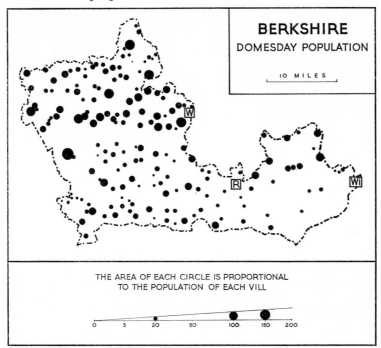

Fig. 82. Berkshire: Domesday population in 1086 (by settlements).

Domesday boroughs are indicated by initials: R, Reading; W, Wallingford; Wi, Windsor.

The miscellaneous category is a small but varied one. One of the most interesting groups is that of the 24 coliberts (*coliberti*) at Barton (58b) and the 18 *buri* at Letcombe (57b);[2] they were in some ways intermediate between serfs and villeins. Among the smaller groups there were the

---

[1] For a discussion of the entries mentioning cottars on holdings rubricated under Ganfield hundred, see F. H. Baring, *op. cit.* pp. 40–1.

[2] It was Maitland who first showed that in the Domesday Book the two terms were synonymous—F. W. Maitland, *op. cit.* pp. 36–7. See also P. Vinogradoff, *op. cit.* pp. 468–9. See p. 314 below.

' 10 traders dwelling in front of the door of the church' (*x mercatores ante portam ecclesiae manentes*) noted in the entry for Barton near Abingdon (58 b), and the 5 *alodiarii* at Swallowfield (63 b).[1] There was also the rad-man with his own plough (*i racheneste cum sua caruca*) at Goosey (59). Radmen are found mainly in the western counties of Gloucester, Hereford,

Recorded Population of Berkshire in 1086

A. Rural Population

Villeins	.	.	.	.	.	.	2,687
Bordars	.	.	.	.	.	.	1,868
Serfs	.	.	.	.	.	.	804
Cottars	.	.	.	.	.	.	734
Miscellaneous	.	.	.	.	.		67
Total	.	.	.	.	.	.	6,160

Details of Miscellaneous Rural Population

Coliberts	.	.	24	Priests	.	.	5
Buri	.	.	18	Knights	.	.	3
Mercatores		.	10	English knight	.	1
Alodiarii	.	.	5	Radman	.	.	1
				Total	.	.	67

B. Urban Population

The apparently rural element in the boroughs—villeins, bordars, and serf—are also included in the table above.

WALLINGFORD	Burgesses mentioned but not enumerated. For details of the contributory properties, see pp. 276–7 below.
READING	30 *hagae*, 29 *masurae*, 64 villeins, 38 bordars; see pp. 278–9 below.
WINDSOR	95 *hagae*, 22 villeins, 2 bordars, 1 priest, 1 serf; see pp. 280–1 below.
OF UNCERTAIN LOCATION	9 *hagae* entered under Faringdon; 51 *hagae* entered under Newbury; 12 *hagae* entered under Thatcham. See p. 273 below.

[1] For a discussion of the meaning of the term *in alodio*, see (1) F. W. Maitland, *op. cit.* pp. 153–4; (2) P. Vinogradoff, *op. cit.* pp. 411–14.

Shropshire and Worcester, and 'it is unusual to find one of this class so far east';[1] they did riding service for their lords and also carried on the agricultural work of their holdings,[2] sometimes with the help of villeins and bordars of their own.[3] The other smaller categories consisted of 5 priests,[4] 3 knights (*milites*) at Bray (57) and an English knight (*miles anglicus*) at Brimpton (62).[5]

(5) *Values*

The value of an estate is usually given in a round number of pounds or shillings, sometimes for three dates (1066, 1086 and an intermediate date), and sometimes only for 1066 and 1086. The following examples illustrate the variation in formulae:

Windsor (56b): *T.R.E. valebat xv libras et post vii libras. Modo xv libras.*
Lollingdon (62): *Valuit c solidos et post xl solidos. Modo lx solidos.*
Fawley (i) (57b): *Valet et valuit xl solidos.*
     (ii) (60): *Valet et valuit semper vi libras.*
Beckett (60): *Valuit iiii libras et modo similiter.*
Southcot (61): *Valuit iiii libras. Modo c solidos.*

For some holdings only one value (*modo*) is given, and it seems that they were valued with other estates at the earlier dates. Thus only a 1086 value was entered for Eling; in 1066 it was held in Hendred and had been placed in Harwell (*misit in Harewelle*) after the Norman invasion (62b). No separate valuation was made of five holdings; three of these holdings were 'appraised' (*appreciata*) with other estates—*Lonchelei* (61b) with Gate-hampton in Oxfordshire, an anonymous holding in Reading hundred (58) with Swallowfield (*Appreciata est cum Solafel quod est capitum manerii*), and a holding at Wokefield (58) with Aldermaston. The omission of a statement about values for two holdings at Chilton (59, 61b) may indicate nothing more than a scribal error.

[1] See J. H. Round in *V.C.H. Berkshire*, I, p. 303.
[2] P. Vinogradoff, *op. cit.* pp. 69–71.
[3] See H. C. Darby and I. B. Terrett (eds.), *The Domesday Geography of Midland England* (Cambridge, 1954), p. 126.
[4] It is sometimes difficult to decide whether to include a priest in our count. Priests at the following places have been so included: Ashbury (59b), Brightwalton (59b), Faringdon (57b), Hampstead Norris (63) and Shrivenham (57b). The priests at Basildon (57) and Cholsey (56b) have been excluded, so have named priests, e.g. Edred the priest at Sparsholt (57). See p. 272 below.
[5] Knights holding land, e.g. the knight (*miles*) at Beedon (58b), have been counted as landholders and excluded from the present totals.

With four exceptions, the Berkshire values are entered as plain statements of money. At Cholsey (56b) and at Sutton Courtenay (57b) payments were reckoned 'by tale' (*ad numerum*); at Hanney (61b) one estate, worth £6, rendered also an ounce of gold—*Valuit et valet vi libras et tamen reddit vi libras et unciam auri*; finally, an estate at Waltham (56b) rendered £15 of weighed money (*ad pensam*).

Many Berkshire estates fell in value after 1066. Some were worth only about 25 to 50 per cent of what they had been worth, and a few had suffered even more (Fig. 162); but no estate in the county was completely wasted at the intermediate date.[1] F. H. Baring attributed the falls in value of some estates at the intermediate date to the passage of the Norman armies.[2] By 1086 many estates had recovered fully or in part, and some were even more prosperous than before. In spite of the general recovery by this date, the values of some estates remained low and a few had decreased further; the figures for Bishop Osbern's estate at Buckland (58b) were £16, £12, £8.

Many of the new landowners were able to obtain from their estates a payment in excess of the value. Fourteen entries for 12 places and one anonymous holding give the value in 1086, and then go on to say that the estate paid a greater sum; the increase was sometimes substantial, as the following examples show:

| | Values | | | Payment |
	1066	Inter-mediate	1086	1086
Bucklebury (57)	£11	—	£11	£16. 10s.
Cookham (56b)	£50	50s.	£36	£45
Sutton Courtenay (57b)	£30	£20	£50	£60

Generally speaking, the greater the number of plough-teams and men on an estate, the higher its value, but it is impossible to discern any constant relationship, as the table on p. 261 for five estates, each yielding £3 in 1086, shows.

It is true that the variations in the arable, as between one holding and another, did not necessarily reflect variations in total resources, but even taking the other resources into account the figures are not easy to explain.

[1] The only mention of waste in the Berkshire folios is that of a waste *haga* in Wallingford—see p. 276 below.
[2] *Domesday Tables*, pp. 48, 210. See p. 569 below.

	Teams	Population	Other resources
Easthampstead (59b)	5	14	Wood
Hodcott (61)	1	3	—
Pusey (59b)	2	3	—
Ufton Nervet (61)	7	14	Meadow, Wood
Ufton Nervet (61b)	3	13	Meadow

It is true that variations in the arable, as between one estate and another, did not necessarily reflect variations in total resources, but even taking the other resources into account the figures are not easy to explain.

Conclusion

The Domesday hundreds, as far as possible, have been adopted in constructing the density maps, but a number of modifications have been made in detail, e.g. the portion of Caversham transferred from Oxfordshire in 1911 has been included with Reading hundred. The result of these modifications has been to produce twenty-three units as a basis for calculating densities.

Of the five standard formulae, those relating to plough-teams and population are most likely to reflect something of the distribution of wealth and prosperity throughout the county in the eleventh century. Taken together, they supplement one another to provide a general picture (Figs. 79 and 81). The essential feature of both maps is the contrast between the north of the county and the south-east. In the northern vales, the densities of both teams and men were high; those of plough-teams ranged mostly between 3 and 4 per square mile, and those of population between 11 and 14 and even up to 18. In the south-east, on the other hand, where the law of Windsor Forest lay heavily on the land, the density of teams was everywhere below 3; that of population was correspondingly low, never rising above 7 per square mile and falling to below 2. Between these two broad areas, in the Downlands and in the Kennet-Loddon area, densities of both teams and men were roughly intermediate.

Figs. 80 and 82 are supplementary to the density maps, but it is necessary to make one reservation concerning them. As we have seen on pp. 242–3, it is possible that some Domesday names may have covered two or more settlements, e.g. the present-day villages of East and West Shefford are represented in the Domesday Book by only one name (62, 62b bis, 63). Then, too, Sonning and its components are represented by only one name.[1] A few of the symbols should therefore appear as two or more smaller symbols, but this limitation does not affect the main pattern of the maps. Generally speaking, they confirm and amplify the information of the density maps.

Types of entries   WOODLAND AND FOREST

The amount of woodland on a holding in Berkshire was normally recorded in terms of an annual rent in swine paid to the lord for the right of pannage in his wood. The usual formula is 'Wood yielding *n* swine' (*Silva de n porcis*). One entry, Windsor (56b), specifically mentions pannage, and it tells first of 'wood rendering 50 swine from pannage' (*Silva de l porcis de pasnagio*) and later of 'as much woodland as renders 5 swine from pannage' (*tantum silvae unde exeunt v porci de pasnagio*).[2] The number of swine rendered ranged from only one pig at a holding in Ufton Nervet (61)[3] to 300 swine at Sonning (58). The Berkshire swine numbers, e.g. 5, 10, 15, 20, 40, 50, 100, 120, are 'suspiciously round',[4] and may indicate estimates rather than numbers actually rendered. Moreover, we cannot tell the relation of these renders to the total number of swine feeding in the woodland.[5]

There are a few entries that record the presence of wood in other ways. Twelve entries mention 'Wood for fencing' (*Silva ad clausuram*), e.g. that for Inkpen (61).[6] A 'small wood' (*parva silva*) was noted for Ashbury (59b), for a holding at Shefford (62b), and also for each of two holdings at Inglewood (62, 63b). The entry for Windsor (56b) refers to the 'third part of one dene' (*terciam partem unius denae*), but we hear nothing at all about the remaining two-thirds. The wood of Caversham (157b)[7] was measured in terms of linear dimensions, the normal method in the Oxfordshire folios; so was that of Charlton (71b), then in Wiltshire.

---

[1] See p. 243 above.

[2] The entry for Windsor (56b) notes also 'other woodland is placed in enclosure' (*alia silva missa est in defensa*); see p. 264 below.

[3] Wood is not recorded for a second holding at Ufton Nervet (61b).

[4] J. H. Round in *V.C.H. Berkshire*, I, p. 308.   [5] See pp. 596–7 below.

[6] The full list is: Calcot (60), Combe (46b), *Ebrige* (63), Enborne (61), Farnborough (59), Faringdon (57b), Ilsley (62), Inkpen (61), Little Coxwell (57b), Remenham (57), Shalbourn (57b) and Shefford (62). Other holdings at Enborne (61, 62b) and at Shefford (63) rendered swine from pannage.

[7] Today Caversham lies partly in Oxfordshire and partly in Berkshire; see p. 187 above. In the present analysis the Domesday woodland of Caversham has been plotted on Fig. 83.

The entry in the Wiltshire folios (72) for Standen records 6 acres of wood (*vi acrae silvae*), and tells also of a wood there which had belonged to Bedwyn, a manor in Wiltshire—*Ibi est silva; pertinuit ad Beduine T.R.E.* The main entry for Bedwyn describes this wood as a 'grove' and records its dimensions—*lucus habens dimidiam leugam longam et iii quarentenas latam* (64b). Finally, it should be noted that no money rent from woodland was recorded in the Berkshire folios.

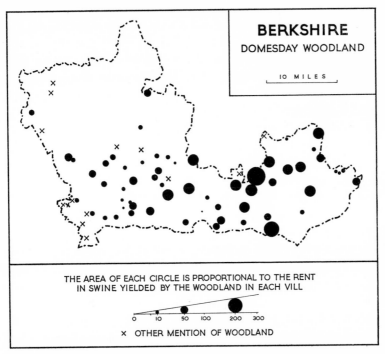

BERKSHIRE

DOMESDAY WOODLAND

10 MILES

THE AREA OF EACH CIRCLE IS PROPORTIONAL TO THE RENT
IN SWINE YIELDED BY THE WOODLAND IN EACH VILL

0   10   50   100   200   300

×   OTHER MENTION OF WOODLAND

Fig. 83. Berkshire: Domesday woodland in 1086.

Where the wood of a village is entered partly in terms of a swine render and partly in some other way, only the swine render is shown.

Distribution of woodland

The outstanding feature of Fig. 83 is the concentration of wood in the south of the county, and on many southern manors there were considerable swine renders for right of pannage. In one area of the south-east, Fig. 83 is misleading. The large symbol of 300 swine for Sonning (58) should be distributed among its several components which were not separately surveyed in the Berkshire folios.[1] Furthermore, Windsor Forest was in this part of the county, and it may well have contained wood that lay outside the scope of the Domesday enquiry.

In contrast to the well-wooded south, the north of the county seems, from Domesday evidence at any rate, to have had but little wood, and there was hardly any at all entered for the northern vales and the higher drift-free portion of the Chalk downland. F. H. Baring thought that there was 'at least strong ground for suspicion' that this lack of mention was due in part to 'omission in the returns'.[2] Several eleventh and twelfth century charters support the view that the Domesday record of wood in northern Berkshire is incomplete.[3] There was wood at Bagley and Cumnor in the great loop of the Thames, where the Domesday Book records none, and this district supplied timber for building in Oxford 'at times throughout the Middle Ages'.[4]

But while fully recognising the possibility of omission from the Domesday record, we must remember that this northern area was certainly the most closely settled part of the county, with the highest densities of teams and population; and we might therefore reasonably expect the woodland to have been largely cleared by 1086. Certainly, in the twelfth century, Letcombe (57b, 62) in the north, for example, was dependent for pannage and timber upon Chaddleworth (59b, 62) to the south, and it is interesting to note that there was no Domesday wood at the former but a render of 10 swine from the wood at the latter.[5]

Forests

The royal forests of Berkshire are mentioned only incidentally in the Domesday Book. Three entries are of particular interest because they refer to Windsor Forest:

Cookham (56b): Wood yielding 100 swine, and the other half is in the forest of Windsor (*Silva de c porcis et alia medietas est in foresta de Windesores*).

Windsor (56b): Wood yielding 50 swine from pannage and other woodland

[1] See p. 243 above.   [2] *Domesday Tables*, p. 41.
[3] See *Chron. Mon. Abingdon* (Rolls Ser. 1858), I, pp. 126, 268–70; II, pp. 10, 113–14, 219–20, 247. Bagley is not a Domesday place-name.
[4] E. M. Jope, 'Saxon Oxford and its region', in D. B. Harden (ed.), *Dark-Age Britain* (London, 1956), p. 247.
[5] *Chron. Mon. Abingdon* (Rolls Ser. 1858), II, pp. 189–90. See also *V.C.H. Berkshire*, I, p. 310.

is placed in enclosure (*Silva de l porcis de pasnagio et alia silva missa est in defensa*).

Winkfield (59): Of this land 4 hides are in the king's forest (*De hac terra sunt iiii hidae in foresta regis*).[1]

Two other entries show that forest law had already been extended to the north and west of the county, and we know that in later times the 'royal forest of Berkshire' included localities north and west of the Kennet.[2] The details are:

Bucklebury (61 b): The same W[alter] (i.e. Walter son of Other) holds Bucklebury for 1 hide; and a certain man of his holds it of him. It belongs to the forest (*In foresta jacet*) and it never paid geld, so the shire [moot] testifies. Aluila Dese held it of King Edward. There is 1 plough-team in demesne. It is and was worth 7s. 6d.

Kintbury (61 b): The same W[alter] (i.e. Walter son of Other) holds half a hide, which King Edward gave to his predecessor out of his feorm, and freed from all dues in consideration of the wardenship of the forest (*propter forestam custodiendam*) except such forfeiture to the king as [is due from] theft (*Latrocinium*), manslaughter (*homicidium*), housebreaking (*Heinfara*) and breach of the peace (*fracta pax*). It is worth 5s.

Finally there is an indirect reference to the royal forests in the account of the customary payments from the county set out on fo. 56b; the fine for failing, when summoned, to drive deer for the king's hunting (*ad stabilitionem venationis*) was 50s.

MEADOW

Types of entries

The entries for meadow in the Berkshire folios are for the most part straightforward. For holding after holding the same phrase is repeated monotonously—'*n* acres of meadow' (*n acrae prati*). The amount of meadow in each vill varied from only one acre at *Ortone* (61 b) to as many as 374 acres at Milton (59). Most of the villages with meadow had substantial amounts; eighteen villages had between 100 and 200 acres apiece, and fourteen had each more than 200 acres. As in the case of other counties, no attempt has been made to translate these figures into modern

[1] The reference in the Abingdon Chronicle is more telling—*de villa Winekefeld, versus Wildesoram sita, regis arbitrio, ad forestam illic amplificandam, iiii hidae tunc exterminatae sunt*. See *Chron. Mon. Abingdon* (Rolls Ser. 1858), II, p. 7.

[2] J. C. Cox, *The Royal Forests of England* (London, 1905), pp. 266 and 287.

acreages. The Domesday acres have been treated merely as conventional units of measurement, and Fig. 84 has been plotted on that assumption.

The entry for Shellingford (59b) mentions a money payment from meadow—*ciiii acrae prati et de aliis pratis xii solidi et vi denarii.* So does that for Steventon (57b) to which had belonged in Oxford one meadow yielding 20s. (*unum pratum de xx solidis*).[1]

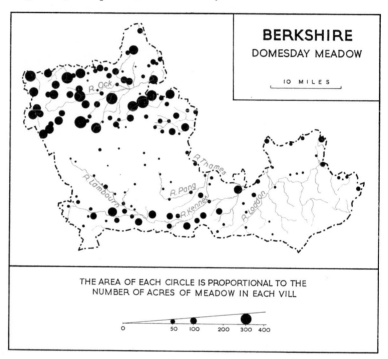

Fig. 84. Berkshire: Domesday meadow in 1086.

Where the meadow of a village is entered partly in terms of acres and partly in some other way, only the acres are shown.

Distribution of meadowland

Fig. 84 shows that by far the greatest amount of meadow lay in the north of the county, especially in the Vale of White Horse watered by the Ock and its tributaries and by the Thames itself; here, for example, was Milton (59) with 374 acres, Sparsholt (57, 57b, 59, 60b, 61b, 63) with 366

[1] See p. 230n. above.

acres, Buscot (60) with 300 acres, Hanney (59, 60 *ter*, 61 b) with 292 acres, and Buckland (58b) with 220 acres. Downstream along the Thames there was a succession of settlements, each with some meadow; Reading (58, 60), near the confluence of the Thames and the Kennet, had as much as 165 acres, but most Thames-side villages had much smaller quantities. In the Kennet valley there were also a number of villages with substantial amounts, e.g. Benham (58b, 63, 63b) with 200 acres, Thatcham (56b) with 147 acres, and Aldermaston (58) with 124 acres. In contrast to these well-watered vales, the valleys of the Berkshire Downs carried very little meadow; in the Lambourn valley, Bockhampton (62b, 63b) and Lambourn (57b, 61b, 62, 63) had only 5 acres apiece. Further east, there were Compton (57b) with 4 acres, Farnborough (59) with 5 acres, Ashridge (60) with 6 acres, and Ilsley (60, 61, 62 *bis*) with 7 acres. There was also very little meadow in the extreme south-east of the county, in the Windsor Forest area.

PASTURE

Pasture is mentioned in connection with only eight settlements in Berkshire. For five of these, money renders were recorded:

Barton (58b): *xv solidi de pastura.*
Goosey (59): *de pastura xvi denarii.*
Reading (58): *De pastura xvi solidi et vi denarii.*
Stanford in the Vale (60b): *pro pastura xxxii denarii.*
Wittenham (60): *pro herbagio v solidi.*

At Charlton (71b), surveyed in the Wiltshire folios, there was pasture, 4 furlongs by one; and at Standen (72), also in Wiltshire, there were 10 acres of pasture. Finally, pasture for horses was mentioned in connection with a claim for land at Kintbury (57b):

Henry de Ferrers holds of this manor 43 acres of land which were in the king's feorm *T.R.E.* according to the testimony of the shire [moot]. They state also that the sheriff Godric made this into pasture for his own horses (*fecit ibi pascua equis suis*), but by what warrant they do not know.

These eight entries stand in great contrast to the regular statements about pasture in Buckinghamshire and Middlesex. It seems that pasture was mentioned in the Berkshire folios only when the grazing was not subject to free common right and had to be paid for, or when it was a matter for special comment.

FISHERIES

Fisheries (*piscariae*) are specifically mentioned in connection with 34 places in Berkshire; one of these places, *Burlei* (60b), cannot be identified. The number of fisheries and their annual rent were normally entered. Generally the rent was paid in money, and the render ranged from 5*d.* yielded by the fishery at Shippon (58b) to 34*s.* 2*d.* by that at Appleton (61b).

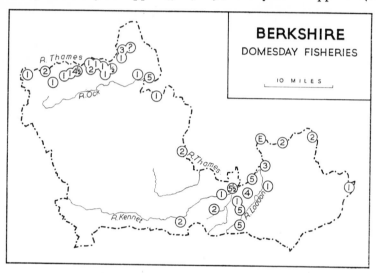

Fig. 85. Berkshire: Domesday fisheries in 1086.

The figure in each circle indicates the number of fisheries; there was also a fishery at *Burlei*.

The entry for Cumnor (58b) does not record the number of fisheries—*de piscariis xl solidi*; no value was entered for the fishery at Draycott (59). At Faringdon (57b) a mill and a fishery were valued jointly—*molinum cum piscaria de xxxv solidis*. At three places the render was paid in eels, and at two of these mills also returned eels:

Shinfield (57): *molinum de v solidis et cl anguillis et v piscariae de quingentibus et l anguillis.*

Wargrave (57): *iii piscariae de iii Milibus anguillarum.*

Whistley (59): *molinum de v solidis et ccl anguillis . . . et piscaria de ccc anguillis.*

Half-fisheries are mentioned in connection with three places, but it is not possible to combine the fractions in any intelligent way. At Fyfield there

were two estates (60b *bis*); one is noted as having half a fishery yielding
11*s.* 8*d.* (*dimidia piscaria de xi solidis et viii denariis*), but the other contains
no reference to a second half. Two entries for Buckland tell respectively
of half a fishery yielding 3*s.* (59b) and of 4 fisheries yielding 20*s.* 6*d.*
(58b). At Reading there seems to have been a total of 5½ fisheries, 3 on
the holding of the king (58) and 2½ on that of the abbey of Battle (60).
In addition to the 34 places for which fisheries were specifically recorded,
there would seem to have been one at Remenham (57), where the mill
paid a rent partly in money and partly in eels—*molinum de xx solidis et
mille anguillarum.*

Fig. 85 shows that the fisheries were along the Thames, mainly above
Wallingford, and along the Kennet and the Loddon and their tributaries.

MILLS

Mills are mentioned in connection with 94[1] out of the 192 Domesday
settlements within the area covered by modern Berkshire. For each
locality the number of mills was entered and also their annual value,
which ranged from one mill yielding 30*d.* at Shellingford (59b) to others
yielding much larger sums; the mill at Boxford (63) yielded 27*s.* 6*d.*, and
another at *Ebrige* (63) rendered 30*s.* Mills at Remenham (57), at Shinfield
(57) and at Whistley (59) paid rent partly in money and partly in eels.[2] At
Faringdon (57b) a mill with a fishery yielded 35*s.* (*molinum cum piscaria
de xxxv solidis*). Three mills did not pay rent (*sine censu*); of these, one
was at Stratfield Mortimer (62b) and the other two were at Barton (58b).
Those at Barton, an estate of the abbey of Abingdon, 'belonged to the
court of the abbot without dues' (*in curia abbatis sine censu*).[3]

Fractions of a mill are occasionally recorded. Thus each of the three
holdings at Coleshill (59b, 61, 63) had one-third part of a mill (*tercia
pars unius molini*) and each third yielded (*de*) 10*s.* At Padworth, there
seems to have been a total of 3 mills, half-a-mill on the holding of William
of Eu (61) and 2½ mills on that of Stephen son of Eirard (63b). But it

---

[1] This figure includes the unidentified *Acenge* (63b) and *Ebrige* (63), but excludes
the unnamed holding of the bishop of Salisbury in Wantage hundred (58); F. W. Ragg
thought that this holding was probably in East Hendred—*V.C.H. Berkshire*, I, p. 335,
n. 6; but it has been counted as an anonymous holding in the present analysis.

[2] For the details of these entries, see under Fisheries above.

[3] There were two other mills yielding 40*s.* at Barton (58b).

is not always possible to assemble the fractions in such a comprehensible manner. Thus 4½ mills were entered under Shefford—one on the holding of Robert d'Oilly (62), a half on that of Roger d'Ivry (62b), one on that of Hugh de Port (63) and two on that of Aiulf the sheriff (63)—but we are given no clue to the missing half. There might also have been an odd half-mill at Burghfield, which consisted of two estates; the folios record

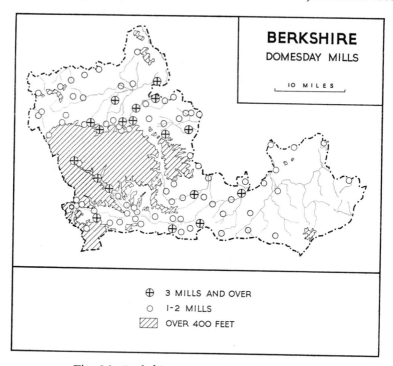

Fig. 86. Berkshire: Domesday mills in 1086.

There were also mills at *Acenge*, at *Ebrige* and on an anonymous holding in Wantage hundred.

one mill on that held by Henry de Ferrers (60b) and half a mill on that of Ralf de Mortemer (62b). But it seems more likely that there was really only one mill at Burghfield, shared equally between the two estates, the more especially as the yields given in the respective entries were the same i.e. 5s. 10d. In the entry for Ralf de Mortemer's portion, the word '*dimid*' is interlined, suggesting that the profits of the mill 'had also been equally divided, and that when Domesday enters a mill as appurtenant to the manor it may only mean a share of a mill'.[1] Finally, there seems to have been an odd fraction at Greenham (60b); for this place the scribe wrote *molinum de xi solidis et ii denarii minus*, but subsequently the words *et dimidia* were interlined.

Three entries in the Berkshire folios refer to disputes about mill ownership. A mill yielding 7s. 6d. on the royal estate at Charlton (57) was held unjustly by Walter Gifard with one of his estates at Hanney (60). At Ardington (62 *bis*), Robert d'Oilly held three mills, one of which was claimed by Cola, an Englishman, who held land at Hendred (63b) nearby; but three Englishmen gave evidence that the mill had always belonged to Ardington (*Aluuin et Goduinus et Aluricus testificantur quod semper jacuit in Ardintone*, 62)

As the following table indicates, nearly two-thirds of the settlements with mills had only one apiece:

Domesday Mills in Berkshire

1 mill	57 settlements	5 mills	1 settlement
2 mills	19 settlements	6 mills	1 settlement
3 mills	10 settlements	7 mills	2 settlements
4 mills	4 settlements		

This table excludes the anonymous holding in Wantage hundred (58).

Six mills were entered under Reading (58, 60), and seven each under Letcombe (57b, 62) and Hanney (59, 60 *ter*, 61b).

Fig. 86 shows that in the northern half of the county mills were aligned along the many small streams of the Vale of White Horse, particularly along the Ock and the Mill Brook and their tributaries; many were situated along the 'fall-line' at the foot of the Chalk escarpment. There were also mills along the Thames itself, but a number of Thames-side villages were without mills. In the south, the Kennet, the Lambourn, the Pang and other smaller streams were also marked by villages with mills.

CHURCHES

Churches (*ecclesiae*) are mentioned in connection with 58 places in Berkshire, including White Waltham (59b) with a small church (*ecclesiola*) and Harwell (62b) with a chapel (*capella*). It is well recognised that the

---

[1] J. H. Round in *V.C.H. Berkshire*, I, p. 304.

mention of churches in the Domesday Book 'is only incidental, and is generally due to the existence of taxable glebe'.[1] Some of the churches in Berkshire were held with substantial amounts of land, e.g. with 5 hides at Shrivenham (57b), and with 3 hides at Thatcham (56b). Sometimes the title to a church was divided; thus at Wantage (57) two-thirds of the church with 4 hides (*ii partes ecclesiae cum iiii hidis ibi pertinentur*) were held by the king and the other third (*Tertiam partem praedictae ecclesiae*) with 1 hide by William the deacon. No church is mentioned in the long account of the borough of Wallingford (56), but the entry for Sonning (58) tells us that, in Wallingford, Roger the priest had a church which belonged of right (*juste pertinet*) to Sonning. We hear of the church of Abingdon only incidentally in the account of Barton (58b) which tells of 10 traders dwelling in front of the door of the church (*x mercatores ante portam ecclesiae manentes*).

Priests (*presbyteri*) are mentioned in connection with churches at seven places in Berkshire,[2] and clerks (*clerici*) in connection with a church at Thatcham (56b). No church is recorded for Windsor (56b) but the priest of the vill (*presbyter villae*) is entered as holding a hide and a half of land.

Generally only one church is mentioned under any one place-name, but two are noted in the entries for Basildon (57), Bray (57, 63b), Brimpton (62, 62b), Hendred (59b, 60), Moreton (61, 63), and Welford (58b). Two may perhaps be inferred at Cholsey (57):

Of this manor the abbey of Mont St Michel holds of the king 1 church (*unam ecclesiam*) with 1 hide, and there is one plough-team with 4 cottars and 7 acres of meadow. It is worth £3.

Two priests also in the same vill hold of the king in tithe and church (*in decima et ecclesia*) what is worth £4.

It would seem, therefore, that 64 churches and 1 chapel are mentioned or implied, and it is clear that this number can represent only a fraction of the parish churches of eleventh-century Berkshire.

[1] J. H. Round in *V.C.H. Berkshire*, I, p. 300.
[2] See p. 259 n. above for a list of these. Named priests (not included in our count) are mentioned in connection with other churches, e.g. at Cookham (56b).

URBAN LIFE

The information about towns is the least satisfactory part of the Domesday evidence, and for Berkshire it is especially unsatisfactory. Only two places in the county—Wallingford and Reading—are specifically styled *burgi*, but J. H. Round also saw an urban element at Windsor, Abingdon, (Great) Faringdon, Newbury, and possibly at Thatcham.[1] In the Berkshire folios, Windsor is styled '*villa*', but it seems to have contained 95 closes (*adhuc sunt in villa c hagae v minus*). Round described Windsor as 'a typical example of a town dependent on a great castle', but A. Ballard did not regard it as a borough since the Domesday entry does not call it one.[2] Abingdon is not described in the Berkshire folios, but there seems to be a reference to it in the entry for Barton (58b), where we hear that 10 traders (*x mercatores*) dwelling in front of the door of the church rendered 40*d.*;[3] Abingdon may already have had an urban element in 1086, but we cannot be certain. The entry for (Great) Faringdon (57b) is difficult, for it says that there were '9 closes in the same vill yielding 40*s.*' (*ix hagae in eadem villam de xl solidis*), and Round concluded that this statement pointed to the beginning of a trading element due to (Great) Faringdon's position at a crossing of routes.[4] But there is no evidence that the *hagae* were geographically as well as legally in the vill; they may have been at Wallingford. There is a reference to (Great) Faringdon in the long account of that borough (56); we are told that the son of Alsi of Faringdon had one *haga* which he claimed the King had given to him (*quam rex ei dedit ut dicit*). The entry for *Ulvritone* (i.e. Newbury, 62b), mentions '51 closes yielding 20*s.* 7*d.*' (*li hagae de xx solidis et vii denariis*), but again we cannot be certain that they were physically as well as legally in Newbury;[5] they may have been either at Wallingford or at Reading.[6] The entry for Thatcham (56b) tells of 12 closes yielding 55*s.* from feorm of the estate (*ibi xii hagae reddentes de firma lv solidos*). Again, it is unlikely

[1] *V.C.H. Berkshire*, I, p. 313.

[2] A. Ballard, *The Domesday Boroughs* (Oxford, 1904), p. 10.

[3] Round wrote: 'Abingdon, of course, is the typical town that rises at the abbey gate; indeed, Domesday describes its ten traders, paying their forty pence, as so situate'—*V.C.H. Berkshire*, I, p. 313.

[4] *Ibid.*

[5] For a discussion of the status of Newbury, see *V.C.H. Berkshire*, I, pp. 313–14.

[6] Aldermaston, some six miles to the east of Newbury, had two closes in Wallingford—*Rex in Ældremanestone ii hagas de v denariis* (56b).

DD

that there was an urban element at Thatcham itself. Because of these uncertainties only Wallingford, Reading and Windsor have been counted as boroughs in the present analysis.

Wallingford

The Domesday folios for Berkshire begin with a long account of the borough (*burgus*) of Wallingford (56). The data which enable us to gain some idea of the size of the borough fall into four groups:

(1) In the first place, we are told that King Edward had 8 virgates[1] of land on which there were 276 *hagae*. By 1086, 6 were quit of dues and service but, more important for our purpose, 8 had been destroyed to make room for the castle, thus leaving 268. Over and above these (*De super plus*) there were 22 *masurae* held by *francigenae*. This makes a total of 290 properties.

(2) Then follows a long and detailed list of properties held by various people. The total amounts to 98 *hagae*, 93 *masurae*, and houses (*domus*) belonging to ten people. If we assume that each of these last held a house apiece, the result is a total of 201 properties;[2] and the grand total so far amounts to 491 properties.

(3) After this comes a shorter list headed 'The following thegns of Oxfordshire had (*habuerunt*) land in Wallingford', but the list itself gives the successors of these thegns in 1086; their possessions amount to 26 houses (*domus*), thus bringing the grand total up to 517 properties.

(4) Some of the properties in the second group above pertained to rural manors, but, in addition to these, others are mentioned in the accounts of some of the rural manors themselves (see p. 276 below). These amount to 39 *hagae*, one of which was waste (*wasta*), but we cannot be sure whether or not they are included in the main account of Wallingford. In one case they may well be included. The entry for Brightwalton, Battle Abbey's only Berkshire manor, says: *In Walengeford v hagae* (59b), and under Wallingford itself we read that the abbot of Battle had 5 *masurae* in Berkshire. If both entries refer to the same property they provide evidence of the equation of *hagae* and *masurae*, but we cannot be sure. If we include all these properties (excluding, of course, the wasted *haga*) the grand total becomes 555.

---

[1] For 8 virgates at Oxford, see p. 227 above.
[2] One holder merely had a plot of land (*unum frustum terrae*) which has been excluded from this total.

Our choice therefore lies between a conservative figure of 491, a likely one of 517, and a possible one of 555. But the occupiers of these properties were not the only inhabitants of Wallingford. King Edward had held 15 acres (*acras*) on which the house-carls (*huscarles*) were settled; twenty years later, these acres (*eas*) were held by Miles Crispin, but we are told nothing of the fate of the house-carls. Nor are we given any information about possible agricultural peasantry; nor, indeed, are we told anything about the agricultural resources of the borough. All that we can safely

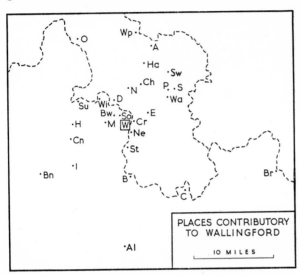

Fig. 87. Places contributory to Wallingford (W).

Berkshire: Al, Aldermaston; B, Basildon; Bn, Brightwalton; Br, Bray; Bw, Brightwell; C, Caversham; Cn, Chilton; H, Harwell; I, Ilsley; M, Moreton; So, Sotwell; Su, Sutton Courtenay; Wi, Wittenham.

Oxfordshire: A, Albury; Ch, Chalgrove; Cr, Crowmarsh; D, Dorchester; E, Ewelme; Ha, Haseley; N, Newington; Ne, Newnham Murren; O, Oxford; P, Pyrton; S, Shirburn; St, Stoke; Sw, South Weston; Wa, Watlington; Wp, Waterperry.

say is that Wallingford seems to have had a population of between 2,000 and 3,000 people. By the standards of the eleventh century, it was an important centre, but a church is mentioned only incidentally (58).

We have scarcely more than a hint of the activity that sustained this urban community. There is a reference to a Saturday market, to a moneyer implying a mint, and to smiths (*fabri*) with properties. That 22 *masurae* were held by *francigenae* suggests trade sufficient to make their presence worthwhile. Some hint of Wallingford's relations with the surrounding countryside is given by the fact that in King Edward's time the burgesses did service for the king with horses or by water (*cum equis vel per aquam*) upstream to Benson and Sutton Courtenay, downstream to Reading, and inland to Blewbury.

Properties contributory to Wallingford

A. *In Berkshire*

Entered under Wallingford	Entered under rural manors
Aldermaston: *ii hagas de v denariis*	
Bray: *una acra et ibi xi masuras de iii solidis*	
Brightwalton(?): *v masuras in berchesire habet abbas de Labatailge de xx denariis*	Brightwalton (59b): *v hagae*
Brightwell: *xxvii hagas de xxv solidis*	Brightwell (58): *de placitis terrae quae in Walingeford huic manerio pertinent xxv solidi*
Ilsley: *iii masurae de iii denariis*	
Sutton Courtenay: *una acra in qua sunt vi masuras (sic) de xii denariis*	Sutton Courtenay (57b): *i haga de xviii denariis sed wasta est*
Wittenham: *Rex Edwardus habuit xv acras in quibus manebant huscarles. Milo Crispin tenet eas; nesciunt quomodo. Una ex his jacet in Witeham*	Wittenham (60): *viii hagae de iiii solidis*
	Basildon (57): *iii hagae de ix denariis*
	Chilton (61b): *vi hagae de ii solidis*
	Harwell (58): *iii hagae de xv denariis*
	Moreton (61): *v hagae de l denariis*
	Sotwell (59b): *viii hagae de xiiii solidis et iiii denariis*

B. *In Oxfordshire*

All entered under Wallingford

Group I

Albury: *unam acram in qua sunt xi masurae de xxvi denariis*
Chalgrove: *i masuram de iiii denariis*
Haseley: *vi masuras reddentes xliiii denarios*
Newnham Murren: (i) *xx masuras de xii solidis et x denariis*; (ii) *iterum unam acram in qua sunt vi hagae de xviii denariis*

Oxford:[1] *ii acras in quibus sunt vii masurae de iiii solidis*
Stoke: *unam masuram de xii denariis*

Group II

Hi subscripti taini de Oxenefordscire habuerunt terram in Walingeford (The holdings are given in the order in which they occur; three holdings were not assigned to a locality)

Newington: *iiii domos reddentes vi solidos*
Dorchester: *unam domum reddentem xii denarios*
(?   ): *unam domum de iiii solidis*
Ewelme: *unam domum reddentem iii solidos*
Pyrton: *i domum reddentem iii solidos*
Caversham:[2] *iii domos reddentes ii solidos*
Watlington: *ii domos reddentes ii solidos*
Waterperry: *i domum de ii solidis*
(?   ): *iii domos de ii solidis*
Crowmarsh:[3] *iii domos reddentes iii solidos*
(?   ): *i domum de xii denariis*
Shirburn and South Weston: *tres domos de iiii solidis*
Ewelme: *i domum de xii denariis*
Ewelme: *unam domum reddentem iii solidos*

As we have noted, one interesting feature that Wallingford had in common with a number of other Domesday boroughs was that several of its properties belonged to rural manors (see p. 274 and Fig. 87). Some of these connections are mentioned in the account of Wallingford itself, others under their respective manors, while three and perhaps four (if we include Brightwalton) are mentioned in both contexts. The two Brightwell entries are, in Round's phrase, 'somewhat difficult'.[4] Under Wallingford we are told of 27 *hagae* yielding (*de*) 25*s*.; but under Brightwell itself the same sum appears not as rent from the houses but as the profits of jurisdiction over them. But Round concluded that, in spite of the identity of the sum, its sources were different.[5] A number of these contributory properties were attached to estates beyond the county boundary in

---

[1] The Latin is *ad oxeneford* and this has been taken to mean the borough of Oxford itself, but it is possible that it may refer to some manor within the shire.

[2] Part of Caversham was transferred to Berkshire in 1911; see p. 241 above.

[3] The Domesday form is *Crem*, which Round identified with a query as being Crowmarsh Gifford (*V.C.H. Berkshire*, I, p. 326); see also M. Gelling and D. M. Stenton, *The Place-Names of Oxfordshire*, I (Cambridge, 1953), p. 47.

[4] *V.C.H. Berkshire*, I, p. 311.   [5] *Ibid.* n. 4.

Oxfordshire; some of them are mentioned in the main list, others appear in a subsidiary list headed: 'The following thegns of Oxfordshire had (*habuerunt*) land in Wallingford.' The list itself gives the 1086 holders, and Round interpreted it to mean that 'this land had been appurtenant to certain manors which these thegns had held and which, at the time of the survey, were in the hands of their successors the Normans whose names follow'.[1] There is no mention of these in the Oxfordshire folios themselves, but, on the other hand, the Berkshire folios record properties in the city of Oxford belonging to Streatley (62) and Steventon (57b).[2]

Reading

Reading is mentioned in two entries—in the account of the lands of the king and in that of those of the abbey of Battle. The former tells of a borough, but describes it apart from the manor of Reading itself. The entries are as follows:

(i) *Terra Regis* (58): The king holds Reading in demesne. King Edward held [it]. Then as now it was assessed at 43 hides. There is land for 40 plough-teams. In the demesne is 1 [plough-team], and 55 villeins and 30 bordars with 55 plough-teams. There, 4 mills yielding (*de*) 35*s*.[3] and 3 fisheries yielding (*de*) 14*s*. 6*d*. and 150 acres of meadow. Woodland yielding (*de*) 100 swine. From pasture 16*s*. 6*d*. *T.R.E.* and afterwards it was worth £40. Now £48.

The king has in the borough (*in burgo*) of Reading 28 *hagae* paying (*reddentes*) £4. 3*s*. from all customary dues (*per omnibus consuetudinibus*). Yet those who hold them render 100*s*. Henry of Ferrers has there 1 *haga* and half a virgate of land in which are 3 acres of meadow. It is worth 6*s*. Godric the sheriff held this land to provide for guests (*ad hospitium*).[4] Therefore Henry holds it.

Reinbald son of Bishop Peter held 1 *haga* there which he transferred (*trahebat*) to Earley,[5] his manor. It is now in the king's hands and is worth 16*d*.

(ii) *Terra ecclesiae de Labatailge* (60): The abbot [of Battle] himself holds a church in Reading with 8 hides thereto pertaining (*ibi pertinent*). Leveva

---

[1] *V.C.H. Berkshire*, I, p. 312.
[2] The details are:
 Streatley (62): *In Oxineford i haga de x denariis*.
 Steventon (57b): *Ad hoc manerium pertinuerunt in Oxeneford xiii hagae reddentes xii solidos et vi denarios et unum pratum de xx solidis*.
[3] In the MS. this figure appears to have been corrected to 55.
[4] See F. W. Ragg in *V.C.H. Berkshire*, I, p. 334, n. 5.
[5] The entry for Earley itself (57) also mentions a *haga* in Reading.

the abbess held [   ]¹ of King Edward. Then it was assessed at 8 hides; now at 3 hides. There is land for 7 plough-teams. In the demesne is 1 [plough-team], and 9 villeins and 8 bordars with 5 plough-teams. There [are] 2 mills yielding (*de*) 40s. and 2 fisheries and a moiety of one yielding 5s. In Reading [are] 29 *masurae*, yielding 28s. 8d., and 12 acres of meadow. Woodland yielding (*de*) 5 swine. From the church £3. *T.R.E.* it was worth £9; afterwards £8; now £11.

If, in fact, both these entries do refer to Reading, we may assume that the community was one of 64 villeins, 38 bordars, 30 *hagae* and 29 *masurae*. These details would seem to imply a total population of at least 650, but the population of Reading in 1086 may have been greater than that. Whatever its size, the community of Reading appears to have been predominantly agricultural in character; this is certainly suggested by its 62 plough-teams and its other agricultural resources. Its position on the Thames, however, must have given it some commercial importance.

Windsor

In the Domesday folios Windsor is styled *villa*, and the account of its activities gives the impression of an agricultural settlement that had acquired something of the flavour of a town. The main entry (56b) is:

King William holds Windsor in demesne. King Edward held [it]. There [are] 20 hides. There is land for [   ]. In the demesne is 1 plough-team and 22 villeins and 2 bordars with 10 plough-teams. There, 1 serf and a fishery yielding (*de*) 6s. 8d., and 40 acres of meadow. Wood rendering 50 swine from pannage dues (*de pasnagio*), and other woodland is placed in enclosure (*missa est in defensa*); and there are, besides (*adhuc*), 100 *hagae* less 5 in the vill. Of these 26 are exempt from rent (*quietae de gablo*), and from the others come 30 shillings. Of the land of this manor Albert the clerk holds 1½ hides and the third part of one dene (*denae*). Walter son of Other [holds] 1½ hides and one virgate and as much woodland as renders 5 swine as dues from pannage (*unde exeunt v porcis de pasnagio*). Gilbert Maminot [holds] 3 virgates, William 1 hide, Alvric 1 hide, and another Alvric half a hide, and the priest of the vill 1½ hides, and 2 sergeants of the king's court half a hide, Eudo the steward 2 hides. *T.R.E.* it was worth £15; afterwards £7; now £15.

---

¹ There is a space left in the MS. between *tenuit* and *de rege E*[*dwardi*], which looks as if a place-name should have been inserted. If so, it may mean that the rest of the entry really describes another place, but Round, Ragg and Baring all assign it to Reading; see (1) J. H. Round in *V.C.H. Berkshire*, I, p. 312; (2) F. W. Ragg, *V.C.H. Berkshire*, I, p. 344; and (3) F. H. Baring, *Domesday Tables*, pp. 68–9.

We are also told, in the entry for Clewer (62b), an adjoining manor, that King William took half-a-hide from the vill and built the castle of Windsor on it:

It (i.e. Clewer) was then assessed at 5 hides, now at 4½ hides; and the castle of Windsor (*castellum de Windesores*) is on the half-hide.

In the Buckinghamshire folios we hear incidentally of the 'guard' of Windsor at a date between 1066 and 1086; Ralf Passaquam, the dispossessed holder of an estate at Drayton Parslow had found (*inveniebat*) 'duos Loricatos in custodiam de Windesores' (151b), but we are not told if this service was also provided in 1086.

It is difficult to be certain about the size of Windsor in 1086, but the 22 villeins, 2 bordars, 1 serf and 95 *hagae* seem to imply a total population of some 500 or so persons.[1]

MISCELLANEOUS INFORMATION

Dairy farms and cheese-making

Three references to dairy-farms and cheese-making constitute an interesting feature of the Berkshire folios:

Buckland (58b): A dairy farm yielding 10 weys of cheese worth 32s. 4d. (*Wica de x pensis caseorum valentes xxxii solidos et iiii denarios*).

Shellingford (59b): from customary dues of cheeses £4. 16s. 8d. (*de consuetudinibus caseorum iiii librae et xvi solidi et viii denarii*).

Sparsholt (57b): Of this manor Henry de Ferrers holds 1 virgate of land and 12 acres of meadow and one dairy yielding 6 weys of cheese (*unam vacariam de vi pensis caseorum*).

These three settlements are in the Vale of White Horse, and J. H. Round showed how a dispute about dues of weys, some thirty years after the Domesday Inquest, enables us to trace further the local production of cheese.[2] Thus we can see in the Domesday Book the early emergence of this well-watered vale as a dairying district.

[1] The Domesday entry for Windsor would seem to relate to Old Windsor and not to the new town, which was already perhaps beginning to grow up near the castle; the first mention of the borough of Windsor is in the Pipe Roll of 1130–1; see *V.C.H. Berkshire*, III, p. 56.

[2] *V.C.H. Berkshire*, I, p. 305.

Markets

Markets are mentioned in connection with only two places in Berkshire —Wallingford (56b) and Cookham (56b). The latter, judged by eleventh-century standards, was a very substantial village, and its 'new' market yielded 20s. in 1086 (*De novo mercato quod ibi est modo xx solidi*).[1] We hear also in the entry for Barton (48b) of traders 'dwelling in front of the door of the church' (i.e. Abingdon Abbey)[2] and paying 40d.

Vineyard

The only mention of a vineyard in the Berkshire folios is under Bisham (60b) where there were 12 arpents of vine (*xii arpendi vineae*).

Castles

The Domesday folios tell us that two castles had been built between 1066 and 1086. At Wallingford (56) 8 *hagae* were destroyed so that the castle could be built—*pro castello sunt viii [hagae] destructae*. The other castle was at Windsor, and had been built on land belonging to Clewer (62b).[3]

Livestock

The Berkshire folios form part of the Exchequer Domesday Book and so do not regularly record information about livestock on the demesne. But two references to livestock have crept into them. At the end of the entry for the unidentified *Ebrige* (63) we hear that the Domesday holder of the estate, Hugo the steersman (*stirman*), had 'transferred the hall and other buildings and the livestock into another manor' (*Ipse quoque transportavit hallam et alias domos et pecuniam in alio manerio*). There is also mention of horses at the end of the account of the royal estate at Kintbury (57b); 43 acres of land held in 1086 by Hugh de Ferrers had earlier been made by Godric the sheriff into pasture for his horses—*Dicunt autem quod Godric vicecomes fecit ibi pascua equis suis*.

Other references

The entry for Appleford (59) contains the curious statement 'from the profit of the demesne land 21s.' (*de lucro terrae dominicae xxi solidi*).[4]

---

[1] J. H. Round suggested that the 'new market' at Cookham may have been connected with Windsor, but he added that this suggestion was 'merely a guess' (*V.C.H. Berkshire*, I, p. 313).   [2] See p. 258 above.
[3] See p. 280 above.   [4] *V.C.H. Berkshire*, I, p. 308.

Round concluded that this formula, which also occurs in the entry for Droxford (41 b) in the Hampshire folios,[1] probably implies that part of the demesne was let at a money rent.

The only record of 'waste' (*wastata*) in the Berkshire folios is of a wasted *haga* in Wallingford belonging to Sutton Courtenay (57b).

REGIONAL SUMMARY

The regional division of Berkshire, shown on Fig. 88, follows in the main that made by William Mavor early in the nineteenth century.[2] Within each of the regions there are variations, but the broad division into five must suffice for the purpose of summarising the geography of the county in the eleventh century.

(1) *Northern Berkshire*

This region, lying to the north of the Berkshire Downs and stretching to the Thames, is, for the most part, below 400 ft. O.D. It comprises four east-west belts of country, with alternating heavy and light soils: (1) Oxford Clay bordering the Thames Valley; (2) Corallian Limestone yielding sandy loams, and forming a ridge that in places reaches heights of 530 ft. and just over; (3) Kimeridge Clay and Gault, drained by the Ock and its streams, and known as the Vale of White Horse; (4) an Upper Greensand and Lower Chalk belt below the main Chalk escarpment.

Taking the area as a whole, it was a well-settled country of numerous villages set mostly just off the clays of the Corallian and on the Upper Greensand and Lower Chalk outcrops. With densities per square mile of 3 to 4 plough-teams and 11 to 18 recorded people, it was the most highly developed part of the county. Perhaps its most outstanding feature was its meadowland; there was scarcely a village without some, and many villages had large amounts. Scattered references in the Domesday folios seem to suggest, moreover, that the Vale of White Horse was already a centre of cheese production. The Thames-side villages were characterised by fisheries. Many settlements were without mills, but below the Chalk escarpment and along Mill Brook there were some settlements with as many as three mills or more apiece. In view of this high development, it is not surprising that the region seems to have contained but little wood.

---

[1] See p. 356 below.

[2] W. Mavor, *General View of the Agriculture of Berkshire* (London, 1808; reprinted in 1809), frontispiece.

The heavy claylands, especially, must once have carried a great deal; the Domesday Commissioners entered wood for only four villages in the region, but the records of Abingdon abbey show that the record of wood in the Berkshire folios was incomplete.[1]

(2) *The Central Downland*

The Berkshire Downlands form the outstanding feature of the relief of the county, and occupy the greater part of its western half. They are

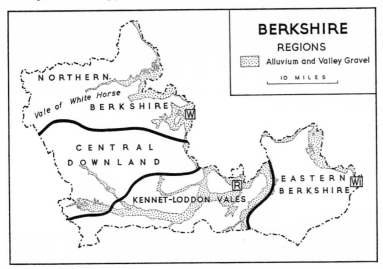

Fig. 88. Berkshire: Regional subdivisions.

Domesday boroughs are indicated by initials: R, Reading;
W, Wallingford; Wi, Windsor.

marked on the north by a steep escarpment which, for the most part, is about 600 ft. above sea-level, but which rises to 856 ft. at Uffington Castle. From this northern edge, a broad dip-slope, falling to below 400 ft., extends southwards towards the valley of the Kennet. Into this sloping Chalk surface various valleys have been incised, notably those of the Lambourn and the Pang, and they lie at about 100 ft. below the general level of the surrounding countryside. The northern and higher portions of the water-less dip-slope have only a thin soil cover. This provides a fine turf well suited for sheep pasture, but, unfortunately, the compilers of the Berkshire

[1] See p. 264 above.

folios omitted all information about sheep, so that we cannot tell to what extent these pastures were grazed in the eleventh century. To the south, much of the Chalk is covered by Clay-with-flints, providing loamy soils.

This contrast between north and south was reflected in the distribution of settlements. In the north, there was a considerable east-west stretch of country without villages; but in the south, where Clay-with-flints appear, and where the relief is broken by the Lambourn and the Pang valleys, villages were numerous. The region as a whole was moderately prosperous, judged by its plough-teams and population densities which were mostly about 3 and about 9 per square mile respectively. As might be expected, there was very little meadow; what there was, lay in the valleys of the Upper Kennet, the Lambourn and the Pang. Mills, too, were few, although some villages along the Lambourn appear to have had three or more apiece. There were no fisheries except for a solitary one along the Thames. The higher Chalk slopes were without wood, but small amounts could be encountered in the southern Clay-with-flints district.

(3) *The Kennet-Loddon Vales*

The two vales, lying to a great extent below 200 ft. O.D., occupy a central position in the county. The rivers themselves meander across marshy flood-plains, separated by higher ground of gravels, sands and clays, which, however, nowhere reach more than 50 ft. above the streams themselves. Villages were moderately numerous, and the densities of plough-teams and of population averaged about 2 to 3 and about 6 to 8 per square mile respectively. Most villages had some amount of meadow, especially those along the Kennet; there were also fisheries both along the lower Kennet and the Loddon. There were only a few valleys without mills. Woodland was fairly widespread, but there was not as much as might be expected from Fig. 83 because the greater part of the large amount entered under Sonning lay to the south-east in the next region.

The parish of Combe, in the extreme south-west, has been included in this region although geographically it forms part of the Hampshire Downs, and was part of Hampshire itself until it was transferred to Berkshire in 1844. It consists of the dry Combe valley cut 350 ft. below the surrounding hills; Walbury Hill to the north-east attains to 974 ft. O.D., and is the highest point in Berkshire.

(4) *Eastern Berkshire*

Within this division, two areas can be distinguished—a richer north and a poorer south. In the north, a great meander of the Thames has separated a small portion of the dip-slope of the Chilterns from the main mass to the north of the river. Clearly defined on three sides by the river, the Wargrave-Waltham upland merges gradually on its southern side into south-east Berkshire. Much of the area lies above 200 ft. O.D., and a few isolated heights rise above 400 ft. Settlements were few; there were about 3 plough-teams and about 6 people per square mile. There was a little meadow, mostly along the Thames, and a few mills and fisheries. Woodland could be encountered, but that entered for some of the vills may well have been situated to the south of the Windsor area.

The southern and larger portion of Eastern Berkshire lies above 200 ft. O.D., and, in the south, it rises sharply to heights of over 400 ft., the highest point being Surrey Hill (427 ft. O.D.). Geologically, the main contrast is between the intractable London Clay and the ungrateful light soils of the Barton, Bracklesham and Bagshot series to the south. In 1086, as now, this region was agriculturally unimportant. Villages were few, and over much of the area the density of plough-teams per square mile fell to below one, and that of population to under two. There was practically no meadow, and hardly any mills or fisheries. Much of the area came within the precincts of Windsor Forest, and, although 'forest' is a legal term, the substantial swine renders from a few of the villages suggest the presence of a fair amount of wood, particularly when we remember that the greater part of the Sonning woodland must have been within this region. Moreover, it is possible that the Forest contained other wood, not recorded by the Domesday commissioners.

BIBLIOGRAPHICAL NOTE

(1) It is interesting to note that D. Lysons and S. Lysons listed the Domesday manors of Berkshire at the beginning of their 'topographical account' of the county which formed the second part of their *Magna Britannia*, I (London, 1813), pp. 167–9.

Towards the end of the nineteenth century, lists of Domesday place-names and of landholders were printed: 'Berkshire—Resumé of Domesday holders and holdings', *Quart. Journ. Berks. Archaeol. and Archit. Soc.* III (Reading, 1894–5, pp. 138–43, 167, 195–200; continued in *Berks., Bucks., and Oxon.*

Archaeol. Journ. I (Reading, 1895), pp. 26–8, 61, 75–8; II (1896), pp. 19–22, 59–60, 86–9, 113–15. These lists were unsigned, but they may well have been compiled by the Rev. P. H. Ditchfield, who was successively editor of both journals.

(2) The only available translation is that by the Rev. F. W. Ragg in *V.C.H. Berkshire*, I (London, 1906), pp. 323–69. It contains a valuable series of identifications and footnotes, and is preceded by one of the famous introductions by J. H. Round (pp. 285–321).

(3) A noteworthy contribution is F. H. Baring's *Domesday Tables for the counties of Surrey, Berkshire, Middlesex, Hertford, Buckingham and Bedford and for the New Forest* (London, 1909). The tables for Berkshire were 'based in part on a table of the hides and holders compiled by the Rev. F. W. Ragg' (*ibid.* p. 39 n.).

(4) A pioneer study of the Domesday geography of the county is F. W. Morgan's 'The Domesday Geography of Berkshire', *Scot. Geog. Mag.* LI (Edinburgh, 1935), pp. 353–63.

(5) The following deal with various aspects of the Domesday study of the county:

W. H. RICHARDSON, 'Notes on Blewbury', *Trans. Newbury District Field Club*, IV (Newbury, 1895), pp. 35–72.

J. E. FIELD: 'Some notes on the Domesday survey of Berkshire', *Berks., Bucks., and Oxon. Archaeol. Journ.* X (Reading, 1904), pp. 81–6.

F. H. BARING: 'The Conqueror's footprints in Domesday', *Eng. Hist. Rev.* XIII (London, 1898), pp. 17–25; reprinted with 'some additions and alterations' in F. H. Baring, *Domesday Tables*, pp. 207–16 (see above).

(6) The English Place-Name Society has not yet published a volume dealing with the county, but two early place-name studies are available: W. W. Skeat, *The Place-Names of Berkshire* (Oxford, 1911); and F. M. Stenton, *The Place-Names of Berkshire* (Reading, 1911).

CHAPTER VII

HAMPSHIRE

BY R. WELLDON FINN, M.A.

Those who planned the record of the Domesday Inquest might well have opened their volume with Hampshire. Here, at Winchester, was the capital of that West Saxon realm which had mastered all England, and whose former system of food-rents to maintain the king and his household was still in evidence when the Inquest was held.[1] It may have been to Winchester that the 'writings', presumably the results of the Inquest, were brought to the king, as the Anglo-Saxon Chronicle tells us; though Salisbury on the occasion of his Lammas visit seems equally likely. But it was certainly at Winchester, the home of the Treasury, that the Domesday Book was long preserved after its making.

The present-day county of Hampshire, in terms of which this study is written, is not exactly the same as the Domesday county. A number of places now in Hampshire are surveyed in the folios for other counties. Damerham (66b, 67b) and Plaitford (74) are described under Wiltshire, and they, together with Martin, Melchet Park and Whitsbury (not described in the Domesday Book) were transferred to Hampshire in 1895. Bramshaw (74 *bis*) is also described under Wiltshire, and Tytherley under both counties (42, 48, 48b, 50 *bis* and 74). Kinson (80b), described under Dorset, was transferred in 1930. Warblington (23b) is described under Sussex; its entry follows that of the manor of Westbourne, and notes: 'To this manor belongs Warblington in Hampshire.' In 1895 Combe (46b) became part of Berkshire, and Mortimer West End was transferred from Berkshire to Hampshire in 1894. Ambersham went to Sussex in 1832.

The outstanding feature of the Hampshire portion of the Domesday Book is the fact that separate sections are devoted to part of the New Forest and the district around it (*In Nova Foresta et circa eam*, 51–51b) and to the Isle of Wight (*Insula de Wit* or *With*, 39b–40 and 52–54). There are, moreover, separate lists of landholders for each of these areas, in addition to the main list for the rest of the country. The Hampshire folios as a whole contain their full share of obscurities and anomalies. Some of

[1] Part of Wellow may also have been in Domesday Wiltshire—see p. 295n. below.

these are mentioned in connection with various matters discussed below, but a number of general points can be noted here. Fo. 42–42b was obviously inserted after the rest had been compiled. It breaks the account of Wootton St Lawrence running from 41b to 43, and on it the entries are written across the page instead of in double column. Other initial omissions have been made good by insertions at the foot of fos. 43, 45b and 48b; there are also various marginal additions, e.g. on fos. 39b and 48; while some passages in the body of the text are postscriptal, e.g. on fos. 43, 43b, 44b, 46b, 48 and 50b. These and other imperfections prepare us for the statistical uncertainties that we encounter in the text.[1] Thus, in some entries, where a figure for plough-lands should be, there is a blank space that was never filled in. Two entries relating to Charford and to *Clatinges* on fo. 44b seem to be repeated on fo. 46, and it is instructive to compare the two versions. The differences between them are not confined to variations in phrasing; the first entry gives the successive value of Charford as £4, £5, £4, the other as £5, £4, £4; the first gives the assessment as 6 hides, the second as 5 hides; but, what is more important from our point of view, both entries on fo. 44b omit any mention of the wood that we are told about on fo. 46.

But there are other and greater difficulties. One of the most important from a geographical point of view is that the Inquest officials often presented their material in terms not of a vill but of a manor. A place with a name of its own in 1086 may therefore be unmentioned in the Domesday Book because the information about it was included within the totals of some large and complex manor of which it formed part. Only once, for Crondall (41), do we seem to be given all a manor's components by name; part of its 50 hides lay at Badley, Cove, Farnborough, Itchell and Long Sutton, forming a tract of country along the north-east border of the county. Normally, only some of the components of a manor are named. Some of the 51 hides of the manor of Alresford (40) were at the unidentified *Bieforde* and at Soberton a dozen miles to the south and in a different hundred; but three other unnamed holdings also formed part of Alresford, and the details of all five subsidiary holdings are grouped together. Not only are we unable to apportion these details, but, moreover, we cannot

---

[1] *V.C.H. Hampshire*, 1 (Westminster, 1900), pp. 456–7 attributes the third line of the original column on fo. 39b to Faccombe (mill, meadow, pasture), but the Domesday text itself shows that this more likely belongs to the Titchfield entry, and that the mill was a duplication of one already entered for Titchfield on the previous folio.

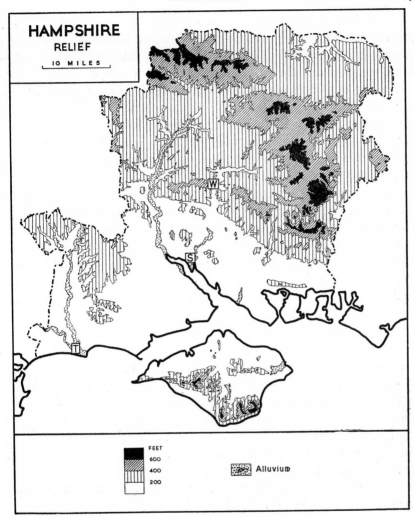

Fig. 89. Hampshire: Relief.

Domesday boroughs are indicated by initials: S, Southampton;
T, Twynham; W, Winchester.

tell whether or not the unnamed holdings were at places named elsewhere
in the Hampshire folios. Or, again, there were eleven subsidiary holdings
attached to the great 106-hide manor of Micheldever (42 b) but only four
of these were named, and the text provides us with no clue to the sites of
the other seven. Similarly, the 50-hide manor of Whitchurch (41) included

six subsidiary holdings, only two of which were named. Chilcomb (41), just outside Winchester, was another substantial manor, and indeed was described by Maitland as 'one of the most interesting estates in all England'. It is true that it was assessed at only 1 hide, but (although the Domesday Book does not tell us this) it was really a 100-hide manor whose assessment had been reduced to the very low rating of 1 hide. Its entry is divided into two parts—a main portion and a summary account of seven unnamed subsidiary holdings; altogether it included 213 recorded adults, 78 plough-teams and 9 churches. We would have no clue to the identity of the subsidiary holdings but for the pre-Domesday documents which reveal that the great Chilcomb estate was scattered over many villages in the Winchester district;[1] even so, we have no means of distributing the Domesday totals among these constituent vills. Among other substantial and complicated manors with subsidiary holdings may be mentioned Odiham (38) with 4 churches, Bishops Waltham (40), Houghton (40b) and Overton (40) with 2 churches each, and Hurstbourne Priors (41). Calbourne (52b), in the Isle of Wight, was another complicated manor with unnamed holdings.

For the purpose of constructing distribution maps, the details of these composite entries have been divided among the holdings concerned, and the resources of the anonymous holdings have been included with those of the main holding. The example of Chilcomb (41) just quoted is an extreme case in that all the resources had to be plotted at Chilcomb itself. Frequently, the divisions are brought together again when the densities are averaged over an area covering a group of villages.[2] These devices are not satisfactory, but it is unlikely that the error greatly affects the general pattern of the distributions.

One further point must be made. We cannot be certain that the existence of subsidiary holdings is always indicated or that the sum of the named and unnamed holdings always gives the total of the dependencies

---

[1] F. W. Maitland, *Domesday Book and Beyond* (Cambridge, 1897), pp. 496–8. A writ of Æthelred II (A.D. 979–1016) shows that the 100-hide manor included parts at least of eleven other villages. Their territory stretched along the Itchen from Kilmeston to Tichborne, then past Ovington, Avington and Easton, and southward by Chilcomb itself, through Twyford, Brambridge, Otterbourne and Bishopstoke. In addition, at some distance away, were Chilbolton near Andover and Nursling near Southampton. All these vills, with the exception of Brambridge and Tichborne, are the subject of independent entries in the Domesday Book, but for all we know their statistics were included in those of the Domesday entry for Chilcomb itself.

[2] See p. 319 below.

of a manor. We can hardly believe, for example, that East Meon (38, 40b), and one unnamed subsidiary holding, were the only settlements in the large hundred of that name. We must assume that the 70 or so hides attributed to East Meon covered a number of small unrecorded settlements, and, indeed, we know from other evidence that this was so.[1] The entry for the 60-hide manor of Chalton (44b) is even more uninformative. It tells us of no subsidiary holdings, and there is nothing to indicate that the substantial resources enumerated were not all at Chalton itself, except possibly for the phrase 'there [are] churches', although this is not conclusive. But we know, from non-Domesday evidence again, that this entry covered not only Chalton but also Blendworth, Catherington, Clanfield and Idsworth, the whole forming a considerable tract abutting on the Sussex border.[2] The entry for the large manor of Neatham (38), with a recorded population of 96, and with 52 plough-teams at work, likewise mentions no subsidiary holdings, but, again, we know from other sources that it must have extended over a number of nearby settlements.[3]

One curious feature, illustrating the difficulty of apportioning manorial totals, is the fact that portions of six manors in the New Forest area had connections in the Isle of Wight:

(1) Eling (38b): *Huic manerio pertinuerunt duae Bereuuicae intra With et tres extra.*

(2) Holdenhurst (39): *Aliae vii hidae sunt in insula.*

(3) Ringwood (39): *aliae [hidae] fuerunt in Wit* (i.e. 18 hides).

(4) Breamore (39): *Huic manerio pertinet una hida in insula de With quam tenet Gherui.*[4]

(5) Stanswood (38b): *Hoc manerium jacet in firma regis quam habet de insula de Wit.*

(6) Twynham (44): The canons of Twynham held *in Wit insula unam hidam.*

The entries for the Isle of Wight do not mention these mainland manors, and we can only speculate about what ancient connection there may have been between them and their distant holdings. Whether the connection affects our figures or not, we cannot be sure. It is possible that duplications lie concealed within these entries, and that the figures for these New Forest

[1] *V.C.H. Hampshire*, III (London, 1908), p. 63. East Meon was in *Mene* hundred, while West Meon was in the hundred of *Menestoches* (40b) and so is counted separately.

[2] *V.C.H. Hampshire*, III, p. 83.   [3] *V.C.H. Hampshire*, I, p. 450.

[4] Among the Isle of Wight entries, Gerin (?Gherui) is said to hold one hide at Ningwood (54); this may be the hide referred to under Rockbourne.

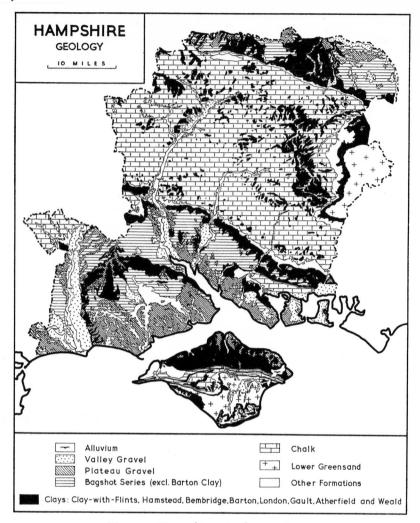

Fig. 90. Hampshire: Surface geology.

Based on Geological Survey One-Inch Sheets (New Series) 267, 268, 282–5, 299, 300, 314–16, 329–31, and the Isle of Wight special One-Inch Sheet.

vills may be too high; the figures for Ringwood seem suspiciously so—86 recorded people for its 16 plough-lands and 17½ teams.[1] Or it may be that in the Isle there were at least 27 hides—some 13 per cent of its total

[1] But see p. 331 below.

assessment—about the inhabitants and equipment of which we are told nothing. Finally, we must note that the Wiltshire folios (64b) say that Bowcombe on the island had, up to 1070 or earlier, been part of the *firma* of Amesbury in Wiltshire.[1] The tenurial arrangements of the island seem to have been very complex.

In addition to the five unnamed berewicks of Eling (38b), three mainland manors also had distant berewicks. Barton Stacey (38b) had one at Kings Worthy; Meonstoke (39) had one at Titchfield; Wolverton (49) had an unnamed berewick somewhere in Titchfield hundred on the other side of the shire.

SETTLEMENTS AND THEIR DISTRIBUTION

The total number of separate places mentioned for the area now within Hampshire seems to be 458, including the boroughs of Winchester, Southampton and Twynham.[2] This figure, for a variety of reasons, cannot accurately reflect the total number of settlements. In the first place, when two or more adjoining villages bear the same surname today it is not always clear whether more than one existed in the eleventh century. There is no indication in the text that, say, the Brown Candover and Chilton Candover of today existed as separate villages; the Domesday information about them is entered under only one name (*Candevre*, 40b, 42), though they may well have been separate in the eleventh century as they certainly were by the thirteenth.[3] That the adjacent village of Preston Candover was already separate by 1086 we may suppose because it is rubricated under a different hundred (44b, 45b, 47, 47b, 49b *bis*). Similarly, as the two entries for *Sireburne* (45) or *Sireborne* (46) were in different hundreds, it seems as if Sherborne St John and Monk Sherborne were separate villages then as now. But the criterion of separate hundreds is not infallible, partly, maybe, owing to faulty rubrication.[4] When the entries are numerous, it is impossible to apportion them satisfactorily; thus the six entries for *Ordie* are now represented by four Worthys, but

[1] Lyndhurst (39), in the New Forest, was also part of the *firma* of Amesbury.

[2] Of this total of 458 as many as 101 were in the Isle of Wight.

[3] The dates of place-names in this section are from E. Ekwall, *The Concise Oxford Dictionary of English Place-Names* (Oxford, 4th ed., 1960).

[4] Thus, although the entries for *Tedorde* or *Todeorde* (46b, 49) are rubricated partly under Andover hundred and partly under Broughton, they have been treated here as one settlement only and plotted at South Tidworth, because North Tidworth is, and was, in Wiltshire and is separately described in the Wiltshire folios (66, 69, 74b).

have been plotted as two settlements on our maps.[1] The seven entries for *Clere* are now represented by three places,[2] but have also been plotted as two. *Anne* or *Anna*, with six entries, also presents a problem, and it also has been treated here as referring only to two settlements.[3] Only occasionally does the Domesday text specifically mention the existence of separate places bearing a name in common. There are four entries for *Tiderlei* or *Tederleg*, all in the same hundred (48, 48b, 50 *bis*); we can only guess which represents East and which West Tytherley, but we can be sure that there were two distinct settlements because a subsidiary entry elsewhere in the text (42) speaks of one chapel in *Tiderlege* and another in *alia Tiderlege*.[4] The distinction between *Wallope* and *alia Wallope* (38b) likewise shows the existence in 1086 of Nether Wallop and Over Wallop; maybe Middle Wallop also existed.[5] Itchen Abbess and Itchen Stoke were certainly distinct, for the first was *Icene* (48) and the second was *Stoche* (43b).[6] *Witesfel* and *alia Witesfel* (53 *bis*), in the Isle of Wight, are represented today not by adjacent parishes but by Whitefield Farm in Brading and Little Whitefield in Ashey; Whitefield Wood now stretches across the parish boundary between Ashey and Brading, but neither of the Domesday entries refers to wood.

There are other reasons why the figure of 458 cannot be taken as the total number of settlements in 1086. One is that, as we have seen, we cannot tell whether or not the unnamed holdings of some large manors were at places named elsewhere in the Hampshire folios.[7] Another reason is that there are, in addition, about 30 major and a dozen or so minor

[1] Headbourne Worthy, Kings Worthy, Martyr Worthy and Abbots Worthy (in Kings Worthy). The Domesday entries are rubricated under three hundreds; Barton Stacey (38b, 46b *bis*, 47b), Meonstoke (41b) and Micheldever (42b). The Meonstoke entry ought perhaps to have been rubricated under Barton Stacey which follows it—hence only two settlements have been plotted here.

[2] Burghclere, Highclere and Kingsclere. The entries under Basingstoke hd. (39), Clere hd. (45, 48b, 50b *bis*) and Mansbridge hd. (43) have been assigned to Kingsclere; that under Evingar hd. (41) to the adjacent parishes of Burghclere and Highclere.

[3] Abbots Ann, Little Ann (in Abbots Ann), Ann Savage (in Amport), Amport, Monxton and Thruxton. The Domesday entries are rubricated under two hundreds: Andover (39, 43, 45b, 47, 49, plotted at Amport), and Welford (44, plotted at Little Ann).

[4] Tytherley (*Tuderlege*) is also mentioned in the Wiltshire folios (74).

[5] Quite separate from these is Farleigh Wallop (50) in the east of the county.

[6] On the other hand, the two entries for *Penitone* (43b, 44b) have been plotted as one although each mentions a church; today they are represented by Penton Grafton and Penton Mewsey. Likewise, the two entries for *Stanham* or *Staneham* (41b, 43), with a church each, have also been plotted as one; today they are represented by North and South Stoneham. [7] See pp. 288–90 above.

entries in which no place-name (though often the relevant hundred) is given;[1] there are two such anonymous entries, for example, under the heading of *Clere* hundred on fo. 50b. These entries, again, may or may not refer to places named elsewhere.

The total of 458 includes some about which very little information is given. Certain places are mentioned incidentally without forming the subject of a detailed entry. Thus, there was a hide in the hundred of King's Somborne which Hugh de Port claimed should belong to his manors of Charford and *Eschetune* (48), the latter of which is nowhere else mentioned. A small estate in Outwick is said to have belonged to *Welle* (48), which may have been Wellow.[2] Then there are other entries that appear to give an incomplete picture. There was half a team without inhabitants at Lea in Bradley (53b). More understandably, perhaps, there were inhabitants without teams at Blackpan (53) and *Sudberie* (50). There were neither inhabitants nor teams at *Abaginge* (53b), but it had half a plough-land and half an acre of meadow. As can be seen, these apparently incomplete entries referred to very small places, but there were other entries, with both population and teams, that also can hardly have referred to true villages; thus both *Celvecrote* (53b) and Huffingford (54) had only one bordar and half a team each. Then, too, there must be added to this list those places about which we know almost nothing except that they were 'in the forest'.[3]

Not all the Domesday names appear on the present-day map of Hampshire villages. Some are represented by hamlets, by individual houses and farms, or by the names of localities. Thus *Abedestune* (40b) is now the hamlet of Abbotstone in Itchen Stoke; *Middeltune* (44) is that of Middleton in Longparish; and *Levintune* (54) is that of Limerstone in Brighstone. *Gramborne* (42b) has survived as Cranbourne, the name of a locality, of a wood and of a number of separate houses (Farm, Grange, Lodge) in Wonston, and *Nortune* (49b) as Norton Manor in the same parish. *Hou* (45) is represented by Hoe Cross, Hoe Gate and East Hoe Farm in

---

[1] A definitive total is impossible because of the form of some entries.

[2] *Welle* is probably not a personal name because we are told who held it in 1066. There may be some connection between these 1½ virgates and those of *Weleue* (50) which Waleran 'put out of the shire and put in Wiltshire' (*misit foras comitatum et misit in Wiltesire*). Before 1895, West Wellow was in Wiltshire and East Wellow in Hampshire—see *V.C.H. Hampshire*, IV (London, 1911), pp. 535 and 598. East and West Wellow have been counted as one place in this analysis.

[3] See p. 327 below.

Soberton. *Emelei* (47b) appears as Embley Wood and Embley House in East Wellow. The name of *Larode* (48b) is preserved in Lyewood and Lyeway Farms in the parish of Ropley, and that of *Wildehel* (48b) in Will Hall in Alton. *Hangre* (50b) and *Derleie* (50b) have become Hanger Farm and Durley Farm, in the parishes of Netley Marsh and Denny Lodge respectively; and *Benverdeslei* (39b) has become Barnsley Farm in Brading. *Snodintone* (45b) appears on the modern map as Snoddington Furze in Shipton Bellinger. These are but some of the changes of fortune among the Hampshire villages. To them must be added forty unidentified names.[1] Fortunately, the majority of these places were only small settlements, and it is often possible to determine the locality in which an unidentified name lay, so that the density figures cannot be greatly in error. Presumably, these small places went out of occupation soon after the eleventh century, or they may have been amalgamated with larger settlements. Whether they will yet be located, or whether the places they represent have completely disappeared leaving no record or trace behind, we cannot say.

On the other hand, many settlements on the modern map are not mentioned in the Domesday Book. Their names do not appear until the twelfth or thirteenth century or even later, and, presumably, if they existed in 1086, they are accounted for under the statistics of other settlements. Thus, so far as record goes, Petersfield was first mentioned in 1182, Aldershot in 1248, Bembridge in 1316 and Cowes as late as 1512. Bournemouth is wholly a recent creation, though the name appeared as early as 1407. Some of the places not mentioned in the Domesday Book must have existed, or at any rate been named, in Domesday times because they are found in pre-Domesday documents. The following names, for example, are found in charters of the tenth and early eleventh centuries

---

[1] The full list of Domesday place-names in Hampshire that have not been located in the present analysis is: NEW FOREST—*Achelie* (Redbridge hd., 51), *Achelie* (Boldre hd., 51b), *Alwinetune* (51), *Bedecote* (39), *Bile* (51 *bis*), *Cildeest* (51b), *Cocherlei* (51b), *Lesteorde* (51), *Mapleham* (51b), *Nutlei* (51b), *Oselei* (51 *bis*), *Oxelei* (51b), *Sanhest* (51b), *Sclive* (51), *Slacham* (39), *Tru(c)ham* (51 *ter*, 51b *bis*), *Wigarestun* (51b); also in the New Forest section of the Domesday Book are *Godesmanescamp* (51b) and *Utefel* (51b), but these are not said to lie wholly or partly 'in the forest'. REST OF MAINLAND—*Aplestede* (45b), *Bieforde* (40), *Chingescamp* (40b), *Clatinges* (44b, 46), *Eschetune* (48), *Finlei* (49), *Gerlei* (46b, 47, 48b), *Hotlop* (50), *Mulceltone* (50), *Sudberie* (50). ISLE OF WIGHT—*Abaginge* (53b), *Abla* (40), *Alvrestone* (53), *Celvecrote* (53b), *Drodintone* (54), *Heceford* (54), *Levegarestun* (53), *Wenechetone* (39b), *Werictetone* (53b), *Witestone* (53), *Witingeham* (53b).

and again in manuscripts of the twelfth century, and yet they do not appear in the Domesday text: Catherington, Grately, Michelmersh, Sparsholt, Swarraton and Tichborne. Occasionally, although a modern parish is not named in the Domesday Book it contains a name or names that are

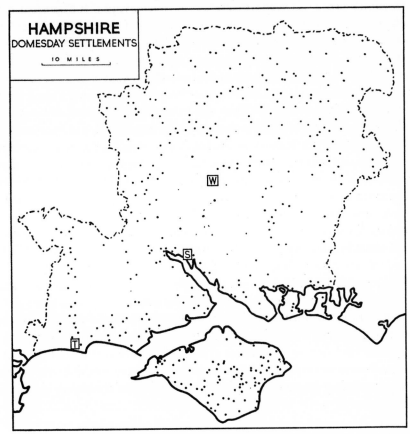

Fig. 91. Hampshire: Domesday place-names.
Domesday boroughs are indicated by initials: S, Southampton; T, Twynham; W, Winchester.

mentioned. Thus the name of Buriton did not appear until 1227, but the parish contains Sunwood Farm which represents the Domesday vill of *Seneorde* (44b). From this account it is clear that there have been many changes in the village geography of the county, and that the list of Domesday names differs considerably from that of present-day parishes.

Yet, except for the considerable extension of settlement around Bournemouth, Portsmouth and Southampton, and for the military development
around Aldershot, the distribution of Domesday names (and probably
also of Domesday settlements, could we but reconstruct the composition
of many manors) was very similar, in a general way, to that of present-day
villages (Fig. 91). This was true even of the New Forest area; settlements
here lay on the fringes of the Forest, and there are today within its com-
pass as few villages as at the time of the Inquest. Over the rest of the
county, most of the Chalk downland stood out as an empty area broken
by valley settlements. The fifth-century invaders had pushed their way up
the valleys of the Avon, the Test, the Itchen and the Meon; and in these
valleys were to be found the majority of the villages. Yet even on the
downland itself, particularly in the north-east towards Basingstoke, there
were some settlements where the Chalk is covered by patches of Clay-
with-flints. Some stood at surprisingly high levels; Dummer and Wield,
for example, were between 500 ft. and 600 ft., and Shalden over 600 ft.
above sea-level. Beyond the Chalk, along the northern and eastern
borders of the county, there were some villageless areas where the surface
is of infertile sand and gravel—the Bagshot Sands to the north of Aldershot, and the Lower Greensand to the east of Selborne. To the south of the
Chalk, and between it and the coast, other stretches of Eocene sand and
gravel continued to lie empty until modern times.

The striking feature of settlement in the Isle of Wight was the absence
of villages over much of the north. Here, both the ill-drained Oligocene
clays and the infertile stretches of gravel were unattractive to early settlement. The more varied and hilly Cretaceous country to the south, on the
other hand, had frequent villages, set at the foot of the downs or in the
valleys.

The Distribution of Prosperity and Population

Some idea of the nature of the information in the Domesday folios for
Hampshire, and of the form in which it is presented, may be obtained
from the entry for Wickham situated in the south of the county on the
River Meon, not far from Portsmouth Harbour. The village was held
entirely by Hugh de Port, and so it is described in a single entry (45):

Hugh himself holds Wickham. Four brothers held [it], as 2 manors, of
King Edward. It was then, as now, assessed at 12 hides (*se defendit pro xii*

hidis). Hugh received [it] as one manor. There is land for 7 plough-teams. In the demesne are 2 plough-teams; and [there are] 15 villeins and 6 bordars with 7 plough-teams. There [are] 5 serfs, and 2 mills yielding (*de*) 20s., and 8 acres of meadow. Wood yielding (*de*) 5 swine. *T.R.E.* it was worth £10, and afterwards £4; now £7.

This entry does not include all the items of information that are given for some other places; there is no mention, for example, of fisheries or salt-pans or pasture. But it is fairly representative and straightforward, and it does set out the recurring standard items that are found in entry after entry. These standard items are: (1) hides, (2) plough-lands, (3) plough-teams, (4) population, and (5) values. Their bearing upon regional variations in prosperity throughout the county must now be considered.

(1) *Hides*

The Hampshire assessment is stated in terms of hides and virgates, and, very occasionally, of what seem to be geld acres; at Blackpan, for instance, there was a holding of 10 acres (53). There are also references to the *ferding*, or quarter-virgate, in the entries for Canterton (50b) and Haldley (52); and two other entries, those for Cholderton (49b) and Langley (50b), also mention quarter-virgates (*quarta parte unius virgatae*). At Aviston (53) there was a holding of 1⅓ virgates; at *Werictetone* (53b) one of 2 hides 3⅓ virgates; at *Drodintone* (54) another of 1½ hides less ⅓ of a virgate; and at Nettlestone (39b, 53b) there were three holdings each of ⅓ of a hide. Two phrases are normally employed to express the assessment: (1) *se defendit pro n hidis* or *se defendebat pro n hidis*; (2) *geldavit pro n hidis*. But there are variants, and we are occasionally told, for example, that *A tenet n hidas in B*, or that *A habet n hidas in B*. No reason seems to govern this variety, and a particular formula is not regularly associated with certain hundreds nor with the holdings of certain tenants-in-chief. For a number of holdings we are told either that each had never been assessed, or that the jurors did not know the hidage. Some of the variations are indicated below:

Andover (39): *De hidis numerum non dixerunt.*
Basingstoke (39): *Nunquam geldum dedit, nec hida ibi distributa fuit.*
Broughton (38b): *De hidis rationem non dederunt.*
Eling (38b): *Numerum hidarum nesciunt.*
Wymering (38): *Nunquam hidatum fuit.*

On some of these unassessed manors, we glimpse the archaic system of the *firma unius diei*, commuted into a fixed rent received by the king.[1]

One feature that the Hampshire folios share with those of the neighbouring counties of Berkshire, Surrey and Sussex is that they so frequently record a reduction in the geld liability of a holding.[2] Thus of Exton (41b) we read: '*T.R.E.* it was assessed at 12 hides, now at 8 hides'; and of Quarley (39): 'It was then assessed at 5 hides, now at nothing.' When the liability had remained unchanged, we are specifically told so; Westbury (45), for example, 'was then and now assessed at 3 hides'. In the entry for Twynham (44) there is a blank space where the 1086 hidage was, apparently, intended to be inserted.

The Land of Earl Roger (fo. 44b)

	Hidage 'then'		Hidage 'now'	
	H	V	H	V
A. *Holdings in demesne*				
Boarhunt	11	o	4	1½
Chalton	60	o	27	o
	71	o	31	1½
B. *Holdings of sub-tenants*				
Candover	5½	o	5½	o
Penton	8	o	5	o
Avon	1	o	1	o
Houghton	2½	o	2½	o
Sunwood	3	o	3	o
In Bosmere hundred	5	o	3	o
Newtimber	3	o	3	o
Hambledon	1	o	1	o
	29	o	24	o

[1] See p. 317 below. The manors were: Barton Stacey (38b), Basingstoke (39), Broughton (38b), Eling (38b), Hurstbourne Tarrant (39), Kingsclere (39), Neatham (38), and possibly Andover (39), Somborne (39b), Breamore (39), Wymering (38). Three other holdings had never paid geld (*nunquam geldavit*), at Bullington (44), at Selborne (38), and at an unnamed place in *Egheiete* hundred (43b); but these do not seem to have belonged to the archaic system of the others.

[2] There is, apparently, one example of the reverse. At Gritnam (51b) a half-hide holding was assessed at 1 hide; but the entry seems confused.

These exemptions recall those of Cambridgeshire, but there the assessments of certain hundreds only were reduced, and the reduction was applied proportionally to the vills within each. In Hampshire we can discern no such principle at work. The amount of the exemption varied greatly within each hundred, and all we can say is that it had taken place largely (but by no means exclusively) on demesne manors, i.e. those without sub-tenants. The changes on the fee of Earl Roger of Shrewsbury, shown on p. 300, illustrate this.

Why such exemptions should have formed such a marked feature of this block of four counties in the south-east is difficult to explain. They could not have been due to damage caused by the Norman armies in 1066 or later, because the manors granted substantial reductions were not those apparently devastated. Other counties (e.g. Buckinghamshire and Hertfordshire) suffered as much as these four from the initial movements of the invading Norman armies, but we hear nothing of a general reduction of assessment in these. In any case, the devastated manors of the south-east seem to have recovered, or even increased, their pre-Conquest values by 1086, so that any reduction in liability need only have been temporary and done with before the Inquest was held. There are, moreover, a number of entries which suggest that the reduction was not always post-Conquest and that it had sometimes already taken place by 1066. These are set out below:

Reductions in Liability before 1066

Bishops Waltham (40): *T.R.E.* it was, as now, assessed at 20 hides; though there might be there 30 hides in number (*T.R.E. et modo se defendit pro xx hidis, quamvis sint ibi xxx hidae numero*).

Bishops Sutton (44b): There are 25 hides. It is now assessed at 10 hides; and it was the same *T.R.E.*, says the hundred court (*Ibi xxv hidae; pro x hidae se defendit modo, et sic fecit T.R.E. ut hundret dicit*).

Calbourne (52b): There are 32 hides. But *T.R.E.* as now, it paid geld for only 17 hides (*Ibi sunt xxxii hidae. Sed T.R.E. et modo non geldavit nisi pro xvii hidis*).

Chawton (45b): There were 10 hides, but King Edward assessed it for service and geld at 4 hides and 1 virgate (*Ibi erant x hidae, sed rex E. misit ad servitium et geldum pro iiii hidis et una virgata*).

Crondall (41): There were 50 hides *T.R.E.*, and then, as now, they paid geld for 40 hides (*Ibi fuerunt l hidae T.R.E., et tunc et modo geldaverunt pro xl hidis*).

Houghton (40b): There are 24 hides. *T.R.E.* it was, as now, assessed at
16 hides (*Ibi sunt xxiiii hidae. T.R.E. et modo se defendit pro xvi hidis*).

Steventon (50b): There were reckoned to be 5 hides there. But it was then,
as now, assessed at 3 hides (*Ibi habebantur v hidae. Sed tunc et modo se
defendit pro iii hidis*).

The reduction was sometimes queried; Hartley Mauditt (47b) was 'then
assessed at 6 hides, and afterwards at 3 hides; but the shire court (*comitatus*)
has not seen the king's writ or seal for this. It is now assessed at 2 hides.'

Some light is thrown on the origin of this double assessment by evidence
from Cornwall, which is another county where the feature is encountered
in the Domesday folios.[1] For that county, it is possible to compare the
Domesday figures with those of the Geld Rolls, and it can be seen that the
difference between the two assessments is the amount of fiscal demesne on
a manor; and it was this which, on occasion, was quit of liability. Some
of the Hampshire entries themselves refer to hides of the demesne:

Alton (43): There were then 10 hides; and the villeins who dwelled there
paid geld for 5 hides. The abbot has now five hides in demesne, but they
have not paid geld (*Tunc erant x hidae, et villani qui ibi manebant geldabant
pro v hidis. Modo habet abbas in dominio v hidas sed non geldaverunt*).

Candover (42): It was assessed at 20 hides; 11 of these are in demesne
(*defendit se pro xx hidis. Ex his xi sunt in dominio*).

Linkenholt (43): It was then assessed at 5 hides, now at 1 hide; the others
are in demesne (*Tunc se defendit pro v hidis, modo pro una hida; aliae sunt
in dominio*).

We may perhaps conclude that these reductions were not intended to be
regular or permanent, but that the demesne was on occasion exempt from
liability to geld. The twelfth-century Pipe Roll figures show that the
total assessments of counties changed very little in comparison with those
of the previous century. Geld was still due from the whole, even though
by favour exemptions had been, and were, granted.[2]

In addition to these general exemptions from the geld, we read of
reductions for particular reasons:

Alvington (52b):[3] [It was assessed] then at 2½ hides. Now at 2 hides because
the castle stands on one virgate (*quia castellum sedet in una virgata*).

---

[1] *V.C.H. Cornwall*, Part VIII, pp. 47–51 (published as a separate part, London, 1924).
[2] See p. 58 for the interesting entry relating to Miswell (138) in Hertfordshire.
[3] In Carisbrooke.

Fareham (40b): *T.R.E.* it was, as now, assessed at 20 hides. However, there are 30 hides in number. But King Edward granted it thus on account of the Vikings, because it is by the sea.

Ovington (43b): It was then assessed at 1½ hides; now at nothing because it is for the support (*de victu*) of the nuns.

Watchingwell (52b): *T.R.E.* it was assessed at 3 hides, now at 2½ hides because half [a hide] is in the king's park (*quia dimidia est in parco regis*).

Viking raids may also have been responsible for the reduction at Alverstoke (41b) nearby on Portsmouth Harbour, although we are not told so. Reduction was also made for land taken into the forest. At Fawley (41b, 51) there were 2 hides in demesne which were assessed at 2 hides, but 'now at 1 virgate only because the remaining 7 are in the forest' (*Ipse episcopus tenet ii hidas...in Falegia...et pro ii hidis se defendebat. Modo non nisi pro una virgata quia vii aliae sunt in foresta*). Or again, Fernhill (51) was assessed 'then at 3 virgates; now at 1 virgate, the remainder being in the forest'. Entry after entry relating to the New Forest reads similarly.[1]

These changes in assessment, whether made before or after the Conquest, masked the five-hide unit. But if we confine ourselves to 1066, the original system of assessment can still be seen clearly. Bishopstoke (40) and Snoddington (45b), for example, were each assessed at 5 hides; and the manor of Fyfield (47b), whose Domesday name (*Fifhide*) recalls the unit of assessment, 'then paid geld for 5 hides, now for 3 hides'. Some entries are difficult to interpret, but it seems that about 36 villages were rated at 5 hides each; another 40 at multiples of 5; and that there were at least a dozen at 2½ hides each.[2] These figures are out of a total of 458, i.e. excluding the 40 or so unnamed holdings. We cannot be far wrong in saying that the five-hide principle is readily apparent in at least one-fifth of the Hampshire villages of 1066. It is clear, moreover, that villages were grouped in blocks as in some other counties. Shipton Bellinger with 1½ and 10½ hides (46b, 47b), and South Tidworth (46b *bis*, 49) with 4, 7 and 2, may have formed a 25-hide block along the north-west border of the county. Or again, a 10-hide block along the eastern border may have comprised Bramshott (46b), Chiltley (38) and Ludshott (45b) with 6, 2 and 2 hides respectively.

[1] See p. 332 below.
[2] Of these, one five-hide vill and one assessed at a multiple of 5, were in the Isle of Wight.

What with the conventional nature of the assessment and the erratic nature of the reduction, it is unlikely that the hidage bore any constant relation to the agricultural resources of a holding. The variation among a representative selection of vills, assessed at 10 hides each in 1066, speaks for itself:

	1086 Hidage	Plough-lands	Teams	Population
Alton (43)	5	4	3	13
Bighton (43)	7	8	8	26
Newton Valence (47 b)	5	12	12	20
Sydmonton (44)	7½	11	11	29
Wonston (41 b)	7	7	7	26

An extreme example of the artificial nature of the assessment is Chilcomb (41). It paid geld, in 1086 as in 1066, for 1 hide, yet it had land for 77 plough-teams and 78 were at work there, while 213 people were recorded.[1]

The form of many entries makes it extremely difficult to arrive at satisfactory totals for the hidage of the county,[2] but the following three sets of figures at any rate serve to indicate the order of magnitude involved:

(a) Assessment (including non-gelding hides): 2,859 hides, 3¾ virgates, 25½ acres.

(b) Gelding hides in 1066: 2,693 hides, 2¾ virgates, 13½ acres.

(c) Gelding hides in 1086: 1,580 hides, $2\frac{5}{12}$ virgates, 5 acres.

F. W. Maitland's totals for the Domesday county in 1066 and 1086 were 2,588 hides and 1,572 hides respectively.[3] But, as Maitland confessed, any total depends upon the individual interpretation of certain entries. Nor, for that matter, could the Domesday clerks have been certain of an exact total because, as we have seen, they did not know the hidage of certain holdings.

(2) Plough-lands

Plough-lands are systematically entered for the Hampshire villages, and the normal formula runs: 'There is land for n ploughs' (Terra est n

---

[1] Pre-Domesday documents show that this was a 100-hide manor whose assessment had been reduced to this nominal figure—see p. 290 above.

[2] The corresponding figures for the Isle of Wight alone are as follows: (a) 196 hides, ¾ virgate, (b) 181 hides, ¾ virgate, (c) 97 hides, 2¾ virgates.

[3] F. W. Maitland, Domesday Book and Beyond, pp. 400–1.

carucis). But there are 17 entries for 17 places in which *Terra est* is followed by a blank space in which a figure was never inserted, e.g. for Andover (39), Rockbourne (50) and Tufton (44).[1] There are also many entries which mention teams but not plough-lands, e.g. for Bramshill (45 b), Houghton (48) and Whippingham (53).[2] Taking these two categories together, there are about 60 places with incomplete figures for plough-lands.[3] An entry for Candover (42) says that there was land for 9 teams, but the figure 18 has been inserted over the 9; this may possibly be a correction, for although only 10 teams were at work on the holding, it was assessed at 20 hides, but in this analysis only 9 plough-lands have been counted.

There are 46 entries relating to land wholly taken into the New Forest, and these sometimes use the unusual formula *Terra fuit n carucis*, but we also find *Terra n carucis* and even the normal *Terra est n carucis*. Of the five entries relating to *Truham* or *Trucham* (51–51 b), two give *fuit*, two *est*, and one neither. Presumably all five entries are providing the same kind of information, and are recording the existence of land suitable for cultivation. Altogether, 122 plough-lands are recorded as having been taken into the New Forest; and on nine holdings the number is not given, which may represent another 20 or so ploughlands.

The relation between plough-lands and plough-teams varies a great deal in individual entries. A deficiency of teams is fairly frequent, being found for just over one-third of the Domesday settlements for which plough-lands were recorded, excluding those places wholly in the Forest. The values on some of these deficient holdings had fallen between 1066 and 1086, but on others they had remained constant, and on yet others they had even increased. No general correlation between plough-team deficiency and decrease in value is, therefore, possible, as the table on the following page shows. These figures are merely indications of unexplained changes on individual manors. We cannot really say whether the plough-land figures are those of teams employed in 1066; but, whatever the implications of the figures, the deficiency seems to indicate understocking.

[1] Three of these seventeen entries, relating to three places, are in the Isle of Wight.

[2] Where teams but not teamlands are entered for the component parts of manors, we have assumed that the manorial figure for teamlands covers the parts.

[3] The total of 'about 60' includes a dozen or so for the Isle of Wight. The figure 60 excludes those places wholly in the Forest (see p. 327 below), and also about half a dozen others for which no information either for teams or plough-lands is given (see p. 295 above).

		Plough-lands	Teams	Value 1066	Value 1086
Decrease in value	Ellisfield (46)	10	6	£10	£5
	Charford (46)	4	3	£5	£4
Same value	Hoddington (41 b)	6	4	£4	£4
	Watchingwell (52 b)	8	5	£3	£3
Increase in value	Alton (43)	4	3	£6	£7
	Tisted (40 b)	8	6	£4	£6

The number of teams at work exceeded the number for which there was land for just under one-third of the Domesday settlements for which plough-lands were recorded, excluding those places wholly in the Forest. Generally speaking, values had risen on these holdings, but not invariably. At Shalden (47b) and at Winslade (45), for example, the value had remained the same; and at Sandown (39b) it had fallen. Very occasionally, the existence of excess teams is emphasised in the text. At Preston Candover (49b), we are told, there was land for half a team, and yet (*et tamen*) there was one team at work: but we are given no reason for this, and we can only conjecture about the excess in general. Or again, at Milford (53b), in the Isle of Wight, there was land for half a team, and yet there was one team on the demesne (*In domino tamen est una caruca*). This excess was general throughout the shire, including the New Forest where, at first sight, we might not expect it. Thus Holdenhurst (39) had 23½ teams for only 20 plough-lands; Ringwood (39) had 17½ for 16; one of the Twynham manors (38b) had 16½ for 13. It may be that teams ploughing the land taken into the Forest were transferred elsewhere to produce an occasional surplus; certainly at Holdenhurst, at Ringwood, and at Twynham, there was forest where there had been 8 and 7 and 3 teams respectively. But this suggestion, while possibly explaining the local excess in the New Forest, does not account for the more general excess throughout Hampshire.

The total number of plough-lands recorded for the area within the modern county is 2,674½. If, however, we assume that the plough-lands equalled the teams on those holdings where a figure for the former is not given, the total becomes 2,844⅝;[1] in making this calculation we have excluded the 40 or so entries for which the information may be con-

[1] The totals in this paragraph include, of course, the figures for the Isle of Wight. The separate figures for the island are: (i) 318 recorded plough-lands; (ii) 335 plough-lands, making allowance for those entries where the figure is missing.

cealed under manorial totals.[1] Furthermore, neither figure includes the 122 plough-lands that had been taken into the New Forest. A grand total for 1066 would, therefore, seem to be 2,966⅝.[2]

(3) Plough-teams

The Hampshire entries for plough-teams, like those of other counties, normally draw a distinction between the teams at work on the demesne and those held by the peasantry. But in an entry for Lessland (39b), in the Isle of Wight, we encounter the most unusual statement that the teams in demesne belonged to the villeins (*Ibi sunt iiii villani habentes in dominio ii carucas et dimidiam*).[3] Occasional entries seem to be defective. That for Sudberie (50), for example, mentions 3 plough-lands and 2 men, but says nothing about any teams; the annual value of the estate had fallen from 40 to 20s., and maybe here was a settlement in decay. Sometimes only demesne teams are entered, e.g. for Bullington (44) where there was land for 6 ploughs, but only two were on the demesne, and the 8 villeins, 4 bordars (and 3 serfs) were apparently without any. An entry for one of the Worthys (42b) records 2 villeins and 9 bordars without a plough (*sine caruca*), but there were 2 on the demesne and there was land for 3. Occasionally, on the other hand, no demesne is mentioned, and the only teams at work were those of the peasants, e.g. on holdings at Oakley (46b) and Silchester (47). Conversely, there was a team in demesne but no people at *Godesmanescamp* (51b), and we are left to wonder who ploughed with it unless it was Ulvric, the sub-tenant, himself. But usually the record of teams is complete and fairly straightforward.

Half-teams are frequently mentioned (e.g. for Cosham, 46), and oxen themselves are sometimes entered, as the examples below indicate:

Barton Stacey (46b): *Ibi sunt ix boves et unus villanus et v bordarii.*
Bishops Waltham (40): *Ibi habet i villanum et iii bordarios cum ix bobus.*
Hurstbourne Priors (41): *habet vii boves in caruca.*
Newtimber (44b): *In dominio ii boves in caruca.*
Preston Candover (49b): *iii villani cum iii bobus in caruca.*
Nether Wallop (45b): *Ibi sunt ii villani et ii bordarii cum ii bobus.*

---

[1] See p. 305 above.
[2] F. W. Maitland's total for the Domesday county amounted to 2,847 plough-lands (*op. cit.* pp. 401 and 410). He made allowance for the missing figures in some entries, but we cannot say exactly how he arrived at his total; presumably it includes the 122 plough-lands that had disappeared into the New Forest.
[3] See p. 311 below for landholding villeins.

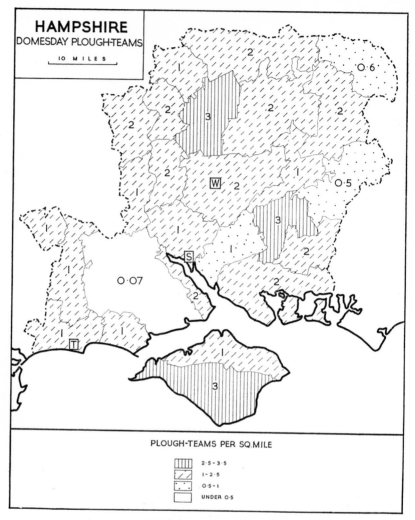

Fig. 92. Hampshire: Domesday plough-teams
in 1086 (by densities).

Domesday boroughs are indicated by initials: S, Southampton;
T, Twynham; W, Winchester.

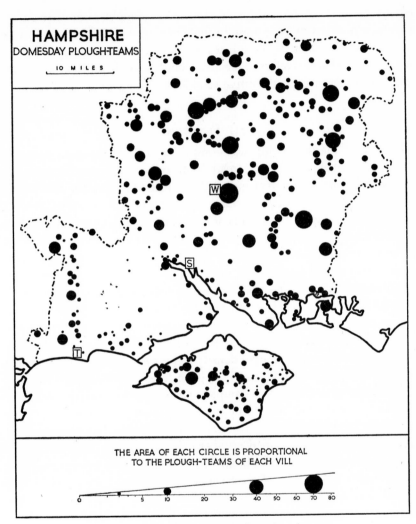

Fig. 93. Hampshire: Domesday plough-teams
in 1086 (by settlements).

Domesday boroughs are indicated by initials: S, Southampton;
T, Twynham; W, Winchester.

At Titchfield (39) there were but 2 'animals' on the demesne (*In dominio nisi ii animalia*); these might have been either draught-oxen or cows, but, from the position of the phrase in the entry, more probably the former.

The total number of plough-teams amounted to 2,779, but it must be remembered that this refers to the area included within the modern county, and that, in any case, a definitive total is hardly possible.[1]

(4) *Population*

The bulk of the population was comprised in the three main categories of bordars, villeins and serfs. In addition to these were the burgesses and a miscellaneous group that included a substantial number of coliberts, together with some coscets, cottars, 'men', radmen, two priests, a *francus homo* and a vavassor. The details of the groups are summarised on p. 314. This estimate is not comparable with that of Sir Henry Ellis, which was in terms of the Domesday county and which included tenants-in-chief, under-tenants and burgesses.[2] In any case, an estimate of Domesday population can rarely be accurate, and all that can be claimed for the present figures is that they indicate the order of magnitude involved. These figures are those of recorded population, and must be multiplied by some factor, say 4 or 5, in order to obtain the actual population; but this does not affect the relative density as between one area and another.[3] That is all that a map such as Fig. 94 can roughly indicate.

It is impossible to say how complete were these Domesday figures. We should have expected, for example, to hear more of foresters; but apart from the mention of those foresters who were landholders,[4] the only reference is to an unspecified number (*forestarii*) who enjoyed rights to honey, pasture and timber for building in the hundred of Broughton (38 b), to the north of the New Forest proper. Or again, there were plough-teams on some holdings, but no mention of men.[5] There must also have been a small garrison and probably some servants in the castle at Alvington

---

[1] F. W. Maitland's total for the Domesday county was 2,614 (*op. cit.* p. 401). Of the present figure of 2,779, the teams in the Isle of Wight numbered 326¼.

[2] Sir Henry Ellis, *A General Introduction to Domesday Book*, II (London, 1833), pp. 449–51: His grand total came to 10,373.

[3] But see p. 589 below for the complication of serfs.

[4] E.g. Herbert the forester at Lyndhurst (39) and Peret the forester at Battramsley (51 b).

[5] See p. 307 above for entries with teams but no men.

(52b), but they are not mentioned. More striking is the small number of priests in relation to the number of churches recorded, but we have no means of knowing to what extent the priests were included amongst the villeins; those priests who were obviously sub-tenants have not been included in the totals.[1] Neither have those freemen, falconers, foresters and huntsmen, who were tenants or sub-tenants, been included.[2] Against the possibility of unrecorded people, we must set that of duplication. Five villeins of the abbey of St Mary of Lyre (52b) had holdings in several manors (*in pluribus maneriis*), and these villeins may have been included in the entries for these other manors.

Bordars constituted the most important element numerically in the population, and amounted to just over 40 per cent of the total; they were followed closely by villeins who numbered just under 40 per cent. At Alverstoke (41b) and at Millbrook (41b) we read of villeins holding directly from the bishop of Winchester without the intervention of under-tenants. Both entries say: 'It was, and is, held by the villeins', and the latter adds: 'There is no hall (*aula*) there.' The villeins numbered 48 and 28 respectively. Moreover, at Lessland (39b) in the Isle of Wight, there were 4 villeins who held 2½ teams in demesne.[3] The statistics relating to bordars present no special feature for our purpose; but we must note the reference to the messuages of 20 bordars at Bowcombe (52) in the Isle of Wight (*xx masurae bordariorum*). The serfs amounted to 18 per cent of the total, and it is interesting to note that they are frequently not grouped with the other categories of population, but are placed after the list of manorial appurtenances such as the church and the meadow, e.g. in the entries for Haldley (52) and for Lomer (43).

In the miscellaneous category, the coliberts are outstanding. There has been some discussion about their status, and they seem in some way to

[1] There were such priests at Bishops Waltham (40), Clere (41), Houghton (40b), Hurstbourne Tarrant (39), Odiham (38), Selborne (38) and Whitchurch (41). The decision whether or not to include them is not always easy.

[2] There were, for example, land-holding freemen at Romsey (43b) and Wield (40b), land-holding huntsmen at Langley (50b) and Ripley (50b), and land-holding falconers at Gorley (49b) and in Basingstoke hundred (50b). For land-holding foresters see p. 310, n. 4 above.

[3] For a discussion of these entries, see J. H. Round in *V.C.H. Hampshire*, I, p. 442. Villeins had similarly held, in 1066, portions of Bishops Waltham (40) and of Stoke Charity (40b). At Chilbolton (41) a certain steward (*praefectus*) had held two hides by villein tenure (*quasi villanus*); and a certain Alvric, in the manor of Crondall, had held 3 virgates *quasi villanus* (41).

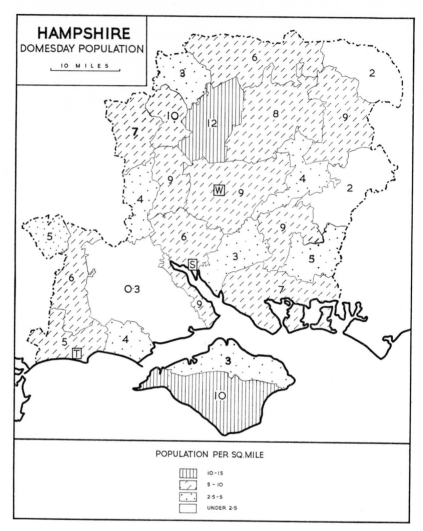

HAMPSHIRE
DOMESDAY POPULATION
10 MILES

POPULATION PER SQ.MILE

10 - 15
5 - 10
2·5 - 5
UNDER 2·5

Fig. 94. Hampshire: Domesday population in 1086
(by densities).

Domesday boroughs are indicated by initials: S, Southampton;
T, Twynham; W, Winchester.

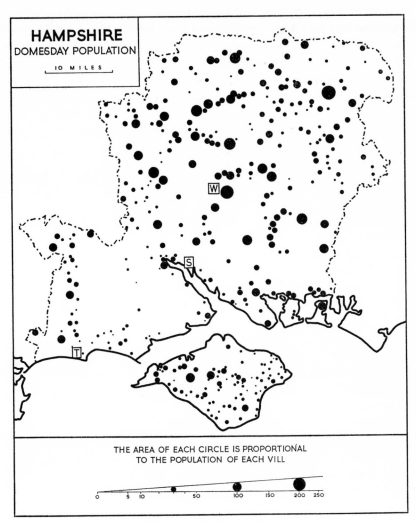

Fig. 95. Hampshire: Domesday population in 1086
(by settlements).

Domesday boroughs are indicated by initials: S, Southampton;
T, Twynham; W, Winchester.

have been intermediate between serfs and villeins.[1] In Hampshire they were to be found only on royal and ecclesiastical manors, and the formula often couples them with serfs; thus in an entry for Meonstoke we read: 'there were 4 serfs and 4 coliberts' (38). Two entries explain that coliberts and 'boors' (*bures* or *buri*) were all one. In that for Nether Wallop (38b), *vel Bures* is interlined above *et coliberti*; and the other, for Cosham (38), speaks of *viii burs i coliberti*, which suggests that the clerk had it in mind

Recorded Population of Hampshire in 1086

A. Rural Population

	Mainland	Isle of Wight	Total
Villeins	3,575	360	3,935
Bordars	3,558	461	4,019
Serfs	1,535	237	1,772
Miscellaneous	167	10	177
Total	8,835	1,068	9,903

Details of Miscellaneous Rural Population

	Mainland	Isle of Wight	Total
Coliberts	136	0	136
Coscets	16	0	16
Cottars	6	0	6
Men (*Homines*)	0	8	8
Radmen	5	0	5
Rustici	2	0	2
Priests	1	1	2
Francus homo	1	0	1
Vavassor	0	1	1
Total	167	10	177

B. Urban Population

Villeins, bordars, radmen, coliberts and serfs are also included above.

WINCHESTER   See p. 353 below.

SOUTHAMPTON   79 *homines*; 65 *francigenae*; 31 Englishmen; 7 houses; 48(?) houses. See p. 351 below.

TWYNHAM   39 houses; 32 villeins; 18 bordars; 4 radmen; 3 coliberts; 3 serfs. See p. 352 below.

[1] See (i) P. Vinogradoff, *English Society in the Eleventh Century* (Oxford, 1908), pp. 468–9; (ii) F. M. Stenton, *Anglo-Saxon England* (Oxford, 1943), pp. 468–70.

to say *viii bures, id est (or vel) coliberti.* It is true that in Anglo-Saxon society the boor (or gebur) was a dependent person, and yet, on the other hand, a few stray Domesday phrases suggest that some coliberts at any rate were not particularly near the servile level. At Barton Stacey (38b), 6 hides had been, and still were, held by coliberts (*quas tenuerunt coliberti et tenent*); the dozen coliberts at Basingstoke (39) seem to have had 4 plough-teams; the pair at Kingsclere (39) rendered 13s. annually; and at Cosham (38), in 1066, there had been 8 coliberts (with 4 plough-teams) making an annual render of 49s. 4d.[1] The coscets and cottars were at Kinson (80b) and at Plaitford (74), places surveyed under Dorset and Wiltshire respectively; no mention of either group is made in the Hampshire folios. The eight 'men' (*homines*) at Bowcombe (52), the 5 radmen (*radchenistri*) at Ringwood (39) and Twynham (38b); the 2 priests in the manor of Basingstoke (43) and at Bowcombe (52), the 2 *rustici* at Tytherley (74),[2] the *francus homo* at Houghton (48) and the vavassor (*vavassorius*) at Aviston (53), complete the total as far as the record goes; the solitary vavassor was, apparently, of humble status, for he had no team but only 2 cows (*ii vaccae*).

(5) *Values*

The value of an estate is normally given for three dates—*tunc, post, modo,* i.e. for 1066, for the year in which a subsequent owner received it, and for 1086.[3] Some entries give only two values, like that for Havant (43) which runs: *Valet et valuit viii libras.* Other entries give but one value, e.g. those for Brockhampton (45b) Midgham (50) and Norton (47); possibly the amount had remained constant, or the figures refer only to 1086. Here, too, must be mentioned those New Forest holdings for which a 1066 value only is stated.[4] No values are given for some holdings because they formed part of a manor, and the valuation was entered for the manor as a whole. The absence of a value in a number of other entries we can only regard as due to straightforward omission.

[1] A virgate in the New Forest (50b) may once have been held by a colibert *in firma regis,* but *Colibt'* appears in the text as possibly a proper name. The coliberts at Nether Wallop (38b) rendered customary dues as others did (*reddunt consuetudinem aliorum*).
[2] Four *rustici* are recorded in a joint entry for Winterslow (Wilts) and Tytherley (Hants).
[3] The customary *post* is sometimes replaced by *Cum recepit,* e.g. in a number of entries on fo. 45. It is interesting to note that in the duplicate entries for Charford, one (44b) has *Cum recepit* and the other (46) has *post.*   [4] See p. 327 below.

The amounts are usually stated to the nearest pound or 10s. or even 30d., but a number of entries suggest greater precision, e.g. Clere (41) paid £12. 3s. 2d. in 1066, and Chiltley (38) paid 53s. at all three dates.[1] We are specifically told that the values of some estates were reckoned by the tale or count (*ad numerum* or *numero*), when the coins were accepted at their nominal value. But in view of the circulation of debased coins, some values were reckoned by weight, and were also tested by assay; the latter were known as 'white money'. East Meon (38), for example, paid its amount by weight (*ad pensam*), while Arreton (39b) paid in white money at 20 pence to the ounce (*reddit xii libras blancas de xx in ora*). At Odiham (38) a change in the mode of reckoning had taken place: '*T.R.E.* and afterwards, it was worth £50 by tale; now £50 by weight.'

One of the outstanding features of the Hampshire valuation is the decrease in the value of very many estates between 1066 and the time when subsequent owners received them, followed by a recovery by 1086. Some of the reductions in payment were considerable, as the following examples show:

	1066	Intermediate	1086
Basing (45)	£12	£8	£16
Bishops Waltham (40)	£31	£10. 10s.	£30
Corhampton (45)	£8	5s.	£8
Ellisfield (46)	£10	£3	£5

F. H. Baring accounted for these temporary decreases by regarding them as marking the passage of Norman armies to and from the Winchester district soon after the Battle of Hastings, and he also discerned the track of a supply force marching inland from the Hampshire coast.[2] It seems a reasonable hypothesis, and it is not surprising that the suggested routes, marked by reductions in value, are interrupted (as they would be when an army was on the march). The majority of manors had recovered, fully or in part, by 1086; some had even become more prosperous than before. Here was a campaign totally unlike that which reduced the north of England to submission.

Another outstanding fact about the Hampshire valuation is that the new landowners frequently obtained from their estates more than what was

[1] Bramshill (48) was worth 40s. in 1066; 20s. 5d. afterwards; and 25d. in 1086. Its mill alone rendered 25d., and, quite possibly, its 1086 figure should read 25s.

[2] F. H. Baring, 'The Conqueror's footprints in Domesday', *Eng. Hist. Rev.* XIII (1898), pp. 17–25. Reprinted with additions and alterations in *Domesday Tables* (London, 1909), pp. 207–16. See p. 569 below.

regarded as a reasonable return. Sixty-nine entries for 74 places and one anonymous holding give the current value in 1086 and then tell us that the estate paid, or was rented at, a greater sum.[1] Some of the revised sums were considerably in excess of those agreed to by the jurors:

	1066	Intermediate	1086	Payment
Bramley (45)	£5	£7	£9	£12
East Meon (38)	£60	£40	£60	£100
Exton (41 b)	£16	£12	£20	£30
Haseley (39 b)	£8	£8	£5	£8
Mapledurham (38)	£25	£25	£25	£32

It is not surprising that both in the entry for East Meon and in that for Exton we are told that the estate could not bear it (*Sed non potest pati*). Many entries record similar complaint, but on one occasion we are told that the amount was just; Newton Stacey (48 b) paid 20s. and it was worth that sum (*est data ad firmam pro xx solidis et tantum valet*).

A few of the valuations show us, wrote J. H. Round, 'an archaic system in the act of passing away. This was the grouping of certain manors to form a unit, from which the king received a fixed rent in kind. Such a rent was known as a *firma unius diei* or *firma unius noctis*, from the Anglo-Saxon word *feorm*.'[2] The manors on which it is found seem never to have been assessed in hides, and we are specifically told this fact in each of the relevant entries. Barton Stacey (38 b) and Eling (38 b) had each rendered half a day's 'farm' in the time of King Edward, and this had been worth £38. 8s. 4d. It would seem as if Broughton (38 b) and Neatham (38) had each been responsible for a whole day's 'farm'; we are not explicitly told so, but the identity of the sums in the following table strongly suggest it:

	T.R.E. et post	T.R.W.	Payment
Barton Stacey (38 b)	£38. 8s. 4d.	£33	£52. 6s. 1d.
Eling (38 b)	£38. 8s. 4d.	£20	£52. 6s. 1d.
Broughton (38 b)	£76. 16s. 8d.	£66	£104. 12s. 2d.
Neatham (38)	£76. 16s. 8d.	£76. 16s. 8d.	£118. 12s. 9d.

The roman figures of the amount for which Neatham was farmed in 1086 may have been misread by a clerk, or the composition of the manor may

---

[1] Included in these totals are 22 entries for 28 places in the Isle of Wight.
[2] *V.C.H.Hampshire*, I, p. 401. See J. H. Round, *Feudal England* (London, 1895; reprinted 1009), pp. 109–15. See also pp. 299–300 above.

have changed. In one entry, the text speaks as if the system were still in force: 'These three manors of Basingstoke, Kingsclere and Hurstbourne Tarrant render one day's "farm"' (39). We are unfortunately not given the money value of this render, but Round was able to show from the evidence of the Hundred Rolls that the group paid £104. 12s. 0d.[1] Other Hampshire manors apparently belonged to the same system, though each had neither its value nor its render stated—Andover (39), Somborne (39b), Breamore (39), and Wymering (38). Like the other seven manors they had belonged to King Edward and they had never been assessed in hides, but the jurors said that part of Somborne ought to be included in the king's demesne 'farm', and that it had been in 1066. The absence of detail about the others is another example of the imperfection of the Domesday text.

Generally speaking, the greater the number of teams and of men on an estate, the higher its value, but it is impossible to discern any consistent relationship. The six estates in the table below each yielded £5 in 1086; the first three show some reasonable relation between value and resources, but the next three are very different:

	Teams	Population	Other resources
East Meon (40b)	4½	21	Meadow, Mill
Lasham (38b)	5	20	Meadow
Penton (44b)	5	21	Meadow, Wood
Compton in Freshwater (52)*	3	11	Meadow
Herriard (45b)	6	11	Wood
Kilmeston (40)	2½	9	Meadow

* 'But it pays 60s. more.'

Or what are we to make of Redbridge (46)? It had a team and 5 people, 2 mills and some meadow, and it yielded 50s., yet the 2 mills alone are said to have yielded 50s.; if the entry is correct, we can only suppose that the mills must have served more than this settlement. Or what of the entry for Milford (51b) which tells us: 'there is nothing there, and yet it is worth 3s.' (*Nichil ibi est et tamen valet iii solidos*)? Or again, what can we understand from the curious entry for Tatchbury (43)? It was waste, but it was worth, and always had been worth, 10s. (*Vasta est et tamen valet et valuit semper x solidos*); no clue is given to any possible resources.

[1] *V.C.H. Hampshire*, I, pp. 401–2.

Conclusion

The Domesday hundreds are unsuitable units for which to calculate densities, partly because of the scattered nature of some of them, and partly because of their imperfect rubrication. The choice of unit areas is also made difficult by the fact that the totals for some manors cover widely separated settlements. We can select areas so as to include, as far as possible, these separate settlements within one unit, but, even so, doubt must remain when some of the components of a manor are anonymous.[1] With these considerations in mind, and also with an eye on the varying nature of soils and relief, twenty-six units have been devised. This does not form as perfect a regional division as a geographer would like, but we must be content with its limitations, and it does provide a rough-and-ready basis for distinguishing broad differences over the face of the county.

Of the five standard formulae, those relating to plough-teams and population are most likely to reflect something of the distribution of wealth and prosperity throughout the county. Taken together, they supplement one another to provide a general picture (Figs. 92 and 94). Among the least prosperous areas, the New Forest stands out with less than a tenth of a team and an average of less than a third of a person per square mile; both its soils and its history account for these low figures. Elsewhere in the county, low densities of teams (under one) and of population (about 2) are to be seen on the infertile sandy soils of the Bagshot district around Aldershot in the north-east, and on those of the Lower Greensand along the eastern border of the county. Some sandy areas are also to be found to the east of Southampton Water, and here also the densities of teams (about one) and population (3 to 4) are below the average for the county. In contrast to these infertile areas, the highest densities are to be found in the middle and upper courses of the Test, the Itchen and the Meon; here, teams average from about 2 to over 3 per square mile, and population from about 9 to nearly 12. In these districts we must envisage belts of settlements in the valleys separated by relatively empty Chalk uplands. In the Isle of Wight, the clays and gravels of the northern plain have low densities—just over one for teams and about 3 for population; these figures stand in contrast to the richer Cretaceous area of the southern hills where there are 3 teams and 10 people per square mile.

[1] See pp. 288–90 above.

Figs. 93 and 95 are supplementary to the density maps, but again it is necessary to make reservations about them. As we have seen on pp. 293–5 some Domesday names covered two or more settlements and several of the symbols should thus appear as two or more smaller symbols. This limitation, although serious locally, does not affect the main impression conveyed by the maps. Generally speaking, they confirm and amplify the information of the density maps.

WOODLAND

Types of entries

The amount of woodland on a holding in Hampshire is normally indicated by the formula *silva de n porcis*, which is sometimes expanded to *silva de n porcis de pasnagio*; and in one entry, for Ellingham (50), this is further expanded to *tantum silvae unde exibant xx porci de pasnagio*. The swine in these entries constituted the rent paid to a lord in return for pannage in his wood. The number varied from one (e.g. at Empshott, 49) to 200 at East Meon (38) and even to 300 at Eling (38b); but it must be remembered that some of the larger amounts were from manors that included more than one settlement. There is no entry that gives us a clue to the relation of these renders to total numbers of swine, and, of course, we can offer no satisfactory answer to the wider question of what acreage of woodland the figures imply. All we can do is to plot them as conventional units in the hope of obtaining some rough guide to the relative distribution of wood over the face of the county.[1]

In addition to the normal formula, there are a number of other expressions that indicate the presence of wood on a holding. Some entries give the render in terms of money; at Marchwood (50b), for example, there was wood yielding 8d. (*Silva de viii denariis*). The amounts are usually small, but part of the wood at Kingsclere (39) rendered 20s., and the wood at Eversley (43b) as much as 30s. At Ashley (51b), some wood, placed 'in the forest', rendered 8 swine, and this render was apparently worth 5s.; but it would be unwise to attempt a general equation on the basis of this one entry. Some entries do not state a render, but tell us that there was 'wood for the fences' (*silva ad clausuram*), e.g. at Upton (38b) and at Gatcombe (52b). This may possibly imply that the wood was reserved for the demesne beasts, and that the villagers had no right to feed their swine in their lord's wood, but only that of removing sufficient timber for

[1] See pp. 596–7 below.

making fences. At Meon in Titchfield (40b) there were 2 acres of wood for fencing (*Ibi duae acrae silvae ad clausuram*), and at Holybourne (38) there was wood both for the fences and with a render of one pig (*Silva ad clausuram et unus porcus de pasnagio*). The wood at some other places was also not entered uniformly. At Crawley (40), some wood yielded 25 swine and other wood 6*d.*; and there was a similar mixture at Mapledurham (38). At Bentley (40b), a swine render and a right to fencing appear together; and at Kingsclere (39, 50b) some wood rendered swine, some rendered money, and some provided fencing materials. At Mottisfont (42), where there was wood for fencing, the king's reeves had taken away, amongst other things, a grove (*grava*).

This does not exhaust the variety of phrasing. Seven entries mention wood without pannage (*Silva sine pasnagio*).[1] Two entries record the presence of useless wood (*Silva inutilis*).[2] Certainly the greater part of the wood at Sunwood (44b) may also have been useless because it had been 'blown down by the wind' (*Silva de iiii porcis. Maxima pars ejus vento corruit*). At Chilworth (47b) the value of the estate had fallen from £10 to £8, and then to only £4 because its owner had no power to use its wood (*quia non habet potestatem in silva sua*).[3] At each of four places there was, so we are told, only 'a small wood' (*parva silva*).[4] In two entries the existence of wood is merely implied. Thus no wood is recorded for Oakhanger (49b), but we are told that the holder could not have 'pasture or pannage in the king's wood, except by authority of the sheriff'. Might the 'king's wood' have been in Woolmer Forest or Alice Holt Forest which the Domesday Book does not mention? Then again, in addition to wood yielding 3 swine in the manor of Broughton (38b), there seems to have been other wood (*una silva*) which was unmeasured and in dispute. Finally, the woods of Damerham (66b) and of Plaitford (74), surveyed in the Wiltshire folios, are measured in a common Wiltshire fashion in terms of length and breadth.[5] By no means all places possessed

---

[1] Quarley (39), Penton (44b), Ann (47), all in the same area; Burgate (50b) in the New Forest; Hardley (*Silva parva*, 52b), Pan (53b) and Sandford and Week (39b) in the Isle of Wight. [2] Littleton (45b) and *Clatinges* (46).

[3] This may mean that the wood of Chilworth (to the north of Southampton) had been taken into a royal forest.

[4] Ann (39), Outwick (48) and South Tidworth (46b); the fourth place is Hardley (52b), in the Isle of Wight, for which we read: *Silva parva sine pasnagio*. It is possible that *parva silva* implies not 'a small wood', but wood not fully grown.

[5] Also the wood in the joint entry (74) for Winterslow (Wilts) and Tytherley (Hants).

wood, but only once, for Botley (47), are we specifically told that it was wanting (*Silva deest*); it is possible that this may mean not that there was no wood but that the wood had been placed in the nearby Forest of Bere. Something similar may also have happened at Durley (50b) on the margin of the New Forest; there, the wood had once rendered 6 swine, but it did so no longer (*Silva de vi porcis fuit sed non est*).[1]

In addition to this variety, there is yet another category of wood entries which refers to wood 'in the forest' (*Silva est in foresta*), i.e. the New Forest; and sometimes we are given the render, either in swine or in money, of the wood so transferred. At Ringwood (39), this wood yielded 189 swine; and at Eling (38b) as many as 280 swine together with 3 sesters of honey, and there was also other wood outside the forest yielding 20 swine; at Milford (51b) the 'forest' woodland yielded 12*d*. At the manor of Broughton with East Dean and Nether Wallop (38b) we hear of timber for house-building (*silva ad faciendas domos*) which the foresters had taken. In a few of these entries, *silva* is replaced by *nemus*, e.g. in those for Avon (44b) and Breamore (39).

Distribution of woodland

The majority of places with large amounts of wood was to be found in the east of the county (Fig. 96). Here are stretches of Gault, of Clay-with-flints, and of London Clay in the north. The Chalk downland (apart from the area with Clay-with-flints in the east) had very little wood. But it is difficult to make any precise correlations because we do not know either the extent of the royal forests at this date, or how much wood was included within them and not recorded in the Domesday folios. At a later date, Alice Holt and Woolmer Forests lay along the eastern border; to the north of Portsmouth harbour was the Forest of Bere; along the western border were the Forests of Clarendon and Chute, amongst others. Although the New Forest features so particularly in the Hampshire folios, it seems likely that not all the wood within it was recorded. But we do hear of some wood, and the villages of the Avon valley, for instance, had substantial tracts of wood for pannage. We may well be surprised that more wood was not recorded for the interior of the New Forest, but we must remember that much of it was probably heathland, and that today wood covers only about one-half of its surface.

[1] For the wood at Botley and at Durley, see the underline to Fig. 96.

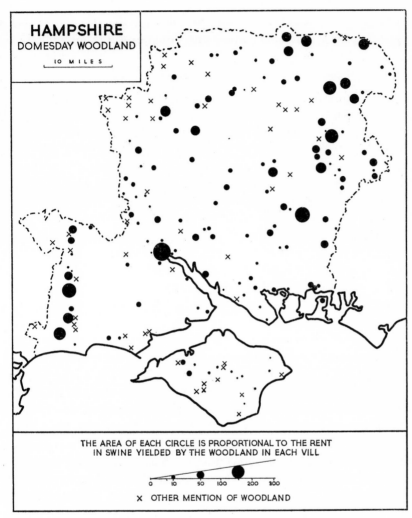

Fig. 96. Hampshire: Domesday woodland in 1086.

Where the wood of a village is entered partly in terms of a swine render and partly in some other way, only the swine render is shown. The wood at Botley has been indicated under the category of 'other mention'; that at Durley in the usual way, i.e. as rendering swine—see p. 322.

There was, apparently, but little woodland in the Isle of Wight, and it is surprising that scarcely any was recorded for the sparsely inhabited Oligocene clays of the north where one would expect to find wood.

THE NEW FOREST

Many royal forests are mentioned in the Domesday Book as a whole, but about only one—the New Forest—are we given any substantial detail. The main account occupies a special section of the Hampshire folios, and is headed *In Nova Foresta et circa eam* (51–51b). Apart from the Isle of Wight, no other district within a county in all England is described in this way with its own schedule of land-holders. From the crowded nature of the pages, J. H. Round came to the conclusion that 'it must have been all written subsequently to those portions of the Survey which come before and after it'.[1] Indeed some part of the account had to be inscribed in a blank space on the preceding folio (50b). Even so, the account is not self-contained, for a number of manors within the relevant area and in the hands of the king are described on fos. 38b–39, and others appear elsewhere, e.g. Ibsley is described on fo. 46, and Sway partly on fos. 51–51b and partly on fo. 44.

This unique section has attracted a great deal of comment. The earlier view, based on the reports of the annalists of the twelfth century, was that the Conqueror had reduced a flourishing district to a waste by evicting a large number of people. But subsequent writers declared this tale of wholesale destruction to be a calumny that finds support neither from the soils of the district nor from the evidence of Domesday Book itself. F. H. Baring, in 1901, discussed the making of the Forest at some length, and showed that the damage done was very much less than the traditional accounts would have us believe. The evidence of the soil is clear enough. The greater part of the area is covered by the most infertile Tertiary sands and gravels which cannot ever have supported a flourishing agriculture and a large population. In the middle of the Forest there are great stretches that seem always to have been virtually uninhabited. The evidence of the Domesday Book likewise shows that the making of the Forest involved no such violent upheaval as that described by the medieval chronicles. By differentiating between the villages wholly 'in the forest' and those only partly so, Baring produced a reasonable interpretation,

[1] *V.C.H. Hampshire*, I, p. 446.

accompanied by a diagram which is an illuminating example of carto-
graphic method applied to Domesday evidence.[1]

The area discussed in the present account extends beyond the New

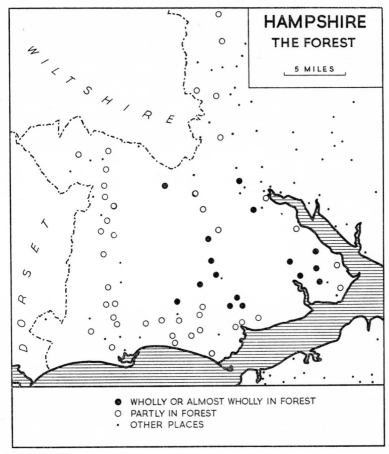

Fig. 97. Hampshire: The Forest.

Forest proper to include the adjacent districts; the afforested northern
villages may well have been not in the New Forest itself but in the Forests
of Clarendon and Melchet which are not mentioned by name in the
Hampshire folios. The villages of the whole area (Fig. 97) fall into three

[1] F. H. Baring, 'The making of the New Forest', *Eng. Hist. Rev.* XVI (1901),
pp. 427–38. Reprinted in *Domesday Tables*, pp. 194–205.

groups: those wholly or almost wholly 'in the forest'; those partially affected; and, lastly, those villages, the entries for which make no reference to forest. The villages of the first two groups are set out in the tables on pp. 327–30, and these, together with those of the third group, must now be separately discussed before some conclusion can be ventured upon.

(1) *Settlements Wholly or Almost Wholly in the Forest*

These settlements are described as being entirely in the forest at each of 46 holdings in 32 named and 5 unnamed places, except occasionally for a few acres of meadow. Nothing is said about the assessment in 1086, or about the people or teams or miscellaneous resources. The following entries are representative:

Gatewood (51b): Godric and Elnod had (*habuerunt*) 2 hides in Gatewood, and it was assessed at that amount. It is now in the forest. There is land for 5 plough-teams (*Terra est v carucis*). It was worth (*Valebat*) 45s.

Wootton (51b): Godric held (*tenuit*) Wootton of the king. Then (it was assessed) at one hide. Now it is in the forest except for 15 acres of meadow which Godric (still) holds. Land for 2 plough-teams (*Terra ii carucis*). It was worth (*Valebat*) 40s.

Cildeest (51b): Brixi had (*habuit*) *Cildeest* of the king in parage. It was assessed at 5 hides. It is now in the forest except for 2 acres of meadow which Alvric the Little holds. There was land for 8 plough-teams (*Terra fuit viii carucis*). It was worth (*Valebat*) £8.

It will be noticed that we are told sometimes that there *is* land, sometimes that there *was* land, and sometimes merely of land for so many teams. Presumably all these entries are providing the same kind of information, i.e. the amount of land available for cultivation. Four entries, the first four of fo. 51, state the value in 1066 and 'afterwards' (*T.R.E. et post*),[1] so does the entry for *Bedecote* (39); one entry, that for Tatchbury (43), also gives two values, one for 1086; the remaining entries apparently give a value only for 1066, except that for Alvric Petit's holding 'in Foresta' (50b) of which it is strange to read: *Valuit vi solidos. Modo xii solidos.*[2]

[1] The entries are for *Achelie*, Fawley, *Truham* and *Sclive*. See p. 333 below for the bearing of similar information upon the date of inclusion in the New Forest.
[2] It may well be that the *xii solidos* is a scribal error for *xii denarios*; a rise in the value of land *in foresta* hardly seems likely.

Holdings Wholly or Almost Wholly in the Forest

.cres; h=hides; hd=hundred; m=meadow; v=virgates. Brackets around the number of ;h-lands indicate the past tense—see p. 326. Unidentified names are shown in italics.

r help with the New Forest names, we are indebted to Mr J. E. B. Gover. *Andret* probably ed to the Hampshire end of the heavily wooded country stretching from Kent to Dorset— . Mawer, F. M. Stenton, J. E. B. Gover, *The Place-Names of Sussex* (Cambridge, 1929), p. 1. *Cildeest* is probably not Yaldhurst in Milford (*V.C.H. Hampshire*, I, p. 514), but nidentified *Childenhurst* recorded in 1339. *Nutlei* (51b), a lost place in Boldre hd, is not confused with *Nutlei* or Netley (on the same folio) in Redbridge hd; the entry for the makes no reference to forest. *Oselei* has been taken as unidentified and not as Ossemsley *V.C.H. Hampshire*, I, p. 511. *Truham, Trucham* is equated in *V.C.H. Hampshire* (I, pp. 510, 514) with Fritham in Bramshaw, where it can hardly have been (it was in Boldre hundred); 3 probably the *Throucham* or *Througham*, recorded between 1539 and 1606, and seems to been on the site of Park Farm in Beaulieu, a much more likely place. It has not, however, marked on Figs. 91, 97 and 98.

Place	1066 Hidage	1066 Value	Plough-lands	Notes
Achelie (51)	1 h	£2. 10s.	4	In Redbridge hd
Achelie (51b)	3 v	£2	—	In Boldre hd
Alwinetune (51)	2 h	£5	(4)	Except 12 ac.m
Battramsley (51b)	2 h	£3	5	Except 4 ac.m
Bedecote (39)	2 v	£1	1	Except 11½ ac.m
Bile (51)	1 h	} £4	—	Except 4 ac.m
Bile (51)	1 h		4	Except 4 ac.m
Bolderford (51b)	1 h	£10	—	Except 2 ac.m
Boldre (51b)	2 h	£3	(4)	Except 6 ac.m
Brookley (51b)	2 h	£1	6	See *Mapleham*
Buckholt (51b)	1 h 1 v	£5	6	
Cildeest (51b)	5 h	£8	(8)	Except 2 ac.m
Cocherlei (51b)	3 v	£3	2	
Eyeworth (39)	1 v	10s.	—	
Gatewood (51b)	2 h	£2. 5s.	5	
Gritnam (51b)	1 h	£2	—	
Hardley (51b)	1 h	£1. 10s.	2	
Hartford (51)	1 h	£1. 5s.	(4)	
Hincheslea (51b)	2 v	£1	2	
Mapleham (51)	Jointly with Brookley above			
Nutlei (51b)	1 v	6s.	1	In Boldre hd
Oselei (51)	1 h	£2	—	Except 1 ac.m
Oselei (51)	1 h	£1	(2)	Except 2 ac.m
Otterwood (51b)	1 h	£1. 1s.	2	
Otterwood (51b)	1 h 1 v	£1. 10s.	3	
Oxelei (51b)	2 h	£2	(4)	Except 4 ac.m
Pilley (51)	1½ v	10s.	(1)	Except 1½ ac.m
Pilley (51b)	1 h	£1. 10s.	—	Except 6 ac.m
Pilley (51b)	2 v	15s.	2	Except 3 ac.m

Holdings *Wholly or Almost Wholly in the Forest* (continued)

Place	1066 Hidage	1066 Value	Plough-lands	Notes
Rollstone (51 b)	1 h	15*s*.	2	
Sanhest (51 b)	2 v	£1	2	
Sclive (51)	3 h	£10	8	Except 8 ac.m
Slacham (39)	2 v	£1. 5*s*.	1	See p. 336
Tatchbury (43)	2 v	10*s*.	—	Waste, but is and was worth 10*s*.
Tatchbury (51 b)	2 h	£2	—	
Truham (51)	2 h 2 v	£3	4	
Trucham (51)	2 h 2 v	£3	(4)	
Truham (51)	1 h	£1. 10*s*.	(2)	Except 1 ac.m
Truham (51 b)	1 h 2 v	£4	4	
Truham (51 b)	1 h	£1. 10*s*.	3	
Wigarestun (51 b)	1 h	5*s*.	(2)	Except 1 ac.m
Wootton (51 b)	1 h	£2	2	Except 15 ac.m
Unnamed holdings:				
Hunta and Pagen (51 b)	2½ v	£1	2	Except 1 ac.m
The king (39)	1 v	7*s*. 6*d*.	1	Except 1½ ac.m
Alvric Petit (50 b)	1 v	6*s*.	1	1086: 1 v, 12*s*.
Sawin (51 b)	1 v	1*s*.	—	Except 1 ac.m
in Andret (44)	8 ac.	—	—	

Holdings *Partly in the Forest*

F=forest; h=hides; m(u)=unmeasured meadow; p=swine; ref=reference; v=virgates; wood; w(u)=unmeasured wood. Unidentified names are shown in italics. Under the heading the forest', the assessment and the value of the portions in the forest are indicated, together any resources. Places with asterisks have other entries that make no mention of the forest. sums in brackets after the 1086 values are the amounts actually paid. The second Fawley entry seems to refer to the same 1 h 3 v as the first, but the values of the portion in the forest (£2. and the remainder (15*s*.) come to more than £3. *Lesteorde* (51), a lost place in Boldre h not to be confused with *Lestred* (Testwood, 46) in Redbridge hd; the entry for the latter m: no reference to forest.

Place	1066 Hidage	Value 1066	Value 1086	In the Forest	Notes
Arnewood (50 b)	1 h 1 v	£1. 10*s*.	£1. 10*s*.	4*s*.	no h in 108(
Ashley (51)	1 h 1½ v	£2. 10*s*.	£1	1 v; 6*s*.	
Ashley (51 b)	1 h	£1	15*s*.	w of 8 p; 5*s*.	1 v in 1086
Avon (44 b)	1 h	£1. 5*s*.	15*s*.	w(u)	Still 1 h in 1
Avon (46)	8 h	£10	£5	1½ h ½ v; w of 4*s*; £5	3½ h in 1086
Baddesley (51) in Boldre hd	1 h	?	3*s*.	3 v	

Holdings Partly in the Forest (continued)

Place	1066 Hidage	Value 1066	Value 1086	In the Forest	Notes
ɔn (51)	1h 3v	£2	£1	2v; 6s.	See pp. 332–3
ɔn (51)	1h	£1	10s.	½h; 6s.	
ːley (51)	1h	£1	15s.	1v; 5s.	
ton (44b)	4h ½v	£5	£3	Pasture; w(u)	2h ½v in 1086
ːrne (51b)	3h	£3	£2	1h	
ːmore (39)	?	?	?	2½h; w of 50p; 51s. 8d.	
ːmore (39)	—	—	—	Indirect ref to F	
ːghton (38b)	?	£76⅚	£66 (£104. 12s. 2d.)	w(u); pasture of 10s.; honey	
ːghton (39)	—	—	—	Indirect ref to F	
ːgate* (39)	1v	?	?	w of 40 p; pasture of 10s.	
ːgate* (39)				Indirect ref to F	
ːterton (50b)	½v	£1	4s.	¼v; w(u); m(u); 16s.	
ːden (51b)	5h	£10	£2. 10s. (£5)	3h	
Dean* (38b)	—	—	—	w(u); pasture of 10s.; honey	
ːg (38b)	?	£38 5/12	£20 (£52. 6s. 1d.)	w for 280p; honey	See p. 336
ːgham (50)	5h 2v	£7	£3. 10s.	1h; w for 20p; 70s.	See p. 336
ːley (41b)	2h	£3	15s.	1h 3v	
ːley (51)	1h 3v	£2. 10s.	—	All in F; 12 plough-lands	
ːhill (51)	3v	13s.	10s.	2v; 3s.	
ːdingbridge (46b)	2h 3v	£3	£3	3v; w(u); 20s.	See p. 333
ːley (49b)	1h	£1	10s.	½h; 7s.	Still 1h in 1086
ːton Admiral (51)	2v	15s.	15s.	½v; 3s.	
ːton Admiral (51)	1h	15s.	15s.	1v; 3s.	
ːdenhurst (39)	29h ½v	£44	£24 (£25)	3½h; w for 129 p; £12. 10s.	See p. 336
ːdle (51)	5h	£8	£5	1h; w(u); £3	See p. 336
ːy (46)	4h	£4	£3	2h; £1	See p. 332
ːeorde (51)	1h	£2	3s.	3¾v	
ːkerley* (45b)	1h	15s.	30s.	1h	See p. 333
ːington (51)	1h	£1	15s.	½h; w(u)	

Holdings Partly in the Forest (continued)

Place	1066 Hidage	Value 1066	Value 1086	In the Forest	Notes
Lyndhurst (39)	2 h	£6	10s.	1 h 3 v	
Milford (51 b)	1 v	?	3s.	w(u); 12d.	See p. 318
Milford (51 b)	1 h	£1	£1	½ h; 10s.	
Milton (50 b)	1 h 2 v	£2	£1	w for 20p; 20s.	See p. 332
Minstead (51 b)	3 h 2 v	£8	£1	3 h	
Nether Wallop* (38 b)	—	—	—	w(u); pasture of 10s.; honey	
Ringwood (39)	10 h	£24	£8. 10s. (£12. 10s.)	4 h; £7. 10s.	See p. 336
Ripley (46)	2 v	£1	15s.	w(u)	Still 2 v in 1086
Ripley (50 b)	5 h	£8	£2. 10s.	3 h; w(u); £5	See p. 336
Rockbourne* (39)	—	—	—	Indirect ref to F	
Rockford (46)	2 h	£3	£1. 10s.	w(u); 30s.	1 h in 1086
Sopley (48 b)	7 h	£10	£2. 10s. (£5)	4 h; w(u); £5. 10s.	See p. 336
Stanswood (38 b)	2 h	£10	£7	1 h	
Sway* (44)	1 h	£1	£1	1 v	
Sway (51)	1 h	9s.	9s.	1 v; 2s.	
Sway (51)	1 h	£1	5s.	3 v; 15s.	
Twynham* (38 b)	1 v	£19	£10 (£12. 10s.)	w(u); £12. 10s.	See p. 336
Walhampton (51)	2 v	15s.	10s.	w(u); 4s.	1 v in 1086
Wellow (50)	5 h	£3	£2	3 v	Still 5 h in 1086
Winkton (48)	7 h	£10	£4. 10s.	1 h ½ v; w(u); £5. 10s.	See p. 335
Unnamed holdings:					
Alvric (51 b)	3 v	10s.	10s.	w for 4 p; 4s.	Still 3 v in 1086
William of Eu (51)	2 h	£2	£1. 10s.	1 v; w(u); 5s.	1¼ h in 1086

The 1066 assessments were low, but, as we have seen, the assessment of a holding does not necessarily provide an indication of its size. The presence of a fair number of plough-lands on many holdings gives us a hint of their former condition; we know from evidence elsewhere that a village with 4 or 5 teams was a sizeable one. It is true that no plough-lands are recorded for 11 holdings, one of which is said to be 'waste', but the total for the rest (35 holdings in at least 27 villages) amounts to 110.[1] Over Hampshire as a whole there were between 3 and 4 recorded people per team, so that the number of male adults these plough-lands represent may be, very roughly of course, between 350 and 500. This implies a total population of, say, 2,000. The figure would be higher if we made allowance for those entries without plough-lands.

What had happened to these people? Had they been driven out as the annalists of the twelfth century said they were? Can we be at one with F. H. Baring in thinking 'that the entries for the main forest entirely agree with the tradition that the ground was cleared of its inhabitants'?[2] Can we be sure that the phrase 'it is now in the forest' implies that the land lay completely waste and that these 32 places and 5 unnamed holdings were entirely ruined and deserted? In that case, who furnished the Inquest officials with information about the former assessments, plough-lands and values? It seems unlikely that this was provided by the men of neighbouring settlements or by former inhabitants transferred from decayed to surviving villages. And if the settlements were entirely deserted, why was it necessary to record their agricultural capacities? Dare we conjecture that the men and their teams (in some settlements at any rate) had disappeared only from the record and not from the land? Did transference into the forest merely mean that they went out of the scope of the Inquest? We cannot say.

If the inhabitants were evicted, where did they go, and what is the significance of the fact that at 21 holdings in 14 named and 3 unnamed places, some meadow still remained within the purview of the Commissioners? Who used this meadow? Can we assume that it provided hay for the horses of the huntsmen? Or, after all, must we be driven to suppose that it continued to be used by those men and for those teams that had passed out of our Domesday ken behind the curtain of forest law.

[1] To this total must be added the 12 plough-lands on a holding at Fawley (51), see p. 329. The entry for this holding follows the pattern of those 'wholly or almost wholly' in the forest.   [2] F. H. Baring, art. cit. (1901), p. 199.

On the other hand, that inclusion 'in the forest' seriously damaged the local economy is suggested by the fact that out of these 32 places, the names of over a dozen remain unidentified, and that the names of others (e.g. Gritnam, Hartford, Hincheslea and Otterwood) are represented to-day by those of farms and localities and not of parishes.

(2) *Settlements Partly in the Forest*

There were 56 holdings in 43 named and 2 unnamed places with only a portion of each 'in the forest'.[1] Some people, with their resources, remained outside the forest, and village life continued, although apparently in a diminished form. The phrasing of the entries varies greatly, but the two following may stand as representative:

> Ibsley (46): Hugh [de Port] himself holds Ibsley, and Ralph of him. Algar held it of King Edward as an alod. It then paid geld for 4 hides, now for 2 hides. There is land for 5 plough-teams. In demesne are 2, and [there are] 6 villeins and 10 bordars with 3 plough-teams. There [are] 3 serfs and a mill yielding (*de*) 10*s*. and 700 eels, and 75 acres of meadow. Wood yielding (*de*) 1 pig. Two hides of this manor are in the forest. *T.R.E.* it was worth £4, and afterwards 40*s*. Now 60*s*. What [is] in the forest, 20*s*.

> Milton (50b): Hugh de Port holds 1½ hides in Milton, and William de Chernet [holds] of him. Alwin held them in parage. There is land for 3 plough-teams. In demesne there is one, and 5 villeins have 2 plough-teams there. There [are] 1 serf and 3½ acres of meadow. *T.R.E.* and afterwards it was worth 40*s*., now 20*s*. *T.R.E.* it was assessed at 1½ hides. Now at 1 hide. In the forest, the king has the wood of this manor yielding (*de*) 20 swine; it is worth 20*s*.

Into this category of partial inclusion, come places like Sway (44, 51 *bis*, 51 b) with three holdings within and one outside the forest.

Sometimes, as in the entry for Ibsley above, we are specifically told that so many virgates or hides had been taken into the forest; but in other entries we are left to assume the amount from a smaller hidage. Another consequence of inclusion in the forest was a decrease in the value of a holding. In the two entries above, the value of the portion affected amounts exactly to the difference between the figures for 1066 and 1086; but very often it is less, and we can only assume that part of the fall in value was due to something else. On one holding at Barton (51) the value had

---

[1] Counting the two Fawley entries as one—see note to table on p. 328.

dropped from 40s. to 20s., but what the king had was said to be worth only 6s. There was an occasional holding, on the other hand, with the same value at both dates, although a part had been taken into the forest. This was true, for example, of Fordingbridge (46b), and it may be that the portion left outside the forest had been improved to such a degree that it was worth what the whole had once been. Indeed at Lockerley (45b) the value seems to have increased from 15s. to 38s., but this is a difficult entry.

There are 31 of these partially afforested holdings for which the values at three dates are given—*tunc, post* and *modo*. On ten of these there was a decline only between *tunc* and *post*; the decline was sometimes very considerable, although it was occasionally followed by recovery. For another twelve holdings, the *tunc* and *post* values were identical, and the decline came only between *post* and *modo*. This immediately suggests the possibility that the extension of the forest was not all of one date, and it may be worth noting that these twelve places with a later decline are on the outskirts of the forest. Another six places show a decline during both periods, and there are three exceptional entries. The details are set out in the table on pp. 334–5.

The information about reduction in assessment or decrease in value, interesting as it is, gives us no clue to what inclusion 'in the forest' meant in terms of resources or population. It is true that we are often told that the wood, or part of it, had been taken into the forest, although we are not always told how much; and, occasionally, we hear of pasture being included. But even this does not take us far towards envisaging what the process of taking land 'into the forest' involved. Are we to assume, for example, that wood taken into the forest was physically still standing in 1086; that is to say, should the wood 'in the forest' appear on our map of Domesday woodland? It is difficult to believe that it had disappeared, and so it has been plotted on Fig. 96.

What of the inhabitants and teams of the affected holdings? How many were they, and what was their fate? Six entries only, set out on p. 336, break the silence of the Domesday Book and tell us a little about them. The total amounts to 51 villeins, 12 bordars and 6 men with 19 plough-teams.[1] They are spoken of in the past tense (*manserunt, erant, manebant*), but their values are given in the present tense (*valet, appreciantur*), and

---

[1] On the assumption that the figures for dwellings at Eling can be taken to represent recorded inhabitants.

Changes in the Value of those Partially Afforested Holdings for which Three Values are Given

The figures in brackets indicate what was paid as
opposed to the value in 1086

Reduction between *tunc* and *post*

	Tunc	Post	Modo
Avon (44b)	25s.	15s.	15s.
Fordingbridge (46b)	£3	30s.	£3
Hordle (51)	£8	£5	£5
Ibsley (46)	£4	£2	£3
Lymington (51)	£1	15s.	15s.
Milford (51b)	£1	10s.	£1
Minstead (51b)	£8	15s.	£1
Sopley (48b)	£10	£2	£2. 10s. (£5)
Stanswood (38b)	£10	£7	£7
Walhampton (51)	15s.	10s.	10s.

Continued reduction *tunc–post–modo*

Avon (46)	£10	£8	£5
Barton (51)	£2	30s.	£1
Dibden (51b)	£10	£8	£2. 10s. (£5)
Holdenhurst (39)	£44	£34	£24 (£25)
Ringwood (39)	£24	£16	£8. 10s. (£12. 10s.)
Winkton (48)	£10	£7	£4. 10s.

Reduction between *post* and *modo*

Ashley (51b)	£1	£1	15s.
Bickton (44b)	£5	£5	£3
Broughton (38b)	£76⅚	£76⅚	£66 (£104. 12s. 2d.)
Eling (38b)	£38 5/12	£38 5/12	£20 (£52. 6s. 1d.)
Ellingham (50)	£7	£7	£3. 10s.
Fawley (41b)	£3	£3	15s.
Lesteorde (51)	£2	£2	3s.
Milton (50b)	£2	£2	£1
Ripley (46)	£1	£1	15s.
Rockford (46)	£3	£3	30s.
Twynham (38b)	£19	£19	£10 (£12. 10s.)
[W. of Eu] (51)	£2	£2	30s.

No reduction *tunc–post–modo*

	Tunc	Post	Modo
Arnewood (50b)	30*s.*	30*s.*	30*s.*
Sway (51)	9*s.*	9*s.*	9*s.*

Increase *post–modo*

Lockerley (45b)	15*s.*	15*s.*	30*s.*

we must ask whether these values were large enough to have covered more than wood. Elsewhere, the swine renders seem to be worth a shilling a pig,[1] and the corresponding figures for these entries are as follows:

	Swine	Value
Eling (38b)	280	520*s.*
Holdenhurst (39)	129	250*s.*
Ringwood (39)	189	150*s.*

On this assumption, or something like it, there may have been no surviving inhabitants or teams left at Ringwood, but there could have been at Eling and Holdenhurst. On the other hand, we must say at once that precise arithmetic based upon a few Domesday entries can be misleading, and we can arrive at no certain conclusion. Although the woodland has been included on Fig. 96, the population and teams have been excluded both from the maps and from the total figures for the county. Had they been included, the relevant symbols on Figs. 93 and 95 would have been larger, and the density maps (Figs. 92 and 94) would have been slightly affected.[2]

If we now look at other entries where this detail is not entered, we occasionally find that the value of the afforested portion is quite high. At Winkton (48), the land *outside* the forest, assessed at 3¼ hides, was valued at £4. 10*s.* in 1086, and it comprised 21 recorded inhabitants with 5½ teams, and 2 mills and 55 acres of meadow. The land *inside* the forest was valued (*appreciatur*) at £5. 10*s.*, and it comprised 1 hide and half a virgate and all the wood (*et totam silvam*). This seems a large sum for

---

[1] At Milton (50b) 20 swine were worth 20*s.*; and on Alvric's holding (51b) 4 swine were worth 4*s.* At Ashley (51b), the figures were 8 swine and 5*s.*, but this ratio only strengthens the argument that follows.

[2] The changes in the maps would be as follows: Fig. 92—the density for the Mid-Avon valley teams would read 2 instead of 1. Fig. 94—the density for the Mid-Avon valley population would read 7 instead of 6, and that for the strip along Southampton Water 10 instead of 9.

The Six Detailed Entries of Holdings Placed in the Forest

Eling (38b): Into the forest were taken (*sunt occupatae*) 16 dwellings (*mansurae*) of villeins and 3 of bordars, and wood yielding 280 swine for the pannage and 3 sesters of honey, all of which are now taken (*sunt minus*) [from the manor] and are together appraised at (*appreciantur*) £26.

Holdenhurst (39): On 7 hides which are in the forest there dwelled (*manebant*) 13 villeins and 3 bordars with 8 plough-teams; and with these hides there is, outside (*foris*) the manor, wood yielding 129 swine for the pannage.... That part which is in the forest is appraised at (*appreciatur*) £12. 10s. (It would seem from the rest of the entry that '7 hides' is a mistake for '3½ hides'.)

Hordle (51): The king holds wood in the forest where dwelt (*manebant*) six men. It is worth (*Valet*) 60s.

Ringwood (39): On 4 hides which are in the forest dwelled (*manserunt*) 14 villeins and 6 bordars with 7 plough-teams, and a mill yielding 30d. and wood yielding 189 swine for the pannage. This part (*Hoc*) which the king has is worth (*valet*) £7. 10s. by tale.

Slacham (39): The king himself holds *Slacham* in his forest.... It then paid geld for half a hide, now for nothing. There is land for 1 plough-team. When Ralph de Limesi received it, there were (*erant ibi*) 3 villeins with 1 plough-team. It was worth (*Valuit*) 25s.

Twynham (38b): The wood is in the forest of the king where there were (*ubi erant*) 5 villeins with 3 plough-teams.... What is in the forest is appraised at (*appreciatur*) £12. 10s.

woodland alone to produce, yet, on the analogy of Eling, Holdenhurst and Ringwood, it is not impossible. The same applies to the woodland within the forest at Sopley (48b) also worth £5. 10s., or to that on a holding at Ripley (50b) where the figure was £5. At Ellingham (50), where there was one hide in the forest and wood that had yielded (*exibant*) 20 swine, the total value was 70s. (*Hoc totum valet lxx solidos*).[1] If our rough equation of 1s. per pig is correct, what was the source of the remaining 50s.? There can be no answer to this question, but it does raise a suspicion, at any rate, that there might have been other things here besides the wood and its swine.

---

[1] In the entries for Sopley and Ellingham, the Latin *val.* has been extended to *valet*. Where the past tense was intended the Domesday scribe usually wrote *valb.* or *valuit*. The entry for Ripley has no verb but merely *Qd in foresta c sol.*

(3) *Settlements Not Specifically in the Forest*

Lastly come those villages the entries for which make no reference to the forest. These have been shown on Fig. 97 in order to indicate the relation of the afforested vills to the distribution of settlement as a whole. Holdings in many of the non-afforested villages were often reduced in value and/or assessment. It is possible that such reductions were associated with other extensions of the forest about which we are not told. But it must be added that the decreases may have been due not to afforestation but to a variety of other causes, and for this reason they have not been indicated on Fig. 97.

Conclusion

Taking the Domesday entries literally, the conclusion that we must come to is that the infertile area of the New Forest was but thinly peopled in 1066; there were villages of moderate size, but many were small. About 30 to 40 of these villages were placed wholly or almost wholly under forest law, leaving no record of their former population. Only about one-half of these appear on Fig. 97 because the rest are unidentified. They lay almost entirely in the centre of the forest or in the district between Southampton Water and Beaulieu River. Varying amounts of some 40 to 50 other villages were also included in the forest, but we have some detail of the affected portions of only six of these. The operation seems not to have been all of one date.

It is possible that yet other villages may also have been affected by the making of the forest, although the Domesday text does not say they were. On the other hand, we must voice the suspicion that perhaps inclusion within it was less destructive than might appear, but there is no proof, and it might well be an unjustified suspicion. Just across the border, at Downton in Wiltshire, the Geld Rolls tell of 'two hides from which the inhabitants have fled because of the king's forest' (*ii hidas de quibus homines ibi manentes fugati sunt propter forestam regis*).[1] The corresponding Domesday entry in the Wiltshire folios (65 b) says nothing of the dispossessed inhabitants.[2] On this analogy there is no reason why we should expect the Hampshire folios to make reference to eviction. But even if we regard at least 32 places as having been obliterated, together with parts

[1] *Liber Exoniensis*, fo. 2b.
[2] The *fugati* might not have been dispossessed but merely lost to the manor.

DD

of at least another 43 places, we must remember that the New Forest was not without some inhabitants and a certain amount of agriculture. Figs. 93 and 95 show what remained in 1086. Brockenhurst (51b), for example, in the very heart of the forest, had its hidage reduced from one hide to a half, but its value doubled from £2 to £4, and it had ten men with 3½ teams on its one plough-land.

MEADOW

Types of entries

The entries for meadow in the Hampshire folios are, for the most part, comparatively straightforward. For holding after holding the same phrase is repeated— 'n acres of meadow' (n acrae prati). The amount of meadow entered under the name of each place varied from as little as half an acre (e.g. at Langley, 50b) to as much as 536 acres at Romsey (43b); in the latter entry quingentae is interlined. Generally, the amount is small, usually below 20 acres, and there are only about a dozen places for which it exceeds 100 acres. As in the case of other counties, no attempt has been made to translate these figures into modern acreages. The Domesday acres have been treated merely as conventional units of measurement, and Fig. 98 has been plotted on that assumption.

The various exceptional methods of measuring meadow that appear for many counties are not to be found in the Hampshire folios, and there are very few unusual entries. One is that for Houghton and Awbridge (45), which records 18 acres of meadow, and then goes on to say that a corner of the meadow (angulum prati) was in dispute. Another peculiarity is that a number of New Forest entries tell us that the whole of a manor 'except the meadow' had been taken into the forest; the amounts of the meadow are then specified in acres, except in the entry for Canterton (50b), and these have been plotted on Fig. 98. Why this New Forest meadow should have been excluded from the forest, if the teams had ceased to exist, is not easy to explain; one possibility is that it grew hay for the huntsmen's horses.[1] At Watchingwell (52b), in the Isle of Wight, an unspecified amount of meadow is said to be in the park (pratum est in parco).[2]

Distribution of meadowland

The valleys that break the Chalk surface were marked by villages with moderate amounts of meadow, each for the most part well below 50 acres

---

[1] See p. 331 above.   [2] See p. 356 below.

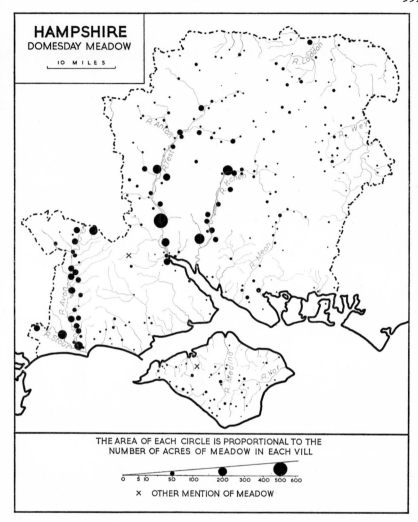

Fig. 98. Hampshire: Domesday meadow in 1086.

(Fig. 98). Along the Test, Romsey (43 b) with 536 acres, Houghton (40 b, 45) with over 160,[1] and Nursling (41) with 140, were outstanding. Along the Itchen, Stoneham (41 b, 43), for example, with 247 acres was also

---

[1] It is difficult to give a precise figure for Houghton because the entry on fo. 45 covers both part of Houghton and part of Awbridge. The figures in each entry are 160 acres (40 b) and 18 acres (45). On Fig. 98, therefore, 169 acres have been plotted for Houghton.

exceptional. The quantities along the narrow valley of the Meon were very much smaller, being mostly below 20 acres. Between these three rivers, the downs were meadowless, but there are some curiosities. Crawley (40), some four miles to the north-west of Winchester and set on the chalk upland between the Itchen and the Test, stands on no stream, and yet it had 26 acres of meadow. Or again, on the Chalk-lands to the south of Basingstoke, some of the high-lying villages away from streams had small quantities entered for them; Farleigh Wallop (50) had 16 acres, Ellisfield (46) had 5, and Dummer (49b) and Woodmancott (42) had an acre apiece. Popham (42b), also in this area, appears on Fig. 98 with 6 acres, but this may be misleading because it is surveyed in a composite entry relating to four places and recording 24 acres of meadow; the Popham meadow may well have been located at one or more of the other three places.

To the north of the Chalk outcrop, small amounts of meadow were associated with the streams of the Loddon and with the tributaries that flow into the Blackwater and the Kennet. To the east, there were also small quantities along the Wey and the Rother and their tributaries.

To the south-west of the Chalk outcrop, there was a certain amount of meadow along the streams of the New Forest district, but the outstanding valley with meadow was that of the Avon; here were many villages with over 50 acres each, and even some with well over 100 acres; Twynham (38b, 44) had 169 acres, Charford (44b, 46, 46b, 50) had 181, and Holdenhurst (39) had 181 acres.

Only small amounts (mostly under 10 acres) are entered for the villages of the Isle of Wight.

PASTURE

Pasture is recorded in connection with only 33 out of the 458 Domesday settlements of Hampshire.[1] This meagre total can only mean that the greater part of the pasture in the county was unrecorded. The usual formula is that so much money is derived *pro* or *de pastura* or *pascua* or *herbagio*, but at Somborne (39b) a distinction seems to have been drawn between the two latter terms, for we read: *Pascua de xvii solidis et x denarii de herbagio*. The renders ranged from 10*d*. at Binsted (41b) to 46*s*. at Barton Stacey (38b). We are never told the size of the pasture either in acres or in linear measurements.

---

[1] Of these, two were in the Isle of Wight and are covered in a joint entry—Sandford and Week (39b).

A number of the entries deserve special mention. At two places, the pastures had names of their own. At Somborne (39b), in addition to the pasture and herbage that rendered 17s. 10d. between them, we hear of a dispute about some other pasture called Down (*pascuam quam vocant dunam*) which rendered 15s.; and at one of the Worthys (42b) we read of a pasture called Moor (*pascua quam vocant moram*), but we are told nothing of its value. At Mottisfont (42) there was one pasture (*una pastura*) which the king's reeves had taken away from the manor but, again, its render is not stated. A reeve of the king also claimed half a hide, for pasturing the king's oxen, in the manor of Oakhanger (49b): *De hoc manerio calumniatur prepositus regis dimidiam hidam ad pasturam boum regis*. Three entries speak of pasture taken into the king's forest; that at Burgate (39) used to yield 10s.; that at Broughton, East Dean and Nether Wallop (38b) is said in a joint entry to yield 10s.; and thirdly, the value of that at Bickton (44b) is unspecified.

FISHERIES

Fisheries (*piscariae*) are mentioned or implied in connection with 23 places in Hampshire. Most of the entries give the number of fisheries and their renders, which range from 2d. from half a fishery at Hurn (46) to 6s. from another at Shirley (46b). The half-fishery at Hurn is the only fraction recorded, and we are told nothing of the corresponding half. Three entries give no render, and imply that the fisheries were appurtenances of manorial lords:

Holdenhurst (39): *iii piscariae servientes aulae.*
Middleton (44): *piscaria ad aulam.*
Perreton (53): *piscaria ad aulam.*

The fishery at Yateley (?*Effelle*, 45b) rendered not money but eels, and it is entered immediately after the mention of a mill: *molinum de v solidis et piscaria de c anguillis*. The total of 23 also includes 5 places with mills that rendered eels but without any mention of *piscariae* as such. These are set out on p. 345, and are also indicated on Fig. 99. Not shown, however, is the fishery that had ceased to exist on an unnamed holding of Milton Abbey (43b): *Piscaria fuit, modo non est.*[1]

Fig. 99 shows that there were some fisheries along the river Avon, and others along the Test, the Itchen and the Meon, and along Southampton

[1] This unnamed Domesday holding was at Twynham—A. J. Robertson (ed.), *Anglo-Saxon Charters* (Cambridge, 1939), pp. 47 and 302.

Water and the coast to the east. There was also another along the Blackwater River—that is if *Effelle* is really to be identified with Yateley.[1] The
solitary fishery entered for the Isle of Wight was at Perreton along the
Yar.[2]

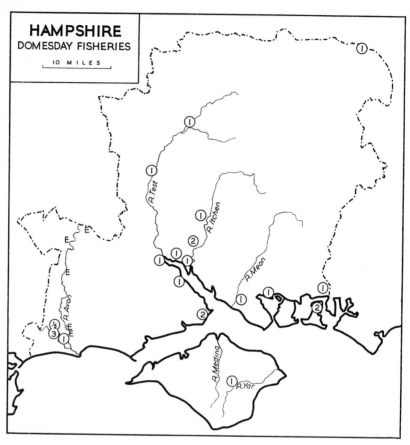

HAMPSHIRE
DOMESDAY FISHERIES

10 MILES

Fig. 99. Hampshire: Domesday fisheries in 1086.

The figure in each circle indicates the number of fisheries.
E indicates renders of eels from mills.

[1] *V.C.H. Hampshire*, I, p. 483.
[2] This is the identification of *Prestetone* given in *V.C.H. Hampshire*, I, p. 520; but
vol. v (London, 1912), p. 191, makes the alternative suggestion that it was Preston
in St Helens near the mouth of the Yar. On Fig. 99 the fishery has been placed at
Perreton.

SALT-PANS

Salt-pans (*salinae*) are entered in connection with 15 places in Hampshire, three of them in the Isle of Wight. The number of pans on a holding is given, and also their render in money. The amounts vary greatly; 6 pans

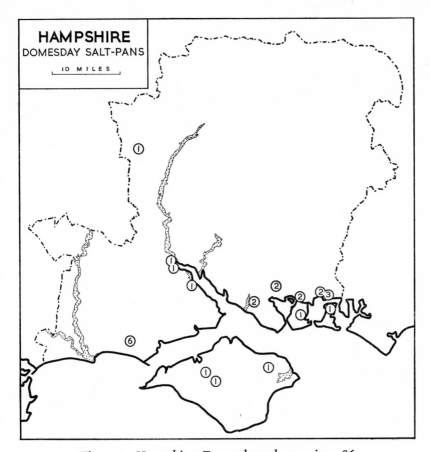

Fig. 100. Hampshire: Domesday salt-pans in 1086.

The figure in each circle indicates the number of salt-pans.
Areas of alluvium are shown (see Fig. 90).

at Hordle (51) yielded only 15*d*., but 2 at Bedhampton (43) yielded as much as 37*s*. 8*d*., That at Eling (38b) was *sine censu*—paying no rent to its lord—and so were those at Bowcombe (52) and Watchingwell (52b).

Fig. 100 shows that the pans were situated for the most part along Southampton Water and especially around the shallows of Portsmouth and Langstone Harbours. There is a curious entry of one salt-pan, yielding 5*d.*, for the inland manor of Nether Wallop (38b), where it would be physically impossible for one to be; we can only suppose that it lay somewhere along the coast; the three in the Isle of Wight must also have been located on the coast.

WASTE

Practically no waste is recorded for Hampshire in 1086, although we might possibly regard some, if not much, of the land taken into the forest as such. In contrast to many other boroughs elsewhere, no waste houses are entered for Southampton or Twynham. So far as we know from the Domesday folios, neither had a castle in 1086, and it was the making of a castle that so often caused the destruction of houses. No waste is entered for Alvington (52b) in Carisbrooke, in the Isle of Wight, but its hidage had been reduced from 2½ to 2 hides because the site of the castle occupied 1 virgate (*sic*). Over the countryside, what damage had been done during the passage of King William's armies was neither total nor enduring. Waste is specifically attributed to only three places:

> Embley (47b): Neither teams nor inhabitants are recorded; the entry concludes: *Tunc geldavit pro dimidia hida, modo pro nichilo. Terra est dimidiae carucae. Valuit x solidos. Modo est Wasta.*

> Tatchbury (43): It was a holding of half a hide upon which neither teams nor inhabitants are mentioned; the entry concludes: *Non geldavit. Vasta est et tamen valet et valuit semper x solidos.*

> Wilmingham (52): This was a royal manor of one hide with villeins, teams and meadow. The entry notes: 'Of this manor of the king, Rainald the son of Croc holds 1 virgate, and says that Earl Roger gave it to his father. It was worth 5*s.*; it is now waste' (*Valuit v solidos. Modo est vastata*).

Another holding at Tatchbury (51b) had been taken into the forest, and it is just possible that the waste entries for Tatchbury (43) and for Embley (47b) to the north may reflect other land taken into the forest. The reason for that at Wilmingham, in the west of the Isle of Wight, is also obscure.

MILLS

Mills are mentioned in connection with 172 out of the 458 Domesday settlements of Hampshire; they also appear in the entries for 7 anonymous holdings.[1] In almost every entry the number of mills is given, and also their annual render, ranging from the mill at Farnborough (41 b) that yielded only 10*d.* to others worth much larger sums; two of the mills at Twyford (40) rendered £4. 15*s.*, the one at Winchester (44), 48*s.*; and the two at Redbridge (46), 50*s.* But only about a dozen or so brought in over £1 apiece; and the renders were very frequently not more than a few shillings. Mills at 3 places in the Isle of Wight are said to render nothing (*sine censu*)—at Huffingford (54), Milford (53 b) and Sheat (53 b). Many mills yielded sums which are multiples or sub-multiples of 50*d.*; values in terms of the *ora* of 16*d.*, or of 20*d.*, were not common. At 5 places the mills returned eels as well as money:

Burgate (39): *Ibi molinum de x solidis et mille anguillis.*
Ibsley (46): *molinum de x solidis et septingentis anguillis.*
Charford (46 b): *molinum de xv solidis et mille ccl anguillis.*
Winkton (48): *Ibi ii molini ad aulam et ccccl anguillae de molino (sic).*
Sopley (48 b): *molinum de x solidis et octingentis lxxv anguillis.*

The two mills at Winkton, it will be noted, were for the use of the hall; so was that at Stratfield (45 b), though we are not given its render. A mill at Ringwood (39) had been taken into the New Forest,[2] and it is not marked on Fig. 101.

Fractions of mills were frequent. Thus each of 2 holdings at Enham (50) had half a mill of 5*s.*, and those at Ovington (40 b, 43 b) also had half a mill apiece rendering 7*s.* Possibly the half-mill at Alton (43) went with the 8½ mills at Neatham (38) nearby on the river Wey. But the fractions do not always so easily combine. We are given no clue to the missing portions of the 1½ mills at Leckford (42) on the Test, or of the 1½ at Itchen Stoke (44) on the Itchen. It is also impossible to see where was the remainder of the half-mill at Bashley (44), of the third part of a mill at Burton (44), of the quarter-mill on a holding at Bramshill (45 b), of another quarter on Alvric's unnamed holding (50 b), and of the fifth part of a mill on a holding at Totton (50 b). No fractions of mills are recorded for the Isle of Wight,

---

[1] See pp. 294–5 above. Twenty of the 172 places, but no anonymous holdings, were in the Isle of Wight.   [2] See p. 336 above.

but before the Conquest, 8 freemen, who shared the royal manor of Knighton and the Down (39b), had each held a part of a mill, each part being worth 22*d.*; we are not told, however, whether the mill was still there in 1086.

About one-half of the Hampshire villages with mills seem to have had only one, or under one, each. But the table below cannot be very accurate because a group of mills on a manor may have been distributed among its component members in a way unknown to us.

Domesday Mills in Hampshire

Under 1 mill	7 settlements		5 mills	2 settlements
1 mill	81 settlements		6 mills	4 settlements
2 mills	46 settlements		7 mills	2 settlements
3 mills	18 settlements		8 mills	2 settlements
4 mills	8 settlements		9 mills	2 settlements

This table excludes the 6 mills on 7 anonymous holdings.

One group of 9 mills appears under Alresford (40). The entry mentions 5 subsidiary holdings; the details of these are set together apart from the main account and they do not include any reference to mills, but some of the 9 mills mentioned in the main account may well have belonged to places other than Alresford.[1] The other group of 9 mills (8½ in fact) was entered under Neatham (38), and, although the entry mentions no subsidiary members, we know from other sources that the manor included holdings in other settlements.[2] The groups of 8 mills each at Clere (39, 43, 45, 48b, 50b) and at Odiham (38)[3] may likewise have been scattered among a number of villages. The groups of 7 mills were at Shide (52b, 53b *bis*) and at East Meon (38, 40b), the latter of which certainly included unrecorded settlements.[4] The four groups of 6 mills were at Andover (39), at Twyford (40 *bis*), at Hurstbourne Priors 141) and at Ann (39, 43, 45b, 47), the two latter probably with unnamed settlements.[5] These examples illustrate the unsatisfactory nature of the table above; indeed we might go so far as to say that a large number of mills entered for one manor immediately creates a suspicion that more than one settlement is involved. This is not to say that the table is without value, because it suggests that there were many villages with more than one mill at work.

[1] See p. 288 above.   [2] See p. 291 above.   [3] See pp. 290 and 294 above.
[4] See p. 291 above.   [5] See pp. 290 and 294 n. above.

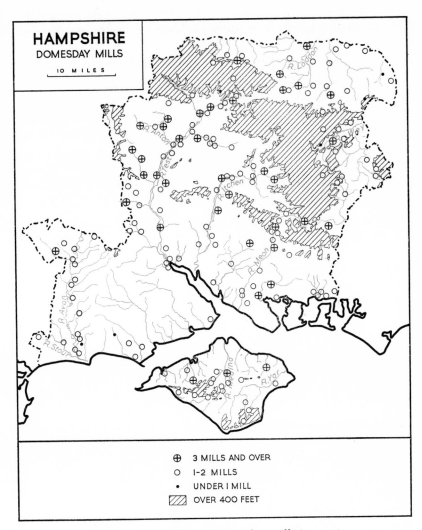

Fig. 101. Hampshire: Domesday mills in 1086.

There were also mills at *Aplestede* and *Bieforde* on the mainland, at *Alvrestone* in the Isle of Wight, and on seven anonymous holdings.

Fig. 101 shows how the mills were associated with the rivers. They were frequent along the upper courses of the Test, the Itchen, the Meon and their various tributaries. In the downland beyond the headwaters of these rivers, there appear to have been no mills; none is entered, for example, for the 8 villages of the hundred of Bermondspit on the high ground to the south of Basingstoke. The nature of the country seems to indicate that these villages were really without water-mills rather than that the inhabitants did not supply the information. To the north, beyond the Chalk outcrop, a number of mills were to be found along the small streams of the Loddon and along the tributaries that flow into Blackwater River and the Kennet. To the east, there were also a number along the Wey and the Rother and their tributaries. On the other side of the county, in the south-west, the course of the Avon was also marked by mills, but they were practically absent from the New Forest itself.

In the Isle of Wight, the mills were again associated with the streams, although some of these streams were very small, sometimes too small to appear on the Quarter-Inch Ordnance Survey map.

CHURCHES

Churches (*ecclesiae*) are mentioned in connection with 92 places, and chapels (*capellae* or *ecclesiolae*) in connection with 12 other places, making 104 places altogether out of the total of 458 recorded for the county.[1] The total of individual churches and chapels is greater than this because some manors had a number obviously situated in associated settlements:

Places in Hampshire with More than One Church or Chapel in 1086

Alresford (40) .	.	3	Overton (40) . .	2
Bishops Waltham (40)		2	Penton (43 b, 44 b) .	2
Chalton (44 b) .	.	?	Somborne (39 b) .	2
Chilcomb (41) .	.	9	*Juxta* Southampton	
Dummer (45 b, 49 b) .		2	(41 b) . . .	2
Easton (40) .	.	2 chapels	Stoneham (41 b, 43) .	2
Houghton (40 b)	.	2	Sutton Scotney (46 b,	
Nether Wallop (38 b) .		1 + 1 chapel	49 b) . . .	2
Odiham (38) .	.	4	Warblington (23 b)	2

[1] Note: (*a*) *Juxta* Southampton has been regarded as part of Southampton; (*b*) there was both a church and a chapel at Nether Wallop; (*c*) there were also 4 other churches at unspecified places in the Isle of Wight (see below).

Of these, Alresford, Bishops Waltham, Chalton, Chilcomb, Houghton, Odiham, and Overton each covered more than one settlement;[1] Penton is today represented by Penton Grafton and Penton Mewsey, and Stoneham by North and South Stoneham.[2] Two churches each at Sutton Scotney and at Dummer seem unlikely; the church at each vill may have been separately recorded for each holding, or each vill may have included separate settlements about which we are not told. Five entries relate to Somborne (39b, 47, 47b, 48b *bis*), but the two churches are given in only one of these; today, Somborne is represented by King's Somborne and by Little Somborne (which includes Up Somborne). The two churches at Warblington are also given in a single entry (the only one for the vill), and it may be relevant to notice that Warblington 'pertained' to Westbourne in Sussex for which no church is entered. It is also just possible that the chapel given under Nether Wallop (38b) was at Over Wallop which again had no church entered for it. The two churches *juxta* Southampton belonged to the mother church of Stoneham; they may have been at different places or they may reflect the influence of the borough. The number at Chalton is indefinite because we are merely told: *Ibi ecclesiae*.

In the Isle of Wight, churches are specifically entered for only four places,[3] but we are also told that 'the abbey of St Mary of Lyre has in the Isle of Wight 6 churches' (52b); two of these are mentioned as belonging to the abbey, in the entries for Bowcombe (52) and Arreton (39b), but of the other four we are told nothing further.

The total of churches is at least 119, and of chapels 14, making a grand sum of at least 133. The only places for which priests are included among the population are Basingstoke (43) and Bowcombe (52), each with one church; but other priests occasionally appear as land-holders;[4] priests elsewhere may have been omitted or, more likely, included in the total of villeins. Clearly, this is not the full tale of churches, and there are well populated districts where we hear of only an occasional church.

We are sometimes told the annual value of the church to the owner of a manor; thus the church at Droxford (41b) was worth 20s. (*ecclesia de xx solidis*), so was that at Crondall (41), while that at Twyford (40) brought in only 5s. In common with holdings in general, some churches

[1] See pp. 288–91 above.   [2] See p. 294 n. above.
[3] Bowcombe (52), Calbourne (52b), Shalfleet (53b), and Arreton (39b).
[4] See p. 311 above.

had to pay more than they were worth. The church at Hinton Ampner (41 b) was valued at 40s., but had to pay 50s. (*Ibi ecclesia de xl solidis. Reddit tamen l solidos*). The three churches at Alresford (40) were worth £4, but they used to pay £6 and had not been able to afford it (*Ibi iii ecclesiae de iiii libris. Hae reddebant vi libras per annum sed pati non potuerunt*). The geld liability of the land appurtenant to a church is sometimes given; thus there was one church possessed of (*cum*) one hide at West Meon (40b); and at Hurstbourne Tarrant (39) Vitalis the priest had the church belonging to the manor (*manerii ecclesia*) with half a hide. But not every church, we may think after studying Domesday Book, possessed a portion of the land of a manor from which it might derive its revenue; the customary dues from the living and the dead (*omnes consuetudines vivorum et mortuorum*), mentioned for Mottisfont (42), must often have formed the main means of support for the priest, apart from his share in the produce of the common fields in which he often laboured. The church at Mottisfont, incidentally, had six dependent chapels (*capellae*) at nearby places which were named—Broughton, Pittleworth, East Tytherley, West Tytherley, East Dean and Lockerley.

Tithes are mentioned sporadically. The abbey of Lyre had the tithe of the vill (*decima villae*) at Clatford (38b), but no church is entered for it; the abbey of Mont St Michael had the tithe of the manor of Basingstoke (43); Richer the clerk had that of Stoneham (41b). The canons of Twynham had all the tithe of Twynham itself (44) and also a third of the tithes of Holdenhurst (*tota decima de Tuinam et tercia pars decimarum de Holehest*); no church is mentioned in the entry for Twynham; and, although a chapel is entered for Holdenhurst, there is no reference to tithe (39). The abbey of Lyre had six churches in the Isle of Wight (52b) and the tithes of all the king's revenues (*Decimas habent de omnibus redditionibus regis*); and tithes are again mentioned for two of these churches—at Bowcombe (52) and Arreton (39b). Both tithe and church-scot are mentioned in a difficult entry for Nether Wallop (38b):

There is a church to which belong 1 hide and a moiety of the tithe of the manor, and the whole church-scot (*totum cirset*), and 46d. from the tithe of the villeins, and a moiety of the lands (*medietas agrorum*). There is besides a chapel (*ecclesiola*) to which belong 8 acres of tithe.

Church-scot (*circesset*) of 14s. is also entered for the manor of Hurstbourne Tarrant (39).

URBAN LIFE

Three places in Hampshire seem to have been regarded as boroughs—Southampton, Twynham and Winchester, which is described as a city (*civitas*). Where we might expect to find an account of Winchester, at the beginning of the Hampshire section, only an empty space precedes the list of landholders in the county. It is curious that the Domesday Book contains no account of Winchester, the ancient capital of the realm, and the place where it was at first kept in the royal treasury, but there are a number of incidental references from which we can glean a little. Southampton is described immediately before a section dealing with the Isle of Wight, but the account is incomplete, and, like that for Twynham, it tells us little about urban activity. No reference is made, for example, to markets or to minting places. The evidence, slender as it is, is set out below. No place in the Isle of Wight was regarded as a borough, but under Bowcombe (52) mention was made of 4 houses (*domus*) and 20 messuages of the bordars (*masurae bordariorum*) which suggests a possible nascent urban development.

Southampton

Southampton is described on fo. 52 at the end of the main account of the shire and before the second instalment of that of the Isle of Wight. The description begins by telling us that the king had in demesne 76 men (*homines*) who paid £7 for land-gafol (*de gablo terrae*) as in 1066. It then goes on to classify these into three groups: 27 who paid 8*d.* each, 2 who paid 12*d.* each, and the 'other 50' who paid 6*d.* each. This makes a total of 79 paying £2. 5*s.*, and provides a good example of the uncertainty of Domesday arithmetic.

This is followed by a statement about land that had been freed from geld in King Edward's day; the land included 4 houses (*domus*) which had passed to Ralph de Mortemer, and 3 which had passed to Bernard Pancevolt. These would seem to be the ones mentioned elsewhere as attached to rural manors:

Fo. 47b Chilworth (Bernard Pancevolt): *iii hagae de xviii denariis.*
Fo. 46b Shirley (Ralph de Mortemer): *iiii masurae de xl denariis.*

We are then told that: 'After King William came into England, there settled in Southampton (*sunt hospitati*), 65 Frenchmen (*francigenae*) and 31 Englishmen. These pay between them £4. 0*s.* 6*d.* for all customary dues.' It seems as if trade with the continent was increasing. Finally, there is a list of 48 houses (*domus*) whose owners were entitled to the dues from them. It is not clear whether these, or some of them, are duplicated in the earlier figures, but it would seem as if the total number of households in Southampton may certainly have been 182, and possibly 230. This implies a minimum population of, say, upwards of 1,200; the actual population may have been much greater.

The entry concludes by saying that the abbess of Wherwell (some 18 miles to the north) had a fishery here and a small piece of land (*parvum terrae*) which rendered 10s., but which had once rendered only 100d. We are told nothing of the trading activity of the port, and, obviously, the Domesday account is very incomplete.[1] Within 70 years the borough was to be 'farmed' for the enormous sum of £300 'blanch'.[2]

Twynham

Two entries are devoted to the holdings of the king (38b) and of the canons of Twynham (44) at Twynham, the modern Christchurch, at the mouth of the river Avon. The general picture that emerges is that of a considerable agricultural settlement with which was associated a small urban element. There were $22\frac{1}{2}$ plough-teams at work; there were two mills, a substantial amount of meadow (169 acres) and some wood. The picture is complicated in that part of the wood and some of the arable (with 3 teams worked by 5 villeins) had been taken into the New Forest.[3] The population in 1086 included 32 villeins, 18 bordars, 4 radmen, 3 coliberts and 3 serfs—that is, a total of 60. To these must be added the inhabitants of the messuages in the borough (*in burgo*):

> Fo. 38b: *xxxi masurae reddunt xvi denarios de gablo.*
> Fo. 44: *vi masurae de xiii solidis et iiii denariis.*

In the account of Burton (44) we are also told of two *masurae* in Twynham, which bring the total to 39. The grand total of 99 implies a population of, say, 500; but how complete this is we cannot say. Nor have we any clue to the activity that went on in the borough.

---

[1] Thus we hear incidentally of two churches *juxta Hantone* (41b), but of none in the town itself.

[2] *V.C.H. Hampshire*, I, p. 433.   [3] See p. 337 above.

Winchester

An incidental reference in the account of Exeter in the Devonshire folios (100) links Winchester with London and York, but, for some reason unknown to us, no account of the city was included in the Domesday Book we now know. There are, however, scattered references to the

Fig. 102. Places contributory to Winchester.

Note: (1) The reference to Basingstoke is in the past tense; (2) Awbridge occurs in a joint entry with Houghton; the properties of Wherwell Abbey are not marked because of their uncertain location. See pp. 339 n. and 354.

city (*civitas*). The abbey of Wherwell is said to have a mill there rendering 48*s*. (44); there is a reference to the king's house in the city (43); and, what is more, some urban properties are recorded as connected with rural manors in the villages around. These are set out on p. 354 (see also Fig. 102). The total amounts to 111 properties together with the 4 inhabitants of the suburbs (*suburbani*) who used to render at Basingstoke, but all these can be only a fraction of the grand total.

There are, however, two early surveys of the city which tell us a little about it. One dates from about 1103–15, the other from 1148; these two form the *Liber Winton* or 'Winton Domesday', as it is sometimes

Places contributory to Winchester

Those marked by an asterisk (*) are said to be paying (*reddentes*) the sums mentioned; the others are said to be worth (*de*) the sums mentioned. The entries marked with a dagger (†) do not specifically mention Winchester, but they seem likely to refer to it.

Holding	Property	£	s.	d.
Awbridge and Houghton (45)†	3 *masurae*	—	—	
Basingstoke (39)	4 *surburbani reddebant*		12	11*
Bramdean (49b)	1 *haga*		3	0
Bramley (45)†	3 *burgenses*		1	10*
Clatford (38b)	7 *hagae*		10	0
Corhampton (45)	1 *domus*		5	0
Dummer (49b)	3 *hagae*		2	0*
Eversley (43b)	1 *haga*		—	7
Faccombe (39b)	6 *domus*	—	—	
Headbourne Worthy (46b)	8 *hagae*	3	5	4
Headbourne Worthy (47b)	1 *masura*			nihil*
Houghton (40b)†	3 *burgenses*		2	6
Minstead (51b)	1 *haga*		1	0
Mottisfont (42)	1 *haga*		2	6
Nether Wallop (38b)	2 *hagae*		5	5
Norton near Wonston (49b)	5 *hagae*		10	0
Preston Candover (44b)	1 *haga*		1	5
Romsey (43b)	14 *burgenses*	1	5	0*
Somborne (47)	9 *mansiones burgensium*		12	2*
Stratfield (48)	1 *haga*	—	—	
West Meon (40b)	8 *hagae*		6	0*
Wherwell Abbey (44)	31 *masurae*‡	—	—	

‡Probably the 'abbess's own house' should be added to these; the entry runs: *Ipsa abbatia tenet in civitate Wintonia xxxi masuras de quibus habet omnes consuetudines quietas excepto geldo regis. A quo etiam geldo est quieta propria domus abbatissae.*

incorrectly called.[1] The earlier is a list of the sums due from the king's tenements and from those of his barons and tenants, street by street, 'in

---

[1] Printed by Sir Henry Ellis in the *Libri Censualis vocati Domesday Book*, IV (London, 1816), pp. 529–62. The documents were discussed by J. H. Round in *V.C.H. Hampshire*, I, pp. 527–37.

the time of King Edward'; the later document is apparently a comprehensive survey of rents. To gauge the number of tenements, either in 1066 or 1086, is a matter of extreme difficulty. An attempt made to estimate the population placed the maximum figure at between 6,000 and 8,000,[1] but this seems very large. Whatever the total may be, even a cursory examination of the documents gives some idea of the life that went on in the city. We hear of the *hantachenesele* or merchants' guildhall, of the halls of the *cnichts* (probably also traders), of a market and shops and stalls, of a sanctuary, of a hospital, of mints, of forges, of the place where thieves were imprisoned, and of shanties (*bordelli*) erected outside the walls. The miscellaneous people mentioned include reeves, 'beadles of the street', tallymen, tanners, a dealer in hay, a swordsmith, and court officials such as the king's cook. Clearly there is a great need for further work on both documents.

MISCELLANEOUS INFORMATION

Markets and tolls

There are three entries relating to markets:

(1) Basingstoke (39): *Ibi mercatum de xxx solidis.*
(2) Neatham (38): *Mercatum de viii libris.*
(3) Titchfield (39): *Mercatum et theloneum xl solidis.*

The first two were on royal manors, and Titchfield was a berewick of the royal manor of Meonstoke. In addition to the toll at Titchfield, there was another toll yielding 15s. entered for the royal manor of Kingsclere (39), and a third yielding 30s. at Bowcombe in the Isle of Wight (52). No markets are entered for the boroughs.

Parks

There was a park for beasts of the chase (*parcus bestiarum*) in the bishop of Winchester's manor of Bishops Waltham (40). Two entries for Soberton nearby also refer to a park:

Fo. 48b. *Tunc se defendebat pro iii hidis. Modo pro ii hidis et dimidia quia in parco Comitis Rogerii est dimidia hida.*

Fo. 49. *Comes Rogerus habet in suo parco unam virgatam.*

---

[1] G. W. Kitchin, *Winchester* (London, 1890), p. 79.

As Earl Roger (of Shrewsbury) seems to have held no land at Soberton, we can only conjecture that the park might have been in his nearby manors of Chalton or Hambledon; but no reference is made to a park in the entries for these or for any other of his holdings (44b); the reduction in assessment suggests that the park was a recent creation. A third park is entered under Watchingwell (52b) in the Isle of Wight: '*T.R.E.* it was assessed at 3 hides; now at 2½ hides because one half [hide] is in the king's park' (*in parco regis*); an unspecified amount of meadow is also said to be in the park, and the entry concludes by saying that what the king had was worth 5*s.* This seems to be a reference to the later royal Forest of Parkhurst.

Other references

Renders of honey are mentioned in two entries. At Eling (38b), wood rendering 280 swine and 3 sesters of honey (*iii sextaria mellis*) had been taken into the New Forest; and at Broughton, East Dean and Nether Wallop (38b) a honey render of 10*s.* was also in the hands of the foresters.

There are no references to vineyards in 1086, but Alward, the holder of an estate at Lomer (43) in 1066, paid 10 sesters of wine (*reddebat abbati per annum x sextaria vini*). We are not told, however, whether the wine was produced on the spot, or whether the render continued to be paid by his successor, Ruald.

Earl William had owned a bakehouse (*furnus*) at Cheverton in the Isle of Wight, and his baker (*pistor*) had held 1½ acres of him (52b).

A castle is entered under Alvington in Carisbrooke (52b): 'Then [it was assessed at] 2½ hides. Now for 2 hides because the castle occupies 1 virgate' (*quia castellum sedet in una virgata*).

The entry for Droxford (41b) contains a reference to 12*s.* as 'the gain arising from the land' (*pro lucro terrae xii solidi*), which, thought Round, referred to a money rent.[1]

Plough-shares (*vomeres*) were returned in connection with three holdings in the Isle of Wight—Adgestone (39b), Aviston (53) and Scottlesford (53). The first rendered 6 and the two latter 3 each, and the formula runs: *unum* (or *quoddam*) *frustum terrae unde exeunt vi* (or *iii*) *vomeres.*

Also at Aviston (53) we hear of a certain vavassor having two cows (*quidam vavassorius habens ii vaccas*).

The only reference to industry is that mentioning a forge (*ferraria*) yielding 2*s.* 2*d.* at Stratfield (45b).

[1] *V.C.H. Hampshire*, I, p. 466 n.

Other perquisites are the soke (*soca*) of two hundreds at Somborne (39b), and certain rights in six hundreds belonging to Nether Wallop in 1066 (38b): 'To this manor belonged *T.R.E.* the third penny of six hundreds; it also had free right of pasture and pannage in all the woods belonging to those six hundreds.' Finally, one curiosity may be noticed. The monks of the bishopric of Winchester had, on the manor of Enham (50), a mortgage of £12 which a man who had died had left to them (*xii libras de vadio quas dimisit eis quidam homo qui mortuus est*).

REGIONAL SUMMARY

The so-called Hampshire Basin extends into eastern Dorset and forms a relatively simple geological and geographical unit surrounded by Chalk; the greater part of Hampshire is therefore occupied by two broad geographical regions—the Hampshire Basin itself and the Chalk downland. In the north and east, the county boundary includes portions of the London Basin and of the western Wealden area; and, to the south, the Isle of Wight, despite its variety of surface, can conveniently be considered as one unit in a broad view. The county as a whole may, therefore, be divided into five regions, varying in size but each possessing some individuality (Fig. 103).

(1) *The Hampshire Basin*

The Hampshire Basin, like the London Basin, is an area of low relief that for the most part lies well below 200 ft. and that only rarely rises more than 300 ft. above sea-level. Like the London Basin again, its rocks consist mainly of Tertiary clays and sands, but there is one important difference in that the tracts of clay are less extensive. A narrow belt of London Clay, with its heavy soils, extends around the northern margin of the Basin, but there is nothing to correspond to the great stretches of London Clay in Middlesex and Essex. There are also other outcrops of clay, but the predominant formations are sands and gravels, which give rise to extensive tracts of light soils, often too sterile to repay cultivation.

The New Forest is the outstanding tract. Today, its surface is, roughly, half wood and half heath; what these proportions were in the eleventh century, we do not know, but there may well have been more wood than is entered in the Domesday Book. Great stretches of the district seem always to have been uninhabited, but it is impossible to say exactly to what degree the extension of forest rights under the Conqueror resulted in eviction and further desolation. In any case, even if we take the Domesday references to holdings 'in the forest' as implying that they were virtually obliterated, we must remember that the New Forest was not without some population or without a certain amount of cultivation. It is

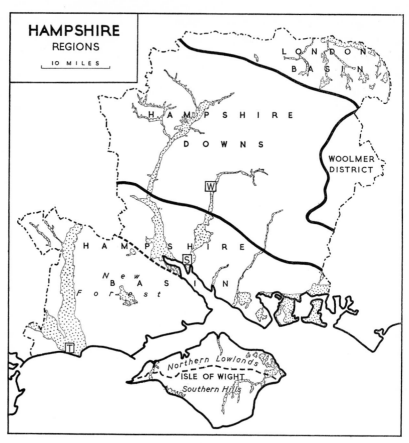

Fig. 103. Hampshire: Regional subdivisions.

Domesday boroughs are indicated by initials: S, Southampton; T, Twynham;
W, Winchester. Areas of alluvium and valley gravel are shown (see Fig. 90).

true that the density of population and of plough-teams over much of the area amounted to less than one-third of a person and less than one-tenth of a team; but higher densities more comparable with those over the rest of the county were encountered along the margins—4 to 9 for population, and 1 to 2 for teams. Villages of varying size pursuing normal agricultural activities were frequent along Southampton Water, along the south coast, especially to the west of Lymington, and along the Avon valley. The resources of the Avon valley villages, in particular, included substantial amounts of meadow, frequent mills and occasional fisheries. There were also fisheries, as well as salt-pans, along Southampton Water. With this region has been included a small portion of the Dorset Downs. In general it resembles the Hampshire Downs, but its position links it with the Avon valley, and it is not separately described here.

The area of light soils continues eastward beyond Southampton Water, but here the countryside is diversified by the alluvial valleys of the lower courses of the Test, the Itchen and the Meon. Densities here were generally higher, being 7 for population and 2 for teams, but there were less prosperous tracts to the east of Southampton Water and along the western borders of the county where densities fell much below these figures; into the latter area, in later times, extended the forests of Melchet and Clarendon. The villages of the lower Test and lower Itchen contained a good deal of meadow and some mills. The economy of the area was diversified by occasional fisheries and by saltpans around Portsmouth and Langstone Harbours.

(2) *The Hampshire Downs*

The Hampshire Downs are highest along their outer margin in the north and east, where much of their surface is over 600 ft. above sea-level and where some localities reach heights of 750 to 800 ft. From this outer irregular rim, the general surface of the Downland slopes southward to dip beneath the beds of the Hampshire Basin. This surface lies for the most part between 300 ft. and 500 ft. above sea-level, and it displays the characteristic landscapes associated with Chalk country in England. Incised into this Chalk dip-slope are the valleys of the Test, the Itchen and Meon; strung along these valleys were the settlements of Domesday times, and between the valleys were the relatively empty Chalk uplands or Downs. We are told practically nothing about these upland pastures in the Domesday Book, but we do hear of pastures called 'Down' and 'Moor' at Somborne and at one of the Worthys—that is in the Winchester district. In spite of the downland, it was in this region that the highest densities of population (9 to 12) and teams (2 to 3) were to be found; and the upper basin of the Test stood out as the most prosperous area. The valley villages had moderate amounts of meadow, a fair number of mills, and a very occasional fishery. In places, especially on the higher portions to the north-east, the Chalk is covered with Clay-with-flints; and associated with these tracts, on the high-lying land to the south of Basing-stoke, there were some villages at surprisingly high levels; Dummer, Shalden and Wield, for instance, were at heights above 600 ft., and, as might be expected, they and the other villages were without mills and had only small amounts of meadow or none at all. It may well be that the wood of the villages along this high eastern margin of the Downs was upon the tracts of Clay-with-flints, but it is difficult to make any very precise correlations. Wood was entered for other villages elsewhere on the Hampshire Downs, but the region as a whole cannot have been well timbered.

(3) *The London Basin*

Below the Chalk escarpment stretches the London Basin with its contrasts between heavy clay soils and light sands and gravels, all infertile to early cultivators. The main spread of sands and gravels is an extension of the sterile Bagshot area of Surrey, and the densities both of population (just over 2) and of teams (below 1) were much below those of the downland. In the west, where there is most clay, the densities were much higher—6 for population and under 2 for teams—but they were still below those of the Downlands. Most of the villages had small amounts of meadow along the streams of the Loddon and of the tributaries that flow into Blackwater River and the Kennet; here, too, were some mills. If *Effelle* is really to be identified with Yateley, there was a fishery in Blackwater River. A few villages seem to have had fairly substantial tracts of wood, but, on the whole, the amounts recorded were small.

(4) *The Woolmer District*

In the east of Hampshire, beyond the outcrop of the Chalk, a variety of formations succeed one another—the Upper Greensand, the Gault, and, covering the greatest area, the various beds of the Lower Greensand. What with the heavy clay of the Gault and the light soils of the Lower Greensand, it is not surprising that the densities of both teams and popula-tion in this district were low—under one and about two respectively. There were only small amounts of meadow along the Wey and the Rother and their small tributaries, and only a few mills. There were, on the other hand, moderate amounts of wood. Here in later times, were Woolmer Forest and Alice Holt Forest; they are not mentioned in the Domesday Book, but there is a reference to the 'king's wood' in the entry for Oakhanger, and it may be that this indicates the presence of a royal forest here in the eleventh century.

(5) The Isle of Wight

The main contrast in the geography of the Isle of Wight is between north and south. In the north, the Oligocene clays (Bembridge Marls and Hamstead Beds) are heavy and ill-drained, and their water-logged surface often passes into boggy tracts and into fresh and salt marsh along the estuaries. This damp countryside, it is true, is relieved by stretches of gravel, but these are infertile and so were unattractive to early settlement. It is not surprising that villages were relatively few here, and that the density of population was only about 3 and that of teams not much above 1 per square mile. Meadow was scarce, and there were only occasional mills, nor were any fisheries recorded along the Medina. A few salt-pans testify to the coastal character of the area. It is curious that scarcely any wood was entered for such a thinly inhabited clayland where one might expect to find much. There is, for example, no reference to the later royal forest of Parkhurst, but we must note that there was a park belonging to the king at Watchingwell not far away.

To the south, the Cretaceous country has a variety of surface, with some localities rising to over 700 ft. above sea-level. Villages were frequent, set at the foot of the Chalk downs or in the valleys. The density of population was about 10, and that of teams about 3 per square mile. The greater number of villages had small amounts of meadow, but mills were relatively infrequent; one fishery was to be found along the Yar. There was some wood of a miscellaneous character, but very little pannage for swine.

BIBLIOGRAPHICAL NOTE

(1) There are two early extensions and translation of the Hampshire folios: Richard Warner, *Hampshire extracted from Domes-day Book: with an accurate English translation; a preface and an introduction*...(London, 1789). This also formed vol. II of D.Y.'s *Collections for the history of Hampshire, and the Bishopric of Winchester*...*with the original Domesday of the county, and an accurate English translation, preface, and introduction* (London, 1795).

Henry Moody, *Hampshire in 1086. An extension of the Latin text, and an English translation of the Domesday Book, as far as it relates to Hampshire; with explanatory notes* (Winchester and London, 1862).

A more recent translation is that by J. H. Round in *V.C.H. Hampshire*, I (Westminster, 1900), pp. 449–526. This is accompanied by an introduction (pp. 399–447) which places much emphasis upon persons and genealogies. Round acknowledges his indebtedness 'for the identification of places' to Henry Moody (see above).

(2) An early study is 'The Domesday Book: Hampshire and Wiltshire', being the second essay (pp. 12–24) of Henry Moody's *Notes and Essays, archaeological, historical and topographical, relating to the counties of Hants. and Wilts.* (Winchester, London and Salisbury, 1851).

(3) The following deal with various aspects:

F. H. BARING, 'The Conqueror's footprints in Domesday', *Eng. Hist. Rev.* XIII (London, 1898), pp. 17–25. Reprinted 'with some additions and alterations' in *Domesday Tables for the counties of Surrey, Berkshire, Middlesex, Hertford, Buckingham and Bedford and for the New Forest* (London, 1909), pp. 207–16.

F. H. BARING, 'Note on Hampshire', being pp. 192–3 of *Domesday Tables* (see above).

F. H. BARING, 'William the Conqueror's march through Hampshire in 1066', *Papers and Proceedings Hants. Field Club*, VII (Southampton, 1915), pt. 2, pp. 33–9.

M. HOFMANN *Die Französierung des Personennamenschatzes im Domesday Book der Grafschaften Hampshire und Sussex* (Murnau, 1934).

J. B. KARSLAKE, 'The water mills of Hampshire', *Papers and Proceedings Hants. Field Club*, XIV (Southampton, 1938), pt. 1, pp. 3–8.

T. W. SHORE, 'Early boroughs in Hampshire', *Archaeol. Rev.* IV (London, 1890), pp. 286–91.

(4) Tables of the New Forest entries are contained in the following early works:

W. Camden, *Britannia*, ed. by R. Gough, I (London, 1789), pp. 129–30.

Richard Warner, *Topographical remarks relating to the south-western parts of Hampshire*, I (London, 1793), pp. 163–215.

P. Lewis, *Historical enquiries concerning forests and forest laws, with topographical remarks upon the ancient and modern state of the New Forest* (London, 1811), pp. 167–72.

Another early account that discusses the New Forest evidence is ch. 3 (pp. 20–38) of J. R. Wise, *The New Forest: Its history and its scenery* (London, 1863; 5th ed. 1895).

A more recent discussion that is accompanied by an interesting diagram, and that refers to earlier work, is F. H. Baring's 'The making of the New

Forest', *Eng. Hist. Rev.* XVI (London, 1901), pp. 427–38; reprinted in *Domesday Tables*, pp. 194–205 (see above).

See also: (i) W. J. C. Moens, 'The New Forest: Its afforestation, ancient area, and law in the time of the Conqueror and his successors', *Archaeol. Journ.* LX (London, 1903), pp. 30–50; (ii) F. H. M. Parker, 'The Forest laws and the death of William Rufus', *Eng. Hist. Rev.* XXVII (London, 1912), pp. 26–38; (iii) F. H. Baring, 'The making of the New Forest', *Papers and Proceedings Hants. Field Club*, VI (Southampton, 1910), pp. 309–17; (iv) F. H. Baring, 'The making of the New Forest', *Eng. Hist. Rev.* XXVII (London, 1912), pp. 513–15.

(5) The Liber Winton was printed by Sir Henry Ellis in *Libri Censualis vocati Domesday Book*, IV (London, 1816), pp. 529–62. It was discussed by J. H. Round in *V.C.H. Hampshire*, I (Westminster, 1900), pp. 527–37.

(6) The student of the Hampshire Domesday is handicapped by the lack of an English Place-Name Society volume for Hampshire, but a study of the place-names of the Isle of Wight is available—H. Kökeritz, *The Place-Names of the Isle of Wight* (Uppsala, 1940).

CHAPTER VIII

SURREY

BY C. W. LLOYD, M.A.

'The Domesday Survey of the county of Surrey', wrote J. H. Round, 'is neither long nor of special interest'.[1] As it raises few points of unusual interest, and is relatively straightforward, the task of making a geographical analysis of the information it contains is comparatively simple. This is not to say that there are no imperfections in the text, for, as will be seen later, information about plough-lands and values is often withheld, and there are numerous omissions. Moreover, the hidage of several estates is only vaguely recorded; and there are a number of duplications;[2] and, furthermore, many holdings are rubricated under the wrong hundreds.

The early nineteenth-century county of Surrey, in terms of which this study has mainly been made, was almost identical with the Domesday county. No significant change in the boundaries of the historic county occurred until 1889, when certain parishes in the north-east were detached to form part of the administrative county of London.[3] In 1086 a great stretch of woodland separated Surrey from Sussex, and the boundary between the two counties seems to have been indefinite.[4] Lodsworth (36b) and Worth (34b), now in Sussex, are described in the Surrey folios. As no other document places them in this county, it seems probable that the county boundary was defined in their neighbourhood within a few decades of the Survey.

Within the eleventh-century county there were thirteen hundreds (Fig. 104), varying in size from Wotton hundred with apparently 60 hides

[1] *V.C.H. Surrey*, I (London, 1902), p. 275.

[2] For a discussion of 'some duplications', see F. H. Baring, *Domesday Tables* (London, 1909), pp. 15–16.

[3] For an early post-Domesday change, see B. F. Davis, 'An early alteration of the boundary between Kent and Surrey', *Archaeol. Cant.* XLIV (London, 1934), pp. 152–5. For change after 1889, see p. 485 n. below.

[4] H. E. Malden, 'The Domesday Survey of Surrey', in P. E. Dove (ed.), *Domesday Studies*, II (2 vols., London, 1888–91), p. 459.

in 1066 to Wallington hundred with 378 hides;[1] their liabilities in 1086 were considerably smaller.[2]

SETTLEMENTS AND THEIR DISTRIBUTION

The total number of separate places mentioned in the Domesday Book for the area included in the nineteenth-century county of Surrey seems

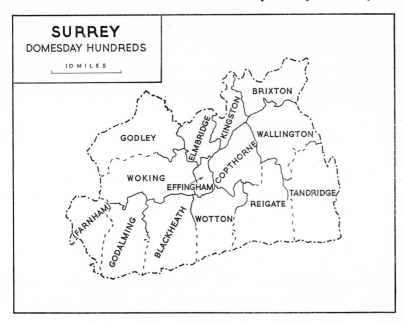

Fig. 104. Surrey: Domesday hundreds.

Any reconstruction of the hundred boundaries can only be hypothetical; the pecked lines indicate the boundaries that are especially so. The manor of Farnham was not rubricated under any hundred in the Domesday Book, but appeared as a separate hundred in the twelfth century.

to be 142, including the boroughs of Guildford and Southwark. This figure, however, does not represent the total number of settlements in the eleventh century. It was Maitland who first showed that the villages

[1] Wotton hundred had 59¼ hides in 1066. In addition to the thirteen named hundreds, there was the 60-hide manor of Farnham, which was not rubricated under any hundred in the Domesday Book, but which appeared as a separate hundred in the twelfth century.

[2] See p. 372 below.

of the later hundred of Farnham may have been grouped together by the
Domesday commissioners in one entry (31); he wrote:

> For example, in Surrey there is now-a-days a hundred called Farnham which
> comprises the parish of Farnham, the parish of Frensham and some other
> villages. If we mistake not, all that Domesday Book has to say of the whole of
> this territory is that the Bishop of Winchester holds Farnham, that it has been
> rated at 60 hides, that it has been worth the large sum of £65 a year and that
> there are so many tenants upon it. We certainly must not draw the inference
> that there was but one vill in this tract. If the bishop is tenant in chief of the
> whole hundred and has become responsible for all the geld that is levied there-
> from, there is no great reason why the surveyors should trouble themselves
> about the vills. Thus the simple *Episcopus tenet Ferneham* may dispose of
> some 25,000 acres of land.[1]

There are also 22 unnamed holdings, including a nameless manor with
14 hides in Tandridge hundred (34b). F. H. Baring suggested that this
might be Warlingham, otherwise not mentioned in the Domesday Book,
but it has been left unassigned in the present analysis.[2] Seven of the
unnamed holdings were in the hundred of Wallington, and five in Copthorne. For the purpose of calculating densities, all these unnamed
holdings have been included in their respective hundreds.

The total of 142 is further complicated by nine pairs of adjoining
villages which have the same surname today, and which may or may not
have been separate units in 1086. Thus, for example, the Domesday
Molesham (35, 36b) is represented today by East Molesey and West
Molesey, but there is no evidence that both units existed in the eleventh
century. The same is true of such pairs of present-day parishes as the
Bookhams (32b, 35b), the Dittons (32, 35) and the Horsleys (31 *bis*, 36);[3]
in each case the distinction between the respective pairs appears later
in time. On the other hand, it is probable that both East Clandon and
West Clandon existed at the time of the Domesday Survey, in spite of
the fact that the Surrey folios name only *Clanedun* (34 *bis*, 36), because

---

[1] F. W. Maitland, *Domesday Book and Beyond* (Cambridge, 1897), pp. 13–14. The
hundred boundaries are identical with those given for the bishop of Winchester's
manor in a pre-Domesday charter. Reference to the hundred appears in the twelfth
century. It included the present parishes of Elstead, Farnham, Frensham, Seale and
Shottermill (formed from Frensham in 1896).

[2] See F. H. Baring, *Domesday Tables*, pp. 2 and 31. See also *V.C.H. Surrey*, I,
p. 315 n.

[3] For the two Horsley entries on fo. 31, see *V.C.H. Surrey*, I, p. 300.

there survives a tenth-century charter which mentions both *Clendone* (East Clandon) and *altera Clendone* (West Clandon).[1] In the present analysis each of these pairs of villages has been counted as a single unit.

The total of 142 includes three places about which very little information is given; the record may be incomplete, or the details may have been

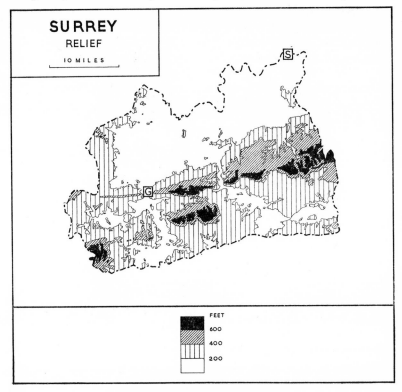

SURREY
RELIEF
10 MILES

FEET
600
400
200

Fig. 105. Surrey: Relief.

Domesday boroughs are indicated by initials:
G, Guildford; S, Southwark.

included with those of a neighbouring village. Thus of Putney (30b) we are merely told that it rendered 20s. from the toll (*de villa putelei xx solidi de theloneo*). Leatherhead is mentioned in the entry for Ewell (30b), but we learn only that its church (*ecclesia de Leret*), together with 40 acres of

[1] For the history of these, and of all other names mentioned in this chapter, see J. E. B. Gover, A. Mawer and F. M. Stenton in collaboration with A. Bonner, *The Place-Names of Surrey* (Cambridge, 1934).

land, belonged to Ewell and was worth 20s.[1] Of *Brameselle* (34), an unidentified place-name, we know only that in 1066 it had belonged (*pertinuit*) to the manor of Limpsfield, but nothing is mentioned about its status or its resources twenty years later.[2]

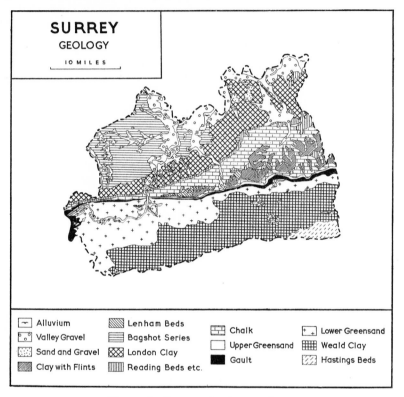

Fig. 106. Surrey: Surface geology.

Based on Geological Survey One-Inch Sheets (New Series) 269, 270, 285, 286, 287; (Old Series) 8, 9.

Not all the Domesday names appear as the names of villages on the present-day map of Surrey. Some are represented by hamlets, by individual houses and farms, or by the names of districts and even of streets and

---

[1] But the present parish of Leatherhead contains Thorncroft which is the Domesday *Tornecrosta* (35b).

[2] 'It may be represented by Broomland in Titsey, a farm'—*V.C.H. Surrey*, I, p. 311, n. 7. This identification has not been adopted in J. E. B. Gover, A. Mawer and F. M. Stenton, *The Place-Names of Surrey*, p. 338.

lanes in some of the suburbs of London. Thus, *Hormera* (36) is now the hamlet of Hurtmore in the parish of Godalming, and *Liteltone* (36b) is the hamlet of Littleton in the parish of Artington. *Losele* (34b) is represented by Loseley House also in Artington, and *Padendene* (36) survives as Paddington Farm and Paddington Tolt in the parish of Abinger. Dirtham Lane in Effingham preserves a trace of the vill of *Driteham* (35, 35b), and *Witford* (31b, 35b) survives as Whitford Lane in Mitcham. These are but some of the changes in the Surrey villages. To them must be added four unidentified names—*Brameselle* (34), *Litelfeld* (36), *Mideham* (35b) and *Pechingeorde* (36b).

On the other hand, there are a number of villages on the modern map that are not mentioned in the Domesday Book. Their names do not appear until the twelfth and thirteenth centuries, and, presumably, if they existed in 1086, they are accounted for under the statistics of neighbouring settlements. Sometimes, although a modern parish is not named in the Domesday Book, it contains a hamlet or farm that is mentioned. Thus, so far as record goes, Puttenham was not mentioned until 1199, but it includes Rodsell Farm which represents the Domesday *Redessolham* (31, 31b); and Ash, first mentioned in 1170, contains the locality of Wyke which is the Domesday *Wucha* (34b). Those parishes which contain no Domesday name lie mainly in the Weald and in the west of the county, but this does not necessarily mean that these districts were entirely without settlements in 1086. Such an assumption is disproved by the existence of pre-Domesday names. In the Weald there are, for example, Lingfield, the name of a parish, and Petridgewood Farm and Thunderfield Castle, both in Horley parish, itself not mentioned until 1199. Indeed, the evidence of place-names suggests that 'the whole of Surrey must have been settled, however thinly in parts, before the conversion of its people to Christianity'.[1] It is, nevertheless, fair to assume that those parts of the county devoid of Domesday names were but thinly peopled in the eleventh century, and that the very nature of the country rendered cultivation negligible—thick woodland on heavy clay soils, and heaths on infertile sands and gravels. It was only later that the real occupation of these areas began, and the earliest names of their parishes date from the twelfth and thirteenth centuries, e.g. Chiddingfold (*c.* 1130), Cranleigh (1166), Pirbright (1166), Ewhurst (1179), Alfold (1227), Dunsfold (1241) and Hascombe (1241).

[1] J. E. B. Gover, A. Mawer and F. M. Stenton, *op. cit.* p. xii.

The distribution of Domesday names was naturally very uneven in
a county with such marked physical contrasts as Surrey (Fig. 107). The
most marked contrast is between the southern third and the rest of the
county. Only two Domesday names, Hartshurst (35 b) and Ockley (35 b
bis), occur on the Weald Clay;[1] and it is clear that in the eleventh century
this region must have been an inhospitable tract separating Surrey from
Sussex. Another strikingly empty area was that of the Bagshot sands and

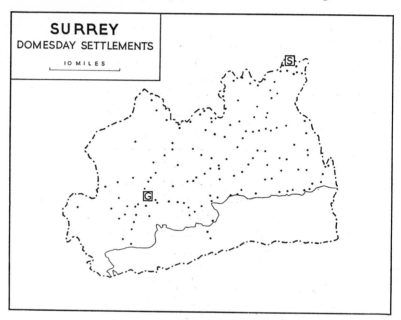

Fig. 107. Surrey: Domesday place-names.

Domesday boroughs are indicated by initials: G, Guildford; S, Southwark.
The northern boundary of Weald Clay is shown (see Fig. 106).

gravels in the north-west. Here, the outlying vill of Chobham (32 b) was in
the valley of the Bourne that crosses the infertile heath. In the settled part
of the county, there were two well-marked lines of villages. One of these
comprised the villages in the Vale of Holmesdale, which runs between the
Weald and the southern edge of the North Downs. The other, to the
north, marked the narrow outcrop of Lower London Tertiaries that

---

[1] It is possible that two nameless manors were also on the Weald Clay (*V.C.H.
Surrey*, I, p. 320 n.).

separates the Chalk from the London Clay. Between these two groups of spring-line villages, settlements on the Chalk itself were largely associated with patches of Clay-with-flints and other superficial deposits. Many of the villages of the plain of north-eastern Surrey were set upon the gravel terraces of the Wey, the Mole and the Thames, but there were some in the London Clay area, mainly upon gravel patches. Southward along the Wey valley, beyond Guildford and towards Godalming, there were a number of villages supported by the fertile loams that the Lower Greensand yields in this locality.

THE DISTRIBUTION OF PROSPERITY AND POPULATION

Some idea of the nature of the information in the Domesday folios for Surrey, and of the form in which it is presented, may be obtained from the entry relating to Cheam (30b), situated on the spring-line along the northern edge of the North Downs. The village was held entirely by the archbishop of Canterbury, and so it is described in a single entry:

The archbishop [of Canterbury] himself holds Cheam for the sustenance of the monks (*de victu monachorum*). In the time of King Edward it was assessed at 20 hides, and now at 4 hides. There is land for 14 plough-teams. In demesne there are 2 plough-teams, and 25 villeins and 12 cottars with 15 plough-teams. There [is] a church and 5 serfs, and one acre of meadow. Wood yielding (*de*) 25 swine. *T.R.E.* and afterwards, it was worth £8. Now £14.

This entry does not include all the kinds of information that appear elsewhere in the folios for the county; there is no mention, for example, of mills or of fisheries. But, although not comprehensive, it is a fairly representative and straightforward entry, and it sets out the recurring standard items that are found for most villages. These are five in number: (1) hides, (2) plough-lands, (3) plough-teams, (4) population, and (5) values. The bearing of these five items of information upon regional variations in prosperity must now be considered.

(1) *Hides*

The Surrey assessment is generally stated in terms of a round number of hides, but virgates and, very occasionally, acres are also employed; thus Weston Green was assessed in 1086 'at 3 hides and 1 virgate' (34) and

Stoke D'Abernon 'at 2 hides and 5 acres' (35). The form of the statement varies, as can be seen from the following representative entries:

> Mickleham (35 b): *se defendit pro ii hidis et una virgata.*
> Esher (34): *tenet...vii hidas et iii virgatas terrae.*
> Bermondsey (34): *habet...i hidam....*
> Mideham (35 b): *jacet i hida.*

At Bramley (31), in addition to the main resources, there were two plough-lands that never paid geld (*Super has est terra ad ii carucas in ipso manerio quae nunquam geldum reddidit*). Another curiosity is the statement that the bishop of Lisieux held, 'in Kent', 2 sulungs (30), a unit of assessment that characterises the Kent folios.[1]

A feature that the Surrey folios share with those of Berkshire, Hampshire, Kent and Sussex is that they so frequently record a reduction in the liability of a holding. Estate after estate gelded in 1086 at only a fraction of its hidage in 1066; thus the total hidage of the three manors of Geoffrey de Mandeville had dropped from 44 to 9½ (36). When the liability had remained unchanged, we are often specifically told so; Wallington (30), for example, was assessed at 11 hides 'T.R.E. et modo'. It is impossible to see, from the Surrey folios, on what principle these sweeping reductions were made.[2] They could not have been due to the damage caused by the Norman armies because they do not generally agree with the depreciations in values between 1066 and 'afterwards'. At Camberwell they almost do, but at Clapham there was a great reduction in geld liability and yet no loss of value, while at Shalford the reverse happened. Or again, both at Bletchingley and at Titsey, the values had fallen to about 60 per cent but the hidage at Bletchingley had been reduced to 30 per cent and that at Titsey to only 10 per cent. Here are the figures themselves:

	Hides		Values		
	1066	1086	*Tunc*	*Post*	*Modo*
Bletchingley (34b)	10	3	£13	£8	£15. 13s. 4d.
Camberwell (36b)	12	6¼	£12	£6	£14
Clapham (36)	10	3	£10	£10	£7. 10s.
Shalford (35 b)	4	4	£16	£9	£20
Titsey (36b)	20	2	£10	£6	£11

[1] See p. 502 below.
[2] But see p. 302 above for the bearing of the Cornish evidence upon the problem.

There are moreover occasional entries which suggest that the reduction was not always post-Conquest, and that it had sometimes already taken place by 1066:

> Pyrford (32): The abbey [of Westminster] itself holds Pyrford. Harold held it of King Edward. Before Harold had it, it was assessed at 27 hides. After he had it, for 16 hides at Harold's pleasure. It now pays geld for 8 hides (*Ipsa abbatia tenet Peliforde. Heraldus tenuit de rege E. Antequam Heraldus habuisset defendit se pro xxvii hidis. Postquam habuit pro xvi hidis ad libitum heraldi. Modo geldat pro viii hidis*).

> Shere (30b): The king holds Shere in demesne. Queen Edith held it. It was then assessed at 9 hides, and yet there were then 16 hides there. Lately, it has not paid geld (*Rex tenet in dominio Sira. Eddid regina tenuit. Tunc se defendit pro ix hidis et tamen erant tunc ibi xvi hidae. Modo non dedit* (sic) *geldum*).

Whatever the cause of the exemptions, and whatever their exact date, it seems clear that they were not permanent, for early in the next century we find the assessments approximating to the figures of 1066.[1]

These reductions in liability greatly obscured the five-hide unit, but, if we confine ourselves to 1066, the system can be clearly seen. Thus, in 1066, Balham had been held for 5 hides (36), Petersham for 10 hides (32b), Walton on the Hill for 15 hides (35), Chivington for 20 hides (34b), Walkingstead for 40 hides (34), and Croydon for 80 hides (30b). Where a village was divided amongst a number of holders, the same feature is sometimes apparent when the several entries are assembled and the village reconstituted. Thus the two holdings that made up Whitford paid geld on 3 hides and on 2 hides, giving a five-hide unit (31b, 35b); and the two that made up Malden paid geld on 2 hides and on 8 hides, giving a ten-hide unit (32b, 35). In 1066 the number of villages assessed at 5 hides, or at a multiple of 5, amounted to 52 out of a total of 142. There were, moreover, a few holdings of 2½ hides. It is also possible that the irregular assessments of some other villages were grouped into blocks that displayed the five-hide principle; and F. H. Baring attempted to show the decimal character of the hidage of each hundred.[2]

What with the conventional nature of the assessment and the erratic nature of the exemption, it is unlikely that the hidage bore any constant

---

[1] *V.C.H. Surrey*, I, pp. 277–8.
[2] F. H. Baring, *Domesday Tables*, pp. 2–4.

relation to the agricultural resources of a vill. The variation among a representative selection of vills, each assessed at 10 hides in 1066, speaks for itself:

	1086 Hidage	Plough-lands	Teams	Popula-tion	Values		
					1066	Inter-mediate	1086
Gatton (31 b)	2½	5	4	9	£6	£3	£6
Petersham (32 b)	4	5	5	17	£5	?	£6½
Tandridge (34 b)	2	10	14	30	£6	£2	£11
Tillingdown (34 b)	1½	4	4½	13	£7	£3	£6*
Westcott (36 b)	3	7	8	22	£9	£8	£8

* 'and yet it renders £7'.

The form of many entries (e.g. that for Cuddington on fo. 31 b) makes it extremely difficult to arrive at satisfactory totals for the hidage of the county, but the following three sets of figures at any rate serve to indicate the order of magnitude involved:

(*a*) Assessment (including non-gelding hides): 2,000½ hides.[1]

(*b*) Gelding hides in 1066: 1,926 hides.

(*c*) Gelding hides in 1086: 698¾ hides, 16 acres.[2]

These totals exclude the two boroughs, Guildford and Southwark; no mention of their assessments is made in the Surrey folios. The figures can only be approximate, for any total depends upon the individual interpretation of a number of entries.

(2) *Plough-lands*

Plough-lands are systematically entered for the Surrey villages, and the normal formula runs: 'There is land for *n* plough-teams' (*Terra est n carucis*). Occasionally, as for Pyrford (32) and Send (36b), this is contracted to *Terra n carucis*. On one estate at Lambeth (34), where there were 12 plough-lands and 6 teams at work, we hear of *una cultura terrae*.

---

[1] F. W. Maitland's total was 1,830 hides (*op. cit.* p. 400). H. E. Malden counted 2,000¼ hides; see his figures quoted by F. H. Baring, whose own total was 1,997¾ hides (*Domesday Tables*, p. 17). Neither Maitland nor Malden appears to have excluded the figures given for duplicated entries. All three made their estimate for the Domesday county.

[2] F. W. Maitland's figure was 706 hides (*op. cit.* p. 401); F. H. Baring counted 698 hides (*op. cit.* p. 17).

On the manor of Bramley (31), with land for 35 teams, we hear also of *terra ad ii carucas*. In no fewer than 20 entries for 17 places the phrase *Terra est* is followed by a blank space in which a figure was never inserted, e.g. for Battersea and for Morden on fo. 32. There are also some entries which make no reference to plough-lands, although they state the number of teams at work, e.g. the entry for Cuddington (31 b). Taking these two categories together, there are about 30 places with incomplete figures for plough-lands.

The relation between plough-lands and plough-teams varies a great deal in individual entries. A deficiency of teams was fairly frequent, being found in about one in three of the Domesday settlements for which plough-lands were recorded. The deficiency was as much as 28 at Egham (32 b), where there were 40 plough-lands but only 12 teams at work. In none of these entries, however, is there any reference to the possibility of further teams being added; the *potest fieri* formula found in the folios of some other counties does not occur for Surrey. An excess of teams, on the other hand, could be found at two in five villages for which plough-lands were recorded. It amounted to as much as 18 at Croydon (30 b), for example, where there were 20 plough-lands but as many as 38 teams apparently at work. Such excess was especially characteristic of the hundred of Woking which straddled the middle Wey valley to the north of the Chalk outcrop; here, there were 99½ plough-lands and as many as 136¼ teams.[1] It is difficult to see why there should have been this great excess here.

There has been considerable discussion as to the exact meaning of the term plough-land. Some scholars have regarded it as a statement of the number of teams that had been at work in 1066. Others have believed it to be an estimate of the potential arable land of an estate; yet others have seen in it a large conventional element. The Surrey evidence is not conclusive on any of these points. Moreover, changes in the values of estates do not throw any light on the problem; the values of estates with fewer teams than plough-lands sometimes fell, but quite often they remained the same, and occasionally they even increased. Similarly on estates with excess teams, the values sometimes rose, but frequently they remained the same, and sometimes they even fell; the entries overleaf are typical of the changes that took place.

---

[1] Lodsworth (36 b), rubricated under Woking, has been excluded from this calculation because it has been counted in Sussex—see p. 364 above.

	Plough-lands	Teams	Value 1066	Value 1086
Bermondsey (30)	8	5	£15	£15
Hambledon (36)	4	7	£5	£5
Lambeth (34)	12	6	£10	£11
Limpsfield (34)	12	19	£20	£24
Pyrford (32)	13	7	£12	£18
Woodmansterne (35)	3	5	£10	£8

The total number of plough-lands for the area included within the early nineteenth-century county is 1,015⅜. If, however, we assume that plough-lands equalled teams on those holdings where a figure for the former is not given, the total becomes 1,259⅝.[1]

(3) *Plough-teams*

The Surrey entries for plough-teams are fairly straightforward, and, like those of other counties, they normally draw a distinction between teams at work on the demesne and those held by the peasantry. Occasional entries seem to be defective. That for Peckham (31b), for example, mentions 4 men, one plough-land and some meadow, but says nothing of a team or teams at work. At Ham in Kingston hundred (32b) there were 2 bordars and land for 1 team, but again no team itself is mentioned, although there is a blank space where the information should have been inserted. On one holding at Chipstead (33) we hear of 3 men, but nothing either of teams or of plough-lands.[2] Occasionally no demesne teams were recorded, e.g. in the entries for Farncombe (31) and Hatcham (31b). Conversely, a few small holdings seem to have had nothing other than demesne teams, e.g. Baingiard's unnamed holding in Copthorne hundred (31b). Oxen are occasionally mentioned (e.g. at Farleigh, 34b), and there is a reference (35) to ploughing-oxen on a tract of land called Ember (*unam terram quae vocatur Limeurde.... Ibi sunt vi boves arantes cum ii bordariis*).

---

[1] F. W. Maitland's total amounted to 1,172 plough-lands (*op. cit.* pp. 401 and 410); that of F. H. Baring was 1,300 plough-lands (*op. cit.* p. 17). Both reckonings made allowance for the unrecorded plough-lands on the assumption that they equalled the existing teams. Both reckonings, unlike the present one, were in terms of the Domesday county.

[2] One of the entries for Apps Court (35) mentions 10 villeins and 6 cottars with 4 cot' (*cum iiii cot'*). In the present analysis this has been taken as a scribal error for *car'*.

The total number of plough-teams in the area included within the early nineteenth-century county amounts to 1,273¼, but it must be remembered that a definitive total is hardly possible in view of the varying interpretations that can be placed upon some entries.[1]

(4) *Population*

The bulk of the population was comprised in the four categories of villeins, bordars, serfs and cottars. In addition to these were the burgesses together with an unusually small miscellaneous group comprising merely one forester at Walton in Elmbridge hundred (36). There were apparently no freemen or sokemen in 1086. The details of these categories are summarised on p. 382. There are three other estimates of the population of the Domesday county. Sir Henry Ellis's figures appeared in 1833,[2] while other estimates have been made by H. E. Malden[3] and F. H. Baring.[4] But no one who counts Domesday population can claim definite accuracy, because varying interpretations of many entries are inevitable. Finally one point must always be remembered. The figures are of recorded population, and must be multiplied by some factor, say 4 or 5, in order to obtain the actual population; but this does not affect the relative density as between one area and another.[5] This is all that a map, such as Fig. 110, can indicate.

It is impossible to say how complete were these Domesday figures. A few entries certainly appear to be incomplete; no population is enumerated in the entries for Chaldon (31b), Leatherhead (30b), Putney (30b), Sutton in Shere (32),[6] and in a small number of entries beginning 'In

[1] F. W. Maitland's total amounted to 1,142 plough-teams (*op. cit.* p. 401); that of F. H. Baring was 1,273. Both reckonings, unlike the present one, were in terms of the Domesday county.

[2] Sir Henry Ellis, *A General Introduction to Domesday Book*, II (London, 1833), p. 494. His grand total for the Domesday county amounted to 4,383, but it included tenants-in-chief, under-tenants and burgesses.

[3] H. E. Malden, 'The Domesday Survey of Surrey', in P. E. Dove (ed.), *Domesday Studies*, II (London, 1891), p. 469. Malden counted 2,382 villeins, 922 bordars, 276 cottars and 503 serfs. Malden's footnote on p. 469 must evoke the sympathy of all fellow-workers on the Domesday text: 'These figures are not quite the same as those given by Sir H. Ellis. I can only say that they are the result of a five times repeated verification by myself and another.'

[4] *Op. cit.* p. 17. Baring counted 2,387 villeins, 820 bordars, 389 cottars and 503 serfs.

[5] But see p. 589 below for the complication of serfs.

[6] But for Sutton in Shere, see *V.C.H. Surrey*, I, pp. 301 and 305.

this hundred...' or 'In this vill....' It may be that their population was included within the descriptions of other places, but we cannot be certain. No priests are mentioned although churches are entered for over one-third of the Surrey vills; to what extent the priests were included amongst the villeins we cannot say. Tenants and sub-tenants have been excluded

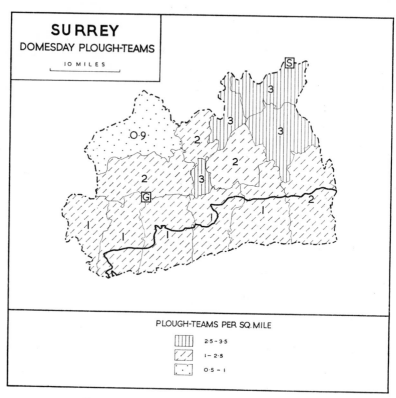

Fig. 108. Surrey: Domesday plough-teams
in 1086 (by densities).

Domesday boroughs are indicated by initials: G, Guildford; S, Southwark.
The northern boundary of Weald Clay is shown (see Fig. 106).

from the totals, and for this reason the king's smith (*quidam faber regis*), who held half a hide at Carshalton (36), does not appear in the table on p. 382.

Villeins constituted the most important element in the population, and amounted to 58 per cent of the total. At Apps Court (35) a villein held

half a hide directly as a tenant. An estate at Clandon (34) was worth
£4 in 1086, but the villeins who held it of Chertsey Abbey paid £6
(*tamen villani qui tenent eam reddunt vi libras*); it was apparently 'at farm',
and it may be worth noting that here there were 7 teams at work on land
for only 5. One of the estates at Chessington (36b) had formerly been

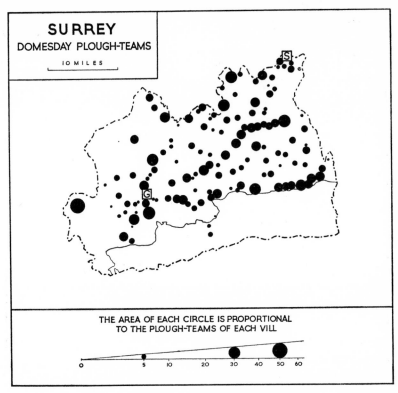

Fig. 109. Surrey: Domesday plough-teams
in 1086 (by settlements).

Domesday boroughs are indicated by initials: G, Guildford; S, Southwark.
The northern boundary of Weald Clay is shown (see Fig. 106).

held by villeins (*Villani tenebant*). Finally, at Gomshall (30b) we read
that the villeins were quit from every sheriff's matter (*ab omni re vice-
comitis sunt quieti*).

Bordars comprised 23 per cent, and cottars only 7 per cent. The
distinction between bordars and cottars is not clear, but the fact that they

occur together only 'once on the same manor, and very seldom in the same hundred' led H. E. Malden to conclude that one or the other tenure prevailed according to local custom.[1] He carefully examined the distribution of cottars in relation to hundreds and to soils, but found that the

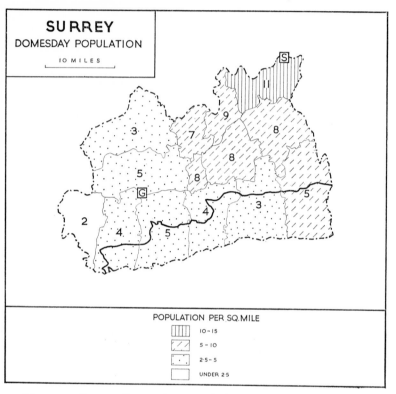

Fig. 110. Surrey: Domesday population in 1086 (by densities).

Domesday boroughs are indicated by initials: G, Guildford; S, Southwark.
The northern boundary of Weald Clay is shown (see Fig. 106).

'only rule for their occurrence' is that there was none on the royal demesne.[2] They were overwhelmingly predominant in the three hundreds of Elmbridge, Godalming and Wallington. They were also in a majority

[1] In P. E. Dove (ed.), *op. cit.* II, pp. 469–70. There seem, however, to have been bordars and cottars on two manors, Godalming (30b) and Mitcham (31b). Separate entries for Molesey (35 *ter*, 36b) record bordars and cottars respectively. Note also the cottar entered under Bramley (31) but apparently belonging to Clandon (34) where there were bordars. [2] *Ibid.* p. 470.

in Blackheath hundred, and there was a solitary cottar entered for Woking hundred. Bordars were entered to the exclusion of cottars in the remaining nine hundreds. F. H. Baring concluded that the use of the term 'cottar' was due only to the returns for the different hundreds being

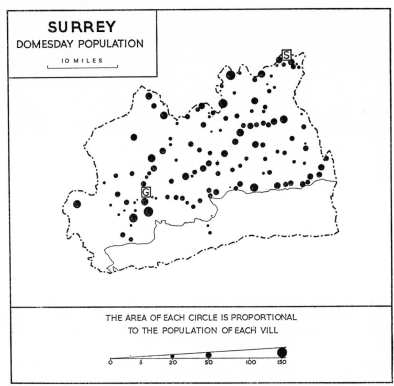

Fig. 111. Surrey: Domesday population in 1086 (by settlements).

Domesday boroughs are indicated by initials: G, Guildford; S, Southwark.
The northern boundary of Weald Clay is shown (see Fig. 106).

made separately.[1] The evidence would certainly seem to suggest that, at least in so far as Surrey was concerned, the terms *bordarius* and *cotarius* were interchangeable.[2] Serfs constituted 12 per cent of the recorded

[1] F. H. Baring, *op. cit.* p. 9.
[2] For a discussion of the differences between bordars and cottars, see F. W. Maitland, *op. cit.* pp. 39 *et seq.*, and P. Vinogradoff, *The Growth of the Manor* (London, 2nd ed., 1911), pp. 338–9. For the interchangeable use of 'bordar' and 'cottar', see H. C. Darby, *The Domesday Geography of Eastern England* (Cambridge, 2nd ed., 1957), pp. 289–90.

population; this is a relatively high proportion when compared with the figures for Kent and Sussex. H. E. Malden drew attention to the small number of serfs on monastic and chapter lands.[1]

No freemen or sokemen are enumerated for 1086, although twenty years earlier there appear to have been a small number living in the county. Thus, in 1066, five freemen held Carshalton of King Edward as five manors, but in 1086 their holdings formed one manor held by Geoffrey de Mandeville (36). At the earlier date, *alodiarii villae*, held 10 hides at Cuddington, and they could seek any other lord for their lands (*qui cum suis terris quo volebant recedere poterant*); but they seem to have been displaced by the time of the Survey (31b). In 1066, six sokemen had held Wandsworth (35b), and three had held Ham in Wallington hundred (34). Such entries as these, together with the absence of any mention of free peasantry in 1086, indicate the lowering of the social and economic position of many of the small Saxon landowners as a result of the Norman Conquest.

Recorded Population of Surrey in 1086

A. Rural Population

Villeins	.	.	.	.	.	2,386
Bordars	.	.	.	.	.	931
Serfs	.	.	.	.	.	503
Cottars	.	.	.	.	.	276
Forester	.	.	.	.	.	1
Total	.	.	.	.	.	4,097

B. Urban Population

The bordar is also included in the table above.

GUILDFORD   175 *homines*; 4 *domus*; 2 *hagae*; see p. 398 below.

SOUTHWARK   42 *mansurae*; 4 *hagae*; 1 *domus*; 1 bordar; see p. 398 below.

(5) Values

The value of an estate is normally given for three dates—*T.R.E.*, *post*, and *modo*. But a number of entries give values only for the first and last dates, and these are especially frequent in the accounts of the lands of

[1] In P. E. Dove (ed.), *op. cit.* II, p. 469.

Chertsey Abbey (32b–34). Occasional entries give only one value, presumably for 1086, e.g. those for Bramley (31) and Esher (32, 34, 36b). An entry for Chipstead (33) also gives only one value, but this seems to refer to a year earlier than 1086, for we are told that when William de Wateville relinquished the land, it was 'at farm' for 40s. (*Quando Willelmus ibiit, erat ad firmam de xl solidis*). The account of an anonymous holding, following that of Bramley (31), specifies that its value was *per annum*. Some entries indicate differences in the method of reckoning, as the following examples show:

> Godalming (30b): In the time of King Edward it was worth £25, and afterwards £20. Now, £30 by tale (*ad numerum*), and yet it renders £30 weighed and burnt (*ad pensum et arsuram*).
>
> Nutfield (34): In the time of King Edward it was worth £13, and afterwards £10. Now, £15 of 20d. to the ounce (*de xx in ora*).
>
> Woking (30): In the time of King Edward and afterwards it was worth £15 by tale (*ad numerum*). Now, £15 by weight (*ad pensum*), and 25s. to the sheriff.

Pechingeorde (36b) was worth 40s., but the men of the bishop of Bayeux claimed two marks of gold or two hawks for the king's use each year. Wadard's estate at Ditton (32) was valued at £4, £2 and £4 respectively, but it was held of Wadard for 50s. and a knight's service (*Ille qui tenet de Wadardo reddit ei l solidos et servitium unius militis*).

The values of a large number of estates had fallen appreciably after the time of the Conquest, but by 1086 the majority of these had recovered, some even to a point exceeding their earlier value. The reduction had often been considerable, as the following examples show:

	1066	Intermediate	1086
Battersea (32)	£80	£30	£75. 9s. 8d.
Camberwell (36b)	£12	£6	£14
Mortlake (30b)	£32	£10	£38
Shalford (35b)	£16	£9	£20

F. H. Baring accounted for these temporary decreases in value by regarding them as marking the passage of Norman armies soon after the Battle of Hastings, and this seems a reasonable hypothesis.[1]

Another feature of the Surrey valuation is that the new landowners

---

[1] *Domesday Tables*, p. 209. See p. 569 below.

frequently obtained from their estates more than what seems to have been
regarded as a reasonable return. Fourteen entries for fourteen places give
the current value in 1086, and then go on to say that the estate paid a
greater sum than this. The increase was often substantial:

	1066	Inter-mediate	1086	Payment
Ewell (30b)	£20	£16	£16	£25
Gomshall (30b)	£15	£10	£20	£30
Horsley (31)	£4	£4	£4	£5
Merton (30)	£25	£16	£35	£43
Sanderstead (32)	£5	£7	£12	£15

At Stoke next Guildford (30), for example, the increase took the form
of a change in the method of reckoning. It was worth £15 (presumably
by tale), and it continued to yield the same sum but by weight (*Modo xv
libras. Tamen qui tenet reddit xv libras ad pensam*). Godalming (30b)
and Woking (30), mentioned above, provide other examples of increase
through change of reckoning. The term 'at farm' is occasionally used;
one holding at Ditton (35) was worth 60s. in 1066, then 30s., and then
50s. in 1086, yet it was farmed out for £4 (*Tamen est ad firmam pro iiii
libris*). The entry for Reigate (*Cherchefelle*, 30), on the other hand, tells
us that it paid what it was worth, but, incidentally, gives only one value
(*Modo appreciatur xl libris et tantum reddit*).

Generally speaking, the greater the number of teams and of men on an
estate, the higher its value, but no consistent relationship can be discerned,
as the following figures for five holdings, each worth £5 in 1086, show:

	Teams	Population	Other resources
Fetcham (36b)	6	18	Meadow, Mill, Wood
Hambledon (36)	7	22	Meadow, Mill, Wood
Hurtmore (36)	3½	5	Meadow, Mill
Ockham (35b)	3	11	Meadow, Wood
Peper Harow (36)	3	7	Meadow, Mill

It is true that the variations in arable, as between one manor and another,
did not necessarily reflect variations in total resources, but even when the
other resources are taken into account, the figures remain difficult to
explain.

Conclusion

The Domesday hundreds have been adopted as the main basis for constructing the density maps, but minor modifications have been made, e.g. where two Domesday names, rubricated under different hundreds, occur in the same modern parish. A division of the county according to physical features or soils would have been preferable, but this is not practicable because so many parishes run north and south, cutting across two or more geological outcrops. In 1086, many of the Surrey hundreds included large areas of inhospitable country which contributed little or nothing to their prosperity; these intractable localities are not readily apparent on the density maps.

Of the five recurring standard formulae, those relating to plough-teams and population are the most likely to reflect something of the distribution of wealth and prosperity throughout the county in 1086. Taken together, they supplement one another; and when they are compared certain common features stand out (Figs. 108 and 110). The most prosperous part of the county was in the north-east, towards the city of London. Here, the line of villages between the Chalk and the London Clay, and those on the gravel terraces of the Thames itself, contributed to relatively high density figures—about 3 teams and between 7 and 11 people per square mile. This prosperous area extended westward to the Hampshire border along the narrowing wedge of Chalk and London Clay, but densities here were lower. Elsewhere in the county, densities were particularly low. The infertile Bagshot area of the north-west had under one team and only 3 people per square mile, and much of it has remained inhospitable up to the present day. In the south, what with the sterile sands of much of the Lower Greensand, and the heavy clayland of the Weald, densities were also low—between one and two for teams and under 5 (often well under) for population.

Figs. 109 and 111 are supplementary to the density maps, but it is necessary to make one reservation about them. As we have seen on p. 366, it is possible that several of the symbols should appear as two or more smaller symbols because some Domesday names may have covered two or more separate settlements; e.g. Great and Little Bookham. This limitation, although important locally, does not affect the general character of the maps, which confirm and amplify the information of the density maps.

WOODLAND AND FOREST
Types of entries

The amount of woodland on a holding in Surrey was recorded in terms of the number of swine paid as an annual rent for the right of pasturage. The formula varies only slightly, as the following entries show:

Bletchingley (34b): *De silva xl porci.*
Epsom (32b): *Silva de xx porcis.*
Hambledon (36): *Silva xxx porcis.*
Henley in Ash (34): *Silva l porcis de pasnagio.*
Limpsfield (34): *Silva de cl porcis de pasnagio.*
Mortlake (30b): *De silva lv porci de pasnagio.*
Mickleham (35): *unus porcus de pasnagio silvae.*
Tadworth (31b): *i porcus de silva.*

The number rendered by each holding varied from only one pig, at Claygate (32) for example, to 200 at Croydon (30b). The round figures of many entries (e.g. 20, 50, 100) suggest estimates rather than precise numbers, but, on the other hand, detailed figures such as 3, 4, 13, 133 and even 150½ at (Farnham, 31) seem to indicate exactness. A few entries record mast swine (*de pasnagio*) and grass swine (*de herbagio*) in a single total, as, for example, in the entry for Fetcham (30b) which notes: 'From pannage and herbage 6 swine' (*De pasnagio et herbagio vi porci*).[1] For the purpose of constructing Figs. 112 and 114, these totals have been divided equally between woodland and pasture.

The Surrey folios give no indication of the ratio between these renders and the total number of swine feeding in the woodland. But four entries relating to grass swine give ratios of one in seven and one in ten.[2] Whether similar proportions characterised the renders of mast swine we cannot say, and, in any case, there is no satisfactory answer to the wider question of what acreage of woodland these figures imply. All we can do is to plot them as conventional units.

The record of wood is only rarely varied by the miscellaneous information that appears in the folios for some other counties, but there are five entries which do provide us with interesting additional detail:

---

[1] Single totals for wood and grass swine are given in the following six entries: Abinger (36), Bookham (35b), Fetcham (30b, 31b), Gatton (31b), and Pyrford (32). A second entry for Bookham (32b) gives separate renders for wood and pasture; and a third entry for Fetcham (36b) states a render for wood alone.

[2] See p. 391 below.

(1) The entry for Ewell (30b) tells us of wood rendering 100 swine, but later in the entry we hear of a dene of wood and a croft (*unam denam silvae et unam croftam*). This is the only 'dene' mentioned for Surrey, as compared with the substantial number that appear in the folios for Kent.[1] There is no indication of where this solitary dene lay.

(2) The entry for Limpsfield (34) records wood yielding 150 swine, and then, later on, refers to '3 nests of hawks in the wood' (*iii nidi accipitrum in silva*).[2]

(3) In the entry for Wallington (30), towards the Kentish border, we read of 'wood which is in Kent' (*Silva quae est in Chent*), but no amount is specified. This entry, incidentally, goes on to say that Richard of Tonbridge held 1 virgate with a wood whence he took away a peasant who dwelt there (*Ricardus de Tonebrige tenet de hoc manerio unam virgatam cum silva unde abstulit rusticum qui ibi manebat*).

(4) On Bishop Osbern's manor of Woking (31)[3] we are told that there was wood yielding 28 swine, and the entry then adds that the manor had the customary right of pasturing 120 swine in the king's wood of Woking, without payment for pannage (*Istud manerium habet et habuit consuetudinem in silva regis de Wochinges. Hoc est quod dominus villae hujus potest habere in ipsa silva cxx porcos sine pasnagio*). The entry is exceptional partly because it is the only one in the Surrey folios that mentions a swine total, and partly because it includes the unusual phrase 'lord of this vill'.

(5) One of the entries for Chipstead (34b) records wood yielding 5 swine and then goes on to say that Richard of Tonbridge (the tenant-in-chief) had retained another wood for himself (*silva v porcis aliud nemus sibi retinuit Ricardus*). But, apparently, we have no record of this other wood.

Distribution of woodland

The greatest stretch of woodland in the eleventh-century county must have been in its Wealden portion, and yet Fig. 112 shows practically none there. The northern boundary of the Weald, however, is indicated approxi-

---

[1] See p. 527 below.
[2] A render of hawks, but not wood, is mentioned in the entry for the unidentified *Pechingeorde* in Effingham hundred (36b); see p. 401 below.
[3] There is reason to believe that the bishop's manor of 'Woking' was at East Horsley nearby, and that the hundred name appears in the entry instead of that of the manor—see (i) *V.C.H. Surrey*, I, p. 300; (ii) F. H. Baring, *Domesday Tables*, p. 35. Woking itself was a royal manor (30).

mately by a line of villages with renders for pannage. It must be remembered that in the absence of information about the location of the wood pastures, it has been necessary to plot the swine renders on the sites of the villages returning them, whereas, in fact, the renders may have referred to swine pastures some distance away.[1] Only one Surrey entry

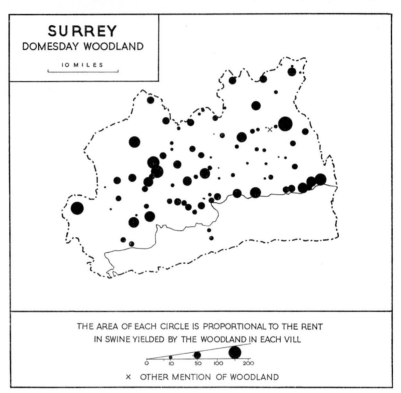

SURREY
DOMESDAY WOODLAND

10 MILES

THE AREA OF EACH CIRCLE IS PROPORTIONAL TO THE RENT
IN SWINE YIELDED BY THE WOODLAND IN EACH VILL

0   10   50   100   200

×   OTHER MENTION OF WOODLAND

Fig. 112. Surrey: Domesday woodland in 1086.

We are specifically told that the wood entered for Wallington, and indicated here as 'other mention', was in Kent (see p. 387). The northern boundary of Weald Clay is shown (see Fig. 106).

(that for Wallington mentioned above) tells us that the wood lay else-where, but we know from other evidence that there were many 'enclaves' within the Weald attached to estates beyond its margins. The symbols on Fig. 112 must therefore be 'spread out' by eye over the adjacent Weald.

[1] For some examples, see F. H. Baring, *op. cit.* p. 14.

The amounts entered for the villages of the northern rim seem small in relation to the size of the Wealden area, and it may well be that some of the Wealden wood went unrecorded.

There appears also to have been a fair amount of wood belonging to the villages just north of the Chalk belt—at Croydon, for example, or in the villages of the middle Wey basin to the south of Woking. It is likely that much of this was located on the London Clay, and some may have been on the Chalk hills themselves, where there were patches of Clay-with-flints. But we cannot press any correlation too closely. The nature of the woodland economy in this part of England means that the woodland map of Surrey is far from yielding itself readily to a geographical interpretation.[1]

Forests

The royal forests of Surrey for the most part go unmentioned in the Domesday Book. In the north-west of the county, certain localities appear to have lain within the royal forest of Windsor, but only one entry actually mentions the word 'forest', although two others seem indirectly to refer to the presence of forest:

Pyrford (32): The king has three hides of this land in his forest (*De hac terra habet rex iii hidas in foresta sua*).

Walton in Elmbridge hundred (36): There [is] a forester yielding 10s. (*Ibi unus forestarius de x solidis*).

Woking (30): Of this land, Walter son of Other holds 3 virgates. A certain forester held this in the time of King Edward, and it was then put out of the manor for King Edward. There is nothing there now (*De hac terra tenet Walterius filius Otherii iii virgatas. Hanc quidam forestarius tenuit T.R.E. et tunc fuit posita extra Manerium pro rege Edwardi. Ibi modo nichil est*).[2]

In addition to these, there is a reference to the king's park at Stoke next Guildford (30), which Round identified as the royal park of Guildford: *Silva* [*de*] *xl porcis et ipsa est in parco regis*.[3] This total of four references does far less than justice to the Norman love of the chase, and to the activity that must have taken place in the localities subject to forest law in Surrey.

[1] See pp. 559–600 below.
[2] Note also the reference to *silva regis* at Woking (31)—see p. 387 above.
[3] *V.C.H. Surrey*, I, p. 296.

Types of entries   MEADOW

The entries for meadow in the Surrey folios are straightforward. For holding after holding the same phrase is repeated monotonously—'*n* acres of meadow' (*n acrae prati*). Only once does it vary, and then but slightly; this is in the entry for Tolworth (35) which records '5 acres and a half of

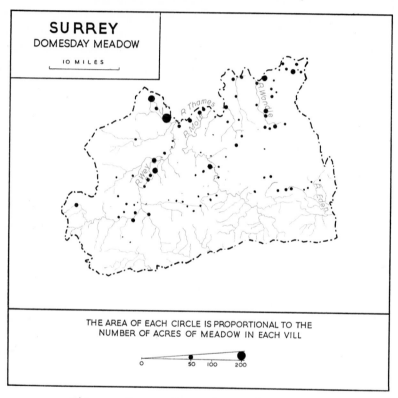

Fig. 113. Surrey: Domesday meadow in 1086.

meadow and half a virgate' (*v acrae et dimidia prati et dimidia virgata*).[1] The amount of meadow entered under the name of each place varied from one acre, at Cobham (32b) for example, to 200 acres at Chertsey (32b). Generally speaking, however, amounts above 50 acres are rare. As in the

---

[1] The Latin is *et dimid v'*. In *V.C.H. Surrey*, I, p. 292, Round expanded it as a half-*virga*, 'probably the eighth of an acre'. The *V.C.H.* text (p. 317), however, translated it as half a virgate.

case of other counties no attempt has been made to translate the figures into modern acreages. The Domesday acres have been treated merely as conventional units of measurement, and Fig. 113 has been plotted on that assumption.

Distribution of meadowland

The most striking fact about the distribution of meadowland was its concentration in the valleys of the Thames, of the Wandle, of the Mole and of the Wey with its tributaries (Fig. 113). Each of these rivers was bordered by villages with substantial amounts of meadow; along the Thames, Chertsey with 200 acres, and Egham with 120, were outstanding. The spring-line villages that border the north and south margins of the North Downs usually had some meadow, but the amounts were very much smaller than those recorded for the villages of the river valleys. Villages on the North Downs themselves were for the most part lacking in meadow. The Weald, owing to the absence of recorded place-names, stands out on the map as an area bereft of meadow; so does the Bagshot area.

PASTURE

Pasture (*pastura*) itself is mentioned only once in the Surrey folios—in the entry for Titsey (36b)—but out of the total of 142 settlements in Surrey, 25 paid a rent in grass swine for *herbagium*. This varied from a rent of 3 swine at Effingham (35b) to one of 43 at Reigate nearby (30). Sometimes, as we have already noted, the renders of grass-swine and pannage-swine are given in a single total.[1] Typical of the references to *herbagium* are:

Abinger (36): *De herbagio et pasnagio xl porci.*
Milton (36): *De herbagio x porci.*

Four entries relate the swine render to the total number of swine, but none of them, incidentally, states the number of swine that was rendered. At Malden and Titsey the ratio was one in seven, but at Battersea and Streatham it was the tenth pig that seems to have been paid:

Malden (35): *De herbagio unus porcus de vii porcis.*
Titsey (36b): *pro pastura septimus porcus villanorum.*
Battersea (32): *De villano habente x porcos unus porcus. Si minus nil dat.*
Streatham (34b): *pro herbagio unus porcus de x porcis.*

[1] See p. 386 above.

We cannot be absolutely certain that the ratio at Battersea does refer to grass swine (as opposed to mast swine), but its position in the text suggests that it does. Whether such ratios were general, and whether they also applied to mast swine, we cannot say.[1]

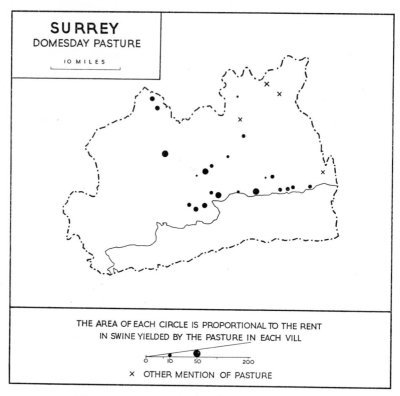

SURREY
DOMESDAY PASTURE
10 MILES

THE AREA OF EACH CIRCLE IS PROPORTIONAL TO THE RENT
IN SWINE YIELDED BY THE PASTURE IN EACH VILL

0   10   50   200

× OTHER MENTION OF PASTURE

Fig. 114. Surrey: Domesday pasture in 1086.

'Other mention of pasture' refers to the swine-ratios. The northern boundary of Weald Clay is shown (see Fig. 106).

In the entries of villages rubricated under seven of the fourteen[2] Domesday hundreds in the county, no reference at all is made to pasture, and we can only speculate why the commissioners did not record it. Furthermore, Surrey has always been famous for its heaths and commons, and they must

---

[1] If these ratios also refer to mast swine, the render of 150½ mast swine at Farnham (31) is difficult to understand in view of the Battersea entry 'If less [than 10 swine], he gives nothing'.   [2] See p. 365 n. above.

have provided a considerable amount of rough-grazing land in the eleventh century. Fig. 114, therefore, cannot be regarded as giving a picture of the Surrey pastures in 1086; it shows merely the disposition of those vills for which there are pasture entries.

FISHERIES

Fisheries (*piscariae*) are recorded in connection with only nine places and one unnamed holding in Surrey. Most entries state the number of fisheries

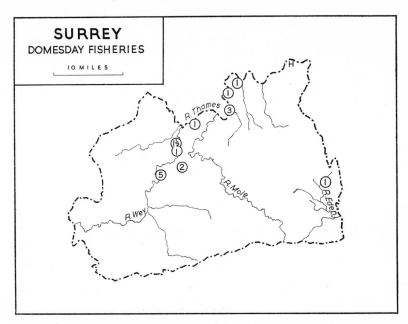

Fig. 115. Surrey: Domesday fisheries in 1086.

The figure in each circle indicates the number of fisheries. There were herring renders (H) at Southwark. There was also a fishery on an anonymous holding in Kingston hundred.

and their render in money or kind, although two of the fisheries are said to be without a render (*sine censu*). The kind of fish is mentioned only three times: at Byfleet (34) and at an unnamed holding in Kingston hundred (36) there were fisheries rendering eels; at Petersham (32b), a rent in eels and lampreys was paid. No eel renders are mentioned in connection with mills. One of the fisheries at Kingston (30b), although without render (*sine censu*), was very profitable (*valde bona*). The fishery at Mortlake had been set up illegally (30b). The complete list of entries is as follows:

Byfleet (34): *Una piscaria et dimidia de cccxxv anguillis.*

Kingston (30b): *Duae piscariae de x solidis et tercia piscaria valde bona sed sine censu.*

In Kingston hundred (36): *i piscaria de cxxv anguillis.*

Limpsfield (34): *una piscaria.*

Mortlake (30b): *una piscaria sine censu. Hanc piscariam habuit comes[1] Heraldus in Mortelaga T.R.E. et Stigandus archiepiscopus habuit diu T.R.W. et tamen dicunt quod Heraldus vi construxit eam T.R.E. in terra de Chingestune* (Kingston) *et in terra Sancti Pauli.*

Ockham (35b): *duae piscariae de x denariis.*

Petersham (32b): *piscaria de mille anguillis et mille Lampridulis.*

Send (36b): *v piscariae reddentes liiii denarios.*

Walton in Elmbridge hundred (35): *piscaria de v solidis.*

Wisley (36b): *piscaria de v denariis.*

No reference is made to a fishery in the main entry for Southwark (32), but the entries of two vills which had contributory properties in the borough mention renders of herrings.[2]

As Fig. 115 shows, all the fisheries were along the Thames and its tributary the Wey, with the exception of an outlying fishery at Limpsfield on a tributary of the Eden in the south-east of the county.

MILLS

Mills are mentioned in connection with 66 out of the 142 Domesday settlements within the area covered by the nineteenth-century county of Surrey; they also appear in the entries for two anonymous holdings.[3] For each locality the number of mills is given, and, generally, their annual rent also; the latter ranged from one mill worth only 20*d.* at an unnamed holding in Blackheath hundred (31) to 7 mills rendering £42. 9*s.* 8*d.* 'or corn of like value' (*aut frumentum ejusdem precii*) at Battersea (32). No value was entered for the mill 'at the hall' (*ad hallam*) in Chertsey (32b), and the mill at Tolworth (35) was said to be 'without render' (*sine censu*). Fractions of mills were sometimes noted. There was 'part of a mill'

---

[1] *Comes* is interlined in the MS.

[2] The places were Ditton and Walkingstead—see p. 400 below.

[3] One mill in Blackheath hundred (31) and half a mill in Copthorne hundred (31b).

pars molini) at Ditton (32); and there were 2 half-mills (*ii dimidii molini*)
at Pachesham in Leatherhead (31b) and a half-mill each at Chessington
(35) and Mitcham (35 b). There was also a half-mill at Baingiard's unnamed
holding in Copthorne hundred (31b), which may have formed part of
Ewell.[1] One entry for Fetcham (31b) tells of 'the sixth part of a mill and

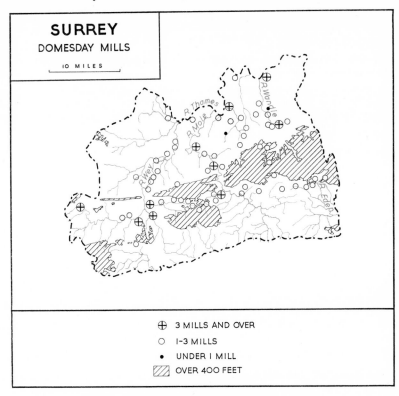

Fig. 116. Surrey: Domesday mills in 1086.
There were also mills on two anonymous holdings in the hundreds of
Blackheath and of Copthorne.

the third part of another mill' (*sexta pars molini et tercia pars alterius
molini*), and there were also 5 other mills there (30b, 36b). It is not possible
to assemble these fractions with any certainty in a comprehensible manner.
The fractions at Fetcham, for example, may have formed part of the mills
at Pachesham on the other bank of the Mole, but we cannot say.

[1] F. H. Baring, *Domesday Tables*, pp. 15 and 27.

Most of the villages with mills had but one or two apiece, and there were only ten villages accredited with more than this, as the following table shows:

Domesday Mills in Surrey

Under 1 mill	2 settlements	4 mills	2 settlements
1 mill	39 settlements	5 mills	2 settlements
2 mills	15 settlements	6 mills	1 settlement
3 mills	3 settlements	7 mills	2 settlements

Note that this table does not include the anonymous holdings for which mills are entered.

One group of 7 mills was at Battersea (32); and the other group was at Fetcham (30b, 31b, 36b) situated at the northern end of the Mole's passage through the North Downs. The group of 6 was at Farnham (31) which, as we have seen, included the resources of other settlements not named in the Surrey folios; the mills were probably on the upper reaches of the river Wey. Bramley (31) and Kingston (30b) each had 5 mills.

Fig. 116 shows the alignment of mills along the main rivers of the county, particularly along the Wey and the Mole and their tributaries. The absence of a mill serving the comparatively prosperous, yet isolated, village of Chobham situated on the Bourne, is suspicious. It may well be that the Domesday record is incomplete, the more so since the entries for nearly one-half of the villages in the Domesday county do not mention a mill. On the other hand, it is difficult to explain the existence of mills in certain villages situated high up on the North Downs far from a stream. Such were the mills at Banstead (31b), Chipstead (34b) and Woodmansterne (35), and we can only conclude that they lay at some distance from the vills themselves.[1]

CHURCHES

Churches are mentioned in connection with 62 out of the 142 settlements in Surrey in 1086;[2] there was also a church on Robert de Watevile's unnamed estate in Tandridge hundred (34b). It is certain that the

---

[1] The Woodmansterne mill was probably on the Wandle at Carshalton, and the Banstead mill may have been as far away as Leigh on the Mole to the south-west of Reigate. See (1) *V.C.H. Surrey*, I, p. 316; (2) F. H. Baring, *Domesday Tables*, pp. 13–14. Carshalton itself is said to have one mill (36), but Leigh is not named in the Domesday Book.

[2] This number includes Malden (35) and Streatham (34b) which had only a chapel apiece.

Domesday record does not give a complete list of all the churches in the county; none is mentioned, for instance, in the entries for Guildford and Reigate, yet both settlements are known to have had pre-Norman churches. Generally, only one church is mentioned in connection with one place-name; but Bramley had three churches (31),[1] and Epsom (32b), Godalming (30b) and Sutton (32b) had two each.[2] Chobham (32b) had one church and 'another chapel' (alia capella). Altogether there were 65 churches and 3 chapels. A render is recorded only from one of the two at Godalming (30b), and from the chapel at Streatham (34b). No priests are enumerated in the Surrey folios.

URBAN LIFE

The information about the towns is perhaps the least satisfactory part of the Domesday evidence, and for Surrey it is even more slender than usual. Two settlements—Guildford and Southwark—appear to have had borough status in 1086, although neither is actually styled a borough (burgus), and Guildford is thrice described as merely a vill (villa). The information about both places is very unsatisfactory, and many details are obscure. Each, for example, must have possessed a market, but we are told nothing of one.

One interesting feature that Surrey shares with some other counties is that some urban houses in both Guildford and Southwark are recorded as being connected with rural manors in the surrounding countryside. The implications of this connection between a borough and the surrounding countryside have been much debated and lie outside the theme of this chapter.[3] In the north-east of the county there were also rural manors with properties contributing to London;[4] some manors held properties in both London and Southwark.

[1] 'Perhaps Bramley, Wonersh and St Martha's' (V.C.H. Surrey, I, p. 301 n.); the two latter places are not mentioned in the Domesday folios.

[2] For the possible location of the additional churches at Epsom and Godalming, see V.C.H. Surrey, I, pp. 308 n. and 299 n.

[3] For a review of the controversy see (1) C. Petit-Dutaillis, Studies Supplementary to Stubbs' Constitutional History, I (Manchester, 1923), pp. 78 et seq.; (2) Carl Stephenson, Borough and Town (Cambridge, Mass., 1933), pp. 81 et seq.

[4] For a complete list and map of Surrey manors with contributory properties in London, see p. 132 and Fig. 47 above.

Guildford

Guildford is the first settlement mentioned in the Surrey folios (30), but the account is very disappointing. At the beginning of the entry we are told that King William had '75 *hagae* wherein live 175 men' (*lxxv hagas in quibus manent clxxv homines*).[1] In the same entry reference is made to another *haga* and to four houses (*domus*), two of which were connected with the manor of Bramley to the south. Under the entry for Shalford (35 b) nearby, we also read of property in Guildford. The three references are as follows:

Bramley (entered under Guildford, 30)
(1) *Altera domus est quam tenet praepositus episcopi Baiocensis de manerio Bronlei.*
(2) *Dicunt etiam homines qui juraverunt de alia domo quae iacet in Brunlei.*
Shalford (35 b)
Huic manerio pertinet una haga in Geldeford de iii solidis.

Thus it would seem that there was a minimum of 81 dwellings in Guildford. On the analogy of 75 *hagae* with 175 men, this figure would imply 189 men or a total population of about 750. But such an estimate is little more than guesswork.

We are told nothing of the economic activities of the borough, yet its position near the northern end of the Wey Gap through the North Downs must have made it of some commercial importance, although much of the countryside around was occupied by wood and heath. Its value rose between 1066 and 1086; at the earlier date it had rendered £18. 0s. 3d., but twenty years later, although valued at only £30, it paid £32.

Southwark

The main account of Southwark (32) is given towards the end of the description of the estates held by the bishop of Bayeux. We are told that in Southwark the bishop had one minster (*monasterium*) and one tide-way (*unum aquae fluctum*). The essential interest of this entry is legal, and it deals primarily with the right of taking toll 'on the strand or near the water' (*in strande vel in vico Aquae*). It is clear from the reference to 'the dues of the stream where ships used to come alongside' (*De exitu aquae ubi naves applicabant*) that Southwark had a tidal creek where ships could

[1] Might not the 75 be an error for 175, or the reverse?

be moored while they discharged their cargoes. Further, since the
tenants-in-chief of two of the manors (Ditton and Walkingstead) holding
contributory properties in Southwark received renders of herrings from
them, the port must have included fishing among its activities.

The full list of manors with contributory properties is given on p. 400,
and they are set out in Fig. 117; the bordar in the account of Battersea has
been included. On the other hand, we must note that the eight *mansurae*
were no longer associated with the manor of Beddington. If the figures

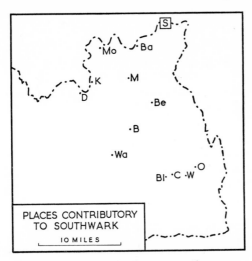

Fig. 117. Surrey: Places contributory
to Southwark (S).

B, Banstead; Ba, Battersea; Be, Beddington; Bl, Bletchingley; C, Chivington;
D, Ditton; K, Kingston; M, Merton; Mo, Mortlake; O, Oxted; W, Walkingstead;
Wa, Walton on the Hill. It is possible that the statement about Mortlake refers to a
date earlier than 1086.

for Bletchingley and for Walkingstead are divided equally between Southwark and London, the total number of properties (including the bordar)
mentioned for Southwark is 48. It is difficult to believe that the Domesday
information gives a complete picture of Southwark in 1086; but whatever
its size and economic position may have been, it was certainly over-
shadowed by the great city nearby, in which, as we have seen, several
Surrey manors had property.

Places Contributory to Southwark

Entered under Southwark

> Kingston (32): *Ipsi homines de Suduuerche deratiocinati sunt unam hagam et theloneum ejus ad firmam de Chingestone.*

Entered under rural manors

> Banstead (31 b): *i domus de xl denariis pertinet huic manerio.*
>
> Battersea (32): *i bordarius de xii denariis.*
>
> Beddington (36b): *De isto manerio [   ] ablatae sunt xxi masurae quas comes Rogerius tenet. In Lundonia xiii. In Sudwerche viii. Reddunt xii solidos.*
>
> Bletchingley (34b): *In Lundonia et Sudwerche vii mansurae de v solidis et iiii denariis.*
>
> Chivington (34b): *iii hagae de xv denariis.*
>
> Ditton (35): *i masura reddit quingenta allecia.*
>
> Merton (30): *xvi masurae de xviii solidis et ii denariis huic manerio pertinent.*
>
> Mortlake (30b): *iiii masurae de xxvii denariis.*[1]
>
> Oxted (34): *i masura de ii denariis.*
>
> Walkingstead (34): *Huic manerio pertinent xv masurae in Suduuerca et in Londonia de vi solidis et ii millen' allecium.*
>
> Walton on the Hill (35): *i masura.*

MISCELLANEOUS INFORMATION

Very little miscellaneous information is recorded in the Surrey folios. There is, for example, no reference to markets; neither are vineyards mentioned, although Walter, a sub-tenant at Wandsworth (36), is described as a *vinitor*.[2] The unusual items are set out below:

Tolls

> Battersea (32): From the toll of Wandsworth £6 (*De theloneo Wandelesorde vi librae*).
>
> Mortlake (30b): 20s. from the toll of the vill of Putney (*de villa putelei xx solidi de theloneo*).
>
> Southwark (32): toll on the strand or near the water (*theloneum in strande vel in vico Aquae*).
>
> Southwark (32): one close and the toll thereof belonging to the feorm of Kingston (*unam hagam et theloneum ejus ad firmam de Chingestone*).

---

[1] This is preceded by a statement about London in the past tense, and it is possible that the information about Southwark also refers to a period earlier than 1086.

[2] See p. 608 below.

Quarries

Limpsfield (34): Two stone quarries rendering 2*s*. (*Duae fossae Lapidum de ii solidiis*).

The village is situated on the Lower Greensand formation.

Other items

Chelsham (34b): one pig for customary payment (*De consuetudine i porcus*).

Chertsey (32b): a forge which serves the hall (*una ferraria quae operatur ad hallam*).

Kingston (30b): Humphrey the Chamberlain had, and has, in his charge a villein to collect the queen's wool (*causa codunandi lanam reginae*).

In Kingston hundred (36): Walter [son of Other] himself holds one man of the soke of Kingston, to whom he had committed the charge of the king's brood mares (*silvaticas equas*), but we know not on what terms (*nescimus quomodo*).

Pechingeorde (36b): The men of the bishop of Bayeux claim from this land every year for the king's use 2 marks of gold or 2 hawks (*duas markas auri vel duos accipitres*).

REGIONAL SUMMARY

Broadly speaking, Surrey includes four distinct areas. The northern portion lies within the London Basin, and the southern portion within the Weald. Between the two come the outcrops of Chalk and of Lower Greensand with distinctive landscapes and economies. Within each of these areas there are variations, but the broad division into four will suffice for the purpose of summarising the geography of the county in the eleventh century (Fig. 118).

(1) *The London Basin*

The countryside along the Thames is low-lying except for the various gravel terraces that provided suitable areas for early settlement above the level of floods. To the south, stretching right across the county, is a belt of London Clay the surface of which is varied by patches of sand and gravel that also provided convenient sites for early villages. Then, too, there are the gravel terraces of the Wey, the Mole, and the Wandle that flow northwards across the clay surface to join the Thames. Taken as a whole, this was the region of greatest prosperity in eleventh-century Surrey. Here were population densities of about 7 to 11 per square mile, and plough-team densities of about 3. How much of this was due to the moderate fertility of the region and how much to proximity to London, it is hard to say. The land was certainly attractive to the medieval culti- vator, and most of the wood had been cleared, although there were still some manors with substantial amounts. There were fair quantities of meadow especially along the Thames and, to a less extent, along the Wey and the Wandle. The rivers themselves were marked by mills, and fishing also entered into the rural economy of the area.

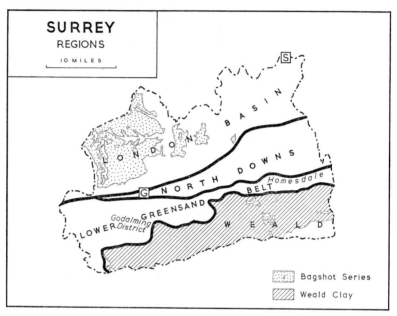

Fig. 118. Surrey: Regional subdivisions.

Domesday boroughs are indicated by initials:
G, Guildford; S, Southwark.

In contrast to this prosperity stood the poverty of the Bagshot plateau in the west. Its infertile sands were unrewarding in the eleventh century as in later times; the density of teams per square mile was below one, and the corresponding density of population was about 3. These figures would be even lower were it not for the Thames-side villages that border the area in the north. The settlement of Chobham stood out in the midst of the Bagshot area. It lay in the valley of the Bourne, and a little meadow and a fairly substantial amount of wood are entered for it.

(2) *The North Downs*

The North Downs form an outstanding feature of the relief of Surrey. Broad in the east, they narrow in the west to the well-known Hog's Back between Guildford and Farnham; they are for the most part over 200 ft. above sea-level, and, along the escarpment that marks their southern edge, they reach heights of between 600 ft. and 800 ft. In the gap formed by the Wey stood the Domesday borough of Guildford, and in that formed by the Mole was the village of Dorking. On the Downs themselves, the superficial deposits of Clay-with-flints and associated superficial deposits provided soils of moderate fertility, and their presence accounts for the existence of a relatively high number of Domesday vills, mostly without mills or meadow but with small quantities of wood. The northern edge of the dip-slope is overlain by a narrow belt of Lower London Tertiaries comprising deposits of sand and clay with some loam. This belt, well endowed with springs, was marked by a line of prosperous Domesday vills whose boundaries extended northwards on to the London Clay and southwards on to the Chalk; these vills usually had mills, meadow and wood. The arrangement of the parish and hundred boundaries makes it difficult to arrive at density figures for the North Downs as such; but it seems clear that, taking the northern belt of spring-line villages into account, here was an area not very much less prosperous than the eastern half of the London Basin in Surrey.

(3) *The Lower Greensand Belt*

Below the escarpment of the North Downs is a narrow belt of Lower Chalk, Upper Greensand and Gault, known as the Vale of Holmesdale. It is not as wide as in Kent, and to the west of Dorking it all but disappears as a separate feature. The Gault is succeeded in turn by the Lower Greensand which yields a variety of soils ranging from good loams to coarse, infertile, hungry sands. The outcrop is disposed in two portions, a narrow belt to the east of Dorking and a fairly extensive tract, drained by the Wey, to the west (Fig. 106).

In the area to the east of Dorking, settlements avoided the Gault Clay and lay to the south on tributaries of the Mole and of the Eden in the Lower Greensand area. Figs. 109 and 111 show a line of villages each with a substantial number of teams and people. The villages had mills and small quantities of meadow and their entries also record considerable amounts of wood. Much of this wood, or most of it, must have been situated to the south, on the Weald Clay plain. It is impossible to give densities because the unit areas (i.e. the hundreds) stretch southward across Lower Greensand and Weald Clay alike.

The Lower Greensand outcrop in the west, like that of the Chalk, presents a steep scarp face to the south, and here are heights such as Leith Hill (965 ft. O.D.) and Hindhead (895 ft. O.D.). Its light soils stand in great contrast with the heavy Weald Clay, yet it, too, formed an undeveloped countryside in 1086, and its sterile heathlands were to gain a notorious reputation. To this generalisation there was one important exception. In the Wey basin to the south of Guildford, in the neighbourhood of Godalming, the Lower Greensand and the Valley Gravels provide rewarding soils. Here was a number of Domesday villages, usually with meadow, sometimes with mills, and of course with wood, although this may have been physically elsewhere. At a much later date William Cobbett, that stern critic of Lower Greensand soils, was able to praise the 'nice light and good lands round about Godalming'.[1] We must remain without a full picture of the extreme west of the Lower Greensand district because the villages of Farnham hundred are not separately described; but the low densities for teams (one) and population (two) leave us in no doubt about the general nature of the countryside.

In this south-west corner of the county, the Hythe Beds of the Lower Greensand are extremely coarse and infertile, and here is Hindhead Common which rises to 895 ft. above sea-level.

(4) *The Weald*

The Weald Clay outcrop occupies almost the whole of the Surrey Weald, apart from a small stretch of Hastings Beds in the south-east corner of the county and patches of gravel and alluvium elsewhere. Only two Domesday names (Hartshurst and Ockley) occur on the Weald Clay, and none on the Hastings Beds. The density figures for teams and population were as high as they are (up to 2 and 5 respectively) because the unit areas include villages to the north. The resources entered for some, if not most, of these villages may have covered outlying portions in the Weald itself, but it is unlikely that the outliers were very large. We can safely suppose

[1] W. Cobbett, *Rural Rides*, I, p. 147 (Everyman's Library).

that the heavy clays carried much wood, some of it entered under the names of the northern villages, but some of it very probably unrecorded. For the Kent and Sussex portions of the Weald, the Domesday evidence provides us with some indications of colonising activity, but the Surrey folios yield no hint of this.

BIBLIOGRAPHICAL NOTE

(1) It is interesting to note that a facsimile copy of the Domesday folios for the county appeared as early as 1804 in Vol. 1 of O. Manning and W. Bray, *The History and Antiquities of the County of Surrey* (3 vols. London, 1804–14).

(2) A translation of the Surrey text appeared as early as 1799, made by S. Henshall and J. Wilkinson. Together with translations for Kent and Sussex, it formed one volume which was intended to be followed by other volumes covering the whole text of both Domesday volumes. No other volumes, however, appeared. The title ran: *Domesday; or, an actual survey of South-Britain, by the commissioners of William the Conqueror, completed in the year 1086, on the evidence of the jurors of hundreds, sanctioned by the authority of the county jurors; faithfully translated, with introduction, notes, and illustrations, by Samuel Henshall and John Wilkinson* (London, 1799).

Another translation appeared in 1862: *A Literal Extension of the Latin text, and an English translation, of the Domesday Book in relation to the County of Surrey* (London, 1862). It was made to accompany the Ordnance Survey photo-zincographed copy of the Surrey folios (Southampton, 1861).

A more recent translation is that by H. E. Malden in *V.C.H. Surrey*, 1 (London, 1902), pp. 295–328. It is accompanied by a useful introduction by J. H. Round (pp. 275–93).

(3) Surrey was one of the counties analysed by F. H. Baring in 1909— *Domesday Tables for the counties of Surrey, Berkshire, Middlesex, Hertford, Buckingham and Bedford and for the New Forest* (London, 1909).

(4) Other works of interest to the Domesday study of the county are:

F. H. BARING, 'The Conqueror's footprints in Domesday', *Eng. Hist. Rev.* XIII (London, 1898), pp. 17–25. Reprinted 'with some additions and alterations' in *Domesday Tables*, pp. 207–16 (see above).

F. H. BARING, 'The hidation of some southern counties', *Eng. Hist. Rev.* XIV (London, 1899), pp. 290–9. See also F. H. Baring's note on this paper in *ibid.* XV (London, 1900), p. 199.

A. HUSSEY, *Notes on the churches in the counties of Kent, Sussex, and Surrey, mentioned in Domesday Book* (London, 1852).

E. H. KENNEDY, 'The Domesday mill at Betchworth', *Surrey Archaeol. Collns,* XL (Guildford, 1932), pp. 120–2.

H. E. MALDEN, 'The Domesday Survey of Surrey' in P. E. Dove (ed.), *Domesday Studies*, II (London, 1891), pp. 459–70. The author refers to a map drawn by himself, but he does not seem to have published it.

H. E. MALDEN, 'Kingsland in Newdigate and Newdigate in Copthorne hundred', *Surrey Archaeol. Collns*, XXXIX (Guildford, 1931), pp. 147–9.

(5) A valuable aid to the Domesday study of the county is *The Place-Names of Surrey* by J. E. B. Gover, A. Mawer and F. M. Stenton in collaboration with A. Bonner (Cambridge, 1934).

CHAPTER IX

SUSSEX

BY S. H. KING, M.A., PH.D.

At the time of the Domesday Inquest, Sussex was apparently divided into five major units, the boundaries of which ran approximately north and south. These were the rapes of Arundel, Bramber, Lewes, Pevensey and Hastings (Fig. 119). The unit of the rape, intermediate between the county and the hundred, is peculiar to Sussex, and both its origin, and the origin of the term itself, have been much discussed. Some scholars have argued that the rapes were a Norman creation,[1] while others have thought that they were ancient institutions of pre-Conquest age.[2]

Within the rapes came the hundreds, and these seem to have numbered some sixty, varying in size from *Tifeld* (29), with apparently only $1\frac{1}{2}$ hides in 1066, to *Staninges*, or Steyning, with 265 hides.[3] The boundaries of the rapes coincided with those of the hundreds, except that the Arundel-Bramber boundary cut through Easewrithe hundred, and the Bramber-Lewes boundary through the hundreds of Wyndham and Fishersgate (*Eldritune*). This has been taken to indicate that the boundaries of the rapes were later in date than those of the hundreds, but this is not necessarily so.

Whatever may have been the origin of rapes as 'districts', they would seem to owe their existence as 'lordships' to the Normans.[4] Before the Conquest, the possessions of the several Saxon lords had been dispersed over more than one rape, and were intermingled one with another, but by

---

[1] F. E. Sawyer, 'The rapes and their origin', *Archaeol. Rev.* I (London, 1888), pp. 54–9. L. F. Salzman, 'The rapes of Sussex', *Sussex Archaeol. Collns*, LXXII (Cambridge, 1931), pp. 20–9.

[2] J. H. Round and H. H. Howorth, 'The Sussex rapes', *Archaeol. Rev.* I (London, 1888), pp. 229–30. J. E. A. Jolliffe: (1) 'The Domesday hidation of Sussex and the rapes', *Eng. Hist. Rev.* XLV (London, 1930), pp. 427–35; (2) *Pre-Feudal England: The Jutes* (Oxford, 1933), pp. 81–6. See also A. Mawer, F. M. Stenton and J. E. B. Gover, *The Place-Names of Sussex*, I (Cambridge, 1929), pp. 8–10.

[3] There is 'no further mention' of *Tifeld* hundred; it was later included in Burbeach hundred—O. S. Anderson, *The English Hundred-Names: The south-eastern counties* (Lund and Leipzig, 1939), p. 85.

[4] *V.C.H. Sussex*, I (London, 1905), pp. 354 *et seq.*

1086 each rape was in the hands of a single Norman lord, except only for
ecclesiastical lands and for the two royal estates. It has been held that these
lordships were created for the defence of a particularly important area,
with its coastline, on the route from London to Normandy; the rapes were
certainly in the hands of relatives or friends of King William, by whose
names they were usually known. The rape of Arundel, for example, was
called also 'the rape of Earl Roger'; Bramber rape was never named as
such in the Domesday folios, but was always known as 'the rape of
William de Braiose'.

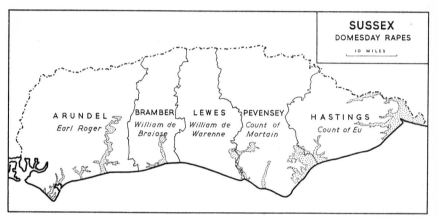

Fig. 119. Sussex: Domesday rapes.

The boundaries of the rapes follow parish boundaries of the nineteenth century, and
can only be conjectural, especially in the Weald. In the thirteenth century the western
portion of the rape of Arundel became the rape of Chichester. Areas of coastal
alluvium are shown (see Fig. 121).

One feature of this Norman reorganisation was that manors that had
included estates in more than one rape were broken up and reconstituted.
There were some 60 to 70 of these manors with outlying estates up to
20 or 30 miles away, and many entries bear witness to the rearrangement
they underwent. Thus, part of the manor of Beeding (28) in Bramber was
said to lie in William de Warenne's rape, i.e. in Lewes; so was part of the
manor of Broadwater (28b) also in Bramber. These two entries do not
tell us exactly where the outlying portions were situated, but fortunately
this is made clear by the account of two holdings at Aldrington (26b) in
the description of William de Warenne's rape. One holding, we are told,
had formed part of (*jacuit in*) Beeding, and the hides of the other had

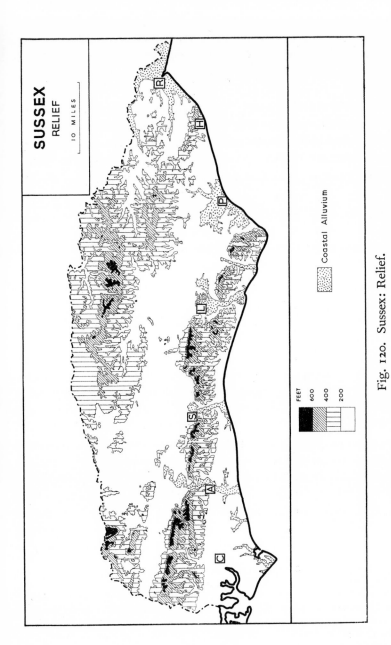

Fig. 120. Sussex: Relief.

Domesday boroughs are indicated by initials: A, Arundel; C, Chichester; H, Hastings; L, Lewes; P, Pevensey; R, Rye; S, Steyning.

formed part of (*jacuerunt in*) Broadwater. What is more, we are also told that on these two estates there was but one hall (*In his duabus terris nisi una halla*). Clearly, the outlying portions of two distant manors in Bramber rape had been joined to form the new manor of Aldrington in Lewes rape.

The information is not always so explicit, and we have to be content not with the exact locality but only with the name of the hundred in which an outlying portion of a manor had lain. Thus portions of the manor of Rodmell, in the rape of Lewes, had been detached because they were in the rapes of Pevensey and Bramber. The entry for Rodmell (26) itself reads:

William [de Warenne] himself holds Rodmell in demesne....In the time of King Edward it was assessed at 79 hides. William received 64 hides because the others [are] in the rape of the count [of Mortain] and [in that] of William de Braiose. These 64 hides are now assessed at 33 hides.

There are references to these two distant holdings in the description of the lands of the count (Pevensey) and of William de Braiose (Bramber). In the former area an unnamed holding of 1½ hides in Hartfield hundred (21 b) had belonged to the manor of Rodmell (*pertinuit manerio de Ramelle*); and in the latter, an unnamed holding of 8 hides in Burbeach hundred (28) had also formed part of (*jacuerent in*) Rodmell.[1] Such anonymous holdings complicate any attempt at mapping on the basis of individual settlements, but in the construction of the density maps the figures for these holdings can be, and have been, included within the relevant hundreds. In view of the complexity of the reorganisation, it is not surprising that the details are not always clear; but, on the other hand, we must remember that the reorganisation (as recorded in the Domesday folios) has revealed to us, in some manors, constituents of which we might not otherwise have known. Curiously enough, the term 'berewick' is used to describe the outliers on only four occasions. An outlier in Burbeach hundred (28) had once formed part of *Berts* (? Berth in Wivelsfield); another at *How*

[1] The main entry (26) implies that 15 hides had been taken away, but the figures in the subsidiary entries (21 b, 28) amount only to 9½ hides. The discrepancy can possibly be explained by the fact that Rodmell manor might have included yet other holdings, in Pevensey and Bramber, which the Domesday text does not specify as having belonged to it. Thus Round thought that one hide on an anonymous holding (21 b) had 'probably' belonged to Rodmell—*V.C.H. Sussex*, I, p. 436 n. Arithmetical difficulties frequently arise when an attempt is made to equate the figures in main entries with the information given for subsidiary holdings.

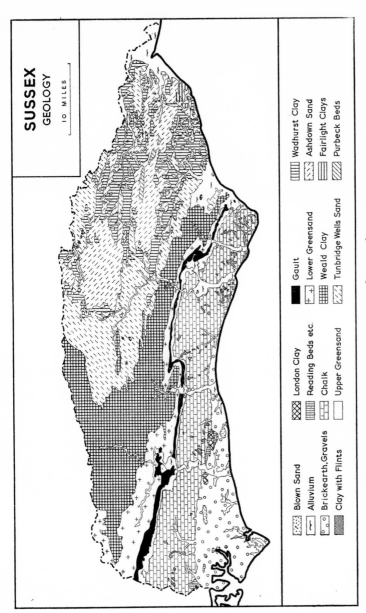

SUSSEX
GEOLOGY

10 MILES

Blown Sand
Alluvium
Brickearth, Gravels
Clay with Flints

London Clay
Reading Beds etc.
Chalk
Upper Greensand

Gault
Lower Greensand
Weald Clay
Tunbridge Wells Sand

Wadhurst Clay
Ashdown Sand
Fairlight Clays
Purbeck Beds

Fig. 121. Sussex: Surface geology.

Based on Geological Survey One-Inch Sheets (New Series) 316–20, 331–4; (Old Series) 5, 6, 8, 9. The Hastings Beds comprise Tunbridge Wells Sand, Wadhurst Clay, Ashdown Sand, and Fairlight Clays.

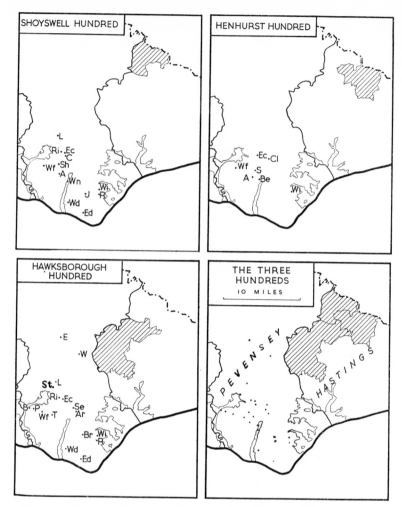

Fig. 122. Sussex: Estates in the rape of Hastings attached to manors
in the rape of Pevensey.

A, Alciston; Ar, Arlington; B, Beddingham; Be, Berwick; Br, Broughton; C,
Chalvington; Cl, Claverham; E, Etchingwood; Ec, Eckington; Ed, East Dean;
J, Jevington; L, Laughton; P, Preston; R, Ratton; Ri, Ripe; S, Selmeston; Se,
Sessingham; Sh, Sherrington; St, Stockingham; T, Tilton; W, Waldron; Wd, West
Dean; Wf, West Firle; Wi, Willingdon; Wn, Winton. The boundary of alluvium is
shown (see Fig. 121).

(Hoecourt Barn in Lancing) had belonged to Hurstpierpoint (29), a third at Tottington to Findon (28), and the fourth at Goring to Steyning (24b, 28). In addition to these there is the place-name of *Berewice* (19b), now Berwick.

Particular attention must be drawn to one group of manors with outlying estates. The three northern—or Wealden—hundreds of the rape of Hastings were Hawksborough, Henhurst and Shoyswell (18b–19b). Only six localities in these hundreds are named,[1] but the account of each hundred also gives details of a number of small unlocated holdings entered under the names of manors situated outside the Weald, in the adjoining rape of Pevensey (Fig. 122). It would seem that these unnamed holdings were estates in the Weald that had once belonged to various Pevensey manors. The manors lie roughly within a triangle formed by Eastbourne, Laughton and West Firle, an area which was early settled and well developed by 1086.[2] The northern portion of Hastings rape, on the other hand, was largely uncleared woodland. 'It seems to me', wrote Mr L. F. Salzman, 'quite probable that, at some uncertain date, claims in the Hastings backwoods were allotted to such of the lords of the Pevensey triangle as would take them up and that this forest district was deliberately colonised.'[3] The totals for the unlocated holdings in each of the three hundreds are shown as open circles on the settlement maps of plough-teams and population (Figs. 125 and 127), and they have, of course, been taken into consideration in calculating the densities on Figs. 124 and 126.[4]

[1] Five of the localities are Burgham (in Etchingham parish), Drigsell (in Salehurst parish) and Salehurst, all in Henhurst hundred; Hazelhurst in Shoyswell hundred; and Warbleton in Hawksborough hundred. There appears to be a sixth named locality because *Borne* and *Burne* may be represented by Bourne Farm also in Salehurst parish—A. Mawer, F. M. Stenton and J. E. B. Gover, *op. cit.* II, p. 458. It is possible, however, that they refer to an unnamed holding belonging to Eastbourne. In this analysis, *Borne* and *Burne* (entries on fo. 19b) have been taken as indicating the locality of Bourne Farm.

[2] One of these Pevensey manors with outliers in the north of Hastings rape was Alciston. The Domesday folios give no clue to the localities where the outliers lay, but we can discover the identity of some of them at any rate from a charter of Henry I —*V.C.H. Sussex*, I, pp. 357–8 and 394.

[3] L. F. Salzman, 'The rapes of Sussex', *art. cit.* p. 23. Mr Salzman suggests that the date of the colonisation might have been 'not long after 1011', the year in which the Danes, according to the Anglo-Saxon Chronicle, ravaged 'Sussex and Kent *and Hastings*'. See also *V.C.H. Sussex*, I, pp. 357–8.

[4] There were also a few holdings in the adjoining hundred of *Ailesaltede* (Hastings rape) which, on fo. 20, are entered under the names of distant manors in the adjoining rape of Pevensey—one under Chalvington which, in addition, had an outlier in

One further general point must be mentioned. The present-day county of Sussex, in terms of which this study has been written, is not identical with the Domesday county. The main differences are in the north and west. It is possible that in 1086 the county possessed no exact northern boundary, the dense wood of Andredesweald making the delimitation of bounds between Sussex and the counties of Hampshire, Surrey, and Kent 'a task of greater difficulty than advantage'.[1] This seems to be suggested by the fact that the vills of Lodsworth (36b) and Worth (34b) were described in the Surrey folios, although in all later documents they are placed in Sussex. One other entry in the Surrey folios (34) should be noted—that for an unnamed outlying estate belonging to Compton in Sussex (*jacet in Contone...in Sudsexe*). There was a similar intermingling of holdings between Sussex and Hampshire, and the Hampshire village of Warblington was said to belong (*pertinet*) to the West Sussex manor of Westbourne (23b). The present parishes of North and South Ambersham, not mentioned by name in the Domesday folios, remained detached portions of the Hampshire parish of Steep until 1832.[2] In the north-east, the boundary with Kent seems to have been indefinite; and there are two, and possibly three, references in the Kent folios to holdings in Sussex.[3] There were also a few nineteenth-century modifications along the Sussex-Kent border. Broadwater Down was transferred to Kent in 1894; and, in the following year, the Sussex portion of Lamberhurst was given to Kent, and the Kent portion of Broomhill to Sussex; none of these three villages is named in the Domesday folios for either county.

The coast of Domesday Sussex was not that we know today. On the one hand, there have been gains from the sea since 1086. A. Ballard thought that the distribution of Domesday salt-pans gives some clue to the former inlets of the sea.[4] Although this is not necessarily so,[5] we can

Shoyswell hundred, and three holdings under *Hectone* which seems to be South Heighton (*Estone* on fo. 21b) to the north-east of Newhaven. Then again there was an unnamed holding (20) which apparently formed part of the manor of Wilmington in the Eastbourne-Laughton-West Firle triangle (*V.C.H. Sussex*, I, p. 399). Whether these were analogous to the unlocated holdings in the three northern hundreds, we cannot really say.

[1] *V.C.H. Sussex*, I, p. 536.

[2] There have also been minor adjustments along the Sussex-Hampshire boundary— *V.C.H. Hampshire*, II (Westminster, 1903), p. 491.   [3] See p. 484 below.

[4] A. Ballard, 'The Sussex coast line', *Sussex Archaeol. Collns*, LIII (Lewes, 1910), p. 15.

[5] See, for example, the discussion of the Norfolk salt-pans in H. C. Darby, *The Domesday Geography of Eastern England* (Cambridge, 2nd ed., 1957), pp. 134–6.

assume that much of what is now alluvium was then beneath water (Fig. 132). On the other hand, there have been losses,[1] and parts of some villages along the coast have been devoured by the sea, e.g. Climping and Wittering in the west; Cortesley and Rottingdean in the east.[2]

Finally, we must note that the Sussex folios contain their share of defective and ambiguous entries. Thus the figure of 1,500 entered for the swine of Stoughton (24) seems to be an error; a place-name seems to have been omitted from an entry in fo. 25; and there are many blank spaces where figures for plough-lands should have been inserted, e.g. in an entry for Graffham (23b). These and other imperfections are noted on the appropriate pages below.

SETTLEMENTS AND THEIR DISTRIBUTION

The total number of separate places mentioned by name in the Domesday Book for the area within the modern county of Sussex seems to be 337, including the seven places which had, or seem to have had, burgesses —Arundel, Chichester, Hastings, Lewes, Pevensey, Rye and Steyning.[3] This figure, for more than one reason, cannot accurately reflect the total number of settlements. In the first place, when two or more adjoining villages bear the same surname today, it is not always clear that more than one existed in the eleventh century. There is no indication in the text that, say, the East and West Wittering of today existed as separate villages; the Domesday information about them is entered under only one name (*Westringes*, 17, 24), though they may well have been separate in the eleventh century as they certainly were by the thirteenth.[4] The same applies, for example, to the three Hartings[5] and to the three Mardens.[6] The distinction between the respective units of each of these groups appears later in time. For some counties the Domesday text occasionally differentiates between the related units of such groups by designating one

[1] Some of the losses as recorded in the Nonae Rolls of 1340 are given in A. Ballard, *art. cit.* p. 21.

[2] For a general discussion see J. A. Steers, *The Coastline of England and Wales* (Cambridge, 2nd ed., 1948), pp. 304–18.

[3] For the complication of the entry relating to Bollington, see p. 471 below.

[4] For the history of these, and of all other names mentioned in this chapter, see A. Mawer, F. M. Stenton and J. E. B. Gover, *The Place-Names of Sussex*, 2 vols. (Cambridge, 1929–30).

[5] East Harting, South Harting and West Harting.

[6] East Marden, North Marden and Up Marden; there is also a West Marden in Up Marden.

unit as *alia* or *parva* or *magna*, but none of the Sussex groups is distinguished in this way. On the other hand, we may infer the separation of East and West Dean in Willingdon hundred from the mention of *Esdene* (19) and *Dene* (19, 19b, 21 *bis*).[1] The adjacent parishes of North Stoke and South Stoke both appear in the Domesday Book as *Stoches*, but they are rubricated under separate hundreds—*Risberg* (24b) and *Benestede* (25)—and so they have been counted here as two settlements.[2] The parish of North Mundham is of some interest. Today, it includes the hamlet of South Mundham, but there is only one entry for *Mundreham* (24) in the Domesday text. That two settlements also existed in Domesday times, however, we may infer from a pre-Domesday reference to *se northra Mundan ham, other Mundan ham*; but by our reckoning they can be counted only as one.

Quite different in category are those places with a surname in common yet situated at some distance from one another, and so appearing under different hundreds, e.g. Horsted Keynes (*Ristone*, 22b) and Little Horsted (*Framelle*, 22); East Chiltington (*Estrat*, 27–27b) and West Chiltington (*Isewerit*, 24b, 29); Tarring Neville (*Flexeberge*, 21b) and West Tarring (*Bradfota*, 16b).[3] Such names have, of course, been counted as indicating separate settlements.

Another reason why the figure of 337 cannot be taken as the total number of settlements in 1086 is that we cannot tell how many of the numerous unnamed holdings were located at places named in a different connection in the Sussex folios.[4] We certainly can assume, however, that

[1] To be distinguished from the East Dean and West Dean of Westbourne hundred in the west of the county. These are not mentioned in the Domesday Book, and are possibly included in the details for Singleton (23)—A. Mawer, F. M. Stenton and J. E. B. Gover, *op. cit.* I, p. xlv.

[2] West Stoke, some ten miles or so to the west, is quite separate, and its name does not appear until the thirteenth century.

[3] The Beedings form an interesting group. 'Upper and Lower Beeding are several miles apart but it is clear that they are to be reckoned as one settlement, for in the Subsidy Rolls we find mention of Beeding alone and yet some persons taxed in this Beeding belong to what we now know as Lower Beeding, and Upper and Lower Beeding formed one parish until modern times. Probably Lower Beeding was the district in the Weald which formed the swine-pastures of the original settlement of Beeding.'—A. Mawer, F. M. Stenton and J. E. B. Gover, *op. cit.* I, p. 205. In the Domesday Book there are two entries for Beeding—one under *Burbece* hundred (28) and the other under *Estrat* hundred (27b). The latter rubrication is open to question and in the present analysis Beeding has been counted as one settlement.

[4] See pp. 410–13 above.

the detached holdings in the north of Hastings rape were not at places otherwise named, but this does not greatly help, for we cannot say how many localities—as opposed to holdings—were involved. In any case, these detached holdings were probably little more than small assarts in Andredesweald.

The total of 337 includes about 30 for which very little information is given. Certain places, for example, are mentioned incidentally without forming the subject of detailed entries. Thus Arlington (19), Berwick (19b), Broughton (19), Etchingwood (19) and Winton (19) appear merely as the parent centres of holdings in the northern part of Hastings rape; they themselves are not surveyed under Pevensey rape where one would expect to find them. Their population and resources may be included in the totals for other places; the details for both Berwick and Winton, for instance, are possibly concealed in the totals for Beddingham.[1] We are specifically told that Compton (21) was appraised (*appreciata est*) in Laughton, and that Standen (22b) was accounted for and appraised (*Computata et appreciata est*) in Tarring Neville, and so we must remain without knowing what was in each. Or again, all that we hear of Shipley (26b–27) is that Fulking had once formed part of it (*jacuit in*); and all that we are told of *Wildetone*[2] (22b) is that *Sp(er)chedene* had been part of it. We are also told nothing about Bechington (22) save that it was assessed at one hide, or about Alchin (16b) save that it was assessed at 1 virgate. We are, on the other hand, given the plough-lands and the values, as well as the hidage, for Hazelden (22b) and *Sp(er)chedene* (22b), but that is all; there is no hint of the resources or the population that might justify even the low values of 1086—5s. and 2s. respectively. Then there are other entries that appear to give an incomplete picture. Thus there were no teams at *Basingeham* (20) or at Birchgrove (22b), though each had a villein and the latter also had half a plough-land. No people are recorded for Hurst (20), Moustone (27b) or Offington (28b), though each had a team at work, and Hurst also had an acre of meadow; the entry for Offington tells us *Nichil plus*. The account of Woolfly (28b) is also explicit: 'There is nothing there except 10 acres of meadow' (*Nichil ibi nisi x acrae prati*); so is that for one holding at Chancton (28b): *Nichil ibi est*, yet it was worth 11s. Finally, some mention must be made of Battle Abbey founded by William, in gratitude for his victory, on the spot

[1] *V.C.H. Sussex*, I, pp. 402 and 403.
[2] For this name see *V.C.H. Sussex*, I, p. 419.

where Harold fell. It appears as one of the land-holders of the county, and some settlement may well have been growing around it by 1086; Battle has been marked on Fig. 123 and included in the total of 337, although we have no information about the resources of the locality.

Not all the Domesday names appear on the present-day map of Sussex villages. Some are represented by hamlets, by individual houses and farms, or even by the names of localities. Thus *Cocheham* (29) is the hamlet of Cokeham in Sompting; *Harditone* (24) is that of Lordington in Racton; and *Pinhedene* (27) or *Pinwedene* (27) is that of Pangdean in Pyecombe. *Trailgi* (26b, 28) appears as Truleigh Farm and Truleigh Sands in Edburton; *Ovelei* (28b) as Woolfly Farm and *Wantelei* (28b) as Wantley Farm, both in Henfield. *Sifelle* (22b) is represented by Sheffield Park and Sheffield Green, and *Bercheham* (22b bis, 24b) by the locality of Barkham, both in Fletchling; *Wiche* (24) by Whyke and Rumbolds-whyke, localities in Chichester. *Drisnesel* (19b) has disappeared from the map, but 'part of Salehurst Park Farm is still called Drigsell'.[1] These are but a few of the changes of fortune among the Sussex villages. To them must be added a number of unidentified names, e.g. *Esmerewic* (26b), *Nonneminstre* (24b)[2] and *Sp(er)chedene* (22b).[3] Whether these will yet be located, or whether the places they represent have completely disappeared leaving no record or trace behind, we cannot say.[4]

---

[1] A. Mawer, F. M. Stenton and J. E. B. Gover, *op. cit.* II, p. 458.

[2] *Nonneminstre* has sometimes been identified with Lyminster, but this is doubtful, and it has not been taken as such in this analysis—A. Mawer, F. M. Stenton and J. E. B. Gover, *op. cit.* I, pp. 169–70. Lyminster appears in the Domesday Book as *Lolinminstre* on the same folio (24b).

[3] In this analysis *Lodintone* (22 *bis*) has been taken as referring to the locality of Wootton House in Folkington, but the identification is uncertain—see A. Mawer, F. M. Stenton and J. E. B. Gover, *op. cit.* II, p. 412.

On fo. 19b we hear of a certain Robert holding one furlong (*unum Ferlang*) of the count of Eu, but there were twelve teams as well as men and a church on the holding. It would seem, therefore, that *unum Ferlang* is a scribal error for *Ferleg'* (Fairlight in Guestling hd.), and it has been so regarded in this analysis (*V.C.H. Sussex*, I, p. 405).

[4] The full list of Domesday place-names in Sussex that have not been located in the present analysis is: *Basingeham* (20), *Borham* (25), *Burgelstaltone* (19b), *Chenenolle* (22), *Esmerewic* (26b), *Evebentone* (19b), *Felesmere* (22b), *Ivet* (19b), *Medehei* (18), *Nonneminstre* (24b), *Ode* (22b), *Pengest* (21b), *Segnescome* (19b), *Sp(er)chedene* (22b), *Storchestone* (24), *Warlege* (22b), *Wildene* (21b), *Wildetone* (22b). The exact location of some other names is also in doubt, but their localities can be assigned to modern parishes, and they have been plotted on the accompanying maps, e.g. *Bogelie* (22) is the lost Bowley in Hailsham, and *Sidenore* (21b) is the lost Sidnor in Selmeston.

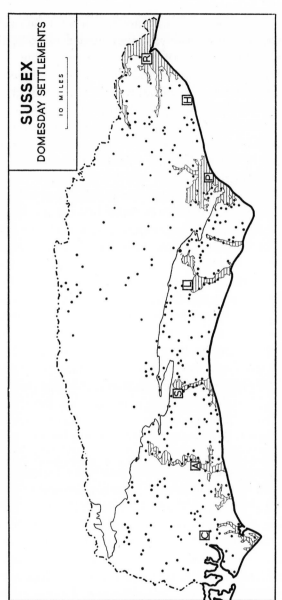

Fig. 123. Sussex: Domesday place-names.

Domesday boroughs are indicated by initials: A, Arundel; C, Chichester; H, Hastings; L, Lewes; P, Pevensey; R, Rye; S, Steyning. Areas of coastal alluvium and the southern boundary of Weald Clay are shown (see Fig. 121).

On the other hand, many villages on the modern map are not mentioned in the Domesday Book. Their names do not appear until the twelfth and thirteenth centuries, and, presumably, if they existed in 1086, they are accounted for under the statistics of other settlements. Thus, so far as record goes, Ardingly was first mentioned about 1107, Slinfold in 1165, Chidham in 1193, Crawley in 1203, Rudgwick in 1210, Newick in 1218, Kirdford in 1228 and Wadhurst in 1253. Some of the places not mentioned in the Domesday Book must have existed, or at any rate been named, in Domesday times, because they appear in pre-Domesday charters and again in documents of the twelfth and thirteenth centuries. Such, for example, are Bersted, Bognor, Earnley, Horsham, Lindfield, Seaford and Telscombe. Sometimes, although a modern parish is not named in the Domesday Book, it contains hamlets or farms that are mentioned. An interesting example of this is East Grinstead in the Weald. The earliest record of it, apparently, is from the year 1271, but the area covered by the present parish includes the Domesday names of Brockhurst (*Biochest*), Fairlight (*Ferlega*), Hazelden (*Halseeldene*), and Shovelstrode (*Calvrestot* or *Celrestius*), all on fo. 22 b. Adjoining East Grinstead, and formed from it as late as 1894, is the parish of Forest Row; the name itself dates from 1467, but the parish contains the two Domesday names of Brambletye (*Branbertie*) and Whalesbeech (*Waslebie*), also on fo. 22 b. Or again, Buxted, likewise in the Weald, is not named in the Domesday Book, but it contains two names that are—Alchin (*Alsihorne*, 16 b) and Etchingwood (*Achingeworde*, 19). From this account it is clear that there have been many changes in the village geography of the county, and that the list of Domesday names differs considerably from a list of present-day parishes.

Fig. 123 shows that there was a marked scarcity of Domesday settlements in the northern half of the county. Hardly a Domesday name is to be found on the outcrop of the Weald Clay itself, and very few in the High Forest Ridge area of the Hastings Beds. But elsewhere on the Hastings Beds, names were to be found around East Grinstead in the north and especially in the district south of the Rother to the east. Here, the juxtaposition of sands and clays provided a basis for village settlement and agricultural exploitation. Fig. 123 does not, however, present a complete picture of settlement in Sussex in 1086 for, as we have seen, the non-occurrence of Domesday names does not necessarily imply absence of settlement; small unnamed holdings bear witness to reclaiming activity that was going on within the Wealden area.[1] But, with this proviso, the fact remains that northern Sussex was largely unsettled in 1086, and the general impression given by Fig. 123 cannot be far wrong.

In contrast to the northern half of the county stood the densely settled south. Names here were frequent, and their villages were set mainly in three characteristic locations: in the scarp-foot zone where the South Downs overlook the Weald, and where springs provide water; on the coastal plain between the Downs and the sea; and, thirdly, along the river valleys that break through the Downs—those of the Arun, the Adur, the Ouse and the Cuckmere. With this last group may be included the villages of the western Rother which runs west-east through Lower Greensand country to join the north-south flowing Arun. Amidst these and other detailed considerations that affect the site of this or that village, the broad contrast between north and south stands out as a striking feature of Fig. 123.

THE DISTRIBUTION OF PROSPERITY AND POPULATION

Some idea of the nature of the information in the Domesday folios for Sussex, and of the form in which it is presented, may be obtained from the entry for Pulborough (24b) in the Arun valley. The village was held entirely by Earl Roger of Montgomery, lord of the rape of Arundel, and so it is described in a single entry:

Robert holds Pulborough of the earl. Ulvric held it *T.R.E.* Then and now it was assessed at 16 hides. There is land for 18 plough-teams. In demesne are 4 plough-teams and [there are] 35 villeins and 15 cottars with 13 plough-teams. There [are] 9 serfs, and 2 mills rendering (*de*) 11s., and 30 acres of meadow, and woodland rendering (*de*) 25 swine, and 2 fisheries rendering (*de*) 3s. There [are] 2 churches.

Of the land of this manor, Tetbald and Ivo hold 2 hides and half-a-virgate, and there [is] on [their] demesne 1 plough-team, and [there are] 3 villeins and 4 cottars with 1 plough-team.

The whole manor *T.R.E.* was worth £16, and afterwards £16. Now Robert's demesne [is worth] £22, [the land] of the men 35s.

This entry does not include all the items that are given for some places; there is no mention, for example, of bordars, of pasture or of saltpans.

[1] See p. 413 above.

But although not comprehensive, it is a fairly representative and straightforward entry, and it does set out the recurring standard items that are found for most villages. These are five in number: (1) hides, (2) ploughlands, (3) plough-teams, (4) population, and (5) values. The bearing of these five items of information upon regional variations in the prosperity of the county must now be considered.

(1) *Hides*

The Sussex assessment is stated in terms of hides and virgates, and, very occasionally, of what seem to be geld acres; there is also a reference to the ferding (*una ferdinga*) in the entry for Sutton (23 b). Sometimes the phrase 'of land' appears; at Duncton (23 b), for example, four Frenchmen held 1½ hides and 1½ virgates and 10 acres of land (*terrae*). The form of the statement varies, as can be seen from the following examples, the first of which is the most frequently encountered:

(1) Catsfield (18): *Tunc se defendit pro una hida et dimidia, modo pro una hida et i virgata.*

(2) Clayton (27): *Tunc et modo se defendit pro vii hidis.*

(3) In *Benestede* hd. (25 b): *In eodem Hundredo tenet Willelmus de comite dimidiam hidam et ii virgatas et pro tanto se defendit semper.*

(4) Bishopstone (16 b): *T.R.E. se defendit pro xxv hidis et modo similiter.*

(5) Preston near Brighton (17): *T.R.E. et modo pro xx hidis se defendit.*

(6) Hurst (20): *T.R.E. pro ii virgatis se defendit et modo facit.*

In Stockbridge hundred, Chetel's holding (24), with land for 1 plough, had never been rated in hides (*Nunquam hidata fuit*); and Alviet's holding (29), in Easewrithe hundred, seems to have been in the same position —*sine numero hidae* (*sic*).

The Sussex assessment is complicated by a strange difficulty, for the axiom that four virgates make a hide has been challenged. The difficulty can be seen in the entry for Frankwell (18) which makes sense only on the assumption that the hide comprised 8 virgates:

The count of Eu holds Frankwell and 6 knights [hold it] of him. One of them, Norman, held it in the time of King Edward, and then as now it was assessed at 1½ hides. There is land for 2 plough-teams.

Of this land, the same Norman has ½ hide, Ralph 2 virgates, Hugh 2 virgates, Osbern 2 vigates, Wenenc 1 virgate, Girard 1 virgate.

A number of other entries seem also to point to a hide of 8 virgates, as the following equations show:

Ewhurst (20):   6h=4h 3v+5v+1h.

Wilting (18b, 17b): 4h=2h 2v+½h 2v+½h+2v+1v+1v.

That a hide comprised more than 4 virgates seems to be indicated by the entry for Brightling (18b). It was assessed at one hide, and, of this, we are told, a certain Robert held 4 virgates.[1] Furthermore, the chronicler of Battle Abbey stated clearly that '8 virgates make one hide'.[2] The Domesday entry for Boxgrove (25b), on the other hand, shows the normal equation:

$$6h=3h \ 1v+1h \ 1v+½h+1h.$$

The problem has been discussed by J. Tait and L. F. Salzman.[3] The latter, in a summary of the evidence, hesitated to go further than to suggest the 'probable existence' of a 8-virgate hide.[4] It certainly seems to have been in use in the rape of Hastings, and all the examples given above are from there.[5] We may even wonder whether the 8-virgate hide might not have been a wider phenomenon in the county when we encounter such quantities as '4 hides and 5 virgates' at Middleton (25), and 'half a hide and 2 virgates' in *Benestede* hundred (25b), both in the rape of Arundel.

One feature that the Sussex folios share with those of the neighbouring counties of Berkshire, Hampshire, Surrey and Kent is that they so frequently record an exemption in the assessment of a holding. Thus of Pagham (16b) we read: *T.R.E se defendit pro l hidis, et modo pro xxxiiii*, and of Wiston (28): *Tunc se defendit pro xii hidis. Modo pro nichilo.* When an assessment remained unchanged we are specifically told so; the entry for

---

[1] On the other hand, we cannot always trust Domesday arithmetic, and the entry for Wellhead in Ewhurst (20) implies that the hide there comprised at least 13 virgates, which we can only explain by assuming a scribal error.

[2] *V.C.H. Sussex*, I, p. 359.

[3] J. Tait, 'Hides and virgates at Battle Abbey', *Eng. Hist. Rev.* XVIII (1903), pp. 705–8. L. F. Salzman, 'Hides and virgates in Sussex', *ibid.* XIX (1904), pp. 92–6. J. Tait, 'Hides and virgates in Sussex', *ibid.* XIX (1904), pp. 503–6. For a summary of the evidence see *V.C.H. Sussex*, I, p. 359. There are more recent discussions in J. E. A. Jolliffe, (1) 'The Domesday hidation of Sussex and the rapes', *Eng. Hist. Rev.* XLV (1930), pp. 431–2; (2) *Pre-Feudal England: The Jutes*, pp. 74–5.

[4] *V.C.H. Sussex*, I, p. 359.

[5] 'In the Rape of Hastings there appears to be an 8-virgate hide in use'—L. F. Salzman, 'The rapes of Sussex', *art. cit.* p. 20. J. E. A. Jolliffe also assumed its existence in north-east Sussex', *art. cit.* p. 431; so did D. K. Clarke, 'The Saxon hundreds of Sussex', *Sussex Archaeol. Collns*, LXXIV (Cambridge, 1933), pp. 214–25.

Clayton (27) reads: *Tunc et modo se defendit pro vii hidis.* Amidst the detail two points emerge. The first is that the degree of exemption varied greatly from lordship to lordship, i.e. from rape to rape. It seems to have been below 10 per cent on the lands of the count of Eu; it was quite appreciable on those of William de Warenne, of Earl Roger and of the count of Mortain (i.e. from about 12 to 24 per cent); and it was very considerable (nearly 70 per cent) on those of William de Braiose. Or again, it was slight (about 5 per cent) on those of the bishop of Chichester, but appreciable (about 25 per cent) on those of the archbishop of Canterbury.[1] The second point is that within each lordship the exemption was not applied uniformly to all holdings, but was limited mainly to the principal demesne manors, i.e. those without sub-tenants. Thus the assessment of the four manors held in demesne by Earl Roger was reduced from $193\frac{1}{2}$ to 101 hides,[2] but as we cast our eye over the rest of the entries for Earl Roger's possessions, we only occasionally encounter an instance of reduction, and the phrase 'then as now' repeats itself monotonously (23–25 b). Similar conditions prevailed upon the lands of William de Warenne and of the count of Mortain. On those of William de Braiose the reduction was more general, but the greatest fall (from 59 hides to nothing) again appeared in a demesne manor—that of Washington (28). The reduction on the count of Eu's lands was also fairly general but the amounts were smaller.

These beneficial exemptions must not be confused with the decreases resulting from the re-arrangement of manors.[3] At Iford (26), for example, a demesne manor of William de Warenne, both factors had been at work:

T.R.E. it was assessed at $77\frac{1}{2}$ hides. When William received it [there were] only 58 hides because the others were in the rape of the count of Mortain. These 58 hides are assessed now at 36 hides.

Then there were also reductions for specific reasons. The assessment of Tortington (25) had been reduced from 4 to 3 hides because Earl Roger had one in his park. Three hides on two holdings at Waltham (25 b *bis*) were also in a park, so was a virgate at Walberton (25) and another at Wilting (18 b). At Shoreham (29) there was half a hide exempt from geld (*quieta de geldo*), but we are not told why.

[1] *V.C.H. Sussex*, I, pp. 360–1.
[2] The four manors surveyed on fo. 23 were Singleton ($97\frac{1}{2}$ hides to 47), Binderton (7 to 3), Harting (80 to 48) and Trotton (9 to 3).
[3] See p. 408 above and p. 425 below.

A number of entries suggest that the reduction in liability was not always post-Conquest, and that it had already taken place by 1066. Such, for example, are the following:

Bosham (16): Then there were 56½ [hides], and it paid geld for 38 hides and now likewise (*Tunc erant lvi et dimidia, et pro xxxviii hidis geldavit et modo similiter*).

Higham (20): *T.R.E.* there were 2½ hides, but it was assessed at 2 hides as [the jurors] say, and now for 2 hides (*T.R.E. fuerunt ii hidae et dimidia, sed pro ii hidis se defendit sic dicunt et modo pro ii hidis*).

Stoughton (24): There are 36 hides, but, then as now, it was assessed at 15 hides (*Ibi sunt xxxvi hidae sed tunc et modo pro xv hidis se defendit*).

Westbourne (23b): There are 36 hides, but it was assessed at 12 hides then as now (*Ibi xxxvi hidae, sed pro xii hidis se defendit tunc et modo*).

The Norman reorganisation of the rapes greatly complicates any consideration of the Sussex hidage. As we have seen, there were many manors, the 1066 assessment of which had covered outlying possessions in other rapes.[1] 'Now before 1086', wrote L. F. Salzman, 'these outlying estates had all been cut off from their manors and formed into separate holdings attached to the rape in which they physically lay; and in almost every case the geld assessment of the parent manor was reduced by an amount equal to that at which the lost member was potentially assessed. This can only point to the geld having been assessed in Sussex at the end of King Edward's reign not by vills but by manors.'[2] Two holdings in Earl Roger's rape illustrate the rearrangement:

Angmering (24b): Then it was assessed at 5 hides. Now one of these hides is in the rape of William de Braiose.

Goring (25): Then it was assessed at 4 hides; now for 2½ because 1½ hides are in the rape of William de Braiose.

Sometimes, the entries for the separated portions themselves make mention of their one-time connection with the parent manor;[3] but frequently we are given no hint of the former connection, and we can reconstitute an

---

[1] See pp. 408–10 above.
[2] *V.C.H. Sussex*, I, p. 358. In support of this theory, Mr Salzman quotes from two entries—(1) Washington (28): *Leuuinus...dedit geldum domino suo et dominus suus nichil dedit*. (2) Westmeston (27): *Non fuit ibi halla neque geldavit ut dicunt*. Subsequently, however, Mr Salzman wrote: 'the original assessment was by vills and not by manors' ('The rapes of Sussex', *art. cit.* p. 21).
[3] E.g. those for the outliers of Rodmell—see p. 410 above.

original manor only with the aid of later documents[1] or not at all. Rearrangement might take place occasionally even within the same rape. Sixteen of the thirty-six hides of Stoughton (24) had been attached, but only temporarily, to Westbourne within the same hundred of *Ghidenetroi: De his fuerunt xvi hidae missae in manerio Burne, modo iterum sunt in Estone.* Or again, the assessment of the archbishop's manor of South Malling (16) had been reduced from 80 to 75 hides because the count of Mortain had 5 hides outside the hundred (*extra hundredum*).

There are many entries which, as well as giving an assessment, state that a holding had never paid geld. *Nunquam geldavit* is a familiar phrase in the Sussex folios, and it seems to imply one of two things. In some entries it may mean that the holding, though assessed, had not paid geld since 1066 and possibly not since an earlier date. Here are examples that include some variations in phrasing:

> Filsham (18): *Wilesham tenuit Rex E. in dominio. Ibi xv hidae sunt, quae non geldant neque geldaverunt.*
> Lyminster (24b): *Ipse comes tenet in dominio Lolinminstre. Rex E. tenuit in dominio. Ibi xx hidae. Nunquam geldavit.*

These statements seem straightforward, and presumably they record beneficial hidation.

But in another context the phrase *nunquam geldavit* indicates a consequence of that reorganisation of manors which we have just discussed; a holding had not been assessed in the particular rape in which it was geographically situated, but the geld had been accounted for with that of its parent manor which lay in another rape. The phrase is characteristic of the entries for the Wealden hundreds and especially for those of the hundred of East Grinstead surveyed on fo. 22b (Pevensey rape). The precise form of the entries differs, but, with the exception of that for Brambletye, each includes a statement: (1) that the holding was outside the rape (*extra rapum*), and (2) that it had never paid geld. Frequently, but not always, we are also told that it had been part of (*jacuit in*) another place, usually a considerable distance away. The following entries are characteristic:

> Whalesbeech: *Isdem Radulfus tenet de comite extra rapum Waslebie. Ibi est i hida. Fulchi tenuit de rege Edwardo. Ad Lovintune* (Lavant near Chichester) *jacuit. Nunquam geldavit.*

---

[1] E.g. the manor of Alciston—see p. 413 n. above.

Hazelden: *Isdem Ansfridus tenet extra rapum dimidiam hidam. Vocatur Halseeldene. Ulwardus tenuit de rege Edwardo. In Alitone* (Allington, near Lewes) *jacuit et nunquam geldavit.*

Warlege: Isdem Willelmus tenet de comite Warlege. Ibi sunt ii hidae. Nunquam geldavit. Extra rapum est.

Somewhat similar entries are found in the descriptions of the nearby hundreds of Hartfield (21b)[1] and Rushmonden (22b). The same phenomenon is encountered to the east, in the three northern hundreds of Hastings rape which, as we have seen, are of especial interest.[2] Almost every one of the small unnamed holdings in the hundreds of Hawksborough and Henhurst had never paid geld although they were assessed; such was the count of Eu's property formerly held by Earl Harold, and attached to the distant manor of Tilton (19) in the adjoining rape of the count of Mortain: *Isdem comes tenet unam virgatam in manerio Telitone. Comes Heraldus tenuit et nunquam geldavit.* In the third hundred (Shoyswell), each holding is assessed, but the separate statements about non-payment are replaced by a general statement at the beginning: *Hoc hundredum nunquam geldum reddidit* (19), followed by another at the end: *Essewelle hundredum nunquam geldum reddidit* (19b).[3] Occasional small estates in the nearby hundreds of Staple and *Hailesaltede* (18b, 20) had also never paid geld; of a virgate at Sedlescombe (20), in the former hundred, we hear: *Nunquam geldavit et semper fuit foris rapum.*

The complications of the Sussex assessment must have obscured greatly the five-hide unit if it had ever existed here. J. H. Round, however, professed to see 'distinct traces' of it, and could point to such 1066 assessments as the 50 hides at Pagham (16b), the 25 at Bishopstone (16b), the 10 at Selsey (17) and the 5 at Donnington (17b).[4] But L. F. Salzman is 'inclined to think that the figures for the reconstituted vills would support either a 5-hide or an 8-hide theory with equal impartiality'.[5] Holdings

---

[1] Here, for example, was one of the unnamed outliers of the manor of Rodmell—see p. 410 above.   [2] See p. 413 above.

[3] The first entry in the account of Shoyswell hundred deals with Hazelhurst (19) and reads: *Tunc et modo iiii hidae et dimidia*; Hazelhurst is itself in the hundred. The other entries refer to the anonymous holdings attached to manors outside Hastings rape, and merely state that *a* had held *b* virgates or hides, e.g. *tenuit Goda dimidiam hidam.*

[4] *V.C.H. Sussex*, I, p. 359, n. 5.

[5] 'The rapes of Sussex', *art. cit.* (1931), pp. 21–2. In an earlier study of 1905 (*V.C.H. Sussex*, I, pp. 359–60), Mr Salzman had said of the 5-hide unit: 'No such unit is observable in Sussex—nor indeed should we expect it during the period when the

of 2, 4, 6 or 8 hides are certainly frequent, and those of 5 or 10 hides are moderately so. But the sums of 2 and 8, and of 4 and 6, are themselves multiples of 5; while therefore the 'five-hide theory' must remain unproved for Sussex, we must always remember the possibility of vills being grouped into blocks for the purpose of assessment as in some other counties. That the assessment was certainly artificial in character is clear from the existence of large groups each forming 'approximately a simple multiple of eighty hides'. This possibility was suggested by L. F. Salzman in 1905.[1] Twenty-five years later, J. E. A. Jolliffe reached the conclusion that an 80-hide unit was an important element in the pre-Conquest assessment of the county.[2] Subsequently, D. K. Clarke attempted a reconstruction of the 80-hide units and showed that there were 41 of them.[3] As Mr Clarke said, such work 'must necessarily be speculative'. Whatever be the exact conclusion, all these brave and ingenious attempts to penetrate the obscurity of the Domesday folios leave us in no doubt about the artificial nature of the Sussex assessment.

The lack of relation between hidage and agricultural resources is very apparent. The variation among a selection of holdings, each assessed at 4 hides both in 1066 and 1086, speaks for itself:

	Plough-lands	Teams	Population
Balmer (26 b)	2	1	5
Barnham (25)	4	5	24
Lordington (24)	4	3	17
Playden (19 b)	7	12½	37
Todham (23 b)	3	2	11

The way in which the assessment of many demesne manors was reduced helped further to reduce the non-coincidence of hidage and resources.

It is even more difficult than usual to estimate the total number of hides. In the first place, the reorganisation of manors has made the interpretation of many entries difficult. We must be careful not to count the same hides

county was assessed by manors and not by vills.' Later (*art. cit.* 1931, p. 21), he came to the conclusion that 'a reconstitution of the vills will be found to reduce considerably the odds against the 5-hide unit'. For assessment by manors, see p. 425 above.
    [1] *V.C.H. Sussex*, I, p. 360.
    [2] J. E. A. Jolliffe, 'The Domesday hidation of Sussex and the rapes', *Eng. Hist. Rev.* XLV (1930), pp. 427–35.
    [3] D. K. Clarke, 'The Saxon hundreds of Sussex', *Sussex Archaeol. Collns*, LXXIV (Cambridge, 1933), pp. 214–25.

wice over—once with those of a main manor and again as those of an
outlier; and, as we have seen, the arithmetic of many entries raises
uncertainty.[1] Then, in the second place, there is the problem of the
8-virgate hide. Fortunately this is not so serious as might at first appear.
The area with many small holdings (i.e. of less than half a hide) lies in
the rape of Hastings where the presence of the 8-virgate hide is fairly
clear. Elsewhere, where the holdings are larger, the adoption of either
four or eight virgates to the hide makes a difference of only a hide or two
in the total for each rape. We have therefore adopted the small virgate
only for the rape of Hastings, and elsewhere have reckoned with the
normal equation of four virgates to the hide. The present count has
yielded a total assessment of $3,192\frac{13}{16}$ hides; gelding hides for 1086 seem
to amount to $2,193\frac{3}{8}$; both figures refer to the area included within the
modern county. F. W. Maitland's totals for the Domesday county were
3,474 and 2,241 respectively, but he thought that these figures might have
been 'too high' because of the reorganisation of the rapes; he seems,
incidentally, to have reckoned throughout on the basis of a 4-virgate hide.[2]
J. E. A. Jolliffe, making allowance for duplication, and adopting an
8-virgate hide for Hastings rape, obtained a total of some 3,139 hides for
1066.[3] D. K. Clarke's estimate, on a somewhat similar basis, amounted
to some 3,224 hides for 1066.[4] All these totals serve at any rate to indicate
the order of magnitude involved.

(2) *Plough-lands*

Plough-lands are systematically entered for the Sussex villages, and the
normal formula runs: *Terra est n carucis*.[5] But there are 16 entries for
14 places and one unnamed holding in which *Terra est* is followed by a
blank space in which a figure was never inserted.[6] There are also many
entries which mention teams but not plough-lands, e.g. for Ashcombe
with 4 teams (27b), for Bellhurst with 2 (20), and for the majority of the

---

[1] E.g. the entry for Rodmell—see p. 410 n. above.

[2] F. W. Maitland, *Domesday Book and Beyond* (Cambridge, 1897), pp. 400, 401
and 409.

[3] J. E. A. Jolliffe, *art. cit.* pp. 432–4.   [4] D. K. Clarke, *art. cit.* pp. 216 and 219.

[5] The phrase *terra ad i carucam* occurs once—for Chetel's holding in Stockbridge
hd. (24).

[6] The sixteen entries are those for Amberley (17), Bishopstone (16b), Bosham
(16, 17), Dallington (18b), Donnington (17b), Elsted (17b), Ferring (16b), Graffham
(23b), Lavant (16b), Preston in Binderton (17b), Tangmere (16b), Wellhead (20), Westhampnett (25b), Woolavington (17b) and an unnamed holding in Henhurst hd. (19b).

small unnamed holdings in the three northern hundreds of the rape of Hastings (18b–19b). Taking these two categories together, there were about 110 entries relating to at least about 60 places with incomplete figures for plough-lands.[1] Fractional parts are recorded only occasionally, and the moieties are stated in terms of simple fractions, such as the land for $7\frac{1}{2}$ teams at Little Horstead (22).

The relation between the number of plough-lands and the number of teams varies a great deal in individual entries. A deficiency of teams was fairly frequent, being found for about one in three of the Domesday settlements for which plough-lands were recorded. The values on many deficient holdings had fallen between 1066 and 1086, but on others they were the same, and on some they had even increased. No general correlation between plough-team deficiency and decrease in value is therefore possible, as the following table shows:

		Plough-lands	Teams	Value 1066	Value 1086
Decrease in value	Keymer (27)	25	19	£14	£12
	Linch (23)	6	3	£8	£5
Same value	Mundham (24)	6	4	£8	£8
	Streat (27)	16	12	£5	£5
Increase in value	Orleswick (26)	4	3	£1. 10s.	£3
	Trotton (23)	36	5	£3	£5

These figures are merely indications of unexplained changes on individual manors. We cannot really say whether the plough-land figures are those of teams employed in 1066.

Excess teams are somewhat less frequently encountered—at about two in seven of the places for which plough-lands were recorded. The excess was occasionally very considerable; thus at Ditchling (26) there were 60 plough-lands with $99\frac{1}{2}$ teams, and at South Malling (16) 50 with 94 teams. Generally speaking, the values had risen on such holdings, but not invariably. At Barnham (25) and at Plumpton (27), for example, the values were the same in 1086 as in 1066, and at Clayton (27) and at Ditchling itself they had even dropped. The attempt to interpret the figure for plough-lands as referring

[1] In addition to the 60 places there were some two dozen places without information either for teams or plough-lands. Very little is said about most of these—see p. 417 above. In the total of 'about 110' are some 40 or so entries relating to the unlocated holdings in the three northern holdings of Hawksborough, Henhurst and Shoyswell.

to 1066 is again frustrated. The places with excess teams are scattered fairly generally throughout the county.

The total number of plough-lands recorded for the area within the modern county is 2,776½. If, however, we assume that the plough-lands equalled the teams on those holdings where a figure for the former is not given, the total becomes 3,130¼. F. W. Maitland did not enter a total for plough-lands because of the large number of omissions.[1]

(3) *Plough-teams*

The Sussex entries for plough-teams, like those of other counties, normally draw a distinction between the teams at work on the demesne and those held by the peasantry. Occasional entries seem to be defective. Thus there were no teams or oxen at *Basingeham* (20) or at Birchgrove (22b), though each had a villein and the latter also had half a plough-land. Sometimes only demesne teams are entered, e.g. for Tortington (25) where there was land for 2 teams, which were on the demesne, leaving the 6 villeins and 2 cottars apparently without any.[2] Occasionally, on the other hand, only the teams of the peasants are mentioned, e.g. for Muntham (29) where again there was land for 2 teams which were in the hands of 5 villeins and 6 bordars. There are entries, however, which specifically draw attention to deficiency on a holding, as the following examples show:

Dankton (29): *In dominio nichil est sed tantum ii villani et iii bordarii et x acrae prati.* There was land for 2 teams, but teams themselves are not mentioned.

Erringham (28): *Ibi ii villani et v bordarii nil habentes.* No plough-lands or teams are mentioned, yet it was worth 40s.

Ifield (29): *In dominio nichil et v villani et iiii bordarii cum i caruca.* No plough-lands, however, are mentioned.

Offington (28b): *Ibi est una caruca in dominio. Nichil plus.* No plough-lands or men to work the team are mentioned. It was worth 26s.

Sakeham (28b): *Terra est ii carucis. Ibi modo nisi ii animalia.* There were 2 bordars and one villein on the holding.

Tilton (21): *Terra est iiii carucis. Ibi nichil modo nisi ii villani et iiii acrae prati.* No teams themselves are mentioned.

[1] F. W. Maitland, *op. cit.* pp. 402 and 410.
[2] An entry for Alfriston (21b) seems obscure: *Terra est v carucis. In dominio modo iii carucae et dimidia, et ii villani et vi bordarii arant ad medietatem.* The *Victoria County History* translates the latter part of this as '2 villeins and 6 bordars do half the ploughing', but a footnote suggests reading *al[iam]* for *ad* (*V.C.H. Sussex*, I, p. 414). If this implies half the ploughing on 5 plough-lands, the demesne teams should be 2½ and not 3½, but it may possibly imply the remaining half of a fourth team.

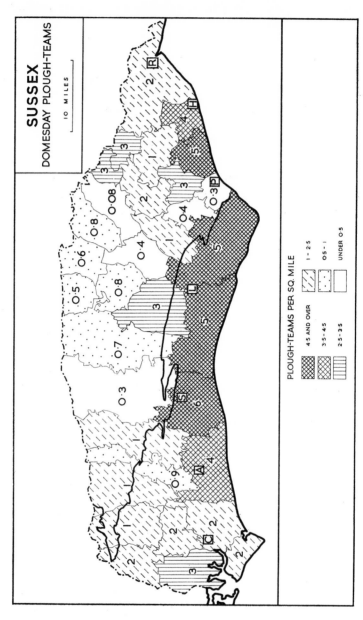

Fig. 124. Sussex: Domesday plough-teams in 1086 (by densities).

Domesday boroughs are indicated by initials: A, Arundel; C, Chichester; H, Hastings; L, Lewes; P, Pevensey; R, Rye; S, Steyning. The southern boundary of Weald Clay is shown (see Fig. 121).

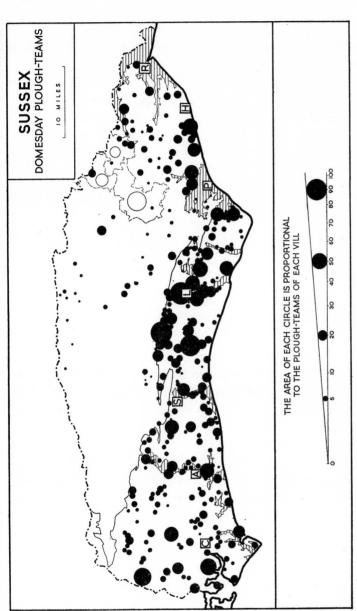

Fig. 125. Sussex: Domesday plough-teams in 1086 (by settlements).

Domesday boroughs are indicated by initials: A, Arundel; C, Chichester; H, Hastings; L, Lewes; P, Pevensey; R, Rye; S, Steyning.

The open circles represent the plough-teams on the unlocated holdings in each of the three northern hundreds of the rape of Hastings. Areas of coastal alluvium and the southern boundary of Weald Clay are shown (see Fig. 121).

In the entry for Hamsey (27b), the scribe wrote 'hides' when, apparently, he meant 'teams': *Terra est xiii carucis. In dominio sunt ii hidae et xvi villani et xiiii bordarii cum x carucis*; these have been counted as teams.

Half-teams are frequently entered (e.g. for Truleigh, 28), and oxen themselves are sometimes mentioned, as the following examples indicate:

Borham (25): *Ibi sunt v boves arantes cum i cotario.*
Marden (24): *In dominio est dimidia caruca et ii villani et iii bordarii cum ii bobus.*
Renching (22): *Ibi ii villani et i bordarius et ii boves arantes.*
Thakeham (29): *Ibi habet v boves cum i bordario.*

At Sakeham (28b), as we have seen, there were but two animals (*ii animalia*).[1]

One Sussex entry is of especial interest because it contains one of the very few explicit Domesday references to colonisation. It is an account of an unnamed estate which Alviet held of William de Braiose in Ease-writhe hundred (29):

Alviet tenet de Willelmo terram ad unam carucam de dominio Willelmi sine numero hidae. Ibi est una caruca, et unum molinum de iii solidis. In Storgetune jacuit in pastura. Modo noviter est hospitata. Valet x solidos.

We can only conjecture whether or not this was an outlier belonging to Storrington and situated in the Wealden backwoods of Bramber rape.[2] The total number of plough-teams amounted to 3,193⅞, but it must be remembered that this refers to the area included in the modern county. Maitland estimated the total for the Domesday county as 3,091.[3]

(4) Population

The bulk of the population was comprised in the four main categories of villeins, bordars, cottars and serfs. In addition to these were the burgesses together with a small miscellaneous group that comprised shepherds and priests. The details of these groups are summarised on p. 438. This estimate is not comparable with that of Sir Henry Ellis which was in terms of the Domesday county and which included tenants-in-chief, under-tenants and burgesses.[4] In any case, an estimate of Domesday population

---

[1] See p. 431 above. [2] Storrington also appears as *Estorchetone* (24).
[3] *Op. cit.* p. 401.
[4] Sir Henry Ellis, *A General Introduction to Domesday Book*, II (London, 1933), pp. 496–8. His grand total for the Domesday county amounted to 10,410.

can rarely be accurate, and all that can be claimed for the present figures is that they indicate the order of magnitude involved. These figures are those of recorded population, and must be multiplied by some factor, say 4 or 5, in order to obtain the actual population; but this does not affect the relative density as between one area and another.[1] That is all that a map such as Fig. 126 can roughly indicate.

It is impossible to say how complete were these Domesday figures. Once, for one holding at Hankham (22), where there was land for one team, we are told that no return had been made—*Inde nullum responsum*. Many other entries make no reference to people; none is recorded, for example, at Hurst (20), Moustone (27b) or Offington (28b) though each had a team at work, and Hurst also had an acre of meadow. There must also have been people living at Battle, but they are not mentioned.[2] Only one entry tells us definitely that no one lived on a holding; this was at Wootton (27b) and was worth 12*s.*, yet almost all we are told about it is *Nullus ibi manet*. Furthermore, the small number of priests in relation to the number of churches is striking, but we have no means of knowing to what extent the priests were included amongst the villeins; those priests who were obviously sub-tenants have not been included in the totals.[3]

Freemen occur quite frequently as occupiers in 1066, and it is difficult to see what had happened to them by 1086. A certain Warin held Rumboldswhyke (24) in 1086 of Hugh who held it of Earl Roger; 5 freemen had formerly held it as five manors. There were 6 villeins and 2 bordars on the holding in 1086, but we can only conjecture whether these were the freemen of 1066 or their descendants. Or again, 2 freemen had held part of Wittering (24) as 2 manors. Were they among the 4 villeins on the estate in 1086? Such entries as these make us wonder to what extent the pre-Conquest freemen had been absorbed into the ranks of the villeins. No freemen are recorded in Sussex for 1086; neither are sokemen recorded for either date.[4]

[1] But see p. 589 for the complication of serfs.   [2] See p. 417 above.

[3] See p. 462 below. The decision whether or not to include them is not always easy. The entry for Mundham (24), for example, records *Presbyter habet dimidiam carucam*, and the priest has been included in the total of 5 (see p. 438). For Compton (24), on the other hand, we read *Presbyter tenet dimidiam hidam*, and, as a sub-tenant, this priest has been excluded.

For a similar reason, the reeve of the manor of Tangmere (16b) has been excluded from the present count: he held land worth 20*s.* out of a total of £6. Knights have likewise been excluded, e.g. at Applesham (28b); so has the *francigena* at Durrington (28b).

[4] Nineteen thegns are entered for 1066, none for 1086—see p. 595 below.

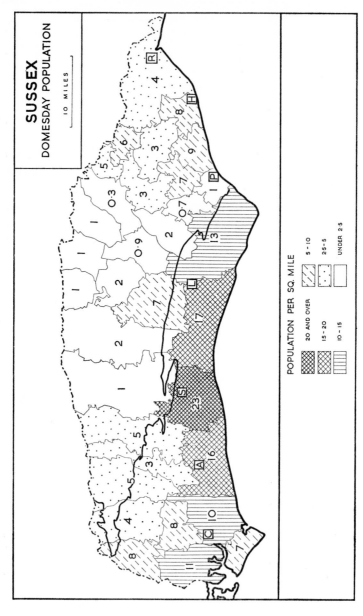

Fig. 126. Sussex: Domesday population in 1086 (by densities).

Domesday boroughs are indicated by initials: A, Arundel; C, Chichester; H, Hastings; L, Lewes; P, Pevensey; R, Rye; S, Steyning. The southern boundary of Weald Clay is shown (see Fig. 121).

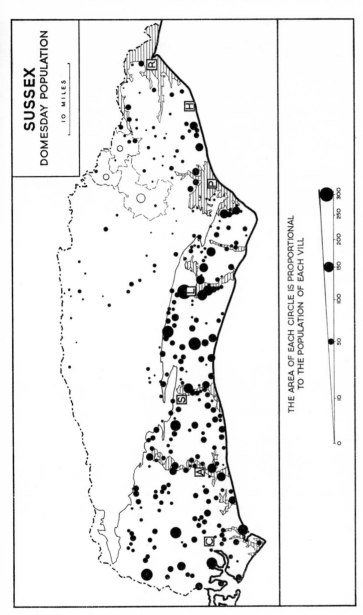

Fig. 127. Sussex: Domesday population in 1086 (by settlements).

Domesday boroughs are indicated by initials: A, Arundel; C, Chichester; H, Hastings; L, Lewes; P, Pevensey; R, Rye; S, Steyning.

The open circles represent the population on the unlocated holdings in each of the three northern hundreds of the rape of Hastings. Areas of coastal alluvium and the southern boundary of Weald Clay are shown (see Fig. 121).

Recorded Population of Sussex in 1086

A. *Rural Population*

Villeins	.	.	.	.	.	.	5,869
Bordars	.	.	.	.	.	.	2,512
Cottars	.	.	.	.	.	.	766
Serfs	.	.	.	.	.	.	410
Miscellaneous	.	.	.	.	.	15
Total	.	.	.	.	.	.	9,572

Details of Miscellaneous Rural Population

Shepherds	.	.	.	10
Priests	.	.	.	5
Total	.	.	.	15

B. *Urban Population*

Villeins, bordars, cottars and serfs are also included in the table above.

CHICHESTER   232½ *hagae*; 60 *masurae*; 9 burgesses; 3 crofts. See p. 463 below.

LEWES   201 *hagae*; 180 burgesses; 57 *masurae*. See p. 464 below.

PEVENSEY   110 burgesses; 1 *domus*. See p. 469 below.

ARUNDEL   13 *hagae*; 4 burgesses. See p. 470 below.

HASTINGS   24 burgesses; 14 bordars. See p. 471 below.

STEYNING   123 *masurae*; 223 villeins; 96 bordars; 9 serfs. See p. 471 below.

RYE   64 burgesses; 103 villeins; 4 cottars. See p. 472 below.

Villeins constituted the most important element in the population, and amounted to 61 per cent of the total. Bordars amounted to 26 per cent, and cottars and serfs came far below with only 8 and about 4 per cent respectively. At Ninfield (18) we hear of a certain villein (*quidam villanus*) holding virgates in 1086, and villeins had also held land at a number of places in 1066.[1] Bordars and cottars are never enumerated in the

---

[1] Villein tenants are recorded for 1066 in the following entries: Aldrington (26b), Balmer (26b), Beeding (27b), Bevendean (26b), Brighton (26b), *Falemere* hd. (26b), *Felesmere* (22b), Iford (26), Westmeston (27). The wording varies; that for Aldrington, for example, runs *Villani tenuerunt T.R.E.*

same entry, and never occur for the same place except for West Chiltington (24b, 29); the distinction between the two categories is obscure.[1] At
Stockingham (19) there was a cottar rendering 12*d*. The serfs present no
special features of interest for our purpose.

The small miscellaneous group comprised only 5 priests[2] and 10 shepherds (*berquarii*); the latter were at Patcham (26) to the north of Brighton,
and constitute a reminder that sheep-rearing must already have been an
important occupation on the South Downs.

(5) *Values*

The value of an estate is normally given for three dates—*tunc, post, modo*,
i.e. for 1066, for the year in which a subsequent holder received it, and
for 1086. Holdings in the hundreds of East Grinstead and Pevensey,
however, have no intermediate values stated for them; neither have many
holdings in the hundreds of *Hailesaltede, Ristone* and Staple, and also
occasional holdings elsewhere, e.g. at Donnington (17b), Felpham (17b)
and Parham (17). Other entries give but one value, e.g. several in the
account of the lands of Battle Abbey on fo. 17b. Then there are a few
entries which give no value; such is one of the two entries for Peelings
(22) and another for Stopham (23b). One holding at Beverington and
Yeverington (20b) was also without a value, but we are told that the
land was appraised (*appreciata est*) in the manor of Willingdon. An
unnamed holding in Totnore hundred (17b) was appraised in another
manor but we are not told which (*Appreciatum est in alio manerio*);
8 hides in this hundred (20b) were also appraised elsewhere (*appreciatae
sunt in alio hundredo*). Or again, 1½ virgates at Standen (22b), formerly
part of Bevendean, were accounted for in the manor of Tarring Neville
(*Ad Bevedene jacuit....Computatur et appreciatur est in manerio de
Toringes*).

In the rearrangement of manors consequent upon the reorganisation of
the rapes,[3] the separate portions of a manor were individually valued.

---

[1] For a discussion of the differences between bordars and cottars, see F. W. Maitland, *op. cit.* pp. 39 *et seq.*, and P. Vinogradoff, *English Society in the Eleventh Century*
(Oxford, 1908), pp. 456 *et seq.*

[2] The priests were at Brambletye (22b), Mundham (24), Selmeston and Sidnor
(21b), Stoughton (24) and West Thorney (17)—see p. 439 below.

[3] See pp. 408 and 424 above.

Only very rarely does the statement about value show us how manors were being broken up or assembled. Half a hide out of the 5 at Sherrington (20b) was in another rape, and the 1086 value is explained by saying that 20s. had been deducted on account of this. On the other hand, Fulking had been part of Shipley, and one holding in Perching had been part of Truleigh (26b, 27). They had come into the hands of a certain Tezelin, and, although they are separately described, they are valued together (*Hae duae terrae Tezelini insimul sunt*). Tezelin was apparently making one manor of them.[1]

The amounts are usually stated to the nearest pound or the nearest 10s. or 5s., but a number of entries suggest precision. Thus the value of West-field (18b) had increased from 20s. to 70s. and then to 72s.; that of Horns (22) had decreased from 13s. to 63d.; and that of an anonymous holding in *Ailesaltede* hundred (20) had decreased from 15d. to 12d. Even more striking is the value of Donnington (17b) which had increased from £4. 10s. 7d. to £6. These details imply that, in these entries at any rate, the 'value' is that of actual receipts rather than an estimate of what the holding was worth. The value of *Lodintone* in Pevensey hundred (22) had increased from 30s. to £6. 11s. 8d., and the description of the hundred ends with a supplementary note saying that 13s. should be added to *Lodiutone*[2] (*sic*) on account of the pasture which the count of Mortain had put into the manor. Occasionally, we hear of a mark of gold entering into the value, e.g. in the entry for Singleton (23). Finally, in the account of Bosham (16), the value of assayed money is contrasted with that of unassayed, and we are told that £50 of the former was worth £65 of the latter (*Tamen reddit l libras ad arsuram et pensam quae valent lxv libras*).

One of the outstanding features of the Sussex valuation is the decrease in the value of very many holdings between 1066 and the time when their subsequent owners received them, followed by a recovery by 1086. Some of the reductions were very considerable, and the values of at least sixteen

---

[1] *V.C.H. Sussex*, I, p. 357. Another holding at Perching (27) seems to have carried the union of two separate portions a stage further. They were surveyed and valued in a single entry as one manor, and we are told: *Tunc fuerunt duae Hallae, modo in uno manerio.* Two portions of Aldrington (26b), belonging to Beeding and to Broadwater in another rape, had also come into single ownership. They were separately described and valued, but, seemingly, they were on the way to being one: *In his duabus terris nisi una halla.*

[2] For *Lodintone*, see p. 418 n. above.

holdings had fallen to nothing (*wasta*).[1] Here are some examples of the changes:

	1066	Intermediate	1086
Ashburnham (18)	£6	20s.	£9
Bexhill (18)	£20	*Wasta*	£18. 10s.
Filsham (18)	£14	*Vastatum*	£22
Netherfield (18b)	100s.	*Vastata*	50s.
Patcham (26)	£100	£50	£80
Wiston (28)	£12	£4	£12

F. H. Baring thought that these temporary decreases indicated the devastation caused by the passage of Norman armies, and this seems a reasonable hypothesis, although it is difficult to determine exact routes in detail.[2] The concentration of wasted holdings in the rape of Hastings is understandable; other holdings in the neighbourhood, although not waste, were very much reduced in value (Figs. 161–2). The majority of these holdings, here as elsewhere in Sussex, had recovered fully or in part by 1086; some had even become more prosperous than before.

Another outstanding fact about the Sussex valuation is that the new landholders frequently obtained, or tried to obtain, from their estates more than what was regarded as a reasonable return. Eighteen entries for seventeen places give the current value in 1086, and then tell us that the holding paid, or was rented at, a greater sum. Part of the manor of Bosham (17), for example, was worth £16. 10s. in 1086, but we are also told that Bishop Osbern of Exeter had 20s. more from the feorm (*et tamen habet de firma xx solidos plus*). Some of the revised sums were considerably in excess of those agreed to by the jurors, as shown overleaf.

---

[1] Thirteen of the places are: Bexhill (18), Broomham (18b), Crowhurst (18b), Drigsell (19b), Filsham (18), Guestling (19b), Hazelhurst (19), Higham (20), Pett (19b), Netherfield (18b), Salehurst (19b), Whatlington (18b), Wilting (18b). To these must be added an unnamed holding in Henhurst hundred (19b) and the two holdings in Shoyswell hundred (19) that are entered under the names of Willingdon and of Winton (see p. 413 above). One entry for Sedlescombe (20) reads: *Valet x solidos. Wasta fuit.* This seems to imply that the holding had been waste *tunc* and *post*, in which case there had been no post-Conquest reduction. It is not clear whether the following were also waste at this time: Hollington (17b), and another holding at Wilting (17b) (see p. 458 below).

[2] F. H. Baring, 'The Conqueror's footprints in Domesday', *Eng. Hist. Rev.* XIII (1898), pp. 17–25. Reprinted 'with some additions and alterations' in *Domesday Tables* (London, 1909), pp. 207–16. See p. 569 below.

	1066	Intermediate	1086	Payment
Burpham (24b)	£8	£8	£8	£10
Pagham (16b)	£40	£40	£60	£80
Shoreham (28)	£25	£16	£35	£50
Stoughton (24)	£40	£30	£40	£50
Westbourne (23b)	£30	£10	£40	£50

It is not surprising that the payment at Pagham was thought to be too heavy (*sed nimis grave est*), and that the amount at Shoreham could not be borne (*sed non potuit pati*). Other entries record similar complaints, and occasionally we hear that an attempt at extortion had failed:

Patching (16b): *Modo xv libras. Dudum fuit ad xx libras sed non potuit pati.*
Preston near Brighton (17): *Modo xviii libras. Olim fuit ad xxv libras de firma sed non poterat reddere.*
Wootton (16b): *Modo iiii libras. Olim reddidit vi libras sed perdurare non potuit.*

Three entries in the Sussex folios show the survival of the ancient rent in kind known as the *firma unius diei* or *firma unius nocti*:

Beeding (28): *T.R.E. reddebat unam diem de firma et valebat quater viginti et xv libras et v solidos et vi denarios, et postea valuit l libras. Modo xl libras.*
Beddingham (20b): *T.R.E. reddebat firmam unius noctis. Quando comes recepit xx libras. Modo xxx libras quod habet comes. Quod homines vi libras.*
Eastbourne (20b): *T.R.E. reddebat firmam unius noctis. Quando comes recepit xxx libras. Modo dominium ejus xl libras. Hominum ejus lxvii solidos.*

Unlike the manors with similar renders in the Hampshire folios, these Sussex holdings were hidated in the usual way.[1]

Generally speaking, the greater the number of teams and of men on an estate, the higher its value, but it is impossible to discern any consistent relationship; the six estates in the table below each yielded £5 in 1086:

	Teams	Population	Other resources
Bepton (23b)	4	23	—
Crowhurst (18b)	15	21	Meadow, Wood
Durrington (28b)	8	22	Meadow, Wood
Linch (23)	3	14	Meadow, Wood
Pangdean (27)	9	23	Meadow, Wood
Rumboldswhyke (24)	3	9	—
Worthing (28b)	3	16	Meadow

[1] See p. 317 above.

Or what are we to make of the one hide at Chancton (28b), when all we are told of it is: *Nichil ibi est. Valet xi solidos?* Or of another hide at Lavant (23) of which we read: *Nichil est ibi; tamen valet et valuit xx solidos?* There was also a holding of half a hide at Erringham (28) worth 40s., and yet all the entry tells us is that there were 2 villeins and 5 bordars who had nothing (*nil habentes*). Then there is the account of the virgate at Laughton (19b): *Walterius nil ibi habet nisi duos solidos.* What produced the 2s. if there was nothing there? To such perplexities the folios offer no answer.

Conclusion

Domesday Sussex contained a large number of small hundreds, and many of these have been grouped together for the purpose of calculating densities. A few other modifications have also been made, and the result is thirty-three units. Although not giving as perfect a regional division as a geographer could wish for, these units provide a useful basis for distinguishing the degree of variation over the face of the county. The boundaries of the Wealden hundreds in particular raise many problems, but any inaccuracy cannot greatly affect the densities in such a relatively empty area.[1]

Of the five recurring standard formulae, those relating to plough-teams and population are most likely to reflect something of the distribution of wealth and prosperity throughout the county. Taken together, they supplement one another to provide a general picture (Figs. 124 and 126). The essential feature of both maps is the contrast between the north and south of the county. In the north, much of the Wealden area, particularly in its higher central portion, had an average of less than a team and not much more than one person per square mile; here was a countryside of broken relief and of hungry sands and ill-drained clays. Westwards, towards the Hampshire border, the figures are higher, reaching to over 2 teams and to 5 and more people per square mile. This is at first sight surprising because a large part of this western area is occupied by an expanse of Weald Clay, unrewarding to agriculture and largely devoid of settlement; but the Clay is bordered on the south by Lower Greensand across which runs the western Rother, and the men and the teams of the villages of the Rother valley accounted for the relatively high densities in the area as a whole. To the east of the central Weald, where the country

[1] For the hundreds, see O. S. Anderson, *The English Hundred-Names: The south-eastern counties*, pp. 66–108.

is lower, and where the juxtaposition of clay and sand provided sites for villages, the densities are also higher—up to 4 or 5 for teams and about 7 or 8 for people. The low densities of some units in this area (e.g. under 1 for teams and about 2 for population) are explained in part by the fact that much of the area was taken up by marsh—the Pevensey Levels and the western edge of Walland Marsh.

Standing in great contrast to these sparsely occupied areas are the districts of the south—the fertile coastal plain and the Downland with its valleys and its scarp-foot zone. Densities of 4 to 6 for teams are frequent, so are population densities of well over 10 and sometimes over 20. The lower valleys of the Arun, the Adur and the Ouse were closely tilled and well-populated. It is probable that the figures for some of these southern units are a little too high because the totals for some southern manors may have included the details of outliers in the Weald, but the number of men so involved, and certainly that of teams, must have been small. The picture given by Figs. 124 and 126 must be broadly correct, and it leaves us in no doubt about the striking contrast within Domesday Sussex.

Figs. 125 and 127 are supplementary to the density maps, but again it is necessary to make reservations about them. As we have seen on pp. 415–16, some names may have covered two or more settlements, e.g. the present villages of North Marden, East Marden and Up Marden are represented in the Domesday Book by only one name. A few of the symbols should therefore possibly appear as two or more smaller symbols. Then again there are those unnamed holdings which we cannot locate in the Wealden hundreds.[1] For three of the hundreds we are able to show their totals as open circles on Figs. 125 and 127; but there may well be other unnamed holdings elsewhere concealed in the entries for some manors. With these limitations, Figs. 125 and 127 serve to amplify the information of the density maps.

WOODLAND

Types of entries

The amount of woodland on a holding in Sussex is normally indicated by the formula *silva de n porcis* or *silva n porcis*, which is sometimes expanded to *de pasnagio silvae n porci* or *silva* [*de*] *n porcis de pasnagio*. The swine in these entries constituted the rent paid to a lord in return for pannage in his wood. The number of swine varies from one (e.g. at

---

[1] See p. 413 above.

Cokeham, 29) to 324 at South Malling (16).[1] The larger amounts are usually in round numbers (e.g. 60, 80, 150) that suggest estimates; but the smaller amounts might be actual numbers (e.g. 3, 4, 6), and for Donnington (17b) the figure is even 'one and a half swine'.

There is no entry that gives us a clue to the relation of these renders to total numbers of mast swine. But swine were also rendered for pasturage, and some of these entries give a ratio of one to seven; it is tempting to assume that the same ratio applied to mast swine.[2] W. H. Legge thought this not so in view of the entry for Ferring (16b) which may suggest that wood and herbage renders were evaluated differently: *silva iiii porcis et pro herbagio unus porcus de vii*.[3] On the other hand, there are a few entries in which a combined figure for wood and grass swine is given, and this would seem to imply similar methods of reckoning, e.g. for Sheffield (22b): *De silva et herbagio xxxii porci*.[4] For the purpose of constructing Fig. 128, these totals have been divided equally between woodland and pasture. We can offer no satisfactory answer to the wider question of what acreage of wood the figures imply. All we can do is to plot them as conventional units in the hope of obtaining some rough guide to relative distribution of wood over the face of the county.

While swine renders form the usual unit of measurement, there are a number of entries that refer to wood in other ways—either as material for fencing or as producing a money rent:

Donnington (17b): *silva ad clausuram*.
Pagham (16b): *parva silva ad clausuram*.
Preston in Binderton (17b): *parva silva ad clausuram*.
Sidlesham (17): *silva ad clausuram*.

Brightling (18b): *silva de v solidis*.

---

[1] The entry for Stoughton (24) says: *De isto Manerio est una hida in Rapo Willelmi de braiose et silva mille quingent' porc'*. J. H. Round's comment was 'These figures must be wrong; I am inclined to think that the scribe misread *silva M(anerii) quinq(ue) porcorum*, as *silva M(ille) quing(entorum) porcorum*' (*V.C.H. Sussex*, I, p. 426 n.). It is possible, of course, that the formula means 'wood for 1,500 swine' (*ibid.* p. 366 n.).

[2] For grass swine, see p. 451 below. In 1273, the king took one swine for every 10 in Ashdown Forest (P.R.O. Rentals and Surveys, 15/46).

[3] *V.C.H. Sussex*, II (London, 1907), p. 293.

[4] Single totals for wood and grass swine are given in the following seven entries: Barkham (22b), Birdham (24), Brambletye (22b), Fletching (22b), Sheffield (22b), Shovelstrode (22b) and an unnamed holding in East Grinstead hundred (22b). Second entries for Fletching (22b) and Shovelstrode (22b) give separate renders for wood and pasture.

Eatons (29): *Silva de v denariis.*

Offham (25): *Ibi habet comes [Rogerius] ii molinos, pasturam et exitum silvae. Val' iiii libras et x solidos.*[1]

Sakeham (28b): *Silva de x denariis.*

West Tarring (16b): *De silva x denarii, de pasnagio xx solidi et ii porci (sic).*

The only reference to forest in the Sussex folios is in the entry for Dallington (18b) where the count of Eu held one hide: *De ista hida habet comes medietatem in foresta et valet v solidos.*[2] But parks are mentioned at five places.[3]

We can occasionally glimpse in the wood entries something of the Norman reorganisation of manors, as the following entries show:

Ditchling in the rape of Lewes (26): *T.R.E. se defendebat pro xlvi hidis. Quando recepit nisi xlii hidae, aliae fuerunt in rapo comitis moritoniensis* (i.e. Pevensey rape), *et vi silvae quae pertinebant ad caput manerii.* But in Pevensey rape we hear only of '6 swine from wood and herbage' that had belonged to Ditchling; they were on an unnamed holding in East Grinstead hundred (22b).

Hollington in the rape of Hastings (17b): *Adhuc est una silva foris rapum de v porcis.* But there is no other reference to this wood in the Sussex folios.

Saddlescombe in the rape of Lewes (27): *Silva fuit de v porcis quae modo est in rapo Willelmi de braiose* (i.e. Bramber rape). But there is no reference to this in the entries for the rape of Bramber.

Stoughton in the rape of Arundel (24): *De isto Manerio est una hida in Rapo Willelmi de braiose* (i.e. Bramber rape) *et silva mille quingent' porc'.* But there is no reference to this in the entries for Bramber rape.[4]

Apart from these specific references to outlying wood, there is also mention of wood in other entries relating to outlying estates as a whole, e.g. the outliers of the Pevensey manors in the hundreds of Hawksborough, Henhurst and Shoyswell.[5]

Distribution of woodland

Fig. 128, showing the distribution of woodland entered under the Domesday place-names of Sussex, has inherent limitations. Its symbols represent not the location of the wood on the ground but only that of the

---

[1] This follows the main entry for Offham which mentions wood yielding three swine.

[2] In 1334 there is reference to a 'wood called the chase of *Dalynton*'. The earliest references to some other Sussex forests are as follows: Ashdown, *c.* 1200; Houghton, 1279; St Leonard's, 1213; Stanstead, 1271; Worth, *c.* 1200—A. Mawer, F. M. Stenton and J. E. B. Gover, *op. cit.* I, pp. 2–3 and 129.   [3] See p. 473 below.

[4] For the figure of 1,500 swine see p. 445 n. above.   [5] See p. 413 above.

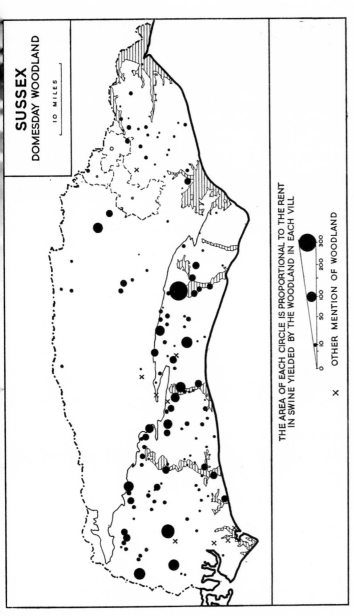

447

Fig. 128. Sussex: Domesday woodland in 1086.

Where the wood of a village is entered partly in terms of a swine render and partly in some other way, only the swine render is shown. The open circles represent the renders in swine from the unlocated holdings in each of the three northern hundreds of the rape of Hastings. Areas of coastal alluvium and the southern boundary of Weald Clay are shown (see Fig. 121).

parent estates to which pannage dues were paid. Thus the 324 swine
recorded in the entry for South Malling (16) were derived from wood that
extended over a considerable tract of territory stretching north-eastwards
to Wadhurst on the borders of Kent.[1] Many of the symbols on Fig. 128
must therefore be 'spread out', so to speak, by eye over the adjacent
Weald. This is especially true of the parent centres situated along the
northern edge of the South Downs, for, without doubt, most of their
appurtenant woodland was situated on the expanse of Weald Clay to the
north (see Fig. 121). Places in eastern Sussex seem to have had fewer
mast swine than those in the west; this may have been due to the fact that
stretches of surface clay were smaller in extent and more broken in
character here, because outcrops of Ashdown Sand and Tunbridge Wells
Sand covered considerable areas. But, both in east and west alike, we may
wonder whether the Domesday entries account for all the wood of the
Weald. It may well be that some unexploited wood—particularly on the
Weald Clay—went unmeasured and so unrecorded in the folios before us.

The Sussex folios, unlike those for Kent, do not contain references to
denes,[2] but both the place-names[3] and the evidence of early charters[4] leave
us in no doubt that in Sussex also there were detached swine pastures,
some already growing into small agricultural settlements by 1086. The
Domesday evidence about this pioneering is disappointingly silent, but,
as we have seen, circumstantial evidence shows that colonisation was
afoot in the Wealden half of the rape of Hastings.[5]

In contrast to the north, the Downs and the coastal plain carried but
a light wood cover. A comparison of Fig. 128 with the map of the
distribution of place-names (Fig. 123) shows that there were many places
in the south (e.g. to the west of Pevensey) for which no wood was
entered.

MEADOW

Types of entries

The entries for meadow in the Sussex folios are comparatively straightforward. For holding after holding the same phrase is repeated—'*n* acres
of meadow' (*n acrae prati*). For Plumpton (27) the word *pratum* is

---

[1] *V.C.H. Sussex*, I, p. 388n.   [2] See p. 527 below.
[3] A. Mawer, F. M. Stenton and J. E. B. Gover, *op. cit. passim.*
[4] E. E. Barker, 'Sussex Anglo-Saxon charters', *Sussex Archaeol. Collns*, LXXXVI
(Oxford, 1947), pp. 42–101; *ibid.* LXXXVII (1948), pp. 112–63; *ibid.* LXXXVIII (1949),
pp. 51–113.   [5] See p. 413 above.

followed by a blank space where a figure should have been inserted. The amount of meadow entered under the name of each place varies from one acre (e.g. at Pangdean, 27) to as much as 233 acres for South Malling (16) with its extensive manor. The entry for Bexhill (18) says specifically that the amount was for the whole manor (*In toto manerio vi acrae prati*). Generally speaking, the amount is usually below 50 acres, and there are only seven places for which it exceeds 100 acres. As in the case of other counties, no attempt has been made to translate these figures into modern acreages. The Domesday acres have been treated merely as conventional units of measurement, and Fig. 129 has been plotted on that assumption.

Distribution of meadowland

The valleys that break the Chalk surface in the south were marked by villages with meadow (Fig. 129). The lower Ouse valley with its substantial alluvial flats was exceptional; here, Hamsey (27b), Iford (26) and South Malling (16) each had 200 or more acres; Rodmell (26) and Southease (17b) each had over 100 acres; and there were other villages with 50 acres or so apiece. Amounts along the Adur were very much smaller, although Steyning (17) stood out with over 100 acres. Along the lower Arun and its west-east tributary, the western Rother, there was a continuous line of villages with moderate amounts, usually under 25 acres. Further west, Singleton (23), on the small stream of the Lavant, had as much as 60 acres, but it was an extensive manor. Or again, it is surprising to find as much as 84 acres for Patcham (26) in the dry area between the Ouse and the Adur, but it again was an extensive manor; J. H. Round thought that this amount, together with the 15 acres at Preston (17) and the 7 acres at Brighton (26b), 'might be accounted for by the stream which once flowed down the London Road valley to the Steyne at Brighton'.[1] Villages along the coast seem to have had little or no meadow, except for Pagham (16b) on its inlet in the west where there was as much as 80 acres. One might have expected more meadow for the villages around Chichester harbour and also, at the other end of the county, for those around the Pevensey Levels and around Walland Marsh, but the relative absence may have been due to flooding by tide-water; the little streams that flow into these eastern marshes were bordered by small amounts, usually not more than 10 or so acres for any village. In the north of the county, the Weald, with its absence of place-names, had practically no meadow entered for it.

[1] *V.C.H. Sussex*, I, p. 365 n.

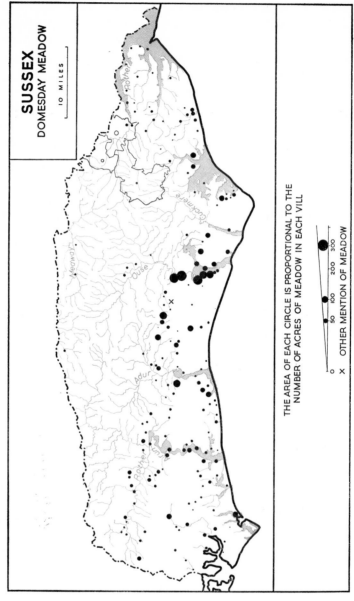

Fig. 129. Sussex: Domesday meadow in 1086.

The open circles represent the meadow on the unlocated holdings in each of the three northern hundreds of the rape of Hastings. Areas of coastal alluvium are shown (see Fig. 121); rivers passing through these areas are not marked.

PASTURE

Pasture (*pastura* or *herbagium*) is mentioned in connection with 35 places and 2 anonymous holdings[1] in Sussex.[2] The two words *pastura* and *herbagium* never occur in entries relating to the same place at the same date; but at Pevensey (20b), 7s. 3d. was due from *pastura* in 1066, and 15s. 4d. from *herbagium* in 1086. The form of the entries varies. About one-half measure pasture in terms of a swine render; *vi porci de herbagio* runs the entry for Alciston (17b). In seven entries a combined render is given for grass and mast swine.[3] Another seven entries provide a ratio between the render and the total number of swine pastured. Five of these give a ratio of one in seven; that for Woolavington does not specify pasturage, but it seems clear that this is meant.[4] In the margin of the entry for Pagham we are told: 'likewise throughout the whole of Sussex'. At Aldingbourne, however, the ratio is given as one in six, and at Bishopstone as one in three; but it may well be that the *vi* and the *iii* are mistakes for *vii*. Here are the entries:

Elsted (17b): *Herbagium de vii porcis i.*
Ferring (16b): *pro herbagio unus porcus de vii.*
Pagham (16b): *De herbagio unus porcus de unocuique villano qui habet vii porcos.*
   In the margin is: *Similiter per totum Sudsex.*
Wittering (17): *Herbagium de vii porcis unus.*
Woolavington (17b): *de vii porcis unus.*

Aldingbourne (16b): *de herbagio i porcus de vi porcis.*
Bishopstone (16b): *de iii porcis unus porcus de herbagio.*

In some entries a money render appears, the amounts varying from 6d. at Perching (*de pastura vi denarii*, 27) to £6 at Eastbourne (20b). At Iford (26), there may have been a render of herrings as well as of money for the pasture.[5] The entry following that for Buncton (29), in the rape of Bramber, mentions 'a small pasture' belonging to *Langemare* (? Angmering): *Ipse Robertus habet parvam pasturam cum ii bordariis qui reddunt*

---

[1] See p. 453n. below for one of these.
[2] This total of 35 includes the unidentified names of *Nonneminstre* (24b) and *Warlege* (22b).
[3] See p. 445n. above.
[4] The Woolavington entry reads: *Silva x porcis et de vii porcis unus*, and on the analogy of other entries, *pro herbagio* seems to have been omitted.
[5] See p. 455n. below.

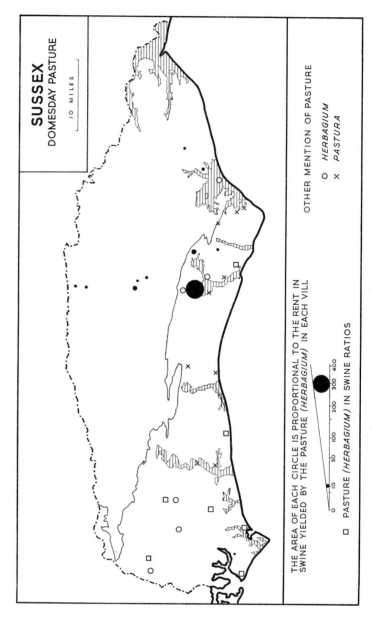

Fig. 130. Sussex: Domesday pasture in 1086.

Areas of coastal alluvium and the southern boundary of Weald Clay are shown (see Fig. 121).

v solidos. Hoc est in Langemare quod tenet comes Rogerius in suo rapo (i.e. Arundel rape); but the main account of Angmering (24b) makes no reference to pasture.[1] At Offham (25) the render was included in a total that also covered mills and woodland: *Ibi habet comes ii molinos, pasturam et exitum silvae. Valent iiii libras et x solidos.* Two entries measure pasture in terms of acres. For Lyminster (24b) and again for *Nonneminstre* (24b) we read: *lx acrae pasturae.*

Fig. 130 shows the distribution of settlements in connection with which pasture is recorded. As in Surrey, the total of these entries cannot have been all the pasture in the county. Almost every village must have had some, but how much we cannot say.

FISHERIES

Fisheries (*piscariae*) are mentioned or implied in connection with 28 settlements in Sussex. Most of the entries give the number of fisheries and their render, usually in money but occasionally in eels. The money renders range from 6*d*. from two fisheries in Henhurst hundred, entered under the name of Berwick (19b),[2] to 5*s*. from one at Arundel (23) and from another at Felpham (17b). At Duncton (23b) two fisheries rendered 360 eels and one at Burton (23b) rendered 280, but in this latter entry the word 'eels' has been left out. Only rarely is no render of any kind given, e.g. for three fisheries at Stopham (23b), for two at Birdham (24) and for one entered under *Borne* in Henhurst hundred (19b).[3] At Henfield (16b) a mill and two fisheries were wanting because they had been made over to William de Braiose: *Molinum et piscaria desunt pro superfacto W. de braiose.* The fishery has been included in our totals and marked on Fig. 131, because, presumably, it was still physically at Henfield or nearby.[4] The total of 28 also includes eight places with mills that rendered eels, but without any mention of *piscariae* as such; these are set out on p. 460 and marked on Fig. 131.

---

[1] It is difficult to decide whether the pasture and bordars were at Buncton or at Angmering or at neither place. On Fig. 130 the pasture has not been marked, and the bordars have also been treated as if they were on an unnamed holding.

[2] See p. 413 above. This entry is not included in the total of 28 settlements with fisheries.

[3] For *Borne*, see p. 413 n. above.

[4] The mill was possibly that mentioned under the neighbouring settlement of Wantley (28b) (*V.C.H. Sussex*, I, p. 390 n.). But the Wantley entry does not mention a fishery.

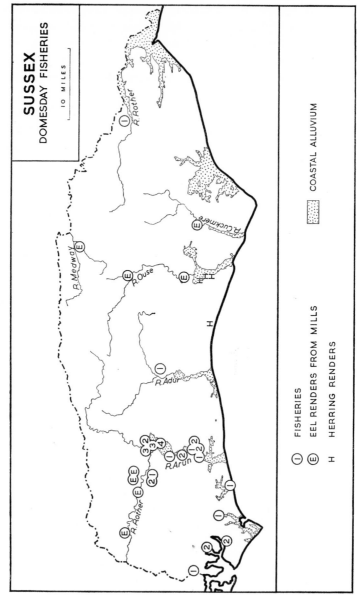

Fig. 131. Sussex: Domesday fisheries in 1086.

The figure in each circle indicates the number of fisheries. In addition to the fisheries marked on this map, there were also two fisheries entered under the name of Berwick but, presumably, situated somewhere along the eastern Rother (see p. 455). There was also one fishery at *Nonneminstre*. Rivers flowing across the alluvium are not marked.

The map shows that most of the fisheries were along the Arun and its tributary the western Rother. It is surprising that the only fishery named along the Adur was the one taken out of Henfield manor (16b), and also that we do not hear more frequently of fisheries and eel renders along the Ouse and the Cuckmere. The two fisheries in Henhurst hundred but entered under the name of Berwick (19b) were presumably somewhere along the eastern Rother. Taking Sussex as a whole, we can only suppose that other fisheries were not mentioned, either because they were not a source of manorial income, or because their render was included in the general total for a manor as a whole. Obviously the Domesday folios do not give us a complete picture.

There was, however, another type of fishing activity along the coast, and there are references to herring renders at four places which have not been included in the total of 28 above. At Brighton, the herrings appear as a gafol rent; at Rodmell we cannot be quite sure whether or not the render was really paid in Lewes; and at Southease we hear of porpoises in addition to the more prosaic herring. The entries are as follows:

Brighton (26b): *De gablo quattuor milia allecium.*
Iford (26): *xvi millenar (sic) allecium.*[1]
Rodmell (26): *In Lewes xliiii hagae de xxii solidis et iiii milia (sic) allecium.*[2]
Southease (17b): *de villanis xxxviii milia allecium et quingenti, pro marsuins iiii libri.*

What fraction this was of the total sea-fishing from the Sussex coast, we cannot tell.

SALT-PANS

Salt was recorded in connection with 34 places, including the unidentified *Medehei* (18) and *Nonneminstre* (24b). We are normally told the number of salt-pans and their render in money. The numbers ranged from as many as 100 pans yielding £8. 15s. at Rye (*Rameslie*)[3] to only one yielding 2s. at Bosham (17); and the render per salt-pan from 41s. 8d. from 5 at Wootton (*Lodintone*, 22) to the 40d. from 4 at Beddingham (20b). No render is

---

[1] At Iford, the herrings might have been part of the render for pasture; the complete entry is: *De pastura xv solidi et viii denarii et xvi millenar allecium.* See *V.C.H. Sussex*, I, pp. 366 and 435.
[2] 'The Rodmell entry looks as if the herrings formed part of the rent due from appurtenant houses, but careful consideration of the entries as a whole favours the view that they were due from Rodmell' (*V.C.H. Sussex*, I, p. 366n.).
[3] See p. 472 below.

stated for the 2 pans at Hunston (24); and the entry for Coombes (28b) does not give a number but merely says *de salinis l solidi et v denarii*. One of the entries for Kingston by Sea, and another for Washington, mention the measure known as the *ambra*:

Kingston by Sea (28b): *vi salinae de viginti solidis et x ambrae (sic) salis.*
Washington (28): *Ibi v salinae de cx ambris salis aut ix solidis et ii denariis.*

An *ambra* was four bushels,[1] and, from the latter entry, we see that an *ambra* of salt was worth 1*d.* In the descriptions of Saddlescombe (27) and Wappingthorn (28), *salinae* are not mentioned, but we hear merely of money renders *de sale*—15*d.* and 20*d.* respectively.[2] Two successive entries for Ratton (21) speak of 'a quarter of a salt-pan rendering 10*d.*', but there is no clue to the other half.

Fig. 132 shows how the salt-pans were associated with the coastal areas of alluvium, much of which must have been flooded in the eleventh century.[3] The very large centre of *Rameslie* (17), with 100 pans, was at or near Rye on the edge of Walland Marsh. To the west, around the Pevensey Levels, there were also salt-making centres, outstanding among which were Hooe (18, 22) with 34 pans, Eastbourne (20b) with 16, Hailsham (22) with 13 and Willingdon (21) with 11. There were also a few centres along the estuaries of the Cuckmere and the Ouse, where Rodmell (26), along the latter, had 11; here, too, may have been the 16 pans of Laughton (22), itself set a little inland. Further west, still along the Adur estuary, was another group of salt villages, among which Lancing (29), with 23 pans, stood out. In the west of the county, salt-making centres could only occasionally be encountered—at Lyminster (24b) along the lower Adur and at East Preston (24b) nearby; in this locality too may have been *Nonneminstre* (24b). We might well have expected to find evidence of greater salt-making activity around the harbours of Pagham and Chichester, but there seems to have been nothing beyond one pan at Bosham (17) and 2 at Hunston (24). To what extent the Domesday folios give us a complete picture, we cannot say.

[1] Sir Henry Ellis, *op. cit.* I, p. 133.
[2] The Wappingthorn entry runs: *De sale xx denarii, et i sextarius mellis.* It is possible to read this as implying a return of honey as well as of money.
[3] For coastal changes, see A. Ballard, 'The Sussex coast line,' *Sussex Archaeol. Collns,* LIII (1909), pp. 5–15.

457

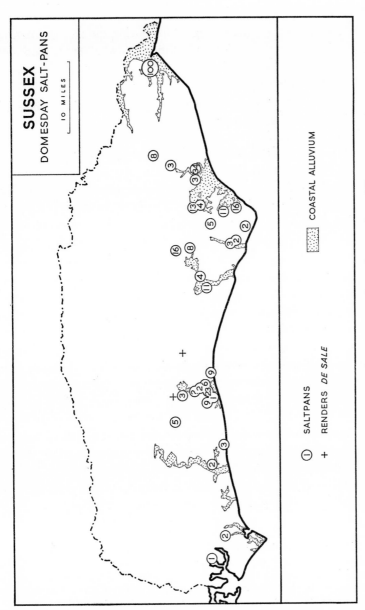

Fig. 132. Sussex: Domesday salt-pans in 1086.

The figure in each circle indicates the number of salt-pans. There were also salt-pans at *Medehei* and *Nonneminstre*.

WASTE

As we have seen on p. 441, the damage done during the passage of King William's armies was not enduring. Localities wasted after the Conquest were flourishing again by 1086,[1] and there are only three references to waste at the time of the Inquest:

> Hollington (17b): *In Holintun quod tenet comes de Ow habet abbas [de Labatailge] unam virgatam terrae wastae.*
>
> West Firle (21): *tenet Gislebertus lx acras terrae vastae.*
>
> Wilting (17b): *In Witinges quod tenet Ingelrannus de comite habet abbas i virgatam terrae wastae.*

There are other holdings on which there was said to be nothing,[2] but these are given a value and so cannot have been waste. Nor do we encounter wasted houses in the boroughs as in those of some other counties.

MILLS

Mills are mentioned in connection with 87 out of the 337 Domesday settlements of Sussex;[3] they also appear in the entries for eight anonymous holdings.[4] In almost every entry the number of mills is given together with their annual render that ranged from 20d. (e.g. at Wantley, 28b) to over 20s. (e.g. at Petworth, 23b). At Chiddingly (22b) there was a small mill as well as a mill (*i molinum cum molinario de iiii solidos*).[5] No renders are stated for mills in the entries for Barlavington (23b), Barnham (25), Catsfield (18), Henfield (16b), Maresfield (22b), Preston near Brighton (17), Steyning (28), West Firle (21). The entry for Barlavington is followed by a blank space which was never filled in; the mill at Catsfield was for the use of the hall (*serviens ad hallam*); that at Henfield, together with a fishery, is described as wanting because it had been made over to William de Braiose (16b);[6] those on one holding at Steyning (28) and on the land

---

[1] For the amount of waste immediately after the Conquest, see Figs. 161–2, and p. 569 below.

[2] See p. 443 above.

[3] The total of 87 includes the unidentified *Nonneminstre* (24b) and *Storchestone* (24).

[4] The unnamed holdings were in the hundreds of Box (25b), Easewrithe (described as part of (*jacuit in*) Washington, 29), Easewrithe again (described as part of Storrington, 29), Henhurst (19b), Henhurst again (under the name of Berwick, 19b), Rotherbridge (23b), Rotherfield (22b), and Totnore (demesne of Battle Abbey, 17b).

[5] Or possibly a site of a mill—*V.C.H. Sussex*, I, p. 418 n. Maybe a miller—Sir Henry Ellis, *op. cit.* I, p. 125, and II, p. 496.

[6] This Henfield mill has been marked on Fig. 133; see p. 453 n. above.

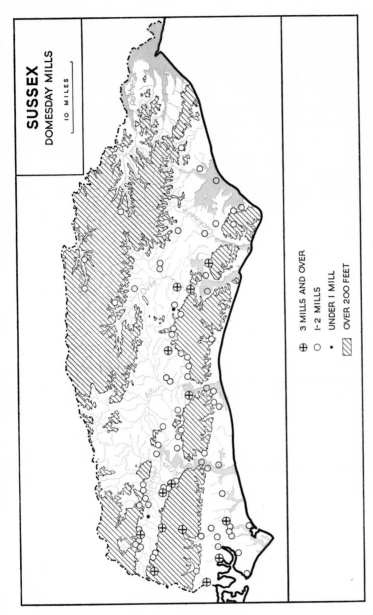

Fig. 133. Sussex: Domesday mills in 1086.

There were also mills at *Nonneminstre* and *Storchestone*. Areas of coastal alluvium are shown (see Fig. 121); rivers passing through these areas are not marked.

of Battle Abbey (17b) were without render (*sine censu*). The render of two mills at Offham (25) was included in a total that also covered pasture and woodland.[1]

There were occasional renders in kind as well as in money. The mill at Arundel (23) rendered corn and mixed grain: *unum molinum reddens x modia frumenti et x modia grossae annonae. Insuper iiii modia.* Swine as well as money were returned for four of the mills at Steyning (17): *iiii molini de xlvii solidis et lxviii porcis insuper.* In eight entries eels appear as part of the render:

Chithurst (23): *i molinum de viii solidis et c anguillis.*
Hartfield (21b): *Ibi i molinum de iiii solidis et cccl anguillis.*
Petworth (23b): *i molinum de xx solidis et clxxxix anguillis.*
Selham (23b): *unum molinum de x solidis et c anguillis.*
Sessingham (21b): *unum molinum de x solidis et quingentis anguillis.*
Sheffield (22b): *Ibi i molinum de xl denariis et quingentis anguillis.*
South Malling (16): *Ibi v molini de iiii libris et x solidis et ii milibus anguillarum.*
Tillington (23b): *i molinum de xx solidis et cxx anguillis.*

At Bignor (25), on the Upper Greensand, there was a quarry for millstones as well as two mills: *ii molini de xxviii solidis et una molaria de iiii solidis.*[2]

Fractions of mills are occasionally encountered. At Perching (26b) two holdings each had half a mill, one rendering 40*d*. and the other 13*s*. 4*d*. One of the entries for East Chiltington (27) also refers to half a mill, but the second entry says nothing about the other half (27). Nearby, at Barcombe (27b), there were 3½ mills, but again we hear nothing of the other half. It is possible that East Chiltington and Barcombe shared a mill on the Ouse or one of its tributaries. At Mundham (24) there were 1½ mills but there is no mention of the other half; and at Todham (23b) there was likewise a third of a mill (*tercia pars molini*).

Domesday Mills in Sussex

Under 1 mill	2 settlements	5 mills	3 settlements
1 mill	55 settlements	8 mills	1 settlement
2 mills	16 settlements	9 mills	1 settlement
3 mills	6 settlements	11 mills	1 settlement
4 mills	2 settlements		

This table excludes the mills of 8 anonymous holdings.

[1] See p. 446 above.
[2] Cf. the entry for Whatton in Nottinghamshire (290b): *Ibi una molaria ubi molae fodiuntur de iii markis argenti.*

Over one-half of the Sussex villages with mills seem to have had only one mill each. But the table above cannot be very accurate because a group of mills on a manor may have been distributed among its component members in ways unknown to us. The group of 11 mills was at Bosham, 8 on the king's manor (16) and 3 on the bishop of Exeter's (17); both were large manors. The group of 9 was at Harting (23); the name today covers three parishes (East, West and South) and, moreover, the Domesday entry may also have included outlying members. The group of 8 was at South Malling (16), another large manor that covered a considerable tract of territory. These examples serve to show the unsatisfactory nature of the table above; indeed we might go so far as to say that a large number of mills entered for one manor immediately creates a suspicion that more than one settlement is involved. But the table is not without value, and it is probably safe to assume from it that there were many villages with more than one mill at work.

Fig. 133 shows that many of the mills seem to have been on the small tributary streams that flow northward from the Chalk escarpment to join the major rivers. There were also many along the western Rother, some along the Ouse, the Adur and the Arun themselves, and some along the small streams that flow into the harbours of Pagham and Chichester. Along the streams of the east there were but few. We may well wonder whether this is the full tale, and what happened to the grain of those many Sussex villages for which the Domesday Book does not record mills?

CHURCHES

Churches (*ecclesiae*) are mentioned in connection with 85 places and one anonymous holding in Sussex;[1] chapels (*ecclesiolae*) are also attributed to 8 other places,[2] making at least 93 places in all. The total of individual churches and chapels is greater than this because some manors had more than one. Eight manors had two churches each;[3] Streat (27) had two chapels; and Rye (*Rameslie*, 17) had as many as five churches. The total

---

[1] The church in the entry for Selmeston and Sidnor (21 b) has been assigned to Selmeston. For Westbourne, see p. 349 above.

[2] The chapels were at Balmer (26b), Catsfield (18), Chithurst (23), Hooe (18), Ovingdean (26b), Sedlescombe (20), Shermanbury (28b) and Streat (27).

[3] The following manors had two churches each: Beeding (28), Bexhill (18), Bosham (16, 16b), Climping (25 *bis*), Kingston by Sea (28b *bis*), Pulborough (24b), Steyning (17) and West Tarring (16b).

number of churches is therefore 98 together with 9 chapels, making a grand total of 107.

Clearly the Domesday record of Sussex churches is incomplete.[1] Contemporary charters mention churches at Lewes, but the Domesday Book is silent about them; and we know also of other places with pre-Conquest churches that are unmentioned. Or again, the entry for Brambletye (22b) does not mention a church, but, as it includes a priest amongst its record of population, we can assume that there was probably a church there also. Four other entries mention priests as well as churches;[2] and in yet other entries priests appear as landowners.[3]

The geld liability of the land appurtenant to a church is sometimes given. At Filsham (18b) Ulward, 'the priest of this manor', held a church with one virgate; at Playden (19b) Tetbald the priest held 3 virgates and one church; at Elsted (17b) Ralph the priest held half a hide which belonged to the church (*quae pertinet ad ecclesiam*); and at Singleton (23) the church had 3 hides 1 virgate of land.[4] Or again, at Compton (24), where there was a church, the priest held half a hide; at Aldingbourne (16b), where there was also a church, the priest held one hide; at Boxgrove (25b) the clerks of the church (*Clerici ecclesiae*) also held one hide; at Bexhill (18), where there were two churches, two clerks held 1 hide as a benefice (*in prebenda*). At Amberley (17), Aeldred the priest held 3 hides, but the entry makes no reference to a church. All these are exceptional entries. Generally speaking, no land is assigned to a church, 'not, probably, because there was no endowment, but because the lands thus set apart were usually exempt from geld'.[5]

At Bosham (17b) the clerks held the tithes of the church (*Decimae ecclesiae clerici tenent*), which amounted to 40s. At Arundel (23) the church of St Nicholas received 24s. from 'the borough, the port of the river and the ship-dues'; in effect this was tithe although it was not so named. Finally, at Iping (29b) church-scot of 40d. was rendered (*de Circet xl denarii*).

[1] H. Poole, 'The Domesday Book churches of Sussex', *Sussex Archaeol. Collns*, LXXXVII (Oxford, 1948), p. 31. See also (1) *V.C.H. Sussex*, I, p. 369; (2) *V.C.H. Sussex*, II (London, 1907), pp. 4–5.

[2] Mundham (24), Selmeston and Sidnor (21b), Stoughton (24) and West Thorney (17).

[3] Land-owning priests have been excluded from the count of population (see p. 435 above); nor can we always be certain that a reference to such a priest implies the presence of a church.

[4] An unspecified number of clerks (*Clerici*), presumably of the church, had 2 teams and 5 bordars.   [5] *V.C.H. Sussex*, I, p. 369. See also *ibid.* II, p. 5.

URBAN LIFE

Seven places in Sussex seem to have been regarded as boroughs. Chichester, Lewes, Pevensey and Arundel are each described in an entry devoted to it alone. Hastings is mentioned only incidentally in connection with other places; it may well be that an account of Hastings should have occupied the blank space on fo. 16 before the beginning of the description of the county. Steyning and Rye were each within the confines of a large manor, and are not described in separate entries; Rye is not mentioned by name but was apparently part of the manor of *Rameslie*. Burgesses are also entered for Bollington, but presumably they were at Hastings. The Sussex boroughs seem to have been flourishing; the number of burgesses at Chichester, Pevensey and even Steyning had increased; and the value of Lewes had also risen. All this is not surprising in view of the stimulus given by the Norman Conquest to trans-Channel traffic. But the information for all seven places is unsatisfactory. We know, for example, that there were mints at Chichester, Hastings and Steyning, but they are unnoticed in the text. The evidence, such as it is, is set out below.

Chichester

The description of Chichester on fo. 23 is brief. Nothing is said about the commercial activities of the burgesses, nor is there any reference to agricultural activity or to the mint which we know existed there in pre-Conquest days.[1] Yet the city must have been prosperous, for its value had increased from £15 to £25, and it was rendering as much as £35:

> In Chichester city, in the time of King Edward, there were 97½ *hagae* (*c hagae ii et dimidia minus*) and 3 crofts (*croftae*) and they returned 49s. less 1d. The city itself is now in the hand of Earl Roger, and there are on the same burgages 60 houses more than there had been earlier (*et sunt in eisdem masuris lx domus plusquae antea fuerant*), and one mill rendering 5s. It used to return £15, £10 to the king and 100s. to the earl. Now it is worth £25, and yet it returns £35. Humphrey Flamme has there one *haga* rendering 10s.

The reference to the additional 60 houses in relation to the *hagae* of 1066 is puzzling, but it may be that in 1086 there was a total of 157½ *hagae* and houses and 3 crofts.[2]

[1] *V.C.H. Sussex*, I, p. 407.
[2] On the relation of *hagae*, houses and burgesses, see A. Ballard, *The Domesday Boroughs* (Oxford, 1904), pp. 13 and 56.

But there were yet other properties in the city. One interesting feature that the city shared with a number of other Domesday boroughs was that some of its burgesses and houses were recorded as belonging to rural manors around; these are specified not in the entry for Chichester but in the entries for their respective manors. Not all these entries mention Chichester by name, but when we read, under Merston (25 b), for example,

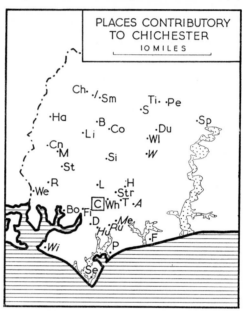

Fig. 134. Sussex: Places contributory to Chichester (C).

Chichester is not specifically named in the entries for those places indicated by italics. *A*, Aldingbourne; B, Bepton; Bo, Bosham; Ch, Chithurst; Co, Cocking; Cn, Compton; D, Donnington; Du, Duncton; F, Felpham; Fi, Fishbourne; H, Halnaker; Ha, Harting; *Hu*, Hunston; *I*, Iping; L, Lavant; Li, Linch; M, Marden; *Me*, Merston; P, Pagham; Pe, Petworth; R, Racton; *Ru*, Runcton; S, Selham; Se, Selsey; Si, Singleton; Sm, Stedham; Sp, Stopham; St, Stoughton; Str, Strettington; T, Tangmere; Ti, Tillington; *W*, Waltham; We, Westbourne; Wh, Westhampnett; *Wi*, Wittering; Wl, Woolavington. Note that the property entered under Pagham consisted of a church, and not of *hagae* or the holdings of burgesses. Areas of coastal alluvium are shown (see Fig. 121).

that there were 'two *hagae* yielding 2s.', we can safely assume that they were located in Chichester. Altogether, 135 *hagae* and 9 burgesses are mentioned; and, in addition, the entry for Pagham (16b) refers to a church at Chichester. Most, but not all, of these appurtenant properties rendered

money payments. The full list is set out below, and the villages concerned
are shown on Fig. 134.

If the total of 144 be added to the information in the main entry, the
grand total of *hagae*, houses, crofts and burgesses amounts to 304½. This
is on the assumption that there is no duplication between the properties
of the main entry and those of the rural entries, and it may imply a total
population of, say, between 1,200 and 1,500. Such an estimate is very
conjectural, and, in any case, it takes no account of any agricultural
population that might have been in the borough.

Appurtenant Holdings in Chichester

Note: (*a*) Those entries which do not name Chichester are indicated by an
asterisk. (*b*) One of the entries for Bosham (16) also refers to 1066. (*c*) The
church entered under Pagham has been included in this list.

Aldingbourne (16b)*: *xvi hagae quae reddunt vii solidos et vi denarios.*
Bepton (23b): *i haga de x denariis.*
Bosham (16): *Ad hoc manerio pertinuit xi hagae Cicestre T.R.E. quae reddebant
  vii solidos et iiii denarios. Modo habet episcopus decem de illis a rege et modo
  est una in manerio.*
Bosham (17)*: *una haga de viii denariis.*
Bosham (17b)*: *i haga de viii denariis.*
Chithurst (23): *i haga de vi denariis.*
Cocking (23): *i haga de xii denariis.*
Compton (24): *ii hagae de ii solidis.*
Donnington (17b): *una haga de iiii denariis.*
Duncton (23b): *una haga de ii solidis.*
Felpham (17b): *vi burgenses de vii solidis.*
Fishbourne (24): *ii hagae de xxi denariis.*
Halnaker (25b): *iii burgenses de v solidis.*
Harting (23): *xi hagae de xv solidis.*
Hunston (24)*: *de i haga vi denarii.*
Iping (29b)*: *Una haga de xx denariis.*
Lavant (23): *i haga de v denariis.*
Linch (23): *i haga de x denariis.*
Marden: (24): *i haga de i denario.*
Marden (24): *iii hagae de xxi denariis.*
Marden (24): *i haga de i denariis.*
Merston (25b)*: *duae hagae de ii solidis.*
Pagham (16b): *una ecclesia in Cicestre reddit lxiiii denarios.*

Petworth (23 b): *ii hagae de xvi denariis.*
Racton (24): *i haga de xx denariis.*
Runcton (25 b)*: *ii hagae de xviii denariis.*
Selham (23 b): *i haga de vii denariis.*
Selsey (17): *vi hagae...de xxxviii denariis.*
Singleton (23): *ix hagae...reddunt vii solidos et iiii denarios.*
Stedham (23): *i haga de vi denariis.*
Stopham (23 b): *i haga de iii denariis.*
Stoughton (24): *xv hagae de vii solidis et viii denariis.*
Strettington (25 b): *iii hagae de ii solidis.*
Strettington (25 b)*: *una haga de iii denariis.*
Strettington (25 b)*: *una haga de viii denariis.*
Tangmere (16 b): *iiii hagae...reddunt xxii denarios.*
Tillington (23 b): *i haga de viii denariis.*
Waltham (25 b)*: *una haga de xvi denariis.*
Waltham (25 b)*: *una haga de vii denariis.*
Westbourne (23 b): *vi hagae de xxx denariis.*
Westbourne (24): *i haga de xii denariis.*
Westhampnett (25 b): *i haga.*
Wittering (17)*: *xiii hagae de xxvi denariis.*
Wittering (24)*: *i haga de vi denariis.*
Woolavington (17 b): *una haga de iii denariis.*
Unnamed, in Box hd. (25 b)*: *ii hagae de ix denariis.*

Lewes

The main interest of the description of Lewes on fo. 26 is legal.[1] There is very little reference to its commercial life, but we hear of a mint (*moneta*) and of toll (*theloneum*),[2] and of trade in horses, oxen and slaves.[3] As the render had risen from £26 to £34, it would seem that the community was flourishing. There are two references to the inhabitants. One tells us that King Edward had held 127 burgesses (*burgenses*) in demesne; and we can only suppose that they or their successors were still there in 1086. The other reference is to 39 inhabited *mansurae* and 20 un-inhabited (*xxxix mansurae hospitatae et xx inhospitatae*). We can there-fore assume a minimum of 166 burgesses and *mansurae* in the borough.

[1] For reference to the castelry and castle of Lewes in the Norfolk folios, see p. 473 below.
[2] Specifically recorded for 1066, but apparently also in existence in 1086.
[3] *Qui in burgo vendit equum dat preposito nummum et qui emit alium. De bove obulum. De homine iiii denarios quocumque loco emat infra rapum.*

But there were yet other inhabitants. In Lewes, as in Chichester and some other boroughs, a number of properties belonged to rural manors around; these are specified not in the entry for Lewes but in the entries for their respective manors. Not all these entries mention Lewes by name, but when we read under Warningore (27b), for example, that there were 'three *hagae* yielding 21*d*.' we may safely assume that the *hagae* were in

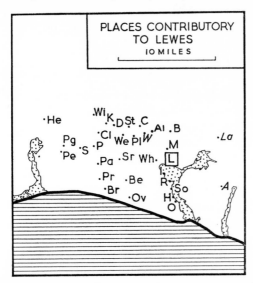

PLACES CONTRIBUTORY
TO LEWES
10 MILES

Fig. 135. Sussex: Places contributory to Lewes (L).

Lewes is not specifically named in the entries for those places indicated by italics. *A*, Alciston; Al, Allington; B, Barcombe; Be, Bevendean; Br, Brighton; C, Chiltington (East); Cl, Clayton; D, Ditchling; H, Harpingden; He, Henfield; I, Iford, K, Keymer; *La*, Laughton; M, Malling (South); O, Orleswick; Ov, Ovingdean; P, Pangdean; Pa, Patcham; Pe, Paythorne; Pg, Perching; Pl, Plumpton; Pr, Preston; R, Rodmell; S, Saddlescombe; So, Southease; Sr, Stanmer; St, Streat; *W*, Warningore; We, Westmeston; Wi, Wickham; Wn, Winterbourne. Areas of coastal alluvium are shown (see Fig. 121).

Lewes. Altogether, 197 *hagae*, 53 burgesses and 18 *mansurae* are mentioned, and there were also 5 vacant *mansurae*. The full list is set out on pp. 468–9, and the villages concerned are shown on Fig. 135.

If the total of 268 be added to the information in the main entry, the grand total of haws, burgages and burgesses amounts to 434, apart from 25 vacant burgages. This is on the assumption that there is no duplication between the properties of the main entry and those of the rural entries, and it may imply a total population of, say, about 2,000. Such an estimate is very conjectural, and, in any case, it takes no account of any agricultural population that might have been in the borough. But clearly, Lewes, situated where the Ouse breaks through the South Downs, was a centre of some importance. Its castle, its mint and its trade, all indicate that here was activity quite different in character from that of the settlements of the surrounding countryside.

Appurtenant Holdings in Lewes

The entries which do not specifically name Lewes are indicated by an asterisk.

Alciston (17b)*: *vii burgenses.*
Allington (27b): *i haga de vi denariis.*
Allington (27b): *iiii hagae de iiii solidis.*
Barcombe (27b): *xviii hagae de viii solidis et vii denariis.*
Bevendean (26b): *ii hagae de xviii denariis.*
Brighton (26b): *iiii hagae.*
Clayton (27): *ix hagae de iiii solidis et vii denariis.*
Ditchling (26): *xi masuras de xii solidis.*
Ditchling (26): *vi burgenses de xliii denariis.*
East Chiltington (27): *i haga de xii denariis.*
East Chiltington (27)*: *una haga et dimidia de viii denariis.*
East Chiltington (27): *i burgensis de vi denariis.*
Harpingden (26): *iiii hagae de xx denariis.*
Henfield (16b): *iii burgenses...reddentes xxi denarios.*
Iford (26): *xxvi burgenses de xiii solidis.*
Keymer (27): *vii hagae de xxvi denariis.*
Laughton (26)*: *xii mansuras, vii hospitatas et v non.*
Orleswick (26b): *ii hagae de x solidis.*
Ovingdean (26b): *x hagae de v solidis.*
Pangdean (27): *ii hagae de ii solidis.*
Pangdean (27): *ii hagae de ii solidis.*
Patcham (26): *xxvi hagae de xiii solidis.*
Paythorne (26b): *iii hagae de xviii denariis.*
Perching (26b): *una haga et dimidia de ix denariis.*
Perching (26b): *dimidia haga de ii denariis.*
Plumpton (27): *ix hagae de iiii solidis et v denariis.*
Preston near Brighton (17): *iii hagae de xviii denariis.*
Rodmell (26): *xliiii hagae de xxii solidis et iiii milia (sic) allecium.*
Saddlescombe (27): *i haga.*

Southease (17b): *x burgenses de lii denariis.*
South Malling (16b): *xxi hagae reddentes viii solidos et viii denarios per annum.*
Stanmer (16b): *vii hagae...reddentes xxi denarios per annum.*
Streat (27): *iii hagae de xviii denariis.*
Warningore (27b)*: *Tres hagae de xxi denariis.*
Westmeston (27): *i haga nichil reddens.*
Wickham (27): *iii partes unius hagae de xv denariis.*
Winterbourne (26b): *iii hagae et tercia pars unius hagae de xviii denariis.*

Pevensey

The account of Pevensey on fo. 20b begins by summarising the state of affairs in 1066:

In the borough of Pevensey, in the time of King Edward, there were 24 burgesses on the king's demesne, and they returned from burgage rents (*de gablo*) 14s. 6d. From toll (*De theloneo*) 20s. From harbour dues (*De portu*) 35s. From pasture (*De pastura*) 7s. 3d.

There were also 28 other burgesses, making a total of 52. We are then told that 'when the count of Mortain received it' there were only (*nisi*) 27 burgesses. It would seem as if there had been a decline immediately after the Conquest.

By 1086 a great change had come. The count of Mortain had 60 burgesses on his demesne, and there were also 50 other burgesses and one house (*una domus*) in the possession of 16 landholders. This total of 111 implies a population of, say, over 500, but such a figure may well be too small. Ballard pointed out that the names of most of the sixteen holders appear among those of the under-tenants of the count of Mortain in the villages around; and he suggested that here may be another example of appurtenant holdings.[1] The yield from toll (*Theloneum*) had increased to £4, and we now hear of 20s. from a mint (*Moneta*), 20s. from a mill and 15s. 4d. from pasturage (*de herbagio*). No mention is made of a castle, but entries for Eastbourne (20b) and West Firle (21) refer to 'the warders of the castle' (*Custodes castelli*), which seems to imply that of Pevensey.

[1] *The Domesday Boroughs*, pp. 23–4. It is difficult to make a satisfactory list of these villages because some of the names appear as those of under-tenants in a large number of villages, and we cannot be sure that Ralph or William, for example, always refers to the same man.

Arundel

Arundel, called *Castrum Harundel,* is described in a single entry on fo. 23. That it was a commercial centre we may assume from the statement that, between the borough and the port of the river and the shipping dues, it rendered £12: *Modo inter burgum et portum aquae et consuetudinem navium reddit xii libras.* We hear also of a toll, or perhaps market dues, from men who were outside the borough (*de hominibus extraneis habet suum theloneum*). There was a fishery yielding 5s., and a mill rendering grain, but there is no mention of agricultural activity.[1] No reference is made to a church, but the entry for Harting speaks of land held by 'the clerks of Saint Nicholas' (23) which was the church of Arundel.[2] The castle had been built by Earl Roger.[3]

The record of inhabitants is brief. The total amounts to 4 burgesses and 13 *hagae.* These are enumerated under the names of seven holders whose names also appear as those of mesne tenants in the nearby villages of Barnham (25), Bignor (25), *Borham* (25), Eastergate (25b), Middleton (25), South Stoke (25), Toddington (24b), Warbleton (25) and Warningcamp (24b). On the basis of this, Ballard suggested that here is another example of appurtenant holdings, although the separate entries relating to these villages make no reference to Arundel.[4] In any case, the combined total of 17 burgesses and *hagae* cannot be complete, and it is impossible to hazard even the roughest estimate of the size of the community. Set where the Arun breaks through the South Downs, Arundel must have been a fairly important centre, and, under eleventh-century conditions of navigation, a port of some substance.

[1] The entry does give us a glimpse of ancient customs as they had been in 1066. In the time of King Edward, Arundel had returned 40s. from a certain mill, 20s. in composition for 3 entertainments, and 20s. for one day's procurage (*de iii conviviis xx solidos et de uno pasticio xx solidos*). 'Convivium appears to have meant the obligation to supply food and entertainment for the lord of the manor and his suite once a year. *Pasticium* seems to be the lay form of "procurage", which was the obligation of the clergy to provide food and lodging for the bishop or his deputy when he was visiting their churches' (*V.C.H. Sussex,* I, p. 421 n.).

[2] *Ibid.* I, p. 422. The main entry also mentions dues to St Nicholas.

[3] J. H. Round, 'The castles of the Conquest', *Archaeologia,* LVIII (London, 1902), p. 332.

[4] *The Domesday Boroughs,* p. 22; Ballard's text is accompanied by a map showing the 'suggested Contributories' to Arundel.

Hastings

There is no Domesday description of Hastings, and J. H. Round suggested that the empty space on fo. 16, before the account of the *Terra Regis*, was intended for such a description which was never inserted.[1] There are, however, two and possibly three references to the borough in the body of the Sussex text:

(1) The entry for *Rameslie* (17) says: 'In Hastings 4 burgesses and 14 bordars render 63s.'

(2) The entry for Bexhill (18) mentions the castelry of Hastings (*castellaria de Hastinges*).

(3) The entry for Bollington (18) says that the count of Eu had 20 burgesses. It is difficult to see where they can have been apart from Hastings, and it has been suggested that their property may have been at Bulverhythe not far to the west of the borough.[2]

In view of the later position of Hastings as head of the Cinque Ports, the absence of a Domesday account is all the more to be regretted.

Steyning

Steyning was the head of two substantial manors. One, held by the abbot of Fécamp (17), was rated at 67 hides in 1086; the other, held by William de Braiose (28) was rated at 18 hides 2 virgates. How large they were can be seen from the following details:

	Abbot of Fécamp	W. de Braiose
Plough-lands	41	21
Plough-teams	55	20
Population	250	78
Value T.R.W.	£100*	£25

* But at feorm for £121. 18s.

The reference to the borough is brief, and it occurs in the first of these entries (17):

In the borough there were 118 *masurae* which used to render £4. 2s. Now there are 123 *masurae* and they render 100s. and 100d., and [the burgesses] have 1½ plough-teams. In the time of King Edward [the burgesses] used to do villein service on the manor (*ad curiam operabantur sicut villani*).

---

[1] J. H. Round, *Feudal England* (London, 1895; reprinted 1909), p. 568.

[2] *V.C.H. Sussex*, I, p. 397.

The inclusion of the borough with such a large manor makes it difficult to interpret the entry and to say, for example, how the agricultural population was distributed between the borough and the rest of the manor. The number of burgesses in 1086 seems to imply a population of at least 600, but the total population may have been very much larger than this. The position of Steyning, commanding the Adur gap through the South Downs, would suggest that it might have been a place of some consequence, but the Domesday folios are exasperatingly silent about its activities. They do not, for example, mention the mint which we know was there.[1]

Rye

A considerable estate held by the abbot of Fécamp in south-east Sussex is described under the name *Rameslie* (17). The name has not survived, and the exact site of the holding is unknown. It was assessed at $17\frac{1}{2}$ hides in 1086, and its size may be gauged from the fact that it had land for 35 plough-teams, that 46 teams were at work, that the agricultural population numbered 107, and that its annual value was £52. 4s. Furthermore, it had, amongst other things, five churches and 100 salt-pans. Embodied in the entry is a reference to a borough: 'In the same manor is a new borough (*novus burgus*), and there [are] 64 burgesses rendering £8 all but 2s. In Hastings [are] 4 burgesses and 14 bordars rendering 63s.' At one time, this *novus burgus* was identified with Hastings,[2] but this is unlikely in view of the reference to Hastings that immediately follows. J. H. Round thought that it was either Rye or Winchelsea, neither of which is mentioned in the Domesday text.[3] A. Ballard thought that it was more likely to be Rye in view of the fact that Winchelsea was the seat of a pre-Conquest mint, and that it could hardly have been a 'new borough'.[4] Subsequent evidence has confirmed the likelihood that it was Rye.[5] But how much of the detail in the *Rameslie* entry should be assigned to Rye itself we cannot say. That it contained at least 300 people seems clear, but it may well have been considerably larger than this.

[1] *V.C.H. Sussex*, I, p. 383.
[2] M. Burrows, *Cinque Ports* (London, 1888), p. 27. Cf. *V.C.H. Sussex*, I, p. 385 n.
[3] *Feudal England*, p. 567.   [4] *The Domesday Boroughs*, p. 9 n.
[5] A. Mawer, F. M. Stenton and J. E. B. Gover, *op. cit.* II, pp. vi–vii.

Castles

Five castles are mentioned, but we are told very little about them:

(1) The castle of Bramber stood on 1 hide of the manor of Washington —*In una ex hidis sedet castellum Brembre* (28).

(2) The castelry of Hastings (*castellaria de Hastinges*) is said to have been given by King William to the count of Eu (18).

(3) Pevensey castle is not mentioned by name, but in entries for East-bourne (20b) and West Firle (21), the warders of the castle (*Custodes castelli*) are said to hold land, and it seems that Pevensey castle is meant.

(4) There is no reference to Lewes castle in the Sussex folios, but in the account of William de Warenne's possessions in Norfolk we hear of land held *de castaellatione lawes* (II, 163) or *ad castellum de lauues* (II, 163b); the various references to *de castello de laquis* (II, 164b, 165) or *pro castellatione aquarum* (162b) also imply the castle of Lewes.

(5) On fo. 23 we also hear of *Castrum Harundel*, and we know from other sources that Earl Roger had built a castle at Arundel.[1]

Parks

Parks are recorded in connection with five places. There was a park in the royal manor of Rotherfield (16); and at Wilting (18b) the count of Eu held 1 virgate in a park. Earl Roger, on the other hand, had imparked land on 3 manors in the west of the county—3 hides at Waltham (25b *bis*), 1 hide at Tortington (25) and 1 virgate at Walberton (25). He also held a park immediately across the border, in Hampshire.[2] J. H. Round pointed out that the park which William de Braiose had formed at Bramber is not mentioned in the Domesday text.[3]

Mineral workings

Only one iron working (*ferraria*) is noted. It was on an unspecified holding in East Grinstead hundred, formerly part of the manor of Ditchling (22b).

Quarries (*quadrariae*) are entered under Grittenham (23b), Iping (29b) and Stedham (23), the renders from each being 10s. 10d., 9s. 4d. and 6s. 8d. respectively. All three places are in the Lower Greensand country

---

[1] See p. 470 above. [2] See pp. 355–6 above.
[3] *V.C.H. Sussex*, I, p. 366.

of north-west Sussex. At Bignor (25) there was a quarry (*molaria*) for millstones rendering 4*s.*; Bignor is near the Upper Greensand outcrop.

Other references

Among other miscellaneous items must be mentioned some renders in kind. There were honey renders of 2 sesters and 1 sester respectively at Beeding (28) and Wappingthorn (28); and at Southease (17b), 3 loads (*summae*) of peas were rendered. There were gafol rents of herring at Brighton (26b) and of swine at Beeding (28). Three crofts (*croftae*) are mentioned for Chichester (23) and 43 for South Malling (16). There was toll (*theloneum*) at Lewes (26) and at Pevensey (20b). Finally, mints are entered for Lewes (26) and Pevensey (20b), but we know from other sources that there were other places in Sussex with mints that the Domesday Book does not mention.[1] There is no specific mention of a market, nor are we told anything of, for example, vineyards.

REGIONAL SUMMARY

Broadly speaking, Sussex may be divided into four main regions—the coastal plain, the Downs, the west Rother valley and the Weald (Fig. 136). Many subdivisions of these regions can be recognised, and the Weald in particular includes areas of widely contrasted soils, ranging from heavy clay to light sand. But a division into four areas serves to give a broad view of the county, and, in any case, the nature of the Domesday information does not warrant any very detailed division.

In addition to these four main regions, the county boundary also includes a small villageless tract in the north-west which is not described here. It is a continuation of somewhat similar country in eastern Hampshire (see Fig. 103) and the south-west corner of Surrey (see Fig. 118). It is composed of the light sandy infertile Hythe Beds of the Lower Greensand formation; much of it lies above the 400 ft. contour, and it rises to 918 ft. in Blackdown Hill.

(1) *The Coastal Plain*

The coastal plain, between the Downs and the sea, widens westward from about Shoreham to a maximum of about 10 miles as the Hampshire border

---

[1] *V.C.H. Sussex*, I, pp. 383 and 407. The other mints were at Chichester, Hastings, Steyning and Winchelsea.

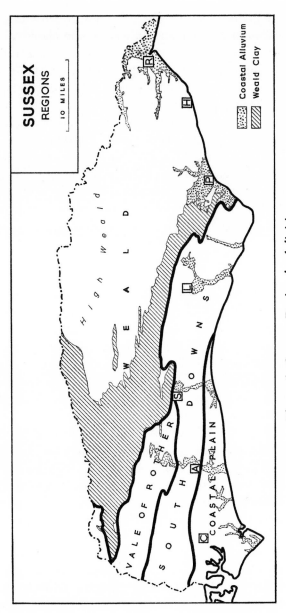

Fig. 136. Sussex: Regional subdivisions.

Domesday boroughs are indicated by initials: A, Arundel; C, Chichester; H, Hastings;
L, Lewes; P, Pevensey; R, Rye; S, Steyning.

is approached. Geologically, as indicated on Fig. 121, it is occupied by Valley Gravels and Brickearth. The fertility of the area has often been praised by eighteenth-century and later writers, and, in places, we might have expected higher densities of teams (2 to 6) and of population (7 to over 20) per square mile than appear on Figs. 124 and 126. On the other hand, we must remember that light soils have only become important agriculturally since the improvements of the eighteenth century, and that much of the plain had relatively few villages. Even so, the densities compare favourably with those of the greater part of England.

Most villages had meadow, but the amounts were small except in the alluvial valleys of the lower Adur, the lower Arun and around Pagham Harbour; the lower Adur valley, in particular, also had many salt-pans. Only about one-half of the villages of the area seem to have had mills. Surprisingly, wood was recorded for many villages, but we cannot be sure that it did not lie physically elsewhere.

(2) The South Downs

The South Downs extend from Beachy Head to the Hampshire border in a belt of about 4 to 6 miles wide. Much of this surface lies over 400 ft. above sea-level, and the northward-facing scarp is usually over 600 ft. and in places even over 800 ft. To the east of Steyning, the narrow scarp-foot zone has been included with the Downs themselves, but to the west, where the outcrop of Lower Greensand broadens, the scarp-foot zone has been included within the Vale of Rother. The belt of the South Downs is divided into separate tracts by the north-south valleys of the Arun, the Adur, the Ouse and the Cuckmere; and in the gaps formed by the first three valleys stood the boroughs of Arundel, Steyning and Lewes. The higher levels of the Downs are characterised by thin soils, but the lower slopes and the valley floors provide soils that are much more rewarding to the plough. Villages were numerous, especially in the valleys and along the scarp-foot zone of the northern edge. The densities of teams over the area as a whole rose up to 6, and those of population to over 20. We cannot say to what extent some of these ploughs and teams were really located in outliers in the Weald; but it does seem clear that the South Downs area must be regarded as among the most fertile districts in eleventh-century England. The alluvial valleys were marked by very substantial amounts of meadow, especially along the Ouse. The Arun valley had many fisheries, and there were also some along that of the

Ouse. Salt-pans, on the other hand, were to be found in the valleys of the Adur and the Ouse. Mills also were associated with the valley villages, but taking the areas as a whole there were many villages without mills. Most villages, on the other hand, had quantities of wood entered for them, but to what extent this really lay in the Weald to the north, we cannot say.

(3) The Vale of Rother

To the west of Steyning the Lower Greensand formation is broad enough to form a distinctive tract of appreciable size between the Downs and the Weald. Here, the Lower Greensand is composed of Sandgate Clays which yield easily-worked and rewarding loam soils. Here, too, is the alluvium of the western Rother which flows along the outcrop to join the Arun. It is not surprising that Figs. 125 and 127 show this to have been an area of frequent and sizeable villages; they lay not only near the Rother itself, but also to the south in a line along the scarp-foot zone below the Downs. It is difficult to calculate densities, because the unit areas stretch into the Weald Clay area, but obviously the prosperity of these Rother villages was reflected in the relatively high densities of the western units of the Weald (Figs. 124 and 126). To what extent the teams and population entered under the names of these villages were disposed in outliers on the Weald itself, we cannot say; but the numbers involved cannot have been great, and there is no doubt that the Rother valley was a fairly prosperous area. Almost all its villages had mills and moderate quantities of meadow; and some had fisheries. Most villages, too, had considerable amounts of wood entered for them, but we can only con-jecture where this was physically situated.

(4) The Weald

Three subdivisions are apparent within the general area of the Sussex Weald—the Weald Clay district, the so-called High Weald, and the eastern part of the Weald where it approaches the coast.

The Weald Clay outcrop is conspicuously devoid of place-names (Figs. 125 and 127). It is a flat plain, generally less than 100 ft. above sea-level, but rising to 200 ft. and more. Its soil is a stiff badly-drained clay or heavy loam which becomes very heavy when wet, and hard and cracked when dry. Locally there are variations, but the outcrop as a whole was uninviting to settlement, and the absence of villages is not surprising.

We can only surmise that much of the wood, entered under the names of villages to the south, was really here; much wood, too, may have gone unrecorded. We cannot be far wrong if we envisage it as a wooded area, with woods and swine pastures attached to settlements elsewhere, and with only occasional centres of cultivation.

Beyond the outcrop of the Weald Clay lies the High Weald, stretching to the northern border of the county. Here are the Hastings Beds which have stood resistant to erosion, and have formed an upland region dissected into narrow steep-sided valleys. Much of the area lies over 400 ft. above sea-level, and it reaches its highest point in Crowborough Beacon (792 ft). The Hastings Beds comprise three groups of strata: (1) Ashdown Sand, (2) Wadhurst Clay, and (3) Tunbridge Wells Sand. The interior of the High Weald is composed largely of the two sandstone formations that yield poor soil. In the eighteenth century the area was repeatedly described as a tract of waste, and here were the heaths of Ashdown Forest and St Leonard's Forest. We can only speculate about its condition in the eleventh century. How much was woodland, and how much heath or waste, we do not know. But there were some settlements here, and there are indications of colonising activity. The small villages of East Grinstead hundred, for example, had, apparently, once belonged to parent centres elsewhere;[1] but the densities of teams (below one) and of population (1 to 2) were still very low. To the east, in the northern part of the rape of Hastings, there are also indications of colonisation from parent centres;[2] and here, where there is much clay as well as sand, the densities were relatively high—2 to 3 for teams and 3 to 6 for population. That there were few mills here, and only small quantities of meadow, is to be expected; but it is surprising that so little wood was entered for the area.

There remains a third district where conditions were quite different; this is the south-eastern Weald, bordered by the sea-coast. This area is still within the outcrop of Hastings Beds, but the Wadhurst Clay division is important, and the juxtaposition of sands and clays, together with the lower elevation, provided a better basis for settlement and agricultural exploitation than did the High Weald. Villages were numerous, and the densities of teams (up to 5) and of population (up to 9) were quite high; the district had obviously recovered from the wasting associated with the campaign of Hastings. Almost every village had a small amount of

[1] See p. 426 above.　　　　　　　　[2] See p. 413 above.

meadow, and most villages had some wood; but there was only an occasional village with a mill. Along the coast there were salt-pans in or around both Walland Marsh and the Pevensey Levels. Finally, on the coast there were no fewer than three Domesday boroughs, Pevensey, Hastings and Rye.

BIBLIOGRAPHICAL NOTE

(1) The earliest published translation of the Sussex section of the Domesday Book is that of S. Henshall and J. Wilkinson in their *Domesday; or, an actual survey of South-Britain* (London, 1799), pp. 109–209. The intention of the translators was to cover both volumes of the Domesday Book in ten parts, but the only part published was that relating to Kent, Sussex and Surrey. The translation was a free one, and no attempt was made to identify the Sussex place-names. An early attempt at the identification of place-names is contained in T. W. Horsfield's *The history, antiquities and topography of the county of Sussex* (London, 1835), 2 vols. This also contains a table showing the hidage totals of the tenants-in-chief (1, p. 77).

(2) Extracts from the Latin text of the Domesday Inquest on the lands subject to the archbishop of Canterbury in Sussex were transcribed and translated in E. Roberts, 'On Mayfield, in Sussex', *Journ. Brit. Archaeol. Assoc.* XXIII (London, 1867), pp. 333–69; the transcriptions and translations are on pp. 335–8 and 341–2.

(3) A later translation, with a facsimile and extension of the Latin text, was edited by W. D. Parish for the Sussex Archaeological Society—*Domesday Book in relation to the county of Sussex* (Lewes, 1886). The work includes an index of tenants, an index of place-names, with notes and suggested identifications, and a glossary of words and phrases. A map of the county in colour shows place-names and the extent of the rapes; this was compiled by F. E. Sawyer, and was reproduced as the frontispiece to the second volume of P. E. Dove (ed.), *Domesday Studies*, 2 vols. (London, 1888–91).

(4) The standard translation now available is that prepared by L. F. Salzman in *V.C.H. Sussex* (London, 1905), I, pp. 387–451. This contains a valuable series of footnotes and identifications and is preceded by an introduction by J. H. Round and L. F. Salzman (pp. 351–85). For an earlier but undated list of identifications see F. E. Sawyer, *Index of names of places in Domesday Survey of Sussex* (?1880).

(5) The following deal with various aspects of the Domesday study of the county, and are arranged in chronological order:

M. A. LOWER, 'Observations on the landing of William the Conqueror, and subsequent events', *Sussex Archaeol. Collns*, II (London, 1849), pp. 53–7.

A. Hussey, *Notes on the churches in the counties of Kent, Sussex, and Surrey, mentioned in the Domesday Book* (London, 1852).

M. A. Lower, 'Notes on watermills and windmills in Sussex', *Sussex Archaeol. Collns*, v (London, 1852), pp. 267–76. This paper contains an interesting table of 'Mills in Sussex at the time of the Domesday Survey, 1086'.

F. E. Sawyer, 'The rapes and their origin', *Archaeol. Rev.* i (London, 1888), pp. 54–9. For comments on this by J. H. Round and H. H. Howorth, see *Archaeol. Rev.* i (London, 1888), pp. 229–30.

H. F. Napper, 'Notes on "Sussex Domesday studies"', *Sussex Archaeol. Collns*, XXXVI (Lewes, 1888), pp. 239–40.

F. E. Sawyer, 'The scope of local elucidation of the Domesday Survey' in P. E. Dove (ed.), *Domesday Studies*, II (London, 1891), pp. 447–57.

F. H. Baring, 'The Conqueror's footprints in Domesday', *Eng. Hist. Rev.* XIII (London, 1898), pp. 17–25. Reprinted 'with some additions and alterations' in F. H. Baring, *Domesday Tables for the counties of Surrey, Berkshire, Middlesex, Hertford, Buckingham and Bedford and for the New Forest* (London, 1909), pp. 207–16.

W. Hudson, 'The hundred of Eastbourne and its six "Boroughs"', *Sussex Archaeol. Collns*, XLII (Lewes, 1899), pp. 180–208.

J. H. Round, 'Note on the Sussex Domesday', *Sussex Archaeol. Collns*, XLIV (Lewes, 1901), pp. 140–3.

J. Tait, 'Large hides and small hides', *Eng. Hist. Rev.* XVII (London, 1902), pp. 280–2.

J. Tait, 'Hides and virgates at Battle Abbey', *Eng. Hist. Rev.* XVIII (London, 1903), pp. 705–8.

L. F. Salzman, 'Hides and virgates in Sussex', *Eng. Hist. Rev.* XIX (London, 1904), pp. 92–6.

J. Tait, 'Hides and virgates in Sussex', *Eng. Hist. Rev.* XIX (London, 1904), pp. 503–6.

E. Sayers, 'The manor of "Dentune"', *Sussex Archaeol. Collns*, L (Lewes, 1907), p. 176.

F. H. Baring, 'Hastings Castle 1050–1100, and the chapel of St Mary', *Sussex Archaeol. Collns*, LVII (Lewes, 1915), pp. 119–35.

W. Page, 'Some remarks on the churches of the Domesday Survey', *Archaeologia*, 2nd series, XVI (Oxford, 1915), pp. 61–102; the Sussex evidence is discussed on pp. 79–81.

L. F. Salzman, 'Some Sussex Domesday Tenants, I. Alvred Pincerna and his descendants', *Sussex Archaeol. Collns*, LVII (Lewes, 1915), pp. 162–79.

L. F. Salzman, 'Some Sussex Domesday Tenants, II. The Family of Dene', *Sussex Archaeol. Collns*, LVIII (Lewes, 1916), pp. 171–89.

J. H. Round, 'The early history of North and South Stoke', *Sussex Archaeol. Collns*, LIX (Lewes, 1918), pp. 1–24.

A. Anscombe, 'The Sussex place-names in Domesday Book which end in "-intun"', *Sussex Archaeol. Collns*, LIX (Lewes, 1918), pp. 76–83.

A. Anscombe, 'The names of the Sussex hundreds in Domesday Book', *Sussex Archaeol. Collns*, LX (Lewes, 1919), pp. 92–125.

E. Sayers, 'The acre equivalent of the Domesday hide', *Sussex Archaeol. Collns*, LXII (Cambridge, 1921), pp. 201–3.

L. F. Salzman, 'Sussex Domesday Tenants, III. William de Cahagnes and the Family of Keynes', *Sussex Archaeol. Collns*, LXIII (Cambridge, 1922), pp. 180–202.

W. D. Peckham, 'Two Domesday Book freeholds', *Sussex Notes and Queries*, II (Eastbourne, 1929), p. 17.

A. Anscombe, 'Segnescombe', *Sussex Notes and Queries*, II (Eastbourne, 1929), pp. 236–37.

Sir Charles Thomas-Stanford, 'Hove in Domesday and after', *Sussex Archaeol. Collns*, LXX (Cambridge, 1929), pp. 86–92.

J. E. A. Jolliffe, 'The Domesday hidation of Sussex and the rapes', *Eng. Hist. Rev.* XLV (London, 1930), pp. 427–35.

L. F. Salzman, 'The rapes of Sussex', *Sussex Archaeol. Collns*, LXXII (Cambridge, 1931), pp. 20–9.

D. K. Clarke, 'The Saxon hundreds of Sussex', *Sussex Archaeol. Collns*, LXXIV (Cambridge, 1933), pp. 214–25.

G. Ward, 'Some eleventh century references to Sussex', *Sussex Notes and Queries*, IV (Eastbourne, 1933), pp. 238–40.

G. Ward, 'A suggested identification of Berts', *Sussex Notes and Queries*, V (Lewes, 1934), pp. 111–12.

M. Hofmann, *Die Französierung des Personennamenschatzes im Domesday Book der Graftschaften Hampshire und Sussex* (Murnau, 1934).

L. F. Salzman, 'The lowey of Pevensey,' *Sussex Notes and Queries*, IX (Lewes, 1944), pp. 3–6.

L. Fleming, 'Pigs in Domesday Book', *Sussex Notes and Queries*, XI (Lewes, 1948), pp. 32 and 34.

W. Budgen, 'The acreage of the Sussex hide of land', *Sussex Notes and Queries*, XI (Lewes, 1948), pp. 73–7.

H. Poole, 'The Domesday Book churches of Sussex', *Sussex Archaeol. Collns*, LXXXVII (Oxford, 1948), pp. 28–76.

(6) Other works of interest to the Domesday study of the county (arranged in chronological order) are as follows:

A. Ballard, 'The Sussex coast line', *Sussex Archaeol. Collns*, LIII (Lewes, 1910), pp. 5–25.

W. HUDSON, 'The ancient deaneries of the diocese of Chichester, and their relation to the rapes of the county of Sussex', *Sussex Archaeol. Collns*, LV (Lewes, 1912), pp. 108–22; inset map, p. 116.

F.B ENTHAM STEVENS, 'The boundary between Sussex and Kent: (i) The Tunbridge Wells area', *Sussex Notes and Queries*, II (Eastbourne, 1929), pp. 10–14; (ii) 'The Lamberhurst area', *ibid.* II, pp. 38–41.

P. MAINWARING JOHNSTON, 'Poling, and the Knights Hospitallers', *Sussex Archaeol. Collns*, LX (Lewes, 1919), pp. 67–91.

E. M. YATES, 'Medieval assessments in north-west Sussex', *Institute of British Geographers, Transactions and Papers*, 1954 (London, 1954), Publication No. 20, pp. 75–92.

L. F. SALZMAN, 'Early taxation in Sussex, Part I', *Sussex Archaeol. Collns*, XCVIII (Haywards Heath, 1960), pp. 29–43.

(7) A. Mawer and F. M. Stenton with the assistance of J. E. B. Gover, *The Place-Names of Sussex*, 2 vols. (Cambridge, 1929–30), is the authoritative study of the place-names of the county. This has superseded the earlier work of R. G. Roberts, *The Place-Names of Sussex* (Cambridge, 1914).

CHAPTER X

KENT

BY EILA M. J. CAMPBELL, M.A.

The description of Kent, with which the Domesday Book opens, is of unusual interest for a variety of reasons. One is that the assessment of the county was unlike that of anywhere else in England. Another is the fact that a great part of the Weald, with its peculiar economy, lay within the county. Yet another reason is the existence, for a number of holdings, of two other compilations derived from the original returns. One of these, conveniently called the Excerpta, is concerned with the lands held or claimed by the abbey of St Augustine at Canterbury together with a number of other estates. The manuscript is a thirteenth-century copy of 'a copy made between 1100 and 1154 (or possibly 1124)'.[1] The other is the so-called Domesday Monachorum, a composite document which includes a variety of information about the churches of eastern Kent and a survey of the estates in Kent belonging to the archbishop of Canterbury and certain other landowners.[2] This portion of the manuscript appears to be a copy made 'about the year 1100'. In both documents, the entries are concerned mainly with assessments and values, and are not as full as those in the Domesday Book itself. All three records include corresponding entries for a few estates.

Detailed collation of these texts raises many points of interest. Generally speaking, the entries in the subsidiary documents pay more attention to local detail than does the Domesday text. Their summary nature means, however, that they hardly ever provide additional information about the

---

[1] The MS. forms part of the Cartulary of St Augustine's Abbey. Its title runs: *Exce(r)pta de compoto solingorum comitatus cancie secundum cartam regis videlicet ea quae ad ecclesiam sancti Augustini pertinent et est in regis domesday.* For the text, with an introduction, see A. Ballard (ed.), *An Eleventh-Century Inquisition of St Augustine's, Canterbury* (British Academy, London, 1920).

[2] This has been edited with an introduction by D. C. Douglas—*The Domesday Monachorum of Christ Church, Canterbury* (Royal Historical Society, London, 1944). There is also a translation with a brief introduction by Nellie Neilson in *V.C.H. Kent*, III (London, 1932), pp. 253–69.

resources of a holding. Even so, they are of great geographical interest for one very important reason. They contain a very large number of place-names not found in the Domesday folios, where, presumably, the information relating to eleventh-century resources is compressed under a more limited range of place-names. Thus these subsidiary documents help us in our attempt to obtain a realistic picture of Domesday conditions.

Not only do the subsidiary documents indicate some of the limitations and imperfections of the Domesday Book, but the Domesday folios themselves frequently bear witness to the human element in their assembling. In as many as ninety-two entries, the formula *Terra est* is followed by a blank space into which a figure was never inserted. These and other imperfections are noted on the appropriate pages below.

This study has been written mainly in terms of the early nineteenth-century county of Kent, which was not identical with the Domesday county. It is possible that in 1086 the boundary between Kent and Sussex, running through Andredesweald, was indefinite. There are two, and possibly three, references in the Kent folios to holdings in Sussex. On fo. 10b we read that the bishop of Bayeux added to the manor of Bilsington three denes which had remained outside the 'division' of the count of Eu (*In hoc manerio misit episcopus iii denas quae remanserunt extra divisonem comitis de Ow*); the count of Eu was a Sussex tenant-in-chief who held no land in Kent. Then again the entry for Leeds (*Esledes, 7b*) tells us that the 'count of Eu has 4 denes of this manor' (*Comes de Ow habet iiii denas de isto manerio*), but does not indicate where they were.[1] The corresponding statement in the Excerpta, however, explains that the denes were in Sussex (*Item de eodem manerio tenet comes Robertus de eu iiii dennas silvarum in Suthsexa*).[2] Thirdly, it is possible that the unidentified *Merclesham* (2) of the Kent folios may refer to Methersham, a locality on the Sussex side of the River Rother, in the parish of Beckley.[3] There were a few nineteenth-century modifications along the Kent-Sussex border: Broadwater Down was transferred to Kent in 1894, and, in the following year, the Sussex portion of Lamberhurst was given to Kent, and the Kent

[1] G. Ward suggested that these 4 denes were entered as 4 virgates in the Sussex folios under the names *Ellede* (18b) and *Eslede* (18b, 19)—'Some eleventh century references to Sussex', *Sussex Notes and Queries*, IV (Eastbourne, 1933), p. 238. *Ellede* and *Eslede* have, in the present analysis, been identified with Eyelid in Ewhurst, Sussex.   [2] A. Ballard, *op. cit.* p. 2.

[3] G. Ward, *art. cit.* p. 239. We are given no details for *Merclesham*; it is named incidentally in a claim of the canons of St Martin of Dover, set out on fo. 2.

portion of Broomhill to Sussex;[1] none of these three villages is named in the Domesday folios for either county. In the north-west, along the border with Surrey, there was no significant change until 1889, when certain parishes were detached to form part of the administrative county of London.[2] The Essex folios include an entry for *Gravesanda* (vol. II, fo. 26 b), but we cannot tell whether or not it refers to Gravesend in Kent; there is separate mention of Gravesend (*Gravesham*, 7 b) in the Kent folios.

The coastline of Domesday Kent was not what we know to-day. On the one hand, there have been substantial gains from the sea. Thus much of Wantsum Strait, between the Isle of Thanet and the mainland, seems to have been reclaimed since the eleventh century.[3] There have also been gains along Thames-side and in Romney Marsh. On the other hand, there have been losses. Parts of some coastal villages have been eroded away, e.g. Hougham near Dover and Seasalter.[4]

One feature of Kent, as of Sussex, was the presence of an intermediate unit—the lathe or lest—between the county and the hundred.[5] The folios for Kent mention five lathes (*lests*) and two half-lathes, but the Domesday Monachorum speaks also of Sandwich as 'a lathe and a hundred in itself' (*est laeth et hundretus in seipso*).[6] Within the lathes came the hundreds, and these numbered sixty-two, ranging in size from Washlingstone with but one 'yoke' to Hoo with 61½ sulungs, or 246 'yokes'; some of the hundreds of later time had not yet appeared, particularly in the Weald.[7] It is not always possible to be precise about the components of each lathe because the Domesday scribe sometimes omitted to give the name of the lathe in which a hundred lay. For this reason, and also because it uses modern parish boundaries, a map such as Fig. 137 can only be conjectural,

[1] F. Bentham Stevens, 'The boundary between Sussex and Kent', *Sussex Notes and Queries*, II (Eastbourne, 1929), pp. 10–14, 38–41.

[2] It is possible that an early post-Domesday change took place along the Kent-Surrey border—see p. 364 above. Since 1889 there have been adjustments along the Kent-Surrey boundary, e.g. Penge was transferred to Kent in 1900.

[3] See (1) G. P. Walker, 'The lost Wantsum channel', *Archaeol. Cant.* XXXIX (London, 1927), pp. 91–111; (2) F. W. Hardman and W. P. D. Stebbing, 'Stonar and the Wantsum channel', *ibid.* LIII (1940), pp. 62–80; LIV (1941), pp. 41–55.

[4] For a general discussion of changes in the coastline of the county, see J. A. Steers, *The Coastline of England and Wales* (Cambridge, 1946), pp. 318–42; 399–402.

[5] J. E. A. Jolliffe, *Pre-Feudal England: The Jutes* (Oxford, 1933), pp. 39–72.

[6] D. C. Douglas, *op. cit.* p. 89. The Domesday text describes Sandwich (3) merely as lying in a hundred of its own (*Sandwice iacet in suo proprio hundredo*).

[7] O. S. Anderson, *The English Hundred-Names: The south-eastern counties* (Lund and Leipzig, 1939), pp. 109–50.

but it does serve to indicate the disposition of the lathes in relation to one another.[1]

One feature of the Kent folios is the frequent reference to the *leuua*, *leuga* or, in English, the lowy of Richard of Tonbridge. The lowy was in effect nothing other than the local fief of Richard, but the term continued to be applied to the district around Tonbridge until recent times.[2] Another example of the Domesday use of the term is in the *Leuga S. Wilfridi* (303 b)

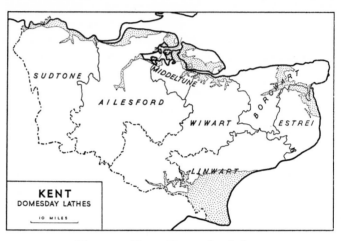

Fig. 137. Kent: Domesday lathes.

The boundaries of the lathes follow parish boundaries of the nineteenth century; boundaries in the Weald are pecked to indicate that they are even more conjectural than those in the north of the county. Areas of coastal alluvium, blown sand and shingle are shown (see Fig. 140).

---

[1] Two other reconstructions of the Domesday lathes are: (1) J. E. A. Jolliffe, 'The hidation of Kent', *Eng. Hist. Rev.* XLIV (London, 1929), pp. 612–18; (2) N. Neilson in *V.C.H. Kent*, III, pp. 179–81. They are not identical, but agree in the main.

[2] For an account of the term, see E. Hasted, *The History and Topographical Survey of Kent*, I (Canterbury, 1782), p. 308: 'It was antiently the custom in Normandy, to term the district round an abbey, castle, or chief mansion, *leuca* or *leucata*, in English the lowy, in which the possessor had generally a grant of several peculiar liberties, privileges and exemptions.

When Richard Fitz-Gislebert (who came into England with the Conqueror), had possessed himself of the manor and castle of Tunbridge, in exchange with the archbishop [of Canterbury] for other lands in Normandy, he procured a grant of several liberties and exemptions to it, as well as to his adjoining manor of Hadlow, probably the same as those he enjoyed with his possessions there, after the example of which he called this district round his manor and castle, the *lowy of Tunbridge*, by which name it has been called ever since.' See also *V.C.H. Kent*, III, p. 190.

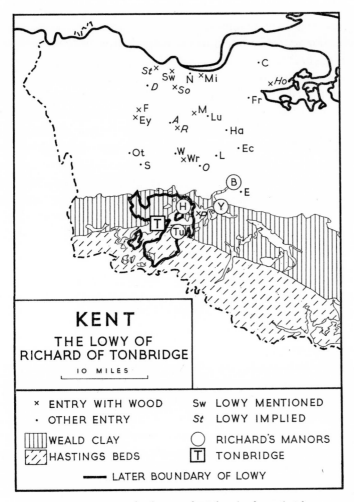

Fig. 138. Kent: The lowy of Richard of Tonbridge.

The later boundary of the lowy is taken from W. V. Dumbreck, 'The lowy of Tonbridge', *Archaeol. Cant.* LXXII (Ashford, 1959), p. 146. Richard's four manors were:
B, Barming; H, Hadlow; Tu, Tudeley; Y, Yalding.

The other holdings were: *A*, Ash; C, Cooling; *D*, Darenth; E, East Farleigh; Ec,
Eccles; Ey, Eynsford; F, Farningham; Fr, Frindsbury; Ha, Halling; *Ho*, Hoo; L,
Leybourne; Lu, Luddesdown; M, Meopham; Mi, Milton near Gravesend; N, North-
fleet; *O*, Offham; Ot, Otford; *P*, Peckham; *R*, Ridley; S, Seal; *So*, Southfleet;
St, Stone near Dartford; Sw, Swanscombe; W, Wrotham; Wr, Wrotham Heath.
Note that the Domesday entry for Darenth does not mention Richard of Tonbridge—
see p. 488 n. below.

of the Yorkshire folios. There is, incidentally, no account of Tonbridge and its castle in the Domesday Book, but an entry in the Domesday Monachorum probably refers to the castle.[1] Richard held Barming (14) and Yalding (14) from the king, and Hadlow (7b) and Tudeley (7b) from the bishop of Bayeux. But descriptions of many other estates contain clauses to the effect that 'what Richard of Tonbridge has in his lowy is worth' a sum of money or, maybe, a swine render; the word lowy is not always mentioned, but it seems to be implied. Once, in the account of Ridley (6), Richard is said to hold a dene of wood. This and the frequent reference to wood suggests that the lowy was composed of the outlying Wealden estates of manors themselves situated to the north of Tonbridge (Fig. 138). They had, apparently, been detached from their parent centres in order to create a compact territory or lowy around Richard's castle.[2]

SETTLEMENTS AND THEIR DISTRIBUTION

The total number of separate places mentioned in the Domesday Book for the area included in the nineteenth-century county of Kent seems to be 347,[3] including the eight boroughs—Canterbury, Dover, Fordwich, Hythe, Rochester, Romney, Sandwich and Seasalter. This figure cannot accurately reflect the total number of separate settlements in the county in 1086. In the first place, when two or more adjoining villages bear the same surname today, it is not always clear whether more than one unit existed in 1086. Thus there is no indication that, say, the East and West Peckham of today existed as separate villages; the Domesday information about them is entered under only one name (Pecheham, 4b, 7b), though they may well have been separate settlements in the eleventh century.[4]

---

[1] D. C. Douglas, op. cit. p. 88. The account of Darenth says that Richard has 10s. from it within his castelry (Et x solidos habet inde Ricardus infra castellum suum). The Domesday entry for Darenth (3) makes no mention of this.

[2] A recent discussion of the lowy is that by W. V. Dumbreck—'The lowy of Tonbridge', Archaeol. Cant. LXXII (Ashford, 1959), pp. 138–47.

[3] This total excludes terra Sophis (i.e. the land of Sophis, 1) from which the king had 12d for 'one inward' (pro uno Ineuuardo). It also excludes Scape (? Sheppey, 4b), and the six anonymous holdings described as 'in the Marsh of Romney' (in Maresch de Romenel, 13 sexiens); Maresc (10b, 11) has been identified with Denge Marsh Farm and has been counted in the total of 347.

[4] The Textus Roffensis (see p. 495) distinguishes between them—Eastpecham and Westpecham; in the present analysis they have been counted only once in the total of 347. For the history of these names, and of other names mentioned in this chapter, see: (1) J. K. Wallenberg, The Place-Names of Kent (Uppsala, 1934); (2) idem, Kentish

The same applies, for example, to the two Bournes in Bridge hundred (9 *bis*, 12), the two Hardres (9 *bis*, 9b), and the two Mallings (3, 5b).[1] For some counties the Domesday Book tells us specifically that there was a second settlement in 1086 by designating one unit as, say, *magna*, and the other *parva*. Something similar occasionally occurs in the folios for Kent. Thus *Broteham* (3) and *Litelbroteham* (8b) are represented today by Wrotham and its hamlet Wrotham Heath, and *Eslinges* (10b) and *Nordeslinge* (10) have become Eastling and its hamlet North Eastling. *Estselve* (8 *bis*) and *Westselve* (8) have survived as two hamlets, Old Shelve and New Shelve in Lenham. Or again, *Estefort* (13) and *Alia Essetesford* (13) have become South Ashford and Ashford, both now in the same parish.[2] *Certh* (5) and *Litelcert* (5) are today Great Chart and Little Chart, but they are not quite comparable with the others because they are rubricated under different hundreds in the Kent folios, and the modern parishes are separated by Hothfield, which is itself recorded in the Domesday Monachorum.[3] Similarly the two Farleighs (*Ferlaga*, *bis*) were rubricated under different hundreds—East Farleigh under Maidstone hundred (4b) and West Farleigh under Twyford (8b)—and they have been counted as separate settlements in the present analysis.

Then again, other names in the Kent folios seem to have covered more

Place-Names (Uppsala, 1931); (3) E. Ekwall, *The Concise Oxford Dictionary of English Place-Names* (Oxford, 4th ed., 1960).

[1] Bekesbourne, Patrixbourne; Upper Hardres, Lower Hardres; East Malling, West Malling. That the names *Borne* (*bis*)/*Burnes*, *Hardes* (*ter*), and *Metlinges*/*Mellingetes* may each have covered more than one settlement apiece is suggested by the fact that the relevant Domesday entries seem to record two churches for each pair. On the other hand, the Domesday Monachorum mentions two churches for *Burna* (*bis*), i.e. Bekesbourne and Patrixbourne, but only one for *Hardan*, i.e. Hardres. It does not record a church at Malling.

[2] There are also the Crays; today four places bear the surname Cray: Foots Cray, North Cray, St Mary *alias* South Cray and St Paul's Cray. In the present analysis the Domesday *Crai* or *Craie* (6b *bis*) has been identified with Foots Cray, *alia Craie* (6b) with St Paul's Cray, and *Sudcrai* (6b) with St Mary Cray. North Cray is not named in the Domesday Book, but the Textus Roffensis records *Northcraei* in addition to *Rodulfes craei* (i.e. St Paul's Cray), and *Fortescraei* (i.e. Foots Cray); the modern parish of North Cray contains the Domesday *Rochelei* (i.e. Ruxley, 6b). The Domesday *Sentlinge* (i.e. Sandlings, 7) is in St Mary Cray.

Among a list of names on fo. 1 there is reference to *Bocheland et aliud Bocheland et tercium Bocheland*. They occur in a context that suggests they may refer to the three *Bocheland* holdings described on fos. 10–10b. All three have been identified with the single vill of Buckland in Faversham hundred.

[3] See D. C. Douglas, *op. cit.* p. 77.

than one settlement apiece. Thus the 7 sulungs entered under Littlebourne
(12) in the Domesday Book were later attributed to Littlebourne and
Stodmarsh. Stodmarsh goes unrecorded in the Kent folios. Similarly, the
Domesday entry for Langport (12) mentions an anonymous holding of
one yoke lying in another hundred, which is later described as 'another

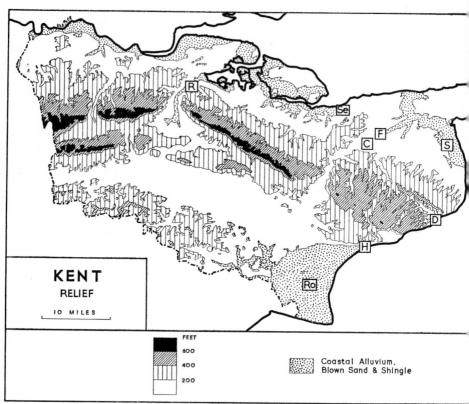

Fig. 139. Kent: Relief.

Domesday boroughs are indicated by initials: C, Canterbury; D, Dover; F, Fordwich;
H, Hythe; R, Rochester; Ro, Romney; S, Sandwich; Se, Seasalter.

yoke in another hundred, called Merton'. Merton, like Stodmarsh, is
unnamed in the Kent folios.[1] To these examples of Domesday names
covering more than one settlement must be added the large composite

[1] These details are included in a list of properties in the White Book of St Augustine's
Abbey—P.R.O. Exchequer Misc. Books (K.R.), no. 27, fo. 15.

manors, for example Adisham (5), Folkestone (9b), Hoo (8b), Maidstone (3), Westgate (3b) and Wrotham (3) which other evidence shows included more than one locality each in 1086. With these must be included the several unnamed holdings in the Weald which were attached to parent centres elsewhere, e.g. the subsidiaries of Milton Regis (2b).[1]

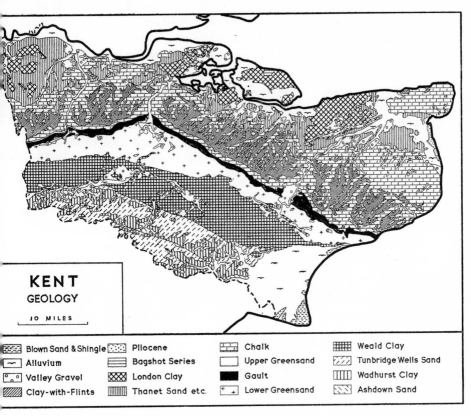

Fig. 140. Kent: Surface Geology.

Based on Geological Survey One-Inch Sheets (New Series)
270–4, 287–8, 290; (Old Series) 3–6.

The total of 347 includes about 20 places regarding which very little information is given; the record may be incomplete or the details may have been included with those of another place. As we have already noted,

[1] See p. 532 below.

there is no account of Tonbridge in the Domesday Book, although the lowy of Richard of Tonbridge is frequently mentioned. We also hear only indirectly of Woolwich; on fo. 14, a brief entry records a holding of 63 acres worth £3 pertaining to Woolwich (*pertinent in Hulviʒ*), but tells us only that there were 12 bordars at the holding paying 41*d*. Then again, all we hear of Barfreston (9b) is that there was a holding of one yoke worth 10*s*. where a poor woman was paying 3½*d*. (*Ibi una paupercula mulier reddit iii denarios et unum obulum*). At Rooting (12) there was a plough-team at work on the demesne, but we are not told who worked it. Or again, the entry for Tudeley (7b) tells of a demesne team, of wood and even of a church, but says nothing about population. Of Hemsted (11b) we hear little more than that there was a villein paying 30*d*.,[1] and of Swetton (14) that there was a bordar paying 12*d*. The entries for six holdings which seem to be rubricated under Somerden hundred on fo. 11b also give us but little information.[2] On the other hand, we are specifically told of a holding at Tottington (7) that 'there was nothing there except 2 acres of meadow' (*ibi nil est nisi ii acrae prati*).[3] We hear incidentally only of pasture (*De pastura*) at Mederclive (2) and of a pasture (*una pastura*) at the unidentified *Scortebroc* (2). Then there are other names which appear on one occasion only—e.g. *Aisiholte* (1b), *Brisewei* (1), *Gara* (1), Harty (1), Hawkhurst (2), *Jaonei* (13b), *Merclesham* (2), *Northburg* (1), *Oslachintone* (1), Penenden (1) and Ripe (2)—and we seem to be told nothing at all about the localities which they represent; most of them appear only in the list of forfeitures set out on fo. 1.

Not all the Domesday names appear on the present-day map of Kent villages. Some are represented by hamlets, by individual houses and farms, or even by the names of topographical features. Thus Crofton (7) is now a hamlet in Orpington, and Hawley (2b, 6) is another in Sutton at Hone. *Popeselle* or *Popessale* (9b *bis*) is represented by the site of Ponshall House in Coldred. *Tevegate* (14) survives as the name of Evegate Manor, a farm in Smeeth, and *Esmerefel* (12) as the name of Ashenfield Farm in Waltham. *Platenovt* (12b) is represented by Wadholt Wood in Coldred. The site of the Domesday *Midelea* (11b) may be indicated to-day by the ruins of a church near Midley House in the parish of Old Romney;

---

[1] *vel x solidos* is interlined in the MS.
[2] See p. 531 below.
[3] This entry follows the main account of Tottington which also mentions meadow, as well as other resources.

Midley itself survived as the name of a parish until the present century. These are but some of the changes in the villages of Kent. To them must be added a number of unidentified names, e.g. *Cildresham/Schildricheham* (10, 1), *Essella* (13) and *Scortebroc* (2).[1] Whether these will yet be located, or whether the places they represent have completely disappeared leaving no record or trace behind, we cannot say.

On the other hand, some villages on the modern map are not mentioned in the Domesday Book. A few of these missing names seem to date from pre-Domesday times. Thus Garlinge occurs in a charter of the ninth century but it does not reappear until 1254. Other names missing from the Domesday record do not make their first appearance until the twelfth and thirteenth centuries, or even later, and presumably, if they existed in 1086, they are accounted for under the statistics of other settlements. Thus, so far as record goes, Knockholt was first mentioned in 1197, Bredhurst in 1240, and Downe in 1283. On the other hand, many of the place-names that go unrecorded in the Domesday folios must have been in existence in the eleventh century because they are named in the subsidiary documents relating to Domesday Kent. Thus, the Excerpta shows that the Domesday Chislet (12), assessed at 12 sulungs, included a holding of six sulungs at Margate (*sex ad margate*),[2] a place that is not recorded by name in the Kent folios. Or, again, an entry for Langport, rubricated under Stowting hundred in the Domesday Book (12b), tells of a holding of 2 sulungs and 1 yoke; the corresponding entry in the Excerpta does not mention Langport, but says that in the hundred of Stowting the abbot of St Augustine's held *elmestede* (i.e. Elmsted) and *hortune* (i.e. Monks

---

[1] The full list of Domesday place-names in Kent that have not been located in the present analysis is: *Aia* (13b), *Afettune* (10b), *Aisiholte* (1b), *Belice* (9b, 13), *Bochelande* in Stowting hundred (9b), *Brisewei* (1), *Cildresham/Schildricheham* (10, 1), *Darenden* in Wye hundred (12), *Eddintone* (6), *Essella* (13), *Gara* (1), *Goslaches* (1), *Jaonei* (13b), *Leveberge* (11 *bis*), *Merclesham* (2), *Northburg* (1), *Oslachintone* (1), *Scortebroc* (2), *Siborne* (13b), and *Soninges* (6). In addition there is *terra Sophis* (1) but it has not been included in the total of 347 places; see p. 488 above. G. Ward has shown that *Aisiholte* may be a variant of *Haeselholte* in the Textus Roffensis or *Haslo* in the Domesday Monachorum; if this is so, then it equates with *Haslow* (i.e. Hadlow, 7b), but we cannot be certain; see G. Ward, 'The list of Saxon churches in the Textus Roffensis', *Archaeol. Cant.* XLIV (London, 1932), pp. 47–9.

The figures for the six holdings 'in the Marsh of Romney' (13) have been totalled and plotted as open circles on Figs. 146 and 148 below. The figures for *in Scape* (? in Sheppey, 4b) have also been plotted as open circles, as have those for the unlocated holdings in Somerden hundred (11b); for a discussion of the latter, see p. 531 below.

[2] A. Ballard, *op. cit.* pp. xxi and 17.

Horton);[1] Elmsted is not elsewhere recorded in the Domesday folios, but there is an entry for another holding in Horton on fo. 13b. The Excerpta also adds to the Domesday record the names *Est monigham* (? Little Mongeham), *Ryple* (i.e. Ripple in Cornilo hundred) and *Walemere* (i.e. Walmer), but it omits the Domesday *Platenovt* (i.e. Wadholt).[2] The survey of the Canterbury estates in the Domesday Monachorum also adds some new names. Here are the corresponding entries for Northwood:

(1) *Domesday Book* (3b): Of this manor Vitalis holds of the archbishop 3 sulungs and 1 yoke and 12 acres of land, and there he has 5 plough-teams and 29 bordars and 5 serfs and 7 salt-pans yielding 25s. 4d. There is a church and 1 small dene of wood. In all it is worth £14. 6s. 6d.

(2) *Domesday Monachorum:*[3] Of these sulungs Vitalis of Canterbury has 1 sulung and 1 yoke, and in Thanet a sulung and a half, and also in *Macebroc* he has 12 acres and half a sulung from the archbishop. And *Ezilamerth* and all this land is valued at £14. 6s. 6d.

Neither *Macebroc* (possibly the lost Makinbrooke in Herne) nor *Ezilamerth* (probably Stourmouth)[4] is mentioned in the Domesday folios. In a similar way the Monachorum account of Adisham mentions Eythorne,[5] also unnamed in the Domesday version (5).[6]

But the main body of new names comes from the lists of churches in the Domesday Monachorum; and as the lists date from 'about the year 1100' we are safe in thinking that the settlements must have been in existence in 1086. These lists of churches refer to those making payments to Christchurch, Canterbury, and so are mainly in the eastern half of the county.[7] But there also survives an early list of churches in the bishopric

---

[1] A. Ballard, *op. cit.* pp. xxi and 30.

[2] See *ibid.* pp. v and 22–3. Other seemingly 'new' names in the Excerpta are but variations on the Domesday spellings; thus the Domesday *Brisewei* (1) and *Northburg* (1) are represented in the Excerpta by *brissegneia* and *Northbreche*; see *ibid.* pp. 32–3.

[3] D. C. Douglas, *op. cit.* p. 84.

[4] But note that Stourmouth is represented elsewhere in the Domesday Monachorum by *Sturmude*; see D. C. Douglas, *op. cit.* pp. 17, 57, 77.

[5] D. C. Douglas, *op. cit.* pp. 89–90.

[6] The other additional names recorded in the Monachorum account of the Canterbury estates are *Broke/Broc* (i.e. Brook), *Cassetuisle* (i.e. Castweazel), *Ordgareswice* (i.e. Orgarswick), *Pette* (i.e. Pett), *Suurtling* (i.e. Swarling), *Tenitune* (i.e. Thanington) and the unidentified *Eadruneland*, *Sturtune* and *Wic*.

[7] For a discussion of the significance of the lists, see D. C. Douglas, *op. cit.* pp. 5–15. See also: G. Ward, 'The lists of Saxon churches in the Domesday Monachorum, and the White Book of St Augustine', *Archaeol. Cant.* XLV (London, 1933), pp. 60–89.

of Rochester in the west—the so-called Textus Roffensis. This list seems to refer to pre-Norman churches,[1] but whether this is so or not, the document itself has been ascribed to the decade 1140–1150,[2] and it seems likely therefore that the places it names were in existence some sixty or so years earlier.

The additional names have been set out on pp. 498–9; they number about 150[3] as compared with the 347 Domesday names[4] and they form a remarkable supplement to the Domesday evidence. The many names in the Weald are striking, but we must note that there is also a general scatter of non-Domesday names beyond its margins. This evidence is reminiscent of that of the Lindsey Survey (1115–18)[5] and of the Leicestershire Survey (1124–29).[6] That additional names are more numerous in Kent is not surprising, for here is a countryside of hamlets. These small scattered settlements may have escaped mention in any summary more easily than the larger and nucleated villages of Lindsey and Leicestershire. What this body of information does is to give us a more realistic picture of the settlement pattern in the eleventh-century county than that furnished by the Domesday Book alone (Figs. 143, 144).

The essential feature of the distribution of Domesday place-names is the contrast between the relatively closely-settled north and east and the sparsely settled south. On Fig. 144, the Weald stands out as an empty area almost devoid of Domesday names. The few Wealden names recorded in the Kent folios relate to villages in the Medway valley and along the inner margin of Romney Marsh. But Fig. 143 supplements the picture of the eleventh-century settlement pattern supplied by the evidence of the Domesday Book alone, and reminds us that there were many small

[1] The list of churches is printed in T. Hearne (ed.), *Textus Roffensis* (Oxford, 1720), pp. 228–31. See also: G. Ward, 'The list of Saxon churches in the Textus Roffensis', *Archaeol. Cant.* XLIV, pp. 39–59.

[2] F. Liebermann, 'Notes on the Textus Roffensis', *Archaeol. Cant.* XXIII (London, 1898), p. 103.

[3] This number excludes the unidentified *Cap. Anfridi* and *Cay. Ho.* in the Textus Roffensis, because it is not certain that they were names of places.

[4] It must be recalled that this number excludes the Domesday *Scape* (? Sheppey) and the *Marescus de Romenel* (i.e. Romney Marsh).

[5] C. W. Foster and T. Longley (eds.), *The Lincolnshire Domesday and the Lindsey Survey* (Lincoln Record Society, 1924). This contains an introduction by Sir Frank Stenton (pp. ix–xlvi), appendices of extinct villages by C. W. Foster (pp. xlvii–lxxxvii), and a map of the additional place-names provided by the Lindsey Survey.

[6] D. Holly in H. C. Darby and I. B. Terrett (eds.), *The Domesday Geography of Midland England* (Cambridge, 1954), pp. 309, 316–17, and fig. 106 (p. 310).

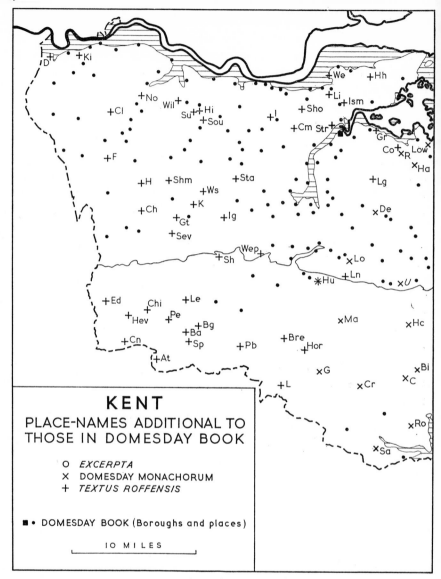

KENT

PLACE-NAMES ADDITIONAL TO THOSE IN DOMESDAY BOOK

O   *EXCERPTA*
X   DOMESDAY MONACHORUM
+   *TEXTUS ROFFENSIS*

■ • DOMESDAY BOOK (Boroughs and places)

10 MILES

Fig. 141. Western Kent: Eleventh-century place-names additional
to those in Domesday Book.

For the key to the initials, see pp. 498–9. Initials in italics indicate uncertain identifications. Note that Hunton occurs in both the Domesday Monachorum and the
Textus Roffensis. Areas of coastal alluvium, blown sand and shingle, and also the
northern boundary of Weald Clay, are shown (see Fig. 140).

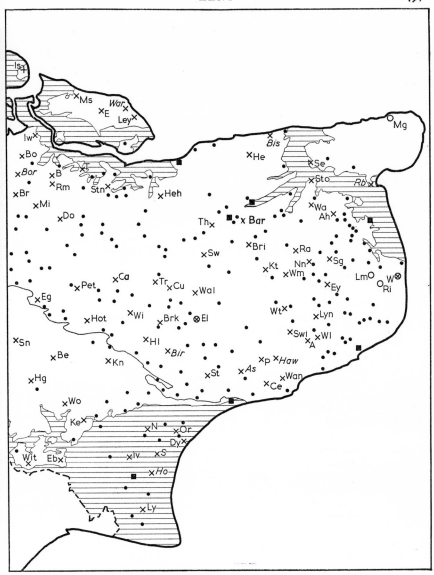

Fig. 142. Eastern Kent: Eleventh-century place-names additional to those in Domesday Book.

For the key to the initials, see pp. 498–9. Initials in italics indicate uncertain identifications. Note that Elmsted and Walmer occur in both the Excerpta and the Domesday Monachorum. Areas of coastal alluvium, blown sand and shingle, and also the northern boundary of Weald Clay, are shown (see Fig. 140).

Eleventh-century Place-names Additional to Those in Domesday Book

A. From the Excerpta

See A. Ballard (ed.), *An Eleventh-Century Inquisition of St Augustine's, Canterbury* (British Academy, London, 1920).

El	Elmsted		Mg	Margate
Lm	Little Mongeham (*Est monigham*)		Ri	Ripple
			W	Walmer

B. From the Domesday Monachorum

See (i) D. C. Douglas (ed.), *The Domesday Monachorum of Christ Church, Canterbury* (Royal Historical Society, London, 1944); (ii) G. Ward, 'The lists of Saxon churches in the Domesday Monachorum and the White Book of St Augustine', *Archaeol. Cant.* XLV (London, 1933), pp. 60–89.

A	Alkham		Hl	Hinxhill
Ah	Ash by Wingham		*Ho*	*Mertumnescirce* (? Hope All Saints)
As	*Achalt* (? Asholt)			
B	Bapchild		Hot	Hothfield
Bar	Barton (in Canterbury)		Hu	Hunton
Be	Bethersden		Iv	Ivychurch
Bi	Biddenden		Iw	Iwade
Bir	*Birichalt* (? Bircholt)		Ke	Kenardington
Bis	*Biscopestune* (? Bishopstone)		Kn	Kingsnorth
Bo	Bobbing		Kt	Kingston (*alia Berham*)
Bor	*Nipecryce* (? Borden)		Ley	Leysdown
Br	Bredgar		Lo	Loose
Bri	Bridge		Low	Lower Halstow
Brk	Brook		Ly	Lydd
C	Castweazel		Lyn	Lydden
Ca	Challock		Ma	Marden
Ce	Cheriton		Mi	Milsted
Cr	Cranbrook		Ms	Minster (*Sexburgamynster*)
Cu	Crundale		N	Newchurch
De	Detling		Nn	Nonington
Do	Doddington		O	Orgarswick
Dy	Dymchurch		P	Paddlesworth (in Lyminge)
E	Eastchurch		Pet	Pett (in Charing)
Eb	Ebony Isle		R	Rainham
Eg	Egerton		Ra	Ratling
El	Elmsted		*Rb*	*Raette* (? in Richborough)
Ey	Eythorne		Rm	Rodmersham
G	Goudhurst		Rn	Rolvenden
Ha	Hartlip		*S*	*Sipoldescirce* (? St Mary in the Marsh)
Haw	*Apoluescyrce* (? Hawkinge)			
Hc	Headcorn		Sa	Sandhurst
He	Herne		Se	Sarre
Heh	Hernehill		Sg	Shingleton (near Nonington)
Hg	High Halden		Sn	Smarden

St	Stanford	Wal	Waltham
Stn	Stone by Faversham	Wan	Walton
Sto	Stourmouth	*War*	*Norðcip* (? Warden)
Sw	Swarling	Wi	Wilmington (in Boughton
Swi	Swingfield		Aluph)
T	Teynham	Wit	Wittersham
Th	Thanington	Wl	Wolverton
Tr	Trimworth	Wm	Womenswold
U	*Delcumepeg* (? Ulcombe Way)	Wo	Woodchurch
W	Walmer	Wt	Wootton
Wa	Walmestone		

The following names are unidentified: *Bellinge, Bilicean, Bracheshala, Brixiestun, Burgericestune, Eadredestun, Eadruneland, Eastweald, Eiscedene, Eiselle, Emmetune, Endleueberga, Hyruuerthestun, Macebroc, Sturtune, Westtune, Wic, Wyttunemersc.*

C. *From the Textus Roffensis*

See: G. Ward, 'The list of Saxon churches in the Textus Roffensis', *Archaeol. Cant.* (London, 1932), XLIV, pp. 35–59.

At	Ashurst	Ism	Islingham
Ba	Barden	K	Kemsing
Bg	Bidborough	Ki	Kidbrook
Bre	Brenchley	L	Lamberhurst
Ch	Chevening	Le	Leigh
Chd	Chiddingstone	Lg	Lidsing
Chi	Chislehurst	Li	Lillechurch (in Higham)
Cm	Cobham	Ln	Linton
Cn	Cowden	No	North Cray
Co	Cozenton	Pb	Pembury
D	Deptford (*West Greneuuic*)	Pe	Penshurst
Ed	Edenbridge	Sev	Sevenoaks
F	Farnborough	Sh	Shipbourne
Gr	Grange (in Gillingham)	Shm	Shoreham
Gt	Greatness (in Sevenoaks)	Sho	Shorne
H	Halstead	Sou	South Darenth
Hev	Hever	Sp	Speldhurst
Hh	High Halstow	Sta	Stansted
Hi	Hilles (in Darenth)	Str	Strood
Hor	Horsmonden	Su	Sutton at Hone
Hu	Hunton	We	West Court (in Cliffe)
I	Ifield	Wep	West Peckham
Ig	Ightham	Wil	Wilmington (near Dartford)
Is	Isle of Grain	Ws	Woodlands

The following names are unidentified: *Cap. Anfridi, Cay. Ho., Comba, Thorndun.* There are two Domesday entries for Peckham (*Pecheham*) and they have been plotted as one symbol over East Peckham on the maps. The Textus Roffensis, however, distinguished between *Est Pecham* and *West pecham*, and accordingly West Peckham has been included in the list above.

settlements in the Weald in 1086 which went unmentioned in the Kent folios because their resources were included with those of their parent manors; they lay to the north and east of the outcrop of Weald Clay.

Beyond the Weald, the scatter of Domesday names is closest in the east of the county on the easily worked soils lying between Sandwich

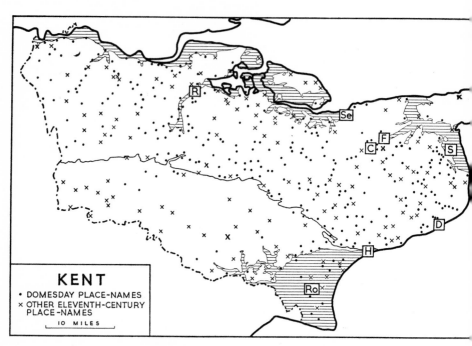

Fig. 143. Kent: Domesday and other eleventh-century place-names.

Domesday boroughs are indicated by initials: C, Canterbury; D, Dover; F, Fordwich; H, Hythe; R, Rochester; Ro, Romney; S, Sandwich; Se, Seasalter. Areas of coastal alluvium, blown sand and shingle, and also the northern boundary of Weald Clay, are shown (see Fig. 140).

and Dover. Other concentrations of Domesday names occur in the valleys of the Cray, the Darent, the Sen, the Medway and the Stour. Fig. 144 shows that many of the coastal villages in the north of the county were situated along the inner margin of the present spread of coastal alluvium which borders the northern shore of the county; similarly there were several Domesday settlements on the so-called ragstone hills overlooking Romney Marsh in the south-east. There is a scatter of Domesday names in Romney Marsh, but only three Domesday names in the 'isles' of Harty, Sheppey and Thanet—Harty itself, and Monkton and Minster in Thanet. But the subsidiary documents show us that in these coastlands, as in the Weald, some eleventh-century settlements were surveyed under the names of their parent estates, e.g. Margate with Chislet.[1]

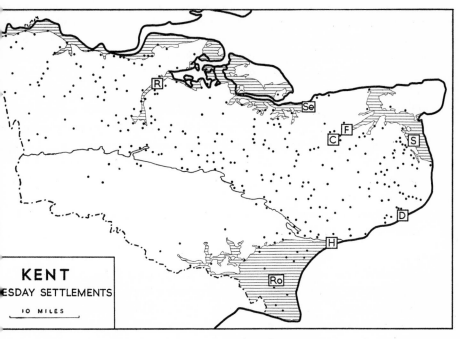

KENT
ESDAY SETTLEMENTS
10 MILES

Fig. 144. Kent: Domesday place-names.

Domesday boroughs are indicated by initials: C, Canterbury; D, Dover; F. Fordwich; H, Hythe; R, Rochester; Ro, Romney; S, Sandwich; Se, Seasalter. Areas of coastal alluvium, blown sand and shingle, and also the northern boundary of Weald Clay, are shown (see Fig. 140).

THE DISTRIBUTION OF PROSPERITY AND POPULATION

Some idea of the nature of the information in the Domesday folios for Kent, and of the form in which it is presented, may be obtained from the account of Aldington. The village itself is situated some 250 feet or so above sea-level on the rising ground that marks the inland border of

[1] See p. 493 above.

Romney Marsh. In 1086 it was held entirely by the archbishop of Canterbury, and so is described in a single entry (4). To what extent this entry covers outliers of the manor, we cannot say.

The archbishop himself holds Aldington in demesne. It was assessed at 21 sulungs *T.R.E.* and now at 15 sulungs. There is land for 100 plough-teams. In demesne are 13 plough-teams, and 190 villeins with (*cum*) 50 bordars have 70 plough-teams. There [is] a church, and 13 serfs, and 3 mills rendering (*de*) 16s., and 3 fisheries rendering (*de*) 21d. There [are] 170 acres of meadow. Woodland [rendering] 60 swine. In all (*In totis valentiis*) it was worth £62 *T.R.E.*, and as much (*tantundem*) when received. Now it pays (*modo reddit*) £100 and 20s.

This entry does not include all the kinds of information that are given for some other places. It does not mention, for example, pasture or saltpans. But, although not comprehensive, it is representative enough, and it does set out the recurring standard items that are entered for most estates. These are five in number: (1) sulungs, (2) plough-lands, (3) plough-teams, (4) population, and (5) values. The bearing of these five items of information upon regional variations in the prosperity of the county must now be considered.

(1) *Sulungs*

The assessment for Kent is normally stated in terms of the sulung (*solin*)[1] and the yoke (*jugum*), units that were peculiar to the county; four yokes made a sulung.[2] Acres are sometimes used, and there is also occasional mention of the *virga* (? virgate),[3] but the virgates are certainly not those of the hidated counties. The word 'hide' occurs in an entry for Little Chart (5) where we read: *T.R.E. se defendit pro iii solins et modo pro ii hidis et dimidia.* That this is a scribal error can be seen from the fact that the corresponding entry in the Domesday Monachorum refers to sulungs only.[4] There is also a reference to a hide in Essex which, we are told,

---

[1] *Solin* is very rarely declined in the Domesday folios. (One example is the plural form *solina* in the account of St Martin's possessions on fo. 2.) In the Domesday Monachorum, it appears as *sullinc* or *sulling*, also not declined. In the Excerpta, it takes the forms *solin*, *solinum* or *solingum*, which are declined. The word 'is variously derived from the Latin *selio* and, more probably, from the Anglo-Saxon *sulh*, a plough' (G. Slater in *V.C.H. Kent*, III, p. 322).

[2] Exemplified in the entry for Eastwell (13): *pro uno solin se defendit. Tria juga sunt infra divisionem Hugonis et quartum jugum est extra.*

[3] The Latin forms are *virga*, *virgā* and *virga⁷*.

[4] D. C. Douglas, *op. cit.* p. 90.

belonged of right (*juste*) to the manor of Chalk in Kent (9). Some indication of the size of the sulung is given in a statement about the common land
of St Martin of Dover: *sunt cccc acrae et dimidia quae fiunt ii solinos* (sic)
et dimidium (2). Vinogradoff argued that it was unlikely that so small an
amount as half an acre would be mentioned alongside 400; and he thought
that 450 acres were implied, which would make the sulung equal to
180 fiscal acres.[1] On the other hand, a comparison of the Domesday
entry for Northbourne (12b) with that in the Excerpta[2] suggests that the
iugum comprised 50 acres, which would make the sulung equal to 200 acres.
The Domesday entry reads: *tenet Gislebertus ii solins dimidium jugum
minus*; and the Excerpta version is: *Gilbertus habet ii solinos xxv agros
minus.*

The assessment is often stated in a very detailed fashion; thus at
Giddinge (5) it was '½ sulung and 1 yoke and 5 acres'; at Northbourne
(12b) it was '3 sulungs less 60 acres'; or, again, at Garrington (12) it was
'½ sulung and 42 acres'. We also hear, for example, of 3½ virgates (13b),
of 3 virgates (12b) and of 1 virgate (13b), all on anonymous holdings.
Then at Lympne (4) there was '½ yoke and ½ virgate'; in Romney
Marsh (13), 'one sulung less ½ virgate'; and in the hundreds of Blackbourne and Newchurch (14), '½ sulung less one virgate'. But nowhere
do the folios for Kent provide us with an equation that might link the
virgate either with the sulung and the yoke or with the acre.[3]

Two assessments, for 1066 and 1086, are sometimes stated. When only
one figure is given, there seems to have been no change between the two
dates; the corresponding entries in the Domesday Monachorum assign the
single figures to *T.R.E.* and then usually add *nunc similiter*. The Domesday folios themselves very occasionally specify no change; thus Boughton
Aluph (14) was rated at 7 sulungs then and now (*tunc et modo*). A marginal
entry for Stuppington (9) gives only the pre-1086 assessment (*T.R.E. et
tunc se defendebat*). Two other entries, on the other hand, provide
information for three dates. Boswell (11) was assessed at one sulung, with
T.R.E. interlined above; but a later sentence in the entry adds: *Quando*

---

[1] P. Vinogradoff, 'Sulung and hide', *Eng. Hist. Rev.* XIX (London, 1904), p. 285 n.
[2] A. Ballard, *op. cit.* p. 21.
[3] J. E. A. Jolliffe reckoned at 4 virgates to the sulung—'The hidation of Kent',
Eng. Hist. Rev. XLIV (London, 1929), p. 614. G. Slater thought that the virgate in
Kent corresponded to the Cornish ferling, which was one-quarter of a Cornish virgate
—*V.C.H. Kent*, III, p. 322. See also J. H. Round, *Feudal England* (London, 1895;
reprinted 1909), p. 108.

herbertus recepit iii juga. Modo ii juga. Of an estate at Eastling (10b), we are told: *pro v solins se defendit T.R.E. et modo pro ii et sic fecit postquam episcopus dedit manerium Hugoni filio fulberti.*

The figures in the Domesday Monachorum are not always the same as those in the Domesday Book, and occasionally they are more detailed, e.g. in the account of Southfleet:

> Domesday Book (5b): *Pro vi solins se defendit.*[1]
> Domesday Monachorum:[2] *in tempore E. regis se defendebat pro vi sullinc et nunc pro v.*

At other times, it is the Domesday entry which is more detailed, as for Trottiscliffe:

> Domesday Book (5b): *T.R.E. pro iii solins se defendit et modo pro uno solin.*
> Domesday Monachorum:[3] *defendit se pro iii sullinc.*

And sometimes it is impossible to guess which entry is giving the correct figure, as in the account of Snodland:

> Domesday Book (5b): *T.R.E. se defendit pro vi solins et modo pro iii.*
> Domesday Monachorum:[3] *in tempore E. regis se defendebat pro vi sullinc et nunc similiter.*

The Domesday Monachorum occasionally amplifies the Domesday information, e.g. in the account of Mersham where an intermediate figure is added:

> Domesday Book (3b): *pro vii solins se defendit T.R.E., et modo pro iii.*
> Domesday Monachorum:[4] *tempore E. regis se defendebat pro vi sullinc et quando archiepiscopus eum recepit pro v et dimidium (sic) et modo pro iii.*

Such examples as these illustrate the margin of error that one must expect in handling Domesday statistics.

It is surprising that J. H. Round could discern only 'some faint traces' of a remission in the assessment of Kent between 1066 and 1086,[5] because reduced figures can frequently be observed as one turns over the folios, especially on the lands of the bishop of Rochester. Almost all show

---

[1] In this, and in subsequent entries on this page, the Domesday form is *defd'* (not *defdb'*), and so has been expanded to *defendit* (not *defendebat*).

[2] D. C. Douglas, *op. cit.* p. 96.   [3] *Ibid.* p. 97.

[4] *Ibid.* p. 91. Note also that the figures for the 1066 assessment differ.

[5] In P. E. Dove (ed.), *Domesday Studies*, I (London, 1888), p. 112.

reduction, and the total decrease was from 66½ sulungs to 40. Here is a complete list of the Rochester estates in the order in which they are entered in the Domesday Book (5b):

	1066	1086		1066	1086
Southfleet	6	5*	Snodland	6	3
Stone	6	4	Cuxton	2½	2
Fawkham	2	2	Denton	2	½
Longfield	1	1	Halling	6	2½
Bromley	6	3	Frindsbury	10	7
Wouldham	6	3	Borstal	2	1½
Malling	3	1½	Rochester†	—	—
Trottiscliffe	3	1	Stoke	5	3

* Corrected from the Domesday Monachorum (see p. 504 above).
† For this entry (5b) see p. 551 below.

We can only suppose that there was some reason, unknown to us, for the favouring of these and other estates.

These beneficial exemptions must not be confused with decreases resulting from the rearrangement of manors. The rating of Brabourne (13b), for example, was reduced from 7 sulungs to 5½ sulungs 1 yoke because part was outside the 'division' of Hugh de Montfort and in the hands of the bishop of Bayeux (*quia alia pars est extra divisionem hugonis et eam tenet episcopus baiocensis*). Or again, the rating of Newington (13b) in Bewsborough hundred had also been reduced because one sulung was *extra divisionem*, so had part of Tinton (13). But we cannot guess, for example, why the 5 sulungs at Sturry (12) should have been discharged (*quietis*) from payment, or why one yoke at Kennington (12b) should also have been discharged from all the king's scot (*quietum ob omni scoto regio*); or, again, why there was 1 yoke of free land (*liberae terrae*) at Shelborough (7b). We hear also of half a sulung of free land at the end of the entry for Wickhambreux (9), and 'of certain free land for 3 oxen' (*quaedam libera terra ad iii boves*) pertaining to Broomfield (8). One sulung and 1 yoke of Langport in Canterbury hundred (12) 'was always acquitted and without customary dues' (*semper quietum fuit et sine consuetudine*).[1]

---

[1] The corresponding Excerpta entry tells us that one sulung in demesne, which lay in the hundred of Canterbury, was always discharged (*semper fuit et est quietum*), and it adds that 'one yoke of land in another hundred was under this sulung' (*Et in alio hundredo est unum jugum terre que subiacet huic solino*); see A. Ballard, *op. cit.* p. 11.

That the brief statements in the Domesday folios conceal many complications may be seen from the example of Chislet (12); it was rated at 12 sulungs, but only from the Excerpta do we learn that 6 of these were at Margate.[1]

It is difficult to establish, with certainty, the basis of assessment in Kent. Factors or multiples of 5, which enter so frequently into the assessment elsewhere in south-east England, are rarely encountered here. Some factor or multiple of 8, on the other hand, seems dominant; 'manors of 4, 6 or 8 sulungs being so common as almost to constitute a rule'.[2] Furthermore, J. E. A. Jolliffe demonstrated 'a surprisingly regular arrangement in groups of 80 sulungs, each group forming a solid block of adjacent hundreds, and one, two, or more such groups exactly occupying the area of each of the lathes according to the hidage of 1066'. It is not always easy to reconstruct the hidage of the lathes because the rubrics of hundreds and lathes are often either misplaced or not given; but, with some adjustment, there emerge eleven units each of which approaches 'within a sulung of the round 80 or 160'. The primitive lathe probably comprised 80 sulungs in east Kent and 160 in the west. Such was the broad framework of the details that meet us in the entries.

The lack of any relation between assessment and agricultural resources is very apparent. The variation among a selection of holdings each assessed at 4 sulungs, both in 1066 and 1086, speaks for itself:

	Plough-lands	Teams	Population
Bilsington (10b)	15	19	74
Chartham (5)	14	17½	75
Cudham (7)	10	10	32
Norton (10)	4	8	24
Sutton (8)	7	6	23

An extreme example of the lack of correspondence is the manor of Dartford (2b); it was assessed at only 1½ sulungs, yet there was land for 40 teams with 55 teams actually at work, and a recorded population of 155.

The form of many entries makes it extremely difficult to arrive at

---

[1] A. Ballard, op. cit. p. 17. See p. 493 above.
[2] The quotations in this paragraph are from J. E. A. Jolliffe, 'The hidation of Kent', Eng. Hist. Rev. XLIV, pp. 612–18. See also J. E. A. Jolliffe, Pre-Feudal England: The Jutes, pp. 44–5.

satisfactory totals for the assessment of the county. There are some entries which, after stating the assessment of a manor, also mention the assessment of anonymous portions of it. It is difficult to know in any particular entry whether or not these portions were included in the main assessment. These secondary figures have been excluded from the totals of the present count:[1]

(a) Assessment (including non-gelding sulungs)—1,151 sulungs, $1\frac{2}{3}$ yokes, 9 virgates, 227 acres.

(b) Gelding sulungs in 1086—1,063 sulungs, $\frac{2}{3}$ yoke, 9 virgates, 227 acres.

The total for 1066 is considerably below that of Maitland, who counted 1,224 sulungs.[2]

(2) Plough-lands

The normal formula in the folios for Kent runs *Terra est n carucis*, with an occasional variant, e.g. the entry for Idleigh and *Soninges* (6) reads *Terra est ibi ad unam carucam*. Fractional parts are occasionally recorded, e.g. at New Shelve (8) there was land for $3\frac{1}{2}$ teams; and at Oakleigh (9), where $1\frac{1}{2}$ teams were at work, there was land for but half a team, and 30 acres besides (*et ibidem sunt adhuc xxx acrae terrae*). At three places we hear of land for oxen—for 3 on a holding at Farningham (6) where 2 oxen were at work, and for 7 at Pinden (6) where a team was at work; there was 'free land for 3 oxen' (*libera terra ad iii boves*) at Broomfield (8). An outstanding feature of the Kent folios is that the phrase *Terra est* is so frequently followed by a blank space in which a figure was never inserted; this is so in no fewer than 92 entries for 84 places. There are also many entries which make no reference to plough-lands, although they state the number of teams at work, e.g. that for Milton Regis (2b) where there were 173 teams at work, and those for the lands of the canons of St Martin of Dover (1b, 2).[3] Including the entries with lacunae, there are altogether about 110 places with incomplete figures for plough-lands.[4]

The relation between plough-lands and plough-teams varies a great

---

[1] Both totals include a figure for Fordwich (12) which was assessed for 1 yoke in 1086; it is the only borough in Kent for which the Domesday Book recorded an assessment.

[2] F. W. Maitland, *Domesday Book and Beyond* (Cambridge, 1897), p. 400.

[3] Where teams but not teamlands are entered for the component parts of manors, we have assumed that the manorial figure for teamlands covers the parts.

[4] The figure 110 excludes some 20 places without information either for teams or plough-lands. Very little is said about most of these—see pp. 491–2 above.

deal in individual entries. A deficiency of teams was fairly frequent, being found for about one-third of the Domesday settlements for which plough-lands were recorded. The deficiency was usually small, but on some of the large manors it was considerable, e.g. at Folkestone (9b) there were 120 plough-lands but only 96 teams seem to have been at work, and at Wye (11b) there were 52 plough-lands but only 26 teams at work. The values on a few deficient holdings had fallen between 1066 and 1086, but on some such holdings they had remained the same, and on most they had even increased. No general correlation between plough-team deficiency and decrease in value is therefore possible, as the following table shows:

		Plough-lands	Teams	Value 1066	Value 1086
Decrease in value	Addington (7)	5	3	£8	£6
	Blean (14)	4	3	£8	£6
Same value	Chart Sutton (6b)	8	7	£12	£12
	Otham (8)	2½	2	£4	£4
Increase in value	Aldington (4)	100	83	£62	£101
	Higham (9)	12	9½	£12	£15

These figures are merely indications of unexplained changes on individual manors. We really cannot say whether the plough-land figures are those of teams employed in 1066. The very brief entry for Rooting (12) does not mention plough-lands, but says that there had been, and still was, one team on the demesne (*Ibi fuit et est una caruca in dominio*); but whether this is telling us, in effect, that there was one plough-land at Rooting, we cannot say. At Yalding (14) there was land for 16 teams but only 7½ were at work; the value '*T.R.E.* and afterwards' had been £30, but it had fallen to £20 by 1086 because the land had been despoiled of stock (*eo quod terra vastata est a pecunia*). This information is consistent with the presence of 16 plough-teams at Yalding in 1066; but whatever the figure for 1066 was, we must remember that plough-beasts cannot have been the only stock on the manor, and that, in any case, it would be unwise to construct a theory out of one apparent hint.

The number of teams at work exceeded the number for which there was land for about just over one-third of the Domesday settlements for which plough-lands were recorded. The excess was sometimes consider-able, e.g. in the manor of *Nortone* (i.e. Whitstable, 3b) there were 66½ teams but only 26 plough-lands, and at Dartford (2b) there were

55 teams but only 40 plough-lands. Generally speaking, the values of such holdings had risen, but they had sometimes remained the same, e.g. at Hadlow (7b); and occasionally they had even dropped, as at *Afettune* (10b); here there were 3 plough-lands with 4½ teams, and the value of the estate had fallen from £5 to £4.

In view of the large number of lacunae, and the absence of any reference to plough-lands in other entries, any total of plough-lands for the county would be misleading. Nor can we hazard an estimate by assuming that plough-lands equalled teams on those holdings for which no figure is available; the omissions are too many. F. W. Maitland, in his county tables, did not enter a figure for plough-lands in Kent.[1]

(3) *Plough-teams*

The plough-team entries for Kent, like those for other counties, normally draw a distinction between the teams at work on the demesne and those held by the peasantry. Occasional entries seem to be defective. Thus there were no teams or oxen at Poulton (13b) which had 2 plough-lands and 3 villeins, or at *Leveberge* (11 *bis*) with no plough-lands, it is true, but with 3 villeins and 3 bordars. Sometimes only demesne teams are entered; at Nurstead (7b) there was land for 2 teams and there was 1 team on the demesne, but the 4 bordars (and 4 serfs) were apparently without a team. Occasionally, on the other hand, only the teams of the peasants are mentioned, e.g. at Newenden (4) where 25 villeins and 4 bordars had 5 teams. On fo. 7b there are three entries (for Fairbourne, Frinstead and Harrietsham) in each of which a blank space is left after the phrase *In dominio*. At Newington near Milton Regis (14b), the demesne was 'at farm', and we are told nothing of its agricultural equipment:

Terra est [   ]. Terra quae fuit in dominio est ad firmam pro lx solidis. In ipso manerio x villani cum xlviii bordariis habent v carucas.

Some entries specifically draw attention to the deficiency on a holding, as the following examples show:

Boughton (8): *Terra est ii carucis. In dominio nichil sed v villani habent i carucam ibi.*

Chillenden (11b): *Terra est [   ]. In domino nichil modo sed ix villani habent ibi ii carucas et dimidiam.*

[1] *Op. cit.* pp. 402 and 410.

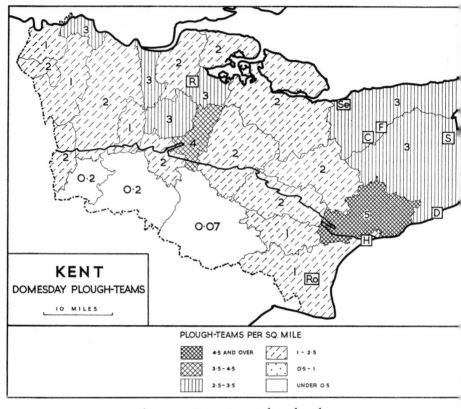

Fig. 145. Kent: Domesday plough-teams
in 1086 (by densities).

Domesday boroughs are indicated by initials: C, Canterbury; D, Dover; F, Ford-wich; H, Hythe; R, Rochester; Ro, Romney; S, Sandwich; Se, Seasalter. The northern boundary of Weald Clay is shown (see Fig. 140).

Crofton (7): *Terra est* [   ]. *In dominio nichil est sed iii villani et iiii bordarii ibi sunt.* But nothing is said about the teams of these seven people.

Haven (9): *Terra est dimidia caruca. In dominio nichil est.* Nothing is said about teams or people, but the preceding entry, also relating to Haven, records one team in demesne and 6 villeins and one bordar with another.

In Hayne hd. (13): *Terra est iii carucis. Ibi unus villanus cum iiii bordariis manet: nulla ibi caruca.*

Offham (7): *Terra est iii carucis. In dominio nichil. Ibi vi villani cum i bordario habent ii carucas.*

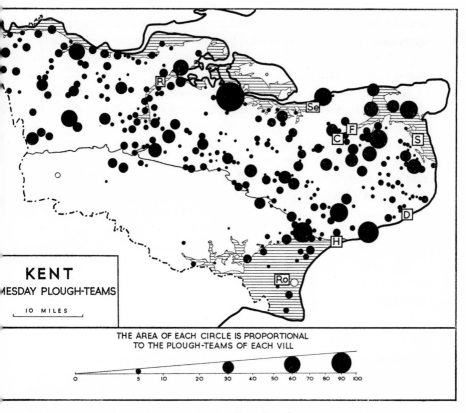

Fig. 146. Kent: Domesday plough-teams
in 1086 (by settlements).

Domesday boroughs are indicated by initials: C, Canterbury; D, Dover; F, Fordwich; H, Hythe; R, Rochester; Ro, Romney; S, Sandwich; Se, Seasalter.
    The open circles represent the plough-teams on anonymous holdings in Romney
Marsh, in the Isle of Sheppey and in Somerden hundred. Areas of coastal alluvium,
blown sand and shingle, and also the northern boundary of Weald Clay, are shown
(see Fig. 140).

Ospringe (10): *Terra est xx carucis. In dominio non sunt carucae. Ibi xxix
    villani cum vi bordariis habent xi carucas.*
Stelling (9): *Terra i caruca et dimidia. In dominio nichil est nisi i bordarius.*
    No teams are mentioned.

A hint of the complications of ploughing arrangements is given in the
account of an anonymous holding of half a yoke with two bordars in

Newchurch hundred (13); here, the land was valued with that of Tinton because it was ploughed with the demesne teams of that manor: *Haec terra appreciatur in Titentone quia illuc arata est cum dominicis carrucis (sic)*. But the entry for Tinton itself, which comes later on the same folio, does not mention this arrangement.

Half-teams are frequently mentioned (e.g. for Bowley, 8), and oxen themselves are sometimes entered. At *Aelvetone* (i.e. Elmstone, 12b), for example, there was one team in demesne and 3 villeins with 3 oxen in a team (*cum iii bobus in caruca*); and on an anonymous holding in Wye hundred (14) there were 5 oxen ploughing (*v boves arantes*) on the demesne as well as 10 teams with the peasantry. At Harbiton (8), on the other hand, there was a team in demesne, and 2 beasts (*ii Animalia*) with the peasantry. An entry for Shelling (11b) reads strangely; there was a team in demesne, and 4 villeins and 3 bordars had 'half a team and 1½ teams' (*habent dimidiam carucam et i carucam et dimidiam*).[1]

The total number of plough-teams amounted to 3,152⅜. Maitland estimated the total as 3,102,[2] but his figures excluded those for the boroughs.[3]

(4) *Population*

The bulk of the population was comprised in the four main categories of villeins, bordars, serfs and cottars. In addition to these were the burgesses, together with a small miscellaneous group that included sokemen, priests, men (*homines*) and others. The details of these groups are summarised on p. 513. This estimate is not comparable with that of Sir Henry Ellis, which included tenants-in-chief, under-tenants, burgesses, and nuns.[4] In any case, accuracy can rarely be claimed for an estimate of Domesday population because varying interpretations of many entries are inevitable; all that can be claimed for the present figures is that they indicate the order of magnitude involved. These figures are those of the recorded male population, and must be multiplied by some factor, say 4 or 5, in order to obtain

---

[1] This may well be a scribal error, but its form is reminiscent of the *potest fieri* formula of some other counties. In that case it should read: *habent dimidiam carucam et i caruca et dimidia possunt fieri*. This would then make a total of 3 plough-lands; but, unfortunately, *Terra est* in the entry is followed by a blank space.

[2] *Op. cit.* p. 401.

[3] The present total of 3,152⅜ teams includes the 2 teams entered for the 'small borough' of Seasalter (5) and the one team *juxta* Canterbury (12).

[4] Sir Henry Ellis, *A General Introduction to Domesday Book*, II (London, 1833), pp. 459–60; his grand total for the Domesday county was 12,205.

the actual population, but this does not affect the relative density as between one area and another.[1] That is all that a map, such as Fig. 147, can roughly indicate.

Recorded Population of Kent in 1086

A. *Rural Population*

Villeins	.	.	.	.	.	6,829
Bordars	.	.	.	.	.	3,372
Serfs	.	.	.	.	.	1,160
Cottars	.	.	.	.	.	309
Miscellaneous	.	.	.	.		83
Total	.	.	.	.	.	11,753

There were also 4 bondwomen (*ancillae*), 4 nuns (*moniales*), a poor woman (*una paupercula mulier*), and a widow (*una vidua*); they have all been excluded from the above total.

Details of Miscellaneous Rural Population

Sokemen	.	.	.	44	Knights (*Milites*)	.	.	3
Men (*Homines*)	.	.	16	Reeves	.	.	.	2
Priests	.	.	12	Freemen (*Liberi homines*)	.		2
Francigenae	.	.	3	*Rusticus*	.	.	.	1
							Total	83

B. *Urban Population*

The bordars are also included in the table above.

DOVER	No record. See p. 546 below.
CANTERBURY	438 burgesses; 142 *masurae*; 15 *hagae*; 4 houses (*domus*). See p. 547 below. For 18 bordars *juxta* Canterbury, see p. 550 n.
ROCHESTER	5 burgesses; 80 *masurae*; 13 *hagae*; 3 *mansiones*; 17 houses (*domus*). See p. 550 below.
SANDWICH	415 *masurae*. See p. 552 below.
HYTHE	231 burgesses. See p. 553 below.
ROMNEY	156 burgesses. See p. 553 below.
FORDWICH	6 burgesses; 80 *masurae*. See p. 554 below.
SEASALTER	48 bordars. See p. 554 below.

---

[1] But see p. 589 below for the complication of serfs.

It is impossible for us to say how complete were these Domesday statistics, but it does seem as if some people had been left uncounted. We hear nothing of the population of Tonbridge although Richard of Tonbridge features so prominently in the Kent folios. We are not told how

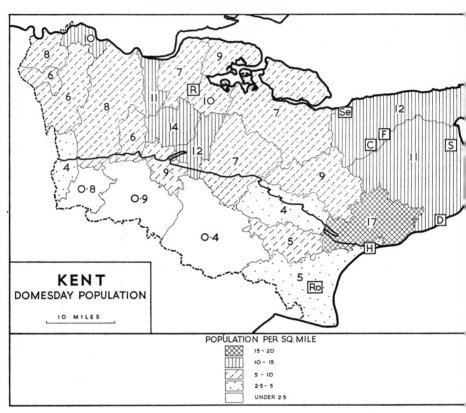

Fig. 147. Kent: Domesday population in 1086 (by densities). Domesday boroughs are indicated by initials: C, Canterbury; D, Dover; F, Fordwich; H, Hythe; R, Rochester; Ro, Romney; S, Sandwich; Se, Seasalter. The northern boundary of Weald Clay is shown (see Fig. 140).

many canons there were in the community of St Martin of Dover (2) although we hear of a payment of 60s. for their sandals (*ad calciamenta canonicorum*). No reference at all is made to the monks of the abbey of St Augustine at Canterbury. Priests are very rarely entered, but it is possible that they were included among the villeins. Ralf de Curbespine held one yoke of the 'land of the sokemen' (*terra sochemannorum*) in the manor of Wye (11b), but we are told nothing of any sokemen there; it is, however, possible that the reference is to sokemen who had disappeared since 1066. Or again, we hear of rent from *rustici* at Lewisham (12b),

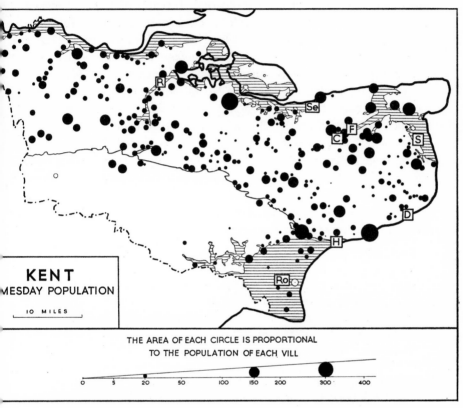

KENT
MESDAY POPULATION
10 MILES

THE AREA OF EACH CIRCLE IS PROPORTIONAL
TO THE POPULATION OF EACH VILL

0   5   20   50   100   150   200   300   400

Fig. 148. Kent: Domesday population in 1086 (by settlements).

Domesday boroughs are indicated by initials: C, Canterbury; D, Dover; F, Ford-wich; H, Hythe; R, Rochester; Ro, Romney; S, Sandwich; Se, Seasalter.

The open circles represent the population on anonymous holdings in Romney Marsh, in the Isle of Sheppey and in Somerden hundred. Areas of coastal alluvium, blown sand and shingle, and also the northern boundary of Weald Clay, are shown (see Fig. 140).

but nothing is said about their number; this payment may refer to one made by the other categories of people enumerated in the entry, but we cannot be certain.[1] Furthermore, as we have seen, some entries seem to

---

[1] The entry records 50 villeins, 9 bordars and 3 serfs.

be defective and contain no reference at all to population. It is impossible to be certain about the significance of these omissions,[1] but they do suggest unrecorded inhabitants.

Villeins constituted the most important element in the population and amounted to about 58 per cent of the total. It is difficult to be certain about the status of the Domesday villeins entered in the Kent folios.[2] At Kennington (12b) villeins had held land in 1066 (*Villani tenuerunt T.R.E.*), and a certain villein had held (*T.R.E. quidam villanus tenuit*) half a dene belonging to Milton Regis (2b). We hear much of the *terra villanorum* in the entries for Folkestone (9b) and Northbourne (12b), and the entry for Leeds (7b) tells of 5 mills belonging to the villeins (*v molini villanorum*). Bordars comprised about 28 per cent of the recorded population, but cottars less than 3 per cent. Bordars and cottars are only once enumerated in the same entry in the Kent folios.[3] As many as 74 cottars are entered under Hoo (8b) and 60 under Ickham (5), but these numbers are unusual, and generally the number of cottars on a holding is below 10. Villeins, and occasionally bordars and cottars, sometimes made money renders, as the following representative entries show:

Buckland (10b): *Ibi est unus villanus reddens vi solidos.*

Macknade (10): *Ibi sunt ii villani reddentes l denarios.*

Oare (10): *Hanc (i.e. unum jugum) tenent iii villani modo ad firmam et reddunt xx solidos et tantundem semper valuit.*

Ringleton (10b): *Ibi ii villani habent i carucam et reddunt vi solidos.*

Shelling (9b): *Ibi habet unum villanum reddentem ii solidos.*

Swalecliffe (10): *In dominio est i caruca cum viii cottaris qui reddunt iiii solidos et vi denarios.*

Swetton (14): *Ibi modo est unus bordarius xii denarios reddens.*

Woolwich (14): *Ibi sunt xi bordarii reddentes xli denarios.*

Serfs comprised nearly 10 per cent of the recorded population, and they were more common in the central part of the county to the south of

---

[1] See pp. 491–2 above.

[2] For some discussion of the *villani* of Kent see: (1) N. Neilson in *V.C.H. Kent*, III, p. 195; and (2) G. Slater in *V.C.H. Kent*, III, pp. 336–8.

[3] At Greenwich (6b), where there were 4 bordars and 1 cottar as well as 24 villeins and 5 serfs. Not quite comparable with the entry for Greenwich is that for Wrotham (3); it tells first of bordars, but in a later section mentions cottars. For a discussion of the differences between bordars and cottars, see: (1) F. W. Maitland, *op. cit.* pp. 39 *et seq.*; and (2) P. Vinogradoff, *English Society in the Eleventh Century* (Oxford, 1908), pp. 456 *et seq.*

Rochester (Fig. 171). The account of Ash (6) gives a combined total for male and female serfs (*viii inter servos et ancillas*), and this figure has been divided equally between the sexes for the purposes of computation; *ancillae* have not been included in the total population.

The miscellaneous category is a small one. The most interesting group is that of sokemen. Forty-four sokemen are enumerated for 1086. The number specifically recorded for 1066 is 61, but in addition there were 26 sokemen entered for 1086 but not for the earlier date. If they had been there in 1066, the total number for that year may well have been 87.[1] Furthermore, on fo. 11b we hear of 'the land of the sokemen' at Wye, which suggests that there were or had been sokemen in the manor. It is sometimes difficult to be certain whether sokemen entered for 1086 had also been there twenty years before. At Tinton (13) it is clear they had been—*Isdem Hugo tenet dimidium jugum quod tenuerunt v sochemanni et modo tenent*—but on a holding in Romney Marsh (13), where the value had increased, it is not so clear: *Isdem Hugo tenet in Maresc de Romenel unum solin dimidia virga (sic) minus; pro tanto se defendit. Terra est iii carucis. Ibi xiiii sochemanni habent iii carucas. T.R.E. valebat iiii libras et post iii libras. Modo c solidos.* From another holding in Romney Marsh it does seem as if the sokemen had disappeared (13):

Isdem Hugo tenet in Maresc de Romenel i jugum. Terra est [   ]. Medietatem hujus terrae tenuerunt ii sochemanni, et ii villani aliam. Ibi sunt modo iiii villani habentes i carucam. Haec terra valuit et valet xii solidos.

It may be that the two sokemen of 1066, or their heirs, had become the additional 2 villeins of 1086. Or again, Orlestone (13b) had been held by 11 sokemen in 1066, but the only population recorded for 1086 is 15 villeins and 9 bordars, and we can only suppose that the sokemen or their successors had been reduced in status.

The remaining miscellaneous groups include 'men' (*homines*) who are mentioned three times; twice in the account of the lands of St Martin of Dover (2)—6 men with 1½ teams, and 8 men dwelling under the mills (*Sub illis molinis manent viii homines*), and once in the entry for Maidstone where we hear of 2 men who paid 20s. a year (3).[2] Twelve priests have

[1] N. Neilson counted 87 for 1066 (*V.C.H. Kent*, III, p. 196).
[2] The man entered under Hoo (8b), the 'certain man' noted under Hastingleigh (14) and the 2 men mentioned in the entry for Ash (6) have been excluded because they seem to be under-tenants.

been counted, but it is a small number in relation to that of churches.[1] There were 3 *francigenae*[2] and 3 knights.[3] We hear of 2 reeves, one at Milton Regis (2b) and the other at Newenden (4). There were 2 freemen at Stocking (7b).[4] One *rusticus* was mentioned at St Margaret's at Cliffe (2), but we also hear of rent from an unspecified number of *rustici* at Lewisham (12b). The decision whether or not to include knights and freemen is not always easy; they have been excluded wherever they seem to be under-tenants.[5] Thegns (*teigni*) have been excluded for the same reason.[6] Women are mentioned on four occasions. There were *ancillae* at Ash (6), 4 nuns (*moniales*) holding 4 acres of land near (*Juxta*) Canterbury (12),[7] one poor woman (*una paupercula mulier*) paying $3\frac{1}{2}d.$ at Barfreston (9b), and a widow (*una vidua*) paying 23d. yearly and living (*manet*) on an unnamed holding in Aloesbridge hundred (11). None of these women has been included in our total of recorded population for the county.

(5) *Values*

The value of an estate is normally given for three dates—*tunc, post, modo,* i.e. for 1066, for the year in which a subsequent holder received it, and for 1086. The possessions of the canons of St Martin of Dover (1b, 2), however, have no intermediate values stated for them, neither have some holdings of the bishop of Bayeux (6), and also other occasional holdings, e.g. at Lympne (4). Occasionally, as in the entry for Tudeley (7b), the form *valet et valuit semper* is found, and this seems to imply a constant value at all three dates. In one of the entries for Lullingstone (6) it is the *T.R.E.* figure that is missing, and in an entry for Cliffe (9) the missing

[1] See p. 544 below for churches and priests.

[2] The *francigenae* were at Boxley (8b), Charlton near Dover (1b), and New Shelve (8); the Boxley reference is to *i franc* which has been taken here to mean *i francigena*. The 'certain Frenchman' at Gillingham (3b) held land and so has not been counted.

[3] At Ash (6), at Fleet (3b) and at Swanscombe (6).

[4] In 1066, there had been other freemen and also *alodiarii* who held *in alodium* or *in alodio* as, for example, those mentioned in the *leges regis* on fo. 1.

[5] Thus the 2 knights at Adisham (5), the 4 French knights who held to the annual value of £12 at Chislet (12), the 'certain knight' at *Cildresham* (10), the 'certain knight' at Ewell (11), the 3 knights at Maidstone (3), the 3 at Minster (12), and the 'certain knight' at Ponshall (9b) have all been excluded from the present count of recorded population. The French reeve at Dartford (2b) has likewise been excluded.

[6] As, for example, the 10 entered under Betteshanger (11).

[7] They held in almoign from the abbot of St Augustine (*in elemosina de abbate*) and paid 2s. and one load of flour (*unam summam farinae*).

figure is that for 1086. The entry for Otford (3) intended to give all three figures, but the phrase *T.R.E. et post* is followed by a blank space. The entry for Tilmanstone (4b) gives two figures but does not specify the date of the earlier figure—*Olim xx solidi. Modo valet xxx solidos.* A number of entries, referring mostly to tiny holdings, give but one value; there is, for example, only a 1086 value given for holdings at Beauxfield (12b), at Hawley (6) and at Upchurch (9). The entry for *Eddintone* (6) gives no specific value for 1066, but merely says that it had been 'small': *Totum manerium appreciatur iiii libris. T.R.E. parvum valebat.* The values for Sturry (12) are 50s., £45 and £50, and it does look as if the 1066 value should read £50. At Court-at-Street (*Estraites*, 13b), the values were 10s., 4s. and £8, which also look strange. Occasional holdings were valued together. Thus Eastry and Giddinge (5) are covered by one set of figures; so are Finglesham and Statenborough (4b). Marley is valued as part of the manor of Bowley (8), and Idleigh and *Soninges* as part of the manor of Ash (6). While the normal form of the entry is *valet n libras*, it is sometimes varied to *appreciatur n libris* as in the account of *Eddintone* (6) mentioned above.[1]

The amounts are usually stated to the nearest pound, but the greater detail of a number of entries suggests precision. Thus the value of a holding at Lullingstone (6) had increased from 60s. to 77s., that of *Asmeslant* (5)[2] was, and had always been, 53s., and *Nortone* (i.e. Whitstable, 3b) paid to the archbishop £50. 14s. 2d. But when we read that the value of Boughton under Blean (3b) had increased from £15. 16s. 3½d. (*T.R.E. et post*) to £30. 16s. 3½d. we may well doubt the precision of an increase of exactly £15; and the same doubt applies to the increase of £10 at Eastry and Giddinge (5)—from £26. 10s. 4¼d. to £36. 10s. 4¼d. Sometimes we hear of payments by weight or of payments tested by assay. The manor of Milton Regis (2b) paid £140 assayed and weighed together with £15. 5s. 10d. by tale (*reddit cxl libras ad ignem et ad pensam et insuper xv libras et vi solidos ii denarios minus ad numerum*); the entry seems to imply that the whole was equal to £200 by tale. The intermediate value of the manor of Wye (11b) was £125. 10s. reckoning at 20d. to the ounce (*de xx in ora*), but by 1086 it had become £100 by tale (*ad numerum*). Occasionally, an ounce of gold (*uncia auri*) entered into the value, e.g. at Southfleet (5b) and at Stone (5b); the latter paid, in 1086, £20 and an

---

[1] In the Excerpta and the Domesday Monachorum, *valet n libras* is almost invariably *est appreciatum n libris*.   [2] Plotted at Gammon's Farm in Newchurch.

ounce of gold and a porpoise (*unum marsum*).[1] Knight-service was included in the valuations of Combe and Sundridge:

> Combe (10b): *T.R.E. valebat lx solidos, et post l solidos. Modo iiii libras et servitium unius militis.*
>
> Sundridge (3): *In totis valentiis T.R.E. valebat xii libras. Quando recepit xvi libras et modo xviii libras. Tamen reddit xxiii libras et unum militem in servitio Archiepiscopi.*

A hint of some complications is contained in the entry for Newington (14b) which includes a note on payments due to it from the manor of Milton Regis:

> From the manor of Milton is paid in Newington a customary due, that is 28 weys of cheese (*una consuetudo idest xxviii pensae caseorum*), and from 28 sulungs of Milton pertaining to Newington £10. 10s., and from the other part, from 9 sulungs pertaining to Newington, 28½ weys of cheese and 58s. as rent (*de gablo*) from these 9 sulungs; and from these 9 sulungs Sigar used to render carrying service at Milton (*reddebat Sigur apud Mildetone Averam*).

But the account of Milton Regis itself (2b) makes no reference to these arrangements.

Many holdings decreased in value between 1066 and the time when their respective owners received them, and F. H. Baring attributed these decreases to devastation caused by the passage of Norman armies.[2] William's forces, after the Battle of Hastings, marched north-east to Dover, and, after staying there for eight days, continued via Canterbury towards London. The Domesday entry for Dover (1) says that the borough had been burnt down so that it could not be properly valued when the bishop of Bayeux received it.[3] The values of the villages around Dover, and in the eastern part of Kent generally, fell considerably, as the examples on p. 521 indicate.[4]

Baring noted that 'amid the general destruction' the estates of the archbishop seem to have escaped unscathed. 'Were they spared to conciliate the church or to tempt the archbishop at a critical moment; or did the

---

[1] The Domesday *unum marsum* is rendered as *i marsuinum* in the Domesday Monachorum (see D. C. Douglas, *op. cit.* p. 96); Stone is on the Thames. Compare the *marsuins* at Southease (17b) in Sussex—see p. 455 above.

[2] F. H. Baring, 'The Conqueror's footprints in Domesday', *Eng. Hist. Rev.* XIII (1898), pp. 17–25. Reprinted with 'some additions and alterations' in *Domesday Tables* (London, 1909), pp. 207–16.

[3] See p. 546 below.   [4] See Figs 162 and 164 below.

	1066	Intermediate	1086
Appleton (11)	100s.	10s.	40s.
Betteshanger (11)	60s.	30s.	50s.
Betteshanger (11)	100s.	30s.	60s.
Coldred (11)	£8	20s.	£6
Northbourne (12b)	£80	£20	£76
Pising and Pineham (10b)	100s.	Nichil	£6

post and *quando receptum* of these entries refer, not to 1067, but to a date after the deposition of Stigand in 1070 or his death in 1072?'[1] But it must be added that even if the archbishop's estates in the east were spared, his holdings in the west of the county sometimes declined in value, e.g. Gillingham (3b) with £15, £12, £23.[2] But, generally speaking, relatively few estates in the west fell in value; thus all the lands of the bishop of Rochester (5b) yielded the same *post* as *T.R.E.* Most of the depreciated holdings in Kent as a whole recovered fully, or in part, by 1086, and some were more prosperous than ever; the figures for a holding at Ponshall (9b) are 60s., 20s., 100s. At Swanton, one holding (13b) had likewise improved —25s., 15s., 30s.—but the other (11) had lagged greatly behind—£10, 30s., 40s. A number of estates had improved steadily, apparently untouched by the troubles of the age; such was Boughton Aluph (14) with values of £20, £30, £40. We must not attribute every decrease in value to the ravages of the Norman armies. Yalding (14) had apparently been untouched; it was worth £30 in 1066 and 'after', but by 1086 its value had fallen to £20 because the land had been despoiled of its stock (*eo quod terra vastata est a pecunia*), but we are not told why.[3]

Some of the sums paid in 1086 were in excess of what was apparently a reasonable return from an estate. Fifty-seven entries for 55 places give the current value for 1086 and then go on to say that in fact a greater sum was paid;[4] Pluckley, valued at £15, paid £20 (*et tamen reddit xx*

---

[1] *Op. cit.* p. 208.

[2] The bishop of Bayeux also held land in Gillingham (8) worth at the three dates 40s., 30s. and 60s. respectively.

[3] Apart from the wasted houses at Canterbury, this is the only specific mention of *vastata* for 1086 in the folios for Kent. Yalding has not been counted as a waste place in the table on p. 615 because *vastata* is merely a comment on the reduction in value. On Figs. 162 and 164, two waste symbols appear for Pising and Pineham (10b) *c.* 1070 because their intermediate value was *nichil*.

[4] The boroughs of Canterbury (2) and Rochester (2) also paid a greater sum, but they have been excluded from the total of 55.

libras); Bilsington, valued at £50, paid £70 from the feorm (*et tamen reddit de firma lxx libras*); Wadholt,[1] valued at only 20*s.*, paid 40*s.* because it was 'farmed out' (*tamen appreciatur xl solidis eo quod sit ad firmam*); Reculver, valued at £35, paid an additional £7. 7*s.* to the archbishop (*Super haec habet archiepiscopus vii libras et vii solidos*). The complete figures for these places are representative of many others:

	1066	Inter-mediate	1086	Payment
Pluckley (3b)	£12	£8	£15	£20
Bilsington (10b)	£10	£30	£50	£70
Wadholt (12b)	20*s.*	20*s.*	20*s.*	40*s.*
Reculver (3b)	£14	£14	£35	£42. 7*s.*

Some details in the entry for Dartford (2b) give a glimpse of the many differences of opinion that must have existed:

T.R.E. it was worth £60, and as much when Haimo the sheriff received it. It is now valued by the English (*ab anglis*) at £60. The French reeve, however, who holds it at feorm, says that it is worth £90. Nevertheless he pays from the manor £70 of weighed money (*pensatas*), and 111*s.* at 20*d.* to the *ora*, and £7 and 26*d.* by tale. Besides this, he pays 100*s.* to the sheriff.

We hear no complaints, as in the Sussex folios, that these payments were too heavy to be borne.[2]

Generally speaking, the greater the number of teams and of men on an estate, the higher its value, but it is impossible to discern any consistent relationship; the five estates in the table below each yielded £5 in 1086:

	Teams	Popula-tion	Other resources
Horton (10b)	1½	14	Meadow, Mills, Underwood
Nashenden (7)	4	25	Meadow
Nurstead (7b)	1	8	Wood
Sifflington (7)	2	13	Meadow, Mill, Pasture
Teston (8b)	3½	22	Meadow, Mill, Wood

Or what are we to make of one of the entries for Haven (9) assessed at one yoke? All we are told of it is thus: *Terra est dimidia caruca. In dominio*

---

[1] Wadholt appears as *Platenovt.*   [2] See p. 442 above.

nichil est. T.R.E. et post et modo valet xx solidos; it had no population or teams, yet it yielded 20s. Or what of the anonymous holding of one yoke in Longbridge hundred (13 b): *Valet et valuit iiii solidos. Nil ibi fuit nec est?* To such perplexities the folios offer no answer.

Conclusion

The hundreds have been adopted as the general basis for calculating densities, but several adjustments have been made. Several hundreds in the eastern part of the county have been grouped together because of their small size. Then again, various adjustments have been made in the Weald, for here the organisation into hundreds seems to have been very rudimentary in the eleventh century;[1] but any inaccuracy cannot greatly affect the densities in this relatively empty area. The result of the modifications has been to produce twenty-six units. Although not giving as perfect a regional division as a geographer could wish for, these units provide a useful basis for distinguishing the degree of variation over the face of the county.

Of the five recurring standard formulae, those relating to plough-teams and population are most likely to reflect something of the distribution of wealth and prosperity throughout the county. Taken together, they supplement one another to provide a general picture (Figs. 145 and 147). The essential feature of both maps is the contrast between the Wealden area and the rest of the county. Much of the Weald had an average of less than a team and under one person per square mile. Over the rest of the county, the density of teams ranged largely between 2 and 3, and that of population between 6 and 12. It is certain, however, that the two maps over-emphasise this contrast, because the totals for many northern manors include the details of outliers in the Weald; the documents subsidiary to the Domesday Book show an appreciable number of Wealden settlements. But even so, the number of men and of teams so involved cannot have been great enough to affect the broad picture given by Figs. 145 and 147.

Figs. 146 and 148 are supplementary to the density maps, but here again we must remember that many Domesday names covered two or more settlements, some nearby, others distantly situated in the Weald. To some extent, the symbols for population and plough-teams, like those for woodland, must be 'spread out' by eye over the adjacent Weald. But

[1] See p. 532 above.

these maps, in spite of their unsatisfactory character, do not err in conveying to us the fact that the main contrast in eleventh-century Kent was between the Weald and the rest of the county.

Type of entries　　　　　　　WOODLAND

The amount of woodland on a holding in Kent was recorded in terms of the number of swine paid to the lord for the right of pannage. The form of the statement varies, as the following entries show:

Brabourne (13b): *Silva de xxv porcis.*
Eastbridge (13): *Silva de iii porcis de pasnagio.*
Eynsford (4): *tantum silvae unde exire possunt xx porci.*
Lewisham (12b): *De silva l porci de pasnagio.*
Mereworth (14): *tantum silvae unde exeunt lx porci de pasnagio.*
Monks Horton (13b): *De silva vi porci.*
West Wickham (6b): *una silva de x porcis.*
Wilderton (12): *v porci de pasnagio silvae.*
Wouldham (5b): *Silva xx porcis.*

The last is the form that occurs most frequently as if the scribe did not think it worth while to write out the statement in full each time; it is the usual formula on fos. 1–11. In the entry for Eastwell (13) the word *silva* is followed by a blank space into which a figure was never inserted. Entries for Barham (9b) and Blean (14) omit the word *silva*, and merely note renders of swine from pannage (*de pasnagio*).

The number of swine due from a holding ranged from only one pig each at Chatham (8b), at Delce (8b) and at Ruckinge (13b), to 500 swine at Wrotham (3); the entry for Wrotham states that the render was due when the wood bore mast (*Silva quando fructificatur quingentis porcis*). One of the entries for Bourne (9)[1] records a fraction of a pig: *Silva vi porcis et dimidio.*[2] There is no entry that gives us a clue to the relation of these renders to total numbers of mast swine. Nor is there a clue to the wider problem of what acreage of woodland the figures imply. All we can do is to plot them as conventional units. There is one entry, however, that tells us something about the value of the swine. At Kennington the render was '40 swine or 54½d.' (*ibi tantum silvae unde exeunt de pasnagio xl porci aut liiii denarii et unus obolus*, 12b).

---

[1] See p. 489 n. above.　　　[2] See F. W. Maitland, *op. cit.* p. 419.

Three entries note a money payment in addition to a swine rent:

Farningham (6): *Silva x porcis et xiiii denariis. Rex habet de silva hujus manerii quod valet viii solidos.*

Maplescombe (6): *silva viii porcis et xvi denariis plus.*

Maplescombe (6): *Silva viii porcis et xvi denariis.*

The entry for Cliffe (4b) records only a money payment (*Silva de xii denariis*); that for Faversham (2b) runs: *Silva c porcis, et de pastura silvae xxxi solidi et ii denarii.* The only other entry with a money payment for pannage is that for Otterpool (14): *silva reddens v denarios de pasnagio.* At *Cildresham* (10), we are told that the wood renders nothing: *Silva est sed nil reddit.* Underwood (*silva minuta*) is mentioned three times:

Horton (10b): *c acrae silvae minutae.*

Nackington (9b): *xvi acrae silvae minutae.*

Wadholt (*Platenovt*, 12b): *Ibi silva minuta.*

The entry for Nackington (9b) also records a small wood with 12 acres of pasture (*Ibi parvum nemus de xii acris pasturae*). The entry for wood in the account of Canterbury (2) is very unusual; we are told that the city had 1,000 acres of wood, not bearing mast, from which came 24s. (*mille acrae (sic) silvae infructuosae de qua exeunt xxiiii solidi*). The corresponding statement in the Excerpta, on the other hand, speaks of 1,000 acres of underwood (*mille agri (sic) minute silve*) which used to render 20s.[1]

The woodland on several holdings is entered in very general terms, e.g. as 'a small wood' or as 'wood for fencing'. The entries are as follows:

Adisham (5): *Silva ad clausuram.*

Easole (9b): *silvula ad clausuram.*

Newington near Milton Regis (14b): *Silvula parva ad clausuram.*

Wingham (3b): *Silva v porcis et duae silvulae ad clausuram.*

Preston near Wingham (12b): *Ibi parva silvula.*

St Martin's in Canterbury (4): *parva silva.*

Tickenhurst (11b): *parva silvula.*[2]

Wood is also recorded in connection with denes, which are discussed on pp. 527–32 below. Finally, there is mention of an alder grove (*unum alnetum*) at Buckwell (10b), and of another that had been withdrawn from the royal manor of Dartford (2b). At Chart Sutton (8), in addition to wood rendering 50 swine, there was a park for beasts of the chase (*parcus*

---

[1] A. Ballard, *op. cit.* p. 7. [2] For Tickenhurst, see p. 531 below.

silvaticus bestiarum). Wickhambreux (9) also had a park, as well as woodland rendering 80 swine and pasture for 300 sheep and 31 animals. The
park at Wickhambreux is also mentioned incidentally in the entries for
Garrington (12), Leeds (7b) and Littlebourne (12).[1]

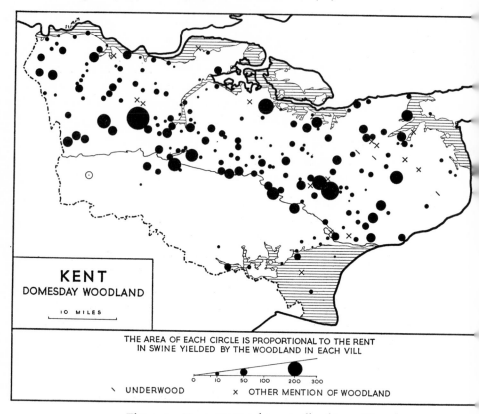

KENT
DOMESDAY WOODLAND

10 MILES

THE AREA OF EACH CIRCLE IS PROPORTIONAL TO THE RENT
IN SWINE YIELDED BY THE WOODLAND IN EACH VILL

0   10   50   100   200   300

↘ UNDERWOOD   × OTHER MENTION OF WOODLAND

Fig. 149. Kent: Domesday woodland in 1086.

Where the wood of a village is entered partly in terms of a swine render and partly
in some other way, only the swine render is shown. The open circle represents the
render in swine from an anonymous holding in Somerden hundred. Areas of coastal
alluvium, blown sand and shingle, and also the northern boundary of Weald Clay, are
shown (see Fig. 140).

Several entries make mention of either the king or Richard of Tonbridge
holding some of the woodland of estates of which they were not the
tenants-in-chief. Thus on the bishop of Bayeux's holdings, the king held

[1] See p. 555 below.

wood yielding 8s. at Farningham (6), and at Lullingstone (6) he held wood yielding 3s. as a new gift (*pro novo dono*) from the bishop. Richard of Tonbridge likewise held wood belonging to eleven manors (Fig. 138).[1] With these may be grouped the wood that Hugh de Montfort held on the bishop of Bayeux's holding at Beamonston (10b): *De isto manerio tenet Hugo de montfort inter silvam et pasturam quod valebat T.R.E. vi libras, et post et modo tantundem.*[2] Finally, in the entry for the royal manor of Dartford (2b) we hear of 6 acres of land and a certain woodland that had been mortgaged for 40s. (*pro quoddam vadimonium, xl solidorum*).

Distribution of woodland

Fig. 149, showing the distribution of woodland entered under the Domesday place-names of Kent, has very great limitations. Its symbols represent not the location of the wood on the ground, but only that of the parent estates to which renders were paid. Thus the 500 swine recorded in the entry for Wrotham (3) must have come from swine pastures in the Weald; or again, so must the 220 swine in the entry for Milton Regis (2b). Many, perhaps most, of the symbols on Fig. 149 should therefore be 'spread out', so to speak, by eye over the adjacent Weald or, maybe, occasionally over small stretches of wood outside the Weald. Even so we may wonder whether the Domesday entries account for all the wood of the Weald. It may well be that some unexploited wood, or extra-manorial wood—particularly on the Weald Clay—went unmeasured, and so unrecorded in the folios before us.[3]

DENES

Pre-Domesday documents show that at an early date many villages in Kent came to regard certain localities in the Weald, often at a long distance away, as their own particular swine pastures; the localities, known as denes or denns, were connected to their parent estates by drove-ways.[4] Here, obviously, was a very unusual economy, but it is one upon which the Domesday Book throws very little light. The lack of information is

[1] See p. 487 above.

[2] This is obscure. As it stands we seem to be told that Hugh's portion was worth £6; but no values are given for the manor as a whole, and perhaps the amounts of £6 really refer to these.

[3] It is possible that the Surrey folios provide us with an example of this; the wood of Wallington (31) is said to be 'in Kent' (see p. 387 above).

[4] N. Neilson (ed.), *The Cartulary and Terrier of the Priory of Bilsington, Kent* (British Academy, London, 1928), pp. 1 *et seq.*

due largely to the fact that the resources of these outliers in the Weald were not set out in separate entries but were included within the entries of their respective home centres. As we have seen, the map of Domesday woodland in Kent is a map of ownership and not of location.

Some Domesday entries, however, do mention denes, and the number so recorded for Kent seems to be 52, together with 3 half-denes.[1] Clearly, from the evidence of the pre-Domesday charters and of thirteenth-century records, this number is only a fraction of the total. Moreover, the frequency of the element 'den' in the place-names of the Weald provides abundant indication of the large number and wide distribution of these early swine pastures. The relatively few mentioned in the Domesday Book were probably inserted either by chance or because of some particular circumstance, e.g. under Postling (10b) we hear of three left out of the 'division' of Hugh de Montfort.

A complete list of the Domesday entries mentioning denes is assembled on pp. 530–1. Fig. 150 shows the parent centres, but we cannot tell where the denes themselves were physically located. Presumably most, if not all, of them were in the Weald (the outline of which is indicated on Fig. 150), but it is possible that some were in small woods outside the Weald. Broadly speaking, the entries fall into two main groups. First come those that mention denes without any reference to population or to teams. This group includes a great variety. There are 'large denes' and 'small denes'; there are denes *de silva*, sometimes with swine renders ranging up to 50 swine from 5 denes; and there are other denes with no mention of wood but with money renders ranging up to 15s. from one dene. The second group of entries mentions denes in connection with population and/or teams. Thus Peckham (7b) had 3 denes where dwelt (*ubi manent*) 4 villeins, apparently without teams; but Tinton (11) had half a dene with 1 villein, and 3 bordars and half a team. An assessment is sometimes stated for these inhabited denes. It is dangerous to argue from silence in the Domesday Book, and it is possible that the denes with no recorded population or teams really had them, but that they were entered under the names of their parent estates. On the other hand, there

[1] The total of 52 is arrived at by (*a*) including the 4 denes at Leeds, said by the Excerpta to have been in Sussex (see p. 484 n. above); (*b*) taking the number in the entry for Newington to be 7—that is 4, together with 3 which had been separated from it since *T.R.E.*; (*c*) including the three denes at Bilsington which may have been in Sussex (see p. 484 above); (*d*) assuming that the two Postling entries refer to the same three denes.

may be a prima facie case for thinking that the denes for which teams are recorded had passed beyond an initial stage of being merely swine pastures.

We might envisage a third stage in the progress of colonisation, represented by those settlements in the Weald with Domesday place-names of their own, some of which end in 'den'. Judged by its entry, Tiffenden (13b) seems to have been only just emerging from a mere swine pasture.

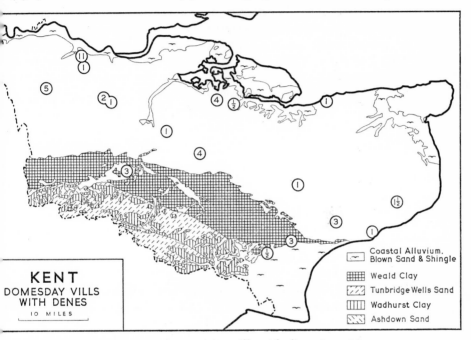

Fig. 150. Kent: Domesday vills with denes in 1086.

There were also unallocated denes in the hundreds of Blackbourne, Newchurch and Rolvenden, and others in the possession of St Martin of Dover. For a complete list see pp. 530–1.

It was assessed at half a yoke; it had 2 villeins with half a team; and it was worth but 100d. a year. On the other hand, Benenden (the dene of Bionna's people) with 3 teams (11) and Newenden (the new dene) with 5 teams (4) had already become 'adult' villages. There was also *Dene* (i.e. Dean Court, 10b) assessed at a sulung, with land for 2 plough-teams on which 1 team was at work, an acre of meadow, wood yielding 7 swine, and a population of 4 bordars and 2 serfs; the entry concludes by telling us that in 1066 Dean 'was divided between three places' (*erat dispertita in tribus locis*).

The Domesday Denes of Kent

A. *Denes without Population or Teams*

(i) *Denes 'de silva'*

Dartford (2b): *De silva viii denae parvae et iii magnae.*

Hawley (6): *una dena silvae de v porcis.*

Milton Regis (2b): *De silva regis habet Wadardus tantum quod reddit xvi denarios per annum, et dimidiam denam tenet quam T.R.E. quidam villanus tenuit.*

Newington near Milton Regis (14b): *iiii denae de silva reddunt xxx porcos de pasnagio.*

Orpington (4b): *v denae silvae de l porcis.*

Ridley (6): *una dena silvae quam tenet Ricardus de Tonebrige.*

Whitstable (*Nortone*, 3b): *Una parva dena silvae.*

(ii) *Other denes*

Allington in Larkfield hd. (7): *una dena de xv solidis.*

Ash (6): *Rex habet inde ii denas quae appreciantur vi solidis.*

Bilsington (10b): *In hoc manerio misit episcopus iii denas quae remanserunt extra divisionem comitis de Ow.*[1]

Ewell (11): *De isto manerio tenet Hugo de Montfort xvii acras terrae et unam denam et dimidiam quod (sic) appreciantur vii solidis.*

Folkestone (9b): *De una Dena et de terra quae data est ab his solins ad firmam exeunt iii librae.*

Leeds (7b): *Comes de Ow habet iiii denas de isto manerio quae valent xx solidos.*[2]

Newington near Milton Regis (14b): *De hoc manerio sunt foris iii denae quae ibi fuerunt T.R.E. sicut hundredum testificatur.*

Postling (13): *De isto manerio tenet Radulfus de curbespine iii denas; extra divisionem sunt et valent xv solidos.*

Wye (11b): *Radulfus de curbespina tenet unam denam et unum jugum de terra sochemannorum hujus manerii; reddit de consuetudine vi denarios.*

B. *Denes with Population and Teams*

In Blackbourne and in Newchurch hds. (14): *Adhuc habet unam denam quae jacuit in Fane[3] manerio Adami. Ibi sunt ii bordarii reddentes xxx denarios. Valet et valuit semper v solidos.*

---

[1] See p. 484 above.

[2] The Excerpta states: *Item de eodem manerio tenet comes Robertus de eu iiii dennas silvarum in Suthsexa quae appreciate xx sol*; see A. Ballard, *op. cit.* pp. vii and 2.

[3] Represented by Fanscoombe in Wye: see J. K. Wallenberg, *The Place-Names of Kent*, p. 386.

Peckham (7b): *Rex habet de hoc manerio tres denas ubi manent iiii villani et valet xl solidos. Comes Leuuinus tenuit.*

Postling (10b): *Isdem Radulfus tenet iii denas quae remanserunt extra divisionem Hugonis de Montfort de pistinges (i.e. Postling) manerio, et ibi est unum jugum terrae et una virga et ibi sunt ii villani. Valet et valuit semper xv solidos.*

In Rolvenden hd. (9b): *In Rolvinden Hundredo Adam filius huberti tenet de episcopo i denam de dimidio jugo quae remansit extra divisionem hugonis de montfort et jacuit in Belice. Ibi habet ii villanos cum dimidia caruca. Valet et valuit haec semper x solidos.*

St Martin of Dover (2): *Ad ista iii solina sunt v denae et vi villani et v bordarii et reddunt ix solidos iii denarios minus; habent iii carucas et dimidiam.*[1]

Tinton (11): *Isdem Robertus tenet de episcopo dimidiam denam de manerio Titentone (i.e. Tinton) quod tenet Hugo de Montfort, et ibi habet terram ad dimidiam carucam et unum villanum cum iii bordariis et dimidiam carucam et ii piscarias de v solidis. Valet hoc totum et valuit xv solidos. Haec terra est extra divisionem hugonis.*

The element 'den' also appears in the names of some Wealden hundreds. On fo. 11b is a heading *In Summerdene hundredo*, and beneath it come six entries, the first for an anonymous holding, and the others for Tickenhurst, Woodnesborough, Each, Marshborough and Elmton. It is difficult to account for this list because the five identified localities are in the east of Kent, far from the Somerden hundred of the western Weald. One possibility is that a hundred heading is misplaced; but, if so, it is not easy to see where the heading should be inserted, because there is not a single Domesday place-name that refers to this part of the Weald, although the names of the modern parishes in Somerden hundred all appear in the Textus Roffensis.[2] Another possibility is that here was a situation comparable with that in eastern Sussex—outposts in the Weald entered under the names of villages elsewhere.[3] There may be yet other explanations.[4]

Another Wealden hundred is that of Rolvenden, but there are only two Domesday entries for this, one anonymous (9b) and the other for

[1] One sulung in each of the hundreds of Blackbourne, Bircholt and Street (2).

[2] The modern parishes are Chiddingstone, Cowden, Penshurst and parts of Hever, Leigh and Speldhurst. See J. K. Wallenberg, *The Place-Names of Kent*, pp. 77–99.

[3] The totals for these places have been indicated by open circles on Figs. 146, 148 and 149, and have also been taken into consideration when calculating the densities on Figs. 145 and 147. For the Sussex outposts, see p. 413 above.

[4] N. Neilson inserted a '?Summerdene' hundred in the east next to Eastry hundred—*V.C.H. Kent*, III, pp. 177 (map), 178n. and 241.

Benenden (11). It may be that the former refers to the village of Rolvenden itself; at any rate, the Domesday Monachorum records a church there at this time.[1] Then again there is the hundred of *Selebrist* (4), which appears in the Domesday Monachorum as *Selebrichtindæne*,[2] and in modern times as Selbrittenden. It consists of two parishes, Newenden and Sandhurst; the former only is named in the Domesday Book (4), but both names appear in the Domesday Monachorum.[3] The names of two other Wealden hundreds end in 'den'—Marden and Tenterden. Neither is mentioned in the Domesday Book. The former almost certainly belonged to the great manor of Milton Regis, near the coast to the north,[4] and we know from the Domesday Monachorum that there was a church at the settlement of Marden itself.[5] The earliest form for Tenterden does not appear until 1119; it means 'the swine-pasture of the men of Thanet'. We know that in the thirteenth century it belonged to Minster in the Isle of Thanet,[6] but whether it was surveyed under the Domesday entry for the large manor of *Tanet* (i.e. Minster, 12) we cannot say.[7] Clearly, the organisation of the Wealden hundreds, as we dimly perceive it in the Domesday Book, was in a very rudimentary condition.

MEADOW

Types of entries

The entries for meadow in the folios for Kent are straightforward. For holding after holding the same phrase is repeated—'*n* acres of meadow' (*n acrae prati*). The amount of meadow entered under the name of each place ranged from half an acre at Ridley (6) to 170 acres at Aldington in Bircholt hundred (4), but amounts above 50 acres are rare. As in the case of other counties, no attempt has been made to translate these figures into modern acreages. The Domesday acres have been treated merely as conventional units of measurement, and Fig. 151 has been plotted on that assumption.

---

[1] D. C. Douglas, *op. cit.* p. 77.　　　　　　　　[2] *Ibid.* p. 92.

[3] *Ibid.* p. 92 (for Newenden) and p. 77 (for Sandhurst).

[4] The entry for Milton (2b) includes the sentence: *homines de Walt reddunt l solidos pro Ineward' et Averis.* The *V.C.H. Kent* translates *homines de Walt* sometimes as 'Walter's men' (p. 209), sometimes as the 'men of the Weald' (p. 180), sometimes as 'the men of the walt' (p. 187).　　　[5] D. C. Douglas, *op. cit.* p. 79.

[6] J. K. Wallenberg, *The Place-Names of Kent*, p. 355.

[7] No swine render is mentioned in the Domesday entry for *Tanet*.

Only one entry records a money payment from meadow. Under Canterbury (2) we read 'There, 8 acres of meadow, which used to belong to the king's messengers, now return 15s. as rent' (*Ibi viii acrae prati quae*

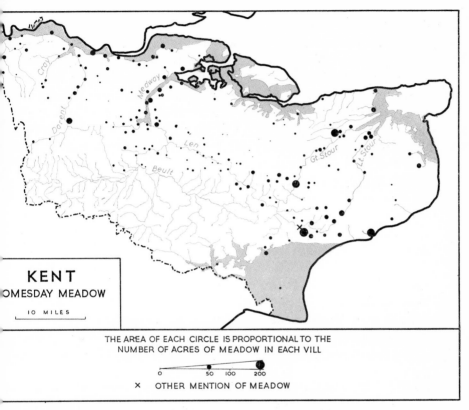

Fig. 151. Kent: Domesday meadow in 1086.

Areas of coastal alluvium, blown sand and shingle are shown (see Fig. 140);
rivers passing through these areas are not marked.

solebant esse legatorum regis, modo reddunt de censu xv solidos).[1] Another unusual entry is that for Stansted (2) in Aldington which merely records 'one meadow'.[2] At Dartford (2b) certain resources had been

[1] The corresponding entry in the Excerpta reads: *viii agri prati unde pascebantur equi regis euntes et redeuntes*—A. Ballard, *op. cit.* p. 7. See p. 550 below.
[2] The full entry states: *Ibi vii villani habent ii carucas et dimidiam et vii bordarios et unum pratum; reddunt xvi solidos et viii denarios.*

withdrawn from the royal estate, and these included not only one meadow (*unum pratum*), but also as much meadow as pertained to 10 acres of land (*adhuc tantum prati quantum pertinet ad x acras terrae*).

Distribution of meadow

The main feature of the distribution of meadow was its concentration along the valleys of the Darent, the Medway and the Great Stour. Thus, in the Darent valley, Stone near Dartford had 72 acres (5 b), and some distance inland, Otford (3) had 78 acres. There were many villages with small amounts along the Medway and its tributaries; standing out among them were Borstal with 50 acres (5 b) and Wouldham with 60 acres (5 b). Along the Great Stour, Chislet with 50 acres (12), Westgate with 134 acres (3 b) and Wye with 133 acres (11 b) also stand out.

Although a number of villages along the Thames estuary had some meadow, it does not seem to have been closely associated with alluvial areas in general; none is entered for either Minster (12) or Monkton (4 b) in the Isle of Thanet, overlooking the Stour. Most of the villages in and around Romney Marsh were either without meadow or had only small amounts; the main exception was Aldington (4), situated on the high ground bordering the Marsh, with as much as 170 acres, but, of course, it does not follow that these were in the Marsh. It is difficult to see where the 140 acres entered under Folkestone (9 b) could have been, because there is no large stream in the neighbourhood.

We cannot say to what extent Fig. 151 gives a realistic picture of the distribution of meadow in 1086. On the one hand, the belt of Weald Clay, with its many streams, could well have carried much meadow; but on the other hand, it is not likely that there were large quantities in such a wooded and poorly developed area. We may therefore conclude that Fig. 151 gives a more realistic picture of meadow in 1086 than Fig. 149 of woodland.

PASTURE

Pastura is mentioned in connection with 23 places in the folios for Kent,[1] and *herbagium* in connection with 3 places. The entries for 10 places record amounts in acres (*n acrae pasturae*), and these range from 1 acre at

---

[1] The total does not include the *pastura* mentioned in connection with wood at Faversham (2 b) and at Nackington (9 b) (see p. 525 above).

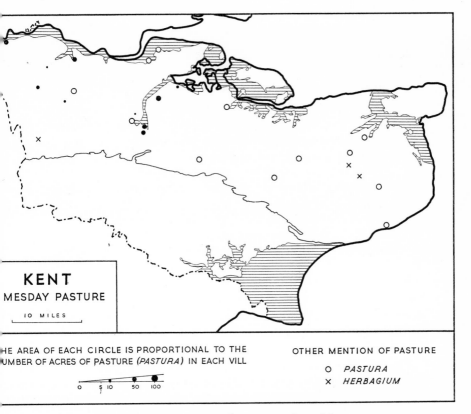

Fig. 152. Kent: Domesday pasture in 1086.

Pastura is also recorded for the unidentified *Scortebroc*. Areas of coastal alluvium, blown sand and shingle, and also the northern boundary of Weald Clay, are shown (see Fig. 140).

Paddlesworth (7) to 60 at Delce (8b).[1] Five entries state the number of animals that could be pastured, and four of these mention sheep:

Birling (7b): *pastura l animalibus.*
Cliffe (9): *Pastura c ovium (sic).*
Farningham (6): *Pastura c ovibus.*
Higham (9): *in Exesse pastura cc ovibus.*
Wickhambreux (9): *Pastura ad ccc oves et ad xxxi animalia.*

[1] The complete list of places with pasture recorded in acres is Dartford (2b), Delce (8b), Ditton (7), Foots Cray (6b), Gillingham (8), Greenwich (6b), Lullingstone (6), Paddlesworth (7), Sandlings in St Mary Cray (7), and Sifflington in Ditton (7).

Money renders are given for 10 holdings; 3 of these are from *herbagium* and 7 from *pastura*:

De herbagio:
  Barham (9b): *De herbagio xxvi solidi.*
  Bishopsbourne (3b): *De herbagio xxvii denarii.*
  Brasted (4): *de herbagio ix solidi et vi denarii.*

De pastura:
  Bourne (9)[1]: *De pastura xl denarii.*
  Broomfield (8): *pastura de xv solidis.*
  Chilham (10): *pastura de xviii solidis et vii denariis.*
  Mederclive (2): *De pastura Medredive et de hortis dovere* (i.e. Dover) *exeunt ix solidi et iiii denarii.*
  Milton Regis (2b): *De pastura xiii solidi et iiii denarii.*
  Scortebroc (2): *Apud scortebroc una pastura reddens ii solidos.*
  Sibertswold (2): *Una pastura in Siberteswalt xvi denarios reddens.*

One of the two entries for Bourne in Bridge hundred (9)[1] tells of 6 acres of pasture which men from elsewhere had ploughed-up (*Pastura unde araverunt extranei homines vi acras terrae*). Finally under Beamonston (10b) we hear of woodland and pasture reckoned together (*inter silvam et pasturam*).[2]

Fig. 152 shows the distribution of holdings in connection with which pasture is recorded. As in Surrey and Sussex, the total of these entries cannot have been all the pasture in the country. Almost every village must have had some, but how much we cannot say.

FISHERIES

Fisheries (*piscariae*) are specifically mentioned in connection with 47 places[3] in Kent, and we can also infer their existence from the references to eel renders for at least three other places. The number of *piscariae* is always stated and their annual value is given, usually in money but sometimes in terms of eels.[4] The two fisheries at Oare (10) and the half-fishery at Pimp's Court (8b) are said to be without render (*sine censu*). No value

---

[1] See p. 489 above.   [2] See p. 527 above.
[3] Luddenham has been excluded from this total because the entry (10b) seems to refer to a sea fishery (see p. 538 below).
[4] Fisheries rendering eels are mentioned in the entries for Birling (7b), East Farleigh (4b), Lyminge (4), Maidstone (3), Preston near Faversham (5), Seal (6b), Wateringbury (8b) and Yalding (14).

is entered for the new fishery (*nova piscaria*) at Monkton in the Isle of Thanet (4b); nor is one stated for the fishery at Wouldham (5b), for that at Blean (14), for that at Reculver (3b), nor for the one in that portion of Richard of Tonbridge's lowy taken from Eynsford (4). At Northfleet (3) the fishery was associated with the mill (*i molinum de x solidis cum una piscaria*) and at Fleet (3b) the fishery and the saltpan were valued together (*una piscaria cum salina de xxx denariis*). Two entries tell of fisheries serving the manor, at Newington near Milton Regis (*serviens Hallae*, 14b) and at Swanscombe (*quae servit ad hallam*, 6).[1] Two fisheries were at half a dene belonging to Tinton (11). There seems to have been a dispute about one fishery which Robert de Romenel withheld from the community of St Martin of Dover (2), but there is no clue to the location of this fishery and it has been excluded from the total above.

Most estates with fisheries had only one apiece, but there were some with 2 or 3, and a few with many more; Barham (9b) had 25 fisheries rendering 34s. 8d., and Milton Regis (2b) had 32 rendering 22s. 8d., but the Domesday Book does not tell us where they were physically situated. Fractions of fisheries were rare; there was the half-fishery at Pimp's Court (8b) noted above, and another half at Eastbridge (13); there were 1½ at Bourne (9)[2] and 4½ at Maidstone (3). It seems impossible, however, to combine the fractions in any comprehensible way.

In addition to the 47 places for which fisheries are specifically recorded, their presence is implied at 3 other places and on an anonymous holding. Renders of eels are recorded from the mill at Lullingstone (6) and from another on the unnamed holding of Haimo the sheriff in Wye hundred (14).[3] Two other entries mention eel renders, but not in connection with mills. At the unidentified *Brisewei* (1) there was a customary render of 2 sticks of eels for bodyguard service to the king (*ii sticas anguillarum pro uno Ineuuardo*);[4] and at the end of the account of the great manor of Wye (11b) we are told that Hugh de Montfort had two yokes rendering 300 eels and 2s.[5]

---

[1] There were 5 other fisheries at Swanscombe; the full statement is: *v piscariae de xxx denariis et sexta quae servit ad hallam*.

[2] See p. 489 above.

[3] For mills with eel renders see p. 541 below. The mill at Birling (7b) rendered eels, but the entry tells also of a *piscaria* yielding eels.

[4] This was linked with a customary service of 2 carts (*ii caretas*).

[5] The statement runs: *Hugo de montfort habet ii juga reddentes ccc Anguillas et duos solidos et sacam et socam in T.R.E. reddebant.*

Fig. 153 shows that most of the fisheries were along the Darent, the Medway, the Great Stour, the Little Stour and the Thames itself. There were also some in and around Romney Marsh. To what extent this map provides a complete picture of the fishing activity along the streams of Kent in 1086 we cannot say.

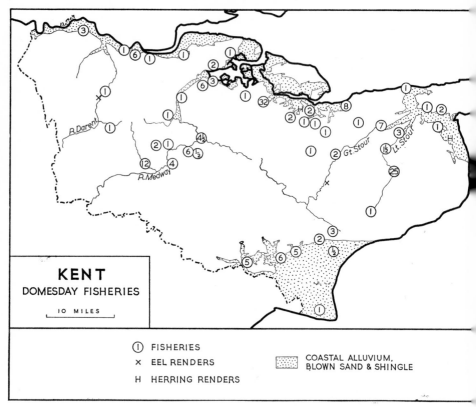

Fig. 153. Kent: Domesday fisheries in 1086.

The figure in each circle indicates the number of fisheries. There were also fisheries at *Brisewei* and on an anonymous holding in Wye hundred. Rivers flowing across the coastal deposits are not marked (see Fig. 140).

There was, however, another type of fishing activity along the coast, and we hear of herring renders in two entries. At Luddenham (10b), on the north coast, there was half a fishery rendering 300 herrings (*dimidia piscaria de ccc allecibus*); and from the borough of Sandwich (3) came

40,000 herrings for the support of the monks (*xl milia de allecibus ad victum monachorum*) in 1086[1] as in 1066. These two places have not been included in the total of 47 above. Whether any of the other *piscariae* really referred to sea fisheries we cannot say;[2] nor can we even guess what fraction of the sea-fishing around the coasts of Kent in 1086 is represented by the herring renders from Luddenham and Sandwich.

SALT-PANS

Salt-pans (*salinae*) are recorded in connection with 24 places. Each of the entries gives the number of pans, and all but three also state their render; the three exceptions are the entries for Arnolton (10), Maidstone (3) and Minster (12). The salt-pan at Fleet (3b) was valued jointly with the fishery there: *una piscaria cum salina de xxx denariis*. At Chislet (12), the render of pans was given not in money but in loads of salt: *xlvii salinae de l summis salis*. At Eastbridge (13) there were not only 8 salt-pans but the third part of a new one: *Ibi viii salinae cum tercia parte novae salinae de xx solidis*. Finally, in the account of the possessions of the canons of St Martin of Dover (2), we hear that a salt-pan had been withheld from them.[3]

Fig. 154 shows how the salt-pans were associated with the coastal areas of alluvium, much of which must have been flooded in the eleventh century. Three main areas of salt-making can be discerned. The first was in the north-east, in the alluvial tract that separates the Isle of Thanet from the mainland. Here were Chislet (12)[4] with 47 pans, Reculver (3b) with 5, Eastry (5) with 3, Wickhambreux (9) with 2, and Bourne (9), Fleet (3b), Minster (12) and Monkton (4b) with one apiece. The second group of places with salt-pans lay along the marshy border of the Swale that separates the Isle of Sheppey from the mainland. Here were Milton Regis (2b) with 27, Whitstable (3b) with 7, Graveney (4) with 4, Arnolton (10) and Faversham (2b) with 2 each, and Boughton under Blean (3b), Oare (10), Ospringe (10) and Tunstall (9) with 1 apiece. The 2 pans of Maidstone (3) must also have been somewhere here, for the village itself was too far inland for them to have been physically situated there. The

---

[1] The Excerpta tells also of 30 *mansurae* paying to the monks 4,000 herrings or 10*s*. (*reddunt monachis iiii millia de allecibus vel x solidos*); see A. Ballard, *op. cit.* p. 20.

[2] For the porpoise (*unum marsum*) rendered at Stone, see p. 520. The Domesday Monachorum mentions this and also another porpoise at Gillingham—D. C. Douglas, *op. cit.* pp. 96 and 98.

[3] This has not been included in the total of 24 places.

[4] The Excerpta shows that part of the manor of Chislet was at Margate (see p. 493).

third salt-making area was in and around Romney Marsh. Here were Bilsington (10b) with 10 pans, Eastbridge (13) with 8 and part of a ninth, and Langport (4b) with 7. Here, probably, were also the pans entered under the names of three more distant places—the 2 pans of Mersham (3b),

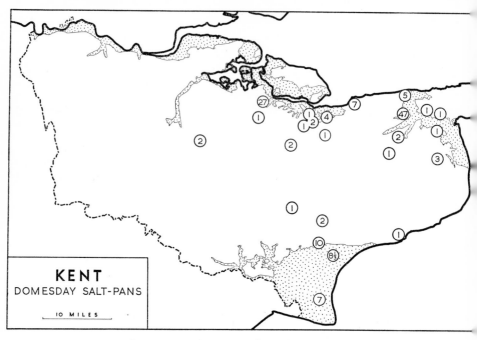

Fig. 154. Kent: Domesday salt-pans in 1086.

The figure in each circle indicates the number of salt-pans. The salt-pan withheld from the canons of St Martin of Dover cannot be marked (see p. 539). Areas of coastal alluvium, blown sand and shingle are shown (see Fig. 140).

and the one each of Folkestone (9b) and Great Chart (5). To what extent the Domesday folios give us a complete picture of the salt-making centres in Kent in 1086, we cannot say.

MILLS

Mills are mentioned in connection with 139[1] our of the 347 Domesday place-names entered in the Kent folios; they also appear in the entries for

---

[1] The total of 139 includes the unidentified *Eddintone* (6) for which 1 mill was recorded.

at least five anonymous holdings.[1] In almost every entry the number of mills is given together with their annual render that ranged from the 10*d*. paid by a mill at Sevington (13) to the £13. 3*s*. 4*d*. paid by twelve mills entered under Ewell (11 *bis*, 13b). The two mills at Horton in Chartham (10b) paid a mark of silver (*una marka argenti*). Half a mill on one holding at Farningham (6) is said to render 5 sulungs, but *de v solins* should obviously be read as *de v solidis*. No render is stated for the mills at eight places,[2] and those at one of these places (Leeds, 7b) are said to belong to the villeins (*v molini villanorum*). At two other places (that is in addition to the eight) the mills are said to render nothing (*sine censu*); these are the 3 mills in the entry for Norton (10) and the one in that for Preston near Faversham (5). The 10½ mills belonging to the canons of St Martin of Dover (2), which paid £7 in 1086, as in 1066, yielded no profit to the canons (*sed non ad proficuum canonicorum*). At Northfleet (3) the mill was associated with the fishery (*i molinum de x solidis cum una piscaria*), and at Lewisham (12b) the profit from 11 mills was linked with rent from the *rustici* (*xi molini cum gablo rusticorum viii libras et xii solidos reddunt*). There were occasional renders in kind. In three entries, mills are said to render eels as well as money:

Birling (7b): *i molinum de x solidis et ccc et xxx anguillis.*
Lullingstone (6): *unum molinum de xv solidis et cl anguillis.*
In Wye hd. (14): *unum molinum de ix solidis et lx anguillis.*

The mill at Dover (11), which caused damage to shipping, rendered 48 measures of corn (*xlviii ferlingels de frumento*).[3]

The entry for Dartford (2b) tells us that a mill, amongst other assets,

---

[1] The five entries with mills at unnamed localities are as follows, but the mills in the first entry may well have been at more than one place: (i) 10½ belonging to St Martin of Dover (2); (ii) one in Bewsborough hd. (13b); (iii) one in Hayne hd. (13); (iv) one in Wye hd. (5); (v) another in Wye hd. (14).

[2] The eight places are: Allington in Larkfield hd. (7), Beckenham (7), Dartford (2b), Hollingbourne (4b), Leeds (7b), Minster (12), Peckham (4b), Sutton (8). Three of the 13 mills at Westgate (3b) also had no values entered for them.

[3] See p. 546 below. The mill was held by 'Hugh' as a sub-tenant of the bishop of Bayeux, and its render is stated in a brief entry on fo. 11. The reference to the damage is given in the main entry for Dover on fo. 1. This says that the mill had been set up by a certain Herbert, and that Herbert's nephew had declared that the bishop of Bayeux had allowed it to be done. The Excerpta entry for Dover gives the name of this nephew as Hugh (A. Ballard, *op. cit.* p. 25). It seems very probable therefore that the mill for which a render is stated on fo. 11 is the same as that which caused the damage.

had been withdrawn from (*ablatum est*) the manor. One of the mills on the manor of Eynsford (4) was held by Richard of Tonbridge in his lowy. On fo. 2 we hear that the canons of St Martin had been deprived of four of their mills; Herbert son of Ivo had given one to the bishop of Bayeux for a mark of gold (*mark auri*) without their consent (*nolentibus illis*), and Lambert, Wadard and Ralf de Curbespine each held one. The Excerpta version of the entry for Canterbury includes an interesting statement (absent from the Domesday version) of the rights of mill-owners and their power to alter their mill-streams.[1]

Fractions of mills are occasionally encounterd. Two entries for Farningham (6 *bis*)[2] record 1½ mills, and that for the adjacent village of Horton Kirby (6b) tells of 2½ mills; it looks as if both may have shared a mill on the river Darent. But fractions do not always so easily combine. We are given no clue to the missing portions of the quarter of a mill (*quarta pars molini*) at Ripton (12), of the half-mill at Allington (7), or of the odd half-mill in the total of 11½ at Folkestone (9b).

About one-half of the villages with mills seem to have had only one mill apiece. But the table below cannot be very accurate because a group of mills on a manor may have been distributed among its component members in a way unknown to us.

Domesday Mills in Kent

Under 1 mill	2 settlements	7 mills	2 settlements
1 mill	66 settlements	8 mills	2 settlements
2 mills	33 settlements	9 mills	1 settlement
3 mills	15 settlements	10 mills	1 settlement
4 mills	7 settlements	11 mills	1 settlement
5 mills	3 settlements	12 mills	2 settlements
6 mills	3 settlements	17 mills	1 settlement

This table includes the mill at the unidentified *Eddintone* (136), but excludes the mills on the four anonymous holdings and the 10½ belonging to St Martin (2).

The group of 17 mills is entered under Westgate (3b) on the Stour; the groups of 12 under Ewell (11 *bis*, 13b) and Folkestone; those of 11 under Lewisham (12b) and in the possession of St Martin of Dover (2);[3]

[1] A. Ballard, *op. cit.* pp. xxvi and 8.

[2] There is no reference to a mill in the entry for another holding belonging to the bishop of Bayeux (6) or in the account of the archbishop's holding there (4).

[3] The St Martin group has not been assigned to a settlement in the table—see p. 541 n.

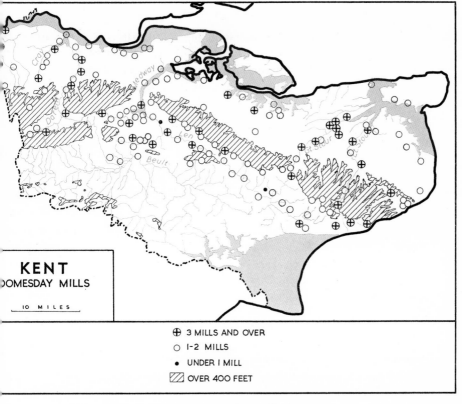

Fig. 155. Kent: Domesday mills in 1086.

There were also mills at *Eddintone* and on four anonymous holdings, and yet others in the possession of St Martin of Dover. Areas of coastal alluvium, blown sand and shingle are shown (see Fig. 140); rivers passing through these areas are not marked.

that of 10 under Sturry (12); that of 9 under Saltwood (4b); and those of 8 under Northgate (5) and Otford (3).

Fig. 155 shows that the mills were aligned along the streams, notably along the Darent, the Medway, the Great Stour, and their tributaries. The western half of the county seems to have been better served by mills than the eastern half.[1] Most of the villages in the streamless area to the north of Dover were without mills.

---

[1] The Domesday record of mills may well be incomplete, for the Excerpta tells of 4 mills paying 29s. 4d. at Langport in Canterbury hundred (A. Ballard, *op. cit.* p. 11); the corresponding Domesday entry makes no reference to mills (12).

CHURCHES

Churches (*ecclesiae*) are mentioned in connection with 145 places and two anonymous holdings; chapels (*ecclesiolae*) are attributed to two other places.[1] The total of individual churches and chapels is greater than this because some manors had more than one. Sixteen manors had two each, five had more than two, and at Milton Regis (2b) we hear that the abbot of St Augustine's held an unspecified number of churches (*ecclesiae*). The details are set out in the table below:

Places in Kent with More than One Church in 1086

Boughton (4, 8)	2 churches	Malling (3, 5b)	2 churches
Bourne (9)[a]	2 churches	Milton Regis (2b)[c]	? churches
Canterbury (2)	? churches	Monkton (4b)	2 churches
Dartford (2b)	1 church and 3 chapels	Norton (10)	3 churches
		Oare (10 *bis*)[d]	2 churches
Dover (1b, 2)[b]	4 churches	Orlestone (13b)	2 churches
Eastbridge (13)	2 churches	Orpington (4b)	2 churches
Eastling (10b *bis*)	2 churches	Petham (3b)	2 churches
Eynsford (4)	2 churches	Postling (13)	2 chapels
Folkestone (9b)	8 churches	Sellinge (13b)	2 churches
Hardres (9 *bis*)	2 churches	Sutton (8 *bis*)	2 churches
Hoo (8b)	6 churches	Whitstable (3b)[e]	2 churches
Lyminge (4)	3 churches	Yalding (14)	2 churches

Notes: [a] See p. 489 above.
   [b] One of these is called a *monasterium* (1b).
   [c] An unspecified number.
   [d] The entries are for one and for half a church, which implies 2.
   [e] *Nortone*, now Whitstable.

The total number of churches is at least 180, together with 6 chapels, making a grand total of at least 186.

Priests are mentioned in only six entries. Four of these also mention churches—at Ashford (13), at Minster (12), at Sevington (13) and at Wickhambreux (9). But at Lympne (4), for which no church is entered, there were 7 priests, and at Elmton (11b) in Eastry hundred there was

---

[1] The two places were Postling (13) with two chapels, and Poulton (13b) with one. Dartford (2b) also had three chapels as well as a church.

a priest dwelling (*Ibi manet unus presbyter*); and we must suppose that there were also churches at these places.

Clearly the Domesday record of churches is incomplete. For only one of the thirteen places rubricated under the hundred names of Bromley, Greenwich and Lessness is there a church mentioned—at Crayford (3).[1] Furthermore, no churches are entered for six of the eight boroughs. Dover (1b, 2) had four, but for Canterbury (2) the number is uncertain. How deficient the Domesday record of churches is, can be seen from the lists of churches in the Domesday Monachorum and the Textus Roffensis. What is more, a large number of these churches were at places that were not even named by the Domesday scribe.[2] These subsidiary documents, moreover, throw light upon the early ecclesiastical organisation of the dioceses of Canterbury and Rochester.

Money payments are sometimes mentioned in connection with churches. At Chislet (12) the church was worth 12s. (*Ibi ecclesia de xii solidis*); three of the churches at Dover (2) paid 36s. 8d. to the canons of St Martin (*Tres ecclesiae apud Doveram reddunt xxxvi solidos et viii denarios*); the other church at Dover (1b) paid (*reddit*) 11s. to the bishop of Bayeux; from five of the eight churches at Folkestone (9b) the archbishop had (*de quibus habet*) 55s.; the bishop of Rochester held the church of the royal manor of Dartford (2b) and it was worth 60s. (*valet lx solidos*). Payments from priests also appear in some entries. The 7 priests at Lympne (4) paid (*reddunt*) £7. 5s.; the priest at Minster (12) gave 20s. a year (*Ibi ecclesia et unus presbyter qui dat xx solidos per annum*); and the priest at Wickhambreux (9), where there was also a church, likewise gave 40s. There is one reference to tithes; at the end of the account of Milton Regis (2b), we are told that the abbot of St Augustine held the churches and tithes (*ecclesiae et decimae*) of the manor, and that 40s. from four of the king's sulungs went to him.

URBAN LIFE

There were eight boroughs in Kent—Dover, Canterbury, Fordwich, Hythe, Rochester, Romney, Sandwich and Seasalter. Three of

---

[1] Crayford represents the Domesday *Erhede*, and was formerly known as 'Eard alias Crayford'.

[2] See G. Ward: (1) 'The lists of Saxon churches in the Textus Roffensis', *Archaeol. Cant.* XLIV, pp. 39–59; (2) 'The lists of Saxon churches in the Domesday Monachorum, and White Book of St Augustine', *Archaeol. Cant.* XLV, pp. 60–89. See pp. 494–9 above.

these are described before the *Terra Regis*—Dover, twice called a *villa*, and Canterbury and Rochester, each called a city (*civitas*). The term borough (*burgus*) is used in entries relating to Hythe, Romney and Sandwich; and the term 'small borough' (*parvus burgus*) in those relating to Fordwich and Seasalter. The information for all eight places is very unsatisfactory, and it provides us with hardly any indication of their life and activities. The evidence, slender as it is, is set out below.

Dover

The Domesday Book opens with an account of Dover. Its burgesses had formerly supplied King Edward each year with 20 ships for 15 days, and in each ship were 21 men; the Excerpta adds *ad custodiendum mare*.[1] Whenever the king's messengers came, they paid 3*d.* for the passage of a horse in winter and 2*d.* in summer, the burgesses providing the steersman and one helper (*stiremannum et unum alium adjutorem*); presumably this was the charge for crossing the Channel. Soon after the arrival of King William, the town had been burnt (*fuit ipsa villa combusta*), but it had obviously recovered and prospered, for its render in 1086 was three times that of 1066.

No attempt is made to list the properties or enumerate the burgesses either for 1066 or 1086; and there is no record of rural contributory properties. We are merely told that the king had lost his customary dues from 29 *mansurae*,[2] but these can have been only a fraction of the total number in the borough. At the entrance to the harbour a mill had been built since 1066, and this was damaging nearly all the shipping because it greatly disturbed the sea (*In introitu portus de Douere est unum molendinum quod omnes pene naves confringit per magnam turbationem maris*).[3] Still, as might be expected, the activity of the town seems greatly to have expanded, and its toll (*theloneum*) had increased from £8 in 1066 to £22. We hear incidentally of a guildhall (*gihalla burgensium*), and of four churches. There is also much interesting information about fines for such offences as housebreaking (*handsoca*), breach of the peace (*gribrige*) and assault in the public ways (*foristel*); but there is nothing that enables us to estimate the size of the community or to form a clear idea of its economic life.

---

[1] A. Ballard, *op. cit.* p. 24.

[2] The total stated is 29, but the sum of the details amounts only to 28. This is because the number assigned to a certain Wadard is only 6, whereas the Excerpta gives the correct figure of 7 (A. Ballard, *op. cit.* p. 24).

[3] For the render of corn at the mill, see p. 541 above.

Canterbury

There are a number of statements about the population and properties of the city which are set out below:

(1) The main account (2) tells us that the king had 'sac and soc' over 212 burgesses in 1066 and in 1086. In addition, there had been 51 other burgesses paying rent to him; but, of these properties, 11 had been destroyed in making the defences of the city (*sunt vastati xi in fossato*

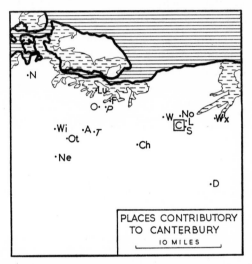

Fig. 156. Kent: Places contributory to Canterbury (C)

Canterbury is not specifically named in the entries for those places indicated by italics. A, Arnolton; Ch, Chilham; D, Denton; F, Faversham; L, Langport; Lu, Luddenham; N, Newington; Ne, New Shelve; No, Northgate; O, Ospringe; Ot, Otterden; P, Perry; S, St Martin's; T, Throwley; W, Westgate; Wi, Wichling; Wx, Wickhambreux. The entries for Langport, New Shelve and Wichling refer to a period before 1086; that for Westgate refers to 1086 and earlier. Areas of coastal alluvium are shown (see Fig. 140).

civitatis),[1] the archbishop had 7, and the abbot of St Augustine's had 14 in exchange for the site of the castle (*pro excambio castelli*). Thus 40 of the original 51 properties were presumably still in existence in 1086.

(2) Two houses of two burgesses, one outside the city and the other within, were situated on the king's highway (*in calle regis*), and had been

---

[1] The Excerpta is more explicit: *et xi sunt perditi infra fossatum castelli*—A. Ballard, *op. cit.* p. 9.

taken away. That these were not in existence in 1086 is confirmed by the Excerpta which says that one had been destroyed and the repair of the other forbidden.[1]

(3) Rannulf de Columbels held 45 *mansurae* outside the city (*extra civitatem*). Ralf de Curbespine had 4 *mansurae* and also another 11 within the city.

(4) On fo. 3, at the beginning of the description of the archbishop's lands, we are told that he held 12 burgesses and 32 *mansurae*.

(5) Finally, there are the contributory properties held by rural manors, set out below (see also Fig. 156). These, for 1086, amounted to 104 burgesses, 50 *mansurae* and 15 *hagae*. Other contributory properties are mentioned in the past tense; thus at Westgate 27 *mansurae* had been destroyed to make room for the new residence of the archbishop. But if we assume that the holdings at Langport, New Shelve and Wichling were still in existence in 1086,[2] we must add 70 burgesses and 4 houses to our list, thus giving a total of 243 appurtenant holdings.

On the assumption that none of these categories overlap, the total becomes 438 burgesses, 142 *mansurae*, 15 *hagae* and 4 houses; and the grand total of 499 suggests a population of about 2,500.

Contributory Properties in Canterbury

The entries which do not specifically name Canterbury are indicated by an asterisk.[3]

A. *In 1086*

Arnolton (10): *i masura de xxi denariis.*

Chilham (10): *xiii masurae pertinentes huic manerio reddunt xv solidos.*

Denton near Barham (11 b): *iiii masurae in cantuaria reddentes vi solidos unum denarium minus.*

Faversham (2b): *iii hagae de xx denariis.*

Luddenham (10b): *v hagae de vii solidis et x denariis.*

---

[1] A. Ballard, *op. cit.* p. 10.

[2] See p. 550 below for the use of the past tense in some of the Rochester entries.

[3] This list does not agree exactly with Ballard's list (see *The Domesday Boroughs* (Oxford, 1904), pp. 12–13) because he identifies *Ernoltun* (i.e. Arnolton, 10) with Elverton, *Dodeham* (i.e. Luddenham, 10b) in Faversham hundred with Doddington in Teynham hundred, *Nordeude* (i.e. Northgate 5) in Canterbury hundred with Little Burton in Kennington, and *Wicheham* (i.e. Wichambreux, 9) in Downhamford hundred with West Wickham in Ruxley hundred.

Newington near Milton Regis (14b): *Ad hoc manerio pertinent in cantuaria civitate iiii hagae[1] et ii in Rovecestre quae reddebant lxiiii denarios.*

Northgate (5): *c burgenses iii minus reddentes viii libras et iiii solidos.*

Ospringe (10): *i masura de xxx denariis.*

Otterden (8): *ii mansurae terrae in cantuaria de xii denariis.*

Perry (10)*: *una masura in civitate de xvi denariis.*

St Martin (4)[2]: *vii burgenses in cantuaria reddentes viii solidos et iiii denarios.*

Throwley (10)*: *in civitate iii hagae de xxxii denariis.*

Westgate (3b)*: *Ad hoc manerium pertinuerunt T.R.E. in civitate lii masurae et modo non sunt nisi xxv quia aliae sunt destructae in nova hospitatione archiepiscopi.*

Wickhambreux (9): *iii masurae reddentes vi solidos et viii denarios.*

B. *In 1066*

Langport (12)[3]: *lxx burgenses erant in cantuaria civitate huic manerio pertinentes.*

New Shelve (8): *Huic manerio pertinebat in cantuaria T.R.E. una domus reddens xxv denarios.*

Westgate (3b): See above.

Wichling (8): *T.R.E. in cantuaria iii domus pertinebant huic manerio reddentes xl denarios.*

Some hint of the life behind these figures is given by the reference in the Excerpta to cobblers, drapers and a porter, and to the making of bread and beer;[4] but for the most part the activity of the city is left to our imagination. The Domesday Book itself mentions churches, toll and foreign merchants.[5] It also enumerates 4 mills, and the Excerpta adds a

[1] These 4 *hagae* have been taken to refer to 1086.
[2] We are fortunate in having three parallel entries for St Martin of Canterbury:
(1) The Domesday Book (4) speaks of a *villa quae vocatur Sanctus Martinus* and goes on to say: *Ad hanc terram pertinent vii burgenses in cantuaria reddentes viii solidos et iii denarios.*
(2) The Domesday Monachorum does not speak of a *villa* but of *apud sanctum Martinum*, and then adds: *Et in Canturberia sunt vii burgenses qui reddunt huic manerio viii solidos et iiii denarios de gablo* (D. C. Douglas, *op. cit.* p. 82).
(3) The Excerpta speaks of *Ad sanctum Martinum*, and later adds: *Infra muros civitatis sunt burgenses qui reddunt huic manerio viii solidos et iiii denarios de gablo—* A. Ballard, *An Eleventh-Century Inquisition of St Augustine's, Canterbury*, pp. 14–15.
[3] This has been plotted at Longport Street, Canterbury.
[4] A. Ballard, *op. cit.* pp. 8–9.
[5] There may also be a reference to a gild. F. W. Ragg translated *in gildam suam* by 'for their gild' (*V.C.H. Kent*, III, p. 206), but in the present analysis it has been taken to mean 'in their geld', i.e. land subject to geld (A. Ballard, *op. cit.* p. xxii).

long paragraph on the rights of mill-owners.[1] Then again the Domesday Book speaks of 8 acres of meadow 'which used to belong to the king's messengers', but the Excerpta tells that it was meadow 'on which the king's horses used to graze, coming and going'.[2] Finally, we hear of 1,000 acres of woodland which did not bear mast (*silvae infructuosae*); the Excerpta describes this as *minutae silvae*.[3] Altogether we have but a meagre amount of information for the ecclesiastical centre of England, and for a city set along the main road from the Continent to London, and at the lowest bridging point of the Great Stour.

Rochester

The account of Rochester on fo. 2 is very brief and it tells us nothing about the inhabitants or the activities of the city:

> The city (*civitas*) of Rochester *T.R.E.* was worth 100s. When the bishop received it a like sum. It is now worth £20, and yet he who holds it pays £40.

But within the city were properties appurtenant to rural manors around, and these are named on pp. 551–2 and set out in Fig. 157. Some of the entries are in the past tense. 'Evidently', wrote Ballard, 'the bishop, in granting these manors to his mesne tenants, reserved the city houses which had been appurtenant to them, in the same manner as a man may sell land to-day, reserving the mines thereunder.'[4] If we assume that all the properties were in existence in 1086, they amounted to 80 *mansurae*, 10 *hagae*, 5 burgesses, 3 *mansiones* and 17 houses (*domus*) together with an unspecified number of houses at Burham. The sum of 115 implies, say 500 people but this number may be only a fraction of the total inhabitants. There is an incidental reference to a castle in the entry for Aylesford (2b); the bishop held land there valued at 17s. 4d. in exchange for the land on which the castle stood (*pro excambio terrae in qua castellum sedet*). One can only conclude that the account of Rochester as a whole is very unsatisfactory.

---

[1] A. Ballard, *op cit.* p. 8.   [2] *Ibid.* p. 7; see p. 533 above.
[3] *Ibid.* p. 7. One other entry on fo. 12 may be necessary to complete the Domesday picture of Canterbury: 'Close by (*Juxta*) the city St Augustine's has ½ sulung which was always discharged from payment, and there is 1 plough-team in the demesne with 15 bordars, and 7 acres of meadow, and there are 4 acres of land which 4 nuns hold of the abbot in almoign and [they] pay 4s. and 1 load of flour. The whole of this *T.R.E.* and afterwards as now, was worth £4.' These details have been excluded from the account of the city.   [4] *The Domesday Boroughs*, p. 16.

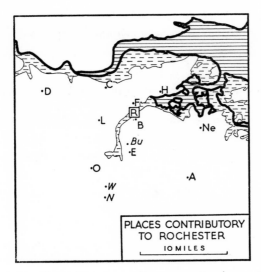

Fig. 157. Kent: Places contributory to Rochester (R).

Rochester is not specifically named in the entries for those places indicated by italics.
A, Allington; B, Borstall; *Bu*, Burham; C, Chalk; D, Darenth; E, Eccles; F, Frinds-
bury; H, Hoo; L, Luddesdown; *N*, Nettlestead; Ne, Newington; O, Offham;
W, Wateringbury. The entries for Chalk, Eccles and Hoo refer to a period before 1086.
Areas of coastal alluvium are shown (see Fig. 140).

Contributory Properties in Rochester

A. *In 1086*

Allington in Hollingbourne (8): *Huic manerio adjacent iii mansiones terrae
in Rovecestre et reddunt v solidos per annum.*

Borstal and Frindsbury (5b): *In Rovecestre habuit episcopus et habet adhuc
quater xx mansuras terrae quae pertinent ad Frandesberie et Borcstele propria
ejus maneria. T.R.E. et post valebant iii libras, modo valent viii libras et
tamen per annum reddunt xi libras et xiii solidos et iiii denarios.*

Burham (7b): *Episcopus de Rovecestre habet domos de hoc manerio et valet vii
solidos.*

Darenth (3): *Ad hoc manerio pertinent v burgenses in rovecestre reddentes vi
solidos et viii denarios.*

Luddesdown (7b): *Episcopus tenet in sua manu juxta civitatem Rovcestre iiii
domos ad hoc manerio pertinentes, de quibus habet ix solidos et x denarios.*

Nettlestead (8b): *De isto manerio habet episcopus xxx solidos pro ii hagas.*

Newington near Milton Regis (14b): *Ad hoc manerio pertinent in cantuaria
civitate iiii hagae et ii in Rovecestre quae reddebant lxiiii denarios.*

Offham (7b): *in civitate Rovecestre i domus reddens xxx denarios.*

Wateringbury (8b): *Huic manerio adjacent iii hagae in civitate reddentes iii solidos.*

B. *Before 1086*

Chalk (9): *In manu sua retinuit episcopus in Civitate Rovecestre iii hagas quae valent l denarios.*

Eccles (7): *in Rovecestre habuit episcopus iii domos de xxxi denariis quas cepit de isto manerio in sua manu.*

Hoo (8b): *Huic manerio pertinebant ix domus in Rovecestre civitate et vi solidos reddebant; nunc ablatae sunt.*

Sandwich

The main account of Sandwich is given on fo. 3. We are told that it was held by the archbishop, that it was assigned to the support of the monks (*de vestitu monachorum*), and that it rendered to the king the same service (*simile servitium*) as Dover rendered.[1] In the year in which the survey was made (*In anno quo facta est haec descriptio*) it rendered £50 from the feorm and 40,000 herrings for the monks (*ad victum monachorum*). The entry concludes with a statement of the properties within the borough: '*T.R.E.* there were 307 occupied properties (*mansurae hospitatae*). Now there are 76 more, that is altogether 383.' Appurtenant holdings are mentioned only in an entry for Woodnesborough (11) where we are told: 'In Sandwich the archbishop has 32 *mansurae* belonging to this manor, and they render 42s. 8d. and Adelwold has 1 yoke which is worth 10s.' It is difficult to tell whether these *mansurae* were in addition to those of the main entry, but on the assumption that they were, the sum of 415 *mansurae* implies a total population of about 2,000.

There are parallel entries in both the Excerpta[2] and the Domesday Monachorum.[3] They are very similar to the main entry in the Domesday Book, but the Excerpta entry concludes with a statement that the abbey of St Augustine had, in the borough, 30 *mansurae* which rendered 4,000 herrings or 10s. to the monks, and also one acre with a church. It is difficult to see exactly how this information fits in with that of the Domesday Book.

---

[1] The Excerpta entry is more explicit and states *servicium in mari*. For the service of 20 ships at Dover, see p. 546 above.

[2] A. Ballard, *An Eleventh-Century Inquisition of St Augustine's*, Canterbury, p. 20.

[3] D. C. Douglas, *op. cit.* p. 89.

Hythe

There is no Domesday account of Hythe, and we hear of it only incidentally in two entries which record contributory properties:

Lyminge (4): *Ibi pertinent vi burgenses in Hede.*
Saltwood (4b): *Ad hoc manerium pertinent ccxxv burgenses in Burgo hedae. Inter burgum et manerium valet T.R.E. xvi libras. Quando recepit viii libras, modo inter totum xxix libras et vi solidos et iiii denarios.*

It thus appears that there were at least 231 burgesses in Hythe, and this suggests a population of over 1,000 people. The Domesday Monachorum lists two churches here.[1] No hint is given even of the maritime life of the borough.

Romney

There is no Domesday account of Romney, and we hear of it only in three entries that record contributory properties:

Aldington (4): In Romney are 85 burgesses who belong to (*pertinent ad*) Aldington, the manor of the archbishop, and they were and are worth £6 to their lord.
Langport (4b):[2] To this manor belong (*pertinent*) 21 burgesses who are in Romney from whom the archbishop receives fines for three offences, theft, breach of the peace, and assault in the public way. But the king has all the service due from them, and they themselves have all customary dues and other fines in return for service at sea (*pro servitio maris*); and they are in the king's hand (*sunt in manu regis*).
In Langport Hundred (10b): The same Robert has 50 burgesses in the borough of Romney, and from these the king has all the service, and they are discharged, in return for service at sea (*pro servitio maris*), from all customary dues except those from these three, theft, breach of the peace, and assault in the public way.

Whether these 156 burgesses were all there were in the borough we cannot say; at any rate they imply a population of at least 800. Of the maritime activities of the port we are told nothing.

---

[1] D. C. Douglas, *op. cit.* p. 78. There is also a parallel entry in the Domesday Monachorum headed *De Hethe et Saltwde* (*op. cit.* p. 93).
[2] This is Langport near Lydd.

Fordwich

Fordwich is termed a small borough (*parvus burgus*), assessed at only 1 yoke (12). There had been 96 *masurae terrae* rendering 13*s*., but in 1086 there were only 73, although they rendered the same amount. There were also 6 burgesses and another 7 *masurae*. This total of 86 suggests a population of at least 400 or so, but how much greater it was, we cannot say. Anyway, the small borough must have been dwarfed by the nearby city of Canterbury.

Seasalter

On the coast to the north of Canterbury was another small borough described in a single entry on fo. 5:

In the same lathe of *Borowart* lies a small borough (*parvus burgus*) named Seasalter which belongs to the archbishop's private kitchen (*proprie pertinet coquinae*).[1] A certain person named Blize holds it of the monks. In the demesne is one plough-team, and [there are] 48 bordars with one plough-team. There (is) a church, and 8 fisheries with a rent of 25*s*. Woodland [rendering] 10 swine. *T.R.E.* and afterwards it was worth 25*s*., and now 100*s*.

Here, apparently, was a borough with no burgesses recorded by the Domesday scribe, and it is difficult to see how its life was distinguished from that of neighbouring villages.

MISCELLANEOUS INFORMATION

Markets

The entries relating to markets in the folios for Kent are three in number:

Faversham (2b): A market rendering £4. (*Mercatum de iiii libras*).
Lewisham (12b): From the profits of the market (*De exitu portus xl solidos*).
Newenden (4): There is a market rendering 39*s*. 7*d*. (*Ibi est mercatum de xl solidos v denariis minus*).

At Milton Regis (2b) we hear of 40*s*. from toll, which may imply a market —*De theloneo xl solidi*. The account of Canterbury (2) also mentions a toll of 68*s*. (*theloneum reddens lxviii solidos*), but the corresponding entry in

[1] The Domesday Monachorum entry begins: *Sæsealtre est burgus monachorum et de cibo et proprie de coquina eorum* (D. C. Douglas, *op. cit.* p. 90).

the Excerpta speaks of a toll of bread that used to render 20s. (*teloneus panis reddebat xx solidos*).[1]

Harbours

There are entries relating to harbours or hithes at four places, all in north-west Kent along the shores of the Thames estuary:

Dartford (2b): There are 2 hithes, that is 2 harbours (*Ibi ii hedae, id est ii portus*).
Gravesend (7b): One hithe (*i heda*).
Milton near Gravesend (7b): A hithe rendering 20s. (*Heda de xx solidis*).
Swanscombe (6): One hithe rendering 5s. (*una heda de v solidis*).

Vineyards

Vineyards are entered for three places:

Chart Sutton (8): There 3 arpents of vine (*Ibi iii arpendi vineae*).
Chislet (12): There 3 arpents of vine (*Ibi sunt iii arpenni vineae*).
Leeds (7b): There 2 arpents of vine (*Ibi ii Arpendi vineae*).

The arpent was a French unit of measurement.[2]

Parks

Parks are mentioned specifically at only two places:

Chart Sutton (8): A park for beasts of the chase (*parcus silvaticarum bestiarum*).
Wickhambreux (9): A park [is] there (*Ibi unus parcus*).

The park at Wickhambreux is mentioned incidentally in connection with three other places. At Garrington (12) and at Leeds (7b)[3] the bishop of Bayeux had given land 'in exchange for his park' (*pro excambio parci sui*); and a portion of the manor of Littlebourne (12), worth 60s., was also included within this park.

Livestock

The folios for Kent, like those for other counties described in the Exchequer Domesday Book, do not make any systematic reference to

[1] A. Ballard, *op. cit.* pp. viii and 7.
[2] For a discussion of the arpent see Sir Henry Ellis, *A General Introduction to Domesday Book*, I, p. 117.
[3] The statement in the Excerpta runs: *de isto manerio habet Abbas sci Augustini dimidium solinum prope ianuam de parco de Wicham et reddebat tempore regis Edwardi x sol.* (see A. Ballard, *op. cit.* p. 2).

livestock apart from the plough-teams and ploughing oxen themselves. But the entry for Yalding (14) refers to livestock when it explains the fall in the value of the estate from £30 to £20 as the result of the destruction of its livestock (*eo quod terra vastata est a pecunia*). We also hear of pasture for sheep at Cliffe (9), at Farningham (6) and at Higham (9), for *animalia* at Birling (7b), and for both sheep and animals at Wickhambreux (9). Finally, a total of 56½ weys of cheese (*pensae caseorum*) appear in the entry for Newington (14b) as a due from the manor of Milton Regis.

Other references

Finally, a few other references may be noted. We hear incidentally of the castle at Rochester at the end of the entry for Aylesford (2b); the king had granted land worth 17s. 4d. at Aylesford to the bishop of Rochester 'in exchange for the land' (*pro excambio terrae*) on which the castle stood. The site of a castle is also mentioned for Canterbury (2). The castle at Tonbridge goes unrecorded in the Kent folios,[1] but the Domesday Monachorum records that Richard had a portion of Darenth worth 10s. 'within his castelry' (*infra castellum*);[2] the Domesday Book says nothing about this arrangement. We also hear incidentally of a payment of 9s. 4d. from gardens (*horti*) at Dover (2).

REGIONAL SUMMARY

The physical features and soils of Kent show marked and fairly clear-cut contrasts, and there have been a number of suggestions for the subdivision of the county into regions based partly on these features themselves and partly on their utilisation.[3] Unfortunately, the nature of the Domesday information does not warrant any detailed division of the county in the eleventh century. All that we can discern, with any certainty, is a broad contrast between the Weald and the northern area of hill and plain; and to these main areas must be added the expanse of Romney Marsh. Within each of the main areas there is a variety of countryside, but we must be content with a few rough generalisations about it (Fig. 158).

[1] D. C. Douglas *op. cit.* p. 40.

[2] *Ibid.* p. 88. See p. 488 n. above.

[3] For a subdivision based on present land-use, see L. Dudley Stamp, *Kent* (London, 1943), p. 597, being Pt. 85 of *The Land of Britain*, ed. L. Dudley Stamp. This may be compared with the subdivision in John Boys, *A general View of the Agriculture of the County of Kent* (London, 1796).

(1) *The Weald*

Within the Weald there is a contrast between the Clay Plain of the north and the so-called High Weald of the south. In the former, the Weald Clay formation itself has given rise to a flat featureless countryside with heavy

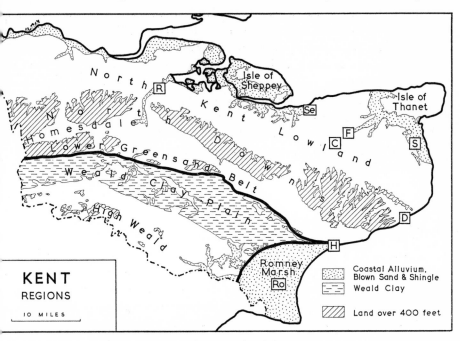

Fig. 158. Kent: Regional subdivisions.

Domesday boroughs are indicated by initials: C, Canterbury; D, Dover; F, Fordwich; H, Hythe; R, Rochester; Ro, Romney; S, Sandwich; Se, Seasalter.

ill-drained soils; the surface generally lies below the 100 ft. contour and nowhere rises above that of 200 ft. The heavy soils are only very occasionally relieved by lighter patches, e.g. in the west where the Medway and its tributaries had spread their loams and gravels. The High Weald rises to over 400 ft. above sea-level and extends across the county boundary into the similar district of northern Sussex. It is formed of Hastings Beds which comprise three groups of strata: (1) Ashdown Sand, represented only in the west, (2) Wadhurst Clay, and (3) Tunbridge Wells Sand. Its soils are accordingly varied and range from heavy to light.

Exactly how much wood was here in the eleventh century and how it was distributed between Clay Plain and High Weald, we cannot say. But even when allowance is made for the fact that much of the wood entered for the villages of northern Kent really lay here, we are still left with the impression that the Domesday entries do not account for all the wood that there must have been. The fundamental fact about the Weald was that its woodland was being exploited and colonised by the villages around, and we can discern stages in the transition from small swine pastures, or denes, in the wood to fully-fledged agricultural settlements. Although the densities of teams and of population may have been a little too low (both under one for much of the area), they could hardly have been greatly so (Figs. 145 and 147). Along the margins, and especially in the east, the densities appear to have been higher, but this was due partly to the settlements of the Medway Valley and those bordering Romney Marsh, and partly to the fact that the density areas include districts outside the Weald itself.

(2) *Northern Hill and Plain*

Northern Kent includes a variety of regions, each of which stretches roughly east-west. Immediately to the north of the Weald Clay, and overlooking it, is the Lower Greensand escarpment which rises in the west to above the 600 ft. contour. The soils over the eastern and central parts of the Greensand dip-slope vary; they can generally be described as light sandy loams, but to the west of the Medway they become coarser and less fertile. The dip-slope descends northwards into the narrow vale of Homesdale which runs west–east along the western part of the outcrops of Upper Greensand, Gault and Lower Chalk; the heavy soils of the blue Gault Clay are modified locally by downwash from the adjacent Chalk. This narrow belt, in turn, is overlooked by the Chalk escarpment, which mostly lies above the 600 ft. contour, reaching to just over 800 ft. near the Surrey border. The Chalk surface is largely covered with Clay-with-flints, and slopes northward to dip beneath the various Tertiary deposits which border the Thames estuary; here the soils vary from light sands to heavy clays, and the coast itself is bordered by wide stretches of marsh.

This varied terrain includes a number of districts with relatively few villages—on the western part of the Lower Greensand outcrop, on the Blackheath beds of north-west Kent, on the London Clay area to the north of Canterbury, and on the Isles of Sheppey and Thanet. But, in general, villages are frequent and widely scattered throughout the area.

Characteristic locations are along the valleys of the Cray, the Darent, the Medway and the Stour, along the spring-lines below the Lower Greensand and the Chalk escarpments, and on the loamy surface of the Chalk to the south-west of Sandwich. The density of teams ranged from 1·3 to 4·8 and that of population from 6·0 to 17·2, but it is difficult to account for the variations when we do not know what proportion of the resources of these northern villages refer to outposts in the Weald. The high figures for the district to the north of Romney were due to the presence of the large composite manors of Aldington, Folkestone and Lyminge, and we do not know what components these included. Assuming that the figures for northern Kent are a little too high, and looking at them generally, we see that they are of the same order as those of, for example, Essex to the north.

How much of the wood entered for these northern villages was really there—on the Clay-with-flints for example—we cannot say. Almost all the villages along the valleys had some meadow; most had mills, and a number also had fisheries. Salt-pans were frequent in the villages that border the Swale Marshes and the Stour Marshes.

(3) *Romney Marsh*

The physiographic history of Romney Marsh and of Dungeness is complicated and has been much debated.[1] What exactly were the physical features of the area in the eleventh century, we cannot say. What is clear, however, is that there were a number of small settlements within the area as well as the borough of Romney itself; and, as Fig. 143 shows, the Domesday record did not exhaust the full tale of named places. The entries for the Marsh villages enumerate population and plough-teams, but only rarely tell us of meadow; the small amounts of woodland we can only suppose to refer to appurtenant holdings in the Weald. Whatever was the precise economy of the area, it is clear that fishing and the making of salt entered into it. The densities of teams (about one) and of population (about 4·5) were not high, but they are sufficient to indicate that life in the Marsh was far from being amphibious.

[1] For a summary of the different views, see J. A. Steers, *The Coastline of England and Wales* (Cambridge, 1946), pp. 318–31.

BIBLIOGRAPHICAL NOTE

(1) It is interesting to note that William Somner's *The Antiquities of Canterbury* (London, 1640) contains a transcription of the Domesday entry for Canterbury (pp. 4–5) and of the section of the Domesday Monachorum relating to the manors of the archbishop and to those of the monks (pp. 425–40).

Early in the next century John Harris made great use of the Domesday Book, occasionally transcribing extracts, in his *History of Kent* (London, 1719); but the first to use the Kent folios systematically was Edward Hasted: *The history and topographical survey of the county of Kent* (4 vols. Canterbury, 1778–99). Hasted reassembled the Domesday information on a parish basis, transcribing and translating the relevant entries. His identifications of the holdings entered in the Kent folios provided a useful basis for subsequent study. A second edition, corrected and continued, was published in 12 volumes with an atlas (Canterbury, 1797–1801).

(2) The first complete translation of the Kent folios was by S. Henshall and J. Wilkinson in *Domesday; or, an actual survey of South-Britain* (London, 1799). This work consisted of translations of the folios for Kent, Sussex and Surrey, together with an introduction and notes; the translation is extremely free. S. Henshall, in his *Specimens and parts: containing a history of the county of Kent* (London, 1798), printed elaborate summary tables of the Domesday entries for Kent. Both this and the work of 1799 are accompanied by a map of Domesday place-names, on which lathes, hundreds and mills are also marked.

In 1869 there appeared a facsimile copy of the Kent folios together with an extension, translation and notes: L. B. Larking, *The Domesday Book of Kent* (London, 1869). The value of Larking's work is increased by the alphabetical list of manors and by the table of Domesday place-names and their modern forms.

The standard translation is that by F. W. Ragg in the *V.C.H. Kent*, III (London, 1932), pp. 203–52. This is accompanied by an introduction by Miss Nellie Neilson (pp. 177–200). It is followed by a translation of the Domesday Monachorum, also by Miss Neilson (pp. 253–69). The index to both works (pp. 437–52) is by Miss Edith M. Kirke.

(3) The following deal with various aspects of the Domesday study of the county, and are arranged in chronological order:

A. Hussey, *Notes on the churches in the counties of Kent, Sussex, and Surrey mentioned in Domesday Book* (London, 1852).

R. Furley, *A History of the Weald of Kent*, 2 vols. (London and Ashford, 1871–74). This work is interesting because Furley discusses the Domesday evidence and prints maps and lists of the Domesday places that lay wholly or partly within the Weald (I, pp. 216–30). He also discusses the pre-Domesday denes (II, pp. 701–28 and pp. 827–32).

P. VINOGRADOFF, 'Sulung and hide', *Eng. Hist. Rev.* XIX (London, 1904), pp. 282–6.

C. I. ELTON, *The Tenures of Kent* (London, 1867), especially pp. 13–58 for tenures in the county before the Norman Conquest; and pp. 113–78 for tenures in burgage etc. of the Domesday Book.

F. H. BARING, 'The Conqueror's footprints in Domesday', *Eng. Hist. Rev.* XIII (London, 1898), pp. 17–25. Reprinted, with 'some additions and alterations', as 'On the Domesday valuations with special reference to William's March from Hastings to London' in F. H. Baring, *Domesday Tables for the counties of Surrey, Berkshire, Middlesex, Hertford, Buckingham and Bedford and for the New Forest* (London, 1909), Appendix A, pp. 207–16, especially pp. 207–9.

R. C. FROST, 'The Domesday Book and its times,' *Woolwich and District Antiq. Soc. Ann. Rpt,* XII (Woolwich, 1907), pp. 67–71.

A. J. PHILIP, 'The long ferry and its foundation', *Home Counties Magazine,* XIV (London, 1912), pp. 56–66. This article includes translations of the Domesday entries for Denton, Gravesend, Higham, Milton, Northfleet and Southfleet.

W. PAGE, 'Some remarks on the churches of the Domesday Survey, *Archaeologia,* 2nd Series, XVI (Oxford, 1915), pp. 61–102; the Domesday churches of Kent are discussed on pp. 82–3.

J. E. A. JOLLIFFE, 'The hidation of Kent', *Eng. Hist. Rev.* XLIV (London, 1929), pp. 612–18.

J. E. A. JOLLIFFE, 'The origin of the hundred in Kent', in J. G. Edwards, V. H. Galbraith and E. F. Jacob (eds.), *Historical Essays in Honour of James Tait* (Manchester, 1933), pp. 155–68.

D. C. DOUGLAS, 'Odo, Lanfranc, and the Domesday Survey', *Historical Essays in Honour of James Tait* (Manchester, 1933), pp. 47–57.

B. W. KISSAN, 'Lanfranc's alleged division of lands between archbishop and community', *Eng. Hist. Rev.* LIV (London, 1939), pp. 285–93.

(4) Other works of interest to the Domesday study of the county (arranged in chronological order) are:

W. A. SCOTT ROBERTSON, 'Romney, Old and New', *Archaeol. Cant.* XIII (London, 1880), pp. 349–73.

J. H. ROUND, 'The attack on Dover, 1067', *The Antiquary,* XII (London, 1885), pp. 49–53.

F. LIEBERMANN, 'Notes on the Textus Roffensis', *Archaeol. Cant.* XXIII (London, 1898), pp. 101–12.

H. W. KNOCKER, '"The Valley of Holmesdale". Its evolution and development', *Archaeol. Cant.* XXXI (London, 1915), pp. 155–77. This article is accompanied by a set of maps, including one of the Domesday fiefs and manors in the west of the county.

F. Bentham Stevens, 'The boundary between Sussex and Kent', *Sussex Notes and Queries*, II (Eastbourne, 1929), pp. 10–14, 38–41. This discusses nineteenth-century boundary changes in the localities of Tunbridge Wells and Lamberhurst respectively.

G. Ward, 'A note on the yokes of Otford', *Archaeol. Cant.* XLII (London, 1930), pp. 147–56.

G. Ward, 'The list of Saxon churches in the Textus Roffensis', *Archaeol. Cant.* XLIV (London, 1932), pp. 39–59. This is of particular value, as Dr Ward made his list from the original MS., and not, as the Rev. Hussey, from Thomas Hearne's edition.

G. Ward, 'The lists of Saxon churches in the Domesday Monachorum, and White Book of St Augustine', *Archaeol. Cant.* XLV (London, 1933), pp. 60–89.

G. Ward, 'The Lathe of Aylesford in 975', *Archaeol. Cant.* XLVI (London, 1934), pp. 7–26, especially pp. 7–11.

B. F. Davis, 'An early alteration of the boundary between Kent and Surrey', *Archaeol. Cant.* XLVI (London, 1934), pp. 152–5.

G. Ward, 'The Manor of Lewisham and its Wealden "dens"', *Trans. Greenwich and Lewisham Antiq. Soc.* IV (London, 1939), pp. 112–17.

G. Ward, 'The origins of Whitstable', *Archaeol. Cant.* LVII (London, 1945), pp. 51–5.

W. V. Dumbreck, 'The lowy of Tonbridge', *Archaeol. Cant.* LXXII (Ashford, 1959), pp. 138–47.

(5) The Domesday Monachorum has been reproduced with an extension and introduction in D. C. Douglas (ed.), *The Domesday Monachorum of Christ Church, Canterbury* (The Royal Historical Society, London, 1944). This was reviewed by Mr Reginald Lennard in *Eng. Hist. Rev.* LXI (London, 1946), pp. 253–60. There is no authoritative translation of the text of the Domesday Monachorum; that printed in *V.C.H. Kent*, III, pp. 255–69, is incomplete.

(6) The Excerpta has been printed, together with the corresponding entries in the Domesday folios and the Domesday Monachorum, by the British Academy; A. Ballard (ed.), *An Eleventh-Century Inquisition of St Augustine's, Canterbury* (London, 1920). The text is accompanied by a useful introduction by A. Ballard (pp. iii–xxvii), which includes also some discussion of the Domesday Monachorum.

(7) The only printed version of the Textus Roffensis is that by Thomas Hearne—*Textus Roffensis* (Oxford, 1720).

(8) In the absence of an English Place-Name Society volume, useful reference may be made to J. K. Wallenberg: (i) *Kentish Place-Names* (Uppsala, 1931); (ii) *The Place-Names of Kent* (Uppsala, 1934). See also P. H. Reaney, 'A survey of Kent Place-Names', *Archaeol. Cant.* LXXIII (Ashford, 1960), pp. 62–74.

CHAPTER XI

THE SOUTH-EASTERN COUNTIES

BY H. C. DARBY, LITT.D.

The Domesday record for the south-eastern counties shows great diversity both in form and in content. Some of these differences arose from varying economic and social conditions. Others may reflect nothing more than the language and ideas of different sets of jurors or clerks. In one respect, however, there was a high degree of uniformity. By far the greater part of the area was assessed in terms of hides and virgates. A reckoning in what are called 'carucates' (*carucatae terrae*) is encountered in the accounts of five manors in Bedfordshire, of four in Buckinghamshire, and of one in Middlesex.[1] But the main exception to hidation in the area is for the county of Kent, where the assessment was recorded in terms of the sulung and the yoke.

In the hidated counties, two exceptional points may be noticed. One is the great detail given in the Middlesex folios; here, not only is the rating of the demesne portion of a holding separately stated, as in some other counties, but detailed assessments are given for the possessions of different groups of the peasantry. The second point is the very considerable exemptions that are encountered in the rating of the five counties of Berkshire, Hampshire, Kent, Surrey and Sussex.

The statement about plough-lands is fairly uniform. It is true that a few entries make no reference to plough-lands, and that in quite a number of entries (for Berkshire, Surrey, Sussex, and particularly Kent) the mention of plough-land is followed by a blank space in which a figure was never inserted. But, generally speaking, the phrase *Terra est n carucis*

---

[1] In Huntingdonshire, we hear of plough-lands on the demesne in addition to the assessment in hides. These Huntingdonshire entries do not expand the form *car'*, e.g. that for Upwood (204) reads *Terra xvi carucis et in dominio terra iii carucis praeter predictas hidas.* See (1) *V.C.H. Huntingdonshire*, 1 (London, 1926), pp. 322–3; (2) H. C. Darby, *The Domesday Geography of Eastern England* (Cambridge, 2nd ed., 1957), p. 324.

F. H. Baring, however, assumed that carucates were implied both in the entries for Huntingdonshire and in these other entries—*Domesday Tables* (London, 1909), pp. 81, 134 and 176. But we might wonder whether these ten entries for Bedfordshire, Buckinghamshire and Middlesex do not refer to plough-lands.

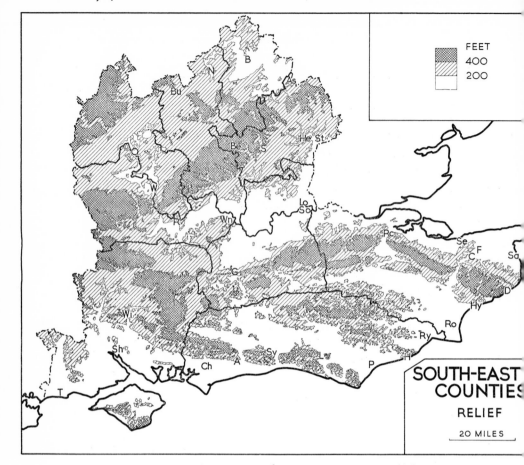

Fig. 159. South-eastern Counties: Relief.

Domesday boroughs are indicated by initials: A, Arundel; As, Ashwell; B, Bedford; Be, Berkhamsted; Bu, Buckingham; C, Canterbury; Ch, Chichester; D, Dover; F, Fordwich; G, Guildford; H, Hastings; He, Hertford; Hy, Hythe; L, Lewes; Lo, London; N, Newport Pagnell; O, Oxford; P, Pevensey; R, Reading; Rc, Rochester; Ro, Romney; Ry, Rye; S, St Albans; Sa, Sandwich; Se, Seasalter; Sh, Southampton; So, Southwark; St, Stanstead Abbots; Sy, Steyning; T, Twynham; W, Wallingford; Wi, Winchester; Wn, Windsor.

is encountered in entry after entry for all counties. There is some doubt about what exactly this information implies. Taken at its face value it seems to denote land fit for ploughing by virtue of past cultivation, present condition or future colonisation.

When the number of teams is smaller than that of plough-lands, we can only infer that a holding was not being tilled to capacity. The entries for the four counties of Bedford, Buckingham, Hertford and Middlesex usually draw attention to the difference between the two figures by stating that other teams could be added. Thus at Kings Langley (136b), in Hertfordshire, there were 16 plough-lands; there were no teams at work on the demesne, but there was room for 2; and the villeins had 2 teams, with room for as many as 12 more. If we suppose the figure for plough-lands to refer to the number of teams in 1066, there had, therefore, been a decrease from 16 to 2, which we should expect to be reflected in a decline in the value of the estate; and, in fact, the value of Kings Langley had fallen from £8 to 40s. But a deficiency in teams is not always accompanied by a fall in value. At Ivinghoe (143b), in Buckinghamshire, for example, there were 25 plough-lands with 23 teams at work, but the value had risen from £15 to £18. This possibility of a decrease in teams and a rise in value is strange, but we must add that even when the figures for plough-lands and teams were identical, the value of an estate often fluctuated, being sometimes greater and sometimes less than in 1066. Changes in value do not seem, therefore, to throw any certain light upon the nature of the plough-land figures. Still, the mere fact that when additional teams are mentioned they are already divided between the demesne and the peasantry, might well indicate past conditions and not future possibilities.

Moreover, a number of entries for Oxfordshire supports the idea that the plough-land figures may refer to the past, and, in particular, to 1066. Instead of telling us about *terra carucis*, three entries on fo. 154b specifically state the number of teams at work *T.R.E.*—at Bampton, at Benson and at Bloxham and Adderbury. Then again, the entries for Banbury, Cropredy and Eynsham on fo. 155, while not as clear, seem to be telling us how many teams had once existed—at Banbury in the time of King Edward, and at Cropredy when Bishop Remigius received the estate. At Waterstock (155b), teams *T.R.E.* seem to be equated with *terra carucis*. Finally, a short entry that may refer to Cadwell (157) does not mention plough-lands but says clearly: *Ibi fuit i caruca*. A similar phrase is also used in the entry for Rooting (12) in Kent.

We must also note the fact that in all counties there were some holdings with an excess of teams, i.e. with more teams than plough-lands. Frequently, the form of the entry draws attention to the excess. At Brize Norton (160b), in Oxfordshire, for example, there was land for half a team, but we are told that nevertheless (*tamen*) there was a whole team at work there. The excess was sometimes very considerable. At Ditchling (26), in Sussex, there were 60 plough-lands with 99½ teams. Clearly we are being told nothing about potential arable here. It might be that the plough-land figure was some traditional estimate of conditions in 1066, and that there had been improvement, great improvement, since then. In that case, we should expect the values in such holdings to have risen. This is often so, but not invariably, and the value of Ditchling itself, for example, had dropped from £80. 5s. 6d. to £72. 10s. 0d. Any correlation eludes us. Could the composition of such manors have changed?

There is another complication. Sometimes it was the total of actual and possible teams that exceeded the number of plough-lands. At Swanbourne (143b), in Buckinghamshire, for example, there were 4 plough-lands; and there were 2½ teams at work but another 2½ could be added. Can it be that here are three estimates of teams—for 1066, for 1086 and for some future year? Or are these obscurities merely the result of scribal error? It is difficult to hazard a guess as to how such figures fit into any general theory about the Domesday plough-land. It is even possible that the phrase *terra carucis* meant different things in different parts of the country. Furthermore, the fact that the number of plough-lands (unlike that of any other item) is so frequently left blank may prompt us to wonder whether the enquiry about plough-lands puzzled the witnesses and jurors of 1086 almost as much as their answers puzzle us. Faced with these uncertainties, we must rely upon the plough-teams themselves in any attempt to construct the economic geography of south-east England in the eleventh century.

One feature of the population statistics is the virtual absence of a free element; it was even completely absent from some counties. There had been a large number of sokemen in Bedfordshire in 1066; they had been reduced to about one-seventh their former number by 1086. The sokemen of Buckinghamshire, Hertfordshire and Kent had also fallen in number, and those of Middlesex and Surrey had completely disappeared. The composition of the unfree population varied, but the most important category was that of villeins, except in the Isle of Wight where villeins were slightly outnumbered by bordars. In Hampshire there was a small but appreciable number of *coliberti*, and there were also some in Berkshire; *buri* occasionally appear in the folios for Berkshire, Buckinghamshire and Oxfordshire. Serfs amounted to between about 10 and 20 per cent of the recorded population of every county but two; the exceptions were Sussex and Middlesex where they formed only about 5 per cent.

The statement about values normally gives information for three dates

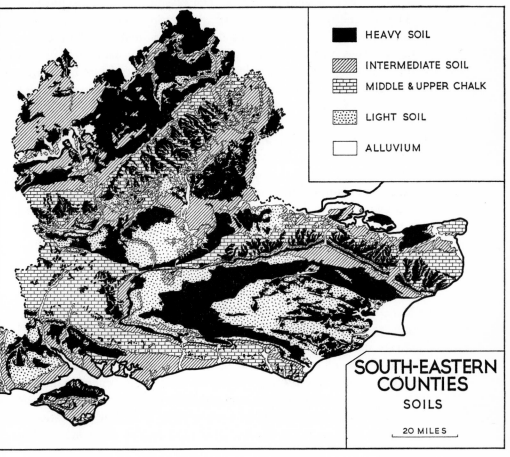

Fig. 160. South-eastern Counties: Soils.

In the compilation of this map I am especially indebted to Dr E. H. Brown.
Information about the Hampshire Basin was kindly supplied by Dr C. E. Everard.

except for Oxfordshire, where the figures for the most part relate only to 1066 and 1086, and for Berkshire where either two or three dates appear. A few entries in most counties give one or even no value. There are occasional renders in kind, and also references to the *firma unius diei.*

When three values are given, the second is often much lower than that of 1066, a result of William's campaign of conquest; but such estates had normally recovered by 1086. Some estates in Hampshire, Kent, Surrey and Sussex were paying more than their reasonable valuation justified.

The miscellaneous resources of the various counties were often measured differently, and the record shows great diversity. The wood of some counties was indicated in terms of swine totals; that of other counties in terms of swine renders; and that of Oxfordshire by means of linear dimensions. The record of meadow also shows diversity, being sometimes in terms of acres, and sometimes in terms of the teams of oxen that the meadow could support. Pasture is entered quite frequently for Hertfordshire, Middlesex and Oxfordshire, but not often for other counties, and for some hardly at all. Fisheries are entered for all counties, but the form of the entry varies. Salt-pans appear in the folios for the three coastal counties; and there are also three references, in the folios for Buckinghamshire and Oxfordshire, to interests in the distant salt-works at Droitwich in Worcestershire. Mills are regularly entered for every county. Churches, on the other hand, are only sporadically mentioned, and hardly any for Bedfordshire, Buckinghamshire, Hertfordshire, Middlesex and Oxfordshire. Among other miscellaneous items were the vineyards that are recorded for places in a number of counties.

Many of these differences are assembled in tabular form on pp. 612–18. These tables do not provide a complete statement of every variation in language and content within the folios for the ten south-eastern counties. They are intended only as a guide to the salient features that have already been discussed in the preceding chapters. While the general framework of the Inquest was the same for all counties, it is clear that the detailed recording of information was far from uniform. The full implications of all these differences cannot be explored until similar tables are available for all the counties of the Survey.

Composite maps have been made not for all items of the Survey but only for those most relevant to an understanding of the landscape and its economic geography—for settlements, plough-teams, population, wood-land, meadow, fisheries and salt-pans. A composite map has also been compiled for that unusual element in the English scene, the vineyard. These maps must now be discussed separately. But before doing so, the depression and recovery of the years 1066–86—as indicated by changes in the valuation of estates—will be considered.

DEPRESSION AND RECOVERY: 1066–86

The folios for every county, except two, normally state annual values for three dates—for 1066, for the year in which an owner of an estate received it, and for 1086; the main exception is formed by the Oxfordshire folios in which values are mostly given only for 1066 and 1086. Even for those counties where information for three dates is normal, there are many entries in which only two dates can be safely assumed. Thus the phrase *valuit et valet*, or something like it, has, for the purpose of our calculations, been taken to imply only two dates; *valet et valuit semper*, on the other hand, seems to be giving information for all three dates. Then again, there are a few entries in which only one value is given, and even some in which no mention is made of a value. When two or more entries relate to one place, they sometimes differ, one entry showing an increase, and the other a decrease. This raises difficulties, but for our purposes the values at each date for each place have been added together, with the result that similar totals at all three dates very occasionally conceal changes.

The values of some estates remained the same, or even rose immediately after the Conquest. Thus the amounts for Edgcott (147b), in Buckinghamshire, were £5, £5, £5, and those for Biggleswade (217), in Bedfordshire, were £10, £15, £17. But very frequently the second value of an estate fell appreciably below that of 1066; occasionally it fell to nothing and the estate was said to be 'waste'. The figures for Burnham (151), in Buckinghamshire, were £10, £6, £10, and those for Bexhill (18), in Sussex, were £20, *wasta*, £18. 10s. F. H. Baring attributed these frequent post-Conquest reductions in value to the passage of William's forces: 'It is obvious that a large army living, as his did, on the country it passes through must move on a wide front and leave a broad strip of ravaged country behind.'[1] Consequently, according to Baring, the great differences in the valuations of many manors just before and after the Conquest mark the footprints of the Conqueror's soldiers. Figs. 161 and 162 set out these differences so far as they can be reconstructed.

The Norman forces landed at Pevensey and, after the Battle of Hastings, marched north-east to Dover, where they stayed for eight days before

[1] F. H. Baring, 'The Conqueror's footprints in Domesday', *Eng. Hist. Rev.* XIII (1898), pp. 17–25. Reprinted with 'some additions and alterations' in *Domesday Tables*, pp. 207–16. Baring attributed the depreciated values in west Sussex and also some of those in Hampshire to reinforcements marching inland 'from Chichester or Portsmouth' (*Domesday Tables*, p. 209).

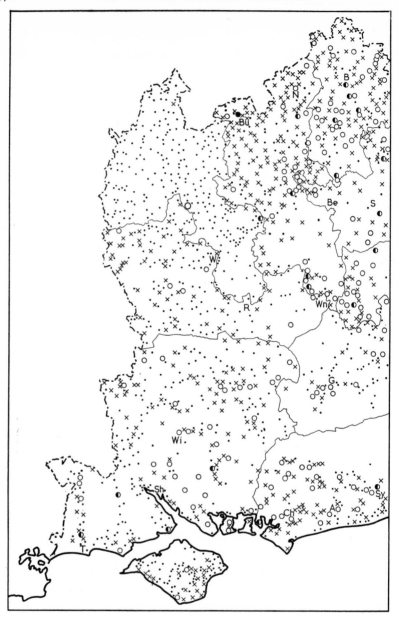

Fig. 161. South-eastern Counties: *Tunc et Post* values in the west.

For the key to the initials of the boroughs see Fig. 159, and for the symbols see Fig. 162. For Oxfordshire, see pp. 208–9.

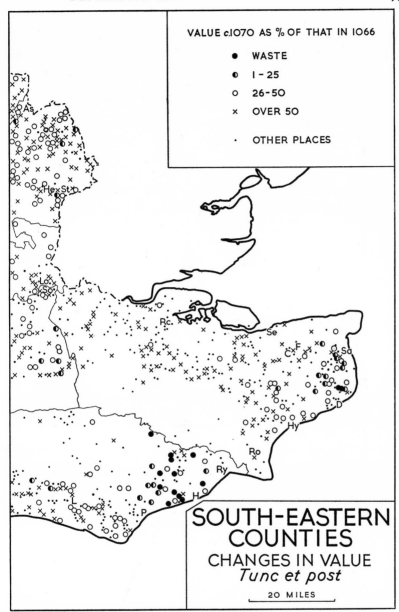

Fig. 162. South-eastern Counties: *Tunc et Post* values in the east.

For the key to the initials of the boroughs, see Fig. 159. Note that the category of 'other places' in the key includes those for which information is lacking as well as those with constant or increased values.

continuing via Canterbury towards London. Places in the neighbourhood
of Hastings suffered considerable reductions in value and some were
completely wasted (Fig. 163). The values of places in eastern Kent,
especially to the north-east of Dover, were likewise greatly reduced

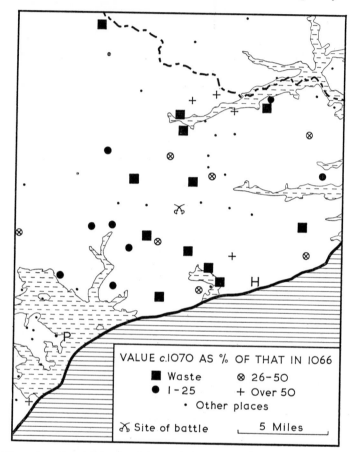

Fig. 163. Depreciated values in the neighbourhood of Hastings.

Areas of coastal alluvium are shown. The boroughs of Hastings (H)
and Pevensey (P) are marked.

(Fig. 164); and there was also a series of depreciated manors in northern
Kent and especially in north-eastern Surrey. William did not cross the
river Thames into London, but, after some of his forces had burnt Southwark, he began a great encircling movement westward and then northward

across the Thames at Wallingford. From here he continued in a general north-eastward direction, and then turned to approach London from the north. A series of depreciated manors extended across Surrey into northern Hampshire and Berkshire. From Wallingford north-eastward there was

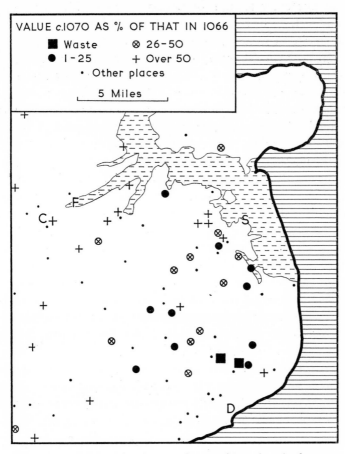

Fig. 164. Depreciated values in the neighbourhood of Dover.

Areas of coastal alluvium and blown sand are shown. The boroughs of Canterbury (C), Dover (D), Fordwich (F) and Sandwich (S) are marked.

a gap in Oxfordshire (for which intermediate values were not given), but heavily depreciated manors were abundant in northern Buckinghamshire and beyond in Bedfordshire and in eastern Hertfordshire. Baring thought that it was near Little Berkhamsted, amid these depreciated manors of eastern Hertfordshire, that William received the submission of the Anglo-Saxon leaders who had come out from London to surrender the city. In support of this view there is the statement of William of Poitiers (who wrote before 1071) that the submission was made at a point where the army had just come in sight of London. From a hill of about 350 ft. above sea-level, to the south-east of Little Berkhamsted, one could have seen the smoke of London some 15 miles away.

The *Anglo-Saxon Chronicle*, under the year 1066, briefly summarises these events by saying that William 'harried all that part which he over-ran, until he came to *Beorh-hamstede*'.[1] Writers before and after[2] Baring have thought that this was not Little Berkhamsted but Great Berkhamsted (called simply Berkhamsted today) in the extreme west of the county, and that William's forces came there more or less direct from Wallingford. Great Berkhamsted is some 27 miles from London Bridge, and it does not fit as conveniently either the statement of William of Poitiers or the postulated wasting of northern Buckinghamshire, Bedfordshire and eastern Hertfordshire. But it has been said that *Beorh-hamstede* obviously refers to the greater rather than to the smaller place, and that William of Poitiers' words must not be taken in too literal a sense. The evidence of the chronicles, which might have thrown light upon the distribution of the depreciated valuations, has instead left room for speculation. We can only venture the opinion that the importance of Great Berkhamsted certainly suggests an almost overwhelming probability that this is the place intended.

Baring's reconstruction of the route of the Norman army involved, as he said, 'an element of conjecture'. The evidence certainly does not lend itself to interpretation in any rigid manner. There was not one army but several forces, and there must also have been foraging bands. Then again, it is most unlikely that the forces always laid waste wherever they went. Moreover, it seems as if the English themselves may have been responsible

[1] The fuller parallel version by Florence of Worcester (which also incorporates the English tradition) says that William ravaged Sussex, Kent, Hampshire, Surrey, Middlesex and Hertfordshire until he came to the *villa* called *Beorcham* (*Chronicon ex chronicis*, I (Eng. Hist. Soc., London, 1848), p. 228. Sir Frank Stenton writes me that *Beorcham* is 'an otherwise unrecorded, but quite possible short form for Berkhamsted'. Note that Florence of Worcester's account omits not only Berkshire, through which the army must have passed to Wallingford, but also Oxfordshire, Buckinghamshire and Bedfordshire.

[2] E.g. E. A. Freeman, *History of the Norman Conquest of England*, III (Oxford, 1869), pp. 544–8; and G. J. Turner, 'William the Conqueror's march to London in 1066', *Eng. Hist. Rev.* XXVII (1912), pp. 209–25.

for some devastation.[1] We know, too (from an entry under 1067 in the *Anglo-Saxon Chronicle*), that some devastation by the Normans took place after William's coronation. Furthermore, the dates when the tenants of 1086 received their lands must have varied. And, as Baring himself wrote in his account of Berkshire, a subjective element may often have entered into the judgement of the juries assessing values.[2] Not least we must remember that many vicissitudes unknown to us may have caused the depreciation of this or that manor, and of this or that district. A number of manors seem to have survived the troubles of the time only to decline in value later; such were Warfield (57), in Berkshire, with valuations of £12, £12, £6, and Yalding (14), in Kent, where the figures were £30, £30, £20. But when all these uncertainties are borne in mind, and while we might well hesitate to mark on a map the exact itinerary of William's forces, the widespread damage that is revealed in the post-Conquest valuations must, in general, be attributed to the campaign and the turbulence by which William won his crown.

By 1086, however, recovery was well on the way. It is true that some manors still remained in their denuded condition. To take but two examples: the valuations of Adstock (148), in Buckinghamshire, are £8, £5, £5, and those of Solton (11), in Kent, are £15, 30s., 30s. But, generally speaking, the devastated manors had recovered either in part or wholly; thus the valuations for Farnham (31), in Surrey, are £55, £30, £47, and those for Gatton (31b), also in Surrey, are £6, £3, £6. Other manors had increased beyond their 1066 value; such was Basing (45), in Hampshire, with figures of £12, £8, £16. The destruction of 1066 was obviously quite different from that of 1069–70 in the northern parts of England. However severely some localities in the south suffered in 1066, agricultural production in general was not impaired for long. In order to put the events of the year into perspective, we must remember that there had been devastation before, and there was to be again. The Pipe Roll of 1156 returned a quarter, and even a half or more of some counties, as 'waste', but by 1162 recovery was almost complete.[3] And so it was in the eleventh century when the countryside was soon yielding almost as much as ever, and in places far more than ever, under its new masters.

---

[1] *Ibid.* p. 211.　　　　[2] *Domesday Tables*, p. 48.
[3] H. W. C. Davis, 'The anarchy of Stephen's reign', *Eng. Hist. Rev.* XVIII (1903), pp. 630–41. H. C. Darby (ed.), *An Historical Geography of England before A.D. 1800* (Cambridge, 1936), pp. 172–3.

SETTLEMENTS

Two reservations must be borne in mind when looking at a map of Domesday names in the south-eastern counties. The first arises from the fact that some Domesday names remain unidentified and so cannot be plotted. Generally speaking this is not a serious omission, and it is always possible that subsequent place-name investigation may clear up even these recalcitrant names. The second reservation is much more important. It springs from the fact that a number of Domesday names covered more than one settlement; the evidence of documents from both before and after 1086 makes this abundantly clear. There are many Domesday names that are represented in later times by groups of two or more adjoining place-names with distinguishing appellations such as Great and Little, East and West, Upper and Lower, or with some more distinctive epithets. Some of these groups may have come into being as a result of post-Domesday colonisation, but we cannot always be sure whether a Domesday name covered only one vill: whether, say, the single name Harting (23), in Sussex, covered three settlements in the eleventh century as it certainly did in the thirteenth—East, South and West. Only occasionally does the Domesday text itself distinguish between the units of such groups, e.g. when it speaks of *Bedefunt* (129, 130) and *West bedefund* (130), that is East Bedfont and West Bedfont in Middlesex.

There may also have been other reasons why eleventh-century settlements are not mentioned in the Domesday Book. The entry for the 60-hide manor of Farnham (31), in Surrey, for example, seems to cover the whole of the later hundred of Farnham where there are now five parishes. Or again, the 60-hide manor of Sonning (58), in eastern Berkshire, included not only Sonning itself but also the adjacent places of Arborfield, Ruscombe, Sandhurst and Wokingham. The whole of Farnham was held by the bishop of Winchester, and the whole of Sonning by the bishop of Salisbury, and for these reasons, apparently, the information about each was summarised in a single entry.

Rather different in character are those great manors that often include within their reckoning holdings at widely separated places. Some examples from Hampshire are striking. The great estate of Chilcomb (41), just outside Winchester, was really a 100-hide manor, but its assessment had been reduced to only one hide. Its entry includes a summarised account of seven unnamed subsidiary holdings and gives no clue to the whereabouts of these. Fortunately, a number of pre-Domesday documents show us that they lay at places mentioned elsewhere in the Hampshire folios, that is all but two—Brambridge and Tichborne; although these two places had been in existence from at least the early part of the tenth century, they went unnamed.[1] The account of the 51-hide manor of Alresford (40) gives details of five subsidiary holdings of which only two are named; that of the 106-hide manor of Micheldever (42b) refers to eleven such holdings of which only four are named; and that of the 50-hide manor of Whitchurch (41) includes six subsidiary holdings of which only two are named. We are left to speculate how many of the unnamed holdings of these three large manors were at places whose names appear nowhere in the Domesday folios. Other examples may be taken from the Oxfordshire folios, which also contain a full share of entries that summarise the resources of large manors. Most of these entries even make no reference to components, named or unnamed, but merely give grand totals for each of their manors as a whole. The first five entries for the lands of the bishop of Lincoln describe large manors (155)—Dorchester with 90 hides, Thame with 60 hides, Great Milton with 40 hides, Banbury with 50 hides and Cropredy with 50 hides. Each of these descriptions must have covered several subordinate holdings, but again we can only speculate whether or not they were at places named somewhere in the Oxfordshire folios. Or again, in Middlesex, the 100-hide manor of Harrow (127) and the 40-hide manor of Fulham (127b) must have been compounded of many units hidden from our eyes.

The most striking indication of the fact that the Domesday Book does not name separately all the settlements in existence at the time comes from Kent. The first part of the Domesday Monachorum seems to date from about the year 1100, and it mentions a large number of places in eastern Kent which do not appear in the Domesday Book yet which must have existed in 1086. The information relating to these was compressed under a more limited range of place-names in the Domesday folios themselves. We can sometimes see how it was done; the Domesday account of Little Chart (5) includes reference to an unnamed subsidiary holding, but the corresponding entry in the Domesday Monachorum assigns this to Pett not far away.[2] There is also another document, the so-called Excerpta,

---

[1] F. W. Maitland, *Domesday Book and Beyond* (Cambridge, 1897), pp. 496–7.
[2] D. C. Douglas (ed.), *The Domesday Monachorum of Christ Church, Canterbury* (Royal Historical Society, London, 1944), p. 90.

dating from shortly after 1100, which adds a few other names in eastern
Kent. What is more, a third document, the Textus Roffensis, gives a large
number of new names for western Kent. The additional place-names of
these three documents lie partly in the north of the county and partly

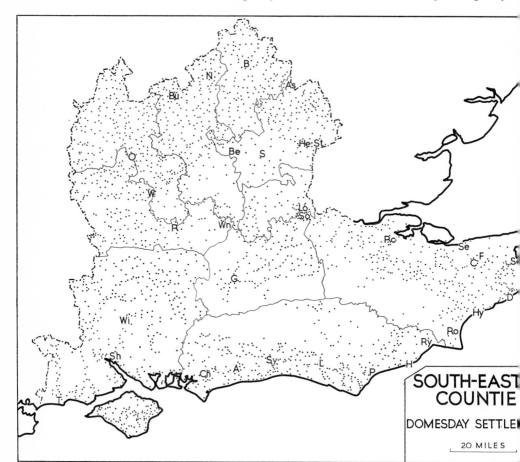

Fig. 165. South-eastern Counties: Domesday place-names.
For the key to the initials of the boroughs, see Fig. 159.

in the Weald (Figs. 141, 142). No similar information is available for
Sussex but, as we shall see, many of the numerous unnamed holdings of
that county were clearly small settlements in the Weald.

In view of these limitations, Fig. 165 cannot give an accurate picture of settlement in the eleventh century. But we might well ask what *is* accuracy in this connection? Are a village and its hamlet to count as one or as two settlements? Or, in an area of dispersed settlement, how are the units attached to names to be defined? The existence of large manors with widely-scattered members, on the other hand, certainly does introduce inaccuracy. But, while not conveying the correct nuance of the intensity of settlement in this or that locality, Fig. 165 probably gives a fair general picture.

The main features of the distribution of place-names are perhaps most easily grasped by considering, in a broad way, the relatively empty, or negative, areas. Three main empty areas stand out in Fig. 165—to the north-west, to the west and to the south of London. There is also a number of smaller areas elsewhere that are largely or entirely without place-names—in the New Forest and on the light soils to the east of Southampton Water, on the Downlands of Hampshire, on the wet clays and sterile gravels of the northern part of the Isle of Wight, on the infertile Blackheath Beds of north-west Kent, and in the Isle of Thanet and the Isle of Sheppey. Over the rest of the countryside, names are distributed in a fairly uniform manner. Characteristic locations are along scarp-foot zones and along river valleys; but, in such a generalised view as this, it is the intensity of settlement and not the detail of siting that must be our concern. The three main negative areas, in particular, demand attention.

The first is that to the north-west of London. Emerging from beneath the chalky Boulder Clay of north-eastern Hertfordshire, the Chilterns stretch from the neighbourhood of Hitchin, through south Bedfordshire and west Hertfordshire, and through Buckinghamshire and Oxfordshire, to the Thames at Goring. Their slope is broken by a series of valleys trending to the south-east, and settlements were more or less restricted to these valleys, between which stretch broad upland tracts covered with Clay-with-flints. It is not surprising that large quantities of wood were entered for the manors of the area. Here were intractable claylands, not favourable for early settlement, and still quite heavily wooded in 1086. Bordering the Chilterns along their south-east margin are other areas also inhospitable to early agriculture. The clays and outwash gravels of the Vale of St Albans yield soils which, whatever their later fertility, cannot have been initially promising; and to the south-west are the sterile gravel spreads of the Beaconsfield and Burnham area. Then again, extending across the boundary from Hertfordshire into north Middlesex, is a fairly

broad stretch of London Clay, the character of which in 1086 can be
summed up in the phrase 'few settlements, much wood'. As late as the
twelfth century here was still a great woodland with wild beasts,[1] and the
name Enfield Chase preserves today a memory of its former condition. The
juxtaposition of these areas of difficult clay and poor gravel formed a large
sparsely occupied tract, separating London from the Midland Plain.

To the west of London was another relatively empty area where Berkshire, Hampshire and Surrey meet in the district to the south of Windsor.
This is the expanse of light dry sterile Bagshot sand and gravel that was
to gain such notoriety in a later age. There were hardly any settlements
here in 1086 except along the Blackwater valley which cuts through the
area. The emptiness continued north and west on to the adjoining outcrop
of London Clay; its heavy ill-drained soils supported a few—but only
a few—villages. Here lay Windsor Forest to which the Berkshire folios
make reference. Taken together, the expanse of very light and of very
heavy soils constituted a substantial area between London and the relatively well-occupied lands of northern Hampshire and western Berkshire.

The third and largest of the lightly settled tracts lay to the south of
London. With the empty area of the Weald itself may be grouped much
of the surrounding outcrop of Lower Greensand. In places, as in the
eastern part of Kent, the Lower Greensand belt supported many villages;
but elsewhere, and especially in Surrey and east Hampshire, its soils are
coarse and unrewarding, with few villages. The great empty interior of
the south-east peninsula is the most striking feature of Fig. 165. There are,
it is true, a number of names in the central portion of the Weald, where the
juxtaposition of sands and clays provided a basis for village settlement and
agricultural exploitation; but there is scarcely a Domesday name on the
outcrop of the sticky Weald Clay itself, which must have been heavily
wooded in 1086. On the other hand, it is certain that the map does less
than justice to the human occupation of the Weald in the eleventh century.
Many of the minor names of the area are of very early date, and they 'dis-
prove, if disproof were needed, the idea that the Weald formed a trackless
wilderness in early Saxon times'.[2] Its shades had been penetrated by
herdsmen with their swine, and its resources had been organised to serve

---

[1] F. M. Stenton, H. E. Butler, M. B. Honeybourne and E. Jeffries Davies, *Norman
London: An Essay* (Historical Association, London, 1934), p. 27.

[2] A. Mawer, F. M. Stenton and J. E. B. Gover, *The Place-Names of Sussex*
(Cambridge, 1929), p. xvii.

the villages around; many of the swine pastures or 'denes' had grown, or were growing, into permanent settlements by 1086. The testimony of independent eleventh-century evidence shows the existence in the Weald of Kent of a considerable number of places that are not mentioned in the Domesday folios. The impression of the Weald given by Fig. 165 must be modified, but not fundamentally changed; even with the additional names, the Weald remains a relatively empty area. Although the Domesday Book does not give a complete picture of the occupation of the Weald, we are able to extract from it some hints of the colonisation that was proceeding.

The folios for Kent mention 52 denes together with 3 half-denes; this number can only be a fraction of the total but it serves to indicate the nature of the economy of the Weald. Amidst much obscurity we can perhaps discern three stages in the process of colonisation. The first is represented by those denes mentioned without any reference to teams or people; we hear of 'small denes' and 'large denes', and, cutting across this division, of denes *de silva*, sometimes with swine renders, and of other denes with no mention of wood but with money renders. A second stage may be reflected by these denes which had teams and people entered for them; thus, attached to Peckham (7b) there were 3 denes where dwelt 4 villeins, and attached to *Belice* (9b) had been a dene with half a team and 2 villeins. The folios do not tell us exactly where the denes at either of these two stages were situated; we hear only the names of their parent estates. But the third stage is represented by those denes which had grown to become ordinary villages with names of their own; Tiffenden (13b) seems to have been only just emerging from a mere swine pasture; it had but half a team and 2 villeins, but, at any rate, it appears in the Domesday Book in its own right and with a name of its own. Places such as Benenden (11) with 3 teams, 13 people and a church, and Newenden (4) with 5 teams, 29 people and even a market, had grown into 'adult' villages. The Domesday Book also gives some details of the Wealden hundreds of Rolvenden (9b, 11), Selbrittenden (4), and Somerden (11b), but in such a form that we can only conclude that the organisation of the Wealden hundreds had barely emerged from a very rudimentary condition. The names of two other Wealden hundreds end in 'den' (Marden and Tenterden), but these are not mentioned in the Domesday Book.

No denes are mentioned in the Sussex folios, but it is possible that the idiosyncrasies of the entries reflect a little of the activity in the Weald.

The Wealden holdings seem to fall into three categories. First, come those tiny holdings mainly in the eastern hundreds of Henhurst, Hawksborough and Shoyswell (18b–19b). They are described under the names of other places in other hundreds outside the Weald; these were presumably their parent manors responsible, incidentally, for the payment of their geld. The second group also includes holdings which were taxed with their main manors but which had names of their own; they are frequently described as having been 'part of' (*jacuit in*) places often a considerable distance away. Such holdings were especially characteristic of East Grinstead hundred (22b) in the middle part of the Sussex Weald; thus Whalesbeech had once been part of Lavant near Chichester, and Hazelden part of Allington near Lewes; the name Hazelden means 'swine pasture where hazels abound'. The third group includes those holdings that were described in their own right, that were much larger, that were responsible for their own geld, and that can be called 'adult' villages. Such were Brambletye in East Grinstead (22b), Hazelhurst in Shoyswell (19), Salehurst in Henhurst (19b), and others elsewhere. The Sussex folios contain one of the very few explicit Domesday references to colonisation, but we cannot say whether it fits into this story of advance in the Weald. The long double-hundred of Easewrithe stretched from the Downs northward across the Weald Clay to the county border; somewhere in the hundred was an unnamed holding to which one team but no people were attributed. 'It was', the entry runs, 'part of Storrington as pasture. Now lately it has been brought into cultivation' (29). But whether it lay in the south of the hundred near Storrington itself, or was an outlier in the woodland of the north, we cannot say.

The Surrey folios mention only one dene of wood, belonging to Ewell (30b), and the entry for Windsor (56b), in the Berkshire folios, refers to a third of a dene, but these entries throw no light upon activities in the Weald. Looking at the Wealden woodland as a whole, we do not know enough about the conditions under which pioneering took place, and we cannot speak with certainty. The possible sequence of events outlined for the Weald of Kent and Sussex is not inconsistent with what is likely to have happened, but when we try to penetrate the silence of the Domesday folios we can only wonder whether we read aright.

When we turn from the countryside to the towns, the incomplete and unsystematic nature of the statistics for the boroughs makes it impossible to discuss the importance of urban life in the south-eastern counties during the eleventh century. Thirty-three places seem to have been regarded as boroughs. Their economic activities are wrapped in such obscurity that it is difficult to arrive at any clear idea of the relative importance of the commercial and agrarian elements in each, but it is safe to say that there was a strong agricultural flavour about most boroughs. Markets are entered for only one of the boroughs—Wallingford—but there were tolls at Ashwell, Canterbury, Lewes, Oxford, St Albans and Southwark. Eleven other places had markets, and we hear of traders at another two places and of tolls at another four. A little information about mints, castles and churches occasionally helps to fill out the detail for this or that borough, but it is usually too vague to be of much value in obtaining a clear picture. Some of the 33 boroughs have no separate entries devoted to them, and we hear of their existence only incidentally in the entries for other places. Such were Hythe and Romney in Kent, and Hastings in Sussex; and, what is surprising, such were Winchester, the city to which the results of the Inquest were brought, and London, the greatest city of the realm.

The neglect of London is a surprising feature of the Domesday Book. Bede in the eighth century had spoken of the city as the market-place of many peoples coming by land and sea.[1] In the ninth century, according to the *Anglo-Saxon Chronicle*, it had been sacked by the Danes in 851 and repaired by Alfred in 886; and it was ravaged by fire in 982 and again in 1077. But in spite of these catastrophes it was obviously a flourishing centre of commerce. The customs of the port of London about the year 1000 show active trade with the Channel ports of the continent, and beyond with the cities of the Meuse valley.[2] Later, in Edward the Confessor's reign (1042–66), it had over 20 moneyers; York came next with over 10; and Lincoln and Winchester had at least 9 each.[3]

Interesting though these facts are, they do not enable us even to guess at the description which might have filled the blank sides of the 126th folio of the Domesday Book, as a prelude to the account of Middlesex. By later standards the city was small. We must picture it as lying almost entirely within its Roman walls. Not far away was the *villa* where stood the church of St Peter (*Villa ubi sedet ecclesia Sancti Petri*, 128). As the

[1] *Historia Ecclesiastica.* Bk. II, chap. 3.
[2] F. Liebermann, *Die Gesetze der Angelsachsen*, I (Halle, 1903), pp. 232–5.
[3] G. C. Brooke, *A Catalogue of English Coins in the British Museum: The Norman Kings*, I (London, 1916), pp. clx–clxxxviii.

contemporary biographer of Edward the Confessor tells us, 'the devout king destined to God that place, both for that it was near unto the famous and wealthy city of London, and also had a pleasant situation amongst

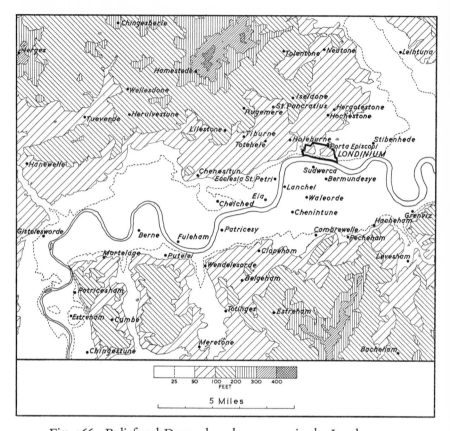

Fig. 166. Relief and Domesday place-names in the London area.

The boundary of *Londinium* or *Lundonia* follows the line of the Roman Wall and the north bank of the Thames.

fruitful fields lying round about it, with the principal river running hard by, bringing in from all parts of the world great variety of wares and merchandise of all sorts to the city adjoining; but chiefly for the love of the apostle, whom he reverenced with a special and singular affection'.[1]
These two centres of London and Westminster were surrounded in the

---

[1] F. Seebohm, *The English Village Community* (Cambridge, 1926), p. 100.

eleventh century by villages, with their plough-land and meadow and wood and pasture. Figs. 166 and 167 give some indication of what has been obliterated by the changes of later times.

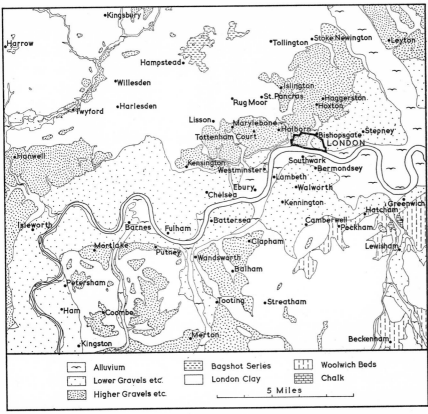

Fig. 167. Surface geology and Domesday settlements in the London area.

The boundary of London follows the line of the Roman Wall and the north bank of the Thames.

POPULATION AND PLOUGH-TEAMS

The density maps in the two earlier volumes dealing with Eastern England and Midland England did not take into consideration the figures for the boroughs. But in the present volume, the assessment, the plough-lands, the plough-teams and the rural population of the boroughs have been included in the calculation both of densities and of county totals. The urban element itself has been disregarded; and, therefore, in estimating the areas of the density units, one square mile has been allowed for London

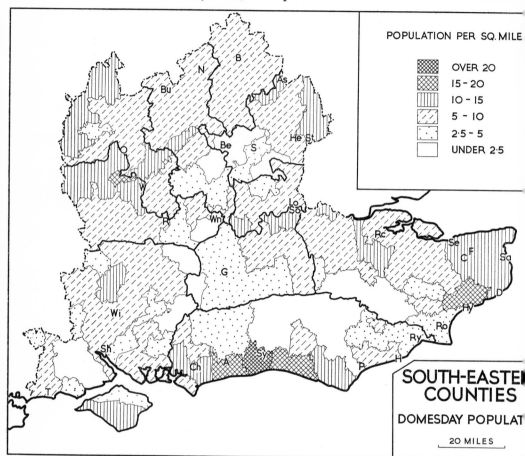

Fig. 168. South-eastern Counties: Domesday population in 1086.

For the key to the initials of the boroughs, see Fig. 159.

and a quarter of a square mile for each of the other boroughs. For the purpose of comparing these maps with those of the earlier volumes, these adjustments make no appreciable difference.[1] As in the other volumes,

---

[1] In the summary volume, the density maps for all counties will be calculated on a uniform basis.

the boundaries between the various density units inevitably have an artificial appearance because they are based upon administrative divisions.

Fig. 168, showing the density of population over the south-eastern

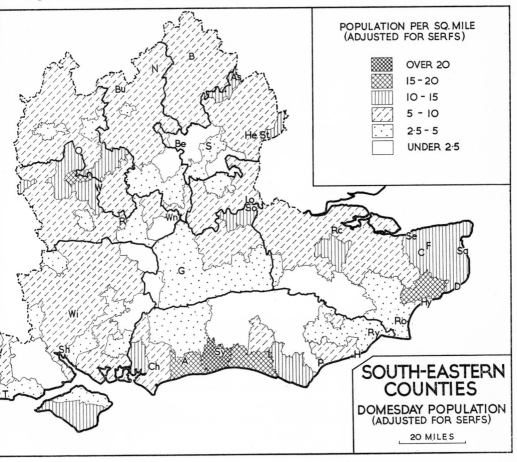

POPULATION PER SQ. MILE
(ADJUSTED FOR SERFS)

OVER 20
15 – 20
10 – 15
5 – 10
2·5 – 5
UNDER 2·5

SOUTH-EASTERN
COUNTIES
DOMESDAY POPULATION
(ADJUSTED FOR SERFS)
20 MILES

Fig. 169. South-eastern Counties: Domesday population
in 1086 (adjusted for serfs).

On this map, the serfs have been regarded as individuals and not as heads of house-holds. Their numbers have been divided by the arbitrary figure of four before calcu-lating densities of population. For the key to the initials of the boroughs, see Fig. 159.

counties, amplifies the general impression given by the map of the distribu-tion of Domesday place-names (Fig. 165). The same three negative areas as in Fig. 165 stand out—the Weald with an extension westward over the

Lower Greensand outcrop, the Bagshot area to the south of Windsor, and the Chilterns together with the adjoining districts of light gravels and heavy clays along the south-east. With the exception of the Oxfordshire Chilterns, these are areas with below 5 people per square mile, and sometimes well below; the average for the Oxfordshire Chilterns is about 8. Among other areas with but few people are the New Forest and the nearby tract of light soils to the east of Southampton Water, parts of the Hampshire Downs, the northern portion of the Isle of Wight, Romney Marsh and the Wychwood Forest area. Over the remaining countryside, densities range for the most part between 5 and 15 per square mile, but the figures are more frequently below 10 than above. The highest densities are to be found in the fertile and long-settled southern part of Sussex where figures of over 20 per square mile are occasionally reached. These figures, like those of Kent, may be a little too high because some of the people recorded for villages here were really in the Weald, but the number so involved cannot have been great; Sussex certainly included some of the most densely occupied districts in eleventh-century England.

It must be remembered that the densities on Fig. 168 refer not to total population but to recorded population. As Maitland said: 'Domesday Book never enables us to count heads. It states the number of tenants of various classes, *sochemanni, villani, bordarii*, and the like, and leaves us to suppose that each of these persons is, or may be, the head of a household.'[1] Whether this be so or not, the fact remains that in order to obtain the actual population from the recorded population, we must multiply the latter by some factor, say 4, or perhaps 5, according to our ideas about the medieval family.[2] This, of course, does not affect the value of the statistics for making comparisons between one area and another. There are, however, a number of other considerations that have to be borne in mind in interpreting the population map.

One reservation arises from the fact that we cannot be sure that all the heads of households were counted. In some entries there are references to unspecified numbers of villeins, foresters, *rustici* and men. Some other entries seem to be incomplete; at any rate we hear of teams and other

---

[1] *Op. cit.* p. 17.

[2] Maitland suggested 5 'for the sake of argument' (*op. cit.* p. 437). J. C. Russell has more recently suggested 3·5—*British Medieval Population* (University of New Mexico Press, Albuquerque, U.S.A., 1948), pp. 38, 52. But for evidence in support of the traditional multiplier of 5, or something near it, see J. Krause, 'The medieval household: large or small?' *Econ. Hist. Rev.* 2nd Ser., IX (Cambridge, 1957), pp. 420–32.

resources but not of people. The entry for Hankham (22), in Sussex, where there was land for one team, specifically tells us that no return had been made (*Inde nullum responsum*). All this seems to indicate the presence of unrecorded householders. A second reservation arises from the fact

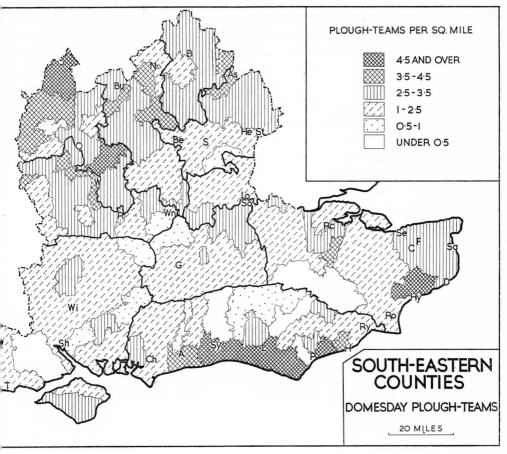

PLOUGH-TEAMS PER SQ. MILE

4·5 AND OVER
3·5 - 4·5
2·5 - 3·5
1 - 2·5
0·5 - 1
UNDER 0·5

SOUTH-EASTERN COUNTIES
DOMESDAY PLOUGH-TEAMS
20 MILES

Fig. 170. South-eastern Counties: Domesday plough-teams in 1086.
For the key to the initials of the boroughs, see Fig. 159.

that *servi* may stand in a different position from other categories of population. They may have been recorded as individuals and not as heads of households. Villages with many *servi* may, therefore, appear to have been relatively more populous than they really were. Maitland put the problem, but gave no answer: 'Whether we ought to suppose that only the heads of servile households are reckoned, or whether we ought to think of the *servi* as having no households but as living within the lord's gates and being enumerated, men, women and able-bodied children, by the head—this is a difficult question.'[1] Vinogradoff also considered the problem, and, as he said, hesitated to construe the numbers of serfs 'as referring to heads of population'.[2]

Whatever the answer, the distribution of *servi* as between one hundred and another, and between one county and the next, is uneven, so that the problem (if there be one) becomes increasingly acute as the county maps are brought together. Fig. 169 has been constructed in an attempt to meet this difficulty. The *servi* of the Domesday entries have been regarded as individuals and not as heads of households. In order to bring them into line with other categories of population, their numbers have been divided by the arbitrary figure of four before calculating densities of population per square mile. To what extent this gives a more accurate picture we cannot say. The detail of the map differs from that of Fig. 168, but the general pattern is very similar. The same negative areas stand out. Over the rest of the countryside, the range of densities is still between 5 and 15 per square mile, but the districts with over 10 are much more restricted, especially in Oxfordshire and northern Berkshire. High densities, reaching to over 20, are still characteristic of southern Sussex, for which few serfs are recorded.

In a general way, the pattern of the population map is confirmed by Fig. 170 showing the distribution of plough-teams per square mile. But there is one difference; the southern part of Sussex is now rivalled as a highly cultivated area by parts of Oxfordshire. Plough-team densities over 5 per square mile are encountered on the North Oxfordshire Uplands where the soil is, as Arthur Young described it, 'uncommonly good',[3] and in the southern part of the Oxford Clay Vale, below the Chiltern escarpment.

Fig. 171 shows the distribution of serfs as a percentage of the total recorded population. The distribution is irregular, but, generally speaking,

---

[1] *Op. cit.* p. 17.

[2] P. Vinogradoff, *English Society in the Eleventh Century* (Oxford, 1908), pp. 463–4: 'I think the serfs entered in the record are those who held *ministeria*, definite offices connected with the estates and farms; both the members of their families and stray personal attendants must have been omitted.'

[3] A. Young, *View of the Agriculture of Oxfordshire* (London, 1809), p. 4.

the percentage is highest in parts of Hampshire, western Berkshire, north-western Oxfordshire, northern Buckinghamshire and Bedfordshire; percentages of over 25 are occasionally reached in these areas. To this generalisation there is one striking exception; similar high percentages are found also in Kent, especially to the south of Rochester. Fig. 172 shows the same information plotted on the assumption that the serfs were recorded as individuals, i.e. the number of serfs was divided by 4 before the percentages were calculated. The same general pattern of distribution appears.

No map has been prepared to show the distribution of the free peasantry (freemen and sokemen) because they amount to less than 10 per cent of the recorded population in every density area except one.[1] But it is abundantly clear that many more sokemen and freemen had been present twenty years earlier. It is not possible to be precise about the numbers of the free peasantry in 1066 because we cannot always be sure whether a sokeman recorded on a holding in 1086 had also been there in 1066. Moreover, as Maitland wrote: 'A little variation in the formula which tells us who held the land in 1066 may hide from us the true state of the case.'[2] Thus two brothers had held equal shares of a holding at Barley (139) in Hertfordshire; one is described as 'a sokeman, the man of King Edward', the other merely as 'the man of Tochi'; both had been able to sell their land (*Utrique vendere potuerunt*). Or again, an entry for Wallington (137), also in Hertfordshire, tells us that '2 sokemen, Eddeva's men, held and could sell this land'; an entry not far below refers to Reed and says that 'Turbern, one of Eddeva's men, held and could sell this land'. Can we be sure that these men, both at Barley and at Reed, were not all sokemen? But even taking the entries exactly as we find them, there is no lack of evidence, and it is apparent that the sokemen, or their successors, had been reduced in status. At Datchworth (140), in Hertfordshire, where there had been 3 sokemen in 1066, there were 3 villeins in 1086. The arithmetic is not often as neat as this, but the implications are clear.

In Bedfordshire, the sokemen of 1066, specifically described as such, amounted to between 600 and 700, but twenty years later they numbered only 90. The sokemen of Hertfordshire had amounted to some 250, but only 43 were left. The number in Kent had fallen from at least 61 to 44. Those of Buckinghamshire had likewise been reduced from some 37 to

---

[1] Counting serfs as individuals, there is no exception. Counting serfs as heads of households, the figure for the hundred of Barford in Bedfordshire is 10·8 per cent.

[2] *Op. cit.* p. 63. See also F. H. Baring, *Domesday Tables*, p. 100.

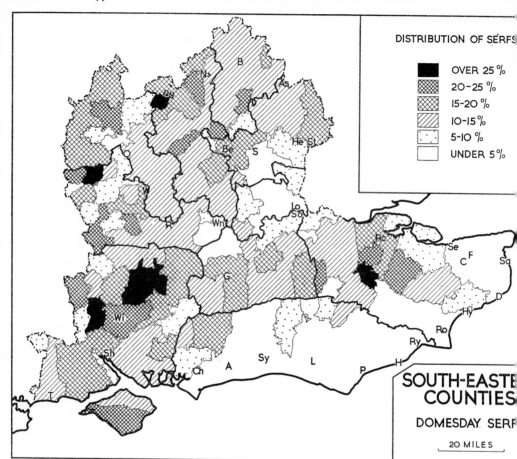

Fig. 171. South-eastern Counties: Distribution of serfs in 1086.

For the key to the initials of the boroughs, see Fig. 159.

20.[1] In Middlesex, the 26 sokemen of 1066 had completely disappeared; so had the 9 in Surrey. No sokemen, either for 1066 or 1086, are entered for Berkshire, Hampshire, Oxfordshire and Sussex.

Some of these facts are set out on Fig. 173, but, in looking at this map, we must remember the very imperfect nature of the evidence, and, in

---

[1] From 37 to 20 is a much smaller reduction than that in the adjoining counties of Bedfordshire and Hertfordshire, but the depression of the free peasantry in Buckinghamshire may well have been much more considerable than the reduction in the number of sokemen indicates. See p. 595 for the Buckinghamshire thegns of 1066.

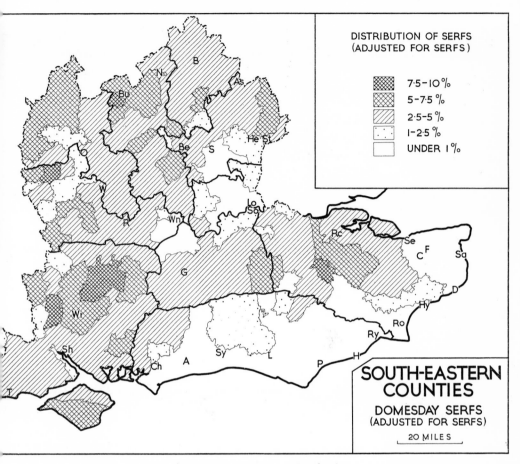

Fig. 172. South-eastern Counties: Distribution
of serfs in 1086 (adjusted for serfs).

On this map, the serfs have been regarded as individuals and not as heads of households. Their numbers have been divided by the arbitrary figure of four before calculating percentages. For the key to the initials of the boroughs, see Fig. 159.

particular, the fact that the distributions are minimum ones. No attempt
can be made to gauge the relative importance of sokemen in 1066 because
we are without any clue to the total population at this time. Sokemen
seem to have been most abundant in the Danelaw—in Bedfordshire and
north-east Hertfordshire. But they were not confined to the Danelaw;
there were some in Buckinghamshire and Middlesex, and even south of

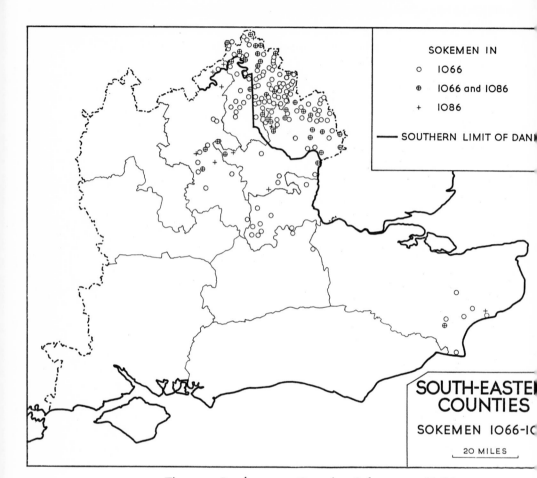

Fig. 173. South-eastern Counties: Sokemen, 1066–86.

The sokemen at unidentified places and on anonymous holdings cannot be indicated. The following is a complete list of these:

1066: Willey hd. (218b) in Beds: *Rodehangre* (140) and *Sapeham* (138) in Herts; *Aia* (13b), Aloesbridge hd. (11), Chart hd. (13b), Longbridge hd. (13b), Blackbourne and Newchurch hds. (14), Somerden hd. (11b), and the lathe of Linwart (13b) in Kent; Ossulstone hd. (129b) in Mdx.

1066 and 1086: *Cudessane* (211b, 214) in Beds; Romney Marsh (13, *quin*) in Kent.

the Thames in Surrey and Kent. The picture given by Fig. 173 may be affected by the fact that the thegns of Buckinghamshire, and maybe of Bedfordshire, were unlike those of other counties. The thegns on many holdings in northern Buckinghamshire in 1066 seem to have been akin to sokemen, and they numbered upward of 200 for the county as a whole. There had also been about 100 thegns in Bedfordshire, many of whom may well have resembled those of northern Buckinghamshire. In each of the other eight counties, the number of thegns in 1066, specifically described as such, was below 50, and sometimes well below;[1] yet there must have been many. When we pass from the sokemen and thegns to the freemen of 1066 in general, the information becomes even more uncertain. Such are the fragments of evidence that remain to us.

Supplementary to the maps are the tables on pp. 617–18 which summarise the relative importance of the different categories of population in each county as a whole for 1086. Any discussion of the significance of these maps and tables lies far beyond the scope of this study. Moreover, their full implications cannot begin to be appreciated until they are set against similar data for the whole of Domesday England.

WOODLAND

The woodland of the south-east counties was measured in one of three different ways, that is apart from the miscellaneous entries that occur for every county—in terms of linear dimensions, of swine totals and of swine renders. Unfortunately it is impossible to reduce these three main units to a common denominator with any certainty, and Fig. 174 has this inherent defect.

The wood of Oxfordshire was normally entered by giving its length and breadth in leagues and furlongs, and, in one entry, in perches. The length of these units is open to doubt,[2] and, in any case, the exact significance of this type of entry is obscure. Is it giving extreme diameters of irregularly-shaped woods, or is it making rough estimates of mean diameters, or is it attempting to convey some other notion? We cannot tell, but we certainly cannot assume that a definite geometrical figure was in the minds of the Domesday commissioners. Nor can we hope to

---

[1] In 1086 there were no recorded thegns but for a few land-holders and under-tenants.

[2] See H. C. Darby and I. B. Terrett (eds.), *The Domesday Geography of Midland England* (Cambridge, 1954), p. 433.

convert these measurements into modern acreages by an arithmetical process. All we can safely do is to regard the dimensions as conventional units, and to plot them diagrammatically as intersecting straight lines. In an entry relating to Crowell (157b) we hear only of 'two furlongs of wood'; such entries have sometimes been regarded as referring to 'areal furlongs', but on Fig. 174 this entry has been plotted merely as a single straight line.[1] Occasional entries in the Oxfordshire folios give dimensions and then go on to state the render of the wood when it bore mast (*cum oneratur*).

For the other south-eastern counties north of the Thames (Bedfordshire, Buckinghamshire, Hertfordshire and Middlesex), wood was measured in terms of the number of swine that could feed upon its acorns and beech-mast. The round figures of the larger entries (e.g. 400, 500, 2,000) may indicate that they are estimates rather than precise amounts; but the detailed figures of other entries suggest precision (e.g. 2, 5, 34, 806). G. H. Fowler attempted to convert the swine totals for Bedfordshire into modern acreages at the rate of $1\frac{1}{2}$ statute acres for each head of swine; he then expressed these acreages as percentages of the areas of the modern parishes (Fig. 14).[2] He was careful to point out the 'difficulties and dangers' of the method, and they are certainly very great. We cannot assume that such an equation was always constant as between one district and another; and, moreover, it is certain that the acreages of many modern parishes have changed since the eleventh century. Fowler's maps consti-tute an extremely interesting experiment; but, in view of the many doubts associated with them, it seems best to plot the swine totals directly on to the map as conventional units.

The wood of the five counties to the south of the Thames was recorded in terms of annual renders of swine in return for pannage. The precise form of the entries varies, and only occasionally is it explicit, e.g. when for Windsor (56b) we read: *tantum silvae unde exeunt v porci de pasnagio*. The round figures of many of these entries again suggest estimates (e.g.20, 50, 100); but, on the other hand, there are many detailed figures that seem to indicate exactness, e.g. 3, 13 and 133. We hear even of $1\frac{1}{2}$ swine from Donnington (17b) in Sussex, of $6\frac{1}{2}$ from Bourne (9) in Kent, and of $150\frac{1}{2}$ from Farnham (31) in Surrey. What was the relation of these renders

---

[1] H. C. Darby and I. B. Terrett (eds.), *op. cit.* p. 434.

[2] G. H. Fowler, *Bedfordshire in 1086: An analysis and synthesis of Domesday Book* (Bedfordshire Hist. Rec. Soc., Aspley Guise, 1922), pp. 62–3 and 107.

to total numbers of swine? It is difficult to give a satisfactory answer to this question. The only Domesday entry that clearly states a ratio is that for Leominster (180) in Herefordshire; there we are told that each villein having ten swine gave one for pannage (*Quisque villanus habens x porcos dat unum porcum de pasnagio*). But in the folios relating to the five southern counties—the very area for which swine renders were characteristically entered—we find no such explicit statement. On the other hand, swine were also rendered for pasturage (*pro pastura* or *de herbagio*) and there are some entries for Surrey and Sussex which give swine ratios for these grass swine. In Surrey it was 1 in 7 at two places and 1 in 10 at another two. In Sussex it was 1 in 7 at five places, 1 in 6 at one place, and 1 in 3 at another; but it is possible that the *vi* and *iii* of the latter entries are mistakes for *vii*. One of the entries with a ratio of 1 in 7 in Sussex is that for Pagham (16b), and a marginal note adds *Similiter per totum Sudsex*. It is tempting to assume that similar ratios applied to mast swine. W. H. Legge thought this unlikely in view of the entry for Ferring (16b) in Sussex, which might be taken to imply that wood and grass render were evaluated differently: *silva iiii porcis et pro herbagio unus porcus de vii.*[1] On the other hand, similar methods of reckoning seem to be indicated by the fact that a number of entries for Kent, Surrey and Sussex link renders of mast swine and grass swine in single totals; thus from Barkham (22b) in Sussex there came *De silva et herbagio ix porci*. To the wider question of what acreages of wood these figures imply we can hazard no reply. All we can do is to plot the figures as conventional units in the hope of obtaining some rough guide to the relative distribution of wood over the face of the countryside.

The miscellaneous references to wood that occur in the folios for every county are very varied in character. It is sometimes measured in acres and occasionally even in hides. Wood for fencing (*ad sepes* or *ad clausuram*) is frequently mentioned, and we also hear of wood for building houses (*ad faciendas domos*). Money renders, usually in addition to swine, but sometimes alone, are quite common; and renders in kind also occur—in the form of plough-shares (*soci*), or of iron for the ploughs (*ferrum carucis*), or (also very strange) of oats or rams. Then there are a few vague references merely to 'a wood' or 'a small wood'. Occasionally the word *silva* is replaced by *nemus*, by *spinetum* or by *grava*. Seven entries for Hampshire mention wood without pannage (*silva sine pasnagio*), and two

---

[1] *V.C.H. Sussex*, II (London, 1907), p. 293.

for the same county speak of useless wood (*silva inutilis*). We also hear of infertile wood in the entry for Canterbury (2) which states that there were as many as 1,000 acres of *silva infructuosa* rendering 24s.; it is an unusual entry for Kent, but it becomes even more interesting when we see that the corresponding entry in the Excerpta refers to 1,000 acres of *silva minuta*.[1] Entries for *silva minuta* occur with moderate frequency in the Domesday folios. Can we assume that they all imply wood not bearing mast?

An important question which we must pause to consider is to what extent the Domesday Book gives a complete record of woodland in England in 1086. F. H. Baring thought that the absence of wood from Cottesloe hundred in Buckinghamshire might have been 'due to mistake in the original return' made by the hundred jury.[2] He also commented on the almost complete absence of wood entries from the hundreds of Biggleswade and Wenslow in Bedfordshire, and again thought 'there may have been a mistake in the preparation of the original returns'.[3] He was struck by the same doubt for Surrey: 'there must surely have been woodland at Ashtead in Copthorne which still has a large and wooded common',[4] and, we might add, this is oakwood on heavy London Clay. Then, again, he noted the absence of wood from the lowland of northern Berkshire and attributed it 'to omission in the returns'.[5] F. W. Morgan thought that the lack of wood here was the result of clearing, and that 'the rich clays were proving agriculturally attractive'.[6] This may well have been true, because the densities of plough-teams and of population were relatively high here. But, even so, there is evidence that some wood, at any rate, in this area went unrecorded. Several charters of the eleventh and twelfth centuries in the Abingdon Chronicle refer to the woods of Cumnor and Bagley in the extreme north, within the great bend of the Thames.[7] There is no reference to wood in the entry for Cumnor (58b), nor is there

---

[1] A. Ballard, *An Eleventh-Century Inquisition of St Augustine's, Canterbury* (British Academy, London, 1920), p. 7.
[2] F. H. Baring, *Domesday Tables*, p. 133.
[3] *Ibid.* p. 177.   [4] *Ibid.* p. 13.
[5] *Ibid.* p. 41.
[6] F. W. Morgan, 'The Domesday Geography of Berkshire', *Scot. Geog. Mag.* LI (Edinburgh, 1935), p. 358.
[7] J. Stevenson (ed.), *Chronicon Monasterii de Abingdon*, II (Rolls Series, London, 1858), pp. 10, 113–14, 219–20 and 247. See E. M. Jope, 'Saxon Oxford and its region' in D. B. Harden (ed.), *Dark-Age Britain* (London, 1956), p. 247.

any Domesday mention of Bagley Wood which later in time was extra-parochial.

A close examination of eleventh- and twelfth-century sources would almost certainly reveal other non-Domesday wood for this or that

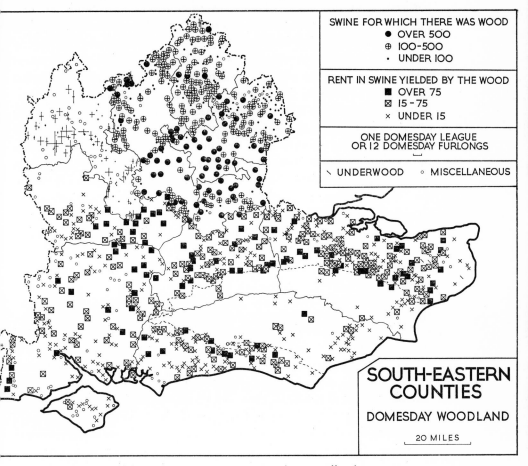

Fig. 174. South-eastern Counties: Domesday woodland in 1086.

The approximate boundary of the Weald (i.e. the outer boundary of Weald Clay) is indicated by a pecked line.

locality. Can we be sure, for example, that all the woodland of the New Forest was entered, or all the wood along the border between north-eastern Middlesex and southern Hertfordshire? There is one area in particular where there must have been much more wood than the Domesday Book reveals, and that is the Weald. Even when the wood entries of the surrounding manors are 'spread out' by eye, we are still left with the impression that they cannot represent all the wood there must have been, particularly on the Weald Clay. It seems clear that a substantial amount of extra-manorial wood or unexploited wood went unmeasured and so unrecorded in the folios before us.

Fig. 174 shows the distribution of woodland as recorded in the Domesday Book. In spite of many uncertainties and difficulties, it is clear that the English countryside in the eleventh century still had a wooded aspect. The Anglo-Saxons had pierced the woodland everywhere with their leys and dens and hursts, and yet almost every page of the Domesday Book shows that a very great deal still remained. What is more, it is clear that the Domesday record does not do justice to the reality. As we have seen, some wood was omitted from the Inquest, and how faithful the record was, we can never say. Later documents show how the clearing, begun so vigorously in Anglo-Saxon times, continued after the eleventh century, but the Domesday Book itself is disappointingly silent about this activity. Paradoxically enough, what hints it gives of clearing come from the Weald,[1] the wood of which appears to have been so imperfectly recorded.

FOREST

In addition to woodland there was forest land about which the Domesday Book normally says very little. The word 'forest' was a legal term, and was far from synonymous with woodland, but forested areas usually contained a nucleus of wood and sometimes large tracts of wooded territory. The character and extent of these forests before 1066 are obscure, but it is certain that after the Norman Conquest the forest law and forest courts of Normandy were introduced into England on a large scale. A rapid extension of forest land took place. These forests, being royal property outside the normal order, rarely appear in the Domesday Book, and it is probable that much wood in the forested areas escaped mention. The existence of a number of forests, however, is indicated by various statements to the effect that a holding, or part of it, or sometimes its wood only, was 'in the forest' or 'in the king's forest'. Some entries do not specifically use the word forest, but merely speak of the king's wood or the king's

----

[1] See pp. 581–4 above.

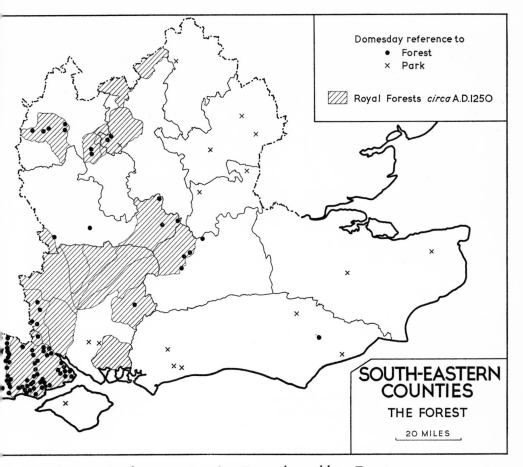

Fig. 175. South-eastern Counties: Domesday and later Forests.

The extent of the royal forests about A.D. 1250 is taken from M. L. Bazeley, 'The extent of the English Forest in the Thirteenth Century', *Trans. Roy. Hist. Soc.* 4th series, IV (London, 1921), p. 148.

The following points must be noted:

1. At Oakley (149) in Buckinghamshire and at Stoke next Guildford (30) in Surrey, the phrase *parcus regis* has been taken to imply forest and is marked as such on the map.

2. At Dallington (18b) in Sussex, the count of Eu is said to have had half a hide *in foresta*, but it is doubtful whether full forest law was in force here.

3. At Kintbury (61b) in the extreme west of Berkshire, half a hide had been freed from dues in King Edward's time *propter forestam custodiendam*; this may refer to Savernake Forest nearby, but we cannot be sure.

4. At Bucklebury (61b) in central Berkshire, one hide lay in the forest (*In foresta jacet*); this was held by Walter son of Other whom we know to have been the king's forester for Berkshire. The forest of Berkshire (apart from that of Windsor) was disafforested early in the thirteenth century—*V.C.H. Berkshire*, I (London, 1906), p. 309; II (London, 1907), p. 167.

enclosure, and these entries may well imply an extension of forest rights. Parks are also mentioned in a number of entries.

The relation of these occasional Domesday references to the royal forests of the thirteenth century is shown on Fig. 175. As can be seen, there is no hint of the existence of some of these forests in the eleventh century. Of the ones it does mention, the most outstanding is the New Forest. The account of the New Forest and its making is unique in the Domesday Book. It constitutes the one exception to the general reticence of the Domesday folios about forests, and it is discussed in detail on pp. 324–38. The afforested villages extended northward from the New Forest along the western border of Hampshire, but the forests of Clarendon, Chute and the like are not mentioned by name in the Hampshire folios. The other forests of which we have hints are Woolmer or Alice Holt Forests in eastern Hampshire, Windsor Forest in Berkshire and Surrey, the forest of western Berkshire, those of Shotover and Wychwood in Oxfordshire, and that of Bernwood in Buckinghamshire, although the name itself does not appear. There is also a reference to half a hide of forest at Dallington (18b) in Sussex but this, in 1334, was called 'the chase' of Dallington and does not appear to have been a royal forest.

MEADOW

The meadow of the south-eastern counties was normally measured in one of two different ways. Unfortunately, it is impossible to reduce these two main units to a common denominator with any certainty, and Fig. 176 has this inherent defect.

One method of measurement was in terms of the number of teams of oxen which the hay of a meadow was capable of feeding; this method was characteristic of the folios of a block of four counties—Bedfordshire, Buckinghamshire, Hertfordshire and Middlesex. Meadow was said to support horses as well as oxen at three places in Buckinghamshire and at one in Hertfordshire, and, occasionally, in addition to supporting oxen, meadow yielded a money render from the hay (*de feno*); we also hear of half a hide of meadow on a holding in Hertfordshire. Only for one place —Orwell in Hertfordshire (141b)—are we explicitly told that there was no meadow (*pratum nil*). G. H. Fowler attempted to convert the figures for Bedfordshire into modern acreages at the rate of 3 statute acres for each ox: he then expressed these acreages as percentages of the areas of the modern parishes (Fig. 16).[1] As we have seen, when discussing Fowler's calculation of woodland acreages, this is a method beset by doubts, and it seems best to plot the plough-team figures directly on to the map as conventional units.

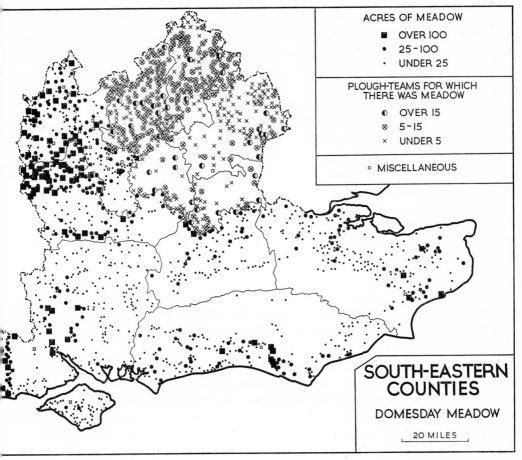

Fig. 176. South-eastern Counties: Domesday meadow in 1086.

The entries relating to meadow in the remaining six counties are in terms of acres. There are also occasional money renders; and, in Oxford-shire, the meadow of five places is measured partly in acres and partly in linear dimensions, and that of nine places entirely in linear dimensions.

[1] G. H. Fowler, *op. cit.* pp. 61–2 and 106–7.

Amounts above 200 acres are quite common; but, in general, the figures are well below this and resemble those of East Anglia and the Midlands rather than the large quantities to be found in the Lincolnshire entries.[1] The round figures of some entries (e.g. 20, 40, 100) may indicate that they are estimates rather than precise amounts, but the detailed figures of other entries (e.g. 2, 7½, 11, 43, 155) suggest precision. In view of the existence of local or 'customary' acres, as distinct from the statute acre, no attempt has been made to convert these Domesday figures into modern acreages. They have been plotted merely as conventional units of measurement.

One of the main facts about Fig. 176 is the large amount of meadow in the lowland that stretches north and west of the Chalk escarpment. Here, on the clays of north Berkshire, Oxfordshire, Buckinghamshire and Bedfordshire, there were few villages without an entry for meadow. Substantial amounts, frequently over 100 acres, and sometimes well over, were to be found along the Ock, the Thames itself, the Windrush, the Evenlode, the Thame, the Ouse, the Ivel, and along the tributaries of these streams. The one part of this area with relatively little meadow was the Oolite belt of northern Oxfordshire.

To the south, where the countryside is dominated by the Chalk-lands, villages with meadow were less generally distributed. Lines of villages with meadow stood out along the Thames and along its tributaries, the Colne and the Lea. Meadow was also to be found along the Chiltern tributaries of the Colne, such as the Misbourne, the Chess and the Gade; but it was much more widely distributed in eastern Hertfordshire, drained by the upper Lea and its tributaries. The southern tributaries of the Thames were bordered by substantial amounts; the meadow along the Kennet was considerable, and, to the east, there were smaller amounts along the Wey, the Mole, the Darent and the Medway, as well as along lesser streams. The rivers draining to the south coast were also bordered by meadow, and sometimes by considerable amounts; from west to east, these were the Avon, the Test, the Itchen, the Arun, the Adur and the Sussex Ouse. With these and their tributaries may be grouped the Great and Little Stour in Kent.

---

[1] For the problem raised by the large figures for Lincolnshire, see H. C. Darby, *The Domesday Geography of Eastern England*, p. 366.

FISHERIES

Fisheries are recorded in a variety of ways. Occasionally, we are merely told that there was one (or more) fishery on a holding; but more usually

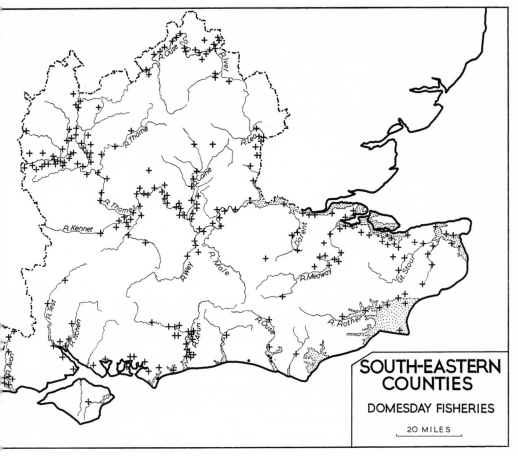

Fig. 177. South-eastern Counties: Domesday fisheries in 1086.

Herring renders at London and Southwark and at places in Kent and Sussex are indicated by small dots. Areas of coastal alluvium are shown; rivers flowing across these areas are not marked.

a render is also stated, either in money or eels or both. The number of eels is normally given as a straightforward figure, but it is sometimes entered in terms of *stiches*, a medieval stick of eels consisting of 25. Moities or halves of fisheries appear for some holdings, but it is not usually possible to assemble the fractions of neighbouring villages together in any comprehensible fashion. A number of entries for Hertfordshire and Middlesex speak of money renders or, more frequently, of eel renders not from fisheries (*piscariae*) but from weirs (*gurgites*). Other entries, for all counties except Surrey, refer to eels in connection with mills, and these eels were presumably from mill-streams or mill-ponds. A few entries in the folios for Kent speak merely of eel renders without any reference to fisheries, weirs or mills. In general, the Domesday Book tells us little or nothing about the gear of the fishermen or about their methods of catching fish; but the entry for Hampton (130), in Middlesex, notes a render of 3*s.* from seins and dragnets in the Thames (*De sagenis et tractis in aqua temisae*). Eels are the only species mentioned except on a holding at Petersham (32b), in Surrey, where there was a fishery yielding 1,000 eels and 1,000 lampreys (*piscaria de mille anguillis et mille Lampridulis*). In a few entries for Oxfordshire, the fishermen themselves are enumerated.

On Fig. 177 the information has been consolidated into one category. An outstanding feature of the map is the number of fisheries along the Thames. Some of its tributaries were also important sources of fish; among the north-bank tributaries were the Lea, the Colne, and the Cherwell; and among the southern tributaries were the Kennet, the Wey, the Darent and the Medway. In the north, there were also numerous fisheries along the Ouse and its tributaries; and in the south, the rivers draining to the coast also provided fishing centres—especially the Avon, the Test, the Itchen and the Arun. With these may be grouped the Great and Little Stour in eastern Kent. To what extent Fig. 177 provides a complete picture of fishing activity along the rivers of the south-eastern counties, we cannot say. But, at any rate, the map leaves us in no doubt about the importance of the fishery in the life and economy of eleventh-century England. A hint of its role meets us in an entry for Iver (149) in Buckinghamshire; there, the fishery provided fish on Fridays for the use of the reeve of the vill.

In addition to the activity along the rivers there was also fishing at sea. An indication of this is provided by the herring renders from London itself, from Southwark in Surrey, and from two places in Kent and four in Sussex. One of these entries for Kent speaks of half a fishery rendering 300 herrings (Luddenham, 10b) and it is possible that some of the *piscariae* with money renders in Hampshire, Kent and Sussex were really sea-

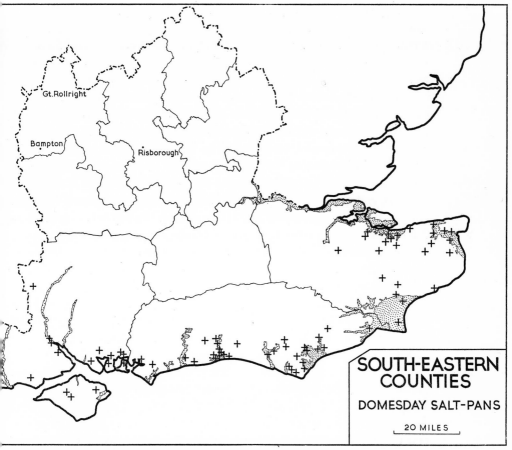

Fig. 178. South-eastern Counties: Domesday salt-pans in 1086.
The entries for Risborough (143 b) in Buckinghamshire and for Bampton (154 b) and Great Rollright (160 b) in Oxfordshire refer to salt-working at Droitwich in Worcestershire. Areas of coastal alluvium are shown.

fisheries; porpoises are mentioned for two places on the coasts of Kent and Sussex. Whether this is so or not, we can safely assume that the Domesday Book reflects only very imperfectly the maritime fishing activity of the age.

SALT-PANS

Salt-pans are recorded in connection with 73 places in the three coastal counties of Hampshire, Kent and Sussex. We are usually told the number of pans on a holding and also their render in money. But occasional entries do not state the number of pans, and a few entries either omit to state a render or state it in terms of *summae* or *ambrae* of salt. There were 8 pans and a third of a new pan at Eastbridge (13) in Kent, and there was half a pan at Ratton (21) in Sussex, but we are given no clues to the remaining fractions. The pans at a few places are said to be *sine censu*.

Fig. 178 shows how the salt-pans were associated with the coastal areas of alluvium—along Southampton Water, around the shallows of Portsmouth and Langstone Harbours, in the estuaries of the Sussex rivers, around the levels of Pevensey and of Romney Marsh, and about the alluvial areas of northern Kent. The number of pans entered for each place varied greatly, and ranged from one upwards to 47 pans at Chislet (12) in Kent, and to as many as 100 at Rye (*Rameslie*, 17) in Sussex. The pans entered for a few inland manors, such as Nether Wallop in Hampshire and Maidstone in Kent, must have been physically situated elsewhere.

We also hear of salt in the entries for Risborough (143b) in Buckinghamshire and for Bampton (154b) and Great Rollright (160b) in Oxfordshire, but these refer to the salt-works at Droitwich in Worcestershire.[1] Such references prompt speculation about the organisation of the salt industry and the way in which salt was distributed among villages and remote hamlets. But the Domesday Book is as silent on these matters as it is about the details of salt manufacture.

VINEYARDS

The folios for the south-eastern counties refer to vineyards at 16 places, and there is also what may be a reference to one in 1066 (Fig. 179). At Lomer (43) in Hampshire, a certain Alward had rendered ten sesters of wine a year, but we are not told whether this wine was produced on the spot or whether the render continued to be paid in 1086 by his successor. Queries are also associated with 2 of the 16 places of 1086. We cannot be absolutely sure that the vineyard entered in fo. 127 was really at Holborn. An even more uncertain allusion appears in the entry for Wandsworth (36) in Surrey. Here, among the sub-tenants, a certain Walter held one hide, and the word *vinitor* is interlined above his name; this has been variously translated, e.g. as 'vineyard keeper' or as 'vintner', but even if the former is implied we cannot be sure that the vineyard was

[1] See pp. 180 and 232 above. See also H. C. Darby and I. B. Terrett (eds.), *op. cit.* pp. 255–6.

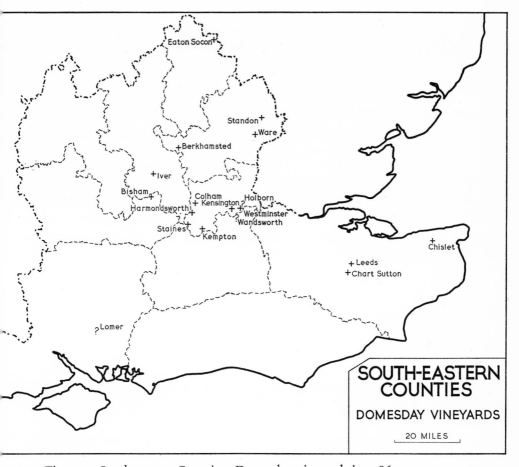

Fig. 179. South-eastern Counties: Domesday vineyards in 1086.

For the uncertainties relating to Holborn, Lomer and Wandsworth, see p. 608.

at Wandsworth itself. J. H. Round argued that the culture of the vine was reintroduced into England by the Normans, and he based his view upon the fact that Domesday vineyards were normally on holdings in the direct hands of Norman tenants-in-chief; that they were usually measured by the foreign unit of the arpent; and that we are sometimes told that they had been planted only recently.[1]

[1] J. H. Round, 'Essex vineyards in Domesday', *Trans. Essex Archaeol. Soc.* N.S. VII (Colchester, 1900), pp. 249–51. See also J. H. Round in *V.C.H. Essex*, I (Westminster, 1903), pp. 382–3.

Round's view cannot be maintained, because we hear of vineyards in England in the eighth, the ninth and the tenth centuries;[1] moreover, the entry for Lomer seems to imply the existence of a vineyard there in Edward the Confessor's day. But, on the other hand, it is true that the vineyards of the south-east were almost all on estates held directly by tenants-in-chief; it is also true that they were measured in arpents, except for that on Eudo the steward's estate at Eaton Socon (212) in Bedfordshire which was measured in acres, and that at Holborn (127) which was unmeasured; and, moreover, we are told that the vineyards at Kempton (129), Ware (138b) and Westminster (128) had but lately (*noviter* or *nuperrime*) been planted. It looks as if the Normans had not so much reintroduced the vine into England as extended, possibly greatly extended, its culture. We may see in the Domesday references to vine-yards, as in the references to forests, symptoms of the new order that the Normans brought to the land they conquered.

[1] George Ordish, *Wine Growing in England* (London, 1953), pp. 20–1.

SUMMARY OF THE DOMESDAY BOOK FOR THE SOUTH-EASTERN COUNTIES

County	Assessment	Plough-lands	Plough-teams
BEDFORDSHIRE	Hides and virgates; occasional acres Frequent 5-hide unit Carucates in demesne at 5 places	Normally *Terra est n carucis*	Teams that could be added frequent Excess teams very ra
HERTFORDSHIRE	Hides and virgates; occasional acres Frequent 5-hide unit	Normally *Terra est n carucis*	Teams that could be added very frequen Excess teams very ra
MIDDLESEX	Hides and virgates; occasional acres Frequent 5-hide unit Carucates in demesne at one place	Normally *Terra est n carucis* Occasionally *Terra est ad n carucas*	Teams that could be added frequent Excess teams rare
BUCKINGHAMSHIRE	Hides and virgates; occasional acres Frequent 5-hide unit Carucates in demesne at 4 places	Normally *Terra est n carucis*	Teams that could be added frequent Excess teams rare
OXFORDSHIRE	Hides and virgates; occasional acres Frequent 5-hide unit	Normally *Terra n carucis* Sometimes *Terra est n carucis*	Understocking very frequent Excess teams frequen
BERKSHIRE	Hides and virgates; occasional acres Frequent 5-hide unit Frequent exemptions 1066–86	Normally *Terra est n carucis* Some lacunae	Understocking very frequent Excess teams frequent
HAMPSHIRE	Hides and virgates; occasional acres Frequent 5-hide unit Frequent exemptions	Normally *Terra est n carucis* Some lacunae	Understocking frequent Excess teams frequer
SURREY	Hides and virgates; occasional acres Frequent 5-hide unit Frequent exemptions	Normally *Terra est n carucis* Some lacunae	Understocking frequent Excess teams frequer
SUSSEX	Hides and virgates; occasional acres 5-hide unit not clear Frequent exemptions	Normally *Terra est n carucis* Some lacunae	Understocking frequent Excess teams frequer
KENT	Sulungs and yokes; occasional acres Frequent exemptions	Normally *Terra est n carucis* Very many lacunae	Understocking frequent Excess teams freque

Population	Values	No. of Place-names
ain groups: villeins, bordars, serfs reat decline of sokemen 1066–86 cord of thegns for 1066	Normally for 3 dates Renders in kind on 3 royal manors	145
ain groups: villeins, bordars, cottars, erfs reat decline of sokemen 1066–86	Normally for 3 dates *Avera* on 5 manors	168
ain groups: villeins, cottars, bordars, erfs kemen of 1066 disappeared	Normally for 3 dates	62
ain groups: villeins, bordars, serfs ecline of sokemen 1066–86 cord of thegns for 1066	Normally for 3 dates	207
ain groups: villeins, bordars, serfs	Normally for 1066 and 1086; sometimes for 3 dates	251
ain groups: villeins, bordars, serfs, ottars. Bordars and cottars mutually xclusive	Sometimes for 3 dates; sometimes for 2 dates	192
ain groups: bordars, villeins, serfs	Normally for 3 dates Frequent decrease *tunc–post* Some payments in excess of 1086 valuations	458
ain groups: villeins, bordars, serfs, ottars kemen of 1066 disappeared ordars and cottars almost mutually xclusive	Normally for 3 dates Frequent decrease *tunc–post* Some payments in excess of 1086 valuations	142
ain groups: villeins, bordars, cottars, erfs. Bordars and cottars mutually xclusive	Normally for 3 dates Frequent decrease *tunc–post* Some payments in excess of 1086 valuations	337
ain groups: villeins, bordars, serfs, ottars. Bordars and cottars almost mutually exclusive. 4 *ancillae* ecline of sokemen 1066–86	Normally for 3 dates Frequent decrease *tunc–post* Many payments in excess of 1086 valuations	347

County	Wood	Meadow	Pasture	Marsh
BEDFORDSHIRE	Normally in swine totals	Normally in plough-teams	Only for 9 places; 4 of these in Herts. folios	None
HERTFORDSHIRE	Normally in swine totals	Normally in plough-teams	For 116 places Usual entry is *pastura ad pecuniam villae*	None
MIDDLESEX	Normally in swine totals	Normally in plough-teams	For 47 places Usual entry is *pastura ad pecuniam villae*	None
BUCKINGHAMSHIRE	Normally in swine totals	Normally in plough-teams	Only for 4 places	None
OXFORDSHIRE	Normally in linear dimensions	Normally in acres Some amounts over 100 acres	For 105 places Either in acres or in linear dimensions	*Morae fo* one plac
BERKSHIRE	Normally in swine renders	Normally in acres Some amounts over 100 acres	Only for 8 places	None
HAMPSHIRE	Normally in swine renders	Normally in acres Amounts over 100 acres rare	For 33 places *Herbagium, Pastura* and *Pascua*	None
SURREY	Entirely in swine renders	Normally in acres Amounts over 50 acres rare	For 26 places *Herbagium* and *Pastura*	None
SUSSEX	Normally in swine renders	Normally in acres Amounts over 50 acres rare	For 35 places *Herbagium* and *Pastura*	None
KENT	Normally in swine renders	Normally in acres Amounts over 50 acres rare	For 26 places *Pastura* and *Herbagium*	Reference to *Mare de Romen*

Fisheries	Salt-pans	Waste	Mills	Churches
[E]el renders from mills for 17 places. Also *vivarium piscium*	None	In 1086 for 2 places	For 63 places	For 4 places
[F]or 8 places; eel renders from mills alone for 2 of these. Also *vivarium piscium*	None	None	For 73 places	For 3 places
[F]or 12 places. Also herring render at London	None	None	For 15 places	For 3 places
[F]or 21 places; eel renders from mills alone for 5 of these	None Reference under Risborough to salt at Droitwich	In 1086 for 3 places	For 78 places	For 4 places
[F]or 26 places: eel render from mills alone for 6 of these. Also *vivarium piscium*	None References under Bampton and Gt Rollright to salt at Droitwich	In 1086 for 5 places. Also waste houses at Oxford	For 116 places	For 2 places Church-scot at 2 other places
[F]or 35 places; eel render from a mill alone for one of these	None	None	For 94 places	For 58 places
[F]or 23 places; eel renders from mills alone for 5 of these	For 15 places	In 1086 for 3 places	For 172 places	For 104 places
[F]or 9 places. Also herring render at Southwark	None	None	For 66 places	For 62 places
[F]or 28 places; eel renders from mills alone for 8 of these. Also herring renders for 4 places	For 34 places	In 1086 for 3 places	For 87 places	For 93 places
[F]or 50 places; eel render from a mill alone for one of these. Also herring renders for 2 places	For 24 places	None in 1086 except waste houses at Canterbury	For 139 places	For 145 places

County	Miscellaneous	Boroughs
BEDFORDSHIRE	Markets for Arlesey, Leighton Buzzard, Luton Vineyard for Eaton Socon	Bedford
HERTFORDSHIRE	Three entries duplicated in *Inquisitio Eliensis* Traders for Cheshunt Vineyards for Berkhamsted, Standon, Ware	Ashwell Berkhamsted Hertford St Albans Stanstead Abbot
MIDDLESEX	Assessment of peasants' holdings given in detail. Vineyards for Colham, Harmondsworth, Holborn (?), Kempton, Kensington, Staines, Westminster	London
BUCKINGHAMSHIRE	Vineyard for Iver Forests for Brill and Oakley. Hawks' eyries at Chalfont	Buckingham Newport Pagnel
OXFORDSHIRE	Hundred headings rarely given. Market for Bampton. Forests for Cornbury, Shotover, Stowood, Woodstock, Wychwood, and possibly for Shipton under Wychwood and Wootton. Quarry for Taynton. Pottery for Bladon. Open-field system for Garsington	Oxford
BERKSHIRE	Markets for Cookham and Wallingford; traders for Barton. Vineyard for Bisham. Forests for Bucklebury, Cookham, Kintbury, Windsor, Winkfield. One third of a dene at Windsor. Castles for Wallingford and Windsor. Cheese-making for Buckland, Shellingford and Sparsholt	Reading Wallingford Windsor
HAMPSHIRE	Special sections on New Forest and Isle of Wight. Markets for Basingstoke, Neatham, Titchfield. Render of wine for Lomer. Castle for Alvington. *Ferraria* for Stratfield	Southampton Twynham Winchester
SURREY	Forests for Pyrford, Walton, Woking. Possible vineyard for Wandsworth. Dene for Ewell. Quarries for Limpsfield. *Ferraria* for Chertsey	Guildford Southwark
SUSSEX	Organisation in rapes. Forest for Dallington. Castles for Arundel, Bramber, Hastings, Pevensey, Lewes. Quarries at Bignor, Grittenham, Iping, Stedham. *Ferraria* for East Grinstead hd. Mints for Lewes and Pevensey	Arundel Chichester Hastings Lewes Pevensey Rye Steyning
KENT	Organisation in lathes. Vineyards for Chart Sutton, Chislet, Leeds. Castles for Canterbury, Rochester, Tonbridge. Markets for Faversham, Lewisham, Newenden. 52 denes and 3 half-denes. Hithes for Dartford, Gravesend, Milton near Gravesend, Swanscombe. Weys of cheese from Milton Regis.	Canterbury Dover Fordwich Hythe Rochester Romney Sandwich Seasalter

SOUTH-EASTERN COUNTIES

Summary of Rural Population in 1086

This summary includes the apparently rural element in the boroughs—see the respective county summaries.

A. *Total Figures*

	Free-men	Soke-men	Villeins	Bordars	Cottars	Serfs	Others	Total
BEDFORDSHIRE	—	90	1,888	1,156	6	480	5	3,625
HERTFORDSHIRE	8	43	1,766	1,120	849	591	125	4,502
MIDDLESEX	—	—	1,163	364	464	112	74	2,177
BUCKINGHAMSHIRE	—	20	2,901	1,314	10	842	8	5,095
OXFORDSHIRE	31*	—	3,699	1,966	—	1,022	66	6,784
BERKSHIRE	6†	—	2,687	1,868	734	804	61	6,160
HAMPSHIRE	6‡	—	3,935	4,019	6	1,772	165	9,903
SURREY	—	—	2,386	931	276	503	1	4,097
SUSSEX	—	—	5,869	2,512	766	410	15	9,572
KENT	2	44	6,829	3,372	309	1,160	37	11,753
Total	53	197	33,123	18,622	3,420	7,696	560	63,668

* Including radmen.
† *Alodiarii* and a radman.
‡ Including radmen and a *francus homo*.

B. *Percentages*

	Free-men	Soke-men	Villeins	Bordars	Cottars	Serfs	Others
BEDFORDSHIRE	—	2·5	52·1	31·9	0·1	13·2	0·2
HERTFORDSHIRE	0·2	0·9	39·2	24·9	18·9	13·1	2·8
MIDDLESEX	—	—	53·4	16·7	21·3	5·2	3·4
BUCKINGHAMSHIRE	—	0·4	56·9	25·8	0·2	16·5	0·2
OXFORDSHIRE	0·5	—	54·5	28·9	—	15·1	1·0
BERKSHIRE	0·1	—	43·6	30·3	11·9	13·1	1·0
HAMPSHIRE	0·1	—	39·7	40·6	0·1	17·9	1·6
SURREY	—	—	58·3	22·7	6·7	12·3	—
SUSSEX	—	—	61·3	26·2	8·0	4·3	0·2
KENT	—	0·4	58·1	28·7	2·7	9·8	0·3
Total	0·1	0·3	52·0	29·2	5·4	12·1	0·9

SOUTH-EASTERN COUNTIES

General Summary

For the various doubts associated with individual figures, see the text. The assessment, plough-lands, plough-teams and rural population of the boroughs are included in these totals, but it must be noted that the information given for the boroughs is often very fragmentary. The assessment is for 1066, and includes non-gelding hides and sulungs.

	Settle-ments	Assess-ment	Plough-lands	Plough-teams	Rural pop.	Boroughs
BEDFORDSHIRE	145	1,198h*	1,610	1,403	3,625	1
HERTFORDSHIRE	168	1,095h	1,707	1,361	4,502	5
MIDDLESEX	62	880h*	677	546	2,177	1
BUCKINGHAMSHIRE	207	2,126h*	2,300	2,056	5,095	2
OXFORDSHIRE	251	2,581h	2,861	2,608	6,784	1
BERKSHIRE	192	2,508h	2,133	1,892	6,160	3
HAMPSHIRE	458	2,860h	2,967	2,779	9,903	3
SURREY	142	2,001h	1,260	1,274	4,097	2
SUSSEX	337	3,193h	3,131	3,194	9,572	7
KENT	347	1,152s‡	—†	3,153	11,753	8
Total	2,309	—	—	20,266	63,668	33

h = hides;   s = sulungs.

* There were also some carucates in demesne—see pp. 16, 106, 149.
† The very large number of lacunae make any realistic total impossible—see p. 509.
‡ There were also some virgates and acres—see p. 507.

APPENDIX II

EXTENSION AND TRANSLATION OF FRONTISPIECE

(Part of folio 136b of the Domesday Book)

EXTENSION

XV. TERRA COMITIS MORITONIENSIS

In Treung hundredo. Comes Moritoniensis tenet Berchehamstede. Pro xiii hidis se defendit. Terra est xxvi carucis. In dominio vi hidae, et ibi sunt iii carucae et aliae iii possunt fieri. Ibi presbyter cum xiiii villanis et xv bordariis habent xii carucas, et adhuc viii possunt fieri. Ibi vi servi, et quidam fossarius habet dimidiam hidam, et Rannulfus i virgatam serviens comitis. In Burbio hujus villae lii burgenses qui reddunt de theloneo iiii libras, et habent dimidiam hidam, et ii molinos de xx solidis. Ibi ii arpendi vineae. Pratum viii carucis. Pastura ad pecuniam villae. Silva mille porcis et v solidis. In totis valentiis valet xvi libras. Quando recepit xx libras. T.R.E. xxiiii libras. Hoc manerium tenuit Edmarus teignus Heraldi comitis.

Rannulfus tenet de comite Scenlei. Pro i hida se defendit. Terra est ii carucis. Ibi est una et altera potest fieri. Ibi ii bordarii. Pastura ad pecuniam. Silva c sol'. Inter totum valet v solidos. Quando recepit iii libras. T.R.E. iiii libras. Hanc terram tenuerunt ii sochemanni. Unus huscarl R.E. et alter homo Leuuini comitis vendere potuerunt.

Ipse comes tenet Aldeberie. Pro x hidis se defendit. Terra est vii carucis. In dominio vi hidae, et ibi sunt iii carucae, et viii villani cum i sochemanno et i francigena habent iiii carucas. Ibi i bordarius et iiii servi. Pratum dimidae hidae. Silva quingentis porcis. In totis valentiis valet cx solidos. Quando recepit viii libras et tantundem T.R.E. Hoc manerium tenuit Aluuinus teignus R.E.

In Pentlai tenet ipse comes ii hidas. Terra est ii carucis. Ibi i villanus cum vi bordariis habent i carucam, et alia potest fieri. Pratum i carucae et dimidae. Valet xxx solidos. Quando recepit xx solidos. T.R.E. xl solidos. Hanc terram tenuit Eddeva monialis de Ingelrico.

TRANSLATION

XV. THE LAND OF THE COUNT OF MORTAIN

In Tring hundred. The count of Mortain holds Berkhamsted. It is assessed at 13 hides. There is land for 26 plough-teams. In demesne 6 hides, and there are there 3 plough-teams, and there could be 3 others. There, a priest with 14 villeins and 15 bordars have 12 plough-teams, and there could be another 8. There, 6 serfs, and a certain ditcher has half a hide, and Rannulf, a serving-man of the count, 1 virgate. In the 'burbium' of this vill 52 burgesses who render £4 from toll, and they have half a hide, and 2 mills yielding 20s. There, 2 arpents of vine. Meadow for 8 plough-teams. Pasture for the livestock of the vill. Wood for 1,000 swine and 5s. In all it is worth £16. When he received it, £20. In the time of King Edward, £24. Edmar, a thegn of Earl Harold, held this manor.

Rannulf holds Shenley of the count. It is assessed at one hide. There is land for 2 plough-teams. There is one there, and there could be another. There, 2 bordars. Pasture for the livestock. Wood, 100s. In all it is worth 5s. When he received it, £3. In the time of King Edward £4. Two sokemen held this land. One, a house-carl of King Edward, and the other, a man of Earl Lewin, were able to sell it.

The count himself holds Aldbury. It is assessed at 10 hides. There is land for 7 plough-teams. In demesne, 6 hides, and there are there 3 plough-teams, and 8 villeins with one sokeman and one 'francigena' have 4 plough-teams. There, one bordar and 4 serfs. Meadow of half a hide. Wood for 500 swine. In all it is worth 110s. When he received it, £8, and likewise in the time of King Edward. Alwin, a thegn of King Edward, held this manor.

The count himself holds 2 hides in Pendley. There is land for 2 plough-teams. There, one villein with 6 bordars have one plough-team, and there could be another. Meadow for 1½ plough-teams. It is worth 30s. When he received it, 20s. In the time of King Edward 40s. Eddeva the nun held this land from Ingelric.

INDEX

Abaginge, 295, 296 n.

Abbots Ann, *see* Ann

Abbots Langley, *see* Langley

Abbotstone, 295

Abbots Worthy, *see* Worthy

Abefeld, 143 n.

Abingdon, 243, 252 n., 258, 272, 273

Abingdon Abbey, 195, 230, 243, 250, 269, 281, 283

Abingdon Chronicle, 239 n., 265 n., 598

Abinger, 386, 391

Abla, 296 n.

Acenge, 245, 251, 269 n., 270

Achelie (Hants., Boldre hd), 296 n., 327

Achelie (Hants., Redbridge hd), 296 n., 326 n., 327

Acres, fiscal, 11, 15, 55, 59, 103, 104, 106, 145, 149, 197, 199, 248, 251, 299, 304, 327, 371, 374, 422, 503, 507, 612, 618

  of arable (*planum*), 33

  of meadow, 36, 170, 214–16, 265–6, 338–40, 390–1, 448–50, 532–4, 568, 614

  of pasture, 218, 220, 267, 340, 453, 534–5, 614

  of underwood, 212

  of vine, 43

  of wood, 31–3, 212, 263, 321, 525, 597

Acton, 101, 102

Adderbury, 189, 193, 197, 198, 200, 201 n., 203 n., 204, 212, 217, 220, 225, 226, 233, 565

Addington (Bucks.), 156

Addington (Kent), 508

Adgestone, 356

Adisham, 491, 494, 518 n., 525

Adlach, 194

Adstock, 147, 575

Adur, R., 421, 444, 449, 455, 456, 461, 472, 476, 477, 604

Adwell, 217

Afettune, 493 n., 509

Affledwick, *see* Beauchamps

Aia, 493 n., 594

Ailesaltede hundred, *see Hailesaltede* hundred

Ailesford, lathe of, 486

Airy, William, 1, 4 n., 9, 19 n., 21 n., 45

Aisiholte, 492, 493 n.

Akeley, 150, 160

Albury (Herts.), 56

Albury (Oxon.), 275, 276

Alchin (in Buxted), 417, 420

Alciston, 412, 413 n., 426 n., 451, 467, 468

Aldbury (Herts.), 56, 57, 58, 80, 619, 620

Aldenham, 61

Alder grove, 525

Aldermaston, 259, 267, 273 n., 275, 276

Aldershot, 296, 298, 319

Aldingbourne, 451, 462, 464, 465

Aldington (Kent, Bircholt hd), 501–2, 508, 532, 534, 553, 559

Aldrington (Sx.), 408, 410, 438 n., 440 n.

Alfold, 369

Alfriston, 431 n.

Alia Berham, *see* Kingston (Kent)

Alice Holt Forest, 321, 322, 361, 602

Alkham, 498

Allington (Kent, Eyhorne hd), 551

Allington (Kent, Larkfield hd), 530, 541 n., 542

Allington (Sx.), 467, 468, 582

Alodiarii, 254, 258, 382, 518 n., 617, 618

Aloesbridge hundred, 518, 594

Alperton, 101

Alresford, 288, 346, 348, 349, 350, 577

Alswick, 52, 73, 78

Alton, 302, 304, 306, 345

Alverstoke, 303, 311

Alvington, 302, 310, 344, 356, 616

Alvrestone, 296 n., 347

Alwinetune, 296 n., 327

Amberley, 429 n., 462

Ambersham, North and South, 287, 414

Ambra of salt, 456

Ambrosden, 199

Amersham, 146, 172

Amesbury, 293

Amport, *see* Ann

Amwell, Great and Little, 49 n., 50 n., 70, 80, 81

Ancillae, 513, 517, 518, 613

Anderson, O. S., 98 n., 407 n., 443 n., 485 n.
Andover, 299, 300 n., 305, 318, 346
Andover hundred, 293 n., 294 n.
Andredesweald, *see* Weald
Andret, 327, 328
Anglo-Saxon Chronicle, 209, 287, 413 n., 574, 575, 583
Angmering, 425, 451, 453
'Animals', 90, 91, 310, 315, 356, 434, 466, 535, 536
Ann, Abbots Ann, Amport, Ann Savage, Little Ann, Monxton and Thruxton, 294 n., 321 n., 346
Annonae, 177, 232–3, 460; *see also* Grain
Anonymous holdings, 166, 217, 220, 224, 225, 226, 239, 243, 251, 259, 269 n., 270, 271, 290, 294–5, 300, 319, 328, 330, 334, 341, 345, 346, 347, 366, 370 n., 376, 383, 394, 396, 410, 413, 414 n., 433, 437, 444, 447, 450, 451, 460, 461, 488 n., 490, 491, 503, 510, 511, 512, 518, 523, 531, 537, 541, 543
Anscombe, A., 481
Aplestede, 296 n., 347
Appleford, 244 n., 281
Applesham, 435 n.
Appleton (Berks.), 268
Appleton (Kent), 521
Apps Court, 376 n., 378
Arborfield, 243, 245, 576
Archaic renders, 25–6, 317–18, 383, 442
Arden, E., 9 n.
Ardingly, 420
Ardington, 253
Ardley, 208
Areal leagues, of meadow, 217
  of pasture, 219–20
  of wood, 32, 211, 595–6
Arkell, W. J., 232 n.
Arlesey, 16, 43, 44, 616
Arlington, 412, 417
Arnewood, 328, 335
Arnolton, 539, 547, 548
Arpent, 43 n., 88, 134, 281, 555, 609
Arreton, 315, 349, 350
Arun, R., 421, 444, 449, 455, 461, 470, 476, 477, 604, 606
Arundel, 415, 438, 453, 460, 462, 463, 470, 473, 476, 616

Arundel, rape of, 407, 408, 421, 423
Asce, 194, 203
Ash (Kent, Axton hd), 487, 517, 518, 519, 530
Ash (near Wingham, Kent), 498
Ash (Surrey), 369
Ash, R., 84, 94
Ashburnham, 441
Ashbury, 250, 259 n., 262
Ashcombe, 429
Ashdown Forest, 445 n., 446 n., 478
Ashendon hundred, 139, 175
Ashenfield, 492
Ashey, 294
Ashford (Kent), 489, 544
Ashford (Mdlx.), 100, 109, 116
Ashley, 320, 328, 334, 335 n.
Asholt, 498
Ashridge, 267
Ashtead, 598
Ashurst, 499
Ashwell, 50, 59 n., 61, 62 n., 70, 85, 86, 88–9, 90, 583, 616
Asmeslant, 519
Aspenden, 73
Aspley, Guise and Heath, 8 n.
Assessment, 11–16, 55–60, 103–10, 145–9, 197–9, 248–51, 299–304, 371–4, 422–9, 483, 502–7, 563, 585, 612, 613, 616, 618
Aston (in Ivinghoe, Bucks.), 142
Aston (Herts.), 58, 61
Aston, North, Middle and Steeple (Oxon.), 192, 207 n., 225
Aston Abbots (Bucks.), 142 n., 150, 166 n.
Aston Clinton (Bucks.), 142 n., 167, 174
Aston Rowant (Oxon.), 143, 189, 192, 208
Aston Sandford (Bucks.), 142 n.
Aston, Tirrold and Upthorpe (Berks.), 243
Astrop, 218
Astwick, 18
Austin, W., 41, 47
Avera, 72, 532 n.
Avington (Berks.), 250
Avington (Hants.), 290 n.
Avisford hundred (Sx.), *see Benestede* hundred
Aviston, 299, 315, 356
Avon, 300, 322, 328, 334

Avon, R., 298, 322, 335 n., 340, 341, 348, 352, 359, 604, 606

Awbridge, 338, 339 n., 353, 354

Aylesbury, 145 n., 157, 161, 170, 176, 179

Aylesbury hundred, 139, 140, 157, 177

Aylesbury, Vale of, 175

Aylesford, 550, 556

Ayot, St Lawrence and St Peter (formerly Montfitchet), 51

Baddesley (Hants., Boldre hd), 328

Badley (Hants.), 288

Bagley, 264, 598

Bagshot (Wilts.), 239

Bagshot District, 319, 360, 402

Bailiffs, see Reeves

Bakehouse, 356

Bakers, 356

Baldock, 53

Baldock, Vale of, 95

Baldon, Marsh and Toot, 198

Balham, 373, 585

Ballard, Adolphus, 131 n., 177 n., 273, 414, 415 n., 456 n., 463, 469, 470, 472, 481, 483 n., 493 n., 494 n., 498, 503 n., 505 n., 506 n., 524 n., 530 n., 533 n., 539 n., 541 n., 542 n., 543 n., 546 n., 547 n., 548 n., 549 n., 550, 552 n., 555 n., 562, 598 n.

Balmer, 428, 438 n., 461 n.

Bampton, 200, 201 n., 203 n., 208, 213, 214, 217, 221, 223, 232, 233, 565, 607, 608, 615, 616

Banbury, 189, 199 n., 200, 201 n., 203 n., 234, 565, 577

Banstead, 132, 133, 396, 399, 400

Bapchild, 498

Barcombe, 460, 467, 468

Barden, 499

Barford hundred, 6, 9 n.

Barfreston, 492, 518

Barham, 524, 536, 537

Baring, F. H., 1, 12 n., 14, 15 n., 19 n., 21, 26, 33 n., 46, 59, 62 n., 63 n., 64, 73, 95, 101, 104, 112, 113, 116, 137, 140 n., 148 n., 149, 154 n., 155, 157, 164, 166 n., 184, 185, 209, 237, 242 n., 245 n., 251, 253, 255, 257 n., 260, 264, 279 n., 286, 316, 324, 325 n., 331, 362,

363, 364 n., 366, 373, 374 n., 376 n., 377, 381, 383, 387 n., 388 n., 395 n., 396 n., 405, 441, 480, 520, 561, 563 n., 569, 573, 574, 575, 591 n., 598

Barker, E. E., 448 n.

Barkham (Sx.), 418, 445, 597

Barking (Essex), 132, 133, 135

Barkway, 67, 77, 81

Barlavington, 458

Barley (Herts.), 63, 69, 81 n., 591

Barming, East and West, 487, 488

Barnes, 585

Barnet, Chipping alias High, East and Friern, 54, 102

Barnham, 428, 430, 458, 470

Barnsley (in Brading, Hants.), 296

Barton (Berks.), 243, 249, 250, 257, 258, 267, 269, 272, 273, 281, 616

Barton (Hants, Boldre hd), 329, 332, 334

Barton (in Canterbury, Kent), 498

Barton, Steeple, Sesswell's and Westcot (Oxon.), 197

Barton Hartshorne (Bucks.), 151, 172

Barton Stacey (Hants.), 293, 300 n., 307, 315, 317, 340

Barton Stacey hundred (Hants.), 294 n.

Barwythe, 4, 5, 20 n., 24, 25, 37, 42, 48

Bashley, 345

Basildon, 249, 259 n., 272, 275, 276

Basing (Hants.), 316, 575

Basingeham (Sx.), 417, 418 n., 431

Basingstoke, 298, 299, 300 n., 315, 318, 340, 348, 349, 350, 353, 354, 355, 360, 616

Basingstoke hundred, 294 n., 311 n.

Battersea, 375, 383, 391, 392, 394, 396, 399, 400, 585

Battle Abbey, 417–18, 435, 439, 458, 460

Battle Abbey Chronicle, 423

Battramsley, 310 n., 327

Bawdwen, William, 95, 136, 184, 237

Bayford, 58, 60, 72, 80, 81 n.

Baylis, C. F., 102, 137

Bayworth, 249 n.

Bazeley, M. L., 600

Beachampton, 145

Beachendon, 149, 154

Beachy Head, 476

Beaconsfield, 143, 579

Beamonston, 527, 536
Beane, R., 86, 94
Beauchamps, 85 n.
Beaulieu, R., 337
Beauxfield, 519
Bechington (in Friston), 417
Beckenham, 541 n., 585
Beckett, 259
Beckley (Hants.), 329
Beckley (Oxon.), 192–3, 221 n.
Beddingham, 412, 417, 442, 455
Beddington, 132, 133, 399, 400
Bedecote, 296 n., 326, 327
Bedfont, East and West, 98, 109, 114, 116, 118 n., 576
Bedford, 6, 7, 13, 16, 17 n., 21, 26, 33, 39, 41, 42, 43, 616
Bedford, Vale of, 10
Bedfordshire, 1–47, 48, 56, 57 n., 60, 73, 104, 139, 157, 563, 565, 566, 568, 569, 573, 574, 579, 591, 592 n., 593, 595, 596, 602, 604, 612–18
Bedhampton, 343
Bedwyn (Wilts.), 263
Beeding, Lower and Upper, 408, 438 n., 440 n., 442, 461 n., 474
Beedon, 244, 249, 259 n.
Beeston, 17, 27, 44
Bekesbourne, *see* Bourne (Kent)
Belice, 493 n., 531, 581
Bellhurst, 429
Bellinge, 499
Bembridge, 296
Bendish, 63
Benenden, 529, 532, 581
Benestede hundred, 422, 423
Bengeo, 57, 63, 81
Benham, 244, 267
Bennington, 62, 63, 71, 77, 91
Bensington, *see* Benson
Bensington half-hundred, 190
Benson, 189, 196, 200, 201, 203 n., 210, 213, 217, 220, 221, 223, 233, 276, 565
Bentley, 321
Beorcham (Kent), 574 n.
Beorh-hamstede, 574
Bepton, 442, 464
Bere Forest, 322
Beresford, M. W., 244 n.

Berewicks, 25, 49–50, 71, 88 n., 99–100, 293, 355, 410, 413
Berham, Alia, see Kingston (Kent)
Berkesden Green, 52, 85 n.
Berkhamsted, 50, 57, 59 n., 62 n., 70, 77 n., 85, 86, 87–8, 90, 91, 92, 574, 609, 616, 619
Berkshire, 187, 190, 230, 231, 239–86, 287, 300, 372, 423, 563, 565, 573, 574 n., 575, 576, 580, 590, 591, 592, 596, 598, 601, 604, 612–18
Berkshire Downs, 246, 261, 267, 282, 283–4
Bermondsey, 132, 133, 372, 376, 585
Bermondspit hundred, 348
Bernwood Forest, 167 n., 602
Berrick Salome, 220
Bersted, 420
Berth (in Wivelsfield), 410
Berwick, 412, 413, 417, 453, 454, 455, 458 n.
Bessels Leigh, 244
Bethersden, 498
Betteshanger, 518 n., 521
Bevendean, 438 n., 439, 467, 468
Beverington, 439
Bewsborough hundred, 541 n.
Bexhill, 441, 449, 461 n., 462, 471, 569
Beynhurst hundred, 257
Bibliographical Notes, 45–7, 95–6, 136–7, 184–5, 237–8, 285–6, 361–3, 405–6, 479–81, 560–2
Bicester, 198
Bickton, 329, 334, 341
Bidborough, 499
Biddenden, 498
Biddenham, 12, 42 n., 43
Biddlesden, 150, 164, 174
Bieforde, 288, 296 n., 347
Biggleswade, 13, 25, 36, 569
Biggleswade hundred, 6, 9 n., 33, 598
Bighton, 304
Bignor, 460, 470, 474, 616
Bile, 296 n., 327
Bilicean, 499
Billington, 10
Bilsington, 484, 506, 522, 528 n., 530, 540
Binderton, 424 n.
Binfield, 242 n.
Binsted, 340
Birchgrove, 417, 431

Bircholt, 498, 531 n.
Birdham, 445 n., 453
Birling, 535, 536 n., 537 n., 541, 556
Biscot, 6, 12
Bisham, 281, 616
Bishopsbourne, 536
Bishopsgate, 98, 100, 108, 585
Bishops Hatfield, 48, 52, 54, 55, 56, 76, 77, 81, 85, 93
Bishops Sutton, 301
Bishopstoke, 290 n., 303
Bishopstone (Kent), 498
Bishopstone (Sx.), 422, 427, 429 n., 451
Bishops Waltham, 290, 301, 307, 311 n., 316, 348, 349, 355
Bispesdone, 194
Bisterne, 329
Bix, 147 n., 209
Blackbourne hundred, 503, 529, 530, 531 n., 594
Black Bourton, 219, 220
Blackdown Hill, 474
Blackheath hundred (Surrey), 365, 381, 394, 395
Blackpan, 295, 299
Blackwater, R., 340, 342, 348, 360, 580
Bladon, 224, 232, 616
Blean, 508, 524, 537
Bledlow, 145, 167, 174
Blendworth, 291
Bletchingley (Surrey), 132, 133, 372, 386, 399, 400
Bletchington (Oxon.), 230, 231
Bletsoe, 40
Blewbury, 276
Blewbury hundred, 257
Bloxham, 189, 193, 198, 200, 201 n., 203 n., 204, 212, 217, 220, 225, 230, 231, 233, 565
Blunham, 21
Boarhunt (Hants.), 300
Boarscroft, 57, 63
Bobbing, 498
Bochelande (Kent, Stowting hd), 493 n.
Bockhampton, 267
Bodicote, 189
Bognor, 420
Bolderford, 327
Boldre, 327

Bollington, 463, 471
Bolney, 207 n.
Bolnhurst, 12
Bondswomen, *see Ancillae*
Bonner, A., 367 n.
Bookham, Great and Little, 366, 385, 386
Bordars, 20, 21, 23, 63, 67, 69, 70, 85, 87, 88, 90, 115, 116, 117, 118, 155, 156, 160, 204, 205, 207, 254, 255 n., 256, 257, 258, 259, 279, 280, 310, 311, 352, 377, 379–81, 382, 399, 434, 435, 438, 439, 453 n., 512, 513, 515, 516, 517, 566, 588, 613, 617, 618
Bordelli, 355
Borden, 498
Borham, 418 n., 434, 470
Boroughs, *see* Urban life
Borowart, lathe of, 486, 554
Borstal, 505, 534, 551
Bosham, 425, 429 n., 440, 441, 455, 456, 461, 462, 464, 465
Bosmere hundred, 300
Boswell, 503
Botley, 322, 323
Botolph Claydon, *see* Claydon
Boughton, Malherbe and Monchelsea (Kent), 509, 544
Boughton Aluph (Kent), 503, 521
Boughton under Blean (Kent), 519, 539
Bourne, Bekesbourne and Patrixbourne (Kent), 489, 524, 536, 537, 539, 544, 596
Bourne (Sx., Henhurst hd), 413 n., 453
Bourne, R., 370, 396, 402
Bournemouth, 296, 297
Bourton (Berks.), 245
Bourton (Bucks.), 149, 154 n., 155 n., 160, 161, 166, 172, 177, 178, 179
Bow Brickhill, *see* Brickhill
Bowcombe, 315, 343, 349, 350, 351, 355
Bowley (Kent), 512, 519
Bowley (in Hailsham, Sx.), 418 n.
Box, Boxbury and Boxfield (Herts.), 62, 63, 71
Boxford (Berks.), 269
Boxgrove (Sx.), 423, 462
Box hundred (Sx.), 458 n., 466
Boxley (Kent), 518 n.
Boycott, 138, 167, 187, 190

Boys, John, 556 n.
Brabourne, 505, 524
Bracheshala, 499
Bradenham, 155
Brading, 294
Bradley (near Hampstead Norris), 243 n.
Bramber, 473, 616
Bramber, rape of, 407, 408, 410, 434
Brambletye, 420, 426, 439 n., 445 n., 462, 582
Brambridge, 290 n., 577
Bramdean, 353, 354
Brameselle, 368, 369
Bramfield, 73, 77 n.
Bramley (Hants.), 317, 353, 354
Bramley (Surrey), 372, 375, 380 n., 383, 396, 397, 398
Bramshaw, 287
Bramshill, 305, 316 n., 345
Bramshott, 303
Bras, 242 n.
Braughing, 83
Braun, H., 137
Bray, 242 n., 272, 275, 276
Bray hundred, 242
Bray, W., 405
Bread, 549, 555
Breamore, 291, 300 n., 318, 322, 329
Bredgar, 498
Bredhurst, 493
Brenchley, 499
Brent, R., 126, 131
Brentford, 101, 102
Brent Pelham, *see* Pelham
Brewing, 549
Bricewolde, 52
Brickendon, 66, 81 n.
Brickhill, Bow, Great and Little, 140, 150
Bridge (Kent), 498
Brighthampton, 193
Brightling, 423, 445
Brighton, 438, 449, 455, 467, 468, 474
Brightwalton, 248, 249, 259 n., 274, 275, 276, 277
Brightwell (Berks.), 250, 275, 276, 277
Brightwell Baldwin (Oxon.), 192, 212, 224
Brill, 145 n., 161, 167, 180, 187, 616
Brimpton, 259, 272
Brisewei, 492, 493 n., 494 n., 537, 538

Brissegneia, see *Brisewei*
Britwell Salome (Oxon.), 192, 203, 208, 212
Brixiestun, 499
Brixton hundred, 365
Brize Norton, 192, 201, 207 n., 208 n., 565
Broadfield, 61
Broadwater (Sx.), 408, 410, 440 n.
Broadwater Down (Kent), 414, 484
Broadwater hundred (Herts.), 50
Broadwell, 198, 208, 217, 221, 223, 225
Brockenhurst, 338
Brockhampton, 315
Brockhurst (in East Grinstead), 420
Bromfield, J. C., 194 n.
Bromham, 39 n.
Bromley, 505, 545
Bromscott, 217, 220
Brook (Kent), 494 n., 498
Brooke, G. C., 583 n.
Brookley, 327
Broom, 25
Broomfield, 505, 507, 536
Broomham (in Catsfield), 441 n.
Broomhill, 414, 485
Broomland (in Titsey), 368 n.
Broughton (Bucks., Moulsoe hd), 175
Broughton (Hants.), 299, 300 n., 317, 321, 322, 329, 334, 341, 350, 356
Broughton (Sx.), 412, 417
Broughton hundred (Hants.), 293 n., 310
Brown Candover, *see* Candover
Brown, E. H., 567
Broxbourne, 73, 80
Bruce-Mitford, R. L. S., 244 n.
Buckholt, 327
Buckingham, 140, 149, 154 n., 155 n., 160, 161, 166, 169, 172, 176, 177, 178–9, 616
Buckinghamshire, 4, 5, 33, 49 n., 60, 91, 104, 138–85, 187, 188, 190, 231, 301, 563, 565, 566, 568, 569, 573, 574, 579, 591, 592 n., 593, 595, 596, 602, 604, 612–18
Buckland (Berks.), 260, 267, 269, 280, 616
Buckland (Herts.), 77, 81
Buckland (Kent, Faversham hd), 489 n., 516
Bucklebury, 244, 260, 265, 601, 616
Bucklow half-hundred, 6, 29
Buckwell, 525
Budgen, W., 481

Bulborne, R., 91
Bullington, 300 n., 307
Bulverhythe, 471
Buncton, 451, 453
Bunsty hundred, 139, 140, 157
Burbeach hundred, 407 n., 410
Bures, Buri, 155, 157, 160, 204, 205, 208, 254, 257, 258, 314, 315, 566
Burford, 230, 231
Burgate, 321 n., 329, 341, 345
Burgelstaltone, 418 n.
Burgericestune, 499
Burgesses, 7 n., 20, 21, 42, 43, 50, 63, 70, 85, 86, 87, 88, 89, 90, 97, 115, 116, 118, 131, 155, 160, 177, 178, 179, 204, 227, 228, 229, 230 n., 254, 258, 276, 310, 377, 415, 434, 438, 463, 464, 465, 466, 467, 469, 470, 471, 472, 512, 513, 546, 547, 548, 550, 553, 554
Burgham (in Etchingham), 413 n.
Burghclere, *see* Clere
Burghfield, 270
Burham, 550, 551
Buriton, 297
Burlei, 245 n., 268
Burnham, 140, 142, 143, 167, 169, 569, 579
Burnham hundred, 139, 142 n.
Burpham, 442
Burrows, M., 472 n.
Burston, 166 n.
Burton (Hants.), 345, 352
Burton (Sx.), 453
Buscot, 250, 267
Bushey, 68, 77, 93
Butler, H. E., 123 n., 131 n., 580 n.
Buxted, 420
Byfleet, 393, 394
Bygrave, 56, 85 n.

C., C. (of Biggleswade), 1 n., 45
Caddington, 4, 5, 31, 37, 48
Cadwell, 201, 203 n., 565
Cainhoe, 31
Calbourne, 290, 301, 349
Calcot, 262 n.
Caldecote (Bucks.), 157, 160 n., 166, 174
Caldecote (Herts.), 63
Cam, Helen M., 190 n., 228 n., 237
Camberwell, 372, 383, 585

Cambridgeshire, 8 n., 14, 24 n., 36, 39 n., 48 n., 56, 57, 67, 68, 73, 94, 146, 157, 221, 249, 301
Camden, William, 244 n., 362
Candover, Brown, Chilton and Preston, 293, 300, 302, 305, 306, 307, 353, 354
Canterbury, 488, 512 n., 513, 518, 520, 521 n., 525, 532, 542, 544, 545, 546, 547–50, 554, 556, 558, 572, 583, 598, 615, 616
Canterton, 299, 329, 338
Cap. Anfridi, 495 n., 499
Cardington, 39 n.
Carucates, 12, 13 n., 16, 104, 106, 149, 563, 612, 618
Carshalton, 378, 382, 396 n.
Cashio hundred, 50, 53 n., 57 n.
Cassington, 212, 223, 225
Cassio (near Watford), 81, 93
Castelry, 466, 471, 473, 488 n., 556
Castles, 88, 274, 281, 310, 356, 466, 468, 469, 470, 473, 488, 550, 556, 583, 616
Castweazel, 494 n., 498
Catherington, 291, 297
Catmore, 244
Catsfield, 422, 458, 461 n.
Caversfield, 139, 187, 190, 223
Caversham, 187, 190, 199 n., 240, 241 n., 261, 262, 275, 277
Cay. Ho., 495 n., 499
Celvecrote, 295, 296 n.
Chaddleworth, 248, 264
Chadlington, 214
Chaldean, 52
Chaldon, 377
Chalfont, St Giles and St Peter, 167, 169, 174, 180, 616
Chalford (in Enstone), 225
Chalgrave, 12
Chalgrove, 199, 217, 226, 275, 276
Chalk (Kent), 503, 551, 552
Challock, 498
Chalton (Hants.), 291, 300
Chalton (Surrey), 348, 349, 356
Chalvington, 412, 413 n.
Chancton, 417, 443
Channell (Beds.), 39 n.
Chapels, 271, 348, 350, 396 n., 397, 461, 462, 544

Charford, North and South, 288, 295, 306, 315 n., 340, 345
Charlbury, 189, 234
Charlton (in Hungerford, Berks.), 240, 262, 267
Charlton (Herts.), 52, 63, 72 n.
Charlton (Kent, Bewsborough hd), 518 n.
Charlton (Mdlx.), 101, 104, 109, 125
Charlton hundred (Berks.), 243, 245
Charlton on Otmoor (Oxon.), 186, 190, 199, 217, 221 n.
Chartham, 506
Chart hundred, 594
Chart Sutton, 508, 525, 555, 609, 616
Chastleton, 224
Chatham, 524
Chauncy, Sir Henry, 95
Chawston, 9
Chawton, 301
Cheam, 371
Checkendon, 209
Cheddington, 164, 174
Cheese, 233, 280, 282, 520, 556, 616
Chellington, 10
Chelsea, 109, 122, 585
Chelsham, 401
Chenenolle, 418 n.
Cheriton, 498
Chertsey, 390, 391, 394, 616
Chertsey Abbey, 379, 383
Cherwell, R., 218, 223, 226, 227, 234, 235, 606
Chesham, 146, 161, 164, 167, 169, 172, 174, 182
Cheshunt, 56, 62 n., 71, 77, 79, 80, 82, 83, 90, 93, 94, 616
Chess, R., 143, 172, 175, 182, 604
Chessington, 379, 395
Chetwode, 147
Chevening, 499
Cheverton, 356
Chichester, 415, 438, 463–6, 474, 569 n., 616
Chichester harbour, 449, 456, 461
Chichester, rape of, 408
Chiddingfold, 369
Chiddingly, 458
Chiddingstone, 499, 531 n.
Chidham, 420
Chilbolton, 290 n., 311 n.

Chilcomb, 290, 304, 348, 349, 576
Childenhurst, 327
Chilham, 536, 547, 548
Chillenden, 509
Chilterns, 10, 33, 36, 45, 76, 91, 92, 143, 165, 167, 169, 170, 172, 175, 182–3, 189, 196, 210, 211, 213, 218, 220, 221, 234, 235, 236–7, 579, 588, 590
Chiltley, 303, 316
Chilton, 259, 275, 276
Chilton Candover, *see* Candover
Chilworth (Hants.), 321, 351
Chilworth (Oxon.), 189
Chingescamp, 296 n.
Chipping *alias* High Barnet, *see* Barnet
Chipstead, 376, 383, 387, 396
Chislehurst, 499
Chislet, 493, 501, 506, 518 n., 534, 539, 545, 555, 608, 609, 616
Chithurst, 460, 461 n., 464, 465
Chivington, 132, 133, 373, 399, 400
Chobham, 370, 396, 397, 402
Cholderton, 299
Cholsey, 259 n., 260, 272
Christchurch (Hants.), *see* Twynham
Christchurch (in Canterbury), 494
Churches, 24, 41–2, 43, 70, 71, 85, 86, 132, 135, 156, 176–7, 208, 228, 233, 271–2, 273, 275, 278, 311, 348–50, 352 n., 367, 378, 396–7, 398, 435, 461–2, 464, 470, 472, 483, 544–5, 549, 552, 553, 568, 583, 614
Church-scot, 233, 350, 462, 615
Chute Forest, 322, 602
Cildeest, 296 n., 326, 327
Cildresham, 493, 518 n., 525
Cities, *see* Urban life
Clandon, East and West, 366, 367, 379, 380 n.
Clanfield, 291
Clapham (Beds.), 12, 15, 31
Clapham (Surrey), 372
Clarendon Forest, 322, 602
Clare Park (Hants.), *see* Badley
Clarke, D. K., 423 n., 428, 429, 481
Clatford, 350, 353, 354
Clatinges (Hants.), 288, 296 n., 321 n.
Claverham, 412
Claydon, Botolph, East, Middle and Steeple, 166

Claygate, 386
Clayton (Sx.), 424, 430, 467, 468
Clerks, 70, 71, 85, 272, 462
Clere, Burghclere and Highclere, 294 n.,
    311 n., 316, 346
Clere hundred, 294 n., 295
Clewer, 250, 280, 281
Cliffe, 518, 525, 535, 556
Clifton (Beds.), 39 n.
Clifton (Bucks.), 146, 147, 150
Clifton hundred (Beds.), 6, 15
Climping, 415, 461 n.
Clophill, 28, 31
Clutterbuck, R., 95
Coastline, changes in the, 414–15, 485
Cobbett, William, 404
Cobblers, 549
Cobham (Kent), 499
Cobham (Surrey), 390
Cocherlei, 296 n., 327
Cockayne Hatley, 8 n., 11, 31, 33
Cockhampstead, 78
Cocking, 464, 465
Codicote, 71
Cogges, 217
Coins, 25, 72, 161, 209, 260, 316, 440; see
    also Mints
Cokeham, 418, 445
Cokenach, 71
Cold Brayfield, 143
Coldred, 521
Coleshill, 240 n., 269
Colham, 101, 109, 112, 119, 128, 609, 616
Coliberts, 157 n., 208 n., 254, 257, 258, 310,
    311, 314, 315, 352, 566
Colmworth, 15
Colne, R., 54, 81, 83, 93, 97, 125, 126, 129,
    130, 131, 136, 143, 165, 169, 172, 173,
    175, 183, 184, 604, 606
Colvin, H. M., 193 n., 194 n.
Comba (Kent), 499
Combe (Berks.), 241, 262 n., 284, 287
Combe (Kent), 520
Combe (Oxon.), 189
Composite entries, 189, 217, 220, 225,
    321 n., 340 n.
Compton (in Freshwater, Hants.), 318
Compton (Sx.), 414, 417, 435 n., 462, 464,
    465

Convivium, 470 n.
Cookham, 249, 260, 264, 272 n., 281, 616
Cooling, 487
Coombe (Surrey), 585
Coombes (Sx.), 456
Coote, H. C., 137
Cop Court, 192 n.
Cople, 22, 31
Copthorne hundred, 365, 366, 376, 394 n.,
    395
Corbett, W. J., 15 n., 59, 149, 185, 199 n.
Corhampton, 316, 353, 354
Cornbury, 214, 616
Cornwall, 302
Cornwell, 197
Cortesley (in Hollington), 415
Coscets, 310, 314, 315
Cosham, 307, 314, 315
Cotswolds, 210, 213, 218, 220, 221, 234–5,
    236
Cottars, 20, 21, 23, 24, 63, 66, 67, 70, 87,
    89, 90, 115, 117, 118, 133, 155, 156,
    160, 254, 255 n., 256, 257, 258, 310,
    314, 315, 377, 379–81, 382, 434, 438,
    439, 512, 513, 516, 613, 617, 618
Cottered, 77
Cottesloe hundred, 139, 142 n., 166, 168,
    169, 175, 598
Cottisford, 186, 190, 204
Court-at-Street, 519
Cove (Hants.), 288
Cowden, 499, 531 n.
Cowes, 296
Cowley (Mdlx.), 108
Cowley (Oxon.), 212, 223, 225, 229
Cox, J. C., 265 n.
Coxwell, Great and Little, 242, 262 n.
Cozenton, 499
Crafton, 166 n.
Cranbourne (in Wonston), 295
Cranbrook, 498
Crane, R., 131
Cranfield, 31
Cranford, 105, 109, 117, 123
Cranleigh, 369
Crawley (Beds.), 16
Crawley (Bucks.), 142, 176, 177
Crawley (Hants.), 321, 340
Crawley (Sx.), 420

Cray, Foots, North, St Mary (formerly South), St Paul's, 489 n., 499, 535 n.
Cray, R., 500
Crem, 277 n.
Creslow, 166 n.
Crochestrope, 245 n.
Crofton, 492, 510
Crofts, 438
Crondall, 288, 301, 311 n., 349
Cropredy, 189, 199 n., 200, 203 n., 212, 226, 565, 577
Crowborough Beacon, 478
Crowhurst (Sx., Baldslow hd), 441 n., 442
Crowell, 201, 208, 211, 212 n., 596
Crowmarsh Gifford, 209, 275, 277
Croydon, 373, 375, 386, 389
Crundale, 498
Cublington, 164, 166 n.
Cuckmere, R., 421, 455, 456, 476
Cuddesdon, 223, 225
Cuddington, 374, 375, 382
Cudessane, 9, 40, 41
Cudham, 506
Culham, 195
Cumnor, 250, 264, 268, 598, 599
Cutslow, 204
Cuxton, 505

Dacorum hundred, 50, 53 n., 57 n.
Dadford, 155
Dairy farms, 280
Dallington, 429 n., 446, 601, 602, 616
Dallington Forest, 446 n., 602, 616
Damerham, 287, 321
Dankton, 431
Darby, H. C., 14 n., 24 n., 39 n., 57 n., 67 n., 94 n., 96, 146 n., 154 n., 209 n., 211 n., 249 n., 259 n., 381 n., 414 n., 563–610, 575 n., 595 n., 596 n., 604 n., 608 n.
Darenden (Kent, Wye hd), 493 n.
Darent, R., 500, 534, 538, 543, 559, 604, 606
Darenth, 487, 488 n., 551, 556
Dartford, 506, 508, 518, 522, 525, 527, 530, 533, 535 n., 541, 545, 555, 616
Datchet, 164
Datchworth, 56, 67, 591

Davies, A. M., 137, 138 n., 140 n., 143, 185, 189, 238
Davis, B. F., 364 n., 562
Davis, E. Jeffries, 123 n., 131 n., 580 n.
Davis, H. W. C., 575 n.
Dawley, 101, 109, 122
Dean (Oxon.), 225
Dean, East and West (Sx., Westbourne hd), 416 n.
Dean, East and West (Sx., Willingdon hd), 412, 416
Dean, Lower and Upper (Beds.), 7, 8, 12, 13, 17, 22, 30
Dean Court (Kent), 529
Deddington, 206 n., 217, 224
Delce, 524, 535
Denge Marsh Farm, 488 n.
Denes, Denns, 262, 387, 484, 488, 527–32, 558, 581–2, 616
Denham, 164, 169, 172, 173
Denton (near Barham, Kent), 547, 548
Denton (near Gravesend, Kent), 505
Deptford, 499
Desborough hundred, 139, 140, 165
Detling, 498
Devonshire, 353
Dibden, 329, 334
Didcot, 245 n.
Digswell, 73, 83
Dileherst, 142
Dinton, 145, 161
Dirtham, 369
Ditchfield, P. H., 286
Ditchling, 430, 446, 467, 468, 473, 566
Ditton (Bucks.), 145, 165
Ditton (Kent), 535 n.
Ditton, Long and Thames (Surrey), 366, 383, 384, 394, 395, 399, 400
Doddington (Kent, Teynham hd), 548 n.
Dogs, 25, 26, 214
Dollis Brook, 126, 131
Domesday Monachorum, 483, 485, 489, 494, 496, 497, 498, 499, 502, 503, 504, 505, 519 n., 520 n., 532, 539 n., 545, 549 n., 552, 553, 554 n., 556, 560, 562, 577
Donnington, 427, 429 n., 439, 440, 445, 464, 465, 596
Dorchester (Oxon.), 189, 199 n., 217, 221, 223, 225, 226, 236 n., 275, 277, 577

Dorchester hundred (Oxon.), 190
Dorking, 403
Dorney, 170
Dorset, 287, 315, 357
Dorset Downs, 359
Douglas, D. C., 483 n., 485 n., 488 n.,
    489 n., 494 n., 498, 502 n., 504 n.,
    532 n., 539 n., 549 n., 552 n., 553 n.,
    554 n., 556 n., 561, 562, 577 n.
Dover, 488, 500, 513, 520, 541, 543, 544,
    545, 546, 552, 569, 572, 573, 616
Down (*Duna*), 341, 359
Down (in Knighton), 346
Downe, 493
Downton (Wilts.), 337
Drag nets, 128
Draitone (in Bruern), 194
Drapers, 549
Draycott, 268
Drayton (Mdlx.), 104, 108, 113, 119, 120,
    128
Drayton Parslow (Oxon.), 160, 169, 280
Drigsell (in Salehurst), 413 n., 418, 441 n.
Drodintone, 296 n., 299
Droitwich, 157, 160, 180, 232, 607, 608, 615
Droxford, 282, 349, 356
Dumbreck, W. V., 487, 488 n., 562
Dummer, 298, 340, 348, 353, 354, 360
Duncton, 422, 453, 464, 465
Dungeness, 559
Dunkin, J., 194 n.
Dunsfold, 369
Dunsley, 57, 58, 59 n., 60
Dunstable, 9
Duns Tew, 192, 201 n.
Dunthrop, 196, 209
Dunton (Beds.), 33
Dunton (Bucks.), 147
Durley (in Denny Lodge), 296, 322, 323
Durrington, 435 n., 442
Duxford, 244
Dymchurch, 498

Each, 531
Eadredestun, 499
Eadruneland, 494 n., 499
Ealing, 101, 102
Earley, 278
Earnley, 420

Easewrithe hundred, 422, 434, 458 n., 582
Easole, 525
East Anglian Heights, 94
East Barming, *see* Barming
East Barnet, *see* Barnet
East Bedfont, *see* Bedfont
Eastbourne, 413, 414 n., 442, 451, 456, 469,
    473
Eastbridge, 524, 537, 539, 540, 544, 608
East Burnham, 135, 140
East Chiltington, 416, 460, 467, 468
Eastchurch, 498
East Clandon, *see* Clandon
East Claydon, *see* Claydon
East Dean (Hants.), 322, 329, 341, 350, 356
East Dean (Sx., Westbourne hd), *see* Dean
    (Sx., Westbourne hd)
East Dean (Sx., Willingdon hd), *see* Dean
    (Sx., Willingdon hd)
Eastergate, 470
East Farleigh, *see* Farleigh (Kent)
East Grinstead, 420
East Grinstead hundred, 426, 439, 445 n.,
    446, 473, 478, 582, 616
East Hagbourne, *see* Hagbourne
Easthampstead, 253, 261
East Hanney, *see* Hanney
East Harting, *see* Harting
East Hatley, *see* Hatley (Cambs.)
East Hendred, *see* Hendred
East Horsley, *see* Horsley
East Ilsley, *see* Ilsley
Eastling, 489, 544
East Malling, *see* Malling (Kent)
East Marden (Sx.), *see* Marden
East Meon, *see* Meon
East Molesey, *see* Molesey
Easton (Hants.), 290 n., 348
Easton (Hunts.), 4
East Peckham, *see* Peckham (Kent)
Eastry, 519, 539
Eastry hundred, 531 n.
East Shefford, *see* Shefford
East Sutton, *see* Sutton (Kent)
East Tisted, *see* Tisted
East Tytherley, *see* Tytherley
Eastweald, 499
Eastwell, 502 n., 524
East Wellow, *see* Wellow

East Wittering, *see* Wittering
Eaton Bray (Beds.), 31
Eaton Socon (Beds.), 39, 43, 609, 610, 616
Eaton, Water Eaton and Woodeaton (Oxon.), 209, 217, 223, 233, 236
Eatons (in Henfield), 446
Ebony Isle, 498
Ebrige, 245 n., 262 n., 269, 270, 281
Ebury, 101, 108, 125, 127, 585
Eccles, 487, 551, 552
Eckington, 412
Eddington, 245, 252
Eddintone, 493 n., 519, 540 n., 542, 543
Eden, R., 394, 403
Edenbridge, 499
Edgcott, 154, 569
Edgware, 102
Edlesborough, 4, 139, 140 n.
Edmonton, 100, 108, 109, 117, 125, 127, 130 n.
Edmonton hundred, 97, 98, 106, 118 n., 119 n.
Edwinstree hundred, 67, 85
Edworth, 20, 24 n.
Eels, 39, 40, 82, 83, 128, 129, 172, 173, 174, 182, 222, 224, 268, 269, 341, 393, 453, 460, 536, 541
Effelle, *see* Yateley
Effingham, 391
Effingham hundred, 365
Egerton, 498
Egham, 375, 391
Egheiete hundred, 300 n.
Eia (Herts.), *see* Rye (Herts.)
Eia (Mdlx.), *see* Ebury
Eight-hide unit, 427–8
Eight-virgate hide, 422–3, 429
Eighty-hide unit, 428
Eiscedene, 499
Eiselle, 499
Ekwall, Eilert, 245 n., 293 n., 489 n.
Elentone, 244
Eletesford hundred, 257
Eling (Berks.), 259
Eling (Hants.), 291, 293, 299, 300, 317, 320, 322, 329, 333, 334, 335, 336, 343, 356
Ellesborough, 182
Ellingham, 320, 329, 334, 336
Ellis, Sir Henry, 21, 24 n., 64, 96, 116, 155

204, 254, 310, 354 n., 377, 434, 456 n., 458 n., 512, 555 n.
Ellisfield, 306, 316, 340
Elmbridge hundred, 365, 380
Elmsted, 493, 494, 497, 498
Elmstone, 512
Elmton, 531, 544
Elstead, 366 n.
Elsted, 429 n., 451, 462
Elthorne hundred, 97, 98, 106, 108, 109, 117, 118 n., 119 n.
Elton, C. I., 561
Elvedon (in Pertenhall), 8
Elverton, 548 n.
Elvey, G. R., 148 n., 185
Ely Abbey, 54, 55, 56, 66
Ember, 376
Embley (in East Wellow), 296, 344
Emmetune, 499
Empshott, 320
Enborne, 248, 262 n.
Endleueberga, 499
Enfield, 109, 115 n., 122, 123, 125, 127, 128, 136
Enfield Chase, 123, 124, 580
Englishmen, 20, 23, 70, 71, 117, 118, 119, 160, 314, 351
Enham, 345, 357
Enstone, 208
Epcombs, 83
Epsom, 386, 397
Epwell, 189, 234
Erringham, 431, 443
Eschetune, 295, 296 n.
Esher, 372, 383
Esmerewic, 418
Essella, 493
Essex, 48 n., 49, 50, 68, 94, 97, 118, 131, 132, 133, 357, 485, 502, 559
Estone (Beds.), *see* Little Staughton
Estrei, lathe of, 486
Etchingwood (in Buxted), 412, 417, 420
Eton, 164
Evebentone, 418 n.
Evegate, 492
Evenlode, R., 218, 226, 227, 234, 235, 604
Everard, C. E., 567
Evershaw, 142
Evershed, H., 93

Eversley, 320, 353, 354
Everton, 3, 28, 33
Evingar hundred, 294 n.
Ewell (Kent), 530, 541, 542
Ewell (Surrey), 367, 384, 387, 395, 582, 616
Ewelme, 275, 277
Ewhurst (Surrey), 369
Ewhurst (Sx.), 423
Excerpta, 483, 484, 493, 494, 496, 497, 498, 502 n., 503, 505 n., 506, 519 n., 525, 528 n., 530 n., 533 n., 539 n., 541 n., 542, 543 n., 546, 547 n., 548, 549, 550, 552, 555, 577, 598
Exeter, 353
Exton, 300, 317
Eyelid (in Ewhurst), 484 n.
Eyeworth, 327
Eynsford, 487, 524, 537, 542, 544
Eynsham, 200, 201, 208 n., 212, 224, 233, 565
Eythorne, 494, 498
Eyton, R. W., 211 n., 220 n.

Faccombe, 288 n., 353, 354
Fairbourne, 509
Fairlight (Sx., Guestling hd), 418 n.
Fairlight (Sx., East Grinstead hd), 420
Falconers, 311
Falemere hundred, 438 n.
Fanscoombe (in Wye), 530
Fareham, 303
Faringdon, Great and Little, 187, 190, 240, 258, 259 n., 262 n., 268, 269, 273
Farleigh, East and West (Kent), 487, 489, 536 n.
Farleigh (Surrey), 376
Farleigh Wallop (Hants.), 294 n., 340
Farnborough (Berks.), 262 n., 267
Farnborough (Hants.), 288, 345
Farnborough (Kent), 499
Farncombe, 376
Farndish, 2, 4
Farnham (Bucks.), 150, 175
Farnham (Surrey), 365, 366, 386, 392, 396, 403, 575, 576, 596
Farnham hundred, 365, 366, 404, 576
Farningham, 487, 507, 525, 527, 535, 541, 542, 556

Faversham, 525, 534 n., 539, 547, 548, 554, 616
Fawkham, 505
Fawler, 196
Fawley (Berks.), 259
Fawley (Bucks.), 147, 164
Fawley (Hants.), 303, 326 n., 328, 329, 331, 332, 334
Felesmere, 418 n., 438 n.
Felmersham, 27
Felpham, 439, 453, 464, 465
Feltham, 109, 113, 120
Ferding, 422
Féret, C. J., 102
Ferling, 503 n.
Fernham, 245
Fernhill, 303, 329
Ferraria, 355, 356, 401, 616
Ferring, 429 n., 445, 451, 597
Fetcham, 384, 386, 395, 396
Field, J. E., 244 n., 286
Fifield (near Benson, Oxon.), 197 n., 248 n.
Fifield (near Idbury, Oxon.), 197
Filsham, 426, 441, 462
Finchampstead, 249
Finchley, 102, 124, 135
Findon, 413
Finglesham, 519
Finlei, 296 n.
Finmere, 186, 190, 205
Finn, R. Welldon, x, 96, 287–363
Finstock, 196
Fish, 82, 172; see also Herrings, Lampreys
Fishbourne, 464, 465
Fisheries, 38–9, 44, 82–3, 94, 128–9, 172–3, 182, 183, 184, 221–3, 235, 236, 237, 268–9, 282, 284, 341–2, 352, 359, 360, 361, 393–4, 402, 453–5, 470, 476, 477, 536–9, 559, 568, 605–7, 614
Fishermen, 39, 204, 205, 208, 221, 222
Fishersgate hundred, 407
Fish-stews, 39, 82, 83, 87, 222, 223
Five-hide unit, 1, 13–15, 56–8, 104–5, 145–7, 197–8, 248–9, 303, 373, 427–8, 612
Flamstead, 58, 77, 92
Fleet, 518 n., 537, 539
Fleming, L., 481
Fletching, 445 n.

Flexmore, 52, 72
Flitt hundred, 6
Flitton, 15, 28
Folkestone, 491, 508, 516, 530, 534, 540, 542, 544, 545, 559
Foots Cray, *see* Cray
Fordingbridge, 329, 333, 334
Fordwich, 488, 507 n., 513, 545, 546, 554, 616
Foresters, 213, 214, 310, 311, 322, 356, 377, 382, 588
Forest Row (Sx.), 420
Forest, 167, 180, 211, 214, 215, 236, 247, 262, 264–5, 285, 306, 321, 322, 324–38, 341, 361, 386, 389, 446, 600–2, 610, 616
Forges, *see* Ferraria
Foristel, 546
Foster, C. W., 495 n.
Fowler, G. H., 2, 6 n., 9 n., 10, 13 n., 15 n., 19 n., 20 n., 21, 24, 26, 27, 33, 34, 35, 36, 37, 38 n., 41, 46, 96, 170, 209 n., 237, 596, 602, 603
Francigenae, 20, 21, 23, 24, 63, 69, 70, 87, 90, 114 n., 115, 116, 118, 119, 157, 160, 205, 274, 275, 314, 351, 435 n., 513, 518
Frankwell, 422
Freeman, E. A., 239 n., 574 n.
Freemen, 63, 69, 70, 114 n., 118, 119, 204, 205, 206, 207–8, 254, 310, 311, 314, 315, 377, 382, 434, 513, 518, 591, 595, 617, 618
Free peasantry, *see* Freemen, Sokemen
Frenchmen, *see Francigenae*
Frensham, 366
Friern Barnet, *see* Barnet
Frindsbury, 487, 505, 551
Frinsted, 509
Fritham (in Bramshaw), 327
Frost, R. C., 561
Fryer, D. W., 180 n.
Fulbrook, 218
Fulham, 99, 102, 108, 114, 116, 117, 118, 119, 121, 122, 124, 125, 126, 128, 132, 133, 577, 585
Fulking, 417, 440
Fulscot, 244
Fulwell (in Mixbury), 209
Furley, Robert, 560
Furlong, 418 n.

Furneux Pelham, *see* Pelham
Fyfield (Berks.), 248 n., 268
Fyfield (Hants.), 303

Gaddesden, Great and Little, 50 n., 58, 88 n.
Gade, R., 45, 54, 81, 83, 91, 604
Gadre hundreds, 190
Gafol rents, 455, 474
Gammon's Farm (in Newchurch), 519 n.
Ganfield hundred, 257
Gara, 492, 493 n.
Gardens, 133, 134, 208, 229, 233, 556
Garlinge, 493
Garrington, 526, 555
Garsington, 197, 616
Gatcombe, 320
Gatehampton, 242, 244, 259
Gatewood, 326, 327
Gatton, 374, 386, 575
Gawcott, 169
Geld Rolls, 302, 337
Gelling, Margaret, 138 n., 192 n., 232 n., 238, 277 n.
Gerlei, 296 n.
Ghidenetroi hundred, 426
Gibons, E., 9 n.
Giddinge, 503, 519
Gihalla, 546
Gillingham, 518 n., 521, 535 n., 539 n.
Gladley, 9
Gloucestershire, 187, 190, 258
Glyme, R., 234
Glympton, 186, 190, 199, 201
Goats, 91
Godalming, 371, 380 n., 383, 384, 397, 404
Godalming hundred, 365, 380
Godesmanescamp, 296 n., 307
Godley hundred, 365
Goldington, 25, 39 n.
Gomshall, 379
Goosey, 253, 258, 267
Gore hundred, 98, 106, 118 n., 119 n., 127
Goring (Berks.), 579
Goring (Oxon.), 208
Goring (Sx.), 413, 425
Gorley, 311 n., 329
Goslaches, 493 n.
Goudhurst, 498
Gould, I. C., 95

Gover, J. E. B., 52 n., 96, 99 n., 125 n., 137, 327, 367 n., 368 n., 369 n., 406, 407 n., 413 n., 415 n., 416 n., 418 n., 446 n., 448 n., 472 n., 482, 580 n.
Graffham, 415, 429 n.
Grafton, 217
Grain, 25; see also Annonae
Grain, Isle of, 499
Grange (in Gillingham), 499
Grately, 297
Graveley, 76
Graveney, 539
Gravenhurst, Upper and Little, 8 n., 28
Gravesend, 485, 555, 616
Great Amwell, see Amwell
Great Barford, 8, 11, 25, 39 n.
Great Berkhamsted, see Berkhamsted
Great Bookham, see Bookham
Great Brickhill, see Brickhill
Great Chart, 489, 540
Great Coxwell, see Coxwell
Great Faringdon, see Faringdon
Great Gaddesden, see Gaddesden
Great Greenford, see Greenford
Great Hampden, see Hampden
Great Hormead, see Hormead
Great Kimble, see Kimble
Great Marlow, see Marlow
Great Milton (Oxon.), 189, 192, 199 n., 200, 208, 217, 233, 577
Great Missenden, see Missenden
Great Munden, see Munden
Greatness (Kent), 499
Great Offley, see Offley
Great Rollright, see Rollright
Great Shefford, see Shefford
Great Stanmore, see Stanmore
Great Tew, see Tew
Great Woolwicks, see Woolwicks
Great Wymondley, see Wymondley
Greenford, Great and Little, 99, 108, 109, 112, 114, 115 n., 116
Greenham, 271
Greenwich, 516 n., 535 n., 545, 585
Gribrige, 546
Griffith, E., 137
Grimsbury, 186, 190
Gritnam, 300 n., 327, 332
Grittenham, 473, 616

Grove, 166 n.
Grundy, G. B., 195 n.
Gubblecote, 57, 58, 59 n.
Guestling, 441 n.
Guildford, 365, 371, 374, 382, 397, 398, 403, 404, 616
Guildford Park, 389

Hackney, 126 n.
Haddenham, 145, 170, 172, 176, 177
Hadham, Little and Much, 48, 50, 60, 73, 78, 85 n.
Hadlow, 486, 487, 488, 509
Hagbourne, East and West, 243, 251
Haggerston, 102, 109, 113, 585
Hailesaltede hundred, 413 n., 427, 439, 440
Hailey, 52, 56, 83
Hailsham, 456
Hainstone, 52
Haldley, 299, 311
Halling, 487, 505
Halnaker, 464, 465
Halstead, 499
Ham (Surrey, Kingston hd), 376, 585
Ham (Surrey, Wallington hd), 382
Hambleden (Bucks.), 145, 161, 182
Hambledon (Hants.), 300, 356
Hambledon (Surrey), 376, 384, 386
Hamilton, N. E. S. A., 48 n., 50 n., 54 n., 66 n., 91 n., 96
Hammersmith, 101, 102
Hampden, Great and Little, 140, 141 n., 167
Hampshire, 241, 242, 282, 284, 287–363, 372, 414, 423, 442, 443, 473, 474, 476, 563, 566, 568, 569 n., 573, 574 n., 576, 577, 580, 591, 592, 596, 597, 598, 602, 606, 607, 612–18
Hampshire Basin, 357–9
Hampshire Downs, 284, 357, 358, 359–60, 579, 588
Hampstead, 108, 109, 119, 585
Hampstead Marshall, 244
Hampstead Norris, 244, 252, 259 n.
Hampton (Mdlx.), 98, 105, 109, 125, 128, 606
Hampton, Gay and Poyle (Oxon.), 207 n., 217, 230
Hamsey, 434, 449
Handborough, 211

Handsoca, 546
Hanechedene, see Radnage
Hanefeld(e), 3, 4 n., 9
Hanger (in Netley Marsh), 296
Hankham, 435, 589
Hanney, East and West, 260, 267, 271
Hanslope, 148, 149
Hanstead, 52, 80, 93
Hantachenesele, 355
Hanwell, 103, 108, 129, 585
Hanworth, 104, 105, 109, 113
Harbiton, 512
Harbours, *see* Hithes
Hardley, 321 n., 327
Hardman, F. W., 485 n.
Hardmead, 150, 155, 177
Hardres, Lower and Upper, 489, 544
Hardwick (Bucks.), 166 n.
Hardwick (in Whitchurch, Oxon.), 193
Harefield, 105, 109, 128
Harlesden, 108, 585
Harlington (Beds.), 18, 31
Harlington (Mdlx.), 109, 115 n.
Harmondsworth, 107, 108, 114, 115 n.,
    118 n., 119, 128, 129, 609, 616
Harpingden, 467, 468
Harrietsham, 509
Harris, John, 560
Harrold (Beds.), 39 n.
Harrow, 99, 104, 105, 108, 111, 114, 118,
    119, 127, 577, 585
Harrowden, 22
Harrow Weald, 101
Hartfield, 427, 460
Hartfield hundred, 410
Hartford, 327, 332
Harting, East, South and West, 415, 424 n.,
    461, 464, 465, 470, 576
Hartley Mauditt, 302
Hartlip, 498
Hartshurst, 370, 404
Harty, Isle of, 492, 501
Harwell, 247, 250, 259, 271, 275, 276
Hascombe, 369
Haseley, 317
Haseleie (Bucks.), 142
Haseley (Oxon.), 275, 276
Haslehangra, Helsangre, 52
Hasted, Edward, 486 n., 560

Hastings, 415, 438, 471, 472, 473, 474 n.,
    479, 572, 583, 616
Hastings, Battle of, 316, 478, 520, 569
Hastings, rape of, 408, 412, 413, 417, 423,
    427, 429, 430, 433, 437, 441, 447, 448,
    450, 478
Hatcham, 376, 585
Hatfield (Herts.), *see* Bishops Hatfield
Hatfield Broadoak (Essex), 49
Hatford, 248, 250, 252
Hatley Cockayne, *see* Cockayne Hatley
Hatley, East and St George (Cambs.), 8 n.
Hatton, 101, 103, 109, 115 n.
Havant, 315
Haven, 510, 522
Haversham, 172, 174 n.
Hawkhurst, 492
Hawkinge, 498
Hawks, 167, 180, 214, 387, 401, 616
Hawley, 492, 519, 530
Hay, 36, 80, 81, 125, 170, 338, 355, 602;
    see also Meadow
Hayes (Mdlx.), 104, 108, 111, 114, 118 n.,
    122
Hayne hundred, 510, 541 n.
Haynes, 15
Hazelden, 417, 420, 427, 582
Hazelhurst, 413, 427 n., 441 n., 582
Hawksborough hundred, 412, 413, 427,
    430 n., 433, 437, 446, 447, 450, 582
Headbourne Worthy, *see* Worthy
Headcorn, 498
Headington, 217, 220, 223, 233
Hearne, Thomas, 495 n., 562
Heceford, 296 n.
Helsthorpe, 166 n.
Helueuuecha, 233
Hemel Hempstead, 52 n., 58, 71, 73, 77,
    81 n., 83, 92
Hempton (in Deddington), 193, 217
Hempton Wainhill, *see* Wainhill
Hemsted, 492
Hendon, 104, 108, 122, 125, 126, 127
Hendred, East and West, 259, 271, 272
Henfield, 453, 455, 458, 467, 468
Henhurst hundred, 412, 413, 427, 429 n.,
    430 n., 433, 437, 441 n., 446, 447, 450,
    453, 455, 458 n., 582
Henley (Surrey), 386

Henley on Thames, 189, 211
Henlow, 35, 38
Henshall, S., 405, 479, 560
Hensington, 198, 212, 217
Herbagia, 122–3
Herbagium, 340, 391, 451, 534, 536, 614
Herdwicks, 71
Herefordshire, 258
Herne, 498
Hernehill, 498
Herriard, 318
Herrings, 129, 393, 394, 399, 455, 474, 538–9, 552
Hertford, 49 n., 50, 55, 56 n., 59 n., 62 n., 70, 72, 83, 85, 86–7, 88 n., 616
Hertford hundred, 50, 83 n., 84, 90
Hertfordshire, 4, 5, 23, 24, 33, 36, 37, 42, 48–96, 97, 98, 104, 124, 135, 140, 148, 156, 157, 301, 565, 566, 568, 573, 574, 579, 591, 592 n., 593, 596, 598, 602, 604, 606, 612–18
Hertingfordbury, 77, 81
Hethe (Oxon.), 186, 190
Hever, 499, 531
Hexton, 61, 62, 72 n.
Heyford, Lower and Upper, 186, 190, 223
Hides, 11–16, 55–60, 103–10, 145–9, 197–9, 248–51, 299–304, 327–30, 371–4, 422–9, 471, 479, 502, 563, 612, 617
Higham (Kent), 508, 535, 556
Higham (Sx., Staple hd), 425, 441 n.
High Barnet, *see* Barnet
Highclere, *see* Clere
Highfurlong Brook, 226
High Halden, 498
High Halstow, 499
High Wycombe, *see* Wycombe
Hilles (in Darenth), 499
Hillingdon, 109, 118, 128
Hinchelsea, 327, 332
Hindhead, 404
Hinksey Ferry, 227
Hinton Admiral, 329
Hinton Ampner, 350
Hinxhill, 498
Hitchin, 5 n., 25, 48, 54, 71, 72 n., 85, 92, 94
Hitchin hundred, 50, 72
Hithes, 555, 616
Hodcott, 244, 261

Hoddesdon, 49 n., 50 n., 68, 71, 83, 85 n.
Hoddington, 306
Hoe, Hoe Cross, Hoe Gate, East Hoe (all in Soberton, Hants.), 295–6
Hoecourt (Sx.), 410, 413
Hofmann, M., 362, 481
Holborn, 100, 585, 608, 609, 610, 616
Holcot, 28
Hollingdon, 166 n.
Holdenhurst, 291, 306, 329, 334, 335, 336, 340, 341, 350
Hollingbourne, 541 n.
Hollington, 441 n., 446, 458
Holly, D., 14 n., 495 n.
Holmesdale, Vale of, *see* Homesdale, Vale of
Holwell, 4, 5, 48
Holybourne, 321
Holywell (Oxon.), 208, 229, 233
Homesdale, Vale of, 370, 403, 558
Honey, 25, 233, 310, 329, 330, 356, 456 n., 474
Honeybourne, M. B., 123 n., 131 n., 580 n.
Honey Hill, 4 n.
Hoo (Kent), 487, 491, 516, 517 n., 544, 551, 552
Hooe (Sx.), 456, 461 n.
Hoo hundred (Kent), 485
Hook Norton, 192, 212
Hope All Saints, 498
Hopgrass, 240 n.
Hordle, 329, 334, 336, 343
Horley (Oxon.), 217
Hormead, Great and Little, 76
Horns (Sx.), 440
Hornsey, 102
Horsenden, 150, 155, 161, 174
Horses, 267, 281, 466
Horsfield, T. W., 479
Horsham, 420
Horsley, East and West, 366, 384, 387 n.
Horsmonden, 499
Horspath, 224
Horsted Keynes, 416
Horton (Bucks., Stoke hd), 169 n.
Horton (Bucks., Yardley hd), 142, 169
Horton (in Chartham, Kent), 522, 525, 541
Horton (Oxon.), 193
Horton Kirby (Kent), 542
Hoskins, W. G., 232 n., 238

Hothfield, 489, 498
Hotlop, 296 n.
Hougham, 485
Houghton (Hants.), 290, 300, 302, 305, 311 n., 315, 338, 339, 348, 353, 354
Houghton Conquest (Beds.), 32
Houghton Forest (Sx.), 446 n.
Houghton Regis (Beds.), 6, 9, 12, 25, 26, 41, 42
Hounslow hundred, 98, 106, 118 n., 119 n.
Howorth, Sir Henry H., 407 n.
Hoxton, 102, 108, 119, 585
Hudson, W., 480, 482
Huffingford, 295, 345
Hughenden, 145
Hundreds, Domesday, 6, 14, 29, 30, 50, 74, 97–8, 105, 121, 139, 140, 164, 165, 190–1, 210, 242, 261, 319, 364–5, 380, 381, 385, 392, 407, 443, 444, 485, 523, 532, 616
Hundred Rolls, 186, 189 n., 193 n., 194 n., 197 n., 318
Hunesworde, 194
Hungerford, 245
Hunsdon, 77 n.
Hunston, 456, 464, 465
Hunter, Joseph, 1
Hunting, 33, 43, 77, 91, 123, 134, 180, 214, 265, 389, 525; *see also* Forests, Hawks
Huntingdonshire, 2, 3, 4, 8 n., 31, 32, 33, 36, 41, 42, 48 n., 563 n.
Hunton, 496, 498, 499
Huntsmen, 214, 311
Hurley, 245 n.
Hurn, 341
Hurst (in Sedlescombe), 417, 435
Hurstbourne Priors (Hants.), 290, 307, 346
Hurstbourne Tarrant (Hants.), 300 n., 311 n., 318, 350
Hurstpierpoint, 413
Hurtmore, 369, 384
Husborne Crawley, 24
Hussey, A., 405, 480, 560
Hyruuerthestun, 499
Hythe, 488, 513, 545, 546, 553, 583, 616

Ibsley, 324, 329, 332, 334, 345
Ibstone, 138, 147, 148, 157, 170, 188, 190
Ickenham, 105, 109, 116

Ickford, 148 n.
Ickham, 516
Idbury, 207 n.
Idleigh, 507, 519
Idsworth, 291
Iffley, 212, 219, 223
Ifield (Kent), 499
Ifield (Sx.), 431
Iford, 424, 438, 449, 451, 455, 467, 468
Ightham, 499
Ilbury, 193
Ilsley, East (formerly Market) and West, 245 n., 262 n., 267, 275, 276
Inglesham (Wilts.), 240
Inkpen, 262
Inland, 197
Inquisitio Comitatus Cantabrigiensis, 96, 97
Inquisitio Eliensis, 48, 66, 90, 96, 97, 616
Intercommoning, 221 n., 229
Inward, 72, 488 n., 532 n., 537
Iping, 462, 464, 465, 473, 616
Iron, 31, 167, 183
Isleworth, 105, 109, 112, 114, 116, 118 n., 119, 122, 127, 128, 131, 585
Isleworth hundred, 98
Islingham, 499
Islington, 104, 105, 108, 109, 112, 114, 119, 585
Islip, 221 n.
Itchell, 288
Itchen Abbess, 294
Itchen, R., 290 n., 298, 319, 339, 340, 341, 345, 348, 359, 604, 606
Itchen Stoke, 294, 345
Ivel, R., 10, 33, 36, 39, 41, 44, 95, 604
Iver, 172, 173, 180, 606, 609, 616
Ivet, 418 n.
Ivinghoe, 150, 151, 164, 166, 565
Ivychurch, 498
Iwade, 498
Ixhill hundred, 139, 142 n.

James, W., 180 n.
Jaonei, 492, 493 n.
Jevington, 412
Johnson, W. B., 96
Johnston, P. Mainwaring, 482
Jolliffe, J. E. A., 407 n., 423 n., 428, 429, 481, 485 n., 486 n., 503 n., 506, 561

Jope, E. M., 186–238, 598 n.
Juga, see Yokes

Karslake, J. B., 362
Kelshall, 48
Kempston (Beds.), 38
Kempton (Mdlx.), 101, 105, 109, 117, 609, 610, 616
Kemsing, 499
Kenardington, 498
Kennedy, E. H., 405
Kennet, R., 246, 261, 265, 267, 269, 271, 283, 284, 340, 348, 360, 604, 606
Kennett, W., 194 n.
Kennington (Berks.), 249 n.
Kennington (Kent), 505, 516, 524
Kennington (Surrey), 585
Kensington, 104, 109, 113, 119, 585, 609, 616
Kensworth, 4, 5, 31, 37, 48
Kent, 372, 382, 387, 388, 403, 405, 413 n., 414, 423, 448, 483–562, 563, 566, 568, 572, 574 n., 577, 578, 579, 580, 581, 582, 588, 591, 595, 596, 597, 605, 606, 607, 608, 612–18
Kenton, 101
Keymer, 430, 467, 468
Keysoe, 2, 4, 25, 31, 36 n.
Kidbrooke, 499
Kiddington, 193
Kidlington, 217
Kilmeston, 290 n., 318
Kimble, Great and Little, 140, 164, 166
Kimbolton, 3, 4 n.
Kimpton, 61
Kingsbury, 108, 109, 126, 127, 585
Kingsclere, 294 n., 300 n., 315, 318, 320, 321, 355
Kingsey, 138, 187–8
Kings Langley, *see* Langley
King's Somborne, *see* Somborne
King's Somborne hundred, 295
Kingsnorth, 498
Kingston (Kent), 498
Kingston (Surrey), 393, 394, 396, 399, 401, 585
Kingston Blount (Oxon.), 200
Kingston hundred (Surrey), 365, 393, 394, 401
Kingston by Sea (Sx.), 456, 461 n.

King's Walden, *see* Walden
Kings Worthy, *see* Worthy
Kinson, 287, 315
Kintbury, 265, 267, 281, 601, 616
Kinwick, 9, 12, 28
Kirdford, 420
Kirke, Edith M., 560
Kirtlington, 193, 213, 217, 220, 233
Kissan, B. W., 561
Kitchin, G. W., 355 n.
Knighton, 346
Knights, 20, 21, 24, 63, 70, 115, 118, 119, 160 n., 133, 204, 205, 208, 258, 259, 435 n., 513, 518
Knocker, H. W., 561
Knockholt, 493
Kökeritz, H., 363
Krause, J., 588 n.

Laleham, 109
Lamberhurst, 414, 484, 499
Lambeth, 132, 133, 374, 376, 585
Lamborn, E. A. G., 237
Lambourn, 248, 250, 252, 253, 267
Lambourn, R., 246, 267, 271, 283, 284
Lampeth, 52
Lampreys, 393
Lamua hundred, 139, 142 n.
Lancing, 456
Langemare, see Angmering
Langford (Beds.), 17, 33, 36, 38
Langford (Oxon.), 187, 190, 240
Langley (Berks.), 243 n.
Langley (Hants.), 299, 311 n., 338
Langley, Abbots and Kings (Herts.), 50 n., 58, 60, 61, 77, 565
Langport (Kent, Stowting hd), 493
Langport (near Canterbury), 490, 505, 543 n., 547, 548, 549
Langport hundred, 553
Langport (near Lydd), 540, 553
Langstone harbour, 344, 359, 608
Larking, L. B., 560
Lasham, 318
Lashbrook, 204, 209, 224 n., 225
Latchford, 194 n.
Lathes, Domesday, 485, 486, 616
Laughton (Sx.), 412, 413, 414 n., 417, 443, 456, 467, 468

Launton, 193
Lavant, 426, 429 n., 443, 464, 465, 582
Lavant, R., 449
Lavendon, 143, 150, 170, 172, 174 n., 175
Lea (in Bradley), 295
Lea, R., 39, 41, 45, 71, 80, 83, 84, 86, 91, 92,
    93, 94, 95, 97, 103, 125, 129, 130, 131,
    135, 136, 574, 604, 606
Leafield, 196
League, Domesday, see Linear measure-
    ments
Leatherhead, 367, 368 n., 377
Leckford, 345
Leckhampstead (Bucks.), 156, 174
Ledwell, 193
Leeds (Kent), 484, 516, 526, 528 n., 530,
    541, 555, 609, 616
Legge, W. H., 445, 597
Leicestershire, 14, 495
Leicestershire Survey, 186, 495
Leigh (Kent), 499, 531 n.
Leigh (Oxon.), 199
Leigh (Surrey), 396
Leighton Buzzard, 6, 8, 12, 13, 25, 36, 41,
    42, 43, 44, 616
Leith Hill, 404
Lenborough, 166
Lennard, Reginald, 107 n., 117, 137, 238,
    562
Leominster, 597
Lessland, 307, 311
Lesteorde (Hants., Boldre hd), 296 n., 328,
    329, 334
Lests, see Lathes, Domesday
Letcombe, Bassett and Regis, 243, 257, 264,
    271
Leveberge, 493 n., 509
Levegarestun, 296 n.
Lewarewiche, 52
Lewes, 415, 438, 455, 462, 463, 466–9, 473,
    474, 476, 583, 616
Lewes, rape of, 407, 408, 410
Lewis, P., 362
Lewisham, 515, 518, 524, 541, 542, 554, 585,
    616
Lewknor, 143 n., 212, 217
Lewknor hundred, 190
Leybourne, 487
Leygreen, 72 n.

Leysdown, 498
Leyton (Essex), 585
Liber Exoniensis, 337 n.
Liber Winton, 353, 363
Liberi homines, see Freemen
Libury, 71
Lidsing, 499
Liebermann, F., 495 n., 561, 583 n.
Lierecote, 245
Lillechurch (in Higham, Kent), 499
Lilley, 68, 72 n.
Lillingstone Dayrell, 139 n., 187
Lillingstone Lovell, 138–9, 167, 187, 190
Limerstone, 295
Limpsfield, 368, 376, 386, 387, 394, 400, 616
Linch, 430, 442, 464, 465
Lincoln, 583
Lincolnshire, 154 n., 604
Lindfield, 420
Lindsey, 495
Lindsey Survey, 186, 495
Linear measurements, of coppice, 212, 215
    of manors, 197
    of meadow, 216–17
    of pasture, 218–20, 267, 340
    of spinetum, 211 n., 212
    of wood, 32, 167, 211–12, 214, 215, 262,
        321, 568, 614
Lingfield, 369
Linkenholt, 302
Linslade, 166 n.
Linton, 499
Linwart, lathe of, 486, 594
Lipscomb, G., 45, 184
Lisson, 105, 109, 122, 127, 585
Litelfeld, 369
Little Amwell, see Amwell
Little Ann, see Ann
Little Barford, 8, 39 n.
Little Berkhamsted, 573, 574
Little Bookham, see Bookham
Littlebourne, 490, 526, 555
Little Brickhill, see Brickhill
Little Burton (in Kennington, Kent), 548
Little Chart, 489, 502, 577
Littlecote, 146, 166 n.
Little Coxwell, see Coxwell
Little Faringdon, see Faringdon
Little Gaddesden, see Gaddesden

Little Gravenhurst, *see* Gravenhurst
Little Greenford, *see* Greenford
Little Hadham, *see* Hadham
Little Hampden, *see* Hampden
Little Hormead, *see* Hormead
Little Horsted, 416, 430
Little Kimble, *see* Kimble
Little Marlow, *see* Marlow
Little Minster (Oxon.), *see* Minster (Oxon.)
Little Missenden, *see* Missenden
Little Mongeham, 494, 498
Little Munden, *see* Munden
Little Offley, *see* Offley
Little Rollright, *see* Rollright
Little Somborne, *see* Somborne
Little Stanmore, *see* Stanmore
Little Staughton (Beds.), 4 n., 13, 32, 33
Little Stoke, *see* Stoke (Oxon.)
Little Tew, *see* Tew
Littleton (Hants.), 321 n.
Littleton (Surrey), 369
Little Whitefield, 294
Little Wittenham, *see* Wittenham
Little Woolwicks, *see* Woolwicks
Littleworth (Berks.), 249
Little Wymondley, *see* Wymondley
Livestock, 90–1, 281, 555–6
Lockerley, 329, 333, 335, 350
Loddon, R., 246, 261, 269, 283, 284, 340, 348, 360
Lodintone (Sx., Pevensey hd), *see* Wootton (Sx., Pevensey hd)
Lodsworth, 364, 375 n., 404
Lollingdon, 259
Lomer, 311, 356, 608, 609, 610, 616
Lonchelei, 242, 244, 245, 252 n., 259
London, 87, 94, 98, 100, 101, 105, 116, 118, 119 n., 123, 131–2, 134, 135, 136, 353, 385, 397, 398, 400 n., 402, 408, 520, 572, 574, 579, 580, 583–5, 586, 605, 606, 615, 616
London Basin, 357, 358, 360, 401–2, 403
Longbridge hundred, 523, 594
Longcot, 245
Long Crendon, 167, 180
Long Ditton, *see* Ditton (Surrey)
Longfield, 505
Longley, T., 495 n.
Long Sutton (Hants.), 288

Long Wittenham, *see* Wittenham
Loose, 498
Lordington, 418, 428
Loseley, 369
Loughton (Bucks.), 160 n.
Lower, M. A., 479, 480
Lower Arncott, 192
Lower Beeding, *see* Beeding
Lower Dean, *see* Dean
Lower Halstow, 498
Lower Hardres, *see* Hardres
Lower Heyford, *see* Heyford
Lower Wainhill, *see* Wainhill
Luckley, 242 n.
Luddenham, 536 n., 538, 539, 547, 548, 606
Luddesdown, 487, 551
Lude, 155
Ludshott, 303
Ludwell, 208, 214
Lullingstone, 518, 519, 527, 535 n., 537, 541
Luton, 6, 8, 12, 13, 25, 26, 30, 31, 33, 39, 41, 42, 43, 44, 45, 616
Lydd, 498
Lydden, 498
Lye, Lyeway and Lyewood (Hants.), 296
Lyford, 230
Lyminge, 536 n., 544, 553, 559
Lymington, 328, 334, 359
Lyminster, 418 n., 426, 453, 456
Lympne, 503, 518, 544, 545
Lyndhurst, 310 n., 330
Lyneham, 220
Lysons, Daniel, 45, 136, 184, 242 n., 245 n., 285
Lysons, Samuel, 45, 184, 242 n., 245 n., 285

Macebroc, 494, 499
Macknade, 516
Madge, S. J., 99 n., 101, 102, 125 n., 126 n., 134 n., 137
Maidenhead, 244
Maidstone, 491, 517, 518 n., 536 n., 537, 539, 608
Maitland, F. W., 6 n., 12 n., 15 n., 19, 20, 24 n., 59, 62, 63, 67 n., 82 n., 87, 97, 107, 113, 117 n., 131, 134 n., 149, 154 n., 157 n., 199 n., 201 n., 204 n., 208 n., 221 n., 233 n., 251, 253, 256 n.,

Maitland, F. W. (*cont.*)
  257 n., 258 n., 290, 304, 304 n., 310 n.,
  365, 366 n., 374 n., 376 n., 377 n.,
  381 n., 429, 431, 434, 439 n., 507, 509,
  512, 516 n., 524 n., 577 n., 588, 589,
  591
Makinbrooke, *see Macebroc*
Malcolm, J., 180 n.
Malden, 373, 391, 396
Malden, H. E., 364 n., 374 n., 377, 380, 382,
  405, 406
Malling, East and West (Kent), 489, 505,
  544
Malt, 174
Manning, O., 405
Mansbridge hundred, 294 n.
Manshead hundred, 5 n., 6, 9 n., 29
Mapledurham, 317, 321
Mapleham, 296 n., 327
Maplescombe, 525
Maran, R., 86
Marchwood, 320
Marden (Kent), 498, 532
Marden, East, North and Up (Sx.), 415, 434,
  444, 464, 465
Marden hundred (Kent), 532, 581
Mares, 90, 401
Maresc, 488 n.
Maresfield, 458
Margate, 493, 498, 501, 506, 539 n.
Market Ilsley, *see* Ilsley
Markets, 43–4, 71, 87, 90, 134, 179, 232, 275,
  281, 351, 355, 397, 400, 554–5, 583,
  616
Marley, 519
Marlow, Great and Little, 166, 169, 172, 182
Marsh, 558, 559, 614; *see also Maresc* and
  Romney Marsh
Marshborough, 531
Marsh Gibbon, 148 n.
Marston Moretaine, 18
Martin, 287
Martyr Worthy, *see* Worthy
Marylebone, *see* Tyburn
Mavor, W., 282
Mawer, Sir Allen, 8 n., 47, 52 n., 96, 99 n.,
  125 n., 137, 138, 167 n., 177 n., 178 n.,
  179 n., 185, 232 n., 327, 367 n., 368 n.,
  369 n., 406, 407 n., 413 n., 415 n.,

416 n., 418 n., 446 n., 448 n., 472 n.,
  482, 580 n.
Meadow, 35–6, 44, 45, 77, 79–81, 87, 88,
  89, 90, 92, 93, 94, 95, 125–7, 133, 135,
  136, 169–72, 182, 183, 184, 214, 215–18,
  234, 235, 236, 237, 265–7, 282, 284,
  327, 328, 329, 338–40, 352, 359, 360,
  361, 390–1, 403, 404, 448–50, 476, 477,
  478, 479, 532–4, 550, 559, 568, 602–4,
  614
Medehei, 418 n., 455, 457
Mederclive, 492, 536
Medina, R., 361
Medmenham, 143
Medway, R., 495, 500, 534, 538, 542, 557,
  558, 559, 604, 606
Meesden, 66, 78
Melchet Park, 287, 325, 359
'Men', 21, 25, 65, 66, 67, 115, 116, 118, 160,
  179, 204, 205, 208, 310, 314, 315, 351,
  382, 398, 512, 513, 517, 588
Mene hundred, 291 n.
Menestoches hundred, 291 n., 294 n.
Mentmore, 166 n.
Meon (Hants., Titchfield hd), 321
Meon, East and West (Hants.), 291, 316,
  317, 318, 320, 346, 350, 353, 354
Meon, R., 298, 319, 340, 341, 348, 359
Meonstoke (Hants.), 293, 314, 355
Meopham, 487
Meppershall, 4, 5, 15, 16, 24, 31, 48, 59 n.
Merchants, *see* Traders
Merclesham, 484, 492, 493 n.
Mereworth, 524
Mersham, 504, 540
Merston, 464, 465
Merthersham, 484
Merton (Kent), 490
Merton (Oxon.), 199, 201
Merton (Surrey), 384, 399, 400, 585
Mertumnes circe, *see* Hope All Saints
Meuse, R., 583
Micheldever, 289, 577
Micheldever hundred, 294 n.
Michelmersh, 297
Mickleham, 372, 386
Middeldene, 8 n.
Middeltune, lathe of, 486
Middle Claydon, *see* Claydon

Middlesex, 53, 56 n., 97–137, 148, 156, 157, 357, 563, 565, 567, 568, 574 n., 579, 583, 592, 593, 596, 598, 602, 606, 612–18
Middleton (Hants.), 295, 341
Middleton (Sx.), 423, 470
Middle Wallop, 294
Mideham (Surrey), 369, 372
Midgham, 315
Midley, 492–3
Milford, 306, 318, 322, 330, 334, 345
Millbrook, 311
Mills, 39–41, 44, 45, 65, 83–5, 87, 89, 90, 92, 93, 94, 95, 129–31, 136, 172, 174–6, 182, 183, 184, 222, 224–7, 229, 234, 235, 236, 237, 268, 269–71, 282, 284, 341, 345–8, 352, 353, 359, 360, 361, 393, 394–6, 402, 403, 404, 453, 458–61, 469, 470, 476, 477, 478, 479, 540–3, 546, 549, 550, 559, 568, 614
Mill-sites, 224 n.
Milsted, 498
Milton Abbey, 341
Milton (Berks.), 265, 266
Milton (Hants.), 330, 332, 334, 335 n.
Milton (Kent, Toltingtrough hd), 487, 555, 616
Milton (Surrey), 391
Milton Ernest (Beds.), 20
Milton Keynes (Bucks.), 150, 151
Milton Regis (Kent, Milton hd), 491, 507, 516, 518, 519, 520, 527, 530, 532, 536, 537, 539, 544, 545, 554, 556, 616
Milton under Wychwood (Oxon.), 192, 209 n.
Minsden, 60, 72 n.
Minstead, 330, 334, 353, 354
Minster, Little and Lovell (Oxon.), 209
Minster (in Sheppey), 498
Minster (in Thanet), 501, 518 n., 532, 534, 539, 541 n., 544, 545
Mints, 178, 229, 275, 351, 355, 463, 466, 468, 469, 472, 474, 583, 616; see also Coins
Misbourne, R., 143, 172, 173, 175, 182, 604
Missenden, Great and Little, 141, 166
Miswell, 57, 58, 81 n., 302 n.
Mitcham, 380 n.
Moens, W. J. C., 363
Mole, R., 371, 391, 395, 396, 401, 403, 604

Molesey, East and West, 366
Mollington, 187, 190
Moneyers, 229, 275, 583
Mongewell, 208 n., 211
Monk Sherborne, 293
Monks Horton, 494, 524
Monks Risborough, see Risborough
Monkton, 501, 534, 537, 539, 544
Monxton, see Ann
Moody, Henry, 362
Moor (*Mora*), 233, 341, 359
Morden, 375
Moreton, North and South, 243, 272, 275, 276
Morgan, F. W., 286, 598
Mortimer West End, 242, 287
Mortlake, 132, 133, 383, 386, 394, 399, 400, 585
Mottisfont, 321, 341, 350, 353, 354
Moulsoe hundred, 139, 142 n., 151, 157, 166, 175
Moustone, 417, 435
Mowat, J. L. G., 194 n., 237
Much Hadham, see Hadham
Mulceltone, 296 n.
Munden, Great and Little, 51, 55, 71, 76
Mundham (Sx., Stockbridge hd), 416, 430, 435 n., 439 n., 460, 462 n.
Muntham (in Findon), 431
Mursley hundred, 139, 175

Nachededorne, 245 n., 249
Nachededorne hundred, 245 n.
Nackington, 525, 534 n.
Napper, H. F., 480
Nares Gladley, see Gladley
Nashenden, 522
Neatham, 291, 300 n., 317, 345, 346, 355, 616
Neilson, Nellie, 483 n., 486 n., 516 n., 517 n., 527 n., 531 n., 560
Nethercote (in Lewknor), 192 n.
Nethercott (in Tackley), 192 n.
Netherfield, 441
Nether Wallop, see Wallop
Netley (Hants., Redbridge hd), 327
Nettlebed, 196
Nettleden, 49 n., 140
Nettlestead, 551

Nettlestone, 299
Newbury, 258, 273
Newchurch, 498
Newchurch hundred, 503, 512, 529, 530, 594
Newenden, 509, 518, 529, 532, 554, 581, 616
New Forest, 287, 291, 293 n., 295, 296 n., 298, 303, 305, 306, 307, 310, 315, 319, 322, 324–38, 340, 345, 348, 352, 356, 357, 358, 579, 588, 599, 602, 616
Newhaven, 414 n.
Newick, 420
Newington (Kent, Bewsborough hd), 505
Newington (Kent, Milton hd), 509, 520, 525, 528 n., 530, 537, 547, 549, 551, 556
Newington (Mdx.), 108, 585
Newington (Oxon.), 212, 219, 231, 275, 277
Newnham Murren, 199, 201, 275, 276
Newton Purcell, 196
Newport Pagnell, 140, 148, 154 n., 155 n., 156, 160, 166, 169, 170, 177, 179, 616
Newsells, 63
New Shelve, see Shelve
Newtimber, 300, 307
Newton Bromswold (Beds.), 2, 4
Newton Stacey (Hants.), 317
Newton Valence (Hants.), 304
Nicholls, G. D., 7
Ninfield, 438
Ningwood, 291 n.
Noke, 221 n., 224
Nomansland (Nanesmaneslande), 98 n., 104, 108, 119
Nonae Rolls, 415 n.
Nonneminstre, 418, 451 n., 453, 454, 455, 456, 457, 458 n., 459
Norðcip, see Warden (Kent)
Norfolk, 48 n., 197, 414 n., 466 n., 473
Normandy, 486 n., 600
Northamptonshire, 2, 4, 36, 85, 186, 187, 190, 204, 209
Northbourne, 503, 516, 521
Northbreche, see Northburg
Northbrook, 201
Northburg, 492, 493 n., 494 n.
North Charford, see Charford
North Crawley, see Crawley (Bucks.)
North Cray, see Cray
North Downs, 370, 371, 391, 396, 398, 403
Northealington, see Pinkneys Green

North Eastling, 489, 544
Northfleet, 487, 537, 541
Northgate, 543, 547, 549
Northill, 40
North Marden (Sx.), see Marden
North Mimms, 100 n.
North Moreton, see Moreton
Northolt, 104, 109
North Stoke (Oxon.), see Stoke (Oxon.)
North Stoke (Sx.), 416
North Stoneham, see Stoneham
North Tidworth (Wilts.), 293 n.
Northwood (Kent), 494
Norton (Kent), 506, 541, 544
Norton (in Selborne, Hants.), 315
Norton (in Wonston, Hants.), 295, 353, 354
Nortone (Kent), see Whitstable
Nuffield, 196
Nuneham Courtenay, 201, 208, 209, 222, 223
Nuns, 512, 513, 518
Nursling, 290 n., 339
Nurstead, 509, 522
Nutfield, 383
Nuthampstead, 53
Nutlei, 296 n., 327

Oakhanger, 321, 341, 361
Oakleigh, 507
Oakley (Beds.), 24 n., 39 n.
Oakley (Bucks.), 145, 166, 167, 180, 601, 616
Oakley (Hants.), 307
Oare, 516, 536, 539, 544
Oats, 31
Ock, R., 266, 271, 282, 604
Ockham, 384, 394
Ockley, 370, 404
Oddington, 221 n.
Ode, 418 n.
Odecroft hundred, 6
Odell, 16, 39 n.
Odiham, 290, 311 n., 316, 346, 348, 349
Odsey hundred, 85
Offham (Kent), 487, 510, 551, 552
Offham (Sx., Benestede hd), 446, 453, 460
Offington, 417, 431, 435
Offley, Great and Little, 50, 71 n., 72, 76

Old Shelve, *see* Shelve
Old Windsor, *see* Windsor
Olney, 157, 172, 174 n.
Open-field system, 197, 616
Ora, Danish, 135, 174, 209, 345, 383
Ordish, George, 610 n.
Orgarswick, 494 n., 498
Orlestone, 517, 544
Orleswick, 430, 467, 468
Orpington, 530, 544
Ortone, 245 n., 265
Orwell Bury, 80, 602
Oselei, 296 n., 327
Oslachintone, 492, 493 n.
Ospringe, 511, 539, 547, 549
Ossemsley, 327
Ossulstone hundred, 98, 106, 109, 116 n.,
    118 n., 119 n., 121, 123, 127, 594
Ot Moor, 210, 221 n., 233, 235, 236
Otford, 487, 519, 534, 543
Otham, 508
Otterbourne, 290 n.
Otterden, 547, 549
Otterpool, 525
Otterwood, 327, 332
Ouse, R. (Beds. and Bucks.), 10, 33, 36, 39,
    41, 44, 173, 175, 604, 606
Ouse, R. (Sx.), 421, 444, 455, 456, 460, 461,
    468, 476, 477, 604
Outwick, 295, 321 n.
Ouzel, R., 39, 41, 175, 180
Overton, 290, 348, 349
Over Wallop, *see* Wallop
Oving, 151, 164
Ovingdean, 467, 468
Ovington, 290 n., 303, 345
Oxelei, 296 n., 327
Oxford, 177, 190 n., 192, 199, 201 n., 204 n.,
    205, 208, 209, 210, 212, 214, 221, 222,
    223, 224, 225, 227–31, 232, 233, 236,
    264, 266, 274 n., 275, 277, 278, 583,
    615, 616
Oxfordshire, 138, 139, 143 n., 177, 186–238,
    240, 241, 242, 274, 276, 277, 278, 565,
    566, 567, 568, 569, 570, 573, 574 n.,
    577, 579, 588, 590, 591, 592, 595–6,
    603, 604, 606, 612–18
Oxted, 399, 400
Oxwick, 71

Pachesham, 395
Paddington (Surrey), 369
Paddlesworth (in Lyminge), 498, 535
Padworth, 251, 269
Page, W., 480, 561
Pagham, 423, 427, 442, 445, 449, 451, 464,
    465, 597
Pagham harbour, 456, 461, 476
Pan, 321
Pang, R., 246, 271, 283, 284
Pangdean, 418, 442, 449, 467, 468
Parham, 439
Parish, W. D., 479
Parker, F. H. M., 363
Parker, James, 237
Park Farm (in Beaulieu), 327
Parkhurst Forest, 356, 361
Parks, 33, 43, 77, 87, 91, 94, 123, 124, 134,
    136, 167, 180, 355–6, 361, 446, 473,
    525, 526, 555
Pasticium, 470
Pasture, 36–8, 77, 81, 88, 89, 90, 127–8, 133,
    172, 218–21, 229, 236, 267, 281, 283,
    310, 329, 330, 340–1, 359, 386, 391–3,
    445, 451–3, 455 n., 460, 469, 534–6,
    568, 614
Patcham, 439, 441, 449, 467, 468
Patching, 442
Patmore, 71, 73
Patrixbourne, *see* Bourne (Kent)
Paythorne, 467, 468
Pearman, M. T., 189 n., 195 n.
Peas, 474
Pechingeorde, 369, 383, 387, 401
Peckham (Surrey), 376
Peckham, East and West (Kent), 487, 488,
    499, 528, 531, 541 n., 581, 585
Peckham, W. D., 481
Peelings (Sx.), 439
Pelham, Brent, Furneux and Stocking, 51,
    78
Pell, O. C., 95
Pembury, 499
Pemscott, 217, 220
Pendley, 52, 57, 58, 59, 619, 620
Penenden, 492
Penge, 485 n.
Pengest, 418 n.
Penshurst, 499, 531 n.

Penton, Grafton and Mewsey, 294 n., 300, 318, 321 n., 348, 349
Peper Harow, 384
Perching, 440, 451, 460, 467, 468
Pereio, 194
Perivale, *see* Greenford
Perreton, 341, 342
Perry, 547, 549
Pertenhall, 2, 3 n., 4, 8
Petersfield, 296
Petersham, 373, 374, 393, 394, 585, 606
Petham, 544
Petit-Dutaillis, C., 230 n., 397 n.
Petridgewood, 369
Pett (Kent), 494 n., 498, 577
Pett (Sx.), 441
Petworth, 458, 460, 464, 466
Pevensey, 415, 438, 448, 451, 463, 469, 473, 474, 479, 569, 572, 616
Pevensey hundred, 439
Pevensey Levels, 444, 449, 456, 479, 608
Pevensey, rape of, 407, 408, 410, 412, 413, 417, 426
Philip, A. J., 561
Pilley, 327
Pimlico, 101
Pimp's Court, 536, 537
Pinden, 507
Pineham, 521
Pinkneys Green, 244
Pinn, R., 129
Pinner, 101
Pirbright, 369
Pirton, 77, 81 n.
Pishill, 196
Pising, 521
Pitstone, 140, 146, 147
Pittleworth, 350
Plaitford, 287, 315, 321
Plantagenet-Harrison, G. H. de S. N., 136
Platenovt, *see* Wadholt
Playden, 428, 462
Plough-lands, 13 n., 16–19, 28, 30, 60–2, 63, 74, 76, 88, 89, 90, 104 n., 107–9, 110–13, 120, 122, 133, 148, 149–51, 154, 162, 165, 169, 199–201, 202 n., 251–3, 304–7, 327, 328, 329, 331, 374–6, 429–31, 471, 472, 507–9, 512 n., 563–6, 613, 618

Plough-shares, 31, 77, 167, 183, 356
Plough-teams, 16, 17, 18, 19, 20, 28, 30, 31, 35, 44, 45, 62, 63, 64, 65, 69, 73, 75, 87, 88, 89, 90, 92, 93, 94, 95, 107, 108, 109, 110, 111, 112, 113–15, 120, 121, 122, 133, 135, 136, 151, 152–5, 164, 165, 180, 182, 183, 184, 201, 202–4, 210, 211, 234, 235, 236, 237, 251, 253, 254, 255, 261, 279, 282, 284, 285, 305, 307–10, 319, 335, 352, 358, 359, 360, 361, 375, 376–7, 378, 379, 385, 401, 402, 403, 404, 413, 429, 430, 431–4, 443, 444, 471, 472, 476, 477, 478, 507, 508, 509–13, 522, 523, 558, 559, 565–6, 568, 585, 589, 590, 613, 618
Plough-team deficiency, *see* Understocking
Pluckley, 521, 522
Plumpton, 430, 448, 467, 468
Podington, 2, 4
Poitiers, William of, 574
Polehanger, 4, 5, 9, 15 n., 30, 48, 57, 59 n.
Ponshall, 492, 518 n., 521
Poole, H., 462 n.
Popham, 340
Population, 11, 20–5, 28, 30, 44, 45, 54, 63–71, 75, 92, 93, 94, 95, 103, 114–19, 121, 122, 135, 136, 143, 155–60, 165, 180, 182, 183, 184, 196, 204–8, 210, 211, 234, 235, 236, 237, 247, 254–9, 261, 282, 284, 285, 298, 310–15, 319, 335, 358, 359, 360, 361, 371, 377, 378, 379, 380–2, 385, 401, 402, 403, 404, 413, 421, 434–9, 443, 444, 471, 476, 477, 478, 512–18, 523, 558, 559, 566, 568, 585–95, 613, 617, 618
Porpoises, 455, 520, 539 n.
Port Meadow, 229
Portsmouth, 298, 569 n.
Portsmouth harbour, 344, 359, 608
Postling, 528, 530, 531, 544
Potteries, 232, 616
Potton, 11
Poulton, 509, 544 n.
Prestetone (Hants.), 342 n.
Preston (in St Helens, Hants.), 342 n.
Preston (Kent, Faversham hd), 536 n., 541
Preston (Kent, Preston hd), 525
Preston (Mdlx.), 101

Preston (Sx., Singleton hd), 429 n., 445
Preston (Sx., Totnore hd), 412
Preston (Sx., Whalesborne hd), 422, 442, 449, 458, 467, 468
Preston, East and West (Sx., Poling hd), 456
Preston Candover (Hants.), *see* Candover
Priestley (Beds.), 20
Priests, 21, 23, 24, 42, 63, 66, 69, 70, 85, 88, 89, 90, 118, 119, 135, 155 n., 177, 205, 208, 254, 258, 259, 272, 310, 311, 314, 378, 397, 434, 435, 438, 439, 462, 512, 513, 514, 517, 544
Primo Gadre, 190 n.
Princes Risborough, *see* Risborough
Prosperity, distribution of, 11–30, 54–76, 103–22, 143–65, 196–211, 247–62, 298–320, 371–87, 421–44, 501–23, 585–95
Pulborough, 421, 461 n.
Pusey, 261
Putney, 367, 377, 585
Putnoe, 9, 39 n.
Puttenham (Herts.), 57, 61, 80
Puttenham (Surrey), 369
Pyrford, 373, 374, 376, 386, 389, 616
Pyrton, 198, 211, 218, 231, 275, 277
Pyrton hundred, 190

Quarley, 300, 321 n.
Quarrendon, 147
Quarries, 232, 401, 460, 473, 474, 616
Quin, R., 94

Racton, 464, 466
Radford, 212
Radmen, 204, 205, 208, 253, 258, 310, 314, 315, 352, 617, 618
Radnage, 148 n.
Radwell, 71, 85 n.
Raette, 498
Ragg, F. W., 1, 6, 45, 46, 71 n., 95, 145 n., 184, 278 n., 279 n., 286, 549 n., 560
Rainham, 498
Rameslie, *see* Rye
Rams, 31
Rapes, Domesday, 407, 408, 618
Ratling, 498
Ratton, 412, 456, 608

Reading, 242, 246, 249, 252, 258, 267, 269, 271, 273, 274, 276, 278–9, 616
Reading hundred, 242, 259, 261
Reaney, P. H., 562
Reculver, 522, 537, 539
Redbornstoke hundred, 6
Redbridge, 318, 344
Reed (Herts.), 67, 591
Reeves, 43, 70, 90, 172, 355, 435 n., 513
Regional divisions, 44–5, 91–5, 135–6, 180–4, 233–7, 282–5, 357–61, 474–9, 556–9
Reichel, O. J., 212 n.
Reigate, 384, 391, 397
Reigate hundred, 365
Remenham, 269
Renching, 434
Rhee, R., 95
Rib, R., 80, 84, 86, 94
Richardson, W. H., 286
Rickmansworth, 61, 62, 77, 83
Ridley, 487, 488, 530, 532
Ringleton, 516
Ringwood, 291, 292, 306, 315, 322, 330, 334, 335, 336, 345
Ripe (Kent), 492
Ripe (Sx.), 412
Ripley, 311 n., 330, 334, 336
Ripple (Kent, Cornilo hd), 494, 498
Ripton, 542
Risborough hundred, 139, 140, 164
Risborough, Monks and Princes, 141, 142, 145 n., 160, 161, 165, 177, 180, 230, 231, 607, 608, 615
Riseley, 20 n., 25
Ristone hundred, 439
Robbins, M., 103 n., 137
Roberts, E., 479
Roberts, R. G., 482
Robertson, A. J., 341 n.
Robertson, W. A. Scott, 561
Rochester, 488, 505, 513, 517, 521, 545, 546, 550–2, 556, 591, 616
Rockbourne, 305, 330
Rockford, 330, 334
Rodehangre, Rodenehangre, 52, 594
Rodmell, 410, 425 n., 427 n., 429 n., 449, 455, 456, 467, 468
Rodmersham, 498

Rodsell, 369
Roeberg hundred, 243 n.
Rofford, 194
Rollright, Great and Little, 192, 232, 234, 607, 608, 615
Rollstone, 328
Rolvenden, 498, 532
Rolvenden hundred, 529, 531, 581
Romney, 488, 513, 545, 546, 553, 559, 583, 616
Romney Marsh, 485, 488 n., 493 n., 495, 500, 501, 502, 503, 511, 515, 517, 534, 538, 540, 556, 558, 559, 588, 594, 608, 614
Romsey, 311 n., 338, 339, 353, 354
Rooting, 492, 508, 565
Rother, R. (Eastern), 420, 454, 455, 484
Rother, R. (Western), 340, 348, 360, 421, 443, 449, 455, 461, 474, 475, 476, 477
Rotherbridge hundred, 458 n.
Rotherfield, 473
Rotherfield hundred, 458 n.
Rottingdean, 415
Round, J. H., 1, 2 n., 4 n., 6 n., 9 n., 10 n., 12 n., 14 n., 20 n., 43 n., 45, 48 n., 50 n., 55 n., 57 n., 58, 59, 72, 77 n., 80 n., 86 n., 87, 88, 95, 96, 104 n., 105, 134, 138 n., 145 n., 146, 148 n., 167 n., 177 n., 178, 184, 187 n., 212 n., 220, 239, 240 n., 243 n., 245, 248, 249, 259 n., 262 n., 271 n., 272 n., 273, 277, 279 n., 280, 281 n., 311 n., 317, 318, 324, 354 n., 356, 362, 363, 364, 389, 390 n., 407 n., 410 n., 427 n., 445 n., 449, 470 n., 471, 472, 473, 479, 480, 481, 503 n., 504, 561, 609, 610
Rowley hundred, 139
Roxborough, 101
Roxeth, 101
Roxford, 85
Roxton, 39 n.
Royston, 53
Ruckinge, 524
Rudgwick, 420
Rug Moor (Mdlx.), 101, 108, 116, 123, 585
Ruislip, 104, 109, 114, 118 n., 123, 136
Rumboldswhyke (Sx.), 418, 435, 442
Runcton, 464, 466
Ruscombe, 243, 245, 576

Rushden, 2, 4
Rushmonden hundred, 427
Russell, Ada, 4 n.
Russell, J. C., 588 n.
Rustici, 70, 71, 314, 315 n., 513, 515, 518, 541, 588
Ruxley, 489 n.
Rycote, 224
Rye (Herts.), 52, 63, 66, 80, 83
Rye (Sx.), 415, 438, 455, 456, 461, 463, 471, 472, 479, 608, 616

Sacombe, 71, 85
Saddlescombe, 446, 456, 467, 468
St Albans, 50, 54, 56 n., 59 n., 62 n., 70, 77, 82, 83, 85, 86, 87, 90, 91, 93, 583, 616
St Albans, Vale of, 91, 92–3, 579
St Augustine's Abbey, Canterbury, 483, 490 n., 514, 552
St Firmin's monastery, 177 n.
St Frideswide's, Oxford, 228
St Frideswide's Cartulary, 229 n.
St Leonard's Forest, 446 n., 478
St Margaret's at Cliffe, 518
St Martha's (Surrey), 397 n.
St Martin of Dover, 484 n., 502 n., 503, 507, 514, 517, 518, 531, 537, 539, 540, 541, 542, 545, 556
St Martin's (in Canterbury), 525, 547, 549
St Mary Cray (formerly South Cray), *see* Cray
St Mary in the Marsh (Kent), 498
St Mary's, Oxford, 228
St Pancras, 108, 118, 123, 127, 585
St Paul's Cray, *see* Cray
St Paul's Walden, *see* Walden
St Peter's, Oxford, 228
Sakeham, 431, 434, 446
Saleshurst, 413 n., 441, 582
Salford (Beds.), 15, 31
Salford (Oxon.), 232
Salford Brook, 41
Salisbury (Wilts.), 287
Salph End, 9
Salt, Salt-making, 180, 232, 455, 456, 539–40, 607, 608; *see also* Salt-pans
Salter, H. E., 189, 194 n., 224 n., 227, 228 n., 230, 230 n., 237

Salt-pans, 343–4, 359, 361, 417, 455–7, 472, 476, 477, 479, 539–40, 559, 568, 607–8, 615
Saltways, 232
Saltwood (Kent), 543, 553
Saltworker, 157, 180
Salzman, L. F., 67 n., 221, 407 n., 413, 423, 425, 427, 428, 479, 480, 481
Sanderstead, 384
Sandford (I.O.W.), 321 n., 340 n.
Sandford St Martin (Oxon.), 211 n., 212
Sandford on Thames (Oxon.), 211, 223
Sandhurst (Berks.), 243, 245, 576
Sandhurst (Kent), 498, 532
Sandlings (in St Mary Cray), 489 n., 535 n.
Sandown, 306
Sandridge, 58
Sandwich, 488, 500, 513, 538, 539, 545, 546, 552, 559, 616
Sandwich hundred, 485
Sandwich, lathe of, 485
Sandy, 17, 32, 33
Sanhest, 296 n., 328
Sapeham, 52, 594
Sarre, 498
Saunderton, 175
Sawbridgeworth, 55, 77, 80, 81, 97 n.
Sawyer, F. E., 407 n., 479, 480
Sayers, E., 480, 481
Scape, see Sheppey
Schildricheham, see Cildresham
Sclive, 296 n., 326 n., 328
Scortebroc, 493, 535, 536
Scottlesford, 356
Seacourt, 244
Seacourt Stream, 244
Seaford, 420
Seal (Kent), 487, 536 n.
Seale (Surrey), 366 n.
Seasalter, 485, 488, 512 n., 513, 545, 546, 616
Seckloe hundred, 139
Seckworth, 244 n.
Secundo Gadre, 190 n.
Sedlescombe, 427, 441 n., 461 n.
Seebohm, F., 137, 584 n.
Segenhoe, 9, 31
Segnescome, 418 n.
Selborne, 298, 300 n., 311 n.
Selbrittenden hundred, 532, 581

Selham, 460, 464, 466
Sellinge, 544
Selmeston, 412, 439 n., 461 n., 462 n.
Selsey, 427, 464, 466
Semibos, 16 n., 20
Sen, R., 500
Send, 374, 394
Serfs, 20, 21, 63, 66, 67, 70, 88, 89, 90, 115, 117, 118, 155, 160, 204, 205, 207, 208 n., 254, 255 n., 257, 258, 280, 310, 311, 314, 352, 377, 381, 382, 434, 438, 439, 512, 513, 515, 516–17, 566, 587, 589–90, 591, 592, 593, 613, 617, 618
Sessingham, 412, 460
Sesswell's Barton, *see* Barton (Oxon.)
Settlements, 7–10, 50–4, 98–103, 140–3, 192–6, 242–7, 293–8, 365–7, 415–21, 488–501, 568, 576–85, 613, 618
Sevenoaks, 499
Sevington, 541, 544
Sewell, 6, 9, 12, 16
Sexintone, 194
Shalbourne (Wilts.), 239, 262 n.
Shalden, 298, 306, 360
Shalfleet, 349
Shalford, 372, 383, 398
Sharnbrook, 38, 39
Sharpe, Sir Montagu, 116, 134 n., 137
Sheat, 345
Sheep, 38, 90–1, 439, 535, 556
Sheffield (in Fletching), 418, 445, 460
Shefford, East (formerly Great) and West, 243, 261, 262, 270
Shelborough, 505
Shelling, 512, 516
Shellingford, 266, 269, 280, 616
Shelswell, 186, 190, 194
Shelton, 23
Shelve, New and Old, 489, 507, 518 n., 547, 548, 549
Shenington, 186, 190, 200, 208
Shenley (Herts.), 53, 57, 77 n., 93, 619, 620
Shenley, Brook End and Church End (Bucks.), 156
Shenlow Hill, 234
Shepherds, 434, 438, 439
Shepperton, 108, 110, 119, 128
Sheppey, 488 n., 493 n., 495 n., 501, 511, 515, 539, 558, 579

Sherborne St John, 293
Shere, 373
Shermanbury, 461 n.
Sherrington, 412, 440
Shide, 346
Shifford, 221, 223
Shillington, 39, 40, 41
Shilton, 187, 190, 240
Shinfield, 268, 269
Shingleton (near Nonington), 498
Shipbourne, 499
Shipley, 417, 440
Shippon, 249 n., 251, 268
Shipton (Bucks., Ashendon hd), 150
Shipton Bellinger (Hants.), 303
Shipton on Cherwell (Oxon.), 186, 190, 219, 220
Shipton under Wychwood (Oxon.), 213, 214, 218, 226, 230, 231, 233, 616
Shirburn, 275, 277
Shirdon, 8
Shirley, 341, 351
Shore, T. W., 362
Shoreditch, 102
Shoreham (Kent), 499
Shoreham (Sx.), 424, 442, 474
Shorne, 499
Shotover, 214, 236
Shotover Forest, 602, 616
Shotover Hill, 236
Shottermill, 366 n.
Shropshire, 259
Shovelstrode, 420, 445 n.
Shoyswell hundred, 412, 413, 414 n., 427, 430 n., 433, 437, 441 n., 446, 447, 450, 582
Shrivenham, 245, 259 n., 272
Sibertswold, 536
Sibford Gower, 186, 190
Siborne, 493 n.
Sidlesham, 445
Sidnor (in Selmeston), 418 n., 439 n., 461 n., 462 n.
Sifflington (in Ditton), 522, 535 n.
Silchester, 307
Silk Stream, 126
Silsoe, 31
Singleton, 416 n., 424 n., 440, 449, 462, 464, 466

Sipoldescirce, 498
Skeat, W. W., 286
Slacham, 296 n., 328, 336
Slapton, 164
Slater, G., 502 n., 503 n., 516 n.
Slaves, 466
Slinfold, 420
Smarden, 498
Smetham, D. J., 96
Smiths, 157, 160, 275, 378
Snoddington (in Shipton Bellinger), 296, 303
Snodland, 504, 505
Soberton, 288, 355, 356
Sokemen, 20, 21, 24, 63, 67–9, 70, 90, 115, 155, 156–7, 160, 206, 254, 377, 382, 512, 513, 515, 517, 566, 588, 591–5, 613, 617, 618
Solton, 11
Somborne, King's, Little and Upper, 300 n., 318, 340, 341, 348, 349, 353, 354, 359
Somerden hundred, 492, 493 n., 511, 515, 527, 531, 581, 594
Somerton, 225
Somner, William, 560
Soninges (Kent), 493 n., 507, 519
Sonning (Berks.), 243, 245, 247, 249 n., 250, 261, 262, 263, 272, 284, 285, 576
Sopley, 330, 334, 336, 345
Sor Brook, 226
Sortelai, 142
Sotwell, 250, 275, 276
Soulbury, 160 n., 166 n.
Souldern, 196
Souldrop, 9
Southampton, 293, 298, 314, 344, 348, 349, 351–2, 353 n., 616
Southampton Water, 319, 335 n., 337, 341, 344, 359, 579, 588, 608
South Ashford, see Ashford (Kent)
South Charford, see Charford
Southcot, 259
South Cray, now St Mary Cray, see Cray
South Darenth, 499
South Downs, 421, 439, 444, 448, 468, 470, 472, 474, 475, 476–7, 582
Southealington, see Maidenhead
Southease, 449, 455, 467, 469, 474, 520 n.
Southfleet, 487, 504, 505, 519

South Harting, *see* Harting
South Heighton, 414 n.
Southill, 32
South Malling (Sx.), 426, 445, 448, 449, 460, 461, 467, 469, 474
South Mimms, 100, 122, 125 n., 127 n., 130
South Moreton, *see* Moreton
South Newington (Oxon.), 206, 224, 225
South Stoke (Oxon.), *see* Stoke (Oxon.)
South Stoke (Sx.), 416, 470
South Stoneham, *see* Stoneham
South Tidworth (Hants.), 293 n., 303, 321 n.
Southwark, 132 n., 365, 374, 382, 393, 394, 397, 398–400, 572, 583, 585, 605, 606, 615, 616
South Weston, 212, 217, 275, 277
Spaldwick (Hunts.), 4
Sparsholt (Berks.), 259 n., 266, 280, 616
Sparsholt (Hants.), 297
Speldhurst, 499, 531 n.
Spelsbury, 186, 190
Spelthorne hundred, 98, 106, 108, 109, 112, 114, 116, 117, 118 n., 119
Sp(er)chedene, 417, 418
Spinetum, 211 n., 212, 215
Staffordshire, 186, 190
Stagsden, 33, 43
Stainer, C. L., 229 n.
Staines, 100, 108, 113, 117, 118, 124, 125, 126, 128, 130, 131, 132, 133, 135, 609, 615, 616
Stamp, L. Dudley, 556 n.
Stanbridge half hundred, 6, 29
Standen (in Hungerford, Berks.), 240, 263, 267
Standen (Sx.), 417, 439
Standlake, 194 n., 196
Standon (Herts.), 69, 79, 80, 84, 91, 94, 609, 616
Stanestaple, 101, 108, 114, 123
Stanford (Beds.), 12, 16, 20, 31, 39, 40, 41
Stanford (Kent), 499
Stanford Dingley (Berks.), 248
Stanford in the Vale (Berks.), 249, 250, 267
Stanmer, 467, 469
Stanmore, Great and Little (*alias* Whitchurch), 99, 109, 123, 127

Stanstead Abbots, 50, 59 n., 60, 62 n., 70, 76, 77, 80, 85, 89–90, 94, 616
Stanstead Forest, 446 n.
Stansted (near Wrotham, Kent), 499
Stansted (in Aldington, Kent), 533
Stanswood, 291, 330, 334
Stantonbury (Herts.), 172, 174 n.
Stanton Harcourt (Oxon.), 192, 223
Stanwell, 109, 113, 114, 118 n., 124, 128, 129
Stanwick, 2, 4
Staple hundred, 427, 439
Statenborough, 519
Stebbing, W. P. D., 485 n.
Stedham, 464, 466, 473, 616
Steep, 414
Steeple Barton, *see* Barton (Oxon.)
Steeple Claydon, *see* Claydon
Steers, J. A., 415 n., 485 n., 559 n.
Steersmen, 281, 546
Stelling, 511
Stenton, D. M. (Lady), 138 n., 192 n., 232 n., 238, 277 n.
Stenton, Sir Frank M., x, 4 n., 8 n., 47, 52 n., 96, 99 n., 123 n., 125 n., 131 n., 137, 167 n., 177 n., 178 n., 179 n., 185, 186 n., 190–1, 193 n., 194 n., 199 n., 202 n., 204 n., 227 n., 232 n., 243 n., 244, 245 n., 246 n., 286, 314 n., 327, 367 n., 368 n., 369 n., 406, 407 n., 413 n., 415 n., 416 n., 418 n., 446 n., 448 n., 472 n., 482, 495 n., 580 n.
Stephenson, Carl, 230 n., 397 n.
Stepney, 99, 102, 108, 109, 112, 114, 117, 121, 123, 124, 125, 126, 127, 129, 130, 585
Steppingley, 15
Stevenage, 71
Stevens, F. Bentham, 482, 485 n., 562
Stevenson, J., 598 n.
Steventon (Berks.), 228, 230, 231, 266, 271
Steventon (Hants.), 302
Steyne, R., 449
Steyning, 415, 438, 449, 458, 460, 461 n., 463, 471–2, 474 n., 476, 477, 616
Steyning hundred, 407
Stiuicesworde, 52, 80
Stockbridge hundred (Sx.), 422, 429 n.
Stocking, 518
Stockingham, 412, 439

Stocking Pelham, *see* Pelham
Stockley, 194
Stodden hundred, 3, 6, 9 n., 15, 29
Stodmarsh, 490
Stoke (Kent), 505
Stoke, Little, North (formerly Basset), and
    South (Oxon.), 208, 221, 223, 275, 277
Stoke D'Abernon (Surrey), 372
Stoke in Amersham (Bucks.), 49 n.
Stoke Basset, *see* Stoke (Oxon.)
Stoke Charity (Hants.), 311 n.
Stoke next Guildford (Surrey), 384, 389, 601
Stoke hundred (Bucks.), 139
Stoke Lyne (Oxon.), 206
Stoke Mandeville (Bucks.), 145, 157
Stokenchurch, 143, 188, 190
Stoke Newington, *see* Newington (Mdlx.)
Stoke Talmage (Oxon.), 199, 218
Stondon (Beds.), 20, 25
Stone (Bucks.), 169
Stone (Kent, Axton hd), 487, 519, 520 n.,
    534
Stone near Faversham (Kent), 499
Stone hundred (Bucks.), 139, 142 n.
Stoneham, North and South, 294 n., 339,
    348, 349
Stonor, 189
Stopham, 439, 453, 464, 466
Storchestone, 418 n., 458 n., 459
Storrington, 434 n., 582
Stort, R., 80, 83, 93, 94
Stotfold (Beds.), 13, 39, 41
Stotfold hundred (Berks.), 139
Stoughton, 415, 425, 426, 439 n., 442, 445,
    446, 462 n., 464, 466
Stour, R. (Kent), 500, 534, 538, 542, 543,
    550, 559, 604, 606
Stourmouth, 494, 499
Stowe, 164, 174
Stowood Forest, 214, 236
Stratfield Mortimer (Berks.), 241, 242, 269
Stratfield, Saye and Turgis (Hants.), 242,
    345, 353, 354, 356, 616
Stratton, 17
Streat, 430, 461, 467, 469
Streatham, 391, 396 n., 397, 585
Streatley (Beds.), 13, 14, 25
Streatley (Berks.), 228, 230, 231, 250, 278
Street hundred, 529, 531 n.

Strettington, 464, 466
Strood, 499
Stuppington, 503
Sturry, 505, 519, 543 n.
Sturtune, 494 n., 499
Suburbani, 353, 354
Sudberie (Hants.), 295, 296 n., 307
Sudbury (Beds.), 8, 25
Sudbury (Mdlx.), 101
Sudcote, 142
Sudtone, lathe of, 486
Suffolk, 48 n., 197
Sugworth, 249 n.
Sulungs, 372, 502–7, 563, 612, 617; *see also*
    Yokes
Sunbury, 108, 110, 112, 119, 120
Sundon, 24
Sundridge, 520
Sunningwell, 249 n.
Sunwood (in Buriton), 297, 300, 321
Surrey, 97, 118, 131, 132, 133, 300, 364–406,
    414, 423, 453, 474, 485, 527 n., 536,
    558, 563, 568, 572, 573, 574 n., 580,
    582, 592, 595, 596, 597, 598, 606,
    612–18
Surrey Hill, 285
Sussex, 287, 291, 300, 364, 370, 372, 375 n.,
    382, 405, 407–82, 484, 522, 528 n., 531,
    536, 556, 563, 567, 568, 569, 574 n.,
    578, 581, 588, 590, 592, 596, 597, 605,
    606, 607, 608, 612–18
Sutton (Beds.), 13, 14, 36
Sutton (Surrey, Blackheath hd), 377
Sutton (Surrey, Wallington hd), 397
Sutton (Sx., Rotherbridge hd), 422
Sutton Courtenay (Berks.), 260, 275, 276
Sutton, East Sutton and Sutton Valence
    (Kent), 506, 541 n., 544
Sutton at Hone (Kent), 499
Sutton Scotney (Hants.), 348, 349
Swale, R., 539, 559
Swalecliffe, 516
Swallowfield, 242, 248, 258, 259
Swanbourne, 154, 161, 566
Swanscombe, 487, 518 n., 536 n., 537, 555,
    616
Swanton, 521
Swarling, 494 n., 499
Swarraton, 297

Sway, 324, 330, 332, 335
Swetton, 492, 516
Swine, 30 ff., 76 ff., 90, 91, 122 ff., 165 ff.,
    262, 320 ff., 386 ff., 391 ff., 401, 444 ff.,
    451, 460, 474, 524–6, 595 ff., 614
Swine renders
    from pasture, 391–2, 451, 597, 614
    from wood, 262, 320, 386, 444–5, 488,
    524, 526, 568, 614
Swineshead, 4, 32, 36 n.
Swingfield, 499
Swordsmith, 355
Swyncombe, 201, 210
Sydmonton, 304

Tadmarton, 230
Tadworth, 386
Tait, J., 227 n., 423, 480
Tallymen, 355
Tandridge, 374
Tandridge hundred, 365, 366, 396
Tangmere, 429 n., 435 n., 464, 466
Tanner, M. E., 116
Tanners, 355
Taplow, 160
Tarring Neville, 416, 417, 439
Tatchbury, 318, 326, 328, 344
Taylor, C. S., 220 n.
Taynton, 218, 220, 225, 230, 231, 232, 616
Telscombe, 420
Temple Dinsley (Herts.), 71 n., 72
Temple Ewell, see Ewell (Kent)
Tempsford, 39 n., 41
Tenterden, 532
Tenterden hundred, 532, 581
Terrett, I. B., 186–238, 259 n., 595 n., 596 n.,
    608 n.
Test, R., 298, 319, 339, 340, 341, 345, 348,
    359, 604, 606
Teston, 522
Testwood, 328
Tetsworth, 196
Tew, Great and Little, 192, 215
Tewin, 77 n.
Textus Roffensis, 488 n., 489 n., 493 n., 495,
    496, 498, 531, 545, 578
Thakeham, 434
Thame, 189, 196, 199, 208, 209, 218, 577
Thame, R., 175, 180, 182, 218, 226, 236, 604

Thames, R., 97, 103, 121, 125, 126, 128, 129,
    130, 131, 136, 143, 165, 172, 173, 183,
    184, 189, 210, 211, 214, 218, 223, 227,
    231, 235, 236, 237, 246, 264, 266, 267,
    269, 271, 279, 282, 284, 285, 371, 391,
    394, 401, 402, 485, 520 n., 534, 538,
    555, 558, 572, 573, 579, 604, 606
Thames Ditton, see Ditton (Surrey)
Thanet, 485, 501, 532, 534, 539, 558, 579
Thanington, 494 n., 499
Thatcham, 258, 267, 272, 273, 274
Thegns, 24, 69, 135, 157, 206 n., 254 n., 274,
    435 n., 518, 595, 613
Theobald, 52, 61 n.
Thepecāpe, see Epcombs
Thomas-Stanford, Sir Charles, 481
Thomley, 208
Thorncroft, 368 n.
Thorndun, 499
Thorney, Red Book of, 193 n.
Thornton, 174
Throucham, 327
Througham, 327
Throwley, 547, 549
Thrupp, 225
Thruxton, see Ann
Thunderfield, 369
Thurrock (Essex), 132, 133
Tichborne, 290 n., 297, 577
Tickenhurst, 525, 531
Tickford, 148, 157, 161
Tifeld hundred, 407
Tiffenden, 529, 581
Tilbrook, 4
Tillingdown, 374
Tillingham (Essex), 128 n.
Tillington, 460, 464, 466
Tilmanstone, 519
Tilton, 412, 427, 431
Tinton, 505, 512, 517, 528, 531, 537
Tiscot, 57
Tisted, East and West, 306
Titchfield, 288 n., 310, 355, 616
Titchfield hundred, 293
Tithes, 177, 350, 462, 545
Titsey, 372, 391
Toddington (Beds.), 13
Toddington (Sx.), 470
Todham, 428, 460

Tollington, 101, 109, 113, 123

Tolls, 86, 87, 88, 89, 90, 179, 229, 232, 355, 398, 400, 466, 469, 470, 474, 546, 549, 554, 555, 583

Tolworth, 390, 394

Tonbridge, 387, 492, 514, 556

Tonbridge, lowy of, 486–8, 492, 537, 542

Tooting, 585

Tortington, 424, 431, 473

Totnore hundred, 439, 458 n.

Tottenhall, 101, 104, 105, 108, 111, 123, 127, 585

Tottenham, 104, 106, 109, 113, 117, 119, 125, 128

Tottenham Court, *see* Tottenhall

Totternhoe, 12, 41

Totteridge, 54

Tottington (Kent), 492

Tottington (Sx.), 413

Totton, 345

Towersey, 138, 187–8, 190, 218

Towns, *see* Urban life

Traders, 63, 70, 71, 90, 94, 258, 272, 273, 281, 355, 549, 616

Trimworth, 499

Tring, 50 n., 57, 58–9, 71, 72, 81, 92

Tring hundred, 50 n., 53 n., 57, 58, 77 n.

Trottiscliffe, 504, 505

Trotton, 424 n., 430

Trucham, Truham, 296 n., 305, 326 n., 327, 328

Truleigh, 418, 434, 440

Tudeley, 487, 488, 492, 518

Tufton, 305

Tunstall, 539

Turner, G. J., 137, 574 n.

Turweston, 148

Tusmore, 206

Twyford (Bucks.), 164, 177, 230, 231

Twyford (Hants.), 290 n., 345, 346, 349

Twyford (Mdlx.), 104, 108, 112, 114

Twynham, 291, 293, 300, 306, 314, 315, 330, 334, 336, 340, 341 n., 344, 350, 351, 352, 616

Tyburn, 109, 113, 123, 127, 585

Tyringham, 166

Tytherley, East and West, 287, 294, 315, 321 n., 350

Tythrop, 138, 170

Uffington, 250, 252, 283

Ufton Nervet, 261, 262

Ulcombe Way, 499

Ulvritone, see Newbury

Understocking, 17–18, 29, 60–2, 73, 75, 76, 88, 110–13, 121, 149–51, 163, 164, 165, 201, 252, 305, 375, 430, 508, 565, 612

Underwood, 76, 212, 215, 525, 550

Upchurch, 519

Up Marden (Sx.), *see* Marden

Upper Arncott, 192

Upper Beeding, *see* Beeding

Upper Dean, *see* Dean

Upper Gravenhurst, *see* Gravenhurst

Upper Hardres, *see* Hardres

Upper Heyford, *see* Heyford

Upper Somborne, *see* Somborne

Upton (Berks.), 252

Upton (Bucks., Stoke hd), 151, 161

Upton (Bucks., Stone hd), 142

Upton (in Hurstbourne Tarrant), 320

Urban life, 21, 42–3, 62, 70, 85–90, 97, 118, 131–4, 149 n., 154 n., 155 n., 160, 177–9, 205, 221, 227–31, 242, 258, 260 n., 273–80, 314, 351–5, 382, 397–400, 438, 458, 463–72, 476, 479, 513, 545–54, 582–5, 586, 616, 617, 618

Utefel, 296 n.

Values, Domesday, 25–9, 71–3, 119–21, 160–4, 208–10, 259–61, 315–18, 327–30, 332–6, 382–4, 439–43, 518–23, 567, 568, 569–75, 613

Vavassores, 157, 310, 314, 315, 356

Ver, R., 10, 45, 54, 81, 91, 92

Verneveld, 194, 224

Villeins, 20, 21, 22, 23, 63, 66, 67, 69, 70, 85, 87, 88, 89, 90, 104, 115, 116, 117, 118, 133, 155, 156, 157, 160, 177, 204, 205, 207, 208 n., 254, 255 n., 256, 257, 258, 259, 279, 280, 310, 311, 314, 352, 377, 378, 379, 382, 434, 435, 512, 513, 514, 515, 516, 517, 566, 588, 613, 617, 618

Vills, *see* Settlements

Vine, Vineyards, 43, 88, 91, 134, 136, 180, 274, 281, 356, 400, 555, 568, 608–10, 616

Vinitor, 400, 608

Vinogradoff, Sir Paul, 24 n., 67 n., 97 n., 107, 108 n., 110, 117 n., 157 n., 256 n., 257 n., 258 n., 259 n., 314 n., 381 n., 439 n., 503, 516 n., 561, 590

Virgates, 11–14, 15 n., 55–7, 103–4, 106, 145, 149, 197, 248, 299, 304, 327–30, 371, 422, 423, 429, 471–2, 502, 507, 563, 612, 618; see also Hides

Waddesdon, 143
Waddesdon hundred, 139, 140, 142 n., 175
Wadholt, 492, 494, 522, 525
Wadhurst, 420, 448
Wainhill, Hempton and Lower, 194
Wain Wood, see Weyley
Walberton, 424, 473
Walbury Hill, 284
Walden, King's and St Paul's, 50 n., 71 n., 72, 76
Waldridge, 145, 157
Waldron, 412
Walhampton, 330, 334
Walker, G. P., 485 n.
Walkern, 58
Walkingstead, 129, 132, 133, 373, 394, 399, 400
Walland Marsh, 444, 449, 456, 479
Wallenberg, J. K., 488 n., 530 n., 531 n., 532 n., 562
Wallingford, 231, 239, 242, 251, 252, 258, 260, 269, 272, 273, 274–8, 281, 573, 574, 583, 616
Wallington (Herts.), 67, 591
Wallington (Surrey), 372, 387, 388
Wallington hundred (Surrey), 365, 366, 380
Wallop, Nether and Over, 294, 307, 314, 315 n., 322, 330, 341, 344, 348, 349, 350, 353, 354, 356, 357, 608
Walmer, 494, 497, 498, 499
Walmestone, 499
Waltham (Essex), 132, 133
Waltham (Kent), 499
Waltham (Sx.), 424, 464, 466, 473
Waltham, St Lawrence and White (Berks.), 243 n., 260, 271
Walton (Kent), 499
Walton (Oxon.), 221, 223
Walton on the Hill (Surrey, Copthorne hd), 373, 399, 400

Walton on Thames (Surrey, Elmbridge hd), 377, 389, 394, 616
Walworth, 585
Wandle, R., 391, 396 n., 401, 402
Wandon, 72 n.
Wandsworth, 382, 400, 585, 608, 609, 616
Wantage, 272
Wantage hundred, 242, 251, 257, 269 n., 270, 271
Wantley (in Henfield), 418, 453 n., 458
Wantsum, R., 485
Wappingthorn, 456, 474
Warbleton, 413, 470
Warblington, 287, 348, 349, 414
Ward, G., 481, 484 n., 493 n., 494 n., 495 n., 498, 499, 545 n., 562
Warden (Beds.), 25
Warden (Kent), 499
Ware, 61, 65, 71, 77, 80, 83, 84, 91, 94, 609, 610, 616
Warfield, 239 n., 250, 575
Wargrave, 268
Warlege, 418 n., 427, 451 n.
Warlingham, 366
Warner, Richard, 361, 362
Warningcamp, 470
Warningore, 467, 469
Warpsgrove, 194
Warwickshire, 186, 187, 190
Washington, 424, 425 n., 456, 473
Washlingstone hundred, 485
Wasing, 245 n.
Waste, 17 n., 27, 44, 73, 164, 174, 208, 223–4, 260 n., 282, 318, 328, 331, 344, 441, 458, 569, 572, 573, 575, 614
    houses, 205, 223, 224, 227, 228, 260 n., 282, 521, 547, 548, 614
Watchfield, 248, 250
Watchingwell, 303, 306, 338, 343, 356, 361
Water Eaton, see Eaton (Oxon.)
Wateringbury, 536 n., 551, 552
Waterperry, 197, 275, 277
Waterstock, 200 n., 565
Watlington, 236, 275, 277
Watton at Stone, 56, 71
Wavendon, 149, 150
Weald, 369, 370, 385, 387, 388, 391, 401, 404–5, 413, 414, 416 n., 417, 420, 421, 443, 444, 448, 449, 474, 475, 476,

Weald (*cont.*)
477–8, 483, 484, 485, 486, 488, 491, 495, 500, 523, 524, 527, 528, 529, 531, 532, 534, 556, 557–8, 559, 578, 580–2, 587, 588, 600
Week (in St Lawrence, Hants.), 321 n., 340 n.
Weirs, 82, 94, 128
Welford, 272
Welford hundred, 294 n.
Wellbury, 72 n.
Welle (Hants.), 295
Wellhead (in Ewhurst), 423 n., 429 n.
Wellow, East and West, 287 n., 295 n., 330
Welwyn, 85
Wembley, 101
Wendlebury, 217
Wendover, 145 n., 161, 165, 170
Wendover Dean, 166
Wenechetone, 296 n.
Wenslow hundred, 6, 10, 33, 598
Werictetone, 296 n., 299
Wessex, 157 n.
West Barming, *see* Barming
West Bedfont, *see* Bedfont
Westbourne (Sx.), 287, 349, 414, 425, 426, 442, 464, 466
West Chiltington, 416, 439
West Clandon, *see* Clandon
Westcot Barton, *see* Barton (Oxon.)
Westcote near Wilshamstead, 31
Westcott (Bucks.), 143
Westcott (Surrey), 374
West Court (in Cliffe), 499
West Dean (Sx., Westbourne hd), *see* Dean (Sx., Westbourne hd)
West Dean (Sx., Willingdon hd), *see* Dean (Sx., Willingdon hd)
West Farleigh, *see* Farleigh (Kent)
Westfield, 440
West Firle, 412, 413, 414 n., 458, 467, 473
Westgate (near Canterbury, Kent), 491, 534, 541 n., 542, 547, 548, 549
West Hagbourne, *see* Hagbourne
Westhampnett, 429 n., 464, 466
West Hanney, *see* Hanney
West Harting, *see* Harting
West Hendred, *see* Hendred
West Horsley, *see* Horsley
West Ilsley, *see* Ilsley

West Malling, *see* Malling (Kent)
West Marden (Sx.), 415 n.
West Meon, *see* Meon
Westmeston, 425 n., 438 n., 467, 469
Westminster, 56, 88, 89, 98, 103, 108, 111, 116, 117, 132–4, 135, 583, 584, 585, 609, 610, 616
West Molesey, *see* Molesey
Weston, 70, 77, 81, 85 n.
Weston Green, 371
Westoning, 4, 5, 15 n., 25, 31, 37, 48, 59 n.
Weston Turville (Bucks.), 170
Weston Underwood (Bucks.), 157
West Peckham, *see* Peckham (Kent)
Westrop, 245 n.
West Shefford, *see* Shefford
West Stoke (Sx.), 416 n.
West Tarring, 416, 446, 461 n.
West Thorney, 439 n., 462 n.
West Tisted, *see* Tisted
Westtune, 499
West Tytherley, *see* Tytherley
West Wellow, *see* Wellow
West Wickham, 524, 548 n.
West Wittering, *see* Wittering
West Wycombe, *see* Wycombe
Wey, R., 340, 345, 348, 360, 371, 375, 389, 391, 394, 396, 398, 401, 402, 403, 404, 604, 606
Weyley, 72, 76
Whalesbeech, 420, 426, 582
Whatlington, 441 n.
Whatton (Notts.), 460 n.
Wheathampstead, 58, 61, 73
Wherwell Abbey, 352, 353, 354
Whippingham, 305
Whipsnade, 45
Whistley, 253, 268, 269
Whitchurch (Bucks.), 166 n.
Whitchurch (Hants.), 289, 311 n., 577
Whitchurch (Mdlx.), *see* Stanmore
Whitchurch (Oxon.), 193
Whitefield, 294
Whitefield Wood, 294
Whitehill (in Tackley, Oxon.), 194, 228, 230, 231
White Horse, Vale of, 246, 266, 271, 280, 282
White Waltham, *see* Waltham (Berks.)

Whitford, 369, 373
Whitsbury, 287
Whitstable, 508, 519, 530, 539, 544
Whyke (Sx.), *see* Rumboldswhyke
Wibalditone, 244
Wic, 494 n., 499
Wichling, 547, 548, 549
Wickham (Hants.), 298–9
Wickham (Sx., Buttinghill hd), 467, 469
Wickhambreux, 505, 526, 535 n., 539, 544, 545, 547, 549, 555, 556
Widford (Herts.), 85 n.
Widford (Oxon.), 186, 190, 200
Widow, 518
Wield, 298, 311 n., 360
Wigarestun, 296 n., 328
Wigginton (Herts.), 57, 58, 59 n., 73, 88 n.
Wigginton (Oxon.), 208 n.
Wight, Isle of, 287, 291, 293 n., 294, 296 n., 298, 303 n., 304 n., 305, 306 n., 310 n., 317 n., 319, 324, 340, 342, 343, 344, 345, 347, 348, 349, 350, 351, 355, 356, 357, 358, 361, 566, 579, 588, 616
Wigram, S. R., 229 n.
Wilden (Beds.), 13, 15, 16, 22
Wildene (Sx.), 418 n.
Wilderton (Kent), 524
Wildetone (Sx.), 417, 418 n.
Wilkinson, J., 405, 479, 560
Will Hall (in Alton), 296
Willesden, 108, 585
Willey hundred, 6, 9 n., 10 n., 29, 594
Willingdon (Sx.), 412, 439, 441 n., 456
Willington (Beds.), 39 n.
Willington (Berks.), 244
Wilmingham, 344
Wilmington (in Boughton Aluph, Kent), 499
Wilmington (near Dartford, Kent), 499
Wilmington (Sx.), 414 n.
Wilting, 423, 424, 441 n., 458, 473
Wiltshire, 239, 240, 287, 293, 294 n., 295 n., 315, 321, 337
Winchelsea, 472, 474 n.
Winchendon, 172, 174 n.
Winchester, 287, 290, 293, 314, 316, 345, 351, 353–5, 359, 583, 616
Windridge, 71
Windrush, R., 218, 227, 234, 236, 604

Windsor, 160, 239 n., 242, 247, 248, 250, 251 n., 258, 259, 262, 264, 272, 274, 279–80, 281, 285, 580, 582, 588, 596, 616
Windsor Forest, 247, 261, 264–5, 267, 285, 389, 580, 602
Wing, 166 n., 172
Wingham, 525
Wingrave, 166 n.
Winkfield, 252, 265, 616
Winkton, 330, 334, 335, 345
Winslade, 306
Winslow, 166
Winterbourne (Sx.), 467, 469
Winterslow (Wilts.), 315, 321 n.
Winton (Sx.), 412, 417, 441 n.
Wise, J. R., 362
Wisley, 394
Wiston, 423, 441
Witestone, 296 n.
Witingeham, 296 n.
Witney, 212
Wittenham, Little and Long, 243, 267, 275, 276
Wittering, East and West, 415, 435, 451, 464, 466
Wittersham, 499
Wiwart, lathe of, 486
Wixamtree hundred, 6
Woburn (Beds.), 17, 36
Wokefield, 259
Woking, 383, 384, 387, 389, 616
Wokingham, 243, 245, 576
Woking hundred, 365, 375, 381
Wolverton (Hants.), 293
Wolverton (Kent), 499
Women, 513, 517, 518, 613
Womenswold (Kent), 499
Wonersh, 397 n.
Wonston, 304
Wooburn (Bucks.), 151, 166, 170, 175, 182
Wood, 30–5, 44, 76–8, 87, 88, 89, 90, 92, 93, 94, 95, 122–5, 133, 135, 136, 165–9, 182, 183, 184, 211–14, 215, 234, 235, 236, 237, 262–4, 282, 283, 320–4, 327, 328, 329, 330, 352, 360, 361, 364, 386–9, 403, 404, 405, 444–8, 476, 477, 478, 479, 488, 524–7, 550, 557, 558, 559, 568, 595–600, 614

Woodchurch, 499
Woodcroft, 6 n.
Woodeaton, see Eaton (Oxon.)
Woodlands (Kent), 499
Woodmancott, 340
Woodmansterne, 376, 396
Woodnesborough, 531, 552
Woodstock Forest, 214, 616
Wool, 233, 401
Woolavington, 429 n., 451, 464, 466
Wooldridge, S. W., 96
Woolfly (in Henfield), 417, 418
Woolley, 250
Woolmer District, 358
Woolmer Forest, 321, 322, 360, 602
Woolstone, 250
Woolwich, 492, 516
Woolwicks, Great and Little, 52
Wootton (Hants., Rodedic hd), 326, 328
Wootton (Kent), 499
Wootton (Oxon.), 186, 190, 200, 213, 214, 233, 616
Wootton (Sx., Pevensey hd), 418 n., 440, 455
Wootton (Sx., Street hd), 435, 442
Wootton St Lawrence (Hants.), 288
Worcestershire, 180, 259, 568
Worminghall, 145 n., 164
Wormley, 72, 83
Worth (Sx.), 364, 375 n., 414
Worth Forest, 446 n.
Worthing, 442
Worthy, Abbots, Headbourne, Kings and Martyr, 293, 294 n., 307, 341, 353, 354, 359
Worton (Oxon.), 186, 190
Wotton hundred (Surrey), 364, 365
Wouldham, 505, 524, 534, 537
Wrestlingworth, 9, 10 n.

Wrotham and Wrotham Heath, 487, 489, 491, 516 n., 524, 527
Wroxton, 198
Wyboston, 18, 24, 27, 44
Wychwood Forest, 196, 210, 213, 214, 218, 235, 588, 602, 616
Wycombe, High and West, 141, 150, 151, 157, 169, 170, 172, 174, 175, 182
Wye, 508, 515, 517, 519, 530, 534, 537
Wye hundred, 512, 537, 538, 541
Wye, R. (Bucks.), 143, 169, 172, 175, 182, 183
Wyke (Surrey), 369
Wykham, 224
Wymering, 299, 300 n., 318
Wymington (Beds.), 13, 17
Wymondley, Great and Little, 51, 72 n.
Wyndham hundred, 407
Wyrardisbury, 170, 172, 173, 174, 184
Wytham, 256 n.
Wyttunemersc, 499

Y., D., 361
Yaldhurst, 327
Yalding, 487, 488, 508, 521, 536, 544, 556, 575
Yar, R., 342, 361
Yardley hundred, 139, 142 n.
Yarnton, 193, 218, 221, 223, 232, 233
Yateley, 341, 342, 360
Yattendon, 251
Yeading, R., 126, 131
Yelden, 24
Yeverington, 439
Yokes (Juga), 502, 507, 563, 612; see also Sulungs
York, 353, 583
Yorkshire, 197, 488
Young, Arthur, 233, 234, 236, 590